Hon. CHARLES G. WALDRON, Mayor of Dover, 1923.

Colonial Era History of Dover, New Hampshire

John Scales

HERITAGE BOOKS
2008

HERITAGE BOOKS
AN IMPRINT OF HERITAGE BOOKS, INC.

Books, CDs, and more—Worldwide

For our listing of thousands of titles see our website
at
www.HeritageBooks.com

Published 2008 by
HERITAGE BOOKS, INC.
Publishing Division
100 Railroad Ave. #104
Westminster, Maryland 21157

Copyright © 1923 John Scales

Other books by the author:
CD: History of Dover, New Hampshire, Vol. 1

All rights reserved. No part of this book may be reproduced or transmitted in any form or by any means, electronic or mechanical, including photocopying, recording or by any information storage and retrieval system without written permission from the author, except for the inclusion of brief quotations in a review.

International Standard Book Numbers
Paperbound: 978-1-55613-192-9
Clothbound: 978-0-7884-7062-2

AUTHORITY.

WHEREAS, the City Councils of 1922, following an exhaustive investigation of all the attendant circumstances, held that "the history of Dover, so essentially a part of the history of the State, should find expression during the Tercentenary Celebration of the Settlement of New Hampshire," but referred final action in the matter to the City Government of 1923, therefore be it

Resolved by the City Councils of the City of Dover:

That the manuscript copy of the history of the City of Dover, prepared by Mr. John Scales and now on file in the office of the City Clerk, be published in book form, and that his Honor the Mayor, the President of the Common Council and the City Clerk, be and hereby are constituted a joint special committee to have full charge of the preparation and arrangement of the text of said history, and to make all necessary arrangements for its publication. Any and all expense incident thereto to be charged to the appropriation to be provided for Contingent Expenses, and all revenues from the sale of the printed volumes to be deposited with the City Treasurer and credited to said appropriation.

Passed January 4, 1923.

Attest:

FRED E. QUIMBY,
City Clerk.

PUBLICATION COMMITTEE.

Hon. Charles G. Waldron, *Mayor.*
Herbert W. Tinker, *President Common Council.*
Fred E. Quimby, *City Clerk.*

EXPLANATION OF THE MAP.

The following data that can be found on the map were collected from various sources, during a search that extended over a period of five years. The search was made in Wills, deeds, depositions, court records, town records, land grants, etc., etc. Every name was located by some land transaction. If other names should be found (no doubt there were others), they can be placed on the map.

Dwellings on the West Side of High Street.

1—William Walderne, 1636/1646.
2—Anthony Emery, 1640/1649. He kept an "ordinary."
3—Thomas Leighton, 1640/1672.
4—Deacon John Hall, 1640/1691.
  Ralph Hall, 1685—
5—FORTIFIED MEETING-HOUSE, 1654/1723.
  This was the second house.
6—Lieut. Thomas Tibbetts, 1680/1720.
7—Capt. John Tibbetts, Sr., 1709—
  Garrison house.
8—Philip Cromwell, 1680/1701.
9—Sylvanus Nock, 1680/1701.
10—Richard Pinkham, 1640/1671.
  John Pinkham (2), 1671/1720.
11—Quaker Meeting-house, 1680/1720.
12—Humphrey Varney, 1659/1673.

Early Householders on the East Side of High Street.

1—Philip Chesley, 1642/1651.
2—Captain Thomas Millett, 1720/1763.
  Millett Appletree, 1720/1913.
3—John Tuttle, Sr., 1640/1662.
  Captain John Tuttle, 1673/1720.
4—George Walton, 1643/1650.
  He kept an "ordinary."
5—Henry Tibbetts, 1643—
6—John Heard, 1640/1650.
7—Richard Walderne, 1636/1655.
8—Ralph Hall, 1650/1664.
  Rev. John Reyner, 1664/1673.
  Hon. Job Clement, 1673/1683.
9—William Storey, 1640—
10—Elder Hatevil Nutter, 1636/1675.

Early Householders on the East Side of High Street.—Concluded.

11—Samuel Haines, 1640—
12—Joseph Austin, 1640—
13—Samuel Cromwell, 1680/1715.
   Nicholas Harford, 1715/1737.
14—Thomas Canney, 1640/1671.
15—Hanson Roberts house built about 1770.

Houses on Low Street, Beginning at the South.

1—Captain Thomas Wiggin, 1633/1650. He lived on "Captain's Hill."
2—William Pomfrett, 1634/1680.
3—John Follett, 1640/1649.
   William Follett, 1649—
4—Captain John Underhill, 1638/1643.
5—Parsonage:
   William Leverich, 1633/1635.
   George Burdett, 1637/1638.
   Hanserd Knollys, 1638/1641.
   Thomas Larkham, 1641/1643.
   Daniel Maud, 1643/1655.
   John Reyner, 1655/1664.
6—Log Meeting-House, 1633/1654.
7—Deacon John Damme, 1634/1693.
8—Richard York, 1640—
9—Robert Nanney, 1640—
10—Jail, 1660/1720.
   Pillory, 1660/1700.
11—James Nute, 1650/1661.
12—Thomas Downs, 1650/1680.
13—Lieut. John Drew, 1675/1699.
   Abraham Nute, 1699/1720.

Dwellings Along Fore River, Beginning at the South.

1—Clement tannery, 1655.
2—Job Clement's house, 1655/1673.
3—Old Brewery, 1640—
4—Edward Colcord, 1640—
5—William Furber, 1637/1642.
6—Charles Buckner, 1657/1668.
7—David Ludecas Edling, 1669—
8—Thomas Beard, 1640/1670.
9—Henry Beck, 1640/1649.

EXPLANATION OF THE MAP. ix

Dwellings Along Fore River, Beginning at the South.—Concluded.

10—John Roberts, Sr., 1650/1700.
Joseph (3) Roberts, 1665/1735.
Stephen (4) Roberts, 1704/1757.

11—Gov. Thomas Roberts, Sr., 1640/1673.
He lived at The POINT before 1640.
12—Jedediah Andrews, 1659—
13—Ralph Twombly, 1659—

Sheep Pasture and Training Ground.

Dwellers Along the Road from High Street to the Log Meeting-House.

1—Elder Edward Starbuck, 1642/1659.
2—Robert Huckins, 1640/1659.

3—Captain Walter Barefoot, 1650/1670.

LIST OF ILLUSTRATIONS.

Hon. Charles G. Waldron (Mayor of Dover, 1923)

John Scales, A. B., A. M. (Editor)............Facing 1

Pomeroy's Cove, Landing Place in 1623........Facing 17

Thomson's Point, the Thomson Grant of 1622....Facing 33

Hilton Hall, site of Edward Hilton's House.....Facing 49

The Bound Oak...........................Facing 81

Site of the Second Meeting-House, 1654.........Facing 129

Confluence of Waters emptying into Great Bay...Facing 177

The Damme Garrison House..................Facing 209

Redding Point, where Town lines converge......Facing 225

Launching of the Ship, "Dover," 1919..........Facing 241

Map of Dover Village, 1834..................Facing 257

In Memory of Governor Thomas Roberts........Facing 305

The Richard Walderne Memorial..............Facing 337

CONTENTS.

	Page.
Map of Hilton Point and Dover Neck Village	Front.
Topographical description of Hilton Point	1
The first permanent settlement of Dover	5
New Hampshire Grants and Patents	5
Biographical sketch of David Thomson	8
David Thomson's Indenture	11
Hilton's petition for Indian Land Grants	24
Thomson's residence at Little Harbor	29
Concerning Thomson's Island	30
What about Mason Hall?	32
The Hilton or Squamscot Patent	36
Biographical sketch of William Hilton	37
Biographical sketch of Thomas Roberts	39
Employments of the first Settlers	40
The Fishery business	41
Contemporaneous Events, 1623-1633	44
Indians about the Pascataqua River	46
Ferries and Ferrymen	52
Brick-making at Dover Point and Dover Neck	56
The Fiske Brick-Making System	60
Dover Ordinaries, or Inns	62
Ship-building on Dover Neck	65
Laws concerning Ship-building	68
Dover's Foreign Commerce	71
Making of Clapboards and Pipe-staves	73
Dover's Intercourse with Barbadoes Island	75
Barbadoes Pond and Vicinity	77
The "Bound Oak"	80
A Wrestling-Match under the Oak	80
The big Elm	82
Captain Millet and his Apple-Tree	82
Muster-roll of Captain Millet's Company	85

	Page.
Dover's Second Foot Company, 1740	87
Corporal Coffin's List of Troopers, 1740	89
First Settlement on Dover Neck, 1633	90
Bristol and Shrewsbury Men	96
Some Causes of the Early Migration	99
Passengers on the Ship "James"	101
Biographical sketch of Thomas Wiggin	102
Biographical sketch of Rev. Wm. Leverich	105
Biographical sketch of Rev. George Burdett	105
Biographical sketch of Captain John Underhill	107
Streets and Lanes of Dover Neck	112
Location of the "Old Brewery"	113
The first Tannery in Dover	113
Biographical sketch of Elder Hatevil Nutter	115
Location of Public Pastures	116
Beck's Slip—Harford's Ferry	117
The Dover Neck Meeting-House	119
The Meeting-House Bell	123
The Old Log Meeting-House	124
Biographical sketch of Richard Pinkham	127
Quaker Missionaries on Dover Neck	128
Stringent Laws against the Quakers	138
Whittier's Poem on "The Quaker Women"	140
School-Masters and Schoolhouses	144
Organization of the First Church	145
Altercation between Mr. Knollys and Mr. Larkham	148
Dover Town Records	151
Double Entry Land Grants	153
William Walderne, the First Town Clerk	162
Places for Holding Courts	164
Elder Edward Starbuck as an Anabaptist	165
Wearing of Long Hair Condemned	165
Dover Fined for not Sending Deputies	166
Campaign of Massachusetts to get Control of Dover	167
Old Dover: Its Boundaries and Divisions	172
Oyster River made a Parish	178

CONTENTS.

	Page.
Somersworth made a Parish	179
Rollinsford set off from Somersworth	181
Madbury made a Parish	181
Lee set off from Durham (Oyster River)	181
Depositions concerning Lampreel River	183
Walter Barefoot, first Resident Doctor in Dover	184
Back River District and Wm. Damme Garrison	201
Dover's Rivers and Landing Places	215
Ship-building on the Pascataqua	220
Important Events in the History of Dover	223
Biographical sketch of Christine Otis Baker	227
Some Early Land Grants	232
Cochecho Marsh, or Great Fresh Marsh	233
The Earliest Tax-Lists, 1648-1675	234
Oyster River (Durham) Tax-Rates, 1661	239
Tax Assessment to pay Rev. Mr. Reyner	241
List of Certain Town Officers	254
Genealogy: The Damme family	263
Guppy family	288
Roberts family	302
Hilton family	310
Nutter family	314
Starbuck family	317
Pinkham family	320
Walderne (Richard) family	324
Waldron (Col. John) family	330
Tibbetts family	335
Page family	341
Coffin family	345
Watson family	352
Tuttle family	357
Clements family	365
Cushing family	368
Austin family	372
Hall (Deacon John) family	375
Hayes family	390
Gage family	396

	Page.
Genealogy: The Edgerly family	400
Wallingford family	405
Evans family	408
Nute family	412
Meserve family	417
Wiggin family	420
Randall family	438
Heard family	444
Otis family	456
Scales family	462
Dore family	478
Twombly family	481
Merrow family	490
Church family	493

JOHN SCALES, A. B., A. M. (Editor).

HISTORY OF DOVER, N. H.

TOPOGRAPHICAL DESCRIPTION OF HILTON POINT.

The first permanent settlement in Dover and New Hampshire was commenced at what is now known as *Dover Point,* which for two centuries was called *Hilton Point,* and before that the Indians called it Wecannacohunt or Wecohamet. That settlement was begun in the spring of 1623 by Edward Hilton, William Hilton, Thomas Roberts and others, a small party whose names are not known. The Hiltons were brothers: it is a tradition that Mr. Roberts' wife was a Hilton, sister to Edward and William. There is no record in regard to this matter of matrimony but various corroborating data indicate that such was probably the fact in the relationship of these three men.

Dover Point is the southern end of Dover Neck and lies nearly northwest and southeast between the Pascataqua River on the west and Fore River on the east. Dover Neck lies in a northerly and southerly direction between Back River on the west and Fore River on the east, the Pascataqua River on the southwest and the Cochecho River on the northeast. It gets its name, "The Neck," because it lies between those bodies of water, the head of it being along a line extending from Sawyer Lower Mill to Campin's Rocks, on the Cochecho River. In local phrase the territory is known as "Upper Neck," "Lower Neck," and "The Point." The Indian name for Fore River is *"Newichawannock,"* which begins at the head of tide water at South Berwick, which the Indians called *"Quamphegan,"* and ends at *Dover Point*, where it unites with the Pascataqua River, which in turn begins at Fox Point, Newington, where the tide water from Little Bay and Oyster River empty into it twice in twenty-four hours.

The Dover and Portsmouth Railroad bridge is at the southeasterly end of "The Point"; the section locally bearing this name extends from Pomeroy Cove to the bridge, a distance of one-third of a mile. The highest part is at the easterly end where the "Kennard" house, so called, stands, the elevation being about fifty feet above high water; at Pomeroy's Cove the surface is only a few feet above tide water, and the width from the cove to the river on the westerly side is about ten rods; while the width just above the bridge is 100 rods. The railroad filling at the Cove and at the Point has changed the original appearance somewhat. It is a beautiful plateau. Pomeroy's Cove is formed by Sandy Point, on the east, and a curve in the land on the west, and is the original harbor, or landing-place used by the first settlers. From the fact that the Card family resided near there during the Nineteenth Century, the cove came to be called "Card's Cove" by the residents of Dover in that period. It is better to preserve and use the original names, *Hilton Point* and *Pomeroy Cove*.

This small and nearly level tract of land is one of the beauty spots of Dover, and of New Hampshire; it is not only delightful in itself, but also in its surroundings. The Pascataqua River, which is on its southerly side, and from the veranda of Hilton Hall can be seen a long distance down stream towards Portsmouth, is broad and deep so that the largest ship in the world could be taken up to the head waters, at Little Bay and Oyster River, and return without difficulty. The channel most of the way is fifty feet deep. It separates *Dover Point* from Newington, which town was a part of Dover until 1714. Newington was made a parish July 16, 1713, but up to that time was known as "Bloody Point in Dover." The name was changed May 12, 1714, the Council Record of which date says: "Bloody Point was named Newington this day by his excellency the Governour."[1]

---

[1] New Hampshire Provincial Papers III: 549-551, 562.

That is all the incorporation the town ever had, but it exercised town privileges from that date, independent from Dover. The Dover and Portsmouth Railroad bridge extends from *Dover Point* to "Bloody Point," a distance of 1700 feet. This name was given to this section of Dover soon after the settlement was commenced on Dover Neck, on account of a contention between Capt. Thomas Wiggin, who was governor or manager of the Dover settlement, and Capt. Walter Neal who was boss at "Strawberry Bank," later called Portsmouth. Capt. Wiggin claimed that what is now Newington belonged to Dover; Capt. Neal claimed that it belonged to his settlement at Strawberry Bank; a meeting was held near where the Newington railway station now is, friends of the two Captains being present. Hubbard, the historian, reports the meeting as follows, on page 217 of his "General History of New England," published about 1680, first speaking of Captain Neal's management of the settlement at Strawberry Bank: "Nor is there anything memorable recorded as done by him, or his company, during the time of his three years' stay, unless it were a contest between him and Capt. Wiggans, employed in like manner to begin a plantation higher up the river for some (men) of Shrewsbury, who being forbidden by him, the said Neal, to come upon a point of land, that lieth in the midway between Dover and Exeter. Capt. Wiggans had intended to have defended his right by the sword, but it seems both the litigants had so much wit in their anger, as to wave the battle, each accounting himself to have done very manfully in what was threatened; so as in respect, not of what did, but what might have fallen out, the place to this day retains the formidable name of Bloody Point."

Directly across the river, from Bloody Point, is Leighton's or Everett's Point in Eliot, off shore from which is Watt's Fort, now only a collection of rocks, but in former years it was an island, like Franks Fort, a short distance below. Above Leighton's Point is Cammock's Creek, also called Shapleigh's Creek. Leighton's Point was so named for its owner, Capt. William Leighton, who bought it of the heirs of William Everett, one of the first settlers there, who kept a tavern there in 1652. It was in Everett's house that, 16th of November, 1652, the articles of agreement were signed.

between the Commissioners of Massachusetts and the citizens of Old Kittery, by which the District of Maine came under the jurisdiction of Massachusetts and so continued until Maine became a State, in 1820.

It was at this point that the first settlement was made in Kittery, about 1634. Kittery was divided in 1814 and this upper part was named Eliot. These facts are here mentioned simply to show the historic neighborhood in which *Hilton Point* is located.

The reader now has a topographical description of *Dover Point*. If he will imagine all of the present houses removed, the railroad torn up, the bridge sunk in the river and the whole ground covered with a magnificent forest, he will then be in a state of mind to understand what the first settlers saw when they came up the river Pascataqua in the spring of 1623, and anchored their ship in Pomeroy's Cove, then unnamed, but which they named in honor of one of their passengers, Leonard Pomeroy, who was a business partner of David Thomson.

THE FIRST PERMANENT SETTLERS OF DOVER.

The first permanent settlers of Dover were Edward Hilton, William Hilton, Thomas Roberts and others whose names have not been preserved. They were of London, England; they came over in the ship *"Providence"* of Plymouth, in the spring of 1623, arriving soon after David Thomson and his party landed at Little Harbor, the southern mouth of the Pascataqua River, on the shore in Rye, opposite the shore in Newcastle on which stands the famous hotel, "The Wentworth." Mr. Thomson's ship was *"The Jonathan"* and was owned by him and his partners, Abraham Colomer, Nicholas Sherwell and Leonard Pomeroy. *"The Providence"* was owned by Mr. Pomeroy, and it is quite probable he came over with the Hiltons to examine his investment in New England territory, hence it came they gave the name "Pomeroy" to the Cove that divides *Dover Point* from Dover Neck. How do we know that these statements are facts? By the dates of various land grants or "patents" issued by the Council of Plymouth, which was organized Nov. 3, 1620, by authority of King James, who granted a Patent or Charter to forty men of note in England; it was incorporated as: "The Council established at Plymouth, in the County of Devon, for the planting, ruling, ordering and governing New England, in America; from the 40th to the 48th degree of longitude, and from the Atlantic to the Pacific Ocean."

Sir Ferdinando Gorges and Captain John Mason were important and influential members of this powerful company. All New Hampshire Patents and Grants were obtained from this Council. There were nine in all:

"The Marianna," to Capt. John Mason, March 9, 1621-2, under which it is claimed that he and Ambrose Gibbons, as his agent, made a small settlement at Cape Ann in 1622 or 1623 and remained there until ousted by the Salem settlement, and Mason lost all control there in 1630.

The Province of Maine, granted to Sir Ferdinando Gorges and Captain John Mason, April 19, 1622. This comprised all the coast from the Merrimack River to the Kennebec River, and back into the country a rather indefinite, or very great distance. So far as New Hampshire was concerned nothing was ever done under this grant.

The third grant was *"A Point of Land in the Pascataway River, in New England,"* given to Mr. David Thomson, Mr. Jobe and Mr. Sherwood. This was what has ever since been known as "Thomson's Point" in Dover. The Council made the grant in July or August, 1622. The Patent, in full, has not been found, but a memoranda of it, and the year in which it was given is now in the archives of the Council, which have been preserved. This point of land is where the first temporary settlement was made in Dover, and New Hampshire, before Mr. Thomson obtained his six-thousand-acre patent in October, 1622; how long before 1622 the settlement was begun is not known; perhaps before the Pilgrims landed at Plymouth.

The fourth grant by the Council was given on the 16th of October, 1622, to David Thomson, alone, consisting of *"Six Thousand Acres of Land and an Island, in New England."* No statement of location, or boundaries, in New England is given. It was under authority of this grant that the settlement at *Hilton Point* was commenced in the spring of 1623.

The fifth grant, *"New Hampshire,"* was given Nov. 7, 1629, to Capt. John Mason. Nothing was ever done under this patent, except that fifty years later, it gave the name to the province which was established, separating Dover, Portsmouth, Exeter and Hampton from Massachusetts, for the purpose of creating new courts which would compel Dover farmers and land owners to pay rent to Captain John Mason's heirs. The name New Hampshire is no where used in connection with these towns, before 1679, so it is a fact that Dover is fifty years older than New Hampshire.

The sixth grant was *"The Laconia,"* made only ten days later, November 17, 1629, to Sir Ferdinando Gorges and Capt. John Mason. This occupied land all around Dover, but no part of it.

Under it the settlement at Portsmouth, then called "Strawberry Bank," was begun in 1630 by Captain Mason, and settlements were commenced in Maine, across the river from *Hilton Point,* a little later. The Laconia Company had nothing whatever to do with Dover. The boundary of the patent extended from the mouth of the Merrimack River along the coast to the Kennebec River, and the side lines extended north and west to include Lake Champlain and territory to the St. Lawrence River. It was designed for a great land speculation, but proved a great failure in everything, except that Capt. Mason founded Portsmouth by sending over Capt. Walter Neal in command of a party, in the ship *"Warwick,"* in 1630. That settlement was called "Strawberry Bank" until the Massachusetts General Court changed the name to Portsmouth, in 1653, at the request of the citizens dwelling therein.

The seventh grant was what is commonly known as the *"Squamscot Patent,"* which was given to Edward Hilton March 12, 1629-30, only four months after the date of the Laconia patent. Mr. Hilton obtained his patent to determine the boundaries of his land and protect his rights from encroachment by the Laconia Company, whose territory surrounded his own, which he had obtained from the Council of Plymouth under David Thomson's grant of October, 1622, and which he had occupied peaceably, and improved, from 1623 to 1630.

The eighth grant was the *"Pascataway"* patent to Sir Ferdinando Gorges and Capt. John Mason, November 3, 1631. The object of this patent was to define more definitely the boundary between Hilton's land and that of Captain Mason's settlers at Strawberry Bank, as disputes had arisen between the inhabitants of these two settlements.

The ninth and last grant was the *"New Hampshire and Masonia"* patent given to Capt. John Mason, April 22, 1635, which in no way concerned Dover. Those who are interested to study these patents further are referred to Mr. Charles W. Tuttle's book on "Captain John Mason," which contains the text of the grants in full, except the patents issued to David Thomson alone, under which the settlement at Dover was begun.

WHO WAS DAVID THOMSON?

Who was David Thomson that he should receive grants of land from the Council of Plymouth? Who was Edward Hilton and what connection had he with Thomson, that he should form a settlement on some part of Thomson's six thousand acres?

David Thomson was born about 1590; he was united in marriage with Amias Cole, of Plymouth, England, July 13, 1613; she was the daughter of William Cole, of that town, who was a ship builder. The wedding took place in St. Andrew's church, and is on record there.

The names of his parents are not known. It is said that he was of Scotch descent, and that he was son of Michael Thomson, but there is no evidence of this. He is nowhere mentioned as connected with any town in Scotland; the inference is that he was born in Plymouth, where he married his wife and was in business a number of years previous to coming to New England. At the time of his marriage, when he was about twenty-three years old, he was called "an apothecary's clerk." His place of residence from 1613 to 1623, was at Plymouth. How long he continued in the apothecary business is not known.

As his father-in-law was a ship builder, he may have engaged in business with him; but up to 1620, there is no record further than above stated, as to what he was employed in doing. But it is quite certain he was a busy man, and became associated with men who were high up in official circles, whose records are well known.

That he was interested in shipping, and had made voyages to New England and the Pascataqua River before 1623, is shown by his knowledge of the localities here and in Boston Harbor and in Massachusetts Bay. The proof that he came here in the ship *"Jonathan,"* in the spring of 1623, will be given in due course. He and his party landed at Little Harbor, the southern mouth of the Pascataqua River. The precise rock on which they set foot, when they landed, cannot be pointed out, as the Plymouth Rock is, on which the Pilgrims stepped, only two and a half years before, but, from the lay of the land, called Odiorne's Point, on which it is probable he built his house, it is quite certain the landing was made in some cove on the south side of Little Harbor, and below the bridge that leads from Rye to the Wentworth Hotel, at Newcastle, as it was not possible to anchor the ship safely any further out toward the open bay.

What interest did Mr. Thomson have in this New England colonization business, that was undertaken by "The Council established at Plymouth, in the County of Devon, (England,) for the planting, ruling, ordering and governing New England in America, etc., etc.?" The Council was chartered November 3, 1620; it was organized soon after, and David Thomson was elected or appointed "Messenger," or confidential "Agent." This is shown by the Records of the Council, when a hot contest was going on in Parliament, to take away the charter, on the ground that the King had exceeded his authority in granting it. The following are excerpts from the Record:

On the 5th of July, 1622: "It is ordered that David Thomson do attend the Lords with A petition to his Majesty for forfeits committed by Thomas Weston; As also to solicit the Lords for procuring from his Majesty a proclamation concerning fishermen in the western parts. Likewise to procure some course for punishing their (the fishermen's) contempt for authority (of the Council.)"

On the 24th of July, 1622: "Mr. Thomson is appointed to attend the Lords, for a warrant to Mr. Atterney-General for drawing the new Patent."

On the 8th of November, 1622: "Mr. Thomson is ordered to pay unto Leo Peddock £10, towards his pains for his last employment to New England."

On the 11th of November, 1622: "Mr. Thomson is appointed to attend Sir Robert Munsell concerning Captain Squebbs' commission."

On the 15th of November, 1622, "Mr. Thomson and the Clerk are directed to see the ton of iron weighed to be sent to Mr. Whitty;" and the same day, "Mr. Thomson is appointed to solicit Captain Love to pay in the £40 for which Sir Samuel Argall standeth engaged," &c.

On the 16th of November:—"It is ordered that Mr. Thomson propoundeth to have an order from the Council for transportation of ten persons, with provisions for New England, And the persons so transported to pay the Council the usual rate for their transportation, after expiration of two years."

David Thomson's name ceases to appear in the records, after December 3d, 1622, as an active agent of the Council. This is easily accounted for, as he was engaged in organizing his emigration party for New England. The agreement with the three merchants, his partners, aforementioned, was drawn up December 14, 1622, and signed that day, which agreement is given on another page.

In the records of the Council of Plymouth it appears that David Thomson was an active agent in helping the Council prevent Parliament from annuling its charter, which it attempted to do. While he was thus engaged in parliamentary work he was granted by the Council the patent of 1622 for "a point of land in the Pascataway River in New England." It was given to himself, Mr. Jobe and Mr. Sherwood. The patent itself has not been found, but a memorandum of such a grant is on record in the Public Record Office in London, and was copied by Mr. Charles Deane of Boston, when he was in London, and later was published in the Massachusetts Historical Register, in 1876; it reads as follows: —"1622. A patent to David Thomson, M. Jobe, and M. Sherwood, for a point (of land) in the Piscataway River, in New England."

In the earliest periods of New England history the term Pascataqua River was applied to the present Pascataqua and the Newichawannock, as the latter continues straight up on the east side of Dover Neck; in later periods to the present time the name Pascataqua is applied to that which flows on the south side of *Dover Point,* extending up to Fox Point, at the mouth of Oyster River, and Little Bay. In the Newichawannock part of what was supposed to be Pascataqua, is a point of land at the junction of the Cochecho River with the Newichawannock, which has always had the name "Thomson's Point" since Dover history began. So that is the only "Point in Pascataqua River in New England" to which this patent of 1622, which was given to Mr. Thomson, Mr. Jobe and Mr. Sherwood, can be applied. It is at this point that

Mr. Thomson made a temporary settlement, for fishing purposes, before 1622, how long before cannot be determined.

The fact that those gentlemen obtained that patent or grant early in 1622, shows that Mr. Thomson was familiar with the river and knew for what purpose that particular "point" could be used, —that was for catching salmon, in the spring time, by stretching a net across the river there, when the fish were going up the salt water to fresh water above the falls, where they deposited their spawn, instinctively, to be hatched. That was what the salmon had been doing for ages until the white men stopped their passage to fresh water by building dams at the lower falls of the Cochecho and the Salmon Falls at South Berwick, the ancient Quamphegan. This last named river gets its very name from the fact that it was the spawning hatchery of the salmon that came up from the salt water in the springtime.

Mr. Thomson had a house there in which his fishermen lived, during the salmon fishing season; that house was standing there for years after he was dead; it is on the tax list of Dover, 1648, in which it is called the "Thomson Point house." The tax lists of the town before that date are lost, but of course it was on the lost lists.

It has been conjectured by some writers that the name came from William Thompson, who was a hired man in a sawmill in Eliot, then Old Kittery, after 1650; this man resided there the rest of his life, and the only land he owned in Dover was a grant given to him by the town of Dover in 1656,—50 acres on Knox Marsh. No house was ever built on it. So the name of Thomson's Point could not have been derived from William Thompson.

DAVID THOMSON'S INDENTURE.

On the 16th of October, 1622, the Council of Plymouth gave a patent, or grant of land to David Thomson, alone, of six thousand acres of land and an island, in New England. The patent for this grant is not extant, but that there was such a patent is proven by an indenture of David Thomson's which was found among the old papers in possession of the late Hon. Robert C. Winthrop, of Boston, which he had inherited from his ancestor, John Winthrop, the founder and first Governor of the Massachusetts Bay Colony. It had lain among the Winthrop papers nearly 250 years, unknown to the historians of New Hampshire, who, in their ignorance, had published a lot of conjectures, suppositions and guesses concerning the beginning of settlements in New Hampshire.

Soon after Mr. Winthrop found the paper he gave it to Mr. Charles Deane, of Boston, who read it before the Massachusetts Historical Society, at a meeting in May or June, 1876, and it was published in the Annual of the Society of that year. In presenting it to the meeting, Mr. Deane first gave a summary of its contents, as follows:

"The Indenture recites that the Council for New England had granted to David Thomson, alone, under date of 16th of October, 1622:

"Six thousand acres of land and one island, in New England, but did not locate it; that Thomson had absolutely conveyed one fourth part of the Island to three merchants of Plymouth, viz. Abraham Colomer, Nicholas Sherwell and Leonard Pomeroy, with covenants to convey, in fee simple, the fourth part of six thousand acres. In consideration whereof it is agreed between the parties, in brief as follows:—"

First. That the merchants Colomer, Sherwill and Pomeroy, will at their own charge,—this present year, 1622,—provide and send two men with Thomson, in the ship *"Jonathan of Plymouth"* to New England, with victuals, provisions, etc., as shall suffice them till they are landed. And if they land there within the space of three months after the ship shall pass Ram Head, (a promontory just outside of Plymouth Sound,) the residue of the three months victuals shall be delivered to Thompson, at his landing, there to be disposed of by him towards finding a fit place for intended habitation, and also to begin the same.

Second. The three merchants will, this present year, 1622, at their own charge, provide and send three men more in the ship *"Providence of Plymouth,"* which ship was owned by Pomeroy, if they may be as soon gotten, or in some other ship with the first expedition that may be to New England; the charges of these three men to be borne equally by all the parties.

Third. Two men more are to be sent this present year, (1622), in the *"Jonathan of Plymouth,"* the charges of them to be borne by all the parties equally.

Fourth. As soon as Thomson and the seven men are landed in New England, Thomson shall, as soon as convenient, find out a fit place to make choice of six thousand acres of land, and a fit place to settle and erect some houses, or buildings for habitations, and to begin the erection of the same. Adjoining these buildings there shall be allotted before the end of five years, six hundred acres of land, which, with all the buildings and everything appertaining to them, shall, at the end of five years, be divided equally between all parties; and all the charges for building, planting, husbanding, &c., during that time shall be equally borne by all. The residue of the six thousand acres to be also divided in a convenient time, between the parties in four parts, whereof Thomson is to have three fourths, and the other three men one fourth.

Fifth. At the end of five years the Island shall be divided into four parts, whereof Thomson was to have three fourths, and the others one fourth.

Sixth. Three fourths of the charge for planting, husbanding and building on the said island, shall be borne by Thomson, and one fourth by his partners.

Seventh. All profits during the five years that may be derived from the six thousand acres, and by fishing and trading, &c. shall be divided equally; the merchants, however, were to have liberty to employ ships to fish at their own charge, if Thomson does not care to participate in the profits of such extra ships.

Eighth. All benefits and profits arising during the five years, on the residue of the six thousand acres, and on the island, shall be divided among the four men, Thomson to have three parts, and the others one part. Each of them shall, on request, deliver a just account of their receipts and payments during the five years.

The above is a summary of the Indenture, which was signed on the 14th of December, 1622, by Thomson, Colomer, Sherwill and Pomeroy, and under which the first settlement of New Hampshire was made. As they then reckoned time, the year 1622 did not end until the 24th of March; so they had ample time to load the ship *"Jonathan of Plymouth,"* and get over here before the end of the year 1622, which was the agreement they would do, and did do; be that as it may, they arrived in the early spring of 1623, as we now reckon the year's beginning, in January instead of March. The Indenture allowed Mr. Thomson to select his "six thousand acres" wherever he might be pleased to settle, in New England. He did make it at Little Harbor, and along the banks of the Pascataqua River. And Edward Hilton, William Hilton and Thomas Roberts were three of the men who settled on that part, at what we now call *"Dover Point."* It seems evident that they came into the transaction through Mr. Pomeroy, who came over in the ship with them. As regards the island, we know it was what is now called Thomson's Island, in Boston Harbor, and has always had that name from the first settlement of Boston. A lawsuit, on record, begun in 1648, to determine the ownership of that island settles the question of who was the first owner of the island,—namely, David Thomson. The suit was brought by his son, who had then become twenty-one years of age; the island had been appropriated by other parties; the Court decided he was the rightful owner, by inheritance from his father, to whom it had been granted in 1622.

We all wish Mr. Thomson had been as gifted in writing as he was in managing business, and had kept a record of his transactions and travels as Gov. Bradford did of Plymouth Colony; unfortunately he left no record or scraps of what he and those with him, did in the years, 1623-1628. We know that he was a young man of twenty-eight or thirty years, by his record in England; from the writings of other men we are able to determine that he commenced his settlement at Little Harbor in the spring of 1623, and the Hiltons commenced that at *Dover Point* at the same time; Thomson remained a year or two at Little Harbor, and then settled permanently on his island in Boston Harbor; the Hiltons remained permanently at *Dover Point.* Following is some of the evidence on which these conclusions are based:

The Rev. William Hubbard, minister of Ipswich, Mass., from 1666 to 1704, wrote his "General History of New England" during the period from 1642, when he graduated from Harvard College, to 1682, when the General Court granted fifty pounds to the author, "as a manifestation of thankfulness" for his history, "he transcribing it fairly that it may be the more easily perused." It was published for the first time in 1815, by the Massachusetts Historical Society; a copy of this first edition is in the Dover Public Library; on page 217 can be found the following:

"Some merchants and other gentlemen in the West of England, belonging to the cities of Exeter, Bristol, Shrewsbury, and towns of Plymouth, Dorchester, etc., incited no doubt by the fame of the plantation begun at New Plymouth in the year 1620, having obtained patents for several parts of New England, from the grand council established at Plymouth, made some attempt of beginning a plantation in some place about Pascataqua River, about the year 1623. For being encouraged by the report of divers mariners that came to make fishing voyages upon that coast, as well as by the aforementioned occasion, they sent over that year one Mr. David Thomson with Mr. Edward Hilton and his brother Mr. William Hilton, who had been fishmongers in London, with some others that came along with them, furnished with necessaries for carrying on a plantation there. Possibly others might be sent in the years following, 1624 and 1625; some of whom first in probability, seized on a place called the Little Harbor, on the west side of Pascataqua River toward or at the mouth thereof; the Hilton's in the meanwhile setting up their stages higher up the river, toward the northwest; at, or about a place since called Dover."

Captain Christopher Levitt, a famous sea Captain, traveller, discoverer, colonizer and historian, left an interesting account, which has been published, of a voyage he made to the New England coast in the summer and fall of 1623; he visited the Isles of Shoals, which he describes very accurately, and in November of that year visited Mr. Thomson and his company at Little Harbor. He calls it "Pannaway," but he is the only writer who has ever so called it; why he used the name has never been explained; Capt. Levitt says:

"The next place I came to was Pannaway, where one Mr. Thomson hath made a plantation. There I staid about a month, in which time I sent my men in the East, (at Agamenticus and York,) who came over in divers ships. At this place I met with the Governor, (of New England, Robert Gorges,) who came thither, (from Plymouth,) in a bark which he had (confiscated) from Mr. Weston about twenty days before I arrived at the land. (Weston had disregarded the orders of the Council of Plymouth.)"

"The Governor then told me that I was joined with him in commission as Counsellor, which being read I found it was so; and he then in the presence of three more of the Council, administered unto me an oath."

"In the time I staid with Mr. Thomson, I surveyed as much as possible I could, the weather being unseasonable and very much snow on the ground."

"In those parts I saw much good timber; but the ground seemed to me not to be good, being very rocky and full of trees and bush wood."

"There is a great store of fowl of divers sorts, whereof I fed very plentifully. About two miles further to the East, (Fort Constitution,) I found a great river and a good harbor, called Pascataway. But for the ground I can say nothing, but by the relation of the Sagamore or King of that place, who told me there was much good ground along the river, about seven or eight leagues above (*Dover Point.*)"

Governor Bradford in his History of Plymouth, under date of 1623, says: "There were also this year some scattering beginnings made in other places, as at Pascataway, by David Thomson, at Monhegan, and some other places, by sundry others."

Thomas Weston, the London merchant who had planned to finance the expense of sending over the *"Mayflower"* and its emigrants, but who backed out of the agreement just as the Pilgrims were on the point of sailing for New England, and left them in great financial straights, was again heard from in the summer of 1622.

At that time he sent over emigrants in two ships, the *"Charity"* and the *"Swan,"* who first landed at Plymouth. There were sixty of these colonists, who appear to have been of a different class of people from those who came over in the *"Mayflower."* They remained there a short time and then selected a place eighteen miles north of Plymouth, at which to begin a settlement, which later was named Weymouth. Weston himself came over in the spring of 1623, with the Maine coast fishing fleet as far as Monhegan, where he left the fleet, and with two men, in a shallop in which he carried a small trading stock. They sailed along the coast, looking for his settlement. When they had reached a point, later known as the Great Boar's Head, a storm capsized the shallop and they barely escaped to the shore alive.

When Weston and his companions gathered themselves up on dry land, with what of their boat had washed ashore, they were attacked by Indians, who were short of guns and clothing. They

POMEROY'S COVE: Landing Place of the First Settlers, in 1623.
(See page 5.)

robbed the men of their guns and most of their clothes, and left them. Weston and his men tramped along the shore, to where they had called on David Thomson, in their journey, a little while before.

Fortunately for the party it was warm summer weather, so they did not suffer, except, may be, with bare feet. Governor Bradford tells the story in his history of affairs and events at Plymouth; he says:—

"He (Weston) got to Pascataquack and borrowed a suit of clothes, and got means, somehow, to come to Plymouth."

It is not recorded what became of Weston's companions; they may have accompanied him to Plymouth, or they may have stayed with Mr. Thomson's hired men and worked in finishing the house at Little Harbor, in which Mr. Thomson had his temporary dwelling, before taking up his permanent residence on the island in Boston Harbor, which has ever since been called Thomson's Island.

The probability is that Weston was taken to Plymouth by Captain Miles Standish, on his return voyage, which is described in Winslow's book,—*"Good News of New England,"* which was published in 1624. In describing the events of 1623, he says:—

"At the same time, Captain Standish, being formerly employed by the Governor to buy provisions for the refurnishing of the colony (at Plymouth) returned with the same, accompanied with Mr. David Thomson, a Scotchman, who also that spring began a plantation twenty-five leagues northeast from us, near Smith's Isles, at a place called Pascataquack, where he liketh well."

This, combined with the preceding quotations, presents unquestionable proof that the settlement, by Thomson and Hilton, was made in 1623. That by Thomson, at Little Harbor, was temporary, as he liked the island in Boston Harbor better. That by Hilton at *Dover Point,* as we call it now, was permanent. In this connection it seems well to explain how Edward Hilton, probably, obtained his title to the town of Dover, through Mr. Leonard Pomeroy, who was a business partner with Mr. Thomson.

The reader will please bear in mind that the year 1622, and all the years before that, and for a century after that, did not end till March 25. So if David Thomson's settlement at Little Harbor is to be counted as the first permanent settlement, then the date for New Hampshire is 1622, instead of 1623, for it is quite certain Thomson arrived at Little Harbor and commenced building his house before March 25.

It is an acknowledged fact that on Nov. 3, 1620, King James granted to certain Englishmen the charter for the . . . "Council of Plymouth for the planting, ordering, ruling and governing New England in America." That corporation was in business fifteen years, and then, 1635, gave back its charter. During those years it granted nine patents, or charters. The first was to Captain John Mason, March 9, 1620-21, four months after the Council commenced business. The last one was also to Capt. Mason, April 22, 1635, from which New Hampshre received its name, and from which the farmers at Dover got, and had to fight, many law suits, which Captain Mason's grandson brought against them, claiming he owned the land, and they were only tenants, like the farmers in England, who had to pay rent to the Lords of the great manors. This grandson claimed he was lord of all present territory of New Hampshire, and the boundary line between it and Massachusetts was not finally settled till in the last decade of the 19th century.

The third grant was given in the spring or early summer of 1622, to David Thomson, who, as the record shows, was then messenger, or special agent, of the Council in its dealings with the King and Parliament. The patent was for . . . "A point of Land in the Pascataway River, in New England, to David Thomson, Mr. Jobe and Mr. Sherwell." This shows that Mr. Thomson had been here and was acquainted with that river and the points of land in it. There is a point of land in Dover, in that river, which has always been called "Thomson's Point" during three centuries. There is no other Thomson from whom it could have received its name. It is the point where a seine, or net, was drawn across the river in the season when salmon and alewives, and other fish went up the river to spawn, in spring time. In that early period, and until the colonists built dams at the falls above, and began to give fish sawdust to feed upon, the Pascataqua River had immense schools of those fish come up the river and the fishermen caught them in that net. No doubt Thomson, Jobe and Sherwell had big crews of fishermen stationed there in the season, and of course they had to have dwellings and "stages" for the workmen, so there was a "temporary" settlement. As late as 1648 "Thomson's Point House" is on the Dover tax list for one pound and four shillings. There is no house there now, and has not been for many years, but Dover can lay claim to the first temporary settlement, as well as for the first permanent settlement, the one in 1622 and the other at *Dover Point* (for a long time called *Hilton's Point*) in 1623.

The fourth grant was issued to David Thomson alone, October 16, of 1622 . . . for "six thousand acres of Land and an island in New England." No mention of the locality of the 6,000 acres, but from later transactions, on record, it is known to have meant an island in Boston Harbor, which has ever since been called "Thomson's Island." It is very evident Mr. Thomson had made up his mind to locate the land on the west side of the Pascataqua River as he had already selected a "point of land in Pascataway River," and had been granted a patent. He wanted some more.

Near the first of December, 1622, an indenture was drawn up between Mr. Thomson and three rich merchants of Plymouth, Abraham Colomer, Nicholas Sherwell and Leonard Pomeroy, in which those gentlemen agreed to join with Mr. Thomson in financing the undertaking, and share in the profits, which seemed to be large. The indenture is published in full in the annual report of the Massachusetts Historical Society, in the summer of 1876. The paper had been read before the Society in the preceding winter by Mr. Charles Deane. It is very interesting, and is one of the most valuable of early documents. In brief:—The merchants agreed to furnish the ship *"Jonathan of Plymouth"* and a crew of men, to take Mr. Thomson and the company across the Atlantic, with provisions and other necessary things for building a house and beginning a settlement, in the winter of 1622. It was also agreed that within three months following, in the year 1622, they would send another ship, the *"Providence of Plymouth"* with another company of men, with provisions, etc., to further aid in making the settlement. On this ship came Edward and William Hilton, and probably Mr. Pomeroy, as the cove where the ship was landed was named "Pomeroy's Cove," and has retained that name to the present day. It is now cut in two parts, by the Dover and Portsmouth railroad. For the first century of Dover that was the shipping point for Dover Neck and *Dover Point*. At one period Major Richard Waldern had a large warehouse there, from which he shipped merchandise to the West Indies, and ports in the Mediterranean sea. Dr. Walter Barefoot, later known as Governor Barefoot, also had a warehouse and dock there, near Waldern's. Barefoot was then a resident physician in Dover.

As is well known the settlement at Little Harbor did not pay, and Thomson went to his island in Boston Harbor in 1625 or 1626, and there resided till his death in December, 1628. That left the 6,000 acres, or such a part of it as belonged to them, by the indenture, on the hands of the Plymouth merchants, and they kept the Hiltons at work at *Dover Point*. That is to say, the three merchants of Plymouth, Colomer, Sherwell and Pomeroy, received their title to the land from David Thomson by indenture; Edward Hilton received his title to it from the Plymouth merchants, who got out of the unprofitable bargain with Thomson as best they could. Hilton had his title renewed and confirmed by the Council of Plymouth, by the Squamscott Patent of 1629, which they gave him. Captain Thomas Wiggin's colonists who came over in 1633, and commenced the settlement on Dover Neck, received their title to the land from Hilton. Those colonists organized a town government, and divided the land amongst themselves and new comers, who might be judged worthy to become citizens. The legal ownership of all land in old Dover was given by that town organization, in the way of "grants." Old Dover consisted of Dover, Somersworth, Durham (Oyster River), Lee, Madbury, and Newington (Bloody Point). Rollinsford was part of Somersworth, till 1849. Of course there was a lot of dickering and trading in which a multitude of names are mentioned in one way or another, but the above statement is the simple way of explanation which leads the reader out of a wilderness of transactions. The organization of New Hampshire was of a later transaction. Dover is fifty years older than New Hampshire. In the old records there is no mention of New Hampshire till 1680 when the scheme was started to separate the Pascataqua towns from Massachusetts, and make them a separate province, in which courts could be organized that might confirm the Mason heirs' claim to ownership of Dover farms, under the 1635 patent given to Captain John Mason, which has the name New Hampshire in it.

Under the circumstances in what better way could Mr. Hubbard state the facts of the beginning of the Pascataqua settlement than he did in the following, copied from his history: "For being encouraged by the report of divers mariners that came to make fishing voyages upon the coast, as well as the afore mentioned occasion (establishing the Plymouth Council), they sent over that year (1623) one Mr. David Thomson with Mr. Edward Hilton and his brother Mr. William Hilton, who had been fishmongers in London, with some others along with them, furnished with necessaries for carrying on a plantation. Possibly others might be sent after them in years following, 1624 and 1625; some of whom, first in probability, seized on the place called Little Harbor, on the west side of Pascataqua River, toward or at the mouth thereof; the Hiltons in the meanwhile setting up their stages higher up the river, toward the northwest, at or about a place since called Dover. But at that place called the Little Harbor, is supposed, was the first house set up, that ever was built in those parts; the chimney and some part of the stone wall (cellar wall) is standing at this day." Mr. Hubbard probably wrote that about 1650, as it is the first part of his manuscript which is now in the possession of the Massachusetts Historical Society.

As regards the name of the settlement of Dover. All the time it was under Edward Hilton's management the settlement is called Pascataqua or Pascataway. When Captain Thomas Wiggin's colonists commenced business they called it Bristol. Later under the pastorate of Rev. Thomas Larkham, who had been minister of the Church at Northam, England, the name changed to Northam, about 1639, and that name was used for a dozen years, or more. At some time under Massachusetts rule the name of Dover came to be used. No reason has yet been found why that name was adopted. None of the old settlers came from Dover, England. Properly the name Pascataqua ought to have been given the State, and it should have extended from the Merrimack to the Kennebec River.

In 1628 Thomas Morton was at the head of a settlement at "Merry Mount," (Wallaston) and was selling firearms and ammunition and rum to the Indians, which caused much trouble. Gov. Bradford of Plymouth ordered him to desist. Morton would not. Bradford sent Capt. Miles Standish, and a company of militia, to arrest Morton. Standish did so and Morton was sent to England for trial and punishment. The expense of the affair was 12 pounds and 7 shillings. The payment was apportioned among the settlements along the coast, from Plymouth to the extreme settlement on the Maine coast, as follows,—Plymouth 2 pounds and 10 shillings;—Naumkeag (Salem) one pound 10 shillings;—Jeffrey and Burselem 2 pounds;—Nan.asket, one pound and 10 shillings; Blackstone at Shawmut (Boston) 12 shillings;—Edward Hilton one pound;—his men at Pascataqua 2 pounds. That shows that Dover was then one of the wealthiest settlements in New England. There was no other settlement, on either side of the Pascataqua River, at that time. This shows the settlement was not a recent affair; they had been in business there five years and had prospered, hand over fist, in trading with the Indians and catching and curing fish. Next to the Isle of Shoals, it was the best place for fishing along the coast.

As previously explained, in speaking of David Thomson, William Hilton came over in the ship *"Providence"* of Plymouth, in the spring of 1623. He did not take his wife and children with him, because they could not be properly cared for, but in 1624, after they had built dwelling houses at *Dover Point* (as we now call it) he went to Plymouth to get his family. He applied to the Church to have his son John, then about two years old, baptized, but the request was denied, on the ground that he was not a member of the Plymouth Church. Thereupon he and his family came up the Pascataqua, and they never had any more dealings with the Plymouth Colony, or Church. So, as William Hilton, Jr., says in his petition of 1660,—"and, in a little tyme following, settled ourselves upon yr River of Paschataq with Mr. Edward and William Hilton, who were the first English planters there." That is to say the "little tyme" was from the summer of 1623 to the summer of 1624. No mystery about that statement. It settles the question beyond doubt that the settlement at *Dover Point* was in the spring of 1623, or it may have been June. Probably David Thomson got his house built at Little Harbor a few months before Edward Hilton had his habitation in order, so Hubbard is correct in saying,—"But at that place, called the Little Harbor, it is supposed was the first house set up, that was ever built in those parts; the chimney and some part of the stone wall, is standing at this day" (about 1650).

William Hilton did not build his house on *Dover Point*, but as soon as he had investigated the territory on both sides of the river he decided to make a bargain with the Indians, then owners of what is now Eliot, and bought their "corn field," and land around it, and built his house there; directly across Pascataqua River from *Dover Point;* there was his residence till 1632, when he was dispossessed by Captain Walter Neal, "governor" of the settlement begun at Strawberry Bank, by Captain John Mason in 1630, the famous "Laconia" company. They claimed their charter gave them the land on the east side of the Pascataqua River, so ousted Mr. Hilton, and gave it to one of the Laconia Company's men. There was no court to protect Hilton in his rights, till 1653. The Province of Maine came under the jurisdiction of Massachusetts in November, 1652, and the Court Records of Oct. 25, 1653, show that William Hilton recovered judgment in the sum of one hundred and sixty pounds against Ann Mason, executrix of the Will of Captain John Mason of London, deceased. Of this sum 50 pounds, were "for the interest for his land, which the defendant took from him, and for the vacancy of one year's time, and cutting down his house, and for other injuries, ten pounds, and for the interest for the whole sixty pounds for the term of one and twenty years, one hundred pounds."—Twenty-one years carries us back to 1632, the time when William Hilton was planting corn just across the river from *Dover Point*. Various old records speak of this "old corn field" as belonging to William Hilton till he was dispossessed by the Laconia Company's Governor, Walter Neal.

After he was driven out of Eliot, William Hilton was busy with business in Dover and vicinity. In 1636, he and his son, William, obtained the grant of land at Pennacook from the Indian Sagamore Tahanto. In 1644, he was Deputy for Dover in the Massachusetts General Court. He received grants of land from the town of Dover. He was in business at Exeter a while. In 1646 he became a resident at Warehouse Point, Kittery, and his residence, for the rest of his life, was in Kittery and York. An honored and able man he died at York in 1656.

William Hilton, Jr., was born in England in 1615, hence was nine years old when he and his mother came to *Dover Point* to live. A boy of that age would have no difficulty in remembering his travels with his parents. Now, what did he say about it? His petition to the General Court was as follows: Date 1660.—"To the Honored General Court, now assembled at Boston, the petition of William Hilton humbly showeth:

Whereas your petitioner's father, William Hilton, came over into New England about the year Anno Dom. 1621, & your petitioner came about one year and a half after (July 1623) and in a little tyme following (one year) settled upon yr River of Paschataq with Mr. Edward Hilton, who were the first English Planters there. William Hilton having much intercourse with the Indians by way of trayed & mutual giving & receiving, amongst whom one Tahanto, Sagamore of Penacooke, for divers kindnesses, received from yr petitioner's Father & himself, did freely give unto ye aforesaid William Hilton, Seniour & William Hilton, Juniour, six Miles of Land lying on ye River Penneconaquigg, being a rivulette running into Penacooke River to ye eastward, ye said Land to be bounded as may bee most for ye best accomodation of yr sd petitioner, his heyeres & assignes. The said Tahanto did also give to ye said father & son & to their heres forever, two miles of ye best Meddow Land lying on ye north east side of ye River Pennecooke, adjoining to ye sd River, with all ye appurtenances, which said tract of Land & Meddow hath, were given in ye presence of Fejld and severall Indians, in ye year 1636. At which tyme Tahanto went with ye aforesaid Hiltons to the Lands and thereof gave them possession. All of wch is commonly known to ye Ancient Inhabitants at Paschatq; and for the further confirmation of ye sd gift or grant your petitioner hath renewed deeds from ye said Tahanto; & since your petitioner understands that there bee many grants of Land lately given, there about, to bee layed out:—And lest any should be mistaken in chooseing their place & thereby intrench apon yr petitioner's rights, for preventing whereof:—Your petitioner humbly craveth that his grant may bee Confirmed by this Court, and that A.—B.—C.—, or any two of them, may be fully Impowered to sett forth ye bounds of all ye above mentioned Lands & make true returne whereof unto this Honored Court. And your Petitioner, as hee is in duty bound, will pray for your future welfare & prosperity.

"Boston June 1, 1660. The Committee having considered the contents of this petition, do not judge meet that ye Court grant ye same, but having considered the petitioner's ground, for ye approbaccon of ye Indian's grant doe judge meet that 300 acres of sd Land bee sett out to ye Petitioner by a Committee chosen by this Court, so as that it may not prejudice any plantation, & this as a finall end & issue of all future claims by virtue of the grant from the Indians."

THOMAS DANFORTH
ELEA LUSHER
HENRY BARTHOLOMEW

The Magists approve of this return if theire ye Depu'ts Consent hereunto.

EDWARD RAWSON, *Secretary.*

Consented to by ye Deputies.

WILLIAM TORRY, *Cleris.*

(Endorsed). The Petition of William Hilton, entered with ye Magistrates, 30 May 1660, & ex.pd'ents Tahanto's Deed and p. Mr. Dant. William Hilton's petition entered & referred to the Committee.

At the time this petition was presented to the Court Mr. William Hilton, Jr., was a resident of Charlestown, Mass., and he was well known by the General Court. For the clearer understanding of the evidence I will give a brief of the career of William Hilton, Jr. He was born in England in 1615. He came over to Plymouth, Mass., with his mother in 1623. He came up to *Dover Point* with his parents in the summer of 1624. He resided with his parents at the farm, just across the river from *Dover*

Point, where his father had purchased an Indian "corn field," as before stated. Of course he lived and worked as all the other boys of the period had to do. When he was twenty-one he was a partner with his father in the purchase of the Tahanto Indian land. About that time he married, and settled in Newbury, Mass. He became one of its prominent citizens, and held various town offices, being Representative for Newbury in the General Court. He had quite a large family of children. His wife died in 1657, and later he married and had another family of children. In 1654 he removed to Charlestown, Mass., and resided there till his death in 1675, aged 60 years. He was a man of much ability. The old records show that among other occupations he was a navigator and a cartographer.

A brief sketch of Rev. William Hubbard, the historian, who declares in his *"General History of New England"* that Edward and William Hilton commenced the settlement at *Dover Point* in 1623, and it was the first permanent settlement in New Hampshire, may very appropriately be inserted at this point:

He was born in England in 1621, and came over to New England when he was a boy, and was educated at Harvard College, graduating in the first class that institution sent out. That was in 1642; there were nine in the class, and Hubbard ranked third, as appears in the catalogue. At graduation he was 21, and like all young graduates engaged in teaching, and soon commenced studying for the ministry. He was a natural born historian, and so commenced collecting and arranging facts, and incidents, as he found them in old records of Gov. Winthrop and others, and also obtained from interviews with the "Ancient Inhabitants." Any one who has engaged in historical, or genealogical work, knows how he had to get his material, and facts, by hard and continual work.

In 1655 he became associate minister of the Church at Ipswich, Mass., and held the office of minister from 1666 till his death in 1704. So he was contemporary with William Hilton, Jr. He was also contemporary with Edward Hilton, uncle of William, Jr., as Edward lived at Exeter during the last thirty years of his life, and died there in December, 1671. It is absurd to suppose

Mr. Hubbard did not consult those gentlemen in his search for facts regarding the beginning of the Dover settlements. There need be no doubt he consulted those men and got the statement direct from Edward Hilton himself, that Edward and William Hilton came to *Dover Point* in 1623. So the statement in his history is correct.

Mr. Hubbard finished the manuscript of the history in 1682, and sold it on October 11 of that year. The General Court voted that day to give him fifty pounds for it. The first publication of it was made in 1815, by the Massachusetts Historical Society. The manuscript had been consulted by all writers after 1682. The Rev. Dr. Jeremy Belknap is among the number. So when it came into the hands of the Historical Society the editors say,— "Of the MS copy a few pages at the beginning and end are mutilated, and the writing in some places is scarcely legible. These passages are given as far as the editors could spell them out. Where they have supplied words, or portions of words, conjecturally, such are printed in italics. Where they were at a loss, they have used asterisks." The MS is well written and has 336 pages. The story of Dover begins on page 141 and occupies ten pages. There are no italics or asterisks in it. The reading is perfect. The MS is in possession of the Massachusetts Historical Society. It was among the first topics Mr. Hubbard wrote, after Plymouth and Boston. Later, when the ecclesiastical troubles began at Dover Neck, Mr. Hubbard gives a more elaborate notice of affairs at Pascataqua. He was always specially interested in Church affairs, so gave only a brief of the beginning at *Dover Point* by the Hiltons. He says, of the beginning of settlements,—"At present therefore (I shall) only insist upon what is most memorable about the first planting thereof, after it came first to be discovered by Captain (John) Smith, and some others, employed on that design, about the year 1614 and 1615."

To give the readers a clear and concise understanding of the evidence presented in this paper, I give the following briefs.

1. Before 1622 David Thomson had been here and located the Pascataqua River, and made up his mind what to do. In June or July, 1622, he obtained from the Council of Plymouth a grant,—

"A Point of Land in the Pascataway River in New England." There is such a point which to this day has always been called "Thomson's Point." It had a house on it, which was on the Dover Tax list as late as 1648, where is the statement,—"Thomson Point House, one pound, 4 shillings," tax.

2. Oct. 12, 1622, the Council of Plymouth gave David Thomson another grant,—*"Six thousand acres and an island."* By later transactions it was shown that the island is in Boston Harbor. No mention of where he was to select his 6,000 acres. Evidently he had settled that question when he was over here and looked out the *"Point of land."* It is on record that he did come over here and make a settlement at Little Harbor, in 1623, but in 1625, or 1626, he changed his permanent residence to the island in Boston Harbor, and there resided till he died in December, 1628. So it appears David Thomson had two temporary residences in New Hampshire, the first of which was in Dover, in 1622. Those who want authority on this matter are referred to the annual report of the Massachusetts Historical Society for 1876. Charles Dean obtained the paper from Hon. Robert C. Winthrop, who inherited it from his ancestors.

3. William Hilton, Jr., gives reliable testimony, that settles the question of date, as in the spring of 1623, by Edward and William Hilton.

4. Rev. William Hubbard, author of,—"A General History of New England," gives record of the fact that Edward and William Hilton commenced the permanent settlement of New Hampshire at *Dover Point* in 1623. Mr. Hubbard had ample opportunity to obtain the information direct from Mr. Edward Hilton, as they were contemporaries, Mr. Hubbard in Ipswich and Mr. Hilton in Exeter. There was constant intercourse between those towns.

5. As further proof that Dover was settled before 1630, is a record of 1628, when Edward Hilton paid one pound as his share of the expense of arresting Thomas Morton and sending him to England, and the other settlers there with him, names not mentioned, paid two pounds, showing that *Dover Point* had the most wealth of any settlement in New England at that time. Of course

they had not then just commenced business. They had been at it five years. At that time there was no other settlement on either side of the Pascataqua River.

6. The Squamscott Patent of 1629, which was given by the Council of Plymouth to protect Hilton from aggressions from the Laconia Company, whose territory was all around his land, acknowledged the land belonged to Hilton and his company. He obtained his original possession, as a part of Thomson's 6,000 acres through the merchants of Plymouth, who financed Thomson's venture at Little Harbor and Thomson's Island, Boston Harbor.

HOW LONG DID THOMSON RESIDE AT LITTLE HARBOR?

To show that the settlement at Little Harbor (Odiorne's Point) was only temporary it is fair to consider the question how long Thomson did remain there. The Historian, Mr. Hubbard, says Thomson settled there in 1623 and abandoned the place "the next year."

Bradford's History of Plymouth says Thomson was at "Pascataway" in 1626, and that he joined with the governor of Plymouth and Mr. Winslow in an expedition to purchase goods at Monhegan (Me.), where the owners broke up their establishment and sold out to the highest bidders.

It appears, in the statement, that when Winslow and Thomson arrived at Monhegan they found other parties bidding for the articles, and when the managers saw there was a lively bidding by the competitors, the prices were put up. Then Winslow and Thomson stopped bidding and withdrew for consultation. The result was that instead of bidding against each other, they decided to purchase the whole lot of material, and then divide it between them, so get the stuff at a much smaller price. Among the lot were some fine animals,—goats, swine, etc. Mr. Thomson took some of these animals with his other selections and carried them to Thomson's Island, not to Little Harbor. At the Island he engaged in the business of raising goats and hogs for sale to the other settlements along the New England coast. It is said he did a flourishing and prosperous business.

As regards the settlement at Little Harbor there is no mention of it in current literature of the period after 1626, till 1630, when Captain John Mason's emigrants came over in the bark *"Warwick,"* and commenced the settlement at Strawberry Bank, under command of Captain Walter Neal, which, in 1653, the Massachusetts General Court honored by giving it the name Portsmouth. This was the beginning of the great Laconia "expectations" grant, which included everything (in New Hampshire territory) outside of Edward Hilton's settlement at *Hilton Point*. To protect his rights Mr. Hilton obtained from the Plymouth Council his "Squamscot Patent."

CONCERNING THOMSON'S ISLAND.

What is there to show that Thomson's Island in Boston Harbor was the permanent residence of David Thomson after 1626? In his personal grant of 1622 it stated the territory to be,—"6,000 acres and an Island, in New England." The indenture does not show the locality of the acres or the island in New England. Evidently Mr. Thomson did not regard that as necessary as he had been over here and settled that question, in his own mind, when he was catching salmon and other fish at Thomson's Point, where the Cochecho flows into the Newichawannock River. The 6,000 acres were on the west bank of the Pascataqua and Newichawannock Rivers. The Island was in Boston Harbor, and has kept the name ever since. Mr. Thomson's contemporaries and later court transactions settle that question.

Mr. Charles W. Tibbetts, editor and publisher of the *"New Hampshire Genealogical Record,"* when in England examined the records in the "Parish of St. James, Clarkenwell, London, England," and found that David Thomson was on record there as son of Richard Tomson and Florence Cramlan, his wife; and was born Dec. 17, 1592. From other records he learned that David Thomson married Amias Cole in 1613. They resided in England ten years. She did not come over with him on the first voyage (1622-3), but did come over about 1624. They had a son born about 1626; they named him John Thomson. David Thomson died in December, 1628, aged 36 years.

It is a matter of record in Shurtleff's History of Boston that in 1627 David Thomson assisted Samuel Maverick in building a house on Nodell's Island (East Boston), which was fortified with four "great guns," when completed. This shows these two men were neighbors and friends. After the death of Mr. Thomson the family friendship was continued by Mr. Maverick's marrying the widow Thomson. To them were born three children, and her son, John Thomson, grew up with the Maverick children. Mr. Maverick was a very able man and a good step-father.

Mrs. Amias (Thomson) Maverick sent the following letter, of date of Nov. 20, 1635, to Robert Trelawney, merchant at Plymouth, England, which is interesting and shows that she had Thomson children in Plymouth at that time.

Nottels Island, 20 Nov. 1635.:—

Good Sir:—I kindly salute you in the Lord. I am given to understand by divers that my father is very much increased against me, but by what means I know not, and that he hath offered to make the sale of his lands, notwithstanding he conveyed it to me, by his deed (whic I doubt not will prove sufficient) and had of me fifty pounds (£50) in consideration of it, that so the land might remain to me and my children, after my father's decease. And now I am informed my father would fain dispose of the land and repay me the fifty pounds. Now my humble request unto your worship is that as you loved my first husband so you would do me and *my fatherless children* the favor to speak to my father concerning this thing, that it may remain with him for my children, etc."

"Amias Maverick."

"Received July 4, 1636."

All the above statements show that Mr. Thomson had ceased to be a resident of Little Harbor (Odiorne's Point). Following is further evidence he was a permanent resident on Thomson's Island, the remaining years of his life.

In 1635, not knowing David Thomson ever had a grant of the Island, the officials of the Bay Colony granted it to the town of Dorchester, which town held possession a dozen years. In 1647 John Thomson, son of David, became of age and entered suit, by petition, to have the Island restored to him, he being the rightful heir of his father, who had received it by grant from the Council of Plymouth. In his petition he states that his father began to occupy it "in or about 1626." Shurtleff's History tells the whole story, which is very interesting, but does not need to be repeated here.

Among the witnesses at the trial were Capt. Miles Standish and William Trevore, who came over in the *"Mayflower,"* in 1620. Trevore visited Boston Harbor in 1621; Trevore testified that he took possession of the island that year, under the name of the Island of Trevore, for Mr. David Thomson, then of London; he also testified that Mr. Thomson obtained a grant of the island from the Council of Plymouth some years before the Massachusetts Bay Colony had its grant.

Captain Standish testified that he knew Mr. Thomson as a resident of the island. Mr. William Blaxton, who was a resident on the peninsula of Boston some years before the Massachusetts Bay Company settled there in 1630, testified that he knew Mr. Thomson well, as a resident on Thomson's Island, where he was prosperously engaged in raising hogs and goats for trade with the Colonists.

There was much other testimony which convinced the authorities and the Court that John Thomson's claim was just and legal; and accordingly the island was restored to him, much to the grief and vexation of the town of Dorchester.

The Court decision, therefore, settles beyond question that David Thomson was a permanent resident of Thomson's Island from 1626 until his death in 1628. It appears from the testimony of Trevore, that he was the person who informed Mr. Thomson about that island, and that Thomson the very next year obtained a patent for it, 16th of October, 1622.

WHAT ABOUT MASON HALL?

In all the histories the story is repeated that David Thomson built a house on what is now called Odiorne's Point; that it was a spacious and elegant house, built in the style of the great mansions in England, in which the Lords of great manors then resided, and in which their descendents reside to this day. How beautiful and grand it seems as you picture it in your mind's eye! The histor-

THOMSON'S POINT: Junction of the Cochecho and Newichawannock Rivers. The Thomson Grant of 1622. (See page 6.)

ians not only say it was a grand mansion, but also that he called it *"Mason Hall."* Well, what about it? There never was any "Mason Hall." In the first place if Mr. Thomson had built such a fine house, there was not the slightest reason why he should name it for Capt. John Mason, who never invested a penny in sending over emigrants before 1630, and had no interest whatever in Thomson's grant of land. Moreover, Mr. Thomson had no time, material or workmen, such as would be absolutely needed for the construction of such an edifice. For example, it is stated as a fact that it took an expert carpenter a year to do the carving and finishing of the Council Chamber in the Governor Wentworth house, at Little Harbor, which was not built till more than a century after David Thomson built the first house at Odiorne's Point, just across the Little Harbor from the Governor's house.

Consider the situation of things when Mr. Thomson anchored his good ship, *"Jonathan of Plymouth,"* in a southwest cove of Little Harbor, in the spring of 1623. The beautiful plateau of Odiorne's Point was covered with a heavy growth of pines, and all the land around was a forest untouched with axe since the forest primeval first started, as the glaciers of the ice age receded and exposed the earth to sunshine.

Evidently the first work the men did was to clear the land of the forest; they had axes and strong muscles, but no saw-mill to cut up lumber, of which there was more than enough.

Mr. Thomson had his men convert those huge trees into a large log house in the quickest time possible; it was capacious and substantial, but there could not have been very ornamental work. The chimney was built of stone, at the north end of the house, and the mortar was tough clay, from a clay bank near by. No doubt they had the house completed before Capt. Levett and Governor Robert Gorges and the Councillors paid Mr. Thomson a visit, in November, 1623, when he entertained them a month, as Capt. Levett says. Whatever the architecture was then, fifty years later the historian Hubbard says on page 214 of his "General History of New England": "But at that place called Little Harbor, it is supposed was the first house set up, that ever was built in those parts; the chimney and some part of the stone wall, is standing at this day (1675)." This is proof that the house had fallen to ruin. At the present time (1923) nothing remains to mark the spot but a few stones that are supposed to have been the foundation on which the chimney stood. These are on the north side of the drive-way leading from the State road to the monument erected by the Society of Colonial Dames in 1894.

EDWARD HILTON.

There is no record of any transactions or business agreements between Edward Hilton and David Thomson; nor has there been found any statement showing why Mr. Hilton settled on a part of Mr. Thomson's grant of six thousand acres in 1623, in nearly the same month; but these facts are known, and give a reasonable explanation of how the arrangement came about. Mr. Leonard Pomeroy, as has already been shown by the "Indenture," had a one-fourth interest in the land venture; Mr. Pomeroy owned the ship *"Providence"* in which Hilton's party came over; a cove at *Hilton's Point* where the *"Providence"* landed, was named Pomeroy's Cove; and probably Mr. Pomeroy was a passenger on the *"Providence"* in its pioneer voyage up the Pascataqua River. So it is a fair inference to draw from this that the *Hilton Point* territory was Mr. Pomeroy's portion of the six thousand acres, and the Hiltons settled there under his management or at his request. Mr. Hilton must have known before he sailed from Plymouth that the Pascataqua River was in the section of New England where Mr. Thomson designed to locate his grant, otherwise he would not have come here, immediately following the ship *"Jonathan."* One thing is certain: he came, and he remained here. Mr. Thomson came, and soon went away to Thomson Island in Boston Harbor.

At this time Edward Hilton was a young man of twenty-two or twenty-three years, and when he commenced the settlement on the Pascataqua River, which later developed into Dover, he was twenty-six or twenty-seven. His brother William was a few years older. Mr. Pomeroy, his coadjutor in the venture, was about fifty years of age. He was member of the local Council of Plymouth in 1612 and later and mayor of that city in 1623, and was a wealthy and active man of business. It appears that he was the financial manager of the founding of Dover as Capt. John Mason was of Portsmouth seven years later, in 1630.

Edward Hilton was no common fisherman as some might erroneously infer from the statement made by all the New Hampshire historians, that he was "a fishmonger of London." While in England in 1873-74 Mr. John T. Hassam visited Fishmongers' Hall in London, which is the headquarters of one of the oldest and wealthiest guilds, or great companies, in that ancient city; its records date far back of the beginning of settlements in New England when the fishing business was very profitable for those who owned ships and had the means to employ men to come over here and catch fish for the English market; that was what the Fishmongers' Guild did; and admission to membership was a very rigid and exclusive operation; none but well-to-do men could get in. Mr. Hassam asked permission to examine the records from 1600 to 1623, with the purpose in view of ascertaining when Edward and William Hilton became members of the guild. The clerk in charge of the old records would not permit him, at first, to look at them, but said he would make an examination and report what he might find. A short time after, Mr. Hassam called again and the official informed him that Edward Hilton was admitted as a Freeman in the year 1621, and what appeared to be "Pawl Hilton" in 1616. Mr. Hassam then asked permission to look at the word "Pawl"; the clerk courteously consented for him to do so; on careful examination, he came to the conclusion that the man who made the record intended it for "William Hilton." There was no question about Edward Hilton's name. This shows the social and business standing of Edward Hilton in London, in 1621.

On November 7, 1629, Captain John Mason received his grant or patent from the Council of Plymouth, which is known as the "New Hampshire Patent" from which the State finally received its name. Its coast boundary was from the Merrimack to the Pascataqua River; and back into the country to Milton Three Ponds, and thence northwestward till three score miles be finished. The other line was the Merrimack River to its source (The Weirs of Winnepesaukee Lake). And then in a direct line to head of the easterly boundary. This, of course, covered every part of Mr. Edward Hilton's grant. So to protect his property he had the Council of Plymouth grant him what is known as the

Squamscot Patent, defining his territory, against any claims Capt. Mason or his heirs might set up. This Patent bears date of March 12, 1629-30, only four months after Mason's date of November, 1629. Here is a copy of the document:

THE HILTON OR SQUAMSCOT PATENT.

Know ye that said President and Council by virtue and authority of his Majesty's said Letters Patent, and for and in consideration that Ed Hilton and his Associates hath already at his and their own proper cost and charge transported sundry servants to plant in New England aforesaid, at a place there called by the natives Wecannecohunt, otherwise Hilton's Point, lying some two leagues from the mouth of the River Paskataquack, in New England aforesaid, *where they have already built some houses and planted Corne.* And for that he doth further intend by God's Divine Assistance to transport thither more people and cattle, to the good increase and advancement, and for the better settling and strengthening of their plantation, as also that they may be better encouraged to proceed in so pious a work which may especially tend to the propagation of Religion, and the great increase of trade, to his Majesty's Realms and Dominions, and the advancement of public plantations—

Have given, granted and Engrossed and confirmed, and by this their present writing, doe fully, clearly and absolutely give, grant, Enfeoffe and Confirme unto the said Edward Hilton, his heirs and Assigns forever: All that part of the River Pascataquack, called or known by the name of Wecanacohunt, or Hilton's Point, with the south side of said River, up to the fall of the River, and three miles into the main land by all the breadth aforesaid; Together with all the shores, creeks, bays, harbors, and coasts alongst the sea, within the limits and bounds aforesaid, with woods and islands next adjoining to the land not being already granted by said Council unto any other person or persons, together also with all the lands, rivers, mines, minerals of what kind or nature soe ever, etc. etc.;

To have and to hold all and singular the said lands and premises, etc. etc. unto said Edward Hilton, his heirs and assigns, etc. they paying unto our sovereign Lord the King, one fifth part of gold or silver ores, and another fifth part to the Council aforesaid and their successors, by the rent hereafter in these presents reserved, yielding and paying therefor yearly forever, unto said Council, their successors or assigns, for every one hundred acres of said land in use, the sum of twelve pence of Lawful money of England into the hands of the Rent gatherer for the time being, of the said Council, for all services whatsoever:— And the said Council for the affairs of England, in America aforesaid, do by these presents nominate, depute, authorize, appoint, and in their place and stead put William Blackston, of New England, in America, aforesaid, Clerk: William Jeffries and Thomas Lewis, of the same place, Gents, and either or any of them jointly or separately, to be their (the Council's), true and lawful Attorney or Attorneys, and in their name and stead to enter into each part or portion of land and other premises with the appointments by these presents given and granted, or into some part thereof in the name of the whole, and peaceable and quiet possession and seisin thereof for them to take, and the same so had and taken in their name and stead, to deliver possession & seisin thereof unto Edward Hilton, the said Edward Hilton, his heirs, associates and assigns, according to the tenor, forme and effect of these presents, Ratifying, Conforming and allowing all & whatsoever the said Attorney, or Attorneys, or either of them, shall doe in and about the Premises by virtue hereof.

In witness whereof the said Councll for the affairs of New England in America aforesaid, have hereunto caused their Common Seal to be put, the twelfth day of March, Anno: Domi: 1629. (1630, N. S.)

Ro. Warwick.

Memo: That upon the seventh day of July, Anno: Domi: Annoq|; R's Caroli pri. Septimo: By Virtue of a warrant of Attorney within mentioned from the Council of the affairs in New England, under their common Seal unto Thomas Lewis, he the said Thomas Lewis had taken quiet possession of the within mentioned premises and livery and seisin thereof, hath given to the within named Edward Hilton in the presence of us:

           THOMAS WIGGIN,
           WM. HILTON.
           SAM'L SHARPE.
           JAMES DOWNE.

Vera copia efficit per nos.
    Tim: Nicholas.
    Pet. Coppur.
Vera Copia, Attest, Rich: Partridge, Cleric.

WILLIAM HILTON.

William Hilton, brother of Edward, was one of the party that settled at *Hilton's Point,* in 1623. What of him? He was five years older than Edward; he was admitted to membership in the Fishmongers' Guild, in London, in 1616, and was an active member until he came to Plymouth, New England, arriving November 11, 1621, in the ship *"Fortune."* He returned in the autumn of 1622, and came over with his brother Edward to Pascataqua, in 1623. His wife and two children came over to Plymouth in the ship, *"Ann,"* in the summer of 1623, and in the summer of 1624 came from Plymouth to *Hilton's Point,* and resided there as long as his brother did, engaged in business with him. He was Deputy to the Massachusetts General Court, in 1644, and probably in other years.

After Exeter was settled he had grants of land there. He also had grants of land in Dover. He had a cornfield, in what is now Eliot, directly across the river from *Dover Point.* It was an old cornfield, which the Indians had used during an unknown period before the Hiltons settled on the Point. Later he built a house and resided there, until he was driven off by Capt. Walter Neal, governor of Capt. John Mason's settlement at Strawberry Bank, who claimed that the land belonged to Mason, under the Laconia grant.

Capt. Neal very summarily destroyed Hilton's house, and granted the land to Capt. Thomas Cammock, June 2, 1633; he designates the grant, as—"Where William Hilton lately planted corne." Hilton brought a suit against Mrs. Mason to recover it; and it was not till twenty years later that the case was decided, after Maine came under Massachusetts rule. It was October 25, 1653, that judgment was given, in his favor, against Mrs. Ann Mason, executrix of Capt. John Mason, and she had to pay him one hundred and sixty pounds, instead of restoring the land which had been occupied by some one during the twenty years. It was his land and his house that Capt. Neal dispossessed him of; the Court so decided, and that, of course, by right of the David Thomson six thousand acres patent. No doubt he began planting corn there soon after the settlement was begun on *Hilton's Point,* as it was an old Indian cornfield, all ready to be worked.

He was assistant justice at Dover in 1642. Later he removed to Kittery Point, where, October 27, 1648, he was licensed to keep a public house at Warehouse Point, near Phyllis' Notch. He had ferry boats which ran to various points on the Great Island and Strawberry Bank side of the river.

In 1650, Mr. Hilton removed to York, where he was one of the signers that made that town come under the rule of Massachusetts, 22 November, 1652, and took the oath of freeman; there were fifty signers. He was one of the Selectmen of York in 1652, '53, '54. He owned the Ferry across York River. He died there in 1655 or '56, as letters of administration are dated, 30 June, 1656, to his son-in-law, Richard White.

THOMAS ROBERTS.

Another man who came over with Edward Hilton in 1623, was Thomas Roberts, who has lineal descendants, in the name, residing on Dover Neck, at the present time (1923), on the very land that he owned two hundred and seventy-five years ago. He was made President of the Court in March or April, 1640, hence Governor of the Colony at Dover, succeeding Capt. John Underhill, which office he held until Dover finally came under the rule of Massachusetts Bay Colony, in 1642-3. His residence at *Dover Point*, after he commenced housekeeping was near that of Edward Hilton's, where Hilton Hall is. After Mr. Hilton removed his residence to the present town of Newfields, Mr. Roberts changed his residence to the Neck, and built his house on the bank of Fore River. The spot has been marked with a granite tablet, which can be easily found, on the easterly side of Mr. William M. Courser's field.

Mr. Roberts was a liberal minded man, and very independent in his views, for that reason he favored giving the Quaker Missionaries a fair hearing when they visited Dover in 1662, and later. His sons took an opposite view, and championed the cause of the First Church. They obeyed the orders of the Court.

Mr. Roberts died Sept. 27, 1673. His grave is in the old burial ground, a short distance above the old meeting-house lot. It has a slate stone properly marked, for visitors to find when desired. It is in the northeast corner of the lot.

WHAT WERE THE EMPLOYMENTS OF THESE FIRST SETTLERS?

What were the employments of these first settlers? Of course the first work was to build houses of logs in which to live, and clear land enough on which to "set up their stages" for curing fish, and then engage in fishing which was then the great money-making occupation. Edward Hilton's house stood where now (1923) is located Hilton Hall. There was another house on the summit of the hill on the southerly side of the *"Point."* As the village grew, other houses were built, as the wants of the new comers demanded.

Just what style of architecture was used in putting the logs together is not known, but we have a description of one that was built near Cape Elizabeth, Portland Harbor, by John Winter, ten years later. He was the agent of Robert Trelawney, at one time mayor of Plymouth, England, proprietor of the settlement at the Cape. In one of his reports Mr. Winter gave Mr. Trelawney the following description of the house; it may have been the same style as Hilton's first house. Mr. Winter says:

"Now for our buildings and planting; I have built a house here at Richmond Island that is forty feet in length, and eighteen foot broad within the sides, besides the chimney (outside); and the chimney is large with an oven in each side of him. And he is so that we can place a kettle within the mantle-piece. We can brew or bake, or boil our kettle within him, with the help of another house that I have built at the side of our house, where we set our sieves and mill and mortar in to break our corne and malt, and to dress our meal in."

"I have two chambers in him, and all our men lies in one of them. Every man hath his close boarded cabin, (bunks like a ship, one above another,) and I have room enough to make a dozen close boarded cabins more, if I have need of them; and in the other chamber I have room to put the ship sails into, and allow dry goods which is in casks; and I have a store house in him that will hold 18 or 20 tuns of casks underneath. Also underneath I have a kitchen for our men to set and drink in, and a stewards room that will hold two tuns of casks, which we put our bread and beer into. And every one of these rooms is closed with locks and keys unto them."

THE FISHERY BUSINESS.

Nine years before the settlement was commenced at *Hilton Point*, Capt. John Smith visited the Isles of Shoals, (July, 1614), and on his return to England gave such a report of it that the locality soon became a famous fishing station for English fishermen, and in 1623, when Capt. Christopher Levett visited there, as already mentioned, he found quite a settlement of fishermen. In passing it may be well to state here that Robert Gorges, son of Sir Ferdinando Gorges, was the first Governor General of New England, and Capt. Levett was one of his Council; when Governor Gorges died, in 1624, Capt. Levett became his successor in office. Capt. Levett, in his published report of his visit in November, 1623, gives a brief description of the Shoals. He saw six fishing vessels there; each of the six carried fifty men, as he informs us was the custom, and he says the shores were inconveniently crowded with fishing stages, and the islands were a place of busy activity, surpassed only by Plymouth, in New England.

It was the usual course of the fishery in those days, for about one-third of each crew to live ashore, and attend to the drying and curing of the catch, while the remainder, in their pinnaces and shallops, cruised about the neighboring ocean in quest of mackerel or cod. Shelter for the large number of shoremen, out of these ships would, of course, be essential, and numerous cabins must have already been built for their accommodation.

The fishing stages, which Capt. Levett speaks of, were floating platforms, projecting from the shore of the Islands into the waters of the harbor, and the rocks at the shore end were roofed over by an open shed, used for the splitting and salting of the fish, which were afterwards dried upon flakes, farther inland. Captain Levett says the harbor was inconveniently crowded with these stages, and that statement gives a clear perception of the extent of business that was being carried on there when the Hiltons came up the Pascataqua and commenced their settlement.

In Captain John Smith's General History, pp. 188, 201, he says: "In March, April, May and half of June here (at the Shoals) is cod in abundance. The salvages (Indians) compare the store in the sea with the hairs upon their heads, and surely there are an incredible abundance of them upon the coast. Then, too, young boyes and girles, salvages or any other, be they never such *idles,* may turne, carry, or return a fish, without shame or any great pain. He is very idle, that is past twelve years of age, and cannot do so much, and she is very old, that cannot spin a threed to make lines to catch fish."

"He is a very bad fisher, that cannot kill (catch) in one day with his hook and line one, two or three hundred cods. And is it not pretty sport to pull up two pence, six pence, and twelve pence, as fast as you can hale and veare a line? And what sport doth yield a more pleasing content, and less hurt or charge, than angling with a hook, and crossing the sweete Ayre from Ile to Ile over the silent streams of a calm sea? wherein the most curious may find pleasure, profit and content."

In 1618 Capt. Smith wrote a letter to the great Lord Bacon in regard to this fishing business. It can be found on page 42, Vol. I, Collection of State Papers, of which the following is a paragraph:

"New England hath much advantage to serve all Europe (with fish) far cheaper than they can (at the Grand Banks, etc.), who have neither wood, salt nor foode, but at a great rate, nothing to help them, but what they carry in their shipps, 2 or 300 leagues from their habitacon, noe Port or harbor, but the mayne sea. Wee (have) the fishing at our dores & the helpe of the land for wood, water, fruites, fowle, corne, or what wee want to refresh us when we list." "That all sortes of Timber for shipping is most plentiful there, all those which return can testifye." "Now if a shippe can gain 59 or 60 pounds in the 100, only by fishing, spending as much time in going and coming, as in staying there, were I there planted, seeing the fish in their seasons serveth the most part of the yeare, and with a little labour I could make all the salt I could use, I can conceive no reason to distrust, but double and triple their gaines, that all the former charge and can fish but two months."

These quotations from such men as Captain John Smith and Capt. Levett show that there was a settlement at the Shoals in 1623, and that it was a profitable business catching cod fish, mackerel and other kinds, of which, in the season, the water was abounding in. It is unreasonable to suppose that the Hiltons and their crews of men would not go there and fish with the other crews in March, April and May. But, aside from all that, the rivers about *Hilton Point* in 1623, and many years following, abounded with fish of various kinds, in their season. So, at times, Edward Hilton and his men had plenty of good fishing without going to Ipswich Bay and the ocean beyond the Isles of Shoals. The fish abounded in these rivers until the settlers placed dams at the lower falls, and built saw mills, which destroyed the natural mode of living, so in time the fish ceased to come up the rivers. The salmon at that time came up the river in the spring time in great abundance, and went up over the Cochecho falls, and the falls at South Berwick, to get into fresh water to lay their spawn; when the dams were placed across those rivers at the falls, the salmon could not get over the dams, and as they could not hatch their spawn in salt water, the result was that in time the species ceased to exist. At the time Edward Hilton came here and settled the salmon were, comparatively, as abundant in the Pascataqua and its branches as they are now in Columbia River, on the Pacific coast. The Salmon Falls River was so named by the first settlers because the salmon fish came up into the fresh water there in great abundance in the spring time. David Thomson found out this fact concerning the salmon before he secured his grant of "Thomson Point."

The soil about their houses on the Point was excellent for raising garden crops and corn, which the Indians soon taught them how to plant and use.

Two or three miles above there, they could get all the oysters they could possibly use; and the clams in Back River were so abundant that they fed their hogs on them. Lobsters, wild ducks, and wild fowl of all kinds were abundant in Little Bay and Great Bay, so that they never lacked for food. As Elder Brewster said of the Plymouth colonists that year, "they were permitted to suck the abundance of the seas and of the treasures hid in the sands."

By the way,—the Indians never, at any tme, troubled the settlers on *Dover Point* or Dover Neck; not even during the fiercest Indian wars. *Hilton's Point* was a most excellent place for meeting and trading with the Indians, for the beaver skins and other Indian products of the forests; and Hilton and his men must have found that branch of their business as profitable as fishing; perhaps more so. That very year, 1623, while Captain Myles Standish and his soldiers were fighting the Indians, hand to hand at Weymouth, all was peace on the Pascataqua, and it continued so all through the troubles at Plymouth, and the Massachusetts Bay Colony.

CONTEMPORANEOUS EVENTS—1623 TO 1633.

It may be of interest just here to chronicle what was happening, in other sections of New England, during the ten years that Edward Hilton was ruler at *Hilton Point;* in this way the reader will get a better understanding of the age in which Hilton lived, and can compare his settlement with others.

During the year 1623, trouble commenced between the Cape Cod Indians and the settlers at Plymouth, and the Pilgrims were having considerable trouble in getting a supply of food and raiment, and many were very thinly clothed, as well as half starved. Squalor and demoralization were everywhere. At Weymouth Captain Miles Standish called four of the Indian conspirators into a room where three of his own men (soldiers) were armed, and shut the door. A hand-to-hand struggle at once commenced, and although the Indians fought desperately, three were killed, and the fourth, who was captured alive, was immediately hanged. Outside, two others were killed, and when Standish himself came out of the room, he killed a seventh. The next day the Weymouth settlers were so thoroughly scared that they got on board their ship, the *"Swan,"* and sailed for Monhegan (Maine) where they got passage to England on one of the fishing fleet. When Captain Standish arrived home at Plymouth, with his warriors, he put the head of the Indian Chief Wituwamat, whom he had beheaded in the fight, upon a pike which was fastened to a corner of the fort, as a warning to all Indians, for the head, with its long, black hair waving in the wind, was allowed to remain for some time—as an object lesson in case another Indian conspiracy should ever be thought of.

From the histories we know this much about Plymouth that year. On the top of the hill was the fort-Meeting-house which played such an important part both in the civil and ecclesiastical life of the colony, so located on the easterly side of the top of the hill that it commanded the brook, the ford and the street. We know that this fort, twenty-four feet square, was built of large, sawed plank; that its flat roof was supported by large oak beams which projected beyond the walls to prevent the building being scaled by Indian warriors; that on the roof were six cannons mounted behind a bulwark, and that underneath, to light the interior, were small windows, like port-holes. We know also that there were one hundred and eighty settlers who had thirty-one small houses, most of them divided into three rooms with a garret of good capacity; that the houses were made of hewn logs, with thatched roofs and outside chimneys of stone, laid in clay; and that the windows were skins of animals, or paper saturated with linseed oil. We know that there were houses on both sides of the street which had been laid out the first year, as well as on a cross street leading from the ford over the brook to the gate in the stockade on the bluff; and that, where the two roads crossed, four small cannon commanded both road ways. Governor Bradford's house was under the hill, at the corner of the two road ways; farther up the hill was Miles Standish's house; and Elder Brewster's house was on the corner diagonally across from the governor's house, where there was a spring of water. We know that the cottages along the main street were enclosed by a fence high enough to be used as a stockade in case of any sudden attack by Indians when within the settlement, and that this gave the street a very trim appearance; that at the foot of the street the building which was used for their first meeting-house, was now used for their trading stock, and had attached to it a large shed made of interwoven boughs chinked with clay; and that under the bluff were three log buildings, where corn, furs, beaver skins, heavy merchandise, salt and the tools of the colony were stored; these buildings being near the pier where their two shallops lay.

Contrast this with Edward Hilton's party as they landed at Pomeroy's Cove in the spring of 1623 and commenced building their houses where now stands Hilton Hall and the village at *Dover Point*. Furthermore, contrast the beautiful approach to it, up the broad Pascataqua, with the crooked channel the Plymouth settlers had to follow to get from Cape Cod Bay into Plymouth Harbor. There was no garrisoned house, or any need of one. In later years, when at its largest, the village there probably had a score of cottages.

It was the Cape Cod Indians that Capt. Miles Standish had to contend with; they did not come up to the Pascataqua. What is known of the Indians in the vicinity of the future Dover? The first man who came up the Pascataqua, and left any description of what he saw, was Captain Martin Pring who came over from Bristol, England, in 1603 on a voyage of discovery. He had two ships, the *"Speedwell,"* of 50 tons, and 30 men; the *"Discoverer,"* a bark of 26 tons, and having 13 men. In Vol. IV. Purchas, published in 1654, is given his report of the voyage, and an interesting description of the coast. Following is what he says of the Pascataqua, as he and his 13 men came up the river in the bark *"Discoverer"*:

"At length coming to the Mayne in the latitude of 43½ degrees we changed our course to the southwest. In which course we found four inlets. (Saco, Kennebunk and York rivers.) The fourth and most westerly was the best, which we rowed up ten or twelve miles. In all these places we found no people, but signs of fires where they had been. Howbeit we beheld very goodly groves and woods, replenished with tall Oaks, Beeches, Pine trees, Firre-trees, Hasels, and Mapels. We saw also sundry sorts of beasts, Stags, Deere, Beares, Wolves, Foxes, Lusernes and Dogges with sharp noses. But meeting with no sassafras we left these places."

As Capt. Pring did not see any Indians, only the place where they cooked their fish at the falls, perhaps the Cochecho in Dover, he left no description of them. But Captain Christopher Levett has left a good description of Indians as he saw them at York, Maine, in 1623, and there can be no doubt that Edward Hilton and his party saw some of the same Indians that Capt. Levett did, and these were the natives with whom he first had intercourse and with whom he engaged in trade. Capt. Levett was His Majesty's woodward, and was one of Gov. Robert Gorges' Council that year, and succeeded him as governor of New England in 1624. His report was published in London in 1628. In his voyage of 1623 he went no farther west than the Isles of Shoals. Following is what he says about the Indians as he saw them at York:

"The next day the wind came fair and I sailed to Quack, which I named York; with me was the (Indian) King, Queen and Prince, bow and arrows, dog and kettle in my boat, his noble attendance rowing by us in their canoes."

"When we arrived at York the masters of my ships bid me welcome and asked what savages those were. I told them and thanked them. The woman or reported Queen asked if those men were my friends, I told her they were; then she drank to them, and told them they were welcome to her country, and so should all my friends be at any time; she drank also to her husband and bid him welcome to her country too; for you must understand that her father was the sagamore of this place, and left it to her at his death, having no more children."

"And thus after many dangers, much labor and great charge, I have obtained a place of habitation in New England, where I have built a house, and fortified it in a reasonable good fashion, strong enough against such enemies as are those savage people."

Captain Levett did not report seeing any Indians when he visited Mr. Thomson at what is now called Odiorne's Point, but here are listed some of the Sagamores he met along the coast at York and elsewhere: Sadaymoyt, the great Sagamore of the East Country, Manawormet, Opparunwit, Shedragussett, Cogawosco, Somerset, Conway and others.

Captain Levett says: "I have had much conference with the savages about our only true God, and have done my best to bring them to know and acknowledge him; but I fear me all the labor will be lost, and no good will be done, except it be among the younger sort."

"I find they have two gods; one they love and the other they hate; the god they love they call Squanto and to him they ascribe all their good fortunes."

"The god they hate they call Tanto, and to him they ascribe all their evil fortunes, as thus, when any is killed, hurt or sick, or when it is evil weather, then they say *Tanto* is hoggery, that is angry. When any die they say Tanto carries them to his *wigwam*, that is his house, and they never see them more."

"I have asked them where Squanto dwells; they say they cannot tell, but up on high, and will point upwards. And for Tanto, they say far west, but they know not where."

"I have asked them if at any time they have seen Squanto, or Tanto; they say no, there is none sees them but their Pawpaws, and they neither but when they dream."

"Their Pawpaws are their physicians and surgeons, and as I verily believe all are witches, for they foretell of ill weather, and many strange things; every Sagamore hath one of them who belongs to his company, and they are altogether directed by them."

"On a time I was at a Sagamore's house and saw a martin's skin, and asked if he would sell it; he told me no; he said the Pawpaw used it to lay under his head when he dreamed, and if he did not have it he could do nothing in his dreams."

"I find them generally to be marvellous quick of apprehension, and full of subtlety; they will quickly find any man's disposition, and flatter and humor him strangely, if they hope to get anything of him; and yet they will count him a fool if he do not show a dislike of it, and say one to another that such a man is "mechecome," that is a fool."

"They are slow of speech, and if they hear a man speak much they will laugh at him and say, he is "Mechecome," that is a fool."

"If men of place (high authority) be too familiar with them they will not respect them; therefore it is to be wished that all such persons should be wise in their carriage."

"The Sagamores will scarce speak to an ordinary man (white), but will point to their men, and say Sanops must speak to Sanops, and Sagamores to Sagamores."

"Their Sagamores are no kings, as I verily believe, for I can see no government or law amongst them but club law; and they call all masters of ships sagamores, or any other man that they see have a command of men."

HILTON HALL: On this site Edward Hilton built his House in 1623.
(See page 1.)

"Their wives are their slaves, and do all the work; the men will do nothing but kill beasts, fish, hunt, etc. On a time I was reasoning with one of their sagamores, about their having so many wives, I told him it was no good fashion; he then asked me how many wives King James had; I told him he never had but one, and she was dead, at which he wondered, and asked me who then did all the King's work."

"They have no apparel but skins, except a few they have obtained from the French. In winter they wear the hair side inwards, in summer outwards. They have a piece of skin about their loins like a girdle. They are all thus apparelled, going bareheaded with long hair; men and women alike."

"Their weapons are bows and arrows; I never saw more than two fowling pieces, one pistol, about four half pikes and three cutlasses amongst them."

"Their houses are built in a half an hour's space, being only a few poles, or boughs stuck in the ground and covered with the bark of trees."

In the above the reader has the descriptions of the Indians about the Pascataqua River as they appeared to eye witnesses in 1623; that was before they had become degenerated by contact and intercourse with wicked and covetous white men.

Edward Hilton, Thomas Roberts and the rest when they came here in 1623, without doubt, met some of the same identical Indians that Captain Levett describes. It is to be regretted that none of those first settlers here had a literary turn of mind. Hilton and the settlers on Dover Neck had no trouble with the Indians until about 1675 when the wars began that continued fifty years.

During 1625 a fleet of not less than fifty vessels was trading along the New England coast, but not many of them took the trouble to go out of their way, up the Pascataqua River to *Hilton Point;* the settlers there, however, kept on fishing and trading with the Indians, in peace and quietness, prosperous and happy.

During this year many of the settlers who had returned to Weymouth, Mass., after their terrible fright from the Indians, left for more desirable localities. Among them was Thomas Walford, a blacksmith who built an "English palisaded and thatched house" at the mouth of the Charles River where Charlestown now is; William Blackstone, a Puritan minister and an eccentric book recluse, who located a mile up the river on the west slope of what is now Beacon Hill, Boston; and Samuel Maverick, a stanch Churchman, who established a trading post and built a sort of fort on Noddle's Island, now East Boston.

This same year a settlement was started at Nantasket, and another at Wollaston, now a part of Quincy, Mass. This settlement was a business venture of one Captain Wollaston, who brought over with him as partners three or four men not without means and some thirty or forty indented servants, or persons who sold their service for a term of years. One of these partners was Thomas Morton, who has been mentioned in previous pages of this history for his conduct at Merry Mount, as he called Wollaston. Members of the Plymouth Colony had established a fishing station at Cape Ann, where they had men, in the season, who attended to fish-drying and fur-buying.

In the year 1626 the English trading post at Monhegan was given up and the stock in trade was purchased by former Governor Bradford and Governor Winslow of Plymouth and David Thomson of Little Harbor, who divided the stock, Thomson taking his share to Thomson's Island, Boston Harbor, where he then resided.

In March, 1628, the Massachusetts Bay Company was organized, having obtained from the Council of Plymouth a grant of that part of New England included between three miles north of the Merrimack River and three miles south of the Charles, and that same fall there arrived at Conant's settlement at Naumkeag sixty emigrants; this was the beginning of a great Puritan exodus from England. Soon after they arrived they changed the name from the Indian Naumkeag to the Hebrew Salem, or peace. John Endicott was deputy Governor of this party. A large accession of immigrants was received here in 1629. The Puritan leaders of this movement in England that year obtained a charter direct from King Charles; under this royal charter the legal title assumed was "The Governor and Company of The Massachusetts Bay in New England."

This charter superseded all grants previously made by the Council of Plymouth, and gave unprecedented liberality in self-government. Under this Endicott was designated as Governor. Among this second lot of emigrants were ninety university men who later gave a high class tone to the community which had much to do in developing the New England type of people.

In 1630 began the Puritan settlement at Boston, of which that at Salem was the advance guard. John Winthrop and his party, in two ships, arrived at Salem, June 12, and he became governor. That summer they settled in localities which now are all included in Greater Boston, except Cambridge. Winthrop settled at Charlestown, but soon crossed over the river to the original Boston, which they named for the old Boston from whence they came in England. During the first year there was much suffering. Winthrop, in a letter to his wife, writing, says: "We may not look at great things here. It is enough that we shall have Heaven, though we pass through Hell for it. We here enjoy God and Jesus Christ: Is it not enough?" In November, 1631, the *"Lion,"* having among her passengers Governor Winthrop's wife and family, arrived at Boston. It was in this year that Captain Thomas Wiggans, usually called Wiggin, came over in one of the Puritan ships and came down from Boston to *Hilton Point,* on the Pascataqua, to look over the settlement; this visit, later, resulted in a trade with Mr. Hilton and his associates, whereby immigrants came over in 1633 and commenced the settlement on Dover Neck.

BUSINESS AT HILTON POINT AFTER 1633.

FERRIES AND FERRYMEN.

Soon after the settlement was begun on Dover Neck they commenced running ferry boats across to Bloody Point and to Everett's Point in Old Kittery now Eliot, which locality was where the first settlement was located about the same time when Captain Wiggin's company arrived in 1633. The first ferry man was Thomas Trickey, the ancestor of the Trickey families of Old Dover and vicinity. Mr. Trickey was one of the first settlers in the Bloody Point section of Old Dover, now Newington, and Captain Thomas Wiggin assigned him a lot on what was known in the nineteenth century as the "Nancy Drew" farm, on the west side of the cove that separates it from the point on which stands the Dover and Portsmouth railway station. He probably was there as early as 1636 and resided there until his death in 1680. Soon after he settled there he commenced running the ferry between that cove and *Hilton Point* and kept control of the business forty years, or more, when his son Zachariah came into control by inheritance and purchase from his sisters. Thomas Trickey also ran ferry boats across the river to Everett's Point, in Old Kittery, now Eliot, from *Hilton Point*. These ferries were in continuous service for a great many years; that to Bloody Point did not cease until the Railroad bridge was built in 1871.

Mr. Trickey was one of the signers of the Combination Government of 1640. In 1641 he was one of the signers of the protest against having Dover, or Northam as it was then called, come under the control of Massachusetts, unless the citizens here could be permitted to manage their own local affairs, and not be obliged to become a member of the Church in order to be admitted a freeman with the right to vote in town-meetings and send a Deputy to the General Court in Boston. In 1643 he was one of the signers to a protest, presented to the Massachusetts General Court, against having what is now Newington classed as belonging to the Strawberry Bank settlement, and the Court granted the request by having a commission restore the boundary, practically as it now is between Newington and Portsmouth. In 1643 there were twelve families living in the Bloody Point section of Dover, or as they called it: "The humble peticon of the inhabitants of Bloody poynt in the Riuer Pascataway;" the heads of families were: James Johnson, Thomas Canning, Thomas ffursen, William Pray, William Jones, Thomas Trickey, John Godard, Henry Longstaffe, John Fayer, Oliuer Trimings, Philip Lewis, Raderic (unreadable)." Some of these families at a later period resided on Dover Neck. The first tax list of Dover of which there is any record is that of 1648. Mr. Trickey is there rated as one of the large tax payers, showing that he was one of the prominent and influential citizens of the town. His son Zachariah managed the ferries until 1705 when he sold his farm and ferry boats to Capt. John Knight. The Trickey family had the ferries seventy years.

John Knight was a Huguenot refugee, who first resided in Portsmouth, and while there changed his French name Chevalier to its English equivalent Knight. On the Portsmouth tax list of 1681 his name is given John Chevalier. October 18, 1702, "John Knight of Portsmouth, alias Chevalier," bought what was known in the nineteenth century as the Carter farm at Pine Point, adjacent to the stream below Bloody Point, and from that date was a citizen of Dover, and one of its prominent men, becoming captain of a militia company in the French and Indian wars, as the following from the town records shows: "27; 1 mo; (March) 1704; Capt. John Woodman (of Oyster River), Capt. John Tuttle (Dover Neck) and Capt. John Knight (of Bloody Point) were ordered to muster their several companies at the Meeting-house on Dover Neck on Wednesday the 5th of April at 10 o'clock, A. M., and Capt. Tuttle there shall take a list of such as shall enter themselves volunteers in the service against the French and Indian enemy." In 1710 Capt. Knight was one of the committee appointed in town meeting to procure a successor to Rev. John Pike who died that year.

The records of the New Hampshire Provincial Assembly for July, 1705, have the following:

"Upon the humble application of Captain John Knight of Dover, near Bloody Point, setting forth that the ferry there kept to *Hilton's Point* belonging to Dover Neck, and the other from said Bloody Point to Kittery Neck, were always holden by the inhabitants of Trickey's farm, which now is his by purchase, and thereupon humbly prays that the right of said ferries may be conferred upon him."

"It is accordingly agreed that the Governor be desired to give him a patent for said ferries, he not demanding more than 12 pence for every horse and man at each ferry, and three pence for every single person without horse, he always taking care that there be Boats always ready, and there be no complaint thereupon."

When Capt. Knight gave up the ferry business it came into possession of the Henderson family whose residence was where Hilton Hall now is on *Dover Point,* Captain Howard Henderson becoming the first owner on the north side of the river (Pascataqua). He was son of William Henderson who came from England to Dover about 1650. He married Sarah Howard, 1668. They resided on Bloody Point. He was engaged in the ship building business, but held some minor town offices. He was constable in 1682 and other years. In the tax list dated 3 July, 1677, he is called Mr. William Henderson and was a large tax payer. In the Massachusetts archives it is the record: "Isaac Waldern of Boston complains, 15th of October, 1679, of William Henderson of Dover for not working on a ship according to agreement, he having paid said Henderson in advance." William and Sarah Howard Henderson had two sons, one born 1670; they named him William; the other, born 1672, they named Howard, in honor of his mother. The elder brother resided on Seavey's Island, after marriage, and Henderson's Point in the Pascataqua River, below the navy yard received its name from him. This point was removed by the United States Government after 1904. The younger son came to reside on *Hilton Point,* where Hilton Hall now (1923) stands, after his marriage, 8 June, 1704, to Miss Sarah Roberts, daughter of Thomas and grand daughter of Governor Thomas Roberts of Dover. Previous to his marriage he had considerable experience as a sailor and soldier. It is recorded that he served in the King's navy and helped capture the fortress of Gibraltar, which for more than two hundred years has remained in possession of Great Britain. He was a ship carpenter and ship builder, as well as sailor. He lived to be one hundred years old. His grave is in the old burying ground on Dover Neck on the southerly side of that of his son Capt. Howard Henderson. The ferry from *Hilton Point* to Bloody Point and from *Hilton Point* to Old Kittery came into possession of Mr. Henderson about 1725, and from him to his son, Capt. Howard Henderson, and remained in possession of the Henderson family during the first part of the nineteenth century. In this connection it is interesting to note what John Adams, second President of the United States, says about Bloody Point ferry in 1770, he then being a young lawyer in Boston who practiced law, from time to time, in the courts of Maine, then a District of Massachusetts. In his published Diary, under date of 29 June, 1770, he says: "Friday. Bagan my journey (on horseback) to Falmouth, in Casco Bay. Baited my horse at Martin's (tavern) in Lynn. Dined at Goodhue's in Salem. Oated my horse and drank balm tea at Treadwell's in Ipswich. After a rest of half an hour rode to Rowley and lodged at Captain Jewett's."

"30. Saturday. Arose not very early, and drank a pint of new milk, and set off; oated my horse at Newbury; then rode to Clark's at Greenland meeting-house, where I gave him hay and oats, and then set off for Newington; turned in at a gate by Colonel March's and passed through two gates more before I came into the road that carried me to my uncle Joseph Adams' house, minister of that town. I found the old gentleman, in his 82d year, as hearty and alert as ever, his son and daughter well, their children grown up, and everything strange to me. I find I had forgot the place; it is seventeen years I presume, since I was there. My reception was as friendly, cordial and hospitable as I could wish; took a cheerful, agreeable dinner, and then set off for York, over *Bloody Point Ferry,* a way I never went before, and arrived at Woodbridge's (in York) a half an hour after sunset."

"By accidentally taking this new route I have avoided Portsmouth, and my old friend, the Governor of it. I have had a very unsentimental journey this day except at dinner with my uncle Joseph at the Newington parsonage. My uncle has been an admirer of Doctor Mather, and was said to affect an imitation of his voice, pronunciation and manner in the pulpit. His sermons, though delivered in a powerful and musical voice, consisted of texts of Scripture, quoting chapter and verse, delivered *memo-*

riter, and without notes. In conversation he was vain and loquacious, though learned and entertaining."

"On my return I must pay my compliments to Governor Wentworth at Portsmouth. It is my duty; he is my friend and I am his. I should have seen enough of the pomp and vanity and ceremonies of that little world, Portsmouth, if I had gone there instead of by Bloody Point Ferry; but formalities and ceremonies are an abomination in my sight."

The future President came over to *Hilton Point* and then was ferryed across to Everett's Point above "Watt's Fort," so called, and then went on to York, and as far east as Falmouth, now Portland. Mr. Adams kept up these annual law visits until the Revolutionary war commenced.

The Cochecho River Boat Company was organized in 1824, and their first meeting for choice of officers was held July 28. At the June session of the Legislature they had secured a charter to build a canal or railway from Winnepesaukee Lake to Dover; also for plying ferry boats to be moved by horse power across the river from *Dover Point* to Newington. It does not appear that this company ever did any more than organize. This is the first mention of a railway in connection with Dover; it was seventeen years after that date when the first passenger train reached here from Boston. The Pascataqua Ferry Company was organized 13 Oct., 1855, for carrying passengers from *Doven Point* to Newington. The ferry was finally displaced by construction of the railroad bridge in 1871.

BRICK MAKERS AND BRICK MAKING AT DOVER POINT AND DOVER NECK.

Brick making in Dover began at a very early period, as the settlers needed that material for construction of chimneys. Who made the first brick, or when, is not recorded, but in the nineteenth century a large and very profitable business was carried on at *Dover Point* and Dover Neck brick yards, and "Dover River Brick" held high rank in Boston markets, commanding the highest price. These yards were located on the south side of The Point, and on both sides of The Neck, on Fore River and Back River.

BRICK MAKING.

The last brick yards operated at The Point were by Seavey & Loughlin, adjoining the south side of the railroad bridge, and that by John E. Pinkham, a short distance above. Work on these was discontinued about 1908. Above Mr. Pinkham's yard, along the bank of the Pascataqua, up to Redding Point, are several old yards that were worked out many years ago. Adjoining Redding Point on the east were yards worked by Henry Card and Benjamin Ford, about 1830, and years following. On Fore River are the old, worked out yards of Aaron Pinkham, Thomas Henderson, James Coleman, Joseph Fernald and Jacob Ford. Next above these are two yards now (1923) worked by Elbridge Gage, formerly worked by George W. Ford, James Parle and James Morang. The next yards above these were three that were started by Hanson Roberts, Joseph Roberts and Jerry Roberts, at an early period in the 19th century. Those yards were worked about two years, when the owners found the clay too hard, and gave it up; they then opened yards on Back River where the clay proved to be satisfactory. It has since been ascertained that the hard clay on Fore River can be worked by the improved methods. The yard which is now (1923) worked by Isaac L. Lucas, on the Upper Neck of Fore River, was opened by Samuel Horne in 1840, who worked it a number of years. Mr. Lucas bought it in 1865 and has worked it every year since then, to a greater or less extent, having opened a new clay bank in 1899; during the whole period of his occupation he has manufactured more than 40,000,000 brick of first class quality. He estimates that there is clay enough along the shore there to last a hundred years more, reckoning on the same basis. In the neighborhood of the Lucas yard are those which were formerly worked by Alonzo and Aaron Roberts.

Still further up the river, at Thomson's Point, David Gage opened a yard about 1836 which he worked for several years and then gave it up as there is a high bank of earth on top of the clay. He then opened a yard on the south bank of the Cochecho River, at Gage's Point, opposite Three Rivers farm, owned by Edward W. Rollins; he worked this yard until 1858, when he gave the business to his son Moses Gage, and devoted his time to the manufacture of a machine which he had invented to make water struck brick. This machine revolutionized the method for the soft mud branch of brick making. The patent was twice renewed, but expired a few years ago. Mr. Gage died at an advanced age, in the year 1900. For several years William M. Courser worked a yard near Mr. Gage's on Cochecho River.

Among the brick makers, in the 19th century, on Back River were Daniel Pinkham, William Clements, John Clements, Hanson Roberts, Joseph Roberts, Jerry Roberts, Alonzo Roberts, Samuel Horne, Giles Horne, Nicholas Varney, Robert Varney, Andrew Varney, John H. Henderson, Howard M. Roberts and Fred Roberts.

Thomas Henderson who owned the first brick yard at *Dover Point,* which was operated in this 20th century by Seavey & Loughlin, sold it to Capt. Thomas Card in 1812 and removed to his new house which he had built on The Neck, now known as the Henderson house, a short distance north of River View Hall, on High Street, now the State Road. Mr. Henderson and his father Howard Henderson were engaged in ship building, as well as brick making, up to 1812, when the war put a stop to the ship business; during that war the British war ships captured several of his vessels. After the war he did an extensive and profitable business in his brick yard on The Neck.

At the time when No. 4 mill of the Cochecho Cotton Manufacturing Company was being constructed, in 1824, Hanson Roberts had his yard in operation on Fore River and furnished a large part of the brick that were used in its construction, his supply being about 1,500,000. The boss mason regarded Mr. Roberts' bricks as the hardest, so used them in the wall next to the water. In this connection it is interesting to note that Mr. Howard M. Roberts informed the writer that Joseph Roberts, his grandfather, built the house, owned and occupied by the late E. P. Kennard, at some date in the 18th century, and he made the bricks for a new chimney at a clay bank on Fore River; when the bricks were dry he hauled them to his house and burned them in a kiln, the marks of which were visible in the present century. After the clay was dug out of the bank Mr. Roberts pulverized it by driving oxen over it. His son, Hanson Roberts, father of Howard M., remembered seeing this brick making done.

Enoch Pinkham was one of the best known of brick men; as early as 1830 his yard was located just at the end of the *Dover Point* bridge. He owned a vessel in which he conveyed his bricks from the yard to Boston. His sons, John E. Pinkham, Ira A. and Richard A. Pinkham, built yards of their own near by on his land up the shore of the river. After his father died his son Richard worked the yard at the bridge, and after Richard's death it was worked by Seavey & Loughlin, the latter being boss of the work and proprietor of the Pascataqua House, at the summit of the hill, later occupied by E. P. Kennard, who refitted it in fine colonial style, and converted the brick yard into a beautiful lawn.

The initial process in preparing the clay, say 250 or 300 years ago, and up to the introduction of the modern horse machine about 50 years ago, was to first dig out the season's clay in the early spring, enough to last for a summer. From this big pile of coarse material each day was wheeled onto the clay dry ground enough to cover to a depth of two or three inches. This was left to dry in the sun and wind. It was then wheeled into soak pits and water bailed on. Clay in a dry state will slack like lime and become fine and in good condition for moulding. From this pit it was shoveled onto a table and put into molds by hand, struck off with a straight edge and left on the yard to dry.

Another way and much practised was to dig out the clay in the fall and leave it to mellow by frost during the winter, turning it frequently to expose it to the action of the atmosphere. In the spring it was thrown into pits where it was soaked and then tempered by the feet of men or oxen, or by means of a pug mill. An edict was issued by a Governor of Massachusettss Bay colony that all brickmakers who sold in Boston must so prepare their clay. By the present method the clay bank is made a gradual slant. Every day, usually in the afternoon, a clay cutter, drawn by horses, back and forth over the sides of the bank, planes off the clay in layers about two inches thick. This is thrown into a pit and soaked in water over night. In the morning it is mixed with one-fourth sand to prevent the clay from shrinking too much in burning, and shoveled into the brick machine. The top of this machine is funnel shaped with an upright revolving shaft, and is fitted with knives which pulverize the clay. Horse power is used. Then it goes down into the press box. To run under the press box is a carriage. On this carriage is placed a brick mold, holding six bricks. By a lever, worked by the foot, this is forced under the press box, filled and drawn out. These molds are placed on a brick-truck and wheeled away to the drying ground where they are skilfully tipped out of the molds onto the ground, where they are left till they are dry enough to handle, when they are turned on edge. After further drying they are wheeled to the kiln ground and arranged for burning. The kiln is built of brick, so spaced as to allow the heat to reach all parts evenly, the spaces acting as flues throughout the whole mass. The kiln is built in arches of 20 or 25,000 brick into which the wood is put for burning. When the setting is finished, poor quality bricks are built up outside and plastered with mud by hand, which renders the kiln air tight. The first few days it must burn slowly until the water, smoke and dampness are gone. Then the heat is increased and must not be allowed to go down. The kiln is dressed once in two hours, that is, the arches are filled with cord wood, spruce, pine or hard wood. The process of burning goes on about a week. This requires all the skill of the maker, and the owner of the yard is rarely absent during this process, as on this depends his profits. Usually one kiln is burned in a season, in August or September.

THE FISKE BRICK MAKING SYSTEM.

In 1902 the Fiske Brick Making System was established in a large plant that was located on the ground north of Sandy Point. This was a large and elaborate construction of machinery so arranged that the clay and sand, the raw materials, entered on a railway at the south end of the building and was dumped into the mixer, and from that the material proceeded systematically through the various processes of molding, stacking, placing in the kiln, and removing from that to the storage room without being touched by the human hands, thus saving a large amount of manual labor.

At the clay beds, on Back River, the clay was cut out by machinery and loaded on box cars, and brought to the factory, where the cars were drawn up an inclined trestle and the material, five cubic yards in each car, was dumped into a hopper at the disintegrator or pug mill and was forced into a brick machine. This machine was standard and no part of the Fiske system. Mr. Fiske's patents covered only the handling. It was called an augur machine, which forced the column of clay, prepared by machinery, through a die. After leaving the die the column of clay passed through an automatic reel where the wires sliced up the bar of clay into bricks which were taken away on a horizontal or off-heaving belt. At this point the special handling machinery began its work. The bricks were handled in masses instead of one by one. As they issued from the molding machine they were placed by hand on setting-up stands, one of which was permanently located on each side of the off-heaving belt. They were placed on these stands in such relative positions that they could be dried, burned, and delivered on the sorting table without re-arrangement, the entire stack of 1500 bricks being lifted as a unit, transported and deposited by suitable machinery, first in the dryer, then in the kiln, and finally in the stock yard. When the first stack was completed the stackers commenced putting bricks on the opposite one so there was no waiting and the brick machine was permitted to run without interruption.

The first stack was removed by the handling machinery which consisted of an overhead electric travelling crane and a special carrier called a brick lift. The crane travelled on tracks supported on an elevated runway near the eaves of the main building and spanned the building completely and travelled its entire length. The crane was driven along the overhead tracks by an electric motor called the "travel motor" and the hoisting and lowering of the load was effected by the hoist motor located on top. Each motor was controlled independently by a lever in the cage of the operator who had at all times an uninterrupted view of the whole floor.

This operator, with one helper, could handle as many bricks as 15 or 20 men with wheel barrows.

The brick lift consisted of two lifting beams braced together to form a girder. To this girder was attached 104 lifting fingers. To transport a load of bricks the lift was brought by the crane in front of the setting-up stand, lowered, and the fingers run into the proper spaces and the entire load was raised by the hoisting motor and carried by the crane to the dryer which was accurately spaced to receive them. The dryer was of brick and steel and fireproof. There were four chambers, each with a cover which could be lifted by the fingers of the brick lift. Each chamber held 18,000 brick. The covers dropped into channels of sand which sealed the chambers. Hot air was forced through the bricks by a powerful fan driven by an electric motor, the air being heated by a Brown Heat Generator. The hot air was forced into a circular tunnel running lengthwise the building and under the floor.

The bricks were carried from the drier to the kiln by the crane and brick lift and there deposited, each chamber having a removable crown so as to leave the entire top open. The crowns were made of fire clay blocks and iron. When a chamber was filled the crown was lowered and sealed around the edge with soft bricks and sand. The fires were fed with coal through holes in the crown. The draft for burning was produced by an exhaust fan driven by an electric motor.

The coal was brought by the crane and brick lift from the storage bin in long iron boxes and deposited near the feed holes. The ashes were taken out in the same way after the bricks were removed. The bricks after burning, were removed by the brick lift to an assorting stand at the end of the kiln.

This plant did good work for several years and the brick from it were used, to a large extent, in construction of the High School House and the Public Library building in Hale Park. Unfortunately this plant was destroyed by fire 28 Dec., 1906, and has not been rebuilt. Debris of the foundations is all that remains to mark the spot where it stood.

DOVER ORDINARIES OR INNS.

The most modern hotels of the present day cannot compare in importance with the ordinaries, or inns, that were opened in the early settlement of New England, which in the Massachusetts Bay Colony were established in every town of much size by order of the General Court and were placed under the direct jurisdiction of the minister and the selectmen. These officials were given authority to enforce the regulations in regard to the sale of intoxicating beverages. The inns of earliest times were located near the meeting-house; so, no doubt, many pleasant moments were passed at the noon hour, between the forenoon and afternoon service; especially in the cold weather when a roaring hot fire was kept burning in the big fire place, where the men from Oyster River, Bloody Point and Cochecho were permitted to warm up externally and internally.

The landlords were men of distinction, being often local magistrates, and the walls of the inn were posted with items of interest, such as notices of calls for town-meetings, elections, new laws, bills of sale and vendues (auctions). With these interesting topics before them, the citizens of the town might sit before the great wood fire and sip their toddy while discussing the news.

Although Dover was under the Massachusetts government for fifty years it was allowed by the Bay Colony General Court to control its ordinaries, or inns, and regulate the sale of liquors, and the town records show what was done in town meetings, and by the Selectmen, and the orders issued by the local court, held at Dover and Portsmouth, at the request of Dover authorities. In 1659; 4 mo; 28. The court being informed of "suffering of persons (in Dover) to continue drinking to excess, as also unto drunkenness, quarreling and fighting, etc."

"This court (held at Portsmouth) taking the same into their serious consideration, accounting it their duty by all means to prevent the like abuses for ye future, do order that henceforth no wine Tavern shall either directly or indirectly suffer or permit any person to have any Wine on the Sabbath day, neither shall they at any time sell any Wine for more than 18 pence a quart, on penalties of forfeiture of ye Licenses, and 5 shillings a pint for selling any on the Sabbath Day, or on evenings of ye Sabbath, excepting only to fishermen who lodge at their house on ye Saturday night, half a pint a man, or to sick persons; and that no ordinary, or house of common entertainment shall sell any strong Liquor on any pretence what ever."

"The Court doth order that henceforth only one Wine Tavern shall be licensed at Dover."

Probably, since 1633, there has always been an inn or tavern of some description on *Dover Point,* for the accommodation of the travelling public as well as for the townspeople.

In 1854, John P. Hanson erected the house now (1923) known as Hilton Hall, at The Point, and for a score of years conducted there a popular inn, known as the "Dover Point House." Mr. Hanson was an expert and successful entertainer and his wife was a popular hostess. The old house which stood there was a spacious story and a half building, covering much ground and affording ample accommodation for a large family. It was erected by Howard Henderson, Sr., at some period early in the 18th century. The last Henderson occupant was his grandson, Thomas Henderson, who removed in 1812 to the house on High Street, which he had erected during the previous year, and has since been known as the "Henderson house." When Mr. Hanson bought the house he did not tear it down but had it removed to another part of the village. That was an occasion of a "great hauling," the boss of which operation was John Sawyer who resided at Garrison Hill and had great fame as manager of moving buildings from one spot to another. The moving power was ox-teams. Sixty years ago every Dover farmer, and the prosperous farmers around, had several yoke of oxen and steers. On this occasion Mr. Sawyer had a long team of these hitched to the building, after he had fixed it properly on moving timbers. Each farmer was teamster for his own oxen, with goad in hand. When all were in line Mr. Sawyer would give the word of command: "Every man to his goad; every ox to his bow! Now go!!" and the house started off on its journey to its new cellar, and reached there in due time amid great cheering.

From 1878 to 1890 Daniel C. Wiggin was proprietor of the Dover Point House. Mr. Wiggin had had much successful experience before that as hotel manager, and during his career at The Point it was a very popular place of resort, beautiful in summer and warm and cosy in winter. Mr. and Mrs. Wiggin never failed to please their patrons, who were many. It was during this period that a local organization of the city, known as "The Hay Jumpers," held a meeting annually in July, when Mr. Wiggin cut his hay on the adjoining land and had it stacked up on his lawn, under the willows. It was their custom to walk down to The Point and partake of a bountiful supper at sunset; but before supper they had an exercise of jumping over several hay cocks in succession, which performance was very amusing; the initiation of new members was especially interesting. At the post prandial exercises there was speech making and songs. All returned home on foot, as they came down.

In 1912 Mr. Harrigan purchased the house and made extensive changes in the interior, producing the present elegant Hilton Hall, which is more popular than the old time inns, receiving not only good local patronage but also a very large patronage of automobile tourists.

SHIP-BUILDING ON DOVER NECK.

Undoubtedly the first vessel of size sufficient to cross the Atlantic ocean, launched from the shores of New England, was "A Faire Pinnace of thirty tons," called the *"Virginia,"* which the historian Strachey says was built by the Popham colony, at the mouth of the Kennebeck River, in 1607, and made a safe voyage to England. Twenty-six years after that is the record of the next launching of a ship in New England which crossed the Atlantic. This was at Plymouth, Mass., on the 4th. of July, 1631; it was christened the *"Blessing of the Bay."* That was the first vessel of any size that was built at Plymouth. When the pirates began to trouble and rob New England ships and shipping along the coast in general, this vessel was converted into a cruiser and did good service in defending New England shipping in general. This is the first American vessel of war on record. Ten years later, January 24, 1641, it is on record that Edward Bangs, ancestor of some of Dover's noted families, launched, at Plymouth, a bark of 40, or 50 tons, estimated to cost 200 pounds; that was the largest vessel that had been launched at Plymouth, up to that date, and that town was ahead of every other town in New England in this business, except Dover.

There is no record of when the first vessel was built in Dover, but it was certainly at a very early period after the lumbermen began to cut the forests. They had the best of ship timber all about the settlement on Dover Neck; they had good facilities for building ships on Fore River; they had the ship carpenters; and there were men of brains with great business capacity to carry on the work successfully; and they did so. Before 1650 a frigate was built in a cove, on the west bank of Fore River, next below Thomson's Point, where the Cochecho empties into that river.

We have the proof of this frigate, singular to say, in two of the early land grants that were made by Dover to two of its citizens. These grants are a part of the ancient records.—Isaac Stokes, in 1661, received a grant of three and a half acres of land on the east side of Dover Neck; one of the specifications of the boundary was this—"near where the Old Friggot was Billed."

The other reference is of an earlier date, as follows:—The town made a grant of three and a half acres of upland to Job Clement 23d, 1omo: 1658, a part of which was below "the highway that goeth from Thomas Canney's into the woods towards Thomson's Point, bounded east by the Fore River, on the northern side of the hollow, where the ship was built." These references show that the building of that "friggot" was one of the remarkable events of that early period.

We do not know how large the vessel was, but probably as big as that one built at Plymouth by Mr. Bangs, as above mentioned. We do not know who built it, but probably Richard Walderne did, as he was in the business and had his mills, at the falls here, in full running operation. But what use did he have for a frigate? The answer is easily found; he was largely engaged in shipping to the West Indies and to England; the pirates were all along the New England coast; they were the scourge of the West Indies; the merchant ships had to be protected by their owners. At one period the pirates were especially troublesome, even so near as the Isles of Shoals; so Captain Walderne had plenty of opportunity to use his frigate. He was elected Representative or Deputy from Dover in 1654, and about every year after that as long as Dover remained under the jurisdiction of the Massachusetts General Court, and was Speaker several years; from the Court records we have the following statement that he was engaged in the shipping business, as he asked to be excused from being present at the meetings of the Court for a few days.

"Upon a motion made to this Courte by Captain Walderne, who hath extraodinary occasions, refering to the leading away of Shippe, The Deputies are willing, for the present, to dismiss him from the Courte, if our honored Magistrates please to consent there to.————————William Torrey, Cleric.

Consented unto by the Magistrates.
Jno. Endicott, Gov'r."

It may have been that Capt. Walderne was specially anxious concerning the pirates, at that time. There is no record that Dover had any poets in the years of its early existence, but in a neighboring town, or perhaps Boston, there was one who produced the following gem which has been preserved to the present day.

> "Ye Pirates. who against God's Law did fight,
> Have all been taken, which is very right.
> Some of them were old and others were young,
> And on the flats of Boston they were hung."

The facts which inspired that poet are these.—Major Stephen Sewall, Capt. John Turner, and 40 volunteers sailed in a shallop from Salem and Fort Pinnace, after sunset, to go in search of some pirates who sailed from Gloucester that morning. The result was Major Sewall and his crew, brought into Salem a galley, Capt. Thomas Lorimore commanding, on board of which he had captured some pirates, and some of their gold, at the Isles of Shoals. Major Sewall carried the pirates to Boston under a strong guard, where Capt. Quelch and five of his crew were hung; thirteen of the ship's crew were placed under sentence of death, to be hung later; the remainder of the lot were cleared.

There is no record that the pirates ever came up the Pascataqua River, but it was certainly near enough when they visited the Shoals, to place Dover sea captains on sharp watch and ready to defend their ships and cargoes.

The pirates of the Spanish Main and the southern coast of the United States, have enjoyed almost a monopoly of popular interest in fact and fiction concerning the works of the pirates. But there was a lot of that sort of robbery all along the New England coast. In 1670 the General Court published in Boston, "beat of the drum," a proclamation against a ship at the Isles of Shoals, suspected a pirate; the commander of that ship took warning and escaped. Three years later another broadside was hurled against "piracy and mutiny." The report of an expedition sent out from Boston, in 1689, in the sloop "Mary" against notorious pirates, Thomas Hawkins and Thomas Pound, has all the dramatic elements and properties of a tale of pure adventure. It is, in detail, quite long, but following is a brief:—

"Being off Woods Hole we were informed that there was a pirate at Tarpolin Cove; soon after we espied a sloop on ahead of us, which we supposed to be the sloop where in said Pound and his company were. We made what sail we could and soon came up with her; we spread our King's Jack and fired a shot athwart her forefoot; upon which a red flag was put out on the head and the said sloop's mast. Then our Capn. ordered another shot to be fired athwart her forefoot; but they not striking we came up with them. Our Capn. ordered us to fire at them, which we did and called to them to strike to the King of England."

Pond standing on the quarter deck, with his naked sword flourishing in his hand, said:—"Come on board you dogs; I will strike you presently, or words to that effect, his men standing by him on the deck, with guns in their hands, and he taking up his gun, they discharged a volley at us, and we met them again; and so continued firing at one another, for some space of time."

"In which engagement our Capn., Samuel Pease, was wounded in the Arme, in the side and in the thigh; but at length wee captured the whole crew and made sayle toward Rhode Island; on Saturday, the 5th, of sd. October, we got our men on shore, who had been wounded, and got a surgeon to care for their wounds. The Capn. died from loss of blood before the doctor could finish dressing his wounds. We carried the pirates to Boston where some of them were hung on the flats, in a few days."

THE LAW TO PREVENT SHAMS IN SHIP-BUILDING.

On the 4th of October, 1641, the following law was enacted by the Massachusetts General Court in regard to having supervision of ship-building:

"Whereas the building of ships is a business of great importance for the common good, and therefore suitable care ought to be taken that it be well performed, according to the commendable course in England and other places:—It is therefore ordered by this Court and authority thereof, that when any ship is to be built within this jurisdiction, or any vessel above 30 tons, the owner, or the builder in his absence, shall before they begin to plank, repair to the Governor, or Deputy Governor, or any two magistrates, upon the penalty of ten pounds, who shall appoint some able man to survey the work, and workmen from time to time, as is usual in England, and the same so appointed shall have such liberty and power as belongs to his office."

"And if any ship-carpenter shall not, upon his advice, reform and amend anything he shall find amiss, then upon complaint to the Governor, or Deputy Governor, or any two magistrates, they shall appoint two of the most efficient ship-carpenters in this jurisdiction, and shall authorize them, from time to time, as need shall require, to take view of all such ships and all thereto belonging, and see that it be performed and carried on according to the rules of their art."

"And for this end an oath shall be administered to them to be faithful and indifferent between the workmen and the owners, and their charges shall be borne by such as may be found in default."

"And those viewers shall have power to cause any bad timber, or other insufficient work, or material, to be taken out and amended at the charge of them through whose default it grows."

As Dover was under Massachusetts rule the Dover ship-builders had to do their work according to law. Dover was then one of the most extensive ship-building localities along the New England coast, for the reason that it had an abundance of the best timber right at hand and had the carpenters who knew how to do good and honest work.

The vessels built here, at Dover Neck, were of all sizes and large for those days, though they would be regarded as the merest cockle-shells in this twentieth century, when travellers cross the Atlantic in palaces, and complete the voyage in as many days as it took the emigrant ship weeks, or in some cases months, to complete the voyage, in 1641. We of the present generation cannot realize the little cock boats in which navigators traversed the ocean two and three centuries ago.

The first American vessels engaged in the slave trade, of which we have any record, sailed from Boston to the coast of Guinea in 1645; they were fitted out by Thomas Keyser and James Smith. Mr. Smith was a member of the First Church in Boston. To the credit of that Church the members revolted at this act of their brother member; Smith was arraigned, and ordered to be punished, when he had returned with a cargo of slaves. The Negroes were returned to their native country, at the expense of the Colony.

It is not on record that Dover sea captains went to Africa and got cargoes of Negroes in exchange for rum, as English captains did, and carried them to the West Indies, and sold them to the sugar planters, but it is a well known fact that they bought some of those men from the slave dealers and brought them to Dover and sold them to the rich men here, who held them as slaves to the end of their lives. Some of these Negroes were living at the beginning of the Revolution, and some of the slaves served with their masters in the army that was fighting for American freedom.

Of course only a few of the wealthier men in Dover could afford to purchase Negro slaves, and those who did were not hard masters, but treated their servants kindly; gave them plenty to eat and, no doubt, gave them plenty of work to do. There is a record of one marriage of slaves in Dover. It can be found on page 174 of the "Dover Historical Collections":—

"December 26, 1774.—Richard, Negro Servant to Mark Hunking, Esq., of Barrington, and Julia, Negro Servant to Stephen Evans, Esq., of Dover, by consent of their respective Masters."

Rev. Jeremy Belknap officiated. Col. Stephen Evans was the most distinguished military officer Dover had in the Revolution. Captain Mark Hunking was a wealthy retired sea Captain of Portsmouth, who spent the last twenty-five years of his life in Barrington. His residence was at "Beauty Hill," near Winkley's Pond.

There is no subject connected with New England's first century, about which so little is known, as is the small vessels employed in the navigation of its waters, of the small craft employed by our ancestors in their coasting, fishing and trading voyages. The "skippers" wrote no books, and the only records they left were the ancient "Log-Books." A few of these are to be found in the possession of old Dover families. They are rather dry reading, though treating of long and tempestuous voyages; some of them covering a period of two years.

In a History of Plymouth is given the following description of a vessel that was built there in 1624:—"She had a little deck over her amidships to keep ye corne dry; but ye men were faine to stand it out in all weathers without shelter." The report says:— "The next year the ship carpenters took one of the biggest of the shallops and sawed her in the middle, and so lengthened her some five or six foote; and strengthened her timbers, and so built her up, and laid a deck on her; & soe made her a convenient and wholesome vessel, very fitte and comfortable for their use, which did serve 7 years after; & they gott her finished, and fitted her with sayles and anchors ye ensuing year."

DOVER'S FOREIGN COMMERCE.

The following statement will give the reader some idea of the commercial business of Dover in the year 1700, at Dover Neck. The ship masters carried merchantable cod fish to the markets of Spain, Portugal, the Straits, and cities along the coast of the Mediterranean Sea. To the West Indies they carried much fish and lumber; the latter being large quantities of pipe staves for the sugar plantations. In return they carried cargos from there to England, of sugar, molasses, cotton, logwood, etc. To England they sent direct quantities of ship timber, various furs, deer, bears, beavers, etc. In return they brought home English goods of various sorts, which were in demand in the home market and in other towns along the coast.

To Virginia the clumsy little sloops and ketches of Dover merchants and ship owners carried molasses, rum, salt, cider, mackerel, wooden bowls, platters, pails, kegs, which were made at the carpenter shops on Dover Neck, and a good supply of salt fish, the product of Dover fishermen. In return they brought back wheat, salt pork, tobacco, furs and hides, Indian corn, old pewter, brass, copper, etc.

The craft which crossed the Atlantic, and made the West Indies in safety were not very large vessels, but they had to encounter the storms that prevailed in that period just as they do in these modern times. Old Ocean was just the same then as now. It is said that some of those old masters made their voyages without sextant or "Practical Navigator." An old writer has described their method in a somewhat exaggerated style as follows:—

"The skippers kept their reckoning with chalk on a shingle, which they stowed away in the binnacle; and by way of observation they held up a hand to the sun. When they got him over four fingers they knew they were straight for Whole in the Wall; three fingers gave them their course to the double headed Shop Key; two fingers carried them down to Barbadoes."

These vessels were of 40 and 60 tons burden, mere cockleshells for deep water voyaging, but they withstood the storms and evaded capture by the pirates who infested the sailing courses of ships of the period. They were commanded by hardy, keen minded and fearless men, in the beginning, and voyaged farther and farther away from Dover, as profitable trade lured them on and on.

In those early days the troublous pirates, or Corsairs, had begun to vex and trouble the New England skippers who boldly crossed the Atlantic in vessels, some of which were not larger than a common brick barge of the 19th century. These "Sallee Rovers" kept watch from the Mediterranean, at the Straits of Gibraltar, to the chops of the English Channel. Many a luckless seaman of Dover was held prisoner in the cities of Algiers, while his friends at home endeavored to gather funds to pay the price of liberty and get him home again.

Dover was a town in Massachusetts till 1680; there was not any New Hampshire before that date. It is on record that in 1661, and for a long time previous, the commerce of Massachusetts was much annoyed by Barbary Corsairs, and that many of its seamen were held in bondage, till the bounty was paid, and they were permitted to return home. In 1700 Benjamin Alford of Boston and William Bowditch of Salem related that—"their friend, Robert Carver of Salem was taken nine years before, a captive into Sally; that contributions had been made for his redemption;

that the money was in the hands of a man in Salem; that if they had the disposal of it they could release Carver." In a time later that was done and Mr. Carver came home.

CLAPBOARDS AND PIPE-STAVES.

Dover Neck did not have any sawmills, but some of its leading residents were largely engaged in building mills and running them in the manufacture of various kinds of lumber. They received grants of falls on several rivers and grants to cut trees in the territory around the mills. The town retained ownership of the land; the mill proprietors paid a certain sum for each tree they cut; there was no clean sweep of small trees as lumbermen now vandalize the forests. These rents were made a fund which was a part of the minister's salary and was so appropriated for many years in the beginning of things. In connection with this mill business was conducted the enterprise of making pipe-staves and clapboards, which were a "merchantable commodity" and a legal tender instead of cash, which was then not very plenty in the pockets of most of the men in Dover.

The lumber from all of these mills, in one way or another, came to Dover Neck and was there used, or loaded onto vessels and transported to towns along the New England coast, or to the West Indies and England. The parts that were suitable for ship building were used in the yards at the Neck, on Fore River; a good deal was cut up into clapboards and pipe staves which kept crews of men at work in cooper shops, and in buildings where clapboards were split out and shaved to the proper dimensions for the foreign markets, as well as for home use. A clapboard was 4 feet long, 6 or 8 inches wide; the thick edge was a half-inch thick and the thin edge about one-eighth of an inch; the ends were beveled so as to lap over when laid, thus making a tight joint. These were made of the best of white pine, of which there was a great abundance around Dover in those early times; some of those old clapboards stood sound and strong on houses, unpainted, for a hundred years; they never rotted, they simply wore out or the nails rusted off and let them fall off. It was quite a nice job to rive out clapboards and pipe staves with the "frow," so as to make the least waste of lumber, and then the material had to be shaved and planed to the correct dimensions, for the market. So it is easy to understand why Dover Neck was a very busy place for a century and more.

The first mention of clapboards in New England is found in Gov. Winthrop's Journal, vol. 1, page 87, as follows:—"Mr. Oldham had a small house near the weir at Watertown, made all of clapboards, burned, August, 1632."—Of course those boards must have been more than four feet long and more than six inches wide, which became the legal dimension a little later. It is said that the origin of the name was from the fact that this sort of boards was first used to cover the clay walls of houses; so the first name was "clay-boards" and in time became changed into "clapboard."

The old English *pipe* was a cask that held two hogsheads, and the hogshead held 63 gallons. As soon as trade began to be brisk with the West Indies and especially with Barbadoes, there was a demand for these pipe staves to make casks for the accommodation of the sugar cane planters to market their sugar, molasses and rum. The enterprising men of Dover at once entered upon the work of supplying this demand, and for many years maintained a large and prosperous business in this line of work. The cooper shops were on Low street, where the staves were finally fitted together into pipes, then taken apart and each lot of staves tied together, and placed on board some ship in waiting, on Fore River. Hoops and heads were also made here to be shipped with the staves. Coopers at Barbadoes put the casks together again. The old town records have mention of this pipe-stave and clapboard business. For example:—

"At a meitting of the Sellecktmen ye 17th. of ye first mo: (March) 1663/4:—Ordered by ye Sellecktmen that Philep Chesle shall go forth in Oyster River to veu and inquire into several psons that doe transgress Towne Orders abut Cuting Tember for pipe staves, boeth in falling Tember by such as have noe right to fell anie tember, but transgress the Towne orders for felling Tember: —Wee, ye Sellecktmen, doe Impower Phelep Chesley to goe into the Woodes to veu the said trespassing and report to us what conditions he finds."

Again in 1665 is the following:—"Att a Publicke Towne meittinge holden ye 25th of ye 8th month, 1665,—Ordered that where as many psons doe fall timber and make staves without order, and take in seveal men to help them for that end, where by the Towne and the Settled Inhabitants are much injured. This order is therefore to Impower John Roberts, Thomas Nock, and Phelep Chesley, or anie two of them, to make diligent search into all the woodes, and where they find anie that have transgressed Towne orders, in making staves and falling tember, what they find they shall cease for the use of the Towne; the informer to have half for his Pauynes, and the other to be returned into the Towne treasury."

These and other records of the town show what importance the town officials placed on this industry, and what safeguards they placed around it. On Dover Neck there was a large and flourishing village, for more than a century; during that time when "Dover" is mentioned in any of the old records, this locality is meant, as all of the town business was transacted there. Its ship building and its shipping of lumber products gave employment to many men. Later the growth of the town in other sections, and new towns around, produced a change in the business center of the town, so "Cochecho" came to be recognized as official "Dover."

DOVER'S INTERCOURSE WITH BARBADOES ISLAND.

Barbadoes, or Barbadoes Island, is isolated from the rest of the Windward and West Indies in more senses than one. It is 95 miles from the nearest point in the Caribbees, which is the southern end of St. Lucia, and the intervening space sinks to a depth of 8,000 feet. It is still further from Tobago, and the continental system of South America. The depth of water between the Islands and the continent is enormous.

Barbadoes is the flattened top of a vast volcanic cone, lifted during the reign of Chaos and Old Night by the Tytanic forces at work in the depths, where Mother Earth had her Electrical Engineering Shop, during the period when the West Indies were being formed. The finishing touches were put on by the corals which built up the enormous reefs.

Barbadoes Island is 21 miles long from north to south, and its widest point about 14 miles across, expanding into a pear shape. It is 55 miles around the shore, not following the indentations, and contains 166 square miles. A low ridge runs through the center from north to south. It has one mountain, Mt. Hillaby, which is

1,145 feet high; the surface generally is undulating, with great variety of hill and dale, of the gentler kind, not having any of the abrupt declivities and wild ravines, such as are characteristic of the Antilles. It is a rolling country and the soil is very prolific; the landscape is variegated with a luxuriant verdure, which makes it look very much like England.

This island was first taken possession of by the English and they settled it, scarcely any other nationality being there, except the negro slaves. The English have always held it, without any contest with other nations, in all the wars and revolutions that have occurred around it. The English began to settle there about the same time that they began business on Dover Neck; some of them may have been neighbors in the old Home; their descendants kept up the acquaintance through several generations, by way of trade, with vessels frequently going back and forth between the island and New England.

The first settlers in Barbadoes raised corn, yams, sweet potatoes, etc. The cultivation of the sugar cane was introduced from South America in 1641; this soon became the chief business and the manufacture of sugar amassed great fortunes for the planters. Indigo, cotton, tobacco and ginger were also largely produced. Molasses and rum, in time, became by-products of the sugar cane, and it is said these were both very popular commodities in Dover for many years. It was fashionable to use that beverage in those days.

The success of the cultivation of the sugar cane soon drew money and men to the island to engage in the business. Dover men not only went down there in their ships to trade, but quite a number invested in the sugar business, by which they acquired much wealth. Robert Nanny, one of the signers of the Combination paper of 1640, in the old log meeting house, purchased a plantation there and settled on it to manage it himself. Thomas Beard, another Dover Neck man, was resident there in 1668, having a large estate on which he resided. It is the tradition that members of the Hanson family made investments there, with satisfactory returns; and one married an English lady who became the maternal ancestor of one branch of the succeeding Hanson family in Dover, and has honored descendants here now.

BARBADOES ISLAND.

One of Dover's historic spots is Barbadoes Pond; most persons, who have thought anything about it, have wondered why in the world such a name was given to that beautiful little pond of water. The explanation is this: Some enterprising merchant, or some thrifty sea captain, who had grown rich in his trade with Barbadoes people, was so pleased that he gave the name to a timber lot that the town had granted to him. It was a custom adopted in the earliest times in Dover to thus name land grants, to fix something for a record where to find it, and locate other lots, as they were granted. Originally the name, Barbadoes, was applied to quite a tract of land, but for a long time has been used only as the name of the pond.

It may interest the reader to know something of what the old records say about this section of Old Dover, called Barbadoes, now in the town of Madbury.

What is known as Kelley's Springs was originally Barbadoes springs. It received its present name from William Kelley, who received a grant of land on which it is located, from the town of Dover. Mr. Kelley was a famous tanner and currier, and built the first Kelley house there. For many years in the 19th century the water from these springs was one of the supplies for Dover citizens on the south side of the Cochecho River.

The locality called Barbadoes is mentioned in various land transfers by Robert Evans of Mendon, Mass. One was June 5th, 1711, when he conveyed to Joseph Meader of Dover, 60 acres of land that was granted to his father, Robert Evans, Sr., and laid out in "Cochecho Swamp" on the south side of the way "that goeth to a place commonly called Barbadoes."

Benjamin Evans, April 10, 1739, sold to Hercules Mooney, then a schoolmaster in that part of Old Dover, now Durham, eleven acres in "ye place commonly called Barbadoes," on the north side of the road from Littleworth to Barrington, beginning at Robert Hanson's bound.

April 6, 1702, the town of Dover granted to Joseph Evans thirty acres of land in—"Barbadoes Woods."

Captain John Wingate made his Will in 1714, and in it he bequeathed to his son Edward thirty acres in—"Barbadoes Woods." This lot is again referred to in a deed from Simon and Joanna

Wingate to their brother Moses, in 1736, and is then spoken of as on the south side of the road that "led from Barbadoes Springs."

Thomas Hanson of Dover in his Will of Sept. 18, 1728, bequeathed to his son Timothy, sixty acres in "Barbadoes Woods."

February 18, 1732-3, Pomfrett Whitehouse conveyed to Nathaniel Hanson thirty-two acres in "Barbadoes Woods," which were granted to his father, Pomfrett Whitehouse, by the town of Dover, in 1702, and laid out to him in 1721. Numerous other quotations might be given, but let this suffice to show the usage of the name in the long ago.

PROOFS OF DOVER'S SHIPPING BUSINESS WITH THE WEST INDIES.

After New Hampshire became a working province, as New Hampshire, separate from Massachusettts, in 1680, Portsmouth became the Port of entry for the province, where custom duties were collected, and the records show facts in regard to Dover's shipping business. The following is the record for one week in the year 1692.

"Arrived,—Sept. 17, 1692, the bark 'Mary,' of Kittery, from Barbadoes, loaded with rum, and limestone for ballast."

"The 'Friends Endeavor' of Portsmouth, from Barbadoes, Nichilas Follett, commander, loaded with sugar, molasses and salt."

"Sept. 19, the brigantine 'Friendship,' of Dover, Samuel Rines commander. from Barbadoes, loaded with salt, rum, molasses and English goods."

So constant was Dover's intercourse with Barbadoes Island, in early times, that business letters and official communications were entrusted to the sturdy commanders of vessels sailing from Dover and Portsmouth, via Barbadoes to England, then a popular and thrifty course of communication with the Home Land. Following is a sample of the official communications that were sent by that route to England. It is found in Vol. I, Provincial Records, page 7.

"By the Governor and Council:

"Whereas frequent complaints are made by merchants, inhabitants of Jamaica, Barbadoes and Leeward Islands, and other his Majesty's plantations, to which pine boards are exported from this Province, of the unreasonable thinness of the boards and the unevan edges of the boards, which unremidied may prove of great detriment to the trade of the Province, and loss of that trade. It is thereby ordered that from henceforth no pine boards shall be accounted merchantable, or delivered in payment, that are not one full inch in thickness, and square edged. And if any boards go out otherwise, such allowance shall be made unto the buyer, or receiver, thereof, as shall be judged reasonable by a sworn surveyor, or collector, to be appointed for that purpose.

"Dated 4th of October, in the 35 th year of the reign of our sovereign lord, King Charles the Second, A. D. 1685."

"R. Chamberlain, Clerk of Council."

Here is another from the Provincial Papers which is of interest in this connection of Dover merchants and ship-masters. It is a petition presented to the General Assembly in 1698, by Captain Richard Gerrish of Dover.

"To ye Honorable Leitt. Governor and Councill & Representatives convened in General Assembly, now sitting att Porttsmouth. The petition of Richard Gerrish of Dover, commander of ye ship 'Benjamin,' humbly sheweth:—

"That wheras your petitioner, an inhabitant of this Province, and now commander off said ship, which was built in this River, at Dover, and now bound for Barbapoes, and coming from Boston, where I paid the duty of 'Powder Money,' which is again here demanded at Portsmouth; and considering the advantage that has accrued to this place (Portsmouth) by means of ye trade used by said ship, and how hard it would bear on my owners to pay 'Powder Money' twice, in one voyage, by my coming here to load;—

"I hymbly pray your honors to remitt ye same, or soe to mitigate itt as may be a furder Incoragement to my Concerne, as also to your Honors' most Humble servant."

"Richard Gerrish."

In Council and Assembly, August 8, 1698:—Ordered that he pay his "Powder Money" here as in Boston.

THE BOUND TREE: PILGRIM OAK OF THE FOREST PRIMEVAL.

There were two historic trees standing on Dover Neck in 1915; one is now living, the other is dead; they were the *"Bound Oak"* and the *"Millet Apple Tree."* The first mentioned stands in the Howard Millet Roberts's orchard, about thirty-five rods east of the Roberts house on the State road. This tree is more than 300 years old, and must have been quite a good sized tree when Edward Hilton and his party landed at Pomeroy's Cove, at *Dover Point,* in the spring of 1623. This oak is twenty-three feet in circumference at the base; at eight feet from the ground it is fifteen feet in circumference; the lowest branch is about twelve feet from the ground. The central part of the tree, when complete, was about ninety feet tall; that central part became decayed and a large part of it fell off a few years ago; the remaining branches encircle a space ninety feet in diameter. It is a grand old monarch now; it was magnificent when in full leaf with its full top and wide spreading branches. It is much regretted there is no picture of it in its prime.

The first owner of the land on which it stands was Gov. Thomas Roberts; the land has always remained in possession of his descendants, coming to the present owners by regular inheritance from father to son; eight generations. It received its name from the fact that it stood on the boundary line between the farms of Governor Thomas Roberts's two sons, Thomas and John; the former's farm was on the north side of the tree and the latter's was on the south side. The house which Thomas Roberts, Sr., built, and in which he lived, after receiving the grant of land from the town, about 1635, stood about thirty rods northeast of the oak, on the bank of the river. Stones that were part of the cellar wall can be seen there now. In the year 1921 a granite stone properly marked was placed there by the Society of Colonial Wars of New Hampshire, and several descendants of Governor Roberts.

A WRESTLING MATCH UNDER THE OAK.

Mr. Howard M. Roberts told the writer an interesting story connected with the "Bound Tree;" he had heard his father tell it

THE BOUND OAK. (See page 80.)

many times. The event took place several years before the Revolutionary war. There were several negro slaves owned by residents of Dover Neck; they were the reminders of the trade that had been carried on a great many years with Barbadoes Island and the West Indies in general, when negro slaves were brought up here on return voyages, and they and their children were held as slaves; they were glad to get here and escape from the cruel masters they had worked under in the islands; they never wanted to leave Dover, where they were kindly treated. Their work here was play compared with what they had to do on the sugar plantations in the West Indies.

Mr. Roberts's grandfather, Joseph Roberts, had a stalwart negro named Caeser; Joseph's kinsman, Thomas Roberts, who lived where Mr. Wm. M. Courser now (1923) lives, also had a negro slave, named Pompy, who was as stalwart as Caeser. One day their masters got to bragging about their colored servants; each claimed his man was the best. Finally, in a friendly way, they agreed to let their men try their strength at a wrestling match, that then being a fashionable sport among the farmers. It was decided to hold it under the *"Bound Oak,"* as that was on the dividing line between the two neighbors. The day was set and the neighbors were invited to attend and witness the contest of strength and skill in wrestling.

At the appointed time the neighbors gathered under the old monarch of the forest primeval, and Caeser and Pompy came prepared to entertain the spectators, with all the strength and agility that was in them. It was argeed that the winner must throw his opponent and hold him to the ground on that side of the dividing line which was his master's land, the oak showing which was Joseph's and which was Thomas's farm.

Caeser took his stand on the south side of the oak; Pompy faced him on the north side; the word was given and the contest began, in accordance with the rules of the game in that period. They did some fine sparring, covering much ground, then clinched for a throw, and Caeser downed Pompy; the crowd cheered; but it was not a win, as Caeser had thrown him on the wrong side of the oak; the men were on their feet almost as quickly as they were down, and renewed their sparring; first on one side of the oak then on the other, then all around it; the spectators cheering continually; each threw the other several times, but in each instance on the wrong side of the tree; which would not count to win. The struggle went on in this way for about an hour, or so. It was a hot day in September; the men began to get weary, but at last Caeser got Pompy onto the south side of the oak and threw him to the ground and held him there firmly until he was declared the winner. The spectators cheered, and then stepped forward and congratulated both of the boxers on the fine work they had done and the good sport they had provided for the dwellers on Dover Neck.

THE BIG ELM.

There is a magnificent elm tree, on the bank of the river, about fifty rods southeast of the oak. Near it the Roberts family had a tannery, which was in active use for more than a century. For quite a period there was a public house near the tannery. The tradition about the origin of this elm is that one day a gentleman rode to this public house on horseback; he hitched his horse and stuck his driving whip into the wet ground of spring-time; when he had finished his business he mounted his horse and drove away, leaving the elm twig where he stuck it in the ground; the twig took root and grew to be the magnificent tree it now is, and has been for nearly two centuries.

CAPTAIN THOMAS MILLET AND HIS APPLE-TREE.

The Millet apple-tree dates from 1720; it bore apples until the year 1913, when it died; its last crop was in 1912; it blossomed in 1913, but the brown tail moths ate every blossom and leaf and the tree died, aged 195 years; its trunk was standing till 1918 when it was cut down; but for the brown tail moths it undoubtedly would have lived to complete two centuries of life.

According to the undeviating tradition in the Millet family, and in the families living in the immediate vicinity, the tree was brought from England in a tub, when but a small shrub; a white rose bush also came in the same tub; the tub was used as a wash tub for many years. Thomas Millet was a young sea captain of Gloucester, Mass., and brought it home in his ship on a return voyage from England, in 1720. Very soon he planted the shrub where the old stump now stands, at the southwest corner of the house that the late Calvin Coleman lived in for more than eighty years, and ate fruit from it nearly every year, as the tree was a thrifty bearer. The Coleman house is not the house in which Capt. Millet lived, which was further back from the road.

The trunk of the tree was about four feet in diameter; it was about eight feet from the ground to where the branches came out, and of uniform size. It was hollow in 1915, one-third of the shell being rotted away, so there was room for two persons to stand inside of the shell, which was sound and ten inches thick. In its prime the tree had wide spreading branches, and a lofty top, magnificent in proportions. Some years it had been known to bear forty and fifty bushels of apples a year; even in its old age it blossomed and bore fruit nearly every year, down to its old age it blossomed and bore fruit nearly every year, down to its death in 1913.

Mr. Howard Millet Roberts, a great grandson of Captain Millet, cut twigs from the old tree and grafted them into a thrifty young tree, in the orchard near his house. The grafted tree bears a large crop of fruit every year. The apples have a mild and delicious flavor, and are of large size.

The large branches of the original tree fell off one by one, from year to year; but smaller branches grew out and took their places and bore fruit; in that way the tree reproduced itself so long a time. The tree stood on the east side of the State road, a short distance below Riverview Hall.

CAPTAIN THOMAS MILLET.

In connection with this tree it seems proper to give a brief sketch of Captain Thomas Millet. He was son of Lieut. Thomas Millet of Gloucester, Mass., where he was born Dec. 20, 1689; he came to Dover to reside in the year 1720; he died here the first week in August, 1761. His father was born in Southwark, England, in 1633, and came to Dorchester, Mass., in 1635, in the ship

"*Elizabeth*"; in 1655 he and his parents removed to Gloucester, Mass. His mother's maiden name was Mary Greenoway. Thomas Millet, Sr., died in 1685; his son, Thomas, Jr., died in 1707. Thomas, Sr., in his Will, gave to his sons and wife, property as follows:—"To my wife, Mary, all of ye my house and upland, about five acres, more or less, situated and lying in Gloucester, in ye county of Essex, near ye mill yt was formerly Mr. John Emerson's; and to my sons, Thomas and John, who now (1706) liveth with me, all my estate lying and being part in Manchester and part in Gloucester." In 1721 (Capt.) Thomas sold his half of this estate to his brother John. In the deed, which is now on file in the archives at Salem, Mass., he is designated as "Captain Thomas Millet of Dover, N. H., late of Gloucester, Mass., and brother of John;" and that "for the sum of 600 pounds conveys to said John Millet all the interest in the estate of his father of which they were joint heirs." His wife, Love (Bunker) Millet signed the deed. This shows that they were married and living in Dover as early as 1720. Probably they were married in 1719. She died Nov. 1, 1763, and was given a grand funeral, at which costly "mourning rings" were given to friends.

It appears that his father, Lieut. Thomas Millet, gave the boy the best education the Gloucester schools afforded and then set him to work as a mariner, in which business he had risen to be captain of a coasting vessel before he was twenty years old. Before he was twenty-five he had become familiar with the routes to the West Indies and to England. In his coasting trade he had visited Dover many times, and had sailed up the Oyster River, to its head waters in pursuit of merchandise. In passing up and down the river he passed Bunker's Creek, on the north side of the river; in sight of the river and on a hill on the west side of the creek, stood Bunker's garrison; in this house Love Bunker was born, A. D. 1700; in some way not explained, but satisfactory in results, Captain Millet made the acquaintance of this young lady and when she was about 19 years old he married her; soon after that they went to live at Dover Neck, which became their home during the remainder of their lives.

Captain John Tuttle died in August, 1720. For more than forty years he had been one of the leading men of Dover and the province of New Hampshire; lumber man, ship builder, high official and a gentleman *"sans peur, sans reproche,"* for more than a half century. Captain Millet came here that same year and took the shipping business which Captain Tuttle had carried on many years, using the old Tuttle ship yard in which to build ships. That yard was on Fore River, not far from the historic apple tree. He was engaged in the work of ship building thirty years or more and became very wealthy. He was also largely engaged in the West India trade, especially with Barbadoes Island.

Captain Millet was a good servant of the public as well as a prudent manager of his private affairs. He was one of the Selectmen of Dover in 1732, and in twenty other years; he was Representative in 1731, and seven other years; he was one of the judges of the supreme court in 1740, 1741, and 1742; but he was always known as Captain Millet; he had won that title before he came to Dover to reside, but he also won that title as commander of the Dover Neck militia company for a number of years. The Millet family became one of the aristocratic branches of colonial society when Governor Benning Wentworth set a pretty high standard for social life.

MUSTER ROLL OF CAPTAIN MILLET'S COMPANY.

Vol. IX, page 173, of the New Hampshire Provincial Papers, has the "List of Training Men under Thomas Millet, Captain of Dover," July 21, 1740.

SERGEANTS:

Daniel Titcomb. Thomas Leighton.

CORPORALS:

John Clement. John Bickford.
John Young. John Leighton.

PRIVATES:

Joshua Perkins. Joseph Daniel.
Paul Canney. John Daniel.
Ephraim Tebbetts. Henry Bussy.
Thomas Ash. Eli Demeret, Jr.
Joshua Canney. John Ham, Jr.
Samuel Holden. Daniel Bunker.

Joseph Bickford.
Timothy Robinson.
John Cromwell.
Solomon Perkins.
John Perkins.
Richard Plumer.
Thomas Canney.
Thomas Canney, Jr.
Otis Pinkham.
Samuel Waits.
Joseph Cromwel.
Abraham Nute.
John Pearl.
Nathaniel Austin.
Thomas Drew, Jr.
Moses Varney.
Hatevil Hall.
James Jackson.
Timothy Moses, Jr.
John Huckins.
David Daniel.
Samuel Chesley.
Stephen Willey.
Anthony Jones.
Joseph Hall, Jr.
Samuel Roberts.
Ebenezer Tuttle.
Joseph Hubbard.
Tobias Randal.
Charles Bickford.
Ichabod Tibbetts.
Stephen Hawkins.
Aaron Roberts.
Thomas Ransom.
Ambrus Bantum.
Isaac Allen.
Clement Ham.
    Total 97.

Zachariah Bunker.
Henry Tibbets.
John Field, Jr.
Samuel Starboard.
Stephen Starboard.
John Tuttle.
James Tuttle.
Thomas Tuttle.
Nicholas Tuttle.
Samuel Hayes.
Joseph Tibbetts.
Shadrach Hodgdon.
John Giles.
James Leighton.
Tristrum Pinkham.
William Allen.
Joseph Allen.
Paul Nute.
Thomas Pinkham, Jr.
Hatevil Laighton.
John Harvey.
Nathaniel Roberts.
Thomas Roberts.
Joseph Dam.
Benjamin Bodge, Jr.
Vincent Torr.
Stephen Pinkham.
James Pinkham, Jr.
Jonathan Daniel.
Jacob Daniel.
Jonathan Harriman.
John Randal.
Joseph Drew.
John Follet.
Solomon Pinkham, Jr.
Robert Wille.
Benjamin Wille.
Clement Harvey.

A LIST OF YE SECOND FOOT COMPANY OF DOVER JULY THE 24, 1740.

SEARGANTS:

John Horn.
Jonathan Young.

Epherem Ham.
John Tasker.

CORPORALS:

Ezera Kimbel.

Natha. Young.
John Demerit.

DRUMMERS:

John Carter.

John Marden.

PRIVATES:

Daniel Plumer.
Job Clement.
Samuel Clement.
Samuel Dam.
Samuel Alley.
John Alley.
John Muckelaroy.
William Whitehouse.
James Withrel.
John Hanson, Jr.
William Horn.
Nathaniel Horn.
Ezekel Wentworth.
Epherem Wentworth.
Joeph Connor.
James Chesley.
John Varney.
Nemiah Kembel.
Thomas Hanson.
John Horn, Jr.
John Waldron.
Nathn. Varney.
Stephen Varney.
Elihu Heays.
John Tenits.
Nathn. Ham.
Daniel Ham.

Samuel Davis.
Samuel Alley, Jr.
William Hill.
Saml. Williams.
Jonth. Ham.
William Perey.
Joseph Hicks.
Francis Dru.
Solomon Emerson.
William Tasker.
Thomas Bickford.
Ezariah Budey.
Derey Pitman.
Zeeberiah Pitman.
Zechariah Pitman.
Zechariah Edgerly.
William Demeret.
Daniel Harvey.
John Bussel.
James Huckins.
Nathl. Davis.
John Fay, Jr.
Ralph Hall.
Joseph Perkins.
Benjn Hall.
John Brown.
Joseph Jackson.

Daniel Horne.
Peter Hayes.
John Hayes, Jr.
Samuel Varney.
Thomas Heays.
Ezekiah Heays.
Mark Gells.
Ichobod Heays.
John Tibbets, Jr.
Jeremiah Tibbits.
Isaac Twombly.
Thomas Young.
Isaac Young.
Robert Evens, Jr.
John Evens.
Nathaniel Hanson.
John Cook.
Henry Bickford.
Nathan Garland.
William Twombly, Jr.
Samuel Young.
Stephen Oats.
Israel Hodgdon, Jr.
John Hanson.
Timothy Hanson.
James Kelley.
Joseph Hanson, Jr.
Ichobod Cenney.
John James.
Joseph Winget.
Jose Joseph Hall.
Richard Scammons.
Jona Church.
Isaac Watson.
Samuel Hoge.
Henry Marshal.
Richard Pinkham, Jr.
Ebenezer Pinkham.
James Biber.

Clement Dru
Meshack Dru.
Elezir Davis.
Daniel Clement.
Richard Clark.
Jonth. Hanson.
Richard Hearn.
Joseph Husings.
James Young.
Jabez Garland
Saml. Heard.
James Richard.
Isaac Horne.
Joseph Ham.
Reuben Heays.
Joseph Heays.
Saml. Hanson.
Danie Evens.
Nathn. Hanson, Jr.
Ezekiah Cook.
Elezer Young.
Benjn. Young.
Joseph Hanson, third.
Joseph Estears.
Isaac Hanson.
Elisha Esters.
Jonth. Chusing.
Saml. Gerrish.
John Winget, Jr.
Saml. Winget.
John Whighthouse.
Benjn. Thrasher.
Saml. Watson.
Saml. Davis, Jr.
Samuel Tasker.
Thomas Harris.
David Dru.
Joseph Evens, third.
Solomon Hanson.

Maul Hanson.
John Twombly, Jr.
Benja. Allen.
Benjn. Pinkem.
Benja Heays.
Job Clement, Jr.

A True Coppey pr. Me William Welland, Clerk.
A true Coppey attested by the Clark, under oath.

Total 153.   John Winget, Left.

THIS IS THE LIST OF THE TROOPERS UNDER THE COMMAND OF CORP'LL TRISTRAM COFFIN IN DOVER, JULY YE 29, 1740.

Corporals:

Benja. Ham.   Jos. Ham.
Jos. Thomas.

Privates:

John Young, Jr.
James Nute, Jr.
Isaac Lebbey.
Paul Gerrish, Jr.
Saml. Heard, Jr.
Ralph Twombly.
Benja. Hanson, JNr.
Dudley Watson.
Benja. Wamouth, Jr.
John Tebbetts, Jr.
Richard Waldron.
Ebenezer Nock.
William Styles.
William Horne, Jr.
Thomas Tebbets, Jr.
Moses Stevens.
Shedrech Walton.
Benja. Robarts, Jr.
Elejah Tuttle.
Spensor Wentworth.
John Drew.
John Heard.
Jonathan Durgen.
John Drew, Jr.
Richard Jones.
Joshua Stagpole.
Daniell Rogers.
Jonathan Watson.
Dodefer Ham.
Ambros Bampton.
Daniell Horne, Jr.
Jos. Drew.
Nathaniel Rendall, Jun.
Jonathan Hanson.
Stephen Jenkins, Jun.
Benja. Jackson.
Samuell Stagpole.

Total—41.—Stephen Robarts, Clark.

BEGINNING OF THE SETTLEMENT ON DOVER NECK.—1633.

In preceding pages it has been shown how Edward Hilton was connected with the three merchants of Bristol, who were the financial backers, and partners of David Thomson in his beginning of the temporary settlement at Little Harbor, in the spring of 1623, and left there for his permanent settlement on Thomson's Island, in Boston Harbor, about 1626. The Little Harbor settlement was a financial failure, and the "three merchants" had the property left on their hands. To partially recompense their loss at Little Harbor they made an arrangement with Hilton to continue his settlement at *Hilton Point*. Then, in 1629-30, Hilton obtained his Squamscott Patent from the Plymouth Council to protect his rights, and define his boundaries, between his land and that which the Council had, four months previously, granted to Captain John Mason, in his "Laconia patent."

That was a period of great land "expectations," by which a colony would be established on the Pascataqua River, which would outrival the Massachusetts Bay Colony at Boston. This Squamscot Patent led Mr. Hilton to engage in a lot of financial schemes to develop his property; this is explained later. One result was that Captain Thomas Wiggin was sent over by those engaged in the new deal, to investigate and report plans for sending over some additional settlers to help Mr. Hilton. He came in 1631, and stayed a year. He learned what was being done in Boston and Salem, and examined Mr. Hilton's territory.

In his surveys he saw what a beautiful place the hill, on Dover Neck, was to establish a village like those he was acquainted with in England. He probably made a complete plan of how he would have the streets and lanes, and may be he engaged Mr. Hilton's employees to cut a road along the shore from Pomeroy's Cove to the foot of the hill. It is not unreasonable to suppose Captain Wiggin, also, engaged those crews to do a lot of preliminary lumbering, in the way of felling trees, and clearing up the ground for the coming pioneer settlers, who were to establish the English village on the hill.

The settlement on Dover Neck began in October, 1633. The colonists who struck the first blows to prepare for habitations came over from the west of England, in the ship *"James,"* and landed at Salem, Mass., 10th of October, 1633. There were "about thirty" in the party, nearly all men; they had been eight weeks on the voyage from Gravesend to Salem; "some of them were of good estates and of some account for religion,"—that is, they were rich men and Puritans, of the same class and religious opinions as the men who settled in Boston, Salem and towns around in the Massachusetts Bay Colony. These colonists did not remain long in Salem but soon came along the coast by water to the Pascataqua River and up to *Hilton Point,* landing at Pomeroy's Cove at the west end of The Point, where the old settlers there cordially greeted them, and gave them the best accommodations their houses afforded; those who could not get a place in which to sleep, on the land, continued to abide at night on the *"James,"* until they could build houses for themselves. In 1634 more men, with women and children, arrived from England and joined the colony, but those who arrived in October encountered and completed the hardest part of the work, as a dense forest then covered Dover Neck. To make the land ready for a village, such as the colonists came from in Old England, required much hard work, chopping down trees, cutting paths, and constructing log houses, for use during the cold weather of the winter. From reports in Massachusetts it does not appear to have been a very severe season, but comfortably mild, so the work of destruction of the forest and construction of roads and houses was carried on rapidly.

There is no record of just what these pioneers did first, but from what we know was done it seems reasonably sure that first of all they cut a path through the woods along the shore from Pomeroy's Cove, where now the railroad crosses the State Road to the rise of the ground a short distance below where stood the old Millet apple tree, in front of the Coleman house.

From the foot of the hill they cut a path northwesterly to the height of land, between what is now (1923) the State Road and

Back Cove, where later they located their first log meeting-house. Also they cut a path a short distance up the hill, where the State Road is. Then, having cleared away the trees, the first houses were built in this section, the meeting-house being the center of business during the first years, as all public meetings were held there, town meetings as well as religious meetings. In a couple of years the village had grown so that the settlement reached the top of the hill, above where the second meeting-house was built in 1654, and its site is now marked by a wall with a bronze tablet. We know this, as Elder Hatevil Nutter's residence was a short distance above the meeting-house, on the east side of the road, in 1636, as he stated in a deposition many years later. They called this road High Street, and the hill was "Nutter's hill." They called the road on which the log meeting-house stood, Low Street, and the minister and many of the prominent citizens lived on that thoroughfare. Later they had other roads, called lanes, connecting with these to enable the dwellers to conveniently reach the log meeting-house, the center of business. But no more will be said now of the village; a description will be given on pages further on. Who were the men who did these things and how were the changes brought about?

The leading man, or at least the chief manager, in this new colony was Captain Thomas Wiggin, but his chief supporters appear to have been Lord Say and Lord Brooke, their official titles, and these men are entitled to credit of being the second founders of Dover, as Captain John Mason was founder of Portsmouth in 1630. When Edward Hilton obtained from the Council of Plymouth, 12th of March, 1630, his Squamscot patent or grant, confirming and defining the bounds of the territory he had acquired under David Thomson's grant of 6,000 acres in 1622, the document was made to begin as follows: "Now, know yee that the said President and Council by Virtue and authority of his Majesty's Said Letters Pattents, and for and in consideracon that Edward Hilton & his Associates hath already at his and their owne proper costs and charges transported sundry servants to plant in New England aforesaid at a place there called by the natives Wecana cohunt, otherwise *Hilton's Point,* lying som two leagues from the mouth of the River Pascataquack in New England aforesaid, where they have *already* built some houses, and planted Corne, etc. etc."

We do not know the names of his "associates," but the actual delivery of this patent was by Thomas Lewis, by power of attorney, to Edward Hilton, on the premises, 7 July, 1631, in presence of Thomas Wiggin, William Hilton, Samuel Sharpe, and James Downe. All that we know about his "associates" is that they were merchants of Shrewsbury, Bristol and other towns of the West of England, particularly of Devonshire County. On a map of New England, in 1634, the *Hilton Point* and Dover Neck settlement is called "Bristol," from the fact that Bristol men owned two-thirds of the joint stock land property under the new patent. It is evident from the history of contemporaneous events that Thomas Wiggin was one of these Bristol associates and they appointed him as their agent; hence he was here and witnessed the signing of the transfer July 7, 1631, and remained here some time making plans for the future. He returned, in 1632, to England and set about the work of getting men to come over here and settle on Dover Neck. He was a hustler, but it took time to find the men and get them interested enough to leave their old home and come over here to plant a new settlement in the wilderness, of what was to be Dover. It required all of the year 1632, and up to June, 1633, to get thirty men ready and on board the ship *"James,"* which set sail from Gravesend, England, about the 10th of that month. While he was doing this work of organizing the emigrant party he had opportunity to show his friendship for the Puritan government of Massachusetts. Governor Winthrop says, in his history of this period:

"Sir Ferdinando Gorges and Capt. (John) Mason had preferred a petition to the lords of the Privy council against us, charging us with many false accusations; but through the Lord's good providence * * * and the good testimony given in our behalf by one Capt. Wiggin, who dwelt at Pascataquack, and had been diverse times among us, their malicious practice took not effect."

From this it appears Mr. Wiggin had attained the title of "Captain" in England, and that he was a Puritan and friend of Governor John Winthrop. In 1641, when the arrangements were made, in October, to place Dover under the rule of Massachusetts, which was carried into effect in 1642, it is stated that "some lords, knights, gentlemen, and others did purchase of Edward Hilton and some merchants of Bristol two patents."

Furthermore, John Allen and partners made a declaration in 1654, that the Bristol men sold their interest in this Dover land to Lord Say, Lord Brooke, Sir Richard Saltonstall, Sir Arthur Heselrig, Mr. Boswell, Mr. Willis, Mr. Whiting, Mr. Hewell, and others, for £2,150. — An old land conveyance on record in Boston, dated 13 May, 1648, says: "Whereas Lords Say and Brooke obtained two patents, now commonly called and knowne by the name of Swampscott and Dover * * * and whereas Robert Saltonstall hath bought twelve shares of twenty-five into which the patent is divided; that is, of Lord Brooke four, of Lord Say one share, etc. etc." In 1634, Gov. Winthrop says: "The Lords Say and Brooke wrote (to him) and to Mr. Bellingham, that however they might have sent a man-of-war to beat down the house at Kenebeck * * * they desired that some of ours (of Boston) might be joined with Captain Wiggin, their agent at Pascataquack, to see justice done." — Again, in Winthrop's Journal, 14 February, 1635, is the statement that: "Capt. Wiggin, governor at Pascataquack under the Lords Say and Brooke, etc. etc." The patent or patents thus appear to have been divided into twenty-five shares; and these were bought and sold, as shown by conveyances still on record, as shares in modern land companies are bought and sold. Lords Say and Brooke held the controlling interest and Captain Thomas Wiggin was their agent and manager in getting the Dover Neck settlers to emigrate in 1633. The historian, Hubbard, says these Lords, "employed Mr. Wiggin to act in their behalf for the space of seven years, the Shrewsbury men still retaining their own shares." That period closed in 1637, when Rev. George Burdett became governor, by popular election, he having succeeded Rev. William Leverich as minister of the parish in 1636.

On the 25th of March, 1633, Edward Howes wrote from London to Governor Winthrop in Boston, Mass., and said: "There are honest men about to buye out the Bristol men's plantation in Pascataqua, and do propose to plant there 500 good people before Michelmas next. T. Wiggin is the chief agent therein." And again, 22 June, 1633, he says: "He (Wiggin) intends to plant himself and many gracious men there this sommer. * * * I have, and you all have cause to bless God that you (will) have soe good a neighbour as Capt. Wiggin." — The Bristol men owned two-thirds interest in the double patent.

The above quotations from contemporary authorities are given to show, and do show, that Edward Hilton had men of Bristol, Shrewsbury, and other towns in England, as his associates in business in 1630; that Captain Thomas Wiggin was leader, or agent, in England; that the Bristol men sold their interests to Lords Say and Brooke; that these gentlemen retained Captain Wiggin seven years in management of the business at Dover Neck, and the Massachusetts authorities recognized him as governor up to 1637, when Burdett was elected governor, Captain Wiggin having commenced his personal plantation on the Greenland shore of Great Bay, which was part of the Squamscott patent. Furthermore, it appears that these Dover Neck settlers were, for the most part, Puritans of the same class as those of Governor Winthrop's colony in Massachusetts Bay, but they came here strictly for business, rather than to have a larger religious liberty. That they were religious men is shown by the fact that they brought the Rev. William Leverich, a Puritan minister, with them, who commenced to officiate as minister of the First Parish as soon as the log meeting-house was completed in the winter of 1633. The proof that they actually came here in 1633 is found in Governor Winthrop's Journal of that year. He says:

"The same day (10 October, 1633), Mr. (Capt.) Grant, in the ship *James,* arrived at Salem, having been but eight weeks between Gravesend and Salem. It brought Capt. Wiggin and about thirty, with one Mr. Leverich, a godly minister, to Pascataquack, which Lord Say and Lord Brooke had purchased of the Bristol men, and about forty for Virginia, and about twenty for this place (Boston), and some sixty cattle." — The historian, Hubbard, writing a half century later, says: "In the interim (1633-1640), several persons of good estate were, by the interests of the Lords and other gentlemen, induced to transport themselves thither, so many as sufficed to make a considerable township."

BRISTOL AND SHREWSBURY.

In the preceding pages there is frequent mention of Bristol and Shrewsbury, so it seems well, at this point, to give the reader an idea of what and where Bristol is in England. It is in the southwest of that island, located on the Lower Avon River, which flows into the river Severn and by that is connected with Bristol Channel, which separates England from Wales. At the quay in Bristol the river Frome unites with the Avon, and this is a large and important shipping point, and has been such from earliest period in history. This river Avon must not be confused with that farther inland, on which Stratford is located, and where William Shakespeare was born, and where he died and was buried, after doing an extensive and lucrative theatre business in London. The Stratford Avon flows into the Severn River fifty miles above Bristol, which is one of the very ancient towns inhabited by the Romans, some marks of whose works can still be traced there. There is sufficient depth of water in the rivers there for ships of large size. It is supposed the name Bristol is derived from the old Saxon word Brigstow, meaning the place of a bridge, as at the junction of the Frome and the Avon is where the first bridge was built in that part of England. There was a town there, built by the Britains, long before the Romans dwelt in it, so its age antedates the Christian era. Its recorded history begins, however, with the subjugation of Gloucestershire by William the Conqueror in 1068. The next year three sons of the king from whom it had been captured came over from Ireland, at the head of fifty-two ships, and sailed up Bristol Channel and the river Avon to Bristol, and as they sailed along Bristol Channel they laid waste the property along the shores. The citizens of Bristol put up a sharp defense and destroyed several ships with their crews, and finally, under the leadership of Geoffry Mowbray, Bishop of Constance, nephew of the famous Tancred, the Crusader, the whole fleet was completely routed.

Bristol has a castle which is famous in the history of several centuries. King Stephen was imprisoned there, until exchanged for the famous Earl of Gloucester, who had been defeated in battle by the army of Stephen's Queen, and captured at Winchester. In Shakespeare's "Richard II" is a scene, laid at Bristol, wherein

Bolingbroke denounced the minions who had bravely defended the town and the castle against the attack of Bolingbroke's northern army, but were finally captured, and Bolingbroke ordered Northumberland to see that a lot of the leaders were speedily dispatched. They were beheaded in the center of the town, where then stood the high cross. The story is told in the drama, "King Richard II."

The *dramatis personae* are King Richard, his two uncles, John of Gaunt, the Duke of Lancaster, and the Duke of York; his two cousins, Henry, surnamed Bolingbroke, son of John of Gaunt, and the Duke of Aumerle, son of the Duke of York; these were, of course, both cousins of the King.

These cousins got into a quarrel about land titles and were going to settle it by fighting a duel; all of the preliminaries were arranged and it was about to begin in the presence of the King, when Richard called a halt, and settled the quarrel by banishing both from England; Bolingbroke to Normandy for six years; the other to some other country for life. John of Gaunt died soon after his son left for Normandy, and his nephew, King Richard, confiscated his Uncle John's estate. Soon after that the King went to Ireland to suppress a rebellion.

While Richard was in Ireland, Bolingbroke came over from Normandy with an army and commenced operations to recover his father's estate, which his uncle had confiscated. It was at Bristol that Bolingbroke began war. He soon captured the King's Lieutenants, Bushy and Greene, and he gave the following order in regard to them, as recorded by Shakespeare:

BOLINGBROKE:
    Bring forth these men!
Bushy and Green, I will not vex your souls,—
Since presently your souls must part your bodies—
With too much urging your pernicious lives,
For 'twere no charity; yet, to wash your blood
From off my hands, here, in the view of men,
I will unfold some causes of your deaths.
You have misled a prince, a royal king,
A happy gentleman in blood and lineaments,
By you unhappied and disfigured, clean:—
You have in manner with your sinful hours,
Made a divorce betwixt his queen and him.

>   Broke the possession of a royal bed,
>   And stained the beauty of a fair queen's cheeks
>   With tears drawn from her eyes by your foul wrongs.
>
>   Myself, a prince by fortune of my birth,
>   Near to the king in blood, and near in love,—
>   Till you did make him misinterpret me,
>   Have stoop'd my neck under your injuries,
>   And sigh'd my English breath in foreign clouds,
>   Eating the bitter bread of banishment;
>   Whilst you have fed upon my signories,
>   Dispark'd my parks and fell'd my forest woods,
>   From my own windows torn my household coat,
>   Razed out my impress, leaving me no sign,
>   Save men's opinions, and my living blood,
>   To show the world I am a gentleman.
>   This and much more, much more than twice all this,
>   Condemns you to death. See them delivered over
>   To execution and the hand of death.
> BUSHY:
>   More welcome is the stroke of death to me
>   Than Bolingbroke to England. Lords, farewell.
> GREEN:
>   My comfort is that heaven will take our souls
>   And plague injustice with the pains of hell.
> BOLINGBROKE:
>   My Lord Northumberland, see them despatched.
>   (Exeunt Northumberland and others with the prisoners)

They were executed on the public square in Bristol, where two centuries later martyrs were burned at the stake for preaching Puritan doctrines.

The doctrines of the Reformation were preached at Bristol by the followers of Tyndale, Cranmer, and Latimer, and our forefathers, by hearing this preaching, became "men of some account for religion," in the settlement they organized on Dover Neck. Some writers of Dover history have been disposed to unjustly sneer at that expression, and belittle the character of the people here in comparison with those of Plymouth and Boston. In speaking of the generation which preceded our forefathers and foremothers, one of the old chronicles says, that after listening to the preaching by the Reformation leaders, the wardens of all the churches in Bristol, and some of the ministers, "brought forth their Roods and other images which were in the churches to the High Cross where they were burnt." Previous to that five martyrs had been burned alive in that public square.

It was from this town that some of the Dover Neck settlers came in 1633, and hence they gave it the name Bristol, which it retained as long as Captain Wiggin was governor; in 1637, when Burdett became governor, by popular election, he changed it to Dover, which name was used until Rev. Thomas Larkham became minister of the parish, who changed it in 1640 to Northam, for the town in the West of England where he had been minister of the church. Soon after the settlement came under Massachusetts, in 1642, the name Dover was again used, but Northam was used frequently for a score of years.

WHY DID THESE PEOPLE COME OVER HERE?

Why did these people come over here? Why expatriate themselves? Why leave the comforts of their old home? Why undertake the hardships of the forests to be subdued? The answer was not given by any one of their number; they left no historical memoranda. Indeed, it is to the Plymouth and Boston historians that we look for the first contemporary record of the settlement of the Pascataqua; and it is to the Journal of Gov. John Winthrop that we are indebted for the record of the fact that they came in the ship *"James"* in 1633. And it is to the stories of the historian, Hubbard, of Ipswich, that we look for the few facts which he gathered forty years after, from the old men, of their coming and their work.

The answer to the question, why they came, cannot be given in a word, or a sentence. There was a spirit of adventure prevalent among the English people of that period. It characterized the Western counties of England in a marked degree. There was a restless feeling among the people, a desire to possess wealthy lands beyond the seas. In addition to this was the political and religious conditions that prevailed from 1620 to 1640, during which was the largest emigration to New England. This was the period in which no parliament met in England. English liberty was struggling against the tyranny of the Stuarts; and at the period of this Pascataqua Emigration, its prospects were gloomy. King

Charles First had, seven years before, levied tonnage, poundage, and ship-money, without a shadow of right, and Hampden's resistance, itself apparently futile, was three years in the future. The King had dissolved parliament after parliament, because none was submissive to his views, and he was ruling without a parliament. He had assented to the Petition of Right in 1628, but he was habitually and shamelessly violating its provisions. So little promise of security in civil rights existed, that many men were driven to the conclusion that the only way out of these difficulties was to emigrate and make new homes in the wilderness of New England; some did emigrate; others remained and fought the battle for freedom in England. Among those who remained at home were Dover's patrons, Lords Say and Brooke. It was a period of intense activity in religious thought. Everybody had been reading King James' new version of the Bible, and put various interpretations upon what they read. The great revolt of the Northern nations against the authority of the Pope of Rome had not come to the settled line which seems to separate the Teutonic and the Latin races; a line which makes a liquid language Roman, and a gutteral tongue Protestant. In fact, there was nothing promising in the broad outlook in England. Many protestants were becoming more protestant. The more they studied the Bible the stronger became their belief that it was not enough to hold that no authority but the Bible should govern's men's faith; none but that should impose rites and ceremonies. In what seemed to them the halfway reformation of the Church of England, they believed that some unscriptural observances were still obligatory. They rejected the requirements of arbitrary command. They were not, like the Plymouth Pilgrims, separatists from the Church of England. They scrupled at its ceremonies, but not at the existence of that Church; not at its doctrines, and scarcely at its polity.

In this period (1629-1640) of rapid emigration to New England there was little hope at home for a purer worship or for liberty of conscience. The tyrannical, bigoted, treacherous Charles was upon the throne. That very summer in which the Dover Neck emigrants set sail from England in the ship *"James,"* Laud was made archbishop of Canterbury and primate of all England. It was itself the threat that the High Commission Court, of which Laud was the moving power, and under whom, says Macaulay, "Even the devotions of private families could not escape the vigilance of his spies," was to be still more powerful. These Dover Neck men had no idea or expectation that King Charles, twelve years hence, would have his head chopped off. So they resolved to be free men in New England, under English law, where they could rear their children in a purer faith. All of these influences combined are the answer to the question: Why did these people come over here?

WHAT WERE THE NAMES OF THE MEN WHO CAME OVER IN THE SHIP "JAMES"?

What were the names of the men who came over in the ship *"James,"* which arrived at Salem, October 10, 1633, and soon after came up here to *Hilton Point* and commenced cutting the forest on Dover Neck? We know for certainty only two, Captain Thomas Wiggin and Rev. William Leverich, but it is quite probable that in the number were the larger part of those who signed the Combination agreement, in 1640, to establish good government, and some of those who were settled at Oyster River, in 1640, and did not sign that important document. But we do know for a certainty that Lord Say and Lord Brooke were practically the second founders of Dover, Edward Hilton being the first. They gave the colonists strong financial aid, hence deserve a brief mention here.

Robert Greville, second Baron Brooke, was a descendant, through female line, of a brother of the great Earl of Warwick, the "King-Maker." His predecessor in the barony was born in that same Alcester, in Warwickshire, in which Richard Walderne, famous in Dover and New Hampshire history, was born. Lord Brooke was a thorough Puritan, an adherent of the great cause of English liberty; he was a soldier rather than a statesman. His name in the current histories of that time is often coupled with that of Lord Say, in a remarkable degree, which indicates they were in close sympathy of sentiment and of action in public affairs. Equally is this so on the map, where Saybrook, in Connecticut, unites the two. In this connection it may be well to suggest that the sea-coast town in Rockingham County, Seabrook, ought to be spelled Saybrooke, as the name was not derived from any "brook" emptying into the sea there, but from the Lords Say and Brooke. Lord Brooke held important commands in the war with King Charles; he was lieutenant-general in rank; he lost his life in the attack upon the massive cathedral at Litchfield, in 1643. An engraved portrait of him is in Clarendon's "History of the Rebellion," edition of 1732.

William Fiennes, whose portrait also appears in Clarendon's history, was the eighth baron Say and Sele, and the first viscount. He was then (1633) forty-eight years of age. Few men were more prominent in the contests that produced the Civil War. "At his house in Broughton," says one writer, " the secret discussions of resistance to the court took place." Whitelocke, Cromwell's ambassador to Sweden, calls him "a statesman of great parts, wisdom and integrity." On the other hand, Clarendon, the historian and advocate of the court, calls Lord Say "a man who had the deepest hand in all the calamities which befell this unhappy kingdom, though he had not the least thought of dissolving the monarchy." "A man of great parts and of the highest ambition." "He had much authority with all the discontented party throughout the kingdom, and a good reputation with many who were not discontented, and who believed him to be a wise man, and of a very useful temper." "He had always opposed and contradicted all acts of State and all laws and impositions which were not strictly legal." "The oracle of those who were called Puritans in the worst sense, and determined all their counsels and designs." He lived until Charles the Second was crowned, and died in the following year, 14 April, 1662.

CAPTAIN THOMAS WIGGIN.

Frequent mention of Captain Thomas Wiggin has been made in the preceding pages. The place of his birth in the West of England is not known, but he was born about 1600, hence was a young man of thirty years when he became interested in the colonization scheme for Dover. His wife's name was Catherine, but her maiden name is not known. They were married about the time the emigration began, and she was a young bride in the wilderness on Dover Neck. They had two sons and a daughter; the eldest, Andrew, was born in 1635 on "Captain's Hill," Dover Neck, where the Wiggin log mansion stood on Low Street, not far from the log meeting-house, of 1633-4. How he acquired the title of captain is not known, but he was so called before he left England. All the Wiggin families of Dover and vicinity are descendants from him. He was governor, or chief manager, of affairs here until 1637, when, by popular election, Rev. George Burdett, who had become pastor of the parish, was placed at the head of affairs except in the matter of land grants, of which Capt. Wiggin yet retained the disposal. Just what state of affairs led to the displacement of the captain is not known, but he continued active in business affairs, although his name does not appear among the signers of the Combination for good government in 1640; nor does Edward Hilton's name appear there. Probably they had removed to their plantations in the vicinity of Exeter. After Dover, Strawberry Bank and Exeter came under Massachusetts in May, 1642, Captain Wiggin again became conspicuous and active in public affairs, and was one of the leading men for a score of years.

On the 9th day of October, 1641, the agreement was enacted whereby Dover, Strawberry Bank, Exeter and Hampton were to come under the rule of Massachusetts. On December 10th, 1641, Captain Wiggin was appointed one of the commission which was to make arrangements to carry the new government compact into effect, which was finally accomplished on the 3d day of May, 1642, on which date commission was granted to Captain Wiggin, Edward Hilton, Mr. Warnerton and William Walderne "to be assistants to (associate judges) such of the magistrates or others as shall be sent either by this Court or by agreement and order of the magistrates (in Boston) or the greater number of them, to keep Court at Pascataqua, and out of Court to see to the preserving of the peace, and to have and exercise such power within our limits at Pascataqua, as any one magistrate of this jurisdiction usually doth and lawfully may exercise out of Court; this commission to continue until this Court take further order, etc."

"At a General Court of Elections held at Boston on the 10th day of the 3rd mo; 1643, it was ordered that Mr. Deputy, Mr. Saltonstall, Mr. Bradstreete, Mr. Symons, or any two of them should go, & keep Court at Pascataqua. Mr. Williams, Capt. Wiggin and Mr. George Smyth to assist them & to be Commissioners there, & Capt. Wiggin's authority is appointed to extend to Hampton as before."

In 1643 a petition was presented by the citizens of Exeter to "The Right Worshipful, the Governor, the Deputy Governor and the Magistrates with the Assistants and Deputies of this honored Court at present (May, 1643) assembled in Boston, etc.," asking to have the boundary line of their town and Dover settled. They say: "And we suppose that Capt. Wiggins, his farme and a good way below it, may well be laid within our Township if this honored Court so please." This shows that Capt. Wiggin then resided on his farm on the shore of Great Bay and claimed to be a resident of Dover. He probably built his house there in 1640. He continued to be associate justice until 1664. In 1651 Governor Endicott sent to him an important letter, saying that he had heard that the citizens of Strawberry Bank were planning to set up an independent government and secede from Massachusetts government, hence he (Endicott) instructed Capt. Wiggin to investigate the affair and report to the General Court in Boston, and gave him authority, meanwhile, to "send one or more of the chiefest, we mean principal actors therein to prison at Boston, who shall answer their rebellion at the General Court." Captain Wiggin attended to Gov. Endicott's order and the threatened rebellion was speedily suppressed. In 1656 Capt. Wiggin was one of the judges appointed to hold court regularly at York and Dover and Portsmouth, and was so continued until 1664, when he declined to serve longer.

This is a brief of Captain Thomas Wiggin's career. He appears to have been a just Judge, and was held in high esteem by the Massachusetts authorities. Of course he did not please everybody in his court decisions, and in one instance Philip Chesley, of Oyster River, was presented at Court in Boston, for contempt of Court, in 1655, "for reproachful speeches against the worshipful Capt. Wiggin." The Court in Boston found him guilty and sentenced him to "make public acknowledgment three times: First at the head of the Train band (in Dover Neck), and at the two next public meeting days at Dover (Neck), when Oyster River people shall be there present—or be whipped ten stripes and pay a fine of 5 pounds."

REV. WILLIAM LEVERICH.

Rev. William Leverich, a native of England, graduated at Emmanuel College, Cambridge, Eng., in 1625; received the degree of A. M. in 1629. He was ordained in England. "An able and worthy Puritan minister," he came here with the Dover colonists in 1633, as already stated. He remained here until May, 1635, when he removed to Boston and was admitted member of the First Church that month. He was minister at Duxbury a short time and then went to Sandwich, where he is shown to be in 1637 by a petition signed by him with others. At Sandwich he became interested in the Indians and made a careful study of their language; being a scholarly man, he was able to do this in an intelligent manner. Having acquired a mastery of the language, the Commissioners of the United Colonies employed him to teach the Indians in civilized ways of living, as set forth in the Gospels of the New Testament. He remained in Sandwich until 1652. In 1653 he went to Oyster Bay, Long Island, where the missionary society of that settlement set him to work doing general missionary work, Indians included.

The Indians became very friendly with him and he did good work among the tribes; in return he received valuable recompense in a land-grant from Assiapum, alias Moheness, the sachem of the region around Oyster Bay; it consisted of a large tract of land in the vicinity of that Bay, and the deed was made to him and Peter Wright, Samuel Mays and a few others, for 4 pounds sterling and various supplies. In 1654 he removed his household goods from Sandwich to Oyster Bay. In 1658 he settled in the nearby town of Huntington, but continued his missionary and school-master work among the Indians in that whole section of Long Island. About 1670 he removed to Newtown, Long Island, where he resided until his death, 19 June, 1677. He left two sons, Eleazer and Caleb; the latter married and has descendants who have won fame and honor in the generations since then.

REV. GEORGE BURDETT.

Sometime in 1636 Reverend George Burdett came to Dover from Salem, Mass., and became minister of the First Parish, which position had been vacant since Mr. Leverich left in May, 1635. He had been a minister of the Church of England, at Yarmouth, before coming to New England. While at Yarmouth he had a disagreement with the Church officials on account of some scruples which he entertained as to performing some of the required rites and ceremonies; in consequence he was suspended by the High Commission Court, in April, 1635, and soon after left Yarmouth and came to New England, landing at Salem, where he was so well received that on September 2, 1635, he was admitted to the Salem Church and became freeman by vote of the officials of the town. He was a man of pleasing address and a ready speaker; there being no opening for another minister in that town, and hearing of a vacancy in the First Parish at Bristol, as Dover was then called, he left Salem and came along the coast and up the Pascataqua to Dover Neck, probably in the spring of 1636. The dwellers in the little village around the log meeting-house, gave him a cordial reception and arrangements were soon made for him to become minister. His conduct as preacher proved to be so popular with the people that at the election in the spring of 1637, they chose him governor, instead of Captain Wiggin, who had been chief magistrate since 1633. Captain Wiggin, however, retained control of the land business for several years more, until the settlement came under control of the Bay Colony in 1642. Under Burdett's administration new rules for better government were formulated by him which were adopted by the people; he speaks of it as a "combination." No record of it has ever been found, and it was superseded by a new one in 1640, under Governor Roberts.

While Burdett was a resident of Salem, in December, 1635, he wrote a letter to Archbishop Laud, then head of the English Church, explaining his course while minister at Yarmouth, and attempted to secure a reconciliation with his old church; but it failed to be successful. The letter is extant in the Public Record Office, London. A second letter, written from Dover, in 1637, is not preserved, but it became known, as did all such documents, to the Massachusetts government, by means of the agents it employed. Its drift was that it was not new church discipline aimed at in Massachusetts, but sovereignty over the settlements on the Pascataqua River. The fact was that Mr. Burdett told the truth, and that very much offended the Bay Colony authorities. The archbishop made a reply in 1638, thanking Burdett for his information. A third letter from Burdett, still preserved, was written from Dover, 29 Nov., 1638, in which he reiterates his declarations as to Massachusetts; he speaks of the Pascataqua River as valuable for a harbor; he says it should be secured for His Majesty, and the plantation is a valuable locality for "loyal" settlers. He says, also, that government ought to be established on the river, there being only "combinations," and that for a year previous "ye helm" had been in his hands. But Captain John Underhill had arrived at the log meeting-house on Dover Neck a few weeks before that letter was written to Laud, and a new atmosphere pervaded the village after the captain arrived straight from Boston. Very naturally Mr. Burdett was not pleased to see the Rev. Hanserd Knollys with Captain Underhill, and consequently forbade him to preach in the log meeting-house. However, Mr. Knollys did preach, and soon after Mr. Burdett crossed the Atlantic and never came back.

CAPTAIN JOHN UNDERHILL.

Captain John Underhill, who came to Dover with Rev. Hanserd Knollys, to establish the First Church, in November, 1638, was born in Warwickshire, England, about 1600; died at Oyster Bay, Long Island, 1672. He was a veteran soldier of high standing in military circles, having served in the army in the Netherlands, and in Ireland and at Cadiz. He held the rank of Captain, and his reputation was so good that Governor John Winthrop secured him to serve as commander of the military company that his Massachusetts Bay Colony would need, when it commenced its settlement at Boston, in 1630. His name is 57th on the list of members of the First Church in Boston.

The first General Court was held in Boston in 1634. Captain Underhill was elected Deputy from Boston, and held that office several years. Governor Winthrop speaks of him as performing creditably, various services in the business routine of the General Court. In 1631, when the mysterious Christopher Gardner had been arrested, and taken into Plymouth, Captain Underhill went to

Plymouth and brought him to Boston for trial. Also, when Roger Williams was to be arrested, that he might be returned to England, for preaching heretical doctrines at Salem, Capt. Underhill served the warrant.

On the 25th of October, 1631, Governor Winthrop, with the officials, went to Saugus and then to Salem, where they were bountifully entertained by Gov. Endicott. Capt. Underhill was one of the honored guests. On the 30th of August, 1632—"ten Sagamores and many Indians," were reported to be assembling at Brookline. Then Capt. Underhill, with twenty muskateers, was sent to investigate, and preserve order, if any trouble should arise; he found the Indians were not making, or intending, any trouble.

In September, 1632, Capt. Underhill gathered his company of militia and exercised them in maneuvres against need if the town were attacked. The report says—"To try how they would behave themselves, he caused an alarm to be given upon the quarters, which discovered a weakness, as the men looked amazed, not knowing what to do." In 1637 he was made one of the officers of the "Ancient and Honorable Artillery Company," of Boston.

Having performed four years of honorable and faithful service for the Colony, Capt. Underhill was granted a leave of absence to visit friends in England and Holland. While in Holland he married a Dutch woman and then returned to Boston, where his wife was admitted to membership in the First Church on the 16th of December, 1636.

In 1636 the Indians murdered John Oldham, at Block Island. The Governor and Council organized an expedition to visit that Island and inflict punishment on the Indians who were guilty of the crime. There were four companies, and Underhill was the senior Captain of the expedition, which was under the command of Gov. John Endicott, of Salem. The complete story of the expedition is quite interesting.

On the 10th of April, 1637, Captain Underhill was sent, with twenty men, by his friend, Governor Henry Vane, to Saybrook "to keep the fort both in respect to the Indians, and especially of the Dutch." The Indian hostilities soon determined the Bay authorities to send a much larger force, but it had not arrived when the work was done. The Connecticut towns had placed ninety men and some Indian auxiliaries under the command of Capt. John

Mason. Underhill united his forces with Mason's and the battle began; the result was that the village was burned and nearly every Indian therein was killled or burned alive. In excuse for all this horrible treatment of the Indians the authorities said: "We had sufficient light from the Word of God for our proceedings."

Thus for seven years Captain Underhill had resided in Boston and never a word of criticism was spoken against him, but many words of commendation had been bestowed on him. But Mrs. Ann Hutchinson, sister-in-law of the Rev. John Wheelwright, the founder of Exeter, a very brilliant woman and a powerful speaker, arrived in Boston this year and commenced preaching a new interpretation of the Gospel: "That the person of the Holy Ghost dwells in the justified person;—that no sanctification can help to evidence of our justification." These theological abstractions stirred up such a commotion in Boston and in all of the towns of the colony, that very strange and far reaching results grew from them in the years that followed. In brief, as follows: Many of the people approved of Mrs. Hutchinson's preaching; among the number were Governor Harry Vane, Rev. John Wheelwright, who was then in Boston, and Captain John Underhill. John Winthrop was a bitter opponent, and carried the magistrates with him in persecuting Mrs. Hutchinson and her supporters. After much disturbance the magistrates won the battle, and banished the eloquent woman preacher, who then went to Rhode Island, where she found all the liberty of speech she desired; Mr. Wheelwright was banished, and in the winter of 1637/8 came to Dover and called on Capt. Wiggin and Edward Hilton and other prominent citizens in the village on Dover Neck, as he came up the Pascataqua River on his way to buy land and found Exeter. Captain Underhill at first went to England and stayed a while; on his return he was accompanied by the Rev. Hanserd Knollys to Boston; they came to Dover in Nov., 1638. The results that soon followed were: the election of Captain Underhill as governor of Dover, displacing Rev. George Burdett; and the organization of the First Church in Dover, and making Mr. Knollys its minister. At the election in May, 1638, Governor Vane was defeated by John Winthrop, who was elected chief magistrate. Boston then elected Vane as their Deputy in the General Court. The authorities refused to admit him to a seat in the legislative body. Soon after that Mr. Vane returned to England where he won great fame in his work for the cause of English liberty.

The meanest thing of all that was done by the government was the disarming of fifty-eight citizens of Boston, and seventeen of other towns; they were ordered to "deliver in at Mr. Cane's house at Boston all such guns, pistols, swords, powder, shot and match, as they shall be owners of, or have in their custody; they were forbidden to buy or borow any more." Of those disarmed Captain John Underhill had the honor of heading the list. On the 12th of October, 1637, there had been a day of thanksgiving kept for the victories against the Pequots, and Captain Underhill and the soldiers who served with him "in the late service" were feasted.

At the close of the theological war, Captain Underhill was compelled to give up his sword, which he had so gallantly wielded at Mystic, when he smote the savages so valiantly.

The citizens in the village on Dover Neck gave Captain Underhill a very cordial welcome; they had all heard of his brave deeds and useful career in the service of the Massachusetts Bay Colony, and entertained no dislike for him on account of his banishment from that jurisdiction. It is said that Captain Underhill "took great pride in his military career and delighted to appear in fine apparel." The Poet Whittier, in his poem, "John Underhill," makes it appear that the captain came to Dover on horseback, and begins his interesting story as follows:

> "A score of years had come and gone
> Since the Pilgrims landed on Plymouth stone,
> When Captain Underhill, bearing scars
> From Indian ambush and Flemish wars,
> Left three-hilled Boston and wandered down
> East by north to Cochecho town.
>
> "He cheered his heart as he rode along
> With screed of Scripture and holy song,
> Or thought how he rode with his lancers free
> By the Lower Rhine and the Zuyder Zee,
> Till his wood-path grew to a trodden road,
> And Hilton Point in the distance showed.

> "Goodly and stately and grave to see,
> Into the clearing's space rode he,
> With the sun on the hilt of his sword in sheath,
> And his silver buckles and spurs beneath;
> And the settlers welcomed him, one and all,
> From swift Quamphegan to Gonic fall."

Captain Underhill's career in Dover will be considered under the topic, "different forms of government"; all that seems necessary to say here is that he failed to be reëlected governor in 1640 because he had favored the authorities at Strawberry Bank in ordering, at their request, the return of a man named Fish, from Exeter, who had been accused of committing some offense for which they wanted to inflict severe punishment. Mr. Fish's friends objected to having him tried before the Court at Strawberry Bank. Captain Underhill was commander of the militia at Exeter, as well as at Dover. He remained in command of the militia here and at Exeter until 1642, when he returned to Boston, and was taken back into the First Church, from which he had been expelled a while before, when the religious troubles were rampant in that colony.

In 1642 he removed to Stamford, Conn. As he had been restored to good fellowship in the church, the authorities furnished a ship to transport him and his family to Stamford, where he at once occupied an influential position; in 1643 he was elected a delegate to the Connecticut General Court. He also held the position of Assistant Justice in the courts of that colony. From Stamford, in 1646, he was called to command the Dutch forces in New York, where the Indians were causing much trouble; he was successful in this campaign and received the thanks of the Dutch people. At the close of that war he removed his family to Flushing, N. Y., where he resided until 1664, when he removed to Oyster Bay, where Rev. William Leverich, the first minister of the First Parish in Dover, was then residing. It is a somewhat notable circumstance that two of Dover's noted first settlers should spend their last days in that historic locality, which in the twentieth century had a world-wide fame as the home of former President Theodore Roosevelt.

In 1665, Captain Underhill was elected delegate from Oyster Bay to the Colonial Assembly held at Hampsted, under Governor Nichols, and he was deputy sheriff for what is now Queen's county, a while. In 1667 the Matinico Indians deeded to him one hundred and fifty acres of land on Long Island, some of which remained in possession of his descendants for two centuries. He died at Oyster Bay in 1672.

Captain John Underhill was one of Dover's Grand Old Men.

STREETS AND LANES.

Mr. Charles W. Hayes, an engineer of fifty years' experience, who had retraced many old lines of farms and ancient timber lots, at the request of the Northam Colonist Historical Society, made a careful survey of the territory which the village on Dover Neck covered during the first century of its history; he commenced the work in 1912 and finished it in October, 1914. Mr. John Scales assisted him in the historical part of the work, that is, of locating the residences of the early dwellers whose houses long ago disappeared. The cellars have been filled, and have been plowed over, from time to time, during the many years since then. These locations were determined by examination of ancient Wills, land grants, deeds, court records, and town records. Of course it was impossible to indicate all of the land transfers during a hundred years, but enough is given to show where prominent men resided at different periods and constituted a large village.

There were two streets and numerous lanes in the village when it was at the height of its prosperity and was "Dover" *per se*. High Street, now the State Road, and Low Street, which was about thirty-six rods west of High Street, and parallel to it, through what is now (1923) fields and gardens of prosperous farmers. The map prepared at that time—1914—and reproduced in this volume, shows where the lanes were, but possibly not all of them.

The road from the Neck to the Point did not go where it now does over the low ground, but at the foot of the hill curved to the bank of Fore River, and so along the bank to Pomeroy's cove, and around it to the road over the Point, which was as it now is, and had no special name. There was a road or lane along the bank of Fore River from the present Riverview Hall to the high and impassable bluff; this lane afforded fine views of the river and on it were the residences of prominent citizens. It was here that the first school master, Mr. Charles Buckner, owned a lot and resided during his service as public teacher, which was about four years; later he was a teacher in Boston or Dorchester.

On this lane the brewery was located; when it was built is not known, but at a very early period, as in 1655, it was alluded to as "the old brewery." Beer was the common beverage, as neither tea nor coffee began to be used until trade with Barbadoes and the West Indies began to be brisk and the people had money to spend; even then beer was a common beverage. But what the first comers looked for, in particular, was a supply of good water; they found it on The Neck in two springs of excellent water; these have long been called "Hall's Spring," at Back Cove, and "Coleman's Spring," on the easterly side of the present Riverview Hall, and not far from where the old brewery stood. No doubt Captain Wiggin began the village at that spot because the springs were handy and saved digging wells.

The first tannery in Dover was on this street; Job Clement, tanner, later known as Hon. Job Clement, came to Dover from Haverhill before 1653, and established a tannery; he was an expert in that business; he was held in such high esteem in Haverhill that they offered him special inducements to remain there; but Dover offered stronger inducements to come here and he came, probably in 1652, and opened his tanpits. The town gave him a grant of land, "4th. 8 Mo: 1653"; it was on Fore River; one bound of which was:—"a stake above the tan house, thence over the spring 5 poles and 4 ft. to a stake 2 poles and 2 ft. to the N. E. corner of the old brew house, upon a straight line to the water side." That land was owned by the late J. Wesley Clements, who was a descendant from the Honorable Job, in the eighth degree. Job Clement, Sr., was one of the leading business men of Dover for thirty years and held important offices; he was member of the Governor's Council when he died in 1682; his son Job and grandson of the same name also held important public offices in the town and provinces; and later generations have a good record.

Another distinguished citizen who lived in a house that stood on the west side of the street, nearly opposite the present Riverview Hall, was Judge John Tuttle, more generally known in his day as "Captain John Tuttle"; he was born in the house that stood where that hall is in 1646; his father lived there, John Tuttle, who came to Dover about 1636. Judge Tuttle was many times one of the selectmen, and representative in the provincial assembly; he was town clerk continuously from 1686 to 1719; he was captain of the Dover Neck military company ten years, from 1692 to 1702; in 1695 Governor Usher appointed him Judge of the Court of Common Pleas, which office he held several years; in the midst of faithfully performing the duties of these public trusts he was one of the great business men of the town for more than forty years; his chief industry was the lumber business and ship-building; he died in 1720; his successor in ship-building was Captain Thomas Millet, who settled there the year Judge Tuttle died, and his house was on the east side of the street, a little below the present hall. A notice of Capt. Millet is given elsewhere. An interesting fact in this connection is that Mr. William Penn Tuttle of Dover Neck, ninth in descent from Judge Tuttle, owns the farm that was granted to the Judge by the town and by him given to one of his sons from whom it has come down in regular succession in the Tuttle family to the present owner.

Low Street was low only in name; it was on the western side of the hill, but was high above Back River. On this street were located the first meeting-house, the parsonage, the prison, the stocks, the pillory, and possibly the whipping-post, but there is no record that they had such a post in Dover; however, as the town was under Massachusetts and the people were subject to the criminal laws of the Bay Colony, the whipping post may have been a necessity required to fulfill the law. On this street also were the cooper shops, where the workmen put the pipe-staves into shape, and headed and hooped the casks, then took them apart and packed them for transportation to Barbadoes Island, where the material was put into shape again by the coopers there, ready for the use of the sugar planters. On this street, also, were the blacksmith-shops and the carpenter shops. So it is manifest that Low Street was a very busy place for many years.

There were at least two lanes that crossed Low Street, leading from High Street to Back River; one was just above the meeting-house and was the much travelled path to the historic Hall's Spring, for a supply of pure water, and to Hall's slip, the landing place at Back Cove; the spring and the slip had their names from Deacon John Hall, one of the noted men of the town and the first deacon of the church.

Nutter's lane was from High Street to Nutter's slip, on Back River; Hall's slip and Nutter's slip were the only good landing places on that side of the river; the channel was then, and is now, very crooked, hence most of the shipping was done on Fore River. This lane was the southern boundary of "the calves pasture," whose northern boundary was a line from Pinkham's Spring (near the garrison) to Back River; the length of the pasture on Low Street was 36 rods. Nutter's lane received its name from Elder Hatevil Nutter, who lived near the second meeting-house.

Hatevil Nutter, Elder and occasional preacher, was born in England, in 1603, or thereabouts, as appears from a deposition of the Elder when he once testified concerning some disputed land titles. He was probably one of the "Company of persons of good estate and of some account for religion," who came over with Captain Wiggin in the ship *"James"* in 1633. He testified in the aforesaid deposition that he was here in 1637, in which year he took a lot of Captain Wiggin, which he had rebounded in 1640 as follows:

"Butting on Fore River on ye East, and upon ye West upon ye High street; on ye North upon ye lot of Samewell Haynes, and on ye South upon ye Lott of William Story."

An old pear tree stands in the hollow where the cellar was; it is about fifteen rods from the nearest corner of the second meeting-house lot.

ELDER HATEVIL NUTTER.

Elder Nutter was a very respectable man. He received various lots of land, and was largely engaged in running saw mills, the lumber business and shipping. His ship yard was on Fore

River at the foot of the hill in the rear of his residence, a beautiful location. Beside being so largely engaged in private business he found time to perform the duties pertaining to offices he held in the town, the church and the colony. He was one of the wealthy men of the town and colony.

Being a stanch supporter of his pastor, Rev. John Reyner, he was active in the defense of the minister when the Quaker women missionaries beset him in times of publc worship and in his private residence. Sewell, the Quaker historian, says:—"and all this (whipping) was in the presence of one Hate Evil Nutwell (Nutter), a Ruling Elder who stirred up the Constabelles to this wicked action and so proved that he bore a wrong name."

Being an able and influential man he stood up boldly and conscientiously for the Church, and the teaching of the sound doctrine as he understood it. He believed the Quakers were wrong and their teachings pernicious, as set forth by those women missionaries who were whipped in front of the second meeting-house. The Quakers had liberty to go elsewhere; as they did not exercise that liberty Elder Nutter believed it was right to force them to go; and they went, but they came back. No doubt both parties were wrong; but the worthy Elder should be judged by the standards that prevailed everywhere then; it would not be just to judge his acts by the standards of the present day. Some of his lineal descendants now reside on Dover Neck, but none of the Nutter name.

PUBLIC PASTURES.

A "calves pasture" has been mentioned in connection with Nutter's Lane. It may be well here to state that the farmers had also an "ox pasture," and a "sheep pasture"; the latter was on the hill north of Mr. Courser's house and was also used for a training ground in Indian war times. The following is from the town records in regard to calves pasture and shows when the grant was made:

"5th. loth. Mo: 1652.—Ordered that the Inhabitants of Dover Necke shall have the land that lyeth waste on the west side of the Necke to make them a calves Pasture; from the lot of John Hall & Philip Lewis to the water side; to be fenced by the Inhabitants."

This lot of land was defined as bounded on the east by Low Street, extending from Pinkham's Spring, near his garrison, to Nutter's Lane, on the south, which lane extended to Back River at Nutter's slip. The north line extended from Pingham's Spring to the river on a line parallel with Nutter's lane. The proprietors of this pasture were:

Thomas Kimball.
Job Clement.
Thomas Downs.
Thomas Roberts, Sr.
Minister's house.
Charles Buckner.
William Pomfrett.
Thomas Beard.
John Tuttle, Sr.
Dea. John Hall.
Thomas Leighton.

John Dam, Sr.
Lieut. Ralph Hall.
Elder Nutter.
Joseph Austin.
Philip Cromwell.
Wm. ffurber.
Jeremiah Tibbetts.
Humphrey Varney.
James Nute.
Richard Pinkham.

The ox pasture land grant appears in the town records as follows:

"5th. 10th. Mo: 1653.—Ordered (in town meeting) that the Inhabitants of the Necke of land of Dover shall have all the necke of Land below the towne which is called the Swampe, and so to *Hilton's Point* to make an ox pasture."

The proprietors of this pasture were nearly the same as the farmers above mentioned. In 1656 a road or lane was laid out through the ox pasture to Redding Point where Back River joins the Pascataqua; opposite to this point on the west, is Cedar Point, where the lines of Dover, Madbury and Durham unite in one point.

BECK'S SLIP.—HARFORD'S FERRY.

Beck's Slip is at Beck's Point on Fore River on land now (1923) owned by the heirs of the late Charles Roberts. It takes its name from Henry Beck, who was one of the signers of the Combination document in 1640. Mr. Beck evidently had a grant of that locality and had a ferry across to Kittery, now Eliot; at least he used it as a shipping point, for which it is admirably fitted by the ledge at the water's edge. It has always retained his name. He may have begun there as early as 1636. About 1660 he appears to have removed to Sagamore Creek, Portsmouth; in the old court records of 1668 "Henry Beck of Sagamore Creek in ye town of Portsmouth, planter" and Ann, his wife, are mentioned. There was a lane or road from High Street direct to Beck's slip which was used a great many years, and the cuttings for it can now be easily traced down over the hill, which, in some parts, is very steep. This was the landing place for "Harford's Ferry." The proprietor was Nicholas Harford, who was a famous ferryman in his day. July 2, 1718, Wm. Parker, of Portsmouth, conveyed to Nicholas Harford a dwelling house and four acres of land on Dover Neck, beginning at a landing place commonly called "Beck's Slip" or "point," and extending west by the highway side to ye High Street, thence south by ye street to Samuel Haines' land, thence east by Haines' land to ye Fore River."

Thomas Cushing of Boston, and Mercy, his wife, Aug. 23, 1736, conveyed to Captain John Gage, five acres of land, with buildings, etc., bought of Nicholas Harford, on the east side of Dover Neck, lying between the land of Joseph Roberts and ye highway that leads down to ye landing place commonly called "Beck's Slip," bounded westerly by the main road over Dover Neck down to *Hilton's Point,* northerly by Roberts' land, south by the said highway from the main road to said landing-place, and easterly by Fore River, including a strip four rods wide running along the river from said highway to the wharf on the river side, built by said Harford; with the privilege of "the ferry from said landing-place over to Kittery Shore." In all of the later years of its use it was in possession of the Hanson Roberts family, but was not much used after 1830.

DOVER NECK MEETING-HOUSES.

The First Parish had two meeting-houses on Dover Neck. The site of the second house is well known and well marked; it is on the summit of Nutter's Hill; a face wall is on the east side of it, on which is a bronze tablet with an inscription which explains what the lot is. The following from the town records explains when and by whom the second house was built:—

"5, 10th. mo: 1652.—Mr. Richard Walderne has accomedation for his mills; in consideration whereof the aforesaid Mr. Richard Walderne doth bind himself, administrators, and his heirs to erect a meeting-house on the hill near Elder Nutter's; the dementions of said house is to be forty foot longe, twenty-six foot wide, sixteen foot stud, with six windows, two doors, fitt for such a house, with a tile covering; and to plancke all the walls; with glass and nails for it; and to be finished betwixt this (Dec. 5) and April next, come twelve months, wch will be in the year 1654."

At that date this distinguished man was simply Mr. Richard Walderne; not long after that date he is called Captain Walderne; in the maturity of his years he became Major Walderne, and is known as such in history. He fulfilled the above contract with the town, and the house was dedicated in April, 1654; of course they had a grand service, with all the town to witness and participate in it. They did not have any bell to call the people together, but Richard Pinkham performed that duty by beating his drum, as he had done for several years, by authority of the town, to summon the people to services in the log meeting-house on the Lord's day. No report of the programme that day has been found; Parson Reyner gave them a good sound sermon and no doubt Elder Nutter and Elder William Wentworth had interesting remarks to add to what their good pastor had said; whether or not Deacon John Hall "deaconed the music" we cannot guess, as there is no record of music in the standard Boston churches of that period. It would be interesting if we knew.

Four years later the town records have the following:—

"At a meeting of the neighborhood of Dover Neck, Cochecho & Bloody Point, ye 20th. day of ye 12 mo: (March) (16)58. Voted by the said inhabitants that the Meeting- House on Dover Neck is to be underpin'd & catted & seeled with Boards; And a pulpet and seats Conveniente to be made & a Bell to be purchased, and this to be paid for by way of Rate upon each man's estate, according to the law of the country."

The repairing and fitting up appear to have been completed in two years, as on the 13th of June, 1660, a tax of one hundred pounds was voted to be assessed to pay the bills.

Although it was voted in 1659 to purchase a bell, the selectmen did not complete the bargain with Captain Walderne, who bought the bell in England and brought it over in one of his ships, until 1664, as is shown by the following town record:—

"At a meeting of the Sellectmen the 15th. 2Mo: (16)65:—Ordered that mr. Peter Coffin shell be Impowered by this meetinge to A gree with some workman to Build a Terrett apon the meeting- house for to hang the Bell wch we have bought of Captain Walderne, and what it cost to pay out of what credit the Necke of Land hathe in your hands; and if it cost moer wee doe in Gage to pay you apon the Towne a Compt.

sellectmen : { Richard Walderne
Will. Wentworth
John Roberts."

The veterans of 1633 had been thirty years in the land, and were growing old, when the Sabbath bell first rang out over that beautiful hill and the surrounding waters, like the bells of Old England; it must have been a day of pleasure and of great rejoicing when Richard Pinkham laid aside his drum and rang that bell for the first time. Mr. Pinkham appears to have been sexton until Deacon John Hall was engaged by the town, 13 January, 1671/2, "to swiep the meeting-house and ring the bell for one year"; his salary was three pounds for the year.

The next move was to build a stockade around the meeting-house; the order for it to be done is in the town records:—

"By ye sellecktmen ye 4th. 5th. Mo: (67.

"It is Agried with Capt. Coffin to Buld the forte about the metting house on Dover Neck, one hundred foot square with two Sconces of sixteen foote square, and all the timber to be twelve inches thick, and the wall to be eight foot high, with sells and Braces; and the sellektmen with the melletory ofecers have agreed to pay him one hundred pounds in days workes, at 2 shillings 6 pence per day, and to all persons concerned in the worke, one day to help Rayse the worke at so many one day as he shall appoint."

That was the order, but when it was completed nobody knows, as there is no record; but as it took six years to get the bell into the turret we may reasonably suppose it took four or five to complete the fortification. Why they issued such an order in 1667 is not explained. It was a time of profound peace; Dover people had not had any trouble with the Indians; and Dover Neck never had any trouble with them during the fifty years of war that was waged all around them. Passaconaway, the great Bashaba, at Penacook, who included the tribes of the Pascataqua in his broad domain, was still alive and in favor of peace. In his old age, indeed, he called his sons and inferior rulers together, and warned them against war with the English. Wonolancet, his son and successor, adhered to his father's counsel, although eventually driven to the homes of the Indians on the Kennebeck. Kankamagus, grandson of Passaconaway, and Mesandowet, also of the Penacook blood, destined to become chieftains of note, had not then appeared in the councils of their nation.

There were Indians on the Cochecho and sachems dwelt at Newichawannock and at Swampscot. Wahowah, better known as Hopehood, was a hereditary sagamore of lands from Exeter to Salmon Falls, and Hopehood's Point is on the western shore of Back River, above the Three Creeks. The historian, Hubbard, calls him Hopehood, the name the English had given him, for what reason is not explained. He was the son of Robinhood, who owned a large area of land around Gonic, which he sold to Peter Coffin January 3, 1686. In that deed the place is called "Squammagonake." This point of land is in plain sight, on the west bank of Back River, to anyone standing on the meeting-house site. According to local tradition, Wahowa was buried on that point, hence the Back River people gave it the name Hope Hood Point. At the time when the town voted to fortify the meeting-house he was only a youngster. In his manhood he was a terror to the white settlers around here; he acted on the plea that the whites had robbed him and his people of their land, hence sought to get his pay by murdering them.

The fortification was completed in some year before 1675, but just when nobody knows. It was not till eight years had elapsed, after the vote to build was taken, that the Indians began war, in 1675, on the Pascataqua River inhabitants; it was in September.

The upright timbers of the fort were set in the earth; at the northwest and southeast corner were the sconces, or projections, which were built higher than the palisade, on the top of which the watchman could see far and wide.

Many important events took place in that house. The town-meetings were held there until about 1720, when the bell was removed and the town-meetings were held at the new meeting-house on Pine Hill. Religious services continued to be held in this house for quite a number of years until the town refused to make necessary repairs to protect the worshipers from the storms of winter and rains of summer. There is no record of when it was taken down, but probably about the time when the Revolutionary War began. Dr. Quint, somewhere, has stated that there was a school-house on the lot after the meeting-house was taken down. We fail to find any proof of that, but on the contrary we have the testimony of an old resident of that school district that the first school-house was built in 1815, by the side of the Quaker burial ground, near the residence of the late Howard Roberts. Before that the schools were kept in private houses. This information was given by Mr. John Clements in a written statement he furnished Mr. John B. Stevens, who was City Clerk of Dover a quarter of a century. Mr. Clements was born in 1810 and died in 1887; his birthplace was in a house that stood near the meeting-house lot; his place of residence was where his son, Mr. J. Wesley Clements, resided until his death, January 26, 1922; his Clement ancestors had resided in that vicinity from the year 1652; he knew all the local traditions. Mr. Clements stated that the first school he attended was kept in a neighbor's house by the "widow Perry"; later he went to school in the first school-house that was built on Dover Neck; that stood by the Quaker burial ground; it was burned down in 1852. Mr. Clements stated that his father, William Clements, who was born in 1776, always attended schools kept in private houses. That was the common custom in Dover, holding public schools in private houses. From this statement by Mr. Clements it appears evident there never was a school-house on that lot, and never any building but the meeting-house; when this was taken down the earth was left undisturbed; and it has remained so to the present time. The soil is not suitable for raising crops of any kind;

so there has been no inducement for any farmer to disturb the ancient mounds. The summer rains and winter snows have never made any material change in the appearance of the earth work; some of the men who came over in the ship *"James"* in 1633 have stood inside of that intrenchment; they helped build the log house in 1633; it was a day of great rejoicing when they were permitted to hold the first meeting in the new house on Nutter's Hill.

THE MEETING-HOUSE BELL.

The reader may be interested to know what became of the bell that Captain Richard Walderne brought over from England and the town had Mr. Peter Coffin build a turret on the meeting-house in which to hang it.

About the year 1712 some of the wealthy men who resided at Cochecho built a meeting-house on Pine Hill, near where the Cushing tomb is, and not far from the mortuary chapel; the town had nothing to do with the job. From that time until 1720, there was a lively contention between the residents of The Neck and those of Cochecho as to which place should have the regular church services and the town-meetings; Cochecho had outgrown Dover and the people of the larger settlement objected to being compelled to travel to Nutter's Hill to attend meetings. The Provincial Assembly was appealed to; a committee was appointed and came here and investigated; they decided in favor of Cochecho. Finally a Parish meeting was held and the following transcript from the records shows what became of the bell.—

"Att a Parrish meetting held att the new meetting:house, at Cochecha the 20th. of February 1720/1.

"2d.—A vote for fencing of the Parsonage Land, or a part thereof. A vote for fencing the whole 20 Acres of Land.

"Att the meetting agreed with John Wingett to fence the sd, Parsonage Land, which is 20 Acres, for 18 pounds, and to be paid out of next year's Rate, and the fence to be well made by the last day of Aprel next Insuing the date hereof; and by the 25th day of December next the money is to be paid to sd. Wingett, or his order, if the fence be made.

"Att the same meetting:—Voted that the meettings on the Lord's Day shall be constantly kept att Cochceha new Meetting-House for the futur, excepting one Sabbath or two att Dover.

"Att the same meeting:—Voted that the bell att Dover shall be brought up to Cochecha."

Some time during that year the bell was brought up and hung on a frame near the meeting-house, as there was no belfry on the house. It will be noticed in this record that the village on the Neck is called Dover and the village at the Falls is called Cochecho. On the Sabbath days for nearly forty years that bell was rung regularly to call the people to meetings. When the new house was completed in 1758 on Tuttle Square, the bell was placed on it, but was first recast, with new metal added. Later it was recast by Paul Revere at the famous bell factory in Boston. When the present brick house of worship was completed in 1829, the bell was placed in its belfry, where it hung and was rung until removed in 1913 to give place to the present bell.

THE LOG MEETING-HOUSE.

The immigrants of 1633 arrived at *Hilton Point* about the middle of October, coming from Salem, where they had arrived in the ship *"James"* from England. As soon as possible they went to work at clearing the ground of trees and building houses for dwellings, on Dover Neck. The tradition during the eighteenth century, and so on to the present time, was that they proceeded at once to build a meeting-house. That seems perfectly natural, and very reasonable; as the record says they were men "of some account for religion" they would build a house for worship as soon as possible; moreover, such a building could be used for general purposes during the time they were building their private dwellings, and no doubt was so used.

Mr. George Wadleigh, in his "Notable Events in the History of Dover," published by his son, Rear Admiral G. H. Wadleigh, says:—"Of the location, as well as the material of which the first meeting-house was constructed, we have no information. The first meeting-house in Boston, built about the same time, is said by the historian, Palfrey, to have had mud walls and a thatched roof. It is reasonable to conclude that in the absence of other material the Dover meeting-house was of a similar character."

We think Mr. Wadleigh is mistaken; the conditions on Dover Neck were entirely different from those in Boston when the two settlements were commenced. Boston had plenty of mud and no trees of any account; Dover had plenty of trees, but no mud of any account. The Dover men had a magnificent forest all over their land; they used the trees to build their houses of logs; it stands to reason they would build the meeting-house of the same material; furthermore, they would not build a small, shanty style structure, after the Boston pattern. No; the logs were large and cut from tall trees; why need they cut them short? They did not, but erected a capacious and substantial edifice, which they used for twenty years. It was a meeting-house for all kinds of public business, not alone for religious purposes.

Where their minister, the Rev. William Leverich, conducted service on the first Sunday we cannot know; perhaps it was in one of the houses on *Hilton Point;* or it may have been under one of the large oak trees whose wide spreading branches were ample to shelter a large audience. According to weather reports in other sections of New England that fall was a pleasant one, and they had plenty of bright sunshine, to worship under the trees and to build the meeting-house, as well as their private residences. And in November they had a delightful "Indian Summer"; the following winter was not particularly severe; so the pioneers were very much favored in their arduous labors.

To this building I have found but two allusions in its own time. Rev. Thomas Larkham, the fourth minister of the First Parish, wrote to Gov. John Winthrop of the Massachusetts Bay Colony, 3 January, 1640/1, giving some account of the difficulty between him and Rev. Hanserd Knollys, with whom he was colleague about one year. In that letter he says:—"He (Knollys) gave forth words that he would deal with one of our magistrates, & me, first of all, before any exercise should goe on, &, indeede was ready in the meeting-house, he to doe, in a marvellous stiff way, had not the magistrates interposed."

The other is of a similar character and need not be quoted here. Many important events took place in and around this house.

It was here that in the affair above referred to by Mr. Larkham, Captain John Underhill, then governor and military commander for Dover, gathered his forces and marched them forth against Mr. Larkham's party, Mr. Knollys carrying a Bible on a halberd, for an ensign, he declaring that they were Scots and the others were English; this was a reference to the contest then going on in England to force the use of the English liturgy in the Presbyterian Churches in Scotland. Mr. Larkham's party beat a hasty retreat to *Hilton's Point* and sent a messenger to Strawberry Bank for Gov. Williams to come up with his militia and help suppress a riot.

It was here that the court was held by Gov. Williams, and Underhill, Knollys and others were convicted of creating a riot, etc. The fact was that Capt. Underhill was only exercising his authority, as military commander, to preserve order in the community.

This meeting-house had no intrenchment, nor need for any; the Indians came there from time to time and exchanged the valuable furs they had collected, the English giving them but small value in return; they were not simply Dover Indians, but some came from as far distant as Penacook, now Concord. Harmony and prosperity prevailed in this intercourse with the red men during the years that they came to this log meeting-house, from 1634 to 1654.

It was in this house that the First Church was organized in December, 1638, by Captain John Underhill and Hanserd Knollys, assisted by local dignitaries, such as Elder Hatevil Nutter, Elder Edward Starbuck, Deacon John Hall, William Pomfrett, William Walderne, Richard Pinkham and others. It was in this house that, one year later, the Combination for better government was completed. It was here that the vote was taken in the fall of 1641 to place the town under the government of Massachusetts; this vote came into force in May, 1642.

This meeting-house had no bell. The following vote in town meeting explains what was used for a substitute to call the people together on the Lord's Day:

"27th. of the 9th. Mo: (16) 48.—It is this day ordered at a publique Towne meiting that Richard Pinckome shall beat ye drumme on ye Lord's Day to give notice for ye time of meiting;

and to sweip ye meiting house; for which he shall be allowed six bushels of Indian Corne, for his pay this year, and be freed from Rates."

In this house successively preached Reverends William Leverich, George Burdett, Hanserd Knollys, Thomas Larkham, Daniel Maud and John Reyner. We have made a careful examination of all the grounds around the second meeting-house and have reached the conclusion that the first meeting-house was located on the hill about six hundred feet west of the State road at the residence of the late Daniel Pinkham, a short distance north of Riverview Hall. It was on what was called Low Street. The parsonage was near it. It is a beautiful location; the western view takes in the territory of Back River and the upper Pascataqua; on the south is a grand view of Fore River and the lower Pascataqua. The first minister who lived in the parsonage was Mr. Leverich; the last was Mr. Reyner.

RICHARD PINKHAM.

Richard Pinkham was one of the respected citizens of Dover Neck; he held various minor offices in town affairs; he received several grants of land from the town; he was prosperous in worldly affairs, and raised a large family of children who maintained the good name of their parents. He came over from England with the first settlers in 1633, or soon after. He has had descendants living on Dover Neck, continuously, to the present year.

The spot where he early dwelt is said to be the same on which stood the Pinkham garrison; this fortified house was built about 1675, or soon after, when the Indians began to make trouble for Dover people. The location of the house is well authenticated; in it the pioneer veteran passed the closing years of his life. Rev. Dr. Quint, in No. 71 of his Historical Memoranda, published in the *Dover Enquirer,* in 1852, says:

"The precise situation of the Pinkham garrison is easily pointed out, inasmuch as it continued to be a dwelling house until one side of it was blown down by a heavy wind seven and twenty years ago (1825). That catastrophe compelled the family to build a new house as soon as possible; the new house is located about five rods easterly from the spot where the garrison stood."

"This new house stands on the north side of a lane leading from the west side of High street towards Back River; it was occupied in 1915, by Elijah Pinkham, a man of more than eighty years, who owned the land once owned by his ancestor, Richard, from whom it came down in regular succession from father to son. About five rods directly west from this house was the garrison house, half of which was taken down about two and a half years after the hurricane blew down the other half."

THE QUAKER MISSIONARIES ON DOVER NECK.

The following accounts of the coming of Quakers to Dover are taken from George Bishop's "New England Judged by the Spirit of the Lord," the first part of which was published in 1661, and the second in 1667, the whole being republished in 1702-3. The reader must remember that the narrative is written by a man who was too deeply interested in the events to be an impartial historian: "In the year 1662, Mary Tomkins and Alice Ambrose, who came from Old England, and George Preston and Edward Wharton, of Salem aforesaid, came to Pascataqua River, and passed up, landed at the town aforesaid (Dover), whither to go it was with them from the Lord, where they had a good opportunity in the inn with the people that resorted to them, who reasoned with them concerning their faith and hope, which to the people being made manifest, some to the Truth thereof Confessed, and others, being not able to gainsay the Truth, ran to Rayner, their Priest, and told him that such a people were come to Town; and that they had discourse with them about their Religion, and were not able to contradict what they said, and therefore desired him to come forth and help them. 'Or else,' said they, 'we are like to be run on ground.' "

"At this the Priest chafed and fretted, and asked the people, 'Why they came amongst them?' To which they answered, 'Sir, it is so we have been amongst them, and if you come not forth to help us we are on ground;' and said the Priest's wife, 'Which do you like best, my Husband or the Quakers?' Said one of them,

SITE OF THE SECOND MEETING-HOUSE, 1654. (See page 118.)

'We shall tell you that after your husband hath been with them.' Whereupon in came Rayner in a fretting and forward manner, saying, 'What came ye here for? see the laws of the country are against such as you are.' 'But what hast thou against us?' replied Mary Tomkins. 'You deny magistrates,' said the priest, 'and ministers and the churches of Christ.' 'How sayest so?' replied Mary. 'And you deny the Three Persons in the Trinity,' said the priest. To which Mary answered, 'Take notice, people, the Man falsely accuseth us, for godly Magistrates and the Ministers of Christ we own, and the Churches of Christ we own, and that there are three that bear Record in Heaven, which three are the Father, Word, and Spirit, that we own, but for the three persons in the Trinity, that's for thee to prove.' 'I will prove three Persons in the Trinity,' said the priest. 'Thou sayest so,' said George Preston, 'but prove it by the Scriptures.' 'Yes,' replied Rayner, 'by that will I prove it where it is said, And he is the express image of his Father's Person.' 'But,' said one, 'that is falsely translated.' 'Yea, it is,' replied a learned man, 'for in the Greek it is not Person but substance.' 'But,' said the priest, 'it is a Person, and so there is one Person.' 'Thou sayest so,' said George. 'But prove thy other Two, if thou canst.' Said the priest: 'There are three Somethings,' and so in a rage flung away, calling to his people from the window to go away from amongst them; but Mary soon after got after him, and spake to him to come back, and not to leave his People amongst them he called wolves; but away packt the priest, whereupon she said unto the people, 'Is not this the hireling that flees and leaves the flock?' So truth came over them all, and there was great service for the Lord, and many were convinced of the truth that day, and notwithstanding the terror of your wicked laws, many waxed bold, and invited them to their houses, and they had at that time a good and great meeting amongst them, and the power of the Lord reached many of them that day. Having had this good service at that time at Dover for the Lord, they passed away into the province of Mayne, being invited to Major Shapleigh's."

If Parson Reyner had "written a book" he would have presented a different view of this theological discussion. The account of his "fretting, etc.," is doubtless drawn from imagination; it is totally opposed to all other accounts of his character. But the Quakers did not remain long in Maine, for "towards the winter it came into the hearts of Alice Ambrose, Mary Tomkins, and Anna Coleman to go and visit the seed of God amongst them that had received the truth in Piscataqua River, where they were not long, but a flood of persecution arose by the instigation of the priest, who caused them to be apprehended by Virtue of your Cart-Law, and order was made to whip and pass them away as followeth:"

"To the constable of Dover, Hampton, Salisbury, Newbury, Rowley, Ipswich, Wenham, Linn, Boston, Roxbury, Dedham, and until these vagabond Quakers are out of this jurisdiction."

"You and every one of you are required in the King's Majesty's name to take these vagabond Quakers, Anna Coleman, Mary Tomkins, and Alice Ambrose, and make them fast to the cart's tail, and drawing the cart through your several towns, to whip them upon their naked backs, not exceeding ten stripes apiece on each of them in each town; and so to convey them from Constable to Constable till they are out of this jurisdiction, as you will answer it at your peril; and this shall be your warrant. Per me, Richard Walderne, at Dover, dated Dec. 22, 1662."

"A cruel warrant, through eleven townships by name and whatsoever else were in that jurisdiction to whip three tender women, and one of them little and crooked, with ten stripes apiece at each place in the bitter cold weather, through such a length of ground, near eighty miles, enough to have beaten their flesh raw and their bones. Oh, the mercies of the wicked, how are thy cruelties! The devil certainly bore through that warrant (and as men used to say) top and topgallant, no interruption. Your warrant was through these towns ten stripes apiece, enough to sink down any man whom God did not uphold; but this outruns the law in the constable, as the proverb is; there is eleven named which, according to the rate of ten in a place, is one hundred and ten apiece laid on so as, if it were possible, the knots might kiss the bones every stroke. And yet this was not enough; if any more towns through them they must go. From whom sprung this unreasonable warrant? Who influenced all this? And through whose instigation were they apprehended? And who drew the warrant? *Omne malum,* saith the proverb, *incipit a sacerdote,* that is all evil begins from the priest; or, from the priest all evil hath its beginning. Priest Raynor aforesaid (who could not evince his own position, but as has been said, instead of proving three persons in the Trinity by the Scriptures, said "They were three Somethings") and so fled away, being not able to stand before the power and force of truth in these servants of the Lord, and sets on this deputy magistrate, Walden, who began to tell them of your law against Quakers. Mary Tomkins replied, 'So there was a law that Daniel should not pray to his God?' 'Yes,' said Walden, 'and Daniel suffered, and so shall you' (see how he appears influenced by this priest's spirit mad and blind), and so demands Alice Ambrose her name; said, 'She is written in the Lamb's book of life.' He answered, 'Nobody here knows this book, and for this you shall suffer.' So, on a very cold day, your Deputy Walden caused these women to be stripped naked from the middle upwards, and tied to a cart, and after awhile cruelly whipped them, whilst the priest stood and looked and laughed at it, which some of the Friends seeing, testified against, for which Walden put two of them (Eliakim Wardell, of Hampton, and William Faurbish, of Dover) in the stocks. Having dispatched them in this town, and made way to carry them over the waters and through woods to another, the women denied to go unless they had a copy of their warrant; so your executioner sought to set them on horseback, but they slid off, then they endeavored to tie each to a man on horseback; that would not do neither, nor any course they took till the copy was given, insomuch that the constable professed that he was almost wearied with them. But the copy being given them, they went with the executioner to Hampton, and through dirt and snow at Salisbury half-way the leg deep, the constable forced them after the cart's tail, at which he whipped them, under which cruelty and sore usage the tender women traversing their way through all, was a hard spectacle to those who had in them anything of tenderness; but the presence of the Lord was so with them (in the extremity of their sufferings) that they sung in the midst of them to the astonishment of their enemies."

"This Walden keeps a Saw Mill, and is a log sawyer, but that day that he sentenced these women, his wife caused him to have hand cuffs put on."

"The tender women they tied with Ropes to the Cart at Dover to be whipped, which being very cruel, James Heard asked whether those were the Cords of the Covenant."

"The constable of Dover's name was Thomas Roberts, who looking pitifully the same night through his extreme toil to bring the servants of the Lord thither to be whipped as they had been at Dover, they were so far above his cruelty that they made some good things for his refreshment, which he took. This disgraceful sentence was executed no farther than Salisbury. But these gentle dealings did not reclaim the wanderers."

"After their release they passed a short time at Maj. Shapleigh's, in Kittery, but when 'after a little space at Maj. Shapleigh's' they returned again to Dover, the place of their late barbarous execution, and there visited their friends who had both received and suffered with them; where being met together on the next First Day of the week after their coming together, whilst they were in prayer, the constables, Thomas Roberts, aforesaid, and his brother John, like sons of Belial, having put on their old clothes with their aprons, on purpose to carry on their drudgery (taking Alice Ambrose), the one by the one arm and the other by the other arm, they unmercifully dragged her out of doors, with her face towards the snow, which was knee deep, over stumps and old trees near a mile; in the way of which, when they had wearied themselves, they commanded two others to help them, and so laid her up Prisoner in a very wicked man's house (Thomas Canny's), which when they had done, they made haste with the rest that were with them to fetch Mary Tomkins, whom, as they were dragging along with her face towards the snow, the poor Father of these two wicked constables followed after, lamenting and crying, 'Wo, that ever he was the Father of such wicked children.' (From this man Thomas Roberts, whose labor was at an end, and who had lived in Dover thirty years, and a member of their church about twenty years, they took his cow away, which gave him and his wife a little milk, for not coming to their worship.)"

"So thither they hauled Mary Tomkins also, and kept them both all night in the same house, and in the morning, it being exceedingly cold, they got into a certain Boat or Canoe, or kind of Trawl hewed out of the body of a tree, which the Indians use on the water, and in it they determined to have the three women down to the harbor's mouth; and they put them in threatening that they would now so do with them that they would be troubled with them no more."

"Whither to go the three women were not willing. They forced them down a very steep place, in deep snow, and furiously they took Mary Tomkins by the arms and dragged her on her back over the stumps of trees, down a very steep hill to the water side, so that she was very much bruised and after was dying away; and Alice Ambrose they plucked violently into the water and kept swimming by the Canoe, being in danger of drowning, or to be frozen to death. (What acts of violence and cruelty are here!) Anna Coleman they put in great danger of her life also, in view of enemies in great hazard, and in all probability they had destroyed them quite according as they had said, viz.: That they would do so now as that they would be troubled with them no more; but on a sudden a great Tempest arose, and so their cruel and wicked purpose was hindered, and back they had them to the House again and kept Prisoners there till midnight, and then they cruelly turned them all out of doors in the frost and snow, Alice Ambrose's clothes being before frozen like boards, and was much and to no other thing could be attributed but to the arm of the Lord that Alice especially and the rest had not been killed;

such unmercifulness to their fellow-creatures lodgest in the Breasts of these wicked men who doubtless thought by these Things to have dispatched them; but the hand of the Lord, who keeps all those who wait upon him, preserved and upheld them, to whom be the glory. Amen."

Another aspirant for martyrdom soon came, — Elizabeth Hooten. Bishop said:

"Then at Dover for asking Priest Rayner aforesaid a Question, she was put in the stocks and kept in prison four days in the cold weather, being an ancient woman which might have cost her her life, but the Lord preserved her; Richard Walden aforesaid (whose wife, it is said, begged the office of Deputy Magistrate for him that he might mischief Friends) being he who executed this cruelty through the instigation of the Priest, as before he had done to others of whom I have made mention; more cold storms she endured and Persecution in the service of the Truth in these Parts than she was able to express, being made a strength to Friends, and leaving the others without excuse."

Elizabeth Hooten says of herself:

"I was imprisoned also at Hampton and Dover where a wicked Constable Came with a warrant and fetched away a poor old man's heifer (Thomas Roberts's probably), who had little else to maintain him, for £ 3 5s. fine imposed on him by fine of five shillings a day for not hearing their teacher which was a horrible oppression, five times worse than the Bishop's law which is but one shilling a day for not coming to hear their Common Prayer. I being present asked him 'who made that warrant?' He said, 'the Treasurer, Peter Coffin.' But he read it 'in His Majesty's name;' I asked him 'Who was that Majesty?' He said 'the King.' Then said I, 'in the King's name restore the poor man his heifer, for he hath made no such law.' But he would not. So I went to Peter Coffin the Treasurer and cleared my conscience unto him and told him 'that he had done contrary to God's law and the King's law in taking away the poor man's cow, for that the King had sent to them That their Church members should not make laws by themselves excluding others.' He told me that he would take away more yet. But the Lord stopped him in that purpose."

"From him I went to Richard Walden the magistrate, to whom I said, 'Yesterday thou and thy wife were at a fast and to-day a poor man's cow is taken away in his Majesty's name by a Warrant.' I asked him if he made that warrant. He said 'no'. I said 'then make a warrant to fetch him again.'"

"But he answered, 'if I had a cow he would fetch her.' I said it was contrary to God's law, and to the King's. Then said he, 'it is the Devil's law.' 'I answered, 'then thou may take it home; as thou sayest it is the Devil's law, so say I, for thou has said it.' Then I bid him repent and turn from these wicked laws and wicked actions, or else God would cut them off. From him I went again to the constable, and bid him return the poor man his cow again, for he did not as he would be done by. But he answered, 'if the magistrate commanded him to take away the man's life he must do it.' So you may see by what law these men act in prosecuting the just, as Walden said himself, 'it is the Devil's law.' So a company of blood-thirsty men are, etc."

"Edward Weymouth was the wicked one that dragged her. Hate-Evil Nutter, a ruling elder, was present stirring up the constables to do this thing, for which no warrant had they as ever could be known, or did appear for procuring none they turned them out at Midnight, as is related."

"In the year 1663, on the 4th day of the 5th Month, Edward Wharton, aforesaid, being at Piscataqua River, and hearing of the cruelties done by your Court at Dover, was pressed in Spirit forthwith to repair to the Court where your Magistrates being assembled, he cryed aloud and said, 'Wo to all oppressors and Persecutors, for the indignation of the Lord is against them, Therefore, Friends, whilst you have time prize the day of his patience and cease to do Evil and learn to do well, ye who spoil the poor and devour the needy, ye who lay Traps and Snares for the innocent.'"

"These words of advice and council and denunciation of Judgment against that which oppresses and persecutes the innocent, were very hard to your Court, and Thomas Wiggins aforesaid (an old bloody Professor) being in a great rage cryed out 'Where is the Constable? Where is the Constable?' The Marshal coming they had him to the stocks and put in his legs and so held him, till having consulted what to do, they had him in again, and then William Hathorne of Salem, who sat at that time Judge of the Court, demanded of him 'wherefore he came thither?' who answered, 'To bear my testimony for the Truth against Persecution and Violence.' Whereupon the said Wiggins fell to raging again, to whom Edward said, 'Thomas Wiggins, Thomas Wiggins, thou shouldst not rage so; thou art old and very gray, and thou art an old Persecutor; its time for thee to give over, for thou mayest be drawing near to thy grave.' Which gave an issue to an order to whip him through three towns, ten stripes at each town."

"Jerry Tibbetts Constable having received the warrant, he was bid to have Edward away and tye him to the Cart tail and whip him through the town. To which Edward answered manfully as he was passing from them, 'Friends, I fear not the worst ye may be suffered to do unto me, neither do I seek for any favor at your hands.' And to William Hathorne he said, 'O William, O William, the Lord will surely visit thee.' So to a pair of cart wheels he was tyed with a great Rope about his middle and a number of People to draw them about, when the Executor cruelly whipped him, told him that he must prepare to receive the like at the next town, which was about fourteen miles from thence through the woods; which being a long way for a man to travel on foot whose back was so torn already, to serve their pleasure in his own Execution, he told them he should not go unless they provided a horse for him or that they dragged him thither, whereupon your Executioner Complaining to your Court, this order according to this copy was issued forth as followeth:"

"'To the Constables of Dover or Either of them: These are to require you That whereas Edward Wharton a vagabond Quaker hath been sentenced according to Law, and at present a Horse, according to that sentence, cannot be obtained, These are in his Majesty's name to and require you to commit the said Edward to the Prison at Dover, there to remain in close Custody till the next second day of the week; and there you are to Execute the said sentence according to Warrant formerly delivered unto you; hereof you are not to fail.'"

"'Dover the 4th of 5th Month 1663.
Thomas Wiggins
William Harthorne
Eliazer Lusher.'"

This sentence was executed.

"At another time Thomas Newhouse, John Liddal, Edward Wharton, Jane Millard, Anna Coleman, on a first day of the week, coming to your worship house in Dover, were by Walden's Command (of whom I have formerly spoken) haled to prison, where after he had caused them to be detained almost two weeks though he confessed, That for aught he knew they might be such as were spoken of in the 11th of Hebrews, yet he must Execute the Law against them, and so set them at Liberty. The people promised that the Priest Rayner should give them a fair reasoning when his Worship was done; but he broke their word and packed away; and though the women followed him to his house yet he would not turn but clapt to his door, having taken out the key and turned Anna Coleman out of the house."

WHAT WERE THE LAWS AGAINST QUAKERS IN THIS PERIOD?

In order that the readers of the Quaker historian's story may not entertain an erroneous idea regarding the people on Dover Neck, and the officials of this town, it may be well to state that they were not any more wicked, to say the least, than the people of Boston and those in England, from whence they had emigrated a few years before. Dover was then a town in Norfolk County, Massachusetts Bay Colony. It was subject to the laws of that colony, and had to submit to the enforcement of those laws, good or bad. The characterization of the Rev. John Reyner as "a wicked and arbitrary priest" is grossly unjust, as appears from other evidence. Calling former Governor Thomas Roberts "a poor man" is absurd, for he was one of Dover's well-to-do citizens. As regards "that wicked man, Thomas Canney," he was not "wicked" in any true sense of that word; he was simply helping enforce a law of the colony. He was one of the respectable citizens of the town. Perhaps the constables, John and Thomas Roberts, were a little too frisky in giving the missionaries a free ride in an Indian canoe on Fore River that cold night, but they were servants of the colony, sworn to enforce the law whenever ordered to do so.

The first Quakers who arrived in Boston, or New England, were Mary Fisher and Mrs. Ann Austin; that was on July 11, 1656. They had a hundred or more books on Quaker doctrines among their baggage. As soon as the ship landed them in Boston the authorities inspected their holdings and confiscated the books; these they burned as soon as fire could consume them. The women were searched and closely questioned for signs of witchcraft by the experts in knowledge of demonology; this was done in court, an institution of great dignity. The court could not find any evidence that they were witches, only Quaker missionaries, so they were ordered to be confined in prison until a ship could be found to take them back to England, whence they had come; they, condemned as "hereticks," were ordered to be exported by the court. They were imprisoned five weeks before a ship could be obtained to take them on board, for England. During the same year eight other Quaker missionaries came over to Boston, were tried in court and condemned as "hereticks" and dangerous persons to have in the community. They were deported to England.

In 1657 and 1658 the General Court of Massachusetts passed laws against Quakers attempting to land in Boston; before that they were simply "hereticks"; the authorities had come to regard Quakers as worse than this class of religious disturbers. The General Court decreed that on the first conviction of anyone preaching Quakerism one ear should be cut off; on the second conviction the other ear should be cut off; on the third conviction the tongue should be bored with a hot iron. Fines were decreed for those who entertained Quakers at their houses, or were present at any of their meetings. Could any law be more frightful?

These awful threats of bodily punishment did not frighten the apostles of George Fox; on the contrary, they rushed to Massachusetts all the more. Then the General Court changed the law and made the penalty that they should be tied to a cart-tail and whipped on their bare backs; then be banished from the colony; if they returned they should be hanged. Under that law three men and one woman were hanged on Boston Common. Other Quaker missionaries were not frightened by this horrible severity of punishment; they came in greater numbers and preached and proselyted with all the greater enthusiasm, manifesting more zeal than ever before. They were persecuted in Old England just as badly, or worse, as in New England: for speaking in churches and interrupting the ministers while speaking; for travelling on the Sabbath; for breach of the peace by preaching on the streets or in the market places; for refusing to pay tythes; for refusing to take off their hats in the presence of officials; for refusing to swear in courts of justice, always affirming, as many persons now do. Such was the state of public sentiment when the Quaker women came to Dover and commenced to shed the rays of that "Inner Light" which they claimed was the inspiration of their souls. They had been persecuted, whipped and imprisoned in England before they came to New England. In fact, the severity of the treatment of the followers of George Fox, the founder of Quakerism, was more severe in England than in New England. The following is the law under which the punishments were inflicted in Dover. It was enacted on the 22nd of May, 1661. It can be found on pages 238-239-240, of volume first of Provincial Papers of New Hampshire:

"This court, being desirous to try all means, with as much lenity as may consist with our safety, to prevent the intrusions of the Quakers, who, beside their absurd & blasphemous doctrine, doe like rogues and vagabonds come upon us, and have not bin restrained by the laws already provided, have ordered that every vagabond Quaker found within any part of this jurisdiction shall be apprehended by any person or persons, or by the constables of the towne wherein he or she may be taken, and by the constable or in his absence by any other person or persons, conveyed before the magistrate of that shire wherein they are taken, or commissioner invested with magistratticall power, & being by the said magistrate or magistrates, or commissioner or commissioners, adjudged to be a wandering Quaker, viz: one that hath not any dwelling or orderly allowance as an inhabitant of this jurisdiction, and not giving civil respect by the usual gestures thereof, or by any other way or means manifesting himself to be a Quaker shall by warrant under the hand of said magistrate, magistrates, commissioner or commissioners, directed to the constable of the towne wherein he or she is taken, or in the absence of the constable by any other meete person, be stripped from the middle upwards, & tyed to a carts tayle, and whipped thro the towne, and then immediately conveyed to the constable of the next towne, towards the borders of our jurisdiction, as their warrant shall direct, & so from constable to constable, till they be conveyed thro any of the outwardmost townes of our jurisdiction.

"And if any such vagabond Quaker shall returne againe, then to be in like manner apprehended & conveyed as often as they shall be found within the limits of our jurisdiction, provided every such wandering Quaker, having been thrice convicted and sent away as above said & returning againe into this jurisdiction shall be apprehended and committed by any magistrate or commissioner as above said to the house of correction within that county wherein he or shee is found untill the next court of that county, when, if the court judge not meet to release them they shall be branded with the letter 'R' on their left shoulder, & be severely whipt & sent away in manner as before; and after this if he or she shall return againe, then to be proceeded against as incorrigible rogues, & ennemys to the common peace, & shall immediately be apprehended & committed to the common jayle of the county, and at the next Court of Assistants shall be brought to their tryall, & proceeded against according to the lawe made Anno 1658, page 36, for their banishment on payne of death. And for such Quakers as shall arise from amongst ourselves, they shall be proceeded against as the former lawe of Anno 1658, page 36, doth provide, untill they have been convicted by a Court of Assistants, & being so convicted, he or shee shall then be banished this jurisdiction; & if after that they shall be found in any part of this jurisdiction, then he or she so sentenced to be banished shall be proceeded against as those who are straingers & vagabond Quakers in manner as is above expressed. And it is further ordered, that whatsoever charge shall arise about apprehending, whipping, conveying or otherwise, about the Quakers, to be laid out by the constables of such townes where it is expended, & to be repaid by the treasurer out of the next country levy; & further, that the constables of the severall townes are hereby empowered from time to time, as necessity shall require, to impress cart, oxen, & other assistance for the execution of this order."

WHITTIER'S POEM ON THE QUAKER WOMEN.

The Quaker Poet, John Greenleaf Whittier, in his beautiful poem, "How They Drove the Quaker Women from Dover," begins his story with the following lines:

> The tossing spray of Cochecho's falls
> Hardened to ice on its icy walls,
> As through Dover town, in the chill gray dawn,
> Three women passed, at the cart tail drawn,
> Dared to the waist, for the north wind's grip
> And keener sting of the constable's whip,
> The blood that followed each hissing blow
> Froze as it sprinkled the winter snow.
> Priest and ruler, boy and maid,
> Followed the dismal cavalcade;
> And from door and window, open thrown,
> Looked and wondered, gaffer and crone."

The poet represents the scene as taking place at Cochecho, that is, in what is now the central part of the city. That is not correct; the stage of action was in front of the church on High Street, Dover Neck, as that was the center of business. There is no mention of the women attempting to preach in this section of the town, where Major Richard Walderne was boss of business; their missionary work was confined to Dover Neck, so far as this town was concerned. The oxen and cart were stationed in front of the meeting-house, which locality is now marked by the bronze tablet on the face wall. It does not appear that the constable struck very hard blows with his whip, or drew any blood; the probability is that he simply went through with the motions, as required by law.

One of the witnesses of this transaction was Dr. Walter Barefoot, who was then a resident of Dover Neck; he was the first praticing physician in this town; he resided here several years, then removed to Newcastle, or Great Island, as it was then called.

He appears to have had a satisfactory record here in Dover, but his record as provincial governor of New Hampshire is one of the worst.

The ox-team did escort duty from the meeting-house to *Hilton Point,* but could go no further. Dr. Barefoot was one of the company that went with the constable; perhaps he went with them to see that the women had proper medical care. The party crossed the Pascataqua River by Trickey's ferry to Bloody Point, and went on to Hampton by paths through the woods, practically as the road now goes. That part of the journey was taken on horseback, with the women riding on pillions behind men, to whom they were tied by ropes. When they arrived at Salisbury, Major Pike interfered in their behalf and would not permit the constable of that town to whip the women. This was a very praiseworthy act on the part of the Major; but his authority extended only to the Merrimack River. He could not keep them in his town; they must pass on. As soon as they should cross the river the authorities of Newbury would take the women, according to law, and whip them. He did not want this to be done; he pitied the poor but zealous missionaries. He consulted with Dr. Barefoot; he consented to give the Quakers into Barefoot's control if he would take them out of the jurisdiction of the Massachusetts Bay Colony. The doctor consented to this arrangement and the Major assisted him in securing boats in which to take them away; so, early one morning, they were placed in the boats and the party went down the river to Ipswich Bay; then along the coast to the Pascataqua; then up the river to Shapleigh's Creek, which is directly across Fore River from the meeting-house on Dover Neck. Major Nicholas Shapleigh lived at the head of that creek. Dr. Barefoot escorted the persistent missionaries to the Major's house, where they were cordially received and were most hospitably entertained for a few weeks, until they had completely recovered from the punishment they had received at Dover and Hampton.

Major Nicholas Shapleigh was one of the great men of Old Kittery, now Eliot. He served as one of the Provincial Councillors from 1644 to 1652, except one year. He held important offices in York County. He was one of the Selectmen of the town for several years, and Deputy in the General Court. In 1656 he was appointed Major of the militia and served all through the Indian wars. But notwithstanding all his greatness and goodness, he was deposed from office as Selectman and disfranchised for entertaining the Quaker women missionaries. But he was enfranchised later and served as Deputy in the General Court.

When they had fully recovered their health and the *"Inner Light"* began to shine in their souls, they took a boat and went up the river to Berwick, at Quamphegan Falls, and began lecturing in private houses, but not meeting with any opposition, they grew weary of doing all of the talking and returned to Dover Neck. They did not go to the meeting-house, nor to Parson Reyner's house, but confined their work to visiting private houses, where they were permitted to speak their minds as they pleased. This annoyed the authorities somewhat, and attempts were made to arrest them; but their friends gave them due warning of any approach of the officers. They then made haste to reach a boat in Fore River and took refuge across the river, to Shapleigh's Cove, where Major Shapleigh always bid them a hearty welcome, and gave them liberty to say what they pleased. The following is a letter written in 1663, by Major Richard Walderne to the authorities in Boston in regard to this matter:

"Major Shapleigh shelters the Quakers that come into our parts, and followeth them where they meet; which is not only a disterber on that side of the river, but also on our side; they come to our town (and lecture) and presently they are gone over the river; and so his house is the harbor of them; and some say he is dictated by the little crooked Quaker (Edward Wharton). Our town will be so disturbed by the Quakers and others that we shall hardly be at peace."

It seems evident that the Quaker missionaries made a serious mistake when they first began work in Dover by using such violent and imprudent methods of proclaiming their doctrines. Had they pursued the same course before being whipped that they did after their return from that vacation they spent at Major Shapleigh's residence, they never would have been whipped; so, in a measure, it was their own fault that they were thus punished.

In time the laws against Quakers ceased to be enforced. Here in Dover the Quakers, eventually, became a third of the entire population, and always industrious, thrifty and of high standing in the community. Their first house of worship stood on Dover Neck, on High Street, near where the cemetery is on the west side of the street. After many years the building was taken down and removed across the river to Kittery, now Eliot, where a society of Friends had existed from the time of Major Shapleigh. The second Quaker meeting-house was built before 1720, at Cochecho, on the southwest corner of Silver and Locust streets. The present house of worship, on Central Avenue, was built in 1768, and is the oldest house of the kind in this city.

SCHOOL-MASTERS AND SCHOOL-HOUSES.

Dover Neck never had a "little red school-house"; in fact, there is no record of one painted red in any part of the town. It seems to have been a fashion that prevailed in the towns remote from the early settlements. Dover came under Massachusetts in 1642; that brought it under the law which required each town of fifty houses to "appoint one within their town to teach all such children, as shall resort to him, to read and write." The Selectmen of every town were required "to have a vigilant eye over their brethren and neighbors, and to see that none of them shall suffer so much barbarism in any of their families, as not to endeavor to teach their children and apprentices so much learning as may enable them to read perfectly the English language, so as to obtain a knowledge of the laws."

The Selectmen of Dover appear to have enforced this law intelligently and faithfully, and thereby the second generation in this town consisted of intelligent men and women. Dover has never since then fallen behind in this regard; its schools and school-masters have always been above the average elsewhere.

Among the school-boys in those early days, it was fashionable to aspire to become mariners; the height of their boyish ambition was to reach the high rank of Captain of a ship, and sail to the West Indies with a cargo of pipe-staves. They had no fear of pirates; but were thrilled with enthusiasm as they heard the stories of the sea captains who had fought them and won victories that were marvels of bravery.

Previous to 1657 the school teaching was done by the ministers, who instructed the public school, free, and received tuition for fitting boys to enter Harvard College. At a town meeting held in August, 1657, the Town Record says,—"Charles Buckner chosen, by vote, a Scoellmaster for this Towne."

Mr. Buckner served several years, and the town had regularly elected schoolmasters after that date, and most of them were graduates of Harvard College, who were first-class instructors in all the branches required to fit the pupils to enter the College, as well as become good accountants.

ORGANIZATION OF THE FIRST CHURCH.

This chapter is not designed to give a complete history of the First Church, but to relate some interesting particulars that occurred in the beginning of the organization. It was in November, 1638, that Captain John Underhill and Rev. Hanserd Knollys arrived at the village on Dover Neck and took the lead in organizing the First Church, in proper Congregational and Puritanical form, according to the rules established at the General Court in Boston. Dr. Belknap's Manuscript History of the First Church states that Mr. Knollys, who had been minister of a church in England, came over in 1638 and was not endorsed by The Massachusetts, because he held "Antinomian tenets," one of which was that he denied that the moral law is binding on Christians, and affirmed that faith alone was necessary to salvation. Captain Underhill was tinctured with this "Antinomian" doctrine, though he was a member of the First Church in Boston, so he endorsed Mr. Knollys and got him to come to Dover and organize a church. That Mr. Knollys was an excellent man and a very able minister is manifest in the fact that after he returned to England, in 1640, he was minister of a large church for forty years, or more. His portrait hangs in the First Parish Church Chapel; it was furnished by Mr. Asa A. Tufts, who was, in his early life, a member of that Church.

The Historian Hubbard says:—

"About the year 1638 the people at Pascataqua attempted to gather themselves into a Church estate. But for want of discretion, if not something else, in them thay were called to this solemn work, they soon after fell into factions, and strange confusion, one part taking upon them to excommunicate and punish the other, in the Church and in the Court; an ordinary effect of loose and pragmatical spirits under any popular government, whether civil or eclesiastical."

For good and sufficient reasons Mr. Burdett had left town before the arrival of Underhill and Knollys. As the town was left without a governor, Captain John Underhill was elected to that office, and held it till the March election of 1640, when Thomas Roberts was elected and held the office till the town came under the rule of Massachusetts, in 1642-43.

Dr. Belknap says in his MS history of the First Church:—

"Being cleared of Burdett, it (the plantation) was ridden by another Churchman, Thomas Larkham. Coming to New England, and not favoring the discipline (at Boston) he removed hither (1640), and the people of Dover were much taken with his public preaching, he being of good parts and well gifted. But not being able to maintain two ministers (Knollys and Larkham) they resolved to cast out Mr. Knollys and embrace Mr. Larkham. Whereupon Mr. Knollys, making a virtue of necessity, gave place, and the other, soon after he was chosen, discovered himself by taking into the Church all that offered, though never so notoriously immoral and ignorant, if they would but promise amendment; and moreover fell into contentions with the people, taking it upon himself to rule all, even the magistrates themselves. This occasioned a sharp dispute between him and Mr. Knollys, who either yet retained, or upon this occasion resumed, the pastoral office. Whereupon they were neither able quietly to divide into two churches, nor live peaceably together in one. The more religious sort still adhering to Mr. Knollys, he, in their name, excommunicated Mr. Larkham, who in return laid violent hands on Knollys, taking the hat from his head, pretending it was not paid for; but he was so civil as to send it to him again.

"In this heat it began to grow a tumult, and some of the magistrates joined with Mr. Larkham and assembled a company to fetch Captain Underhill before the Court. Underhill also gathered some of their neighbors together to defend themselves and keep the peace, and so marched out (from the log meeting house) to meet Mr. Larkham, one carrying a Bible on a halberd, for an ensign, Mr. Knollys being armed with a pistol. When Mr. Larkham saw them thus provided, he withdrew his party, and went no further, but sent down to Mr. Williams, Governor of Strawberry Bank, for assistance, who came up with a company of armed men and beset Mr. Knolly's house (on Low street) where Capt. Underhill was, kept a guard upon him night and day till they could call a Court; and then Mr. Williams, sitting as Judge, they found Underhill and his company guilty of riot, and set great fines upon them, and ordered Knollys and some others to depart out of the plantation."

Captain Underhill and Mr. Knollys appealed to the authorities in Boston and the Governor and Assistants commissioned Mr. Bradstreet, Hugh Peters of Salem, and Mr. Dalton of Hampton, who came hither on foot to inquire into the matter and endeavor to make peace. They succeeded so well that Mr. Larkham was released from his excommunication and Capt. Underhill and the rest from their sentences.

Another account of these troubles is given by the historian Lechford:—

"They two (Larkham and Knollys) fell out about baptizing children, receiving of members, burial of the dead; and the contention was so sharp that Knollys and his party rose up and excommunicated Mr. Larkham and some that held with him; and further, Mr. Larkham flying to the magistrates, Mr. Knollys and Captain Underhill raised arms and expected help from the Bay, Mr. Knollys going before the troop with a Bible upon a pole's top, and giving forth that their side were Scots and English. Whereupon the gentlemen of Sir F. Gorges' plantation at Portsmouth came in and kept court with the magistrates of Pascataqua, who fined all of those who were in arms for riot, by indictment, jury and verdict, formally; nine of them were censured to be whipped, but that was spared; Mr. Knollys and the Captain, their leaders, were fined 100 pounds apiece, which they were not able to pay."

Governor Winthrop makes mention of the affair in his Journal and says:—

"In this heat it began to grow to a tumult; some of their magistrates joined with Mr. Larkham and assembled a company to fetch Capt. Underhill (one of their magistrates and their Captain) to their court; and he (Underhill) also gathered some of his neighbors to defend himself and to see the peace kept so they marched toward Mr. Larkham's company, one carrying a Bible upon a staff for an ensign, and Mr. Knollys armed with a pistol. At their approach Larkham's company withdrew and sent to Strawberry Bank for Gov. Williams to come up and help them."

ALTERCATION BETWEEN REV. MR. KNOLLYS AND MR. LARKHAM—1640.

The reader should bear in mind that these events took place in and around the log meeting-house, which stood on Low Street, on a hill about six hundred feet from High Street, at the residence where the late Daniel Pinkham lived for many years, which house is six hundred feet from the southeast corner of the second meeting-house lot. It is a beautiful location, commanding a fine view of Back River and the upper Pascataqua and also of Fore River and the lower Pascataqua.

The regular annual election for governor of the Massachusetts Bay Colony was held in March, 1638. There were two candidates: Gov. Harry Vane asked for another term; former Governor John Winthrop was the candidate against him. The reason for this opposition was that Governor Vane had favored the views which Mrs. Ann Hutchinson had been preaching in Boston in the months preceding, which views Mr. Winthrop and his party violently opposed, and secured her expulsion from the colony. Mr. Winthrop won the election; Boston people then turned around and elected Gov. Vane as one of the Deputies to the General Court. He was refused a seat in that august body, on some technical ground. Soon after Gov. Winthrop was installed in office Mr. Vane and Capt. John Underhill, who were great friends and entertained like views regarding Mrs. Hutchinson's preaching, left for England; Mr. Vane never visited Boston again. At about the same time they left for England Mrs. Hutchinson left and went to Rhode Island; Rev. John Wheelwright left Boston for the same reasons, and came to *Hilton Point* and visited the leading men in Dover to consult with them about organizing a colony of his own somewhere in this vicinity. He obtained information from them where he could meet Indian sagamores from whom he could obtain a grant of land, which investigation finally resulted in the founding of Exeter.

Captain Underhill did not remain in England very long; he returned to Boston in the fall of 1638. Rev. Hanserd Knollys came over at the same time, perhaps in the same ship. They soon got acquainted and came to Dover, together, in November, 1638. We do not know just what was said and done when they arrived, but the results that soon followed were the resignation of Rev. George Burdett as minister of the parish and his resignation from the office of governor, which he had held about a year and a half, and his departure to Agamenticus; following which Captain Underhill was elected governor and the First Church was organized, with Mr. Knollys as minister. They served in those offices two years, and then were succeeded by Thomas Roberts, as governor, and Thomas Larkham, as minister.

Mr. Larkham arrived in Dover in the summer of 1640; he came from Boston, to which place he had come from Northam, England, a few months before, in which town, near the Bristol Channel, he had been a Puritan minister a few years. He was a young man of thirty-nine years; a graduate of one of the English Universities; a good speaker; pleasing in his address and social in his intercourse with the people. Why he came nobody has explained; no one had invited him to come; perhaps it was merely a chance visit to see what kind of a settlement there was on *Hilton Point* and Dover Neck. Anyway, he did not stop at Strawberry Bank in his journey to Dover. Being here, he was invited to preach occasionally, as a matter of ministerial courtesy. He appears to have liked here, as he prolonged his visit. There does not appear to have been any trouble between Mr. Knollys and Mr. Larkham until late in the fall of 1640; then it appears that a difference of opinion on certain religious points had produced hard feelings between them. Mr. Knollys was much more radical in his demands for reforms in the liturgy of the English church than was Mr. Larkham, who was striving to reform that church, not to establish a new one.

It may be of interest to say something further concerning the differences between Mr. Knollys and Mr. Larkham, which started the trouble between them. Mr. Larkham baptized the children of members of the Parish, as well as those who were members of the Church; Mr. Knollys would not baptize the children of those parents who were not members of the church; Mr. Larkham used the sign of the cross in baptizing; Mr. Knollys would not make that sign. Mr. Larkham admitted to church membership all members of the parish who were willing to come in, regardless of their doctrinal beliefs; Mr. Knollys would not admit any who were not sound in the profession of the Puritan faith. As regarded burial of the dead: Mr. Larkham used the burial service given in the Church of England Liturgy; Mr. Knollys would not use any service at the grave. These disputes began in the fall of 1640 and the final battle was fought in the winter of 1640/1.

Mr. Lechford in his statement of the altercation, says: "Master Knollys going before the troop with a Bible upon a pole's top, and he, or some one of his party, giving forth that their side were Scots and the other English." The explanation of that is found in the contention going on between the Presbyterians of Scotland and the Church men in England. In 1637 the canons for liturgical worship in Scotland were published and a great commotion of revolt ensued among the Presbyterians, who were largely in preponderance in Scotland. On the 23d of July, 1637, the new liturgy pressed upon Scotland by the English Bishops was read for the first time in Edinburgh. A great riot ensued. Finally Scotland took up arms in opposition. War ensued. In the beginning of the year 1639 the English forces moved northward and soon occupied Berwick. A temporary pacification was announced 17 June, 1639; but the conflict was renewed in 1640, and the little war known as "the Bishops' war," ended with the battle at Newburn-on-Tyne, 28 August, 1640, which Clarendon calls "that infamous, irreparable rout at Newburn." With this defeat of the English, the attempt to establish in Scotland the liturgy of the Church of England utterly failed. This conflict was well understood at Dover, in 1640; hence the expression used that the two parties were Scots and English.

DOVER TOWN RECORDS.

There is nothing to show when Captain Thomas Wiggin ceased to manage the business of disposing of the land, and the town took it in hand to make land grants. Probably the change was made about 1638, as then, or soon after, he removed to his plantation on the east shore of Great Bay, in what is now Stratham. That was then regarded as a part of Dover. It seems advisable to give here a list of the Town Records, to show on what our information is based regarding the beginning of business. All the records were kept at Dover Neck during the first century. These records may be described as follows:

I. The oldest book extant is marked on the cover: "Dover Old Book of Records." It bears marks of much usage and of less care; but it is now carefully preserved by the City Clerk. It contains 197 pages, nearly entire, with a tolerable index. Its first record shows that it was commenced in 1647, but it has copies of matter earlier than that date, all of which have been published in the *"Dover Enquirer,"* and later were republished in a volume of "Historical Memoranda of Old Dover," except the land grants, votes relating to the ministry, preservation of trees, etc. These records extend regularly to about 1660, and here and there are interspersed matters as late as 1753. The Town Clerks who made those records were: William Walderne, probably from 1635; certainly from December, 1641, until his death, September, 1646. — George Smith, appointed by Massachusetts court in November, 1646; he served one year. — William Pomfrett, who was chosen by the town November, 1647, and served until about 1685. In his writing is our oldest extant volume of town records, and it is marked: "No. 7" on its parchment cover.

II. A fragment containing 17 loose leaves, paged 13-29. It contains two lists of freemen and various votes which are crossed, as if copied into some other book, though into what book does not appear. They bear date of 1653 and thereabout.

III. A fragment of 16 leaves, commencing page 5; it contains regular records of elections; — instructions to deputies in the General Court; — parish quarrels; — land grants, etc. The business is within the dates 1661-1670.

IV. Tax book, 1661, 1672 (1669 missing). It contains 32 pages in tolerable order, chiefly valuable for its names, all of which are published in the Genealogical Register, Boston, July, 1850.

V. Sixteen leaves, loose, torn, corner burned off, edges worn, beginning and ending defective; mostly taken up with sales of land; it has tax lists for 1675 and 1677, but not complete; and a few scraps of records of an earlier date.

VI. Records from 1686 to 1689, but containing scattered entries up to 1726; it consists of land grants, elections, etc., for sixty pages; deficient at beginning and ending, and twin brother to the preceding, if looks prove any relationship.

VII. A gathering of fragments; being ten leaves or pieces of leaves saved from destruction and varying in size from a square inch up to nearly the size of a whole page.

VIII. A volume marked *"Dover Town Records." "No. 8."* It contains 458 pages of the usual record matter; it commences with March 1693/4 and extends to 1757. This volume is in very good condition, except that the ink is faded in some places; the leaves show that they have been handled by the fingers of many persons.

IX. A "Highway" fragment of six pages, 1733/8.

X. A volume of births and marriages, commencing about 1690; it contains a good deal of valuable genealogical information, all of which can be found in Vol. One, *"Dover Historical Collections."*

XI. The records since 1757 are in good condition. None of them have been published. About the year 1820 a volume of highways matter disappeared; it has never been found. The Town Clerk, James Richardson, said he lent it to one of the Selectmen; that official denied ever having received the book. Both were agreed that the book was lost. Also a volume of Dover matter was reported to have been burned in the fire which destroyed a large part of the New York State Library, at Albany, a few years ago. How this Dover matter got into that library has not been explained; neither is it known what class of matter it was or the date. Nobody in Dover knew there were any such records in existence until the New York Library officials announced they were burned.

DOUBLE ENTRY LAND GRANTS.

In 1729, December 16, Captain Paul Gerrish, Representative from Dover in the General Assembly of New Hampshire, presented a petition to the Assembly, signed by nearly three-score of "ye Principal men in Dover, praying an order to rectify some abuses suffered by Dover Town Books of Records by the fault of the late Town Clerk (Thomas Tebbetts), as they apprehend."

At that time Captain Gerrish was also Town Clerk. In volume four of the Provincial Papers of New Hampshire, page 554, is the record of the order of the House that day on which the petition was presented:—

"Voted that the Clerk of the said town of Dover, for the time being, be hereby prohibited entering any old Committee Grants that are suspected not to be legally obtained and to enter only such grants as have been or may be allowed by said town or the Selectmen thereof until the next sitting of the General Assembly and that there be a committee chosen by the Assembly to go to the Town Clerk for the time being who is hereby required to show unto such committee such entry matters and things as he, or any of said town supposed to be done by ill practice, and the said committee shall by virtue hereof summon before them all such persons that give any light explaining any matters or things which they may see occasion to examine into for discovering the truth and detecting such vile practices and to give such person or Persons their oaths and to make return of their doings there in to the General Assembly, next session, and that Nathaniel Weare Esq. and Theo. Atkinson Esq. be a committee of this house to join such as shall be appointed above for that end and that the Petitioners pay the charges."

The Council concurred and appointed Jotham Odiorne and Henry Sherburne to be members of the committee.

That committee came to Dover and made an examination of the land-grants record and made a report to the Assembly Nov. 28, 1730. The Council on Dec. 1st, 1730, Voted:

"That another committee be chosen to make a more Exact and particular Inquiry into the several grants and returns in said book, supposed to be corrupt and vicious; and that they have full power to summon & examine any person or Persons upon oath, in order to discover the truth as far as may be, and any Person or Persons duly convened by summons before the said committee, & refusing to declare upon oath what he or they knew of the affair, shall be committed to prison by said Committee, or the major part of them, there to remain till they comply to take their oaths, and that then the said committee give public notices on all the meeting- houses in Dover, with convenient time for all persons that have any claims to any land by virtue of the aforesaid supposed vicious grants and returns, to make out the same before the Committee, at a certain day, and when the said Committee have made a strict examination in the Towne-Book & fully heard all the claimers upon their Grants and their returns, they to make a particular report how many corrupt and vicious grants and returns they find on the said Book, with the dates there of; in what folios of the Book they stand recorded, and who are the respective grantees; & return, in order, to the General Assembly; proceeding thereon as to justice doth pertain; and that Mr. Odiorne and Mr. Sherburne be of the Committee to joyne with such as the House shall appoint to Act in the above affair."

"R. Waldron, Sec'y."

In House of Representatives
Epdem die.

"The above vote was read and concurred, with this amendment:—That the whole Towne of Dover pay the charge of the committee, and that Nathaniel Weare & Theodore Atkinson, Esq. be a Committee of the House to joyne with the above Committee to act in the above affaire."

"Jam. Jeffrey, Cler. Assem."

In the report of the proceedings in the House, May 6th, 1731, is the statement:—"The report of the committee about Dover Towne Book read and sent down by the Secretary (to the Council)."

The first report of the committee, made in 1730, was in substance: That they found by examination of the book of records numerous forgery and fraud entries of land grants and returns thereof; grants were entered in the interspaces in the records many years back; that the book had often been left open and exposed, so that anyone could make entries as they pleased; that large tracts of land had been entered in these ways and the town had been defrauded of 15,000 pounds worth of land, according to their best judgment.

On page 163 of Volume IX, Povincial Papers of New Hampshire, is given the full report of the committee, as follows:

Whereas the General Assembly of this his Maj's Province upon reading the report of the Committee formerly appointed by sd. Assembly to Examine Town book: Wee, whose names are hereunto Subscribed were appointed by the General Assembly to make a more exact and particular Inquiry into the several Grants & returns in sd. book, supposed to be Vicious and Corrupt as pr. sd. Vote of the 30th. of December, 1730, will appear & having Strictly examined sd. Town Books & files as alsoe the former Town Clerk & other persons from whom we could receive any Insight or Information & do report that all the Grants & returns mentioned in this report we Imagine to be fraudulent Corrupt & Vicious for the reasons mentioned with Each record herein recited as:

First.—In the old Book Page (120) a grant made in the 10th. of the 11th. month (59) & a return made and entered by Capt. Thomas Tibbets, the late Clerk & in a space amongst the records made many years before he was Clerk & the time of his recording it was entered with the sd. Grant & return & afterwards erased & the Clerk acknowledged he recorded it, beside we view the originall & find it all of one hand and signing.

Secondly.—In the New book Page (9) a grant made by a committee whereof William Furber was clerk of 60 acres of Land made to the Rev. Mr. John Pike, Dated the 23d of June, 1701, & confirmed by the Town the 23d. March, 1702. This Capt. Thomas Tibbets swears he doth not know how it came upon record & that Dr. Pike had been with him to get the sd. Grant &c recorded but he refused to enter it, being as he believed not good. Notwithstanding it is entered in a Vacancy Left in sd. book formerly, & in a Different hand from the records of that Time & some obliterations.

Thirdly.—In sd. book Page (16) a grant made by sd. committee for (30) acres of land to Capt. Thomas Tibbets on the third of June, 1701, because entered by Capt. Tibbets son Samuel, as he himself declares upon oath, amongst the records made by Capt. Tuttle, &

we observed that the Date of the record, in the same page both before and after were in the year (1694) but we could not obtain any originall.

Fourth.—In page (19) a grant made to Nich. Harrison for 60 acres on the 19th. 1693/4 and confirmed by the town in the month of April following, Entered in a space amongst the records made by Capt. Tuttle & not in his hand, and differing from his sd. Tuttle's method.

5th.—In ye (27th) a grant made by sd. Committee to Captain Samuel Tibbets in the year 1694, recorded in an unusual hand & crowded in a vacancy amongst the records, the original Samuel Carl Swears he had of one Burnham, & Capt. Tibbets swears he refused to record it, believing it not good, yet we find it recorded.

6th.—Page (32) a grant made to Nathaniel Tibbets for thirty acres Dated the 11th April 1694, & confirmed on the 16th. of the same month by the Town, Crowded in between Tuttle's record in an unusuall hand & by the original it appears that Furbur, the Clerk of the Committee's name neither wrote or spelt as he used to do & the Grant and confirmation of the same hand writing.

7th.—In Page (57) Grant to Francis Pittman, by the Town, of April 6th 1702, for forty acres crowded in with Tuttle's record in an unusual hand; Thomas Tibbets Swears that he doth not know whether he recorded it or not, but he did enter some Grants & returns in Capt. Tuttle's vacancy in sd. book.

8th.—In Page (62) June the 23d. 1701, a grant by sd. Committee to Jeremiah Burnum for 50 acres entered in one of Tuttle's vacancys & by Tibbets himself, as he swears, but is not signed by any Clerk.

9th.—In page (75) June 23d. 1701, a grant to Nathanl. Landers by the sd. Committee & entred by Tibbets in the Bottom of a Leaf with the Tuttle records, as appears by the hand writing & his acknowledgement & the Different Inck & the originall appears not to be the writing of Furbur, the Clerk of the committee, which we received from Tibbets.

10th.—In Page (76) grant to Roger Vose for three score acres of land & meadow by sd. committee the 19th. March 1693/4 & confirmed by the Town the 2d April 1694, crowded in amongst Tuttle's entries in a different hand and different Collered Inck from the entry before & after.

DOUBLE ENTRY LAND GRANTS. 157

11th.—86th. Page grant to Eli Dimerrest for 30 acres of land, the 11th of April, 1694, & confirmed the 16th of April, 1694; Tibbets acknowledges he entered a vacancy left by Tuttle since was Clerk.

12th.—91 Page a grant by the sd. committee to John Tuttle & Ezek Wentworth for 30 acres of Land by sd. Committee, June 23d. 1701, entered by Capt. Tibbets at the Bottom of Tuttle's entries, not confirmed by the Town, nor signed by the clerk of the committee for Town.

13th.—93d Page a grant to Jere Barnum for 40 acres, April 11th 1694, crowded in at the bottom of Tuttle's record & supposed to be Vicious, it being in an unusuall hand writing.

14th.—Page 94 a grant by sd. committee for forty acres to Jere Barnum & not confirmed by the Town. This Tibbets, upon oath, says he recorded in a Vacancy of Tuttle's record about seven years since.

15th.—Page 95 a grant made by the committee to Thos. Roberts the 11th. of April 1694 & confirmed 16th. April following & we find the Grant was made to Thomas Roberts, *tertius*, which is left out in the record, & Tibbets swears that he entered it himself; James Hanson swears he got the originall of Ebenr. Young who told him, sd. Hanson, if he would get it recorded he would have half of it, and accordingly the sd. Hanson swears he went to Capt. Tibbets and gave him two gall'ns rum & ord'rd Abner Young to pay him twenty shillings in money for recording it.

16th.—Page 98 granted by said committee fifty acres to Richard Hussey & confirmed, 16 April 1694, crowded among Tuttle's writing in an unusual hand and in different Collered Inck.

17th.—Page 101, granted to Abraham Clark the 23d. of June 1701 & confirmed the 6th. of April 1702. Tibbets swears he recorded about three years since & the sd. Clerk swears that Mishack Drew & William Hill asked him about that time if he would sell him his grant of land if they could find it upon record; I promised them that they should have it & sometime after they told him it was recorded & then, bargained with him for Ten pounds & about this time the sd. Clark asked Capt. Tibbets if he had any grant & he told him he did not love to enter such falce things.

18th.—Page 103; a grant by sd committee to Pumphret Whitehouse June 23, 1702, for 50 acres entered amongst Tuttle's records, and Tibbets he recorded it himself and by the original it appears not to be Furbur's writing, it being different from his hand & his name not spelt right.

19.—Page 104; a grant by sd. committee of 50 acres on the 19th of March 1693/4; confirmed the 11th. of April 1694, made to Bryant Higgins. This Tibbets swears he recorded amongst Tuttle's records and that Thomas Davis brought to him about five years past to have it recorded.

20.—Page 105; a grant by sd. committee to Robert Allen in the year 1701 & confirmed 6th. April, 1702 for 40 acres; Tibbets swears he recorded it amongst Tuttle's records about four years past.

21.—Page 113; 11th. 1701, a grant by sd. Committee for forty acres of land. This Tibbets swears he entered about five or six years since & in a vacancy in Tuttle's entries; the original appears to be altered & not writ by Furbur, the clerk; it differs both in writing and spelling.

22.—Page 120; June 3d. 1701; granted by sd. Committee to George Chesley & Confirmed by the 23d. March 1702—50 acres of Land, entered by Tibbets as he swears about five years Since & the originall it appears that the Grant & Confirmation to be both of one hand & yet neither Furbur's nor Tuttle's writing.

23.—Page 130; In the year 1699 & no day or month, a Grant made by the Selectmen to Jos. Jenkins 40 acres which Tibbets swears he entred himself & amongst Tuttle's record & swears he signed the originall, not as Selectman, but as a witness, he remembering the grant to have been made about the year above sd., which Induced him to write the Grant and record it.

24.—Page 131; April 11th. 1694; Granted by sd. Committee to Jos. Smith, Junr. & Confirmed the 16th. of April, 1694. Tibbets swears he recorded it amongst Tuttle's records & that the originall was altered & obliterated before he entred it from 60 acrs to 40 acres.

No.—25 is missing.

26.—Page 132; granted June 23d. 1701, by the Committee aforesaid 30 acres to Nathl. Pittman. Tibbets entered it amongst Tuttle's records about five or six years ago & the original appears not to be Furbur's writing & much interlined.

DOUBLE ENTRY LAND GRANTS. 159

27.—Page 136; June 23d. 1701, granted by sd. committee to John Rand forty acres of Land which is not Confirmed by this town. This Tibbets Entred 10th. in Tuttle's records about five or six years since.

28.—Page 139; June 23d. 1701, a grant to Joseph Jenkins by said Committee. Tibbets swears he entred it about seven years ago.

29.—Page 144; May 28th. 1701, a grant to John Pinkham for twenty acres, the original appearing not to be the writing of said Furbur, nor his signing his name, not spelled right.

30.—Page 147. April 11th. 1701; a grant by the Committee to John Hanson for 60 acres, not confirmed by the Town, & ye originall neither wrote nor signed by the Clerk.

31.—Page 149; April 11th 1694, granted by the committee to Joseph Joanes, 40 acres who says that he had the originall from Barnum and that he Got it allowed by the Sellectmen since & had recorded for the common fees.

32.—Page 157; a grant by the Committee of the 11th April 1693/4 Richard Rendall for 30 acres. This grant Nathanl. Rendall swears he had of Burnum; & Captain Tibbets swears he recorded it but the originall appears not to be the hand writing of Furbur nor signed by him.

33.—Page 152; June 23d. 1701. Granted to James Davis 60 acres of land Entred by Tibbets, the original grant being much interlined & scratched. Colonel Davis says upon oath that Burnum asked him what he should give him for a grant of land & sd. Davis said he knew of no Grant but what was upon record & that his son Sometime after went to Burnum and got the grant and carried it to Capt. Tibbets to record.

34.—Page 153; granted by sd. committee to Saml. Chesley 40 acres April 11th 1694, but not confirmed. Entred by Tibbets but the original not Furbur's writing nor signing.

35.—Page 154; June 23d. 1701. Granted by the sd. Committee to Richard Clark, not confirmed nor wrote nor signed by Clerk of sd. Committee.

36.—Page 154; April 16th. Day, 1702; granted at a Town meeting to Samuel Perkins 30 acres of Land; the original not wrote nor signed by the Committee.

37.—Page 153; June 23d. 1701; granted by the Committee to Ely Demerret for 10 acres of Land under the same circumstances as the above grant to Perkins.

38.—Page 155; June 23d. 1701, granted by the Committee to Amos Pinkham, 40 acres, not confirmed by the Town, & the originall not signed by the Committee or any Clerk, and yet in the record William Furbur is Entred as Clerk.

39.—Page 155; June 23d. 1701; a grant by the Committee to James Nute of 40 acres not wrote or signed by Furbur, the Clerk.

40.—Page 156; March 19th. 1693/4,; a grant by sd. Committee to Tristram Heard for 30 acres; Vicious for the reasons mentioned in James Nute's grant aforesaid.

41.—Page 157; May 2d. 1701; granted by the Committee to Jos. Ham 20 acres, Vicious for the same reasons.

42.—Page 158; April 11 1694; granted by the Committee to Robt. Higgins, 30 acres; the originall interlined and otherwise Vicious for the reasons above said.

43.—Page 158; June 23 1701; a grant by the Committee to Josh. Richards for 60 acres; confirmed the 23d. March 1702; both Grant & Confirmation in the same hand & neither Furbur's nor Tuttle's.

44.—Page 158; March 29th. 1693/4; Granted by the Committee to Stevenson thirty acres of Land; Vicious because not signed nor wrote by the Clerk.

45.—Page 162; June 23d. 1701; a grant by the Committee for 30 acres of Land to Wm. Hill & confirmed the 23d. of March 1702; because interlined and altered, the Grant & Confirmation both by one man's writing & neither of them by Furbur's nor Tuttle's writing.

46.—Page 162; April 11 a grant to John Davis by the Committee for 30 acres; no Conformation of the Town and by Furbur's writing, nor signing.

47.—Page 164; June 23d 1701; a grant to David Kinckad by the Committee & Confirmed the 6th. of April 1702; both of the same hand writing, & it appearing by the records that the sd. Kincad had a grant of the same Date & Quantity of Land recorded before.

48.—Page 164; March 19, 1693/4; a grant made by the Committee to Thos. Drew & Confirmed the 2d. of April 1694. Tibbets swears Mishack Drew brot. the grant to him to record, but Drew Denies he ever carryd any grant to him to record.

49.—Page 165; March 19th. 1693/4; a grant made to Elias Cretchet for three score acres of land, not confirmed Because wrote upon a new ps. of paper, appears to have been cut off from a ps. of paper we find a grant made to Abraham Benneck seven years after the stamp of the paper being partly one & partly on the other & not of the Clerk's writing.

50.—Page 165; June 23d. 1701; a grant of sd. Committee to Abraham Bennick, wrote on the ps. of paper above mentioned & wrote by the same, except the Date of the Grant & Some few words besides.

51.—Page —; June 23d. 1701 In Page 167 a grant by sd. Committee to Ichabod Rollins for 50 acres, Confirmed 23d. March 1702, because not signed by the Committee nor their Clerk nor by the Town Clerk.

52.—Page 121; A grant by sd. Committee of 30 acres to Nicho. Harford; no date & the Grant & Petition for sd. grant being on the same ps. of paper & wrote by the same hand & Differs from the record because the Record is Dated & the originall not.

53.—Page 106; March 19, 1693/4; a grant by the Committee to the estate of Joseph Field for ten acres; Confirmed the 16th. April 1694; because all wrote by one hand & neither of them the Clerk, either of the Committee or the Town.

54.—Page —; June 23d. 1701; a grant by the Committee to Capt, Tibbets for a small Gore of Land; the originall was all of his own writing & Furbur's name alsoe & he, sd. Tibbets hath Entred in the records a Confirmation of the Town & on the originall there is no such thing.

We alsoe report that many things appear Very Dark by the record, which we have omitted because we could not come at the originall Grants nor finde any particular information about them; we alsoe, by James Barnum's own oath, report that he purchased a bundle of these Grants from the widow of the sd. Furbur, the Clerk of the

Committee & since that hath sold them to many persons & they have got them recorded.

April 30 1731.

Henry Sherburne
Nathl. Weare
Theod. Atkinson

No action appears to have been taken on the report at that time. The next mention of it in the Journal was on May 11, 1732. A meeting of the Council was held "at Captain Wibird's house in order to have a quorum of five." At that meeting it was voted:—"To suspend ye affair of ye Dover Town Books." On the next day, the record says, "His Excellency concurred" with the action of the Council. It does not appear that any of the offenders in the land grant book-keeping were prosecuted.

The first mention in town-meeting, ordering the land grants to be recorded was in November, 1647, as follows:—

"Primo. die, Nov. Mensis, (47.—At a publique Towne meeting it is this day ordered yt William Pomfrett shall keep the Records of the Towne, and to record the lands and the Acts of the Towne, as hath bin given, heretofore, to p'ticular persons, or that shall bee, hereafter."

WILLIAM WALDERNE, THE FIRST TOWN CLERK.

William Walderne came over from England with his brother Richard, later known as Major Richard, in 1635. They were sons of William and Catherine (Raven) Walderne of Alcester, England. Two other brothers, George and Edward, came over here later, being younger than Richard. William was the eldest of a family of twelve children, of which Major Richard was eighth. In 1637 Richard went to England and returned again in about one year; while in England he married a "Gentlewoman of very good family;" the names of her parents are not known; she did not come over on his return, but came about 1640. He had his house lot on the east side of High Street, a short distance north of the present Riverview Hall; he purchased this lot of Captain Thomas Wiggin, and resided there until he removed to Cochecho, after he built his saw mill at the falls.

THE FIRST TOWN CLERK.

William Walderne resided on Dover Neck, neighbor to his brother, and was engaged in business with him, in sawmills, shipbuilding and general shipping to the West Indies and to England. It did not take much time to do the town clerk work, so he kept the records from about 1635, when they began to have need of a clerk, until his death, by accidental drowning, in September, 1646. It would be very interesting and very helpful if the editor could consult those first records kept by Mr. Walderne, but much to the regret of everybody the first book of records was lost, or in some way destroyed, during the period of the Mason heirs' law suits. Mr. Walderne was not so noted as his brother, the distinguished Major Richard, but he manifestly was an able man and held the confidence and esteem of his fellow townsmen. He left no children. The following from the Massachusetts Colony records may be of interest in this connection.

Massachusetts Records.

To The Honored Court of Magistrates & Deputyes.

The humble petition of the inhabitants of Dover is, that Mr. George Smyth may be voted for one of the three men appointed to end small cases under 20 s.

And also that you will make an act for the recording of sale of lands at Dover as at Ipswich & so a transcript as is ordered by Court to be sent to Boston & to appoynt a Recorder.

William Waldern.

In behalfe of the Towne

Dover, 7th. of ye 5th. Mo: 1645.

The House of Deputies have passed this bill & have nominated Wm. Waldern as Recorder there till the Court shall take further order, with reference to our honored magistrates concurrence herein.

Edward Rawson.

John Winthrop, Gov.

Consented to by the magistrates.

June 4, 1647 Upon the petition of the inhabitants of Dover it is ordered that Mr. Bellingham & Mr. Bradstreete shall keepe Courte at Pascataqua for this year, & if either of them shall faill through any unexpected providence, the Governor & Deputy Governor & one of the magistrates shall appoint some other in their place.—C. Rec., Volume 2, page 167.

Upon the petition of the inhabitants of Dover the Court doth grant commission to Mr. Bellingham, Mr. Saltonstall & 2 or three more of the neerest &c. together with Captain Wiggin, Mr. George Smyth & Ambrose Gibbens to keepe Court at Pascataqua when they or any two of the magistrates see fit, & that any three of them may keepe Court so as one of them be a Magistrate, which shall be President.

And further the inhabitants of Dover are granted exemption from serving at the General Courte except it be at the Courte of election & so long as that session shall continue, and their fine for not appearing is remitted.—C. Rec., vol. 2, p. 188.

27 October, 1647   Vol. 3, p. 120.—

In answer to the petition of Wm. Ballew, Hateevill Nutter, Richard Parker, John Maning, Robt. Knight, Hugh Gunnison, Edmond Grenlefe, Tho. Burton, Xtopher Lawson, Wm. Furber, Wm. Bacon, & John Butler, who desire, in pursuance of an order of the last Courte held at Dover, that all the creditors of William Walderne, deceased, should attend the General Courte for to make demands of their debts, & proclamation being both made at Boston & Dover to that purpose wee desire that wee may be putt into some course by the estate of the sd. Wm. Walderne to be divided amongst proportionably according to our debts.

It is ordered by this Courte that the estate of the said Wm. Walderne be delivered into the hands of Capt. Wiggin & Edward Rawson, who are hereby authorized to call any before them that may give evidence concerning his estate, & where it lyeth, to administer oath to the full discovery & delivery thereof to them, & to examin all the bills and debts that shall in any way by the petitioners be claimed as dew from the said Wm. Walderne; & what they shall find to be justly dew, to make an equal distribution of the estate of the said Wm. Walderne to the severall creditors, making return of what they shall do herein, under their hands, to the next General Courte; provided the charge of the Commissioners shall be defrayed & borne by the estate before the division. By both.

11 November, 1647. Vol. 2, p. 225.—Towne Marks agreed upon by the General Courte for Horses, ordered to be set upon one of the nere quarters. S(trawberrybanke). N(ortham). H(ampton). E(xeter).

PLACES FOR HOLDING COURTS.

At a session of the Generall Courte the first month (March), 1647 or 1648.

Upon the petition of Norfolk, the Court doth think fitt that the shire town of Norfolke be refered to further consideration, & the magistrates to agree some of themselves to keep Courte, as is desired and that they have liberty to choose gentlemen of worth in or out, of their shire for associates, & that they be not called out of their shire for general training there; Provided they train 8 times a year according to law, & be under command of the Serjeant Major of Essex to general trainings in their shire, or otherwise in times of danger.

It is ordered that the first Courte in Norfolk shall be kept the last third day of the 2d. mo: (April), at Salsberry, & to have the same magistrates that Keepe Court at Dover, & in the meanwhile liberty to choose their Commissioners, & to take their oathes before the same magistrates.—C. Rec. vol. 2, p. 193.

16 May, 1648.—Vol. 2, p. 242.

Mr. Samu. Dudley, Capt. Wiggin, Robt. Clements, have commission to keepe Courte in that (Norfolk) County, according to order of Courte, & Mr. Dudley hath commission to give oath to the three commissioners for small causes in the several towns in the said County of Norfolk.

It is ordered that the same magistrates that keepe courte at Dover should be desired to keep Courte at Salsberry & Hampton this year ensuing.

ELDER EDWARD STARBUCK AN ANABAPTIST.

October 18, 1648.

This Courte being informed of great misdemeanor Committed by Edward Starbuck of Dover with profession of Anabaptism, for which he is to be proceeded against at the next Courte of Assistants if evidence can be prepared by that time, & it being very far for witnesses to travel to Boston at that season of the year,—It is therefore ordered by this Courte that the Secretary shall give commission to Captain Thomas Wiggin & Mr. Edward Smyth to send for such persons they shall have notice of, which are able to testify in this case, & to take their testimony upon oath & certify the same to the Secretary as soone as may be, that further proceedings may be therein if the cause shall so require. By both. C. Rec., vol. 3 p. 151.

WEARING OF LONG HAIR CONDEMNED.

In the year 1648 the wearing of long hair was condemned as sinful. The Governor, Deputy Governor and Magistrates entered into an association to prevent the growing evil. They said and decreed:—
"Forasmuch as the wearing of long hair, after the manner of ruffians and barborous Indians, has begun to invade New England, contrary to the rule of God's word, which it is a shame for a man to wear long hair, as also the commendable custom generally of all the godly of our nation, until within these few years; We, the Magistrates, who

have subscribed to this paper (for the showing of our innocency in this behalf) do and declare and manifest our detestation against the wearing of such long hair, as against a thing uncivil and unmanly, whereby men do deform themselves, and offend sober and modest, men; and do corrupt good manners: We do, therefore, earnestly entreat all the elders of this jurisdiction (as often as they shall see cause) to manifest their zeal against it in their public administrations, and to take care that the members of their respective churches be not defiled therewith." Ad. Ann., p. 34.

DOVER FINED FOR NOT SENDING DEPUTIES.

Oct. 14, 1651. There being no Deputy appearing from the Towne of Dover, neither this nor the last session of this Court, the Deputies think meet that the said Towne of Dover shall be fined 10 pounds, for neglect with referenc to the consent of our honored magistrates hereunto   William Torrey, Cleric.

Consented to by the magistrates,

Edward Rawson, Sec.

III, pp. 252/4. The inhabitants of Dover being under a fine of 10 pounds, for neglecting to send a Deputy to this Courte, upon the request of Mr Maud (minister at Dover) hath their fine respited, & not to be levied till the next Court of Election, that the Courte may judge of Dover's answer.

May 27, 1652.—p. 273.—The Towne of Dover desiring that Mr. Bellingham may be Judge of that Court this yeare, as also that Mr. George Smythe, Mr. Richard Walderne & Mr. Valentine Hill, might be associates, have their request granted provided Mr. Hill may be exempted, according to his desire, & also that Mr. Bellingham be desired to attend they keeping the holding of the County Courts of Norfolk, Hampton & Salsbury, as well as Dover & Straberry Banke, for the ensuing year.

October 19, 1652:—Whereas upon the submission of the inhabitants upon the River Pascataqua to this jurisdiction, this Court did grant them among other privileges liberty to send two Deputies from said River & whereas the freemen of Dover are increased to that number that by another law they have liberty to send two Deputies to this Courte:—This Courte doth order & declare that the said Towne of Dover shall henceforth enjoy their liberty to send two deputies according to law, & that Straberry Banke shall have liberty to send one according to former agreement.

Courte Rec., vol. 3, p. 361.

THE MASSACHUSETTS BAY CAMPAIGN TO GET CONTROL OF THE DOVER SETTLEMENT.

In 1638 The Massachusetts Bay Colony commenced its campaign to get control of the Dover settlement. The negotiations make an interesting combination of religious doctrines and political designs.—Politics and religion were very much mixed everywhere in the world at that time. They had banished John Wheelwright, Hanserd Knollys, Anne Hutchinson, Capt. John Underhill, and others for entertaining heterodox religious opinions. Mrs. Hutchinson went to Rhode Island and dwelt in Roger Williams's domain of free thought and free speech; Mr. Wheelwright was given two weeks, in November, 1637, in which to leave the territory controlled by The Massachusetts Bay Colony, and he came round to Dover and made his headquarters here, while he was searching for some land, owned only by the Indians, and outside of The Bay Colony territory. Captain John Underhill took a vacation in England, with his friend, Ex-Governor Henry Vane, who had been defeated for re-election, on account of his opinions.

The story in brief: Rev. John Wheelwright arrived in Boston in May, 1636, and became a popular preacher, for a while. His wife came with him; she was sister of William Hutchinson, whose wife, Anne Hutchinson, was a very capable woman, a fine speaker, and a keen thinker, whose personal character was never questioned. She had a fondness for theological speculations, which were characteristic of that age. She had adopted some opinions not in unison with the majority of Puritan ministers of The Massachusetts Bay Colony. She made bold to enunciate them in the way of criticisms on their sermons and doctrines, at weekly meetings of the sisterhood held at her house in Boston. These heterodox opinions were the merest theoretic abstractions imaginable, such as that "a person of the Holy Ghost dwells in a justified person"; and that "no sanctification can help to evidence to us our justification," and such like, which had no possible relation to the practical concerns of life. The common name for it all was—"Antinomian," which means, literally, against law; one who denies that the moral law is binding on Christians, and affirms that faith alone is necessary to salvation.

While Mr. Wheelwright was stopping here at Dover, and surveying the head waters of the Squamscot River, he made a bargain with "Wehanownowit, Sagamore of Piskataquake and his son Pummadockyon," for the Exeter plantation, and obtained a deed from them, dated April 3, 1638. He proceeded to organize his colony of about a score of persons, who held to the same opinion in religious matters as he did. One of the persons was Dover's distinguished citizen of a later period, Elder William Wentworth.

When Captain Underhill returned from his visit in England, in the fall of 1638, he took Rev. Hanserd Knollys and came to Dover and they organized the First Church. Probably Mr. Wheelwright and Elder William Wentworth came down the river from Exeter and assisted in the ceremonies. It is an interesting fact that a dozen years later Mr. Wentworth came up from Wells, where he went with his friend Wheelwright, who was obliged to leave Exeter on account of that old decree of banishment from Massachusetts rule, and became a permanent citizen of this town. He always retained a kind regard for Exeter, which he helped establish.

As soon as the First Church was organized the citizens elected Captain Underhill its governor, as Gov. Burdett had left town previous to the arrival of Knollys and Underhill. The Massachusetts rulers were offended with the people of Dover for electing Underhill governor and entertaining Wheelwright and making Knollys minister of the new church. Governor Winthrop wrote to Captain Thomas Wiggin, to this effect:—"That whereas there had been good correspondence between us formerly, we could not but be sensible of their entertaining and countenancing, etc. some that we had cast out, etc. and that our purpose was to survey our utmost limits and make use of them."

Governor Winthrop and his assistants kept a watchful observation over the Pascataqua River settlements. The Pascataqua had a harbor superior to that of Boston, and they were fearful it might rival that town, and be dangerous if left independent. Moreover, banished citizens from Boston could find a safe retreat here as long as this territory was independent.

The new Church here at Dover sent communications to the First Church in Boston, commending Underhill, and styling him as their right worshipful and honored governor, and were highly pleased with Mr. Knollys as their minister, but the Boston Church would not forgive the Captain till he should come before that Church and make proper confession of his heterodox views, and amendment for letters he had written.

Winthrop says of these letters: "The General Court wrote to all the chief inhabitants of Pascataquack and sent them a copy of his (Underhill's) letters (wherein he professed himself to be an instrument ordained of God for our ruin), to know whether it were with their privity and consent that he sent us such a defiance, etc., and whether they would maintain him in such practices against us, etc."

The substance of the replies, as given by Winthrop, was this: The Dover "plantation disclaimed to have any hand in his miscarriages, etc., and offered to call him to account, etc., whensoever we would send any to inform against him,"—evidently a reply mildly declining any acknowledging of Massachusetts authority. "The others at the river's mouth," says Winthrop, "disclaimed likewise, and shared their indignation against his insolences, and their readiness to join in any fair cause for our satisfaction; only they desired us to have some compassion of him, and not to send any forces against him," which, being interpreted, probably objected to any attempt of Massachusetts to carry out by force its threatened extension of boundary.

At a General Court in 1639 some of the people of Dover wrote to Massachusetts, proposing that Dover come under that jurisdiction. Who led in this movement no records show. It was, of course, the Puritan element, and Underhill's proceedings later in the year indicate a probability that he, the chief magistrate, was concerned in it. Answer was returned that if the people would send "two or three" with full powers, it was likely the court would agree to their proposal. Governor Underhill then wrote, 12th October, 1639, asking a safe-conduct for such as should be sent from Dover, but taking the opportunity to refer to his own affairs, and intimating that he was endeavoring to help forward the business.

At the court of November, 1639, three commissioners appeared from Dover, whose names are not preserved. The court appointed three persons to treat with them. The appointment and result is recorded thus:

"The Deputy Governor.

"Mr Emanuel Downing, & Capt. Edward Gibons were appointed to treate with the three committees from the towne of Dover upon Pascataqua, wth whom they did agree, and certified the same."

A particular account of this transaction is given by Winthrop:

"And now at this Court, came three with commission to agree upon certain articles annexed to their commission, which being read, the court appointed three to treat with them; but their articles not being reasonable, they stand not upon them, but confessed that they had absolute commission to conclude by their discretion. Whereupon the treaty was brought to a conclusion to this effect: That they should be as Ipswich and Salem, and have courts there, etc., as by the copy of the agreement remaining with the recorder doth appear. This was ratified under our public seal, and so delivered to them; only they desired a promise from the court, that, if the people did not assent to it, (which yet they had no fear of,) they might be at liberty, which was granted them."

Hanserd Knollys was now pastor of the church. He was born in Cawkwell, Lincolnshire, England, in 1598, of pious parents; educated at the University of Cambridge; after graduation was chosen master of the free school at Gainsborough; ordained June 30, 1629; received from the bishop of Lincoln the living of Humberstone; was indefatigable in labor; became scrupulous as to "the lawfulness of using the surplice, the cross in baptism, and the admission of persons of profane character to the Lord's Supper"; and therefore resigned his living after holding it "two or three years"; preached two or three years longer in various churches by the bishop's good nature; in or about 1636 he renounced his Episcopal ordination and joined the Puritans; was imprisoned, released, harassed, and left England.

Knollys came to Boston in 1638. His child had died on the passage. He was very poor. Some money of his wife's had paid their passage, he having on embarking "just six brass farthings left." The Boston ministers represented to the magistrates that he was an Antinomian, and advised that he be not allowed to remain.

At Boston, he says, "I was necessitated to work daily with my hoe for the space of almost three weeks." Two persons from Dover happened to be in Boston, and invited him to go to Dover. He did so, but by Rev. George Burdett, then ruler, was forbidden to preach.

From Dover Knollys, incensed by his treatment by the Bay Government, early wrote to England, inveighing against that power, comparing it especially to the High Commission Court in England. This letter excited great resentment with Winthrop and his associates in Boston, as they saw it was very harmful to their desires to get control of affairs at Pascataqua. A copy of this letter, in some way, was sent to Boston. The Bay authorities kept agents on the watch in London, all the time, to get news of this character for their inspection.

The commissioners returned to Dover. Their agreement was not ratified by the people. Underhill was afterwards charged with being chiefly instrumental in its rejection, while "he had written to our governor and laid it upon the people, especially upon some among them; and for this they produced a letter from our Governor, written to one of their commissions in answer to a letter of his, where he discovered the captain's proceedings in this matter."

It does not appear that any further proceedings were had in the Dover Court, or that any copy of Knollys' letter to England was forwarded to them. Instead of that it appears to have been the steady policy of Governor Winthrop and his assistants to compel the governor and minister at Dover to appear in person in Boston and face the Church and the Colonial authorities, and submit to the *"argumentum ad hominem"* which they were so fond of administering to their opponents. This course was in tacit harmony with the yet quiescent claim of jurisdiction.

The result was that both persons went to Boston, each having a guarantee of safe conduct, dated 29 January, 1640. The only report of the interview that Underhill and Knollys had with the authorities is a one-sided affair written by Governor Winthrop, who was always careful to give a properly colored story. He says regarding Knollys, date not given, but apparently in March: "Upon a lecture day at Boston (most of the magistrates in the Bay being there assembled) he (Knollys) made a very full and free confession of his offence, with much aggravation against himself, so as the assembly were well satisfied. He wrote also a letter to the same efect to his friends in England, which he left with the Governor to be sent to them." A copy of this letter is preserved.

It is difficult to account for the intensity of feeling manifested in this letter, by the language he used; he must have been under a sort of terror when in the presence of Winthrop and the elders of the Church. Had he committed murder he would have found it difficult to find stronger expressions of remorse. There may be two explanations. One is the exaggerated and morbid style of writing in that period of intense religious thought; the other is that he may have come to the conclusion that Massachusetts Bay authority was the only bulwark for the preservation of Puritanism in New England, and he was a real Puritan, hence he wrote the letter with that impression strong upon him. The people at Strawberry Bank, under Governor Williams, were largely anti-Puritans; those at Newichawannock were partly so, and some of the Dover citizens were worldly sort of people. So it may have been that Mr. Knollys concluded that the safest way to advance the Puritan cause was not to help its enemies in England. But certainly most of his original letter, even as reported to us, was but the simple truth concerning the way they had of conducting government in the Bay Colony in 1638-40.

OLD DOVER; ITS BOUNDARIES AND DIVISIONS.

The first mention we find of any particular boundaries of the town is recorded in Belknap, page 12, where it is said that in 1634,—"Neal and Wiggin joined in surveying their respective patents and laying out the towns of Strawberry Bank and Bristol." The authority for this statement is found in a letter which describes the town in a way that might do very well when nobody lived above the town, except Indians and wolves, but which is somewhat indefinite as to the exact line between this town and the future towns of Barrington and Rochester. It was while Captain Wiggin and Captain Neal were making this survey that they had the historic altercation which gave to Newington the formidable name—*"Bloody Point."* They had a hot dispute as to which settlement the Newington territory belonged, and drew swords, and were about to fight a duel. Historian Hubbard says:— "Both the litigants displayed so much wit in their anger that they waived the battle, each accounting himself to have done very bravely, so as not in what did, but what might have fallen out, the place to this day bears the formidable name of *Bloody Point."* Neal claimed that his territory extended up to Little Bay and the Pascataqua River; Wiggin disputed the claim, and won, retaining the boundary practically as it is now between Newington and Portsmouth. The settlement at Strawberry Bank retained that name till 1653, when the inhabitants petitioned the General Court of Massachusetts Bay, humbly desiring—"that the name of the plantation, being Strawberry Banke, (accidentally soe called by reason of a banke where Strawberries were found in this place) might be called *Portsmouth,* beinge a name most suitable for the place, it beinge at the River's mouth, and a good harbour as any in the land." The MS petition is on file in the archives, in the State House at Boston. The petition was granted.

Strawberry Bank held possession of the *Bloody Point* territory from 1641 till 1643. The people there did not like the arrangement and that year petitioned The Massachusetts General Court to have their territory restored to Dover. The petition reads as follows:

"The humble peticon of the inhabetants of Bloody Poynt, in ye Rieur Pascataway, Humbly showinge unto your good Worshipps that your peticonrs, the inhabitants of Bloody Poynt, being as they are informed ordered to be within ye Towneship of Strawbarry Banke, which was done altogeather against our consent, wee euer hauing beene within the Towneship of Dover & in combination with them at our entrance under your gouerment, and had promise from you to injoy all our lawful liberties, for felling timber & the wch your peticoners are debarred, of which upon record in your books, and have been formerly to their great loss and damage.

"Alsoe your peticoners further show unto your good Worshipps that Strawberry Bancke lieth 4 miles from them, or thereabouts, whereby they are all debarred from hearing The Word, by reason of the tide falling out, that we cannot goe but once a fortnight, and then can stay but part of the day, wch will rather be a day of toyle & labour, than rest unto the Lord, & yet must be forced to pay for the maintenannce of their minister. And since the Court placed us under Strawberry Bancke controll, they (Strawberry Bancke Townsmen) have laid out to themselves 20,100 or 200 Acres in pts around us, penning us up & denying us falling any timber without their leave, & making every one that will have of said land to pay yearly 50 shillings for a 100 acres, & so after the rate for more or lesse, they being some 14 or 15 families, living remote from one another, scateringe upon the River 2 miles & 4, 5 or 6 myles from us, yet have taken to themselves all our best land adjoyning to us."

"Humbly Beseeching your good Worshipps to be pleased to take our case into your pious consideration & to take some order for us that we may enjoy our former liberty, and may be in the same Towneship (Dover) we were of. And that the oder of Court may be confirmed wch was, that our Neck should be in Dover Towne, otherwise wee shall be forced to remove, to our undoing, being 12 poor familyes, And your poor peticoners shall be bound to pray your Worshipps." Signed,

*James Johnson	John Godard
*Thomas Canning	Henry Langstaffe
*Thomas Ffurson	*John Fayer (?)
William Pray.	Oliver Trimings.
William Jones	Philip Lewis.
Thomas Trickey	Radieric (unreadable)

*These made their mark.

The petition was granted and the inhabitants remained citizens of Bloody Point in Dover till 1713, when the Assembly conferred upon the territory the name of Newington, and gave it the full parish rights.

The inhabitants of the Oyster River territory first petitioned to be made a separate parish May 17, 1669; they did not succeed in getting the grant from the Massachusetts General Court; later they were granted the right to have a separate parish for holding religious services if they would build a meeting-house for the purpose and pay their own minister.

Before that in town meeting, an agreement was made, 14 July, 1651, that two ministers should be employed, each at £50 salary, Mr. Daniel Maud to remain at Dover Neck, and another be called for Oyster River. A voted dated 16 April, 1655, provides for the "comfortable maintenance of the ministry of Dover and Oyster River," by devoting to that purpose all the rents of the saw-mills, and a tax of two pence in the pound upon all inhabitants. A meeting-house was built upon Durham Point in 1655, and it was voted 30 March, 1656, that "thear shall be a house at Oyster Reuer Billd neier the meeting house for the use of the menestrey, the demenshens as follareth, that is to say 36 feet long, 18 foett Brod, 12 foot in the wall, with too chemneyes and to be seutabley feneshed." There was also a minister there. On the 17th of June, 1657, "Mr. Flecher and the towne hauing had some discorse whether he will leaue them, he willingly manifested that he was not minded to stay aney longer, but to Prepaer himselfe for old England and could not justly lay Aney Blame Apon the Towne."

The following shows how the differences between the two parts of the town were settled:—

"Wee hose names are heir under writen being chosen By the towne of Douer ar Appoynted by thear order to heire and Determine all such Differences as apier Betwixt the inhabetants of the too thierds of the towne of Douer and the on thierd of the towne in Oyster Riuer Doe Conclude at Present as followeth that is to saye

"1ly That from the first of Aprill 1657 and soe forward from yeir to yeir it is heirby mutually a greed upon that the naigeborhoed of Oyster Riuer shall inioy full Righte and intrest of twenty pounds out of the Rents of the towne to be from lamprell Riuer grant Rent performed as allsoe the sayd neagberhoed shall inioy thear full Right of the too peney Rate Rising from within themselfes boeth wich twenty pounds and too peney Rate is for the supply of the minestrey within themselfes and to be ordered by themselfes for the End Exprest

"2ly It is Agried and determined that the sayd naighberhoed shall haue leberty from time to time to make Choyse of a minestrey for thear accomodations, prouided that thay haue the approbations of the sayd towne or of anie three oidasent Elders

"3ly That in Case the nieghberhoed of Oyster Riuer shall bee without a ministrey aboue fower moenthes theay shall Returne the twenty pounds aboue sayd into the Coman tresseurey with Proper anabell (?) Contrebution theay of Douer doeing the like to them in proportion in the like Case and this mutually to be Donn soe longe as thear is Defeekte of Eather sied

"4ly (It (is) Ordred for the minestry of Douer Necke thear is sett aparte fifty fiue pounds of Towne Rents with the two penie Rate appon all the inhabetants Except oyster Riuer is set apart. for the ministry thear and in Case this Doe not make up the Sallarey, then to be maed up by a Rate uppon the sayd Inhabetants, Blody poynt Excepted only paying the two penneo Rate

"5ly It is ordered for the suppley of Cochechoe thear is set apart fiftien pound of towne Rents for the ministrey thear in the winter seasone

"6ly It is agreed that the house of mr Vallintin Hill wich is his nowe dwling house at Rockey point shall be within the line of Deuetion to Oyster Riuer

"Witnes oure hands this 17th of July 1660

"Vallintine Hill William ffurber
Richard Walderne John Daues
William Wentworth Robert Burnom
Raphfe hall William Willyames
Richard Otes William Robords"

Rev. Joseph Hull also served a brief time at Oyster River. Our records make no mention of him, but Bishop's "New England Judged by the Spirit of the Lord," a thoroughly partisan work, mentions him. "George Preston, Edward Wharton, Mary Tomkins, Alice Ambrose (alias Gary)," says this work (published in 1667), "having been at Dover, . . . passed from thence over the water to a place called Oyster River, where, on the first day of the week, the women went to Priest Hull's place of worship, who standing before the Old Man, he began to be troubled." After the usual interruption, the Quakers were "led out of the place of worship, but in the afternoon they had their meeting, unto which came most of the Priest's hearers, when truth gave the Priest such a blow that day," says Bishop, "that a little while after the Priest left his Market place, and went to the Isles of Shoals, three leagues in the sea."

The people at Oyster River, being dissatisfied, sent a petition to the General Court at Boston, 17 May, 1669, signed by John Bickford and thirty-eight others, desiring incorporation as a town. They represented "the intolerable inconvenience of our traveil many myles, part by land, part by water, manie tymes by both,

CONFLUENCE OF WATERS: Back River, Pascataqua River and Oyster River, emptying into Great Bay.

to the public worship of God and the necessarie stay of manie of us from public worship, who cannot undergo the difficulties of traveil to it"; that they comprised two hundred and twenty souls, near fifty families, and seventy and "odd" soldiers, and they hope the Court would find "our hearts and hands strengthened in the work of God, our case more vigorous for an able, Orthodox minister, our families instructed according to law, ourselves growing in truth and peace to God's glory." A strange argument this would be with which to appeal to a modern legislature in behalf of a division of a town.

The movement was successful only in causing the town by action 6 October, 1669, to decide that Oyster River may "build a meeting-house" at their own expense, and appropriate their tax for the ministry.

It was agreed in 1675 that two of the five selectmen should be selected from Oyster River. Under this arrangement the people there for many years had their own minister, who was paid by the town, but with the taxes imposed upon that people for the purpose. John Buss was both physician and minister from, perhaps, 1684. He was living there at the time of the great Indian and French massacre of 18 July, 1694, when ninety-four of his parishioners were killed or carried away captive. He was not at home that morning, and his family escaped to the woods; but his valuable library was burned. In his petition laid before the Governor and Council in 1718, are the words "your petitioner who for forty years successively has labored in the work of the ministry in that place"; and, "But being now advanced to seventy-eight years of age, and unable to perform the usual exercise of the ministry, the People have not only called another minister but stopp'd their hands from paying to my subsistence, whereupon he is greatly reduced, having neither bread nor sufficient clothing to encounter the approaching winter." He had, indeed, been in some straits earlier. Fifty-five persons in Oyster River petitioned the General Assembly, 11 November, 1715, stating that "whereas by mutual agreement the inhabitants of Oyster River have for many years past made choice of their own minister and paid his salary . . . and that the selectmen of the town in generall (two whereof have been annually chosen within the district of Oyster River) have all along made rates (i. e., taxes) for the several ministers," and, as there has been lately some neglect either in making or collecting the tax, they ask that they have, practically, parish powers. The papers show that there was a division of sentiment at Oyster River. But the result was an order that the selectmen of Dover "call to an account Joseph Davis, the last year's constable in Oyster River, and oblige him to pay the money he should have collected; and that the selectmen make the legal assessment as formerly, on the inhabitants of Oyster River, for the support of the present minister, Mr. Buss, until another minister be called and settled in his room."

On the 4th of May, 1716, Oyster River was made a parish,— "The new meeting-house built there (to) be the place of the public worship of God in that district." That parish was incorporated as Durham, 15 May, 1732, and took from parish and town the present towns of Durham and Lee and part of Madbury,—all then Durham.

The church was organized 26 March, 1718. "This day (through the smiles of Heaven upon us)," wrote Nathaniel Hill and Stephen Jones to the *"Boston News Letter"* of that time, "we had a Church gathered here, in the Decency and Order of the Gospel, and our Teacher, the Reverend Mr. Hugh Adams was then consecrated and Established the Pastor thereof, who then preached from that Text in Cant. 3, 11; we being then favored with the Presence and Approbation of some Reverend Pastors of the next Neighboring Churches, with the Honored Messengers thereof at the said Solemnity, in our New Meeting-House, wherein they gave the Right Hand of Fellowship."

The first meeting-house in Durham was built by the town of Dover in 1655, near the lower end of Durham Point. The second, "new" in 1716, was farther up, on land owned (in the nineteenth century) by Hamilton A. Mathes, and under its pulpit was concealed a portion of the powder taken from Fort William and Mary, 14 December, 1774, in the daring attack on that royal fortress by John Sullivan and others, of Durham, in connection with John Langdon, and from which place the powder was taken to Bunker Hill and used in that battle. The third house was the huge one built at Durham Falls in 1792, which was taken down in 1848. It was noticeable for its immense windows and general lack of beauty. It stood upon the triangular piece of ground just south of the bridge. The fourth and present house was dedicated 13 September, 1849.

SOMERSWORTH.—The Somersworth, which became a parish 19 December, 1729, not only included Rollinsford, but Rollinsford was largely Somersworth. Its centre of population was at the present Rollinsford Junction. The venerable meeting-house (third in time there) stood in the burial ground, and was destroyed by an incendiary.

But Rollinsford was an ancient settlement when the waters were running to waste at the Great Falls. Its south line was the present north line of Dover until it met Fresh Creek easterly, and then it followed that stream to the Newichawannock. Its soil began, therefore, but a mile from Walderne's mills and trading post. Anthony Emery's farm is mentioned, over that line, before 1646, and a grant of marsh to him 2 May, 1642. The mill privilege on Fresh Creek was granted 6 December, 1652, for £6 annual rent, to William Furbur, Elder William Wentworth, Henry Langstar, and Thomas Canney. In that year Elder William Wentworth received land in that vicinity, and may have been living there in 1653 on land a part of which is still in possession of his descendants, on the turnpike to South Berwick. The river lots, from St. Alban's Cove to Quamphegan, were granted in 1656, and ranged upward as follows: Lieut. Ralph Hall, John Roberts, Deacon John Hall, Henry Magoun, James Grant, Thomas Canney, Joseph Austin, Henry Tebbetts, John Damme and Thomas Beard; and there they reached the land of Thomas Broughton. In 1658, a second and interior range was granted, going northward, to Jeremy Tebbets, Thomas Hanson, and Ralph Twombly; and, interior of these, to Job Clement. While only a few of these persons settled on the above grants, their children did to a great extent, and not a few names are recognized there in this twentieth century.

Saw-mills at Quamphegan and at what now is Salmon Falls gathered a population. It was at that latter place occurred the savage massacre by French and Indians, 18 March, 1689-90; surprised in the darkness before dawn, when, as the pastor of the parish wrote in his sad journal, "The whole place was destroyed with fire, twenty-seven persons slain, and fifty-two carried captive." It was less than nine months after the desolation of Cochecho, 28 June, 1689, when the same pastor recorded, "Killed twenty-three persons, carried captive twenty-nine." The two massacres swept everything from the edge of Cochecho to the northern line. "Heard's Garrison at Cochecho," wrote Frost, 26 March, 1690, "being the frontier and the only Garrison on the north side of that River, . . . having now left three men." Such was Old Dover in 1690. But such was its people that not a foot of land was yielded in all that fifty years of war, even when people of Dover petitioned, as in 1722, regarding the law as to grammar schools, because "For at the time fit for children to go and come from schools is generally the chief Time of the Indians doing Mischief, so that the Inhabitants are afraid to send their children to Schoole, and the Children dare not venture." Such was once the conditions in Dover.

So greatly had Somersworth (Rollinsford really) grown in 1729, that a petition for separation as a parish was presented that year. It gave the usual reasons: "That the Dwelling places of yor Petitioners are at a great distance from the house of Publick Worship of God in the Town of Dover, where yor Petitioners live, by which their attendance thereon is rendered very difficult, more especially to the women and children of their Families, and that in the Winter Season and in Stormy Weather they cannot pay that Honour and Worship to God in Publick as it is their hearts desire they could, therefore for the advancing the Interest of Religion," etc.

The petition was granted, and the parish of "Summersworth" established 19 December, 1729.

There had been some public service there earlier. James Pike, teaching in South Berwick, preached there in 1727. On the 28th of October, 1730, he was ordained pastor of the church there. "This day," said a correspondent of the *Boston News Letter*, "the Rev. Mr. James Pike was ordained Pastor of the Church in this Place. The ceremony was opened by the Rev. Mr. Tufts. The Rev. Mr. Wise preached from the 9th Chapter of Matthew, 37 and 38 verses. The Rev. Mr. Cushing gave the charge, and the Rev. Mr. Rogers the Right Hand of Fellowship."

The Parish of Summersworth was incorporated with a change of orthography to Somersworth, 22 April, 1754. No one knows why the spelling was changed; it is certain the petitioners never asked to have it spelled "Som" instead of "Sum." Probably Theodore Atkinson was the guilty person, as he was the grand scribe who drafted most of the bills for the General Assembly.

Rollinsford was taken from Somersworth and incorporated July 3d, 1849. It was granted that name because the Rollins family was numerous and influential within its borders for many years.

Madbury was made a parish, for religious purposes, May 31, 1755. The people had petitioned for it in 1743, but the request was not looked upon favorably by Dover and Durham, and the petitioners were given leave to withdraw. They presented another petition to the General Assembly 17 January, 1754, and this was granted, as above stated. They built a meeting-house, in which meetings were held during many years. In answer to a petition the parish was made a town 26 May, 1768.

Lee was separated from Durham, by mutual consent in town meeting, as "The Parish of Lee" in 1766, and was incorporated by the General Assembly 16 January, 1767, with full powers as a township.

During the first decade under Massachusetts there was much discussion and no little contention about the boundary line between Dover and Exeter. Consequently on the 8th, 7th Mo: 1652 the Massachusetts General Court appointed certain men to "settle the limits" of Dover. Those men attended to the duty assigned them. Following is a brief of their report in 1656:—

"That the utmost bound on the west is a Creeke on the east sied of Lamprill River; and from the end of that Creeke to the Lamprill River first fall; and soe from this fall on a north and by east line fower miles from a creeke next below Thomas Canne, his house, to a certain cove near the mouth of Great Bay, called Hogstye Cove, and all the marsh and meadow ground lyinge and buttinge on Great Bay with conveniente upland on which to salt their hey."

On the 19th of October following the north boundary was fixed as it now is. Between Dover and Exeter (which included Newmarket) it was decreed "that the line formerly laid out shall stand."

In 1654 the middle of the river was fixed as the boundary line between Dover and Kittery, now Eliot.

DOVER PETITION CONCERNING BOUNDS.

October 20, 1652—To the honored General Courte now assembled in Boston:—The humble petition of Dover showeth that whereas some that were formerly entrusted & employed at the General Courte have neglected what we betrusted them with, among other things in a special manner the recording of our Township according to the granting of said Courte, we therefore in the behalf of the aforesaid town of Dover doe crave this favor that the sayd limits according to our grant may be confirmed to us by this honored Courte now assembled, & your petitioners shall rest ever engaged in all humble service to be commanded.

Val. Hill.
Richard Waldern.
In behalf of the Towne of Dover.

For the settling of these rights & bounds of Dover consider these things:

1.—A purchase from the Indians of Lampreele River 1635, two witnesses.

2—Possession & use of it by plantinge, fishinge & fellinge of timber.

3.—When taken into the government of the Bay this was one of their peculyar agreements that they should enjoy all such lawful liberties of fishinge, plantinge, & fellinge of timber as formerly, 2 booke of laws title Pascattua; this was 1641.

4. Anno 1642 in ye old Booke No. 538 by order of General Courte, to Dover granted the liberty which other Townes have, & foure commissioners appoynted to settle the limits thereof.

5—There is 3 of the foure commissioners met & agreed & did settle the bounds of Dover as appeare under their hands, upon which Dover granted several proppertyes.

6—The bounds of Lampreel river was by consent of Dover & Exeter men as Captayne Wiggans remembers & it appears by the boundaryes for a neck of land is reserved to Exeter on the north side of the River.

7.—Lampreel river is about six miles from Dover, northeast, & is alsoe about six miles from Exeter, southard, as Capt. Wiggins affirms.

8.—Dover cannot be enlarged as Exeter may be, for ye River between Kittery & Dover bounds them northard, & Lampreel River & Exeter bounds them southard, & the commissioners have bound them eastward and southard.

9.—Exeter besides the bounds towards Lampreel River may be enlarged to the westward & southward to their other limits.

10.—Between Lampreel River & Oyster River Dover hath settled a ministry; it is ere long like to become a towne of itselfe in respect to accommodation of Lampreel River, it being but about 3 miles between the two rivers.

11.—For Exeter yr. purchase of the Indyans was anno 1638, yn. they began to be a towne, after they submitted to the Bay, anno 1644, without any agreement at all, except that they are in the condition of other townes, but Dover's former Rights are confirmed to them, upon agreement besides the grants of courte, which were before Exeter submitted to this Government.

The utmost bounds of Dover was the utmost of the bounds of this pattent, where any person or towne did then submit unto this jurisdiction.

DEPOSITIONS ABOUT LAMPREEL RIVER.

The deposition of John Ault taken the 18th. of the 8th. mo: 1652.

Deponent sayeth that in the yere 1635, that the land about Lampreel river was bought of the Indanes & made use of by the men of Dover & myself both for planting & fishing & feling of timber.

John Ault.

sworne to before me, George Smyth.

Richard Yorke doth testify the same above specified.

Richard Yorke sworne, who affirmed upon his oath that what he doth testifie above written was trew.

Sworne before me, George Smyth.

The deposition of Hateevil Nutter taken the 18th. of the 8th. month, 1652.

Deponent sayeth that in the year 1636 the land about Lampreel River was in the posession of the inhabitants of Dover on both sides of the River both for fishing & plantinge & feling of timber.

Hateevil Nutter sworne, who affirmed upon his oath that the primeses was trew.

Sworne before me, George Smyth.

In the year 1637 Will. Furbur doth testifie the same about Lamp-rill Ryver.

William Furbur sworne on the 18th. of the 8th. month (52) who affirmed upon his oath that what he doth testify next above written was trew.

Sworne before me, George Smyth.

These are to certify that being one of them deputed by the General Courte about 7 or 8 years since to lay out the bounds betweene Exeter & Dover, It was always intended by us that Lamprey River as it naturally runs up into the country should be the bounds betweens, & what Line is recorded if it proves to give anything to Dover on the west side of Lamprey River, it was upon a mistake, & utterly besides our instructions. And for the confirmation hereof I have put to my hand this 27th. of May 1652. John Baker.

Att John Baker's request I testify that he did his endeaver to procure the bounds of Dover recorded, but the many urgent occasions of the Country were such that it came not to Issue.

Per Edward Rawson.

DR. WALTER BAREFOOT, FIRST RESIDENT DOCTOR IN DOVER, AND SOME OF HIS COMPEERS.

The first practicing physician (chirurgeon as they called them) in Dover was Dr. Renald Fernald, who resided on Great Island (Newcastle), and came up the river when there was need for a doctor. He died in 1656, and soon thereafter Dr. Walter Barefoot came to Dover Neck and resided there about twenty years. He arrived in New England that year, as he stated in a letter to the Privy Council, of date March 6, 1683:—"I have been an inhabitant here above twenty-five years." He was educated as a chirurgeon, in England, and went first to Barbadoes Island, and shortly after came to New England. Merchants of Dover had great trade with that Island at that time; some of its citizens had plantations there, others owned part interests in the sugar-making business. It may be, and probably was the fact, that Barefoot made his voyage from that island in one of Major Richard Walderne's ships, of which he had several at that time engaged in carrying on the trade with the sugar planters.

At that date Captain Thomas Wiggin, who had first resided on Dover Neck,—having his house on "Captain's Hill," which still retains that name,—had removed to his plantation on the shore of Great Bay, and his son Thomas had possession of the old home on "Captain's Hill." About 1660 Thomas Wiggin, Jr., married Sarah Barefoot, sister of Walter. She survived both her husband and her brother, the latter bequeathing much of his property to her in his will.

Just when Dr. Barefoot settled in Dover and commenced practice of his profession is not a matter of record, but judging from all the subsequent events in his career it seems more than probable it was not long after Dr. Fernald died; a physician was needed, and he came just in time to fill the vacant place. Moreover, there is no mention of his opening an office in any other place. That is the way young doctors begin practice now.

Probably his sister Sarah came to Dover with him; if not, certainly soon after, and in that way made the acquaintance of young Thomas Wiggin, whom she married, being his second wife. The lumber business was then very brisk and profitable; and very naturally Dr. Barefoot made investments in it. This is evident from various transactions on record.

At a town meeting held on the 2d of the 3d month (May), 1662, the records of the town say:

"Granted unto Captain Walter Barefoott fowerscoer foott in Breath of flates belowe hie water marke at Sande poynt, below the marke, and 24 foott of upland, not intrenching apon anie former grant, to be belt apon within one hole yer after the date heirof, or else to be voyd."—Dr. (Capt.) Barefoote complied with the terms of the grant.

Same date:

"Granted unto Cap. Richard Walderne 24 foot of upland to jine to his former grant of flats at Sande poynt."

The "former grant" was that which gave to Richard Walderne Pomeroy's Cove (which is between *Dover Point* and Dover Neck), *"from Sande poynt right over to the other side of the Cove, to make a Docke."* He was then only a Captain; later he was promoted to Major of the Dover militia.

These two grants (to Barefoot and Walderne) adjoined each other. The Cove is on the south side of Sandy Point, where Walderne had his dock, and did an immense lumber business. On the east of Sandy Point is Fore River (Newichawannock). The shore on that side is almost at right angle with the shore on the cove side, where Walderne had his wharf and store-houses. Barefoot had his wharf and dock on the Fore River shore, close neighbor to Walderne.

The reason why the town of Dover made this grant to Dr. Barefoot is manifest in the following transactions: In 1650 the town of Dover granted to Capt. Thomas Wiggin "a site for a sawmill at the second fall of the Cochecho River with accomodation of timber, near adjacent," on land about one mile square. The sawmill was built. It was about one mile above the first fall in the city, where the great cotton mills now are.

About ten days before the town made the Sandy Point grant to Barefoot the following land and mill transfer is on record as having taken place in Dover.—Thomas Wiggin of Squamscott, and Thomas, Jr., of Dover, for 400 pounds, sold to Captain Walter Barefoot, of Dover, one-half of sawmill on Cochecho River, with half of all buildings, timber accommodations, etc., etc., connected therewith, half of six hundred acres granted by Dover to Thomas Wiggin; also, they sold one-half of the 200-acre grant made to Thomas, Sen., by the Massachusetts Government; also, twenty acres of salt marsh near Sandy Point in Exeter; also, one-half of ten mares, one colt, three oxen, and three cows, 21 April, 1662. Ralph Hall and others afterwards testified that they were present and witnessed the transaction.

This transaction shows why he asked for the grant from the town, and it was given him in town meeting on the second day in the following month. He then began work in the lumber business on a grand scale.

On June 27, 1662, Walter Barefoot made a sale to Thomas Wiggin, Jr., of Dover, and in the deed he calls him his brother-in-law. After the death of his father, Captain Thomas, the son removed to that section where his parent had lived.

In 1664, Barefoot tried to get possession of what is known as Wadleigh's Falls, in Lee, which was then in the town of Dover.

He inveigled Harlakenden Symonds of Ipswich, Mass., brother-in-law of John Winthrop, Jr., afterwards Governor of Connecticut, into an exchange of lands, which was to give Barefoot several hundred acres of timber and the mill privilege at the above named falls. This sale was made 12 Sept., 1664. On 11 May, 1666, Barefoot sold his half (of the original grant to Samuel Symonds, Sr., by Massachusetts, in 1654), to Robert Wadleigh (then of Kittery). Samuel Symonds, Sr., then owned the south side of the river and Wadleigh the north side. The first saw-mill was built there in 1667, by Wadleigh. These falls are about eight miles from Barefoot's dock at Sandy Point, in Dover. This was his shipping point for his lumber till he became interested in getting bigger dividends by assisting in the attempts to enforce the Mason claims against Dover farmers and others. Various other land and lumber transactions might be mentioned, but it seems unnecessary in this connection.

Barefoot had numerous law suits and altercations, which go to show that he was a resident of Dover up to about 1678, when he is on record as a practicing physician and lively politician in Portsmouth, with residence in Newcastle.

The Puritans, when colonizing Massachusetts and Connecticut, looked upon this region as a refuge for their religious and political party, should it be defeated in Great Britain; and did in fact use it as such after the Restoration of the Stuarts, for a few decades. The aristocratic party in Church and State, on the contrary, naturally wished to establish here their system of a State Church, of lands held in large estates, and of titles of honor, rising in rank from the simple Knight and Baronet to the higher degrees of Baron, Earl, Marquis, Duke, and even Prince. Had Charles II succeeded in his scheme of uniting Maine and New Hampshire in one province, under the control of his bastard son, the Duke of Monmouth, he would probably have conferred on so large a landlord the rank of "Prince." Charles's brother, the Duke of York, did for a time exercise seigniorial rights over the Province of New York and the Elizabeth Islands in Buzzard's Bay, whence that jurisdiction, when it became a part of Massachusetts, retained its name of "The Duke's County." Care was taken in the unrealized Charter granted by Charles I, in 1635, to Captain

John Mason and his heirs, but which never "passed the seals," that the inferior titles could be bestowed by the ruler of the proposed County Palatine, or by the Governor-General of all New England;—the reason assigned being "lest the way to honor and renown might seem difficult and hard to find in so remote and far distant a country." Mason and his heirs were to have power, also, to create villages into boroughs, and boroughs into cities; and to hold

"all the advowsons and patronages of churches whatsoever, to be erected within the said tracts; with license and ability there to build and found churches, chapels and oratories, and to cause the same to be dedicated or consecrated according to the ecclesiastical laws of England . . . And we do declare and ordain that the said Province of New Hampshire shall be immediately subject to our Crown of England, and dependent upon the same forever."*

Although this scheme never took effect, and though John Mason soon died, and his partner, Sir Ferdinando Gorges, was never able, after 1635, to follow up his opportunities in New England, the wills of these grantees provided for church glebes, for submission to English Bishops, and for the holding of land in enormous estates, with ground-rent for purchasers, and tenant-service for such as lived on the estate without purchase.

Captain John Mason himself, a vigorous and wealthy person, expected to double and treble his wealth by disposing of his early grants of New England territory, which had been given him to satisfy debts that James I had incurred by employing Mason in the naval service around Scotland. Charles I further paid him by giving him the governorship of Portsmouth Castle, which commanded the important naval station and channel town of Portsmouth; and it was at Mason's house there that Buckingham, the unprincipled favorite of James and Charles, was assassinated in August, 1628. Seven years later, Mason, now appointed Vice-Admiral of New England, was coming over to look after his lands and his Portsmouth colony, and to keep the Puritans in order. But his ship met with an accident and he died himself, before he

---

*Sanborn, *History of New Hampshire*, 13, 15.

could set sail. He left his American lands to his grandson, Robert Tufton, who was to take the name of Mason, and come over here to look after the property. Sir Ferdinando Gorges had already sent over a kinsman to take charge of his Maine property, which was to have a fine manor, or capital town, near Agamenticus, called Gorgeana. The Revolution of 1640 intervened (called by Clarendon "the Great Rebellion"); Sir Ferdinando lost his ready money, upholding the King's cause, and soon died himself. The Mason property suffered in the same period, and it was under the government of Oliver Cromwell, in 1651, that Mrs. Mason, the widow of John and grandmother of Robert, sent a kinsman, Joseph Mason, to Portsmouth and Boston, to revive the family interests in New England. He made little headway, and it was not till the Restoration of the Stuarts under Charles II, that Robert Mason saw a way to recover and profit by his inherited estate in New Hampshire. By that time (1659-60) Massachusetts had full possession of Maine and New Hampshire, as parts of her jurisdiction, and had no inclination to restore Mason or the Gorges family to their charter privileges. Accordingly, the restored king was urged, and consented, to appoint, in 1664, a royal commission, to hear and pass upon the complaints of colonists as to the misgovernment to which they were subjected by the Puritans of Massachusetts. These commissioners, who were Maverick, a former planter near Boston, and Nicolls, Carr and Cartwright, official persons in other Colonies, came over in 1665. They found here, or brought with them, either at once or in their train, several active promoters of the cause of Mason, Gorges and their heirs,—of whom the chief were, named alphabetically, though not in the order of coming over, Colonel John Archdale, Captain and Dr. Walter Barefoot, Captain Francis Champernowne, Dr. Henry Greenland, Robert Mason, Esq., and Nicholas Shapleigh; who for the next twenty-five years, along with Edward Randolph, a distant cousin of Mason, continued to give trouble to the Massachusetts and New Hampshire Puritans, until the last of the seven ceased, either by death or departure, to contest the Massachusetts right to govern the three provinces, now constituting Maine, New Hampshire and Massachusetts. Of these persons and their acts and characters, the following is a historical summary:

I. *Col. John Archdale.* He was a country gentleman, whose sister had married one of the Gorges family. Born about 1640, he came over to Pascataqua in 1664, to look after the possessions and claims of his sister's kinsmen in Maine. He soon bought land in Kittery and elsewhere, and seems to have resided in that neighborhood, perhaps with occasional visits to England and the West Indies, until he sold his Maine property, and became one of the proprietors of South Carolina, about 1680. He held property there in the right of his son and in his own right, and late in the seventeenth century he was made Governor of South Carolina, to end the quarrels among the factious people settled there, as he successfully did. At some time before 1680 he became a Quaker, as Major Shapleigh did, and was one of those who gravely resented the persecution of the Quakers by Massachusetts. He sided with Barefoot, Champernowne and Randolph, in their efforts to throw off the Puritan domination in the Pascataqua region, but took no active part therein; being, apparently, a peaceable, judicious person, of learning and property, who took the part of good government wherever he dwelt. Originally a Churchman, he joined the Dissenters as a Quaker, and stoutly maintained their cause in Carolina against the factious Anglicans, who there refused to the Dissenters all civil office, and made trouble in various ways. He outlived all his Pascataqua associates, and died in England about 1710.*

---

*Much light has been thrown on the career of John Archdale by recent publications in South Carolina and in England. He published pamphlets in his later English life, describing the troubled years of the Carolinas while he was a proprietor there; and was aided in this paper controversy by the novelist Defoe, himself a Dissenter, who introduced elements of fiction into his writings of every sort. Dr. Rufus Jones, of Haverford College, Philadelphia, has made much mention of Archdale in his excellent volume, ''The Quakers in the American Colonies,'' in which he shows him as ''the chief gentleman of Chipping Wycombe'' when at home, but active also in Carolina affairs for some twenty-five years. It is worth mentioning that several Pascataqua families, connected with Champernowne by his marriage with the widow of Robert Cutt,—the Elliotts, Scrivenses, etc., migrated to South Carolina, along with Mrs. Champernowne, after the Captain's death and burial in the spring of 1687. By his will, in 1686, when he was seventy-two years old, Champernowne made his wife's grandson, C. Elliott, his heir, giving to him ''all the lands of right belonging unto me, or that may belong unto me either in Old England or in New England, not by me already disposed of,'' showing that he still had property and expectations in his native Devonshire.

II. *Dr. Walter Barefoot.* This notable personage, a real thorn in the flesh to the Puritans of Ipswich, Dover, Portsmouth and Boston Bay, would seem to have been the grandson of a Puritan minister of some note in England, and to have lived either in London (where his father, John, was a merchant), or in the county of Essex near London, before coming over to Kittery about 1656-57. He was a surgeon ("chirurgeon") by profession, a captain by title, and may have held that rank in Cromwell's navy, or else served as surgeon there. He had ready money on his first appearance in the Maine records, having bought for cash the pay-certificates of seamen in the navy (at Kittery), and soon after was a buyer of land in York County.†

He was the scion of a mercantile family in London, the head of which for more than a century held the ancient manor of Lambourn on the Roding River in Essex; was a free liver and jovial, who soon established himself as a physician at Dover, near his brother-in-law, Thomas Wiggin, Jr., who had married Sarah Barefoot, Walter's sister. They were Anglicans, and friends of Champernowne and Randolph, the former going bail for Barefoot in one of his frequent arrests for debt, assault or other offense. He was accused by the Puritans of having left a wife in London when he migrated, to which a certain Davis testified, in 1676 (when Massachusetts wished to make out a case against Barefoot), as follows:

"In the year 1662, being in England, there came to my lodging a woman who said she was the wife of one Walter Barefoote in New England: . . . said she was in a very low condition and desired me to get him to send her some maintenance, for she had two children to maintain, and had no subsistence for them. Further, there came an ancient man to me, who said Walter Barefoote was a very knave, in that, desiring him to be security for him to a merchant in Mark Lane, for linens he had of him, Barefoote did never send pay for the same; so that the old man was forced

---

†The date of Barefoot's birth is not known, but it must have been as early as 1630. From 1657 to his death in 1688, he was the most litigating and scandal-raising personage connected with the Pascataqua region, whether as doctor, captain, prisoner or prison-keeper, deputy-governor, land speculator or chief justice. His education was good, he wrote a good hand, and was fond of signing his unusual name—otherwise Barford in England—with a flourish of the pen.

to lie in the King's Bench, a prisoner, as he said. These things I acquainted Mr. Barefoote with, when I came over; who owned the linens he had taken up."

In his will of 1688 Barefoot made no mention of any wife and children, though he left a large estate, mainly to his sister, Mrs. Wiggin. He is probably buried among the Wiggins, at Sandy Point in Stratham, having no other near relatives in America. He died at Great Island (New Castle) in his own house, the island where he had many adventures, guarding prisoners of the Province, and being a prisoner there himself, as well as at Hampton and Dover, in some of his many lawsuits and affrays. He was from the first a landholder, as well as a practising physician of note; bought land of Colonel Archdale and of Captain Champernowne, leased land of Mason, bought saw-mills of Harlakenden Symonds, the brother-in-law of John Winthrop the younger, and was mixed up in suits with many of the prominent planters of New Hampshire, Maine and Massachusetts. In a dispute of 1674, while Barefoot was still a practising physician at Dover, he became involved with the Hiltons of Exeter, and was carried away to the Hampton jail, after a scene in the Dover jail which is depicted with much liveliness in the depositions on record at Concord, New Hampshire. The Hampton constable, Christopher Palmer, acting for the Hiltons, went with an arresting *posse* to Dr. Barefoot's house in Dover, and persuaded him to go along with them to the jail, and release upon bail two Hiltons there imprisoned, under Jeremiah Tibbetts, the jailer. With great good-humor the Doctor went along, and took a gallon of perry, to celebrate the armistice in the lawsuit by treating the company. Young Tibbetts, the jailer's son, then testified:

"They brought with them a runlet of perry, which Capt. Barefoote brought to drink with them, as he said; and so long as it lasted they were very merry. But presently, after it was ended, there was a great noise,—Captain B. lying on the ground, saying, he would not go, for he was in a prison already, where he would abide; but said Christopher Palmer answered, he was *his* prisoner, pulling him very rough and rudely."

Palmer himself described the scene by saying that when he arrested Barefoot upon a proper warrant, "he laid himself along the floor at Jeremiah Tibbett's house, *more like a pig than a captain.*" Pig or captain, Palmer put him in a boat, and as he sailed up the stream and came near Captain Champernowne's great farm of "Greenland," on the Great Bay, Champernowne brought the party to, and offered bail for his friend, which Palmer refused; and then carried him across the country to Hampton jail, whence Barefoot wrote an indignant protest to the Massachusetts authorities, quoting their own statutes to them and demanding his release. He was taken to Hampton, September 21, 1674, and, as John Souter, the Hampton jailer, testified: "I saw him lockt up into the Hampton prison of Norfolk County; and Christopher Palmer bade me go with them and lock the said Barefoote into the common gole, and bade me have a care of him, lest he should give me the slip."

A queer complication of this affair is that, in the May preceding, Dr. Barefoot had sued Palmer, in the same Hampton court, for "several physical and chirurgical medicines and visits, to the value of six pounds." In a previous controversy with the Hiltons, the old lady, Mrs. Katharine Hilton (born Shapleigh) swore that in Exeter (1670) "Captain Barefoote got a pistol or a sword or rapier, and drove the marshal away." Such affairs had early brought him into collision with the Massachusetts Puritans, who in 1671-73, tried to send him back to England. In 1671 the magistrates fined Barefoot 20 shillings "for his profaneness and horrid oaths," and went on to decree thus: "It appearing that he left a wife and two children in England, we do sentence him to return to England by the first ship, and that he shall henceforth be debarred to practise chirurgery or physic in any part of this jurisdiction."

To this sentence Dr. Barefoot paid no regard, but continued to practise and send in bills, which were paid. The wonder is, that when they had him in prison, in 1674, they did not undertake to enforce their own decree. But he seems to have been a chartered libertine, who could get into scrapes of all kinds without being seriously discredited by them. In the year 1678 the selectmen of Portsmouth, where Barefoot's political foes were in full control, and where Barefoot was then a citizen, made a singular agreement with him for the cure of one Richard Harvey, who had lately broken his leg, with this condition:

"If said Barefoote make a perfect cure, providing and finding all means at his own cost, except rum for steeps, which the Town is to find, and if he shall perfect the cure, he is to have for the same 20 pounds, all in money or merchantable white oak pipe-staves, at £3. 10s. per thousand; and if in case he performs not a perfect cure, he agrees to have nothing for his pains, more than the 20 shillings in money already paid him for what he has done for him this day."

It was a case of first aid to the injured, and indicates that Barefoot had reputation as a good surgeon, although so litigious and so ready to draw sword or pistol, and to swear great oaths, like other captains. His recalcitrancy against the persecuting Puritans, one of whom was his Dover neighbor, Major Waldron, a shrewd old Indian trader and Indian fighter, first showed itself in 1662, when, by tradition (for I have found no written record of it), he interfered in Salisbury to have Major Pike, a magistrate of another county, discharge the three Quaker women, whom Waldron had sentenced to be whipped at the cart's tail in every town from Dover to the Rhode Island line. Such was the intent of his barbarous order; but Dr. Barefoot, by tradition, followed or met this lamentable procession in Salisbury, and there, with the connivance of Major Pike, took the women from the constable of Salisbury, under pretence of delivering them to the Newbury constable, and in Newbury, with the aid of another physician, Dr. Henry Greenland, bound up their wounds and set them free. About the same time Waldron (December, 1662) implicated another of my list of Churchmen, Major Nicholas Shapleigh, living in what is now Eliot, with the Quakers, writing thus:

"Major Shapleigh shelters all the Quakers that come into our parts, and followeth them where they meet. Which is not only a disturber upon that side [of the Pascataqua] but also on our side, where is but the river between. And so they come into our town, and presently they are gone over the river; and so his house is a harbor for them. And some say he is dictated by the little crooked Quaker [Edward Wharton]. Our town will be so disturbed with the Quakers and others that we shall hardly be at peace."

These "others" were the members of the Anglican Church, who kept insisting, under the restored Stuarts, that they were deprived of the rites of their religion and the use of the Book of Common Prayer. It can hardly be supposed that Barefoot and Greenland suffered greatly from lack of the Anglican ordinances; but others probably did. At any rate, a considerable number of the residents on both sides of the river united in a petition that they might have the use of the Prayer Book and other ordinances of the English Church. Moreover, in 1664-65, when Charles II sent over his first royal Commission, many of these residents signed a petition to Carr, Cartwright and Maverick, alleging that:

"Your petitioners for several years last past have been kept under the Government of the Massachusetts by an usurped power whose laws are derogatory to the laws of England; under which power five or six of the richest men of this parish [Portsmouth] have ruled, swayed and ordered all offices, both civil and military, at their pleasures. . . . And at the election of such officers the aforesaid party, or the greatest part of them, have always kept themselves in offices for the managing of the gifts of lands and settling them; whereby they have engrossed the greatest part of the lands, within the precincts and limits of this plantation, into their own hands. . . . The parties we petition against are Joshua Moodey, Minister; Richard Cutt, John Cutt, Elias Stileman, Nathaniel Fryer, Brian Pendleton, Merchants."

Barefoot did not sign this petition, being then a citizen of Dover; but he took the same view of the situation, and there was too much reason for it. He was himself accused, a few years later, of getting unjust possession of some 6,000 acres in New Hampshire, which one Captain Littlebury, in the North of England, alleged as belonging to himself, to cover an advance of three hundred pounds sterling to Mason and his associates in colonizing New Hampshire:

"as an adventure there; for which in 1663 the survivors, Gardner and Eyres, had agreed to give him a fourth part of their property, —his promised share being 6,000 acres; but now he hath been deluded 3 years to his great hindrance and damage, by Capt. Champernowne, Major Shapleigh, Dr. Barefoot, and other grand incendiaries to the present government."

Littlebury meant the government by Massachusetts, by which he was probably incited to make this claim, never heard of afterward, I think. He added, this Holy Island Captain, as an aggravation of his conduct, that "Shapleigh hath lately made leases of lands for 1,000 years, to Mr. Hilton of Exeter, Dr. Barefoote and others."

This introduces into political and religious controversy the celebrated Masonian claim to the whole of New Hampshire and parts of Maine and Massachusetts; which kept the courts of New England busy for a century and a half, until it was finally settled, soon after the Revolution, by a compromise with the State government of New Hampshire. Shapleigh, in making leases with ground-rent, was acting as the agent of Robert Mason in England; and by accepting his leases, Hilton and Barefoot placed themselves on the side of the English system of land tenure, with primogeniture and Episcopal church government, against which the Puritans were struggling. From that time forward—say 1666—Barefoot was a sturdy and quarrelsome supporter of the Stuart policy.

Upon his arrest by Palmer of Hampton, Barefoot, in his long protest, quoted the following passage from the printed Body of Liberties of the Bay Colony:

"Forasmuch as the free fruition of such Liberties, Immunities and Privileges as humanity, civility and Christianity call for, as due to every man in his place and proportion, without impeachment and infringement, hath ever been, and ever will be, the tranquility and stability of churches and Commonwealth; and the denial or deprival thereof, the disturbance if not ruin of both,—"

"It is therefore ordered by this Court, and the authority thereof, that no man's life shall be taken away, no man's honor or good name shall be stained, no man's person shall be arrested, restrained, banished, dismembered, nor any way punished; no man shall be deprived of his wife or children, no man's goods or estate shall be taken away from him, nor any way indamaged, under color of law, or countenance of authority, except it be by virtue or equity of some express law."

"Consider [Barefoot goes on] whether a deputy named Christopher Palmer have not broken every tittle of this wholesome and express law. He cannot plead ignorance of the law, for it is well known that he hath been and is a known attorney and a malicious one; for in this very case, his malice—not regarding God nor the word of God, nor the authority who made these express bounds and laws,—he endeavored all in him lay to take away not only my honor or credit, but struck at my life,—if he could a' prevailed with the prison-keeper of Hampton, to a' kept me in the close dungeon, far remote from any house,—and said prison-keeper not able or willing to give me bread or anything to support life.

"Nextly I shall instance the subtlety of this Deputy,—coming to my habitation, pleading friendship; so I entertained him as a friend with the best in the house. Then he invited me to go see Sam. and Charles Hilton in the prison, where they were prisoners; and I very willingly went with him to give them a visit, and carried along a two-gallon runlet of Perry. And when we were come to the prison-keeper's house, where the said Sam. and Charles Hilton were prisoners, I treated them civilly, and likewise they spoke civilly and courteously to me; and this Deputy still pretended great love to me till the Perry was all drank out, and then suddenly said Deputy claps hold on me, as if he meant violence to my person. I, being not willing to resist, but rather to expose by life than give occasion of offence to authority, did submit to his will,—he declaring he arrested me in an action of Sam. Hilton. Said Hilton being then by [present], did declare he never did give order to him for any such thing, nor did he know of it; and showed his dislike of what was done by said Deputy."

This meek submission of Barefoot to constituted authority, contrasts vividly with his previous conduct in 1670-71, towards an honest Dogberry of a constable in Portsmouth, Henry Dering, who tried to arrest and imprison him upon an action of attachment brought by Abraham Corbett, for two suits, one for £1000 and the other for £150, and declined to take bail for either, in fear of being swindled by Barefoot, who did not inspire confidence by his promises. With tiresome prolixity Dering tells the story of one eventful night on Great Island, while yet Barefoot lived in Dover, and only came down occasionally to the Piræus of old Portsmouth, which New Castle then was. But the upshot of it was thrilling. After an attempt to escape in a canoe, with the help of the aforesaid Charles Hilton, and while Dering mistrusted his prisoner;

"the more by reason of his banishment out of the Jurisdiction, and his also telling me that he must be gone, and would ere long, but would return and answer that action; hearing that said Barefoote was ordered by the General Court to depart the Jurisdiction by a certain time, on the penalty of £20, and also not to practise physic under a fine of £100; and he having forfeited both."

Therefore, Dering resolved to put Barefoot in prison; and was leading him along the island road for that purpose, when his *posse* was assaulted by Charles Hilton and his crew, trying to rescue Barefoot; who, grasping Dering by the neck-band, threw himself backward with so much force as almost to strangle Dering, who thus goes on:

"And when said Swett had pulled Barefoot from me, I went to take hold of his shoulder again; and he going backward I missed my hold; and his band coming in the way of my closing, my hands took hold of it, and he going from me, it tore. Whereupon he was very angry, and began to come towards me, and to lay hands on me. And I, seeing him ketch at my neckcloth, which was twice about my neck, I went backward to shun that danger. But he making use of that advantage (I also having a candle and lanthorn in one of my hands) followed me to take hold of my neckcloth; but I went backwards till Charles Hilton came behind me and kept me up to Barefoote. And then said B. took hold of my neckcloth, and going from me that he might have the better advantage to pull and choke me, I bid him let go, and requested Hilton to loose his hands from my neckcloth. But neither would he let go, nor Hilton cause him; and immediately either Hilton or George Swett struck the lanthorn out of my hand, with such force that, although it was a new one scarcely used before, it broke,—I holding one piece in my hand and put it in my pocket, and showed it to the people after help came."

"So when the light was out, I had more hands about me than Barefoot's, and I received a blow on the side of my head, so that it was swelled from the crown to my ear,—and very sore it was— and a great portion of the hair was pulled off. And how it came to pass I know not, for I was in a great measure deprived of my senses and understanding by reason of my being almost choked by Barefoot, with my neckcloth. But I presume it was this,—that B. preceiving that he, standing, could not quite choke me, fell down with his back on the ground, and up with one of his feet, and placing it aaginst my breast, he, the said Barefoot, did with his hands pull my neckcloth, and thrust me away with his foot, so that he had almost made an end with me. I mean that he had almost killed me, whereby he might attain his purpose of escape from under the two said arrests. And when I perceived that Charles Hilton stood close by me, and would not help me; neither Barefoot let go, nor ease his force that he used to choke me, and that my life was even almost spent,—the Lord put it into my thoughts that, unless I could cry 'Murder,' I was there like to perish,—for indeed then my life required haste,—I bent myself down and pulled the said Barefoot's arms toward me. Whereby I got a little ease, and but a little; for, as I remember, in straining to get my wind out of my throat, the blood gushed out of my nose."

Yet this nose-bleeding Dogberry not only saved his own life, but took Barefoot away as his prisoner, by the help that came to him upon his outcry. All this Dering deposed before Elias Stileman, a kinsman of the Cutts, and one of the magnates of Portsmouth, in a Court of Associates held there, January 1, 1673.

III. *Capt. Francis Champernowne.* Earlier, and still more pronounced, was the support given by Champernowne, into whose ancient Norman family both Sir Humphrey Gilbert and Sir Walter Raleigh had married in the sixteenth century. They were all Devonshire people; and Gawen Champernowne, a cousin of Raleigh, was the grandfather of Francis, who was therefore a third cousin of Raleigh; the younger son of a titled family, who came to New England hoping to begin a titled family here. For, under the draft of a charter for Mason's Colony, made in 1635, but never in force, Capt. John Mason was to be a Count Palatine in New England, after the pattern of the Bishop of Durham in England. As such (as already quoted) Mason was to have this imperfect charter (which bears the marks of Laud's contriving brain and the grasping despotism of Charles I), and had it gone into full effect, and been followed up by a similar charter for Gorges in Maine, it would have developed a landed and titled aristocracy, a church with tithes and rents, endowed schools dependent on the clergy, and the whole glittering parade of Church and State, which was the ambition and the unfulfilled dream of Charles, of Buckingham, of Wentworth and of Laud.*

*In the copious Memoir of Francis Champernowne by C. W. Tuttle, it is shown that his grandfather, Gawen Champernowne, married to the daughter of that Count Montgomery who had the misfortune to give the king of France, Henry II, a mortal wound in a tournament, was first cousin of Raleigh, and served with him in the religious wars of France. Arthur Champernowne, father of Francis, was Raleigh's second cousin, and Francis himself, third cousin of Raleigh and his half-brother Gilbert, became, by Sir Ferdinando Gorges' second marriage, a nephew of that colonizer and grantee of Maine. When Francis was twenty-two years old, his father, Arthur, received from his brother-in-law, Gorges, grants of a thousand acres of land on or near Champernowne's Island in Maine. The following year, 1637, Francis came over (probably in company with young Lord Ley, with whom he afterward sailed as a naval captain in the fleet of Charles I), and took possession of his father's grant, half of which afterward became the property of Walter Barefoot. His own estate, for a few years after, was a tract of 400 acres on the Great Bay, which he called Greenland, long within the limits of Portsmouth; and he seems to have been residing there in October, 1640, when he was one of the signers of a "combination" for maintaining order and government, before New Hampshire came under the control of Massachusetts. After 1641 he disappears from the Pascataqua region for six or seven years, during which he probably served as captain under the command of the third Lord Ley, who had become Earl of Marlborough, by the death of his grandfather.

Champernowne had come over to Portsmouth with wealth enough to buy large tracts on both sides of the river. His farm, Greenland, on the Bay above Portsmouth, afterwards furnished a name for the parish and town so designated. His estate in Kittery included the island since known by the name of Cutts, and he is commemorated in the name of the hotel that now stands in Kittery by the waterside opposite New Castle. Though twice married, he left no surviving sons; his widow migrated to South Carolina, where she might have been more at home than among the yeomanry and merchants of the Pascataqua. He left his romantic name to his region, and the reputation of a genial, good citizen, to whom no scandals attached. He was technically and habitually a gentleman, void of the unscrupulous ambition that brought his distinguished cousin Raleigh to grief and to the scaffold.

THE BACK RIVER DISTRICT.

THE WILLIAM DAMME GARRISON.

Hilton's Point, now known as *Doven Point,* was settled in the spring of 1623; Dover Neck began to be settled in the fall of 1633; Back River District in 1642. *Hilton's Point* is about a mile below the mouth of Back River, at Royal's Cove. Dover Neck is on the eastern side of Back River and the western side of Fore River (Newichawannick is the Indan name). The Back River District is one of the best farm land sections of the town or the State, and the dwellers therein have always been among the best citizens of the town. And their sons and daughters who emigrated from there have made good records, near and far.

History of the so-called 20-acre lots.

The oldest record of the town of Dover, now in existence, was recorded by the town clerk, William Walderne, on a piece of paper, in 1642, and that paper was copied into the earliest record book now extant, by William Pomfrett, who was chosen clerk in 1647, and served nearly a quarter of a century. There were record books before this one, which is marked on the cover "No. 7," but they have all been lost. Perhaps someone destroyed them to prevent their being used in the land lawsuits which the Mason heirs brought against the large land owners in Dover. Town Clerk Pomfrett was an interested party in having the contents of that piece of paper preserved, hence he recorded it in the first book he kept. It reads and spells as follows:

The west sied of ye Back Reue or ouer ye Back Riuer

A Record of ye 20 Ackes loets as theay waer in order given and layed out to ye inhabetance hoes names are here under menshened with the nomber of the loet to each pertickler man. As it was fowned Recorded by William Walden in a Pec of paper in ye yeir (16)42, wich lots ar in Breadth at ye water sied 40 poell and in lenketh 80 poll up into ye woods.

Names
Thomas Roberts, 1
Henry Tebbets, 3
Edward Colcord, 5
John Tuttle, 7
Barthey Smeg, 9
John Dam, 11

Richard Roggers, 2
Mr. Larkham, 4
George Webe, 6
William Story, 8
John Ugrove, 10

William Pomfrett, 12. This 12th lott is exchanged with Dea. Dam for ye 17th lott.
Wm. Hilton, Sr., 13   Edward Starback, 14
Samewell Haynes, 15. This 15th lott was Resined to John Hill, and by him sold unto Wm. ffollett as was acknowledged.
Robert Huggins, 16
John Crosse, 17. This 17th Lott is Exchanged by John Dam with Lt Pomfret for ye 12th Lott.
Thomas Layton, 18   John Hall, 19
Hatabell Nutter, 20   Henry Beck, 21
John Westell, 22   No name, 23
Richard Pinkham, 24

Bear in mind these lots on the river bank were 40 rods in width and 80 rods in depth; as there were 24 lots, the distance from Royal's Cove, at the mouth of Back River, was three miles to lot No. 24, close to the head of tide water where Back River begins and Bellamy River ends, or empties into it.

Soon after the grants were awarded the owners began trading and exchanging. Deacon John Dam (who was not deacon until 30 years later), who drew No. 11, soon received No. 12 from his father-in-law, William Pomfrett, the town clerk. And in 1656 Deacon Dam bought lot No. 13, so he then owned Nos. 11, 12 and 13, and he settled his son, William Dam, on the land, when he became of suitable age; his other son, John, was located on the east shore of Little Bay, which to this day bears the name, Dame's Point.

William Dam was born 14 October, 1653; his wife was Martha Nute, also born in 1653. She was daughter of James, who owned the lots next south of Deacon John Dam's. They were married about 1679. He probably had been living on his father's land there three or four years before marriage and had built a garrison house, as the Indians were getting to be troublesome. Anyhow, he had a garrison, as the Provincial records show. The Nute and Dam families have a common burying ground on the bank of Back River, where there are three headstones with inscriptions, and others without name. These three are the graves of James Nute, founder of the Nute family in America, Martha Dam and her husband, William Dam.

It was before 1648 that James Nute bought lots No. 9 and 10 from the grantees, John Ugrove and Barthey Smeg. And much, if not all, of that land is now owned by the Nute family, his descendants, having remained in the name 275 years.

In Volume 17 of the Provincial Papers are the following references to the Dam garrison. From 7 January to 6 February, 1695, it says, John Cross served as one of the guards at Will. Dam's garrison; from 12 May to 8 June, 1695, John Bickford was watchman; from 4 November to 5 December, 1695, John Tucker and John Miller were guardsmen; from 5 December, 1695, to 7 January, 1696, Ephraim Jackson was the special soldier on duty. That period was very perilous, and no man or crew of men dared to go to the fields or the woods to work without carrying their loaded guns, for use in case an Indian appeared.

For more than a hundred years the house was called the "Drew garrison." It came into the possession of Joseph Drew, Jr., about 1771, and remained in possession of his descendants till it came into the possession of the Woodman Institute, by the gift of Mrs. Ellen S. Rounds, as will be explained later. In 1912 the author received information from Mr. N. W. Davis of Winchester, Mass., to the effect that the garrison then stood on a 20-acre lot at the west end of Dea. John Damme's lot, No. 13 of the Back River district. This lot, No. 13, was originally granted to William Hilton, Sr., and was purchased by Deacon Damme in 1656, who gave it to his son William Damme, when he came to be "one-and-twenty." The son was married, in 1679, and had his log house built, ready for house-keeping, just as you can see it at the Woodman Institute.

Mr. Davis, who gave the information as to the locality of the original site, was a gentleman of much experience in historical research; he was a member of the New England Historical and Genealogical Society, and lived in Dover several years when a boy. He is a lineal descendant of Capt. John Drew, who was supposed to have been the man who built the garrison. Mr. Davis, in his researches for other matter, ran across the legal documents which are given in connection with this history of the garrison. This discovery aroused a suspicion in Mr. Davis's mind that he and others were mistaken in supposing the garrison was built by

John Drew, Sr. Mr. Davis felt reluctant to give up the idea that it was built by his ancestor, as he had entertained much pride in having the old house belong in his family. To dispel all doubt in the matter he employed an engineer to measure the shore line on the west side of Back River, to ascertain as nearly as possible the dividing line between the lots. The engineer surveyed the ground carefully and found that the garrison is on the west of lot No. 13, and Drew's lot, No. 14, on the height of land beyond, up the river. Hence the conclusion that the old garrison was built by William Dam, between 1675 and 1679, and is at least 234 years old, and is the oldest house in Dover. In further confirmation of the correctness of the engineer's survey, and that the garrison stood in the rear of lot No. 13, is the fact that the old Dam burial ground is on this lot, between the garrison site and the river, whereas the Drew burial ground is on the lot No. 14, next above on the river bank, where the inscription of Sergt. John Drew's headstone may be read, even now. He died 23 October, 1723, aged 73 years.

But how does it come to be called the Drew garrison? It took its name from Joseph Drew, father of William Plaisted Drew; it came into his possession through the inheritances of his wife, Leah Nute, to whom he was married in 1771, and they came to reside in the house that year, so it came into possession of the Drew family 152 years ago. Joseph Drew was great-grandson of John Drew, Sr.

The ownership, previous to 1771, appears to have been nearly in this line. Built by William Dam, 1675; he died in the garrison 20 March, 1718; his son, William Dam, Jr., inherited it and resided there several years; his sister, Leah, married Samuel Hayes in 1720; at sometime prior to 1740, Mr. and Mrs. Hayes came into possession of the garrison and resided there until his death about 1770. Jacob Allen, who married Martha Dam, sister of William Dam, Jr., also had an interest in the house after the death of her father in 1718. One of their daughters married James Tuttle and she inherited her parents' interest in the house, and this was "quit-claimed" to Joseph Drew in 1786. Joseph Drew's wife, Leah Nute, obtained her interest in the house from her mother, Mary Hayes, who married James Nute, and Mary was the daughter of Samuel and Leah (Dam) Hayes.

This old garrison is one of the most interesting houses in New Hampshire. Dea. John Dam, with other worthies across the river, on Meeting House Hill, must have been a frequent visitor there, as he was living in 1693, and he was one of the men who came over from England in 1633. So this old house takes us back to the very first settlers on Dover Neck. The following briefs of certain real estate transfers are convincing evidence that the Drew garrison is the original William Dam garrison. It does not appear there was any other "Drew garrison," and this did not become such until after 1770.

1. On June 7, 1712, William Dam, Sr., of Dover, in consideration of the love, good-will and affection which he bore to his son, William Dam, conveyed to him one-half of the *new house* he was then building, and half of the land on which it stood, with one-third of his orchard, and three acres of land, being all his land on that side of the creek.

2. William Dam, Jr., on the same day, June 7, 1712, bound himself to be at one-third of the charge of moving the house in which he then dwelt at the "west end" of the Dam lands, the said house being 24 feet long and 30 feet wide, "up to the *logg house* and set it there."*

3. On April 7, 1724, William Dam (not called Jr., but he was son of the above William, Sr.) conveyed to Jacob Allen, his brother-in-law, who had married his sister, Martha, "one-half of the *dwelling logg house,* set in Dover, on the westerly side of ye back river, which was formerly ye dwelling house of William Dam, Sr.," together with part of "ye upper orchard," and four and one-half acres lying in ye *spruce pasture.*†

4. On January 17, 1786, James Tuttle (b. 1711, d. 1790) for £9 lawful money, quitclaimed to Joseph Drew all his right,

---

*(NOTE.—The garrison is built differently from most of the garrison houses, being built of square beams, or logs, and not boarded on the outside.)

†(NOTE.—The present garrison stood on what was anciently, as now, known as Spruce Lane.)

title and interest in the house where the said Joseph Drew "now lives" (this is known to be the garrison), being the west end of the house and the room at the east end, that was allowed in the return of the division of the estate of Samuel Hayes of Dover, deceased.‡

5. Joseph Drew (5), son of Joseph (4), dwelt in the garrison from the time of his marriage, in 1771, to Leah Nute, granddaughter of Samuel and Leah (Dam) Hayes, by daughter, Mary. As shown in deed 4, he was enjoying possession of the Hayes part of the garrison in 1786, when James Tuttle conveyed to him the Jacob and Martha Allen interests for £9.

Abstract of Deed
John and Sarah Drew
to son Francis of
Dover Apr. 9, 1712.

To all whom it may concern, this deed of gift, John Drew of Dover, together with and through the consent of Sarah, my wife, for and in consideration of a good settlement, in order to his further comfort and well being in this world, and for the natural love, good wish and fatherly affection which I do own and bear to my now only son, Francis Drew of said town and Province (i. e., Dover, N. H.). Three lots of land which I bought of Thomas Austin, Joshua Winget and Israel Hodgdon, lying on the southward side of the way that leads from my house to the Queen's Road, which three lots contain by estimation 56 acres or thereabouts, all within fence beginning at a division fence at the west of a 20-acre lot bought of Wm. Brackstone, from that southward and westward till it comes to a join with Zachariah Field's land hard by, excepting unto myself and Sarah, my present wife, full power and free liberties of firewood, fencing stuffs and pasturing in lots bought of Winget and Hodgdon; one small piece of salt marsh which I bought of Wm. Brookin, being one-half acre more or less, with the privileges and appurtenances thereunto belonging lying on the west side of Johnson's creek; one-half of 20 acre lot which I bought of John Derry taking it at the southward and west of Zachariah Field's land; one-half of the 20 acre lot which I bought of Zachariah Pitman, together with half of the vacancies

‡(NOTE.—A perusal of the Tuttle Genealogy will show that the only possible way James Tuttle could have any interest in this property was through his wife, Mary, daughter of Jacob and Martha Allen, said Martha being daughter of William Dam. Samuel Hayes owned and occupied part of the garrison for a great many years and died there, about 1770. His wife was Leah, daughter of William Dam.)

granted to me in the Dry Pines; one-half of the 20-acre lot granted to me by the town between William Hill's plantation and Maharrimet's Hill, the eastward part thereof; all which said parcels of land and marsh above mentioned, with the privileges and appurtenances to each and every of them belonging or in any ways appertaining except above excepted and reserved, shall be for and to the whole and sole use and benefit of my aforesaid son Francis Drew, To Have and to Hold, etc.

In witness whereof I have hereunto set my hand and seal this ninth day of April in the year of our Lord God 1712.

(Signed:) JOHN DREW.

Signed sealed and
delivered, etc., in
the presence of us.
JOHN TUTTLE Sen.
PAUL GERRISH
SAM'L PEARL.

It is well to keep in mind that the Indians did not trouble Dover people before 1675, more than 30 years after the grants of land were made. So there were no garrisons before that date. Another point to bear in mind is that there was no call for building garrisons after 1725, when the Indian wars ceased here, having continued fifty years. The last Dover man who lost his scalp was John Evans, the Poet Whittier's great-grandfather. The Indians performed that surgical operation in the vicinity of the Knox Marsh road beyond the road to Bellamy mill. Mr. Dam had good reason for building a garrisoned house when he did. The Oyster River massacre had occurred only four years before, when his father and one brother were killed, and other members of the family were carried captives to Canada.

In the records of about 1700 a highway is mentioned between Dam's land and that of James Nute, just south, which led to a landing place at the head of James Nute's creek, about a mile from the Dam garrison. This creek is above Hope-Hood's Point. The name of this point is derived from a noted Indian chief, said to have belonged to the Abenaki tribe. Doctor Quint says he was the Sagamore, Wahowah, or Wohawa, chief of all the lands from Exeter to Salmon Falls. The historian, Hubbard, in his Narrative, calls him "Hope Hood," and says he was son of Robin Hood. The two are mentioned together in signing a deed of land at "Squammagonak" to Peter Coffin, January 3, 1688. It was Hope Hood who led the attack on Newichawannick settlement in 1690, as well as that on Fox Point shore soon after. So noted did he become for his ferocity to the English settlers that Mather, in his "Magnolia," calls him "that memorable tygre," and "that hellish fellow," etc. The tradition is that he was killed in 1690, and buried on this point of land which bears, and will ever bear, his name. No headstone marks the exact spot where he was buried, but it is affirmed that the groans of the old Indian warrior are still to be heard there from time to time among the moaning branches of the trees, when great storms prevail. It is supposed he died of his wounds received in the fight at Fox Point, and his friends brought him across the river to this Point and buried him.

Hope Hood was one of the occasional neighbors of William Dam and James Nute. No wonder they had a garrison and soldiers to defend them, although the doughty old Indian chief seems never to have troubled them. Probably he was in his peaceful moods when he lived on Hope Hood Point, and they treated him kindly.

Cotton Mather, in his "Magnolia," commenting on Hope Hood's treatment of James Key, son of John Key of Quochecho, a child of about five years of age who was captured by the Indians at Salmon Falls, says: "That hellish fellow, Hope Hood, once the servant of a Christian master in Boston, was made master of him, and treated him in a very cruel manner."

In another passage Mather says, in regard to the Indian attack on Wells, that Hope Hood and his party, "having first had a skirmish with Captain Sherborn, they appeared the next Lord's Day at Newichawannick, or Berwick, where they burned some houses and slew a man. Three days after they came upon a small hamlet on the South side of the Pascataqua River, called Fox Point, and besides the burning of several houses, they took half a dozen prisoners, and killed more than a dozen of the too securely ungarrisoned people; which was as easy to do as to have spoiled an ordinary hen-roost. But Captain Floyd and Captain Greenleaf coming (from Salisbury) upon these Indians made some slaughter among them, recovered some captives, with

THE DAMME GARRISON: Now (1923) enclosed within a Colonnade at the Woodman Institute. (See page 201.)

much plunder, and bestowed a good wound upon Hope Hood, who lost his gun (which was next to his life) in this action." The unfortunate thing about these Indian wars is that the Indians left no record of their side of the history.

It may be noticed, from the list of lot owners, that John Tuttle had "No. 7." Mr. Tuttle was the first of the name to settle in Dover, and his residence was on Dover Neck, on the east side of High Street and about a quarter of a mile below the meetinghouse, where now is Riverview Hall. He did not come over to Back River to reside, but one son did, and that lot, No. 7, remained in possession of the Tuttle family and the Tuttle name until a few years ago.

What a beautiful locality Back River is, and always has been. Directly across the river from the Dam garrison is Huckleberry Hill, the ancient training ground of Capt. John Tuttle's valiant soldiers. Further down the ridge, at the extreme right, is the site of the old meeting house. All along the river bank, at suitable spots, are the burial lots of the Back River families; there lies the dust of brave men and devout women. There are no ancient burying grounds back so far from the river as this old garrison. Those men and women had eyes that appreciated the beautiful in life, and the "Sleeping Place" in death.

Another noticeable thing about this Back River locality is the location of the dwellings a half mile back from the river; each land owner built his house and his barn as near to the river bank as the nature of the ground would permit, to secure good drainage and good spring water. The houses were nearer to the river than the barns and outbuildings. This arrangement was because of the fact that the chief travel was done by boats on the river. There were roads to the river where each family had its boats. The great business center then, was on the Neck, just across the river. When the farmers wanted to trade they went there in their boats, or to Portsmouth. This custom of travelling by boats was in use as late as seventy years ago. The old houses all fronted square to the south, as the garrison did. The reason for this is apparent when we consider the fact that clocks were scarce, and, when they had them, were not very accurate timekeepers. The sun always keeps correct time; when it cast a shadow square with the east and west ends of the house the housewife knew that it was high noon, and would toot her dinner horn accordingly, to call the workmen from afar in the fields. A noon mark on the window sill was kept to show the time, also. You can find the noon mark now, if you search carefully in the front windows of very old houses. Now no housewife thinks of blowing the dinner horn, or the conch shell, which antedated the horn, because every day laborer carries a Waterbury or a Waltham watch in his vest pocket, and has it regulated by an electric stroke from the Observatory in Washington or Cambridge at noon every day. Why, the day laborers now have for every-day fare what would have been luxuries for the aristocrats of Dover Neck and Back River in those early days.

Persons driving along the Garrison road no doubt wonder at the fashion that prevails of having the barns nearer the road then the houses which seem to be behind them; that is the barns appear to be in front of the house. The reason of that is that the barns were built long before the roads, and were *behind* the houses, because the great thoroughfare was the river, and, moreover, they did not want the beautiful view to the river, and Dover Neck beyond, obstructed by old barns and out buildings. They had an eye for the beautiful, as well as the useful.

Speaking of garrisons it may be well to mention one more in this section, which stood on the height of land, a short distance west of the Back River school house. It was built by Zachius Field, who was taxed at Oyster River in 1664 and owned land at Back River as early as 1670. It was probably built soon after the Indians squared their accounts with Major Walderne at Cochecho, June 28, 1689. In connection with that garrison Rev. John Pike, for many years pastor of the First Church, relates that July 8, 1707, John Bunker and Ichabod Rawlins were going with a cart from Lieut. Zach Field's garrison to James Bunker's, at Oyster River, for a loom, when they were slain by the Indians. This incident shows what lively times they had about here in those days.

In conclusion of this Back River-Garrison story it seems well to give a resumé of the important historical points to help the reader understand the whole situation, and how the garrison came to be removed from its original foundation to its present location in the Woodman Institute, where it can be kept for ages, that future generations can see what sort of houses they had on Dover Neck village, in the years following 1633. When the business men got things well in hand, their houses were of the same style as this William Damme garrison.

The house was built by Deacon John Dam for his son William about 1675; it was surrounded by a stockade (which made it a garrison) before 1680, which remained standing for thirty years, or more. In 1642 Deacon Dam received (from the town) a grant of the 20-acre lot, No. 11; his father-in-law, William Pomfrett, at the same time had given him lot No. 12, and William Hilton, Sr., had No. 13. A few years later Deacon Dam bought lot No. 13; he also bought a 20-acre lot on the west end of lot No. 13; on the west end of this last mentioned lot he located this Garrison for his son; he placed it on top of a steep hill, at the foot of which, on the north, is a brook; and on the west of it was made the lane, known as Spruce Lane, until Mrs. Rounds changed it to "Garrison Road." It is one-half mile from Back River. It was one of the best built houses of that period, the walls being massive hewn logs, twenty feet long and more, making the house forty feet long by twenty-two feet in width; in the rear of the house can be seen the manner in which the carpenters joined the timbers, in the framing. The oak timbers were never clapboarded. The large garret afforded ample room for the family beds, with "trundle beds" for the children. Many of the first settlers on Dover Neck (1633) were guests in this house, from time to time.

"Will Dam's Garrison" is mentioned in the Provincial Papers. The Government sent soldiers there to assist in guarding it against any possible attack by the Indians. From 7 January to 6 February, 1695, John Cross was guardsman there. John Bickford was on guard there from 4 November to 5 December, 1695. John Tasker and John Miller were stationed there by the Government from 5 December, 1695, to 7 January, 1696. Ephraim Jackson and others were on watch there from time to time. Of course, Mr. Dam had his guns all ready for use, but there is no mention of any attack being made by the Indians. The visitors can see some of the port-holes, made in the walls, through which the guns could be fired in case an enemy got inside of the stockade. These apertures were closed with plaster after the wars were over, and so remained until taken down, when the building was removed to its present location.

William Dam was born on Dover Neck 14 October, 1653; married Martha Nute soon after the house was completed for habitation. Martha Nute was daughter of James Nute, who lived on lot No. 10. They resided in this house till his death in 1718. His son, William Dam, inherited the house and farm, and resided there till about 1740. At his death it came into possession of his sister, Leah Dam, who had married Samuel Hayes. Samuel and Leah resided there (and raised a family), up to about 1770. Soon after that it came into possession of their grand-daughter, Leah Nute, who married Joseph Drew in 1771. Leah took her husband home, to the Garrison, and there they lived the rest of their married life until 1810. Up to 1770 it was known as the *"Dam Garrison."*

Joseph Drew was a man of much ability and prospered. In 1810 he built the former mansion house in which Mrs. Rounds lived, until Mr. Rounds died in 1916. When Joseph Drew built the mansion house, his son, William Plaisted Drew, was sixteen years old; at the death of the father this son inherited the house and farm. At that time the Garrison had come to be known as the "Drew Garrison," as it had long been in possession of the family.

William Plaisted Drew was born in 1794; he died in 1868. He was a prominent citizen of Dover and had prospered in business. At his death his son, Edwin Plaisted Drew, came into possession, and held it until 1883, when it came into possession of Deacon Bryant Peavey; he gave it to his daughter, Ellen S. Peavey, who had married Mr. Holmes B. Rounds. Mr. Rounds's mother was a Drew, descendant of Joseph and Leah Nute (Dam) Drew, so the old Garrison remained in possession of a descendant of William Dam, the original owner, till it came into possession of the Woodman Institute, a period of two hundred and forty years.

When Mrs. Rounds came into possession of the property the garrison was very much out of repair, and but for her care and forethought it would have gone to ruin. She took it in hand and had it repaired; not only that, she commenced collecting antique articles of historic interest and value. The collection increased slowly at first, but when her friends saw what a good beginning she had made they took hold and helped, as opportunity enabled them to do. The result of thirty years' labor, by Mrs. Rounds and her friends, can be seen in the garrison, in which she has arranged the various articles, consisting of more than eight hundred pieces. During the last twenty years of her ownership many persons visited the garrison; before that no one thought it of any account to visit, and but comparatively few Dover people knew there was such a house.

The house remained in possession of the Dam family for nearly a century. It remained in possession of the Drew family one hundred and twelve years. Mrs. Rounds owned it thirty-two years, and then negotiations commenced for the transfer to the Woodman Institute, which was being put into shape for business of entertaining the public. It had been in possession of the Drew family so long that it had come to be called the "Drew Garrison."

Col. Daniel Hall, for the trustees of the Institute, made a satisfactory agreement with Mrs. Rounds for the transfer whereby she gave the building and contents to that institution, if the trustees would have it removed to the grounds of the Institute, and put it in proper repair for preservation, and permit her to arrange the articles in the various apartments, as she saw fit, and retain control of them as long as she may live. Daniel Chesley was entrusted with the job of moving the garrison to its present home. He completed the work in the last of October, 1915; it took him one week to roll it up to town; one horse furnished the motive power; four men kept the rollers in place and watched the movements. The moving attracted much attention. One young man wanted to know why they did not build it up here instead of at Back River. Mr. Chesley kindly informed him why.

In this connection it seems well to make a record of certain real estate transactions which are connected with the history of the old house.

1—June 7, 1712, William Damme, Sr., of Dover, in consideration of the love, good-will and affection which he bore to his son, William Damme, conveyed to him one-half of the *new house* he was then building, and one-half of the land on which it stood, with one-third of his orchard, and three acres of land, being all his land on this side of the creek. The creek was on the north side of the garrison.

2—William Damme, Jr., on the same day bound himself to be at one-third charge of moving the house, aforementioned, in which he then dwelt at the "west end of the Damme land," the said house being 30 by 24 feet, *"upp to ye logg house and sett it there."* Just where he "sett it" is not known, but probably on the spot where the mansion house stood, which was built in 1810. It was ten feet shorter than the garrison and two feet wider, so, of course, could not be fitted on to the old house.

3—April 7, 1724, William Damme (not called "Jr." as his father had died in 1718) conveyed to Jacob Allen, who had married Martha Damme, sister of William, "one half of ye dwelling logg house set in Dover, on ye westerly side of ye Back River, which was formerly ye dwelling house of William Damme, Sr.," together with part of "ye upper orchard and four and one half acres lying in *ye Spruce pasture."* The name of the road, *Spruce Lane,* was derived from this pasture.

4—January 17, 1786, James Tuttle (born 1711, died 1790), for £9 lawful money, quitclaimed to Joseph Drew, who married Leah Nute, "all his right, title and interest in the house where the said Joseph Drew now lives," (this is known to be the garrison), being the west end of the house, and the room at the east end of the house, that was allowed in the return of the estate of Samuel Hayes, who died in 1770. This interest came from the fact that Tuttle had married Mary, the daughter of Jacob and Martha (Damme) Allen; Martha was sister of William, Jr., and daughter of William, Sr. Samuel Hayes and family had lived in the garrison many years. His successor in the garrison was Joseph Drew. The garrison was occupied as a dwelling house till after the close of the Civil War.

In its original position the garrison faced to the south, as was the custom of that period, so as to get the noon mark on the window casing. In its present location it faces nearly to the east. What was the east end is now to the north, and the effects of the storms of 240 years are apparent on that end more than on any other part of the building. In the present locality the building is precisely as in the old; the chimney is an exact reproduction of the old one, which had to be taken down.

DOVER'S RIVERS.

Dover Neck is bounded by four rivers: Back River on the west; Pascataqua on the south; Newichawannock on the east (for convenience, and in contrast with Back River, also called Fore River); and the Cochecho River on the north. As the "crow flies," it is less than a mile between the head of tide water at Back River and that at Cochecho. The territory has always been called "Lower Neck and Upper Neck." They are all tide-water rivers. The fresh-water river above the Cochecho Falls is also called "Cochecho," and has its source in ponds in New Durham and Middleton. The Indians applied the name only to the Falls, and Dr. Quint said the word means,—"Swift foaming water."

The name "Back River" extends only to the head of tide-water; the fresh water river is now called Bellamy River. For more than 200 years it was called "Belleman's Bank," and is so mentioned in deeds of 1658, and in the years following; in later years the town records have it "Bellamy Bank." The late William Hale was the first to introduce the present spelling—"Bellamy River."

As to the origin of the name. Down to the time of Mr. William Hale's abbreviation, the name always ended with the word "Bank." That word had reference to the high bank that is on the northeast side of the river at the lower falls. On the field, extending back towards the road, was, anciently, an Indian cornfield, handy for planting the fish, as well as the corn, in spring time. The Indian Sagamore who had charge of the cornfield, when the first settlers came to Dover Neck (1633), was a large man, with a large abdomen, so the white men, in speaking of the locality, called it "Belleman's Bank."

Miss Mary P. Thompson, in her wonderful book,—"Landmarks in Ancient Dover"—says on page 20: "The name is suggested by the term of *'ye old planting-ground'* in the following deed. Thomas Beard, of Dover, August 6, 1654, conveyed to Richard Walderne a quarter part of the sawmill (at the falls where the lower mill of the American Woolen Company now is), with all the iron works, ropes, wheels and all implements and housings, with all the logs and the grant of timber by the town, and likewise *ye old planting-ground,* commonly called *Bellemies Bank,* with 20 acres more, granted by the town of Dover." Miss Thompson adds,—"The word is evidently a corruption, and one that is ignoble to the ear." The river has its source in Swayne's Pond, near Beauty Hill, in Barrington.

In common parlance the name "Fore River" was applied to the Newichawannock up as far as the mouth of the Cochecho River, at Thomson's Point. Beyond that the name Newichawannock extends to Quamphegan Falls, at South Berwick. That name is not applied to the fresh water river, which has always been called "Salmon Falls River," from the time when the English settlers commenced to catch salmon, as they were trying to get into the fresh water to lay their spawn, about 1634. Its head water is at Milton Three Ponds. It is the best river in New Hampshire for manufacturing purposes, except the Merrimack River.

At Thomson's Point is the locality where the *"Thomson Poynt house"* stood that is on the tax list of 1648, as will be seen by reference to the tax lists in another part of this book. On pages 151-152 of "Landmarks in Ancient Dover," Miss Thompson says: "This point is mentioned again, the 15th, 10 mo, 1652, when orders were given to begin at *Tomson's Pointe* to mark the three hundred pines and 100 oak trees granted Capt. Thomas Wiggin and others, and thence upward into Mr. Walderne's grant. Thomas Canney had a grant of 16 acres of upland the 6th, 10 mo, 1656, to be laid out adjoining *his perches at Tomson's poynt.* This land was laid out from the utmost point turning up to Cochecho 50 rods to the *long creek* westward below *Tomson's poynt,* butting on Fore River, thence running three score and ten rods up the *long Creek side,* reserving a cartway from the woods to the water side at the head of the creek, and up Cochecho River three score and ten rods, and thence on a straight line over to the bound at the head of *long creek."*

Job Clement had a grant of 3½ acres of upland 23d, 10 mo, 1658, part of which was below "the highway that goeth from Thomas Canney's into the woods towards *"Thomson's Poynt,"* bounded E. by the Fore River, on the northern side of the hollow, *where the ship was built.* This ship was the frigate built by Major Richard Walderne, as referred to elsewhere. A lane from Parson Reyner's land to Thomson's Point is mentioned in 1675. Thomas, eldest son and rightful heir of Thomas Canney, Jr., and his wife, Grace, conveyed to his brother Samuel, August 12, 1703, forty-five acres of land in tenure of said Samuel, adjacent to *Thomson's Point* and next to Henry Tibbett's land. Joshua Canney, son of Samuel, conveyed to John Gage, December 17, 1745, a tract of land extending to the mouth of the Cochecho River and westerly on said river to *Thomson's Point,* adjoining Gage's land on the south, along Fore River. Mr. Gage had a famous brick yard there, as long as the clay bank continued to serve him for that purpose.

The Pascataqua River begins at Fox Point, Newington, where the Oyster River unites with the tide-water from Little Bay, which was so called as early as 1642. At the upper extremity of Little Bay is the Narrows (strait) between *Adams Point* and *Furber's Point,* where the tide passes into Great Bay, which, at high tide, is a beautiful basin of water, four miles wide in one part, enclosed between Durham and Newmarket on the north and Greenland and Newington on the south. It was so named as early as 1643. Three river empty into it,—the Squamscot, the Lamprey and the Winnicot. So much for the source of the Pascataqua River.

The Pascataqua River was discovered by the very earliest explorers along the New England coast, but the first one to make mention of his sailing on its waters was Martin Pring, who came up as far as its headwaters at Dover in June, 1603. He was searching for "sassafras," that being regarded as one of the great remedies then popular in the medical world. He did not find any, but says he saw huge forest trees, various kinds of wild animals, and the camping-place of the Indians at the head-waters, where they had cooked their fish and feasted in the spring of the year, when the salmon and other fish were plenty about the falls. This fishing and feasting season was over a few weeks before Captain Pring arrived, but he saw and reported the fresh fire brands, which the Indians had left when they started on a hunting excursion up country, among lakes Winnepesaukee, Suncook, Pennacook, and other favorite summer resorts which they had, something as the civilized mortals now spend their hot-weather vacations.

It is not known at what place Captain Pring saw the "fire brands" the Indians left, after their feasting, but it is quite probable that he went straight up the Newichawannock to the head of tide water, at Quamphegan Falls. The Indian camping, and cooking place, was probably on the Rollinsford shore. There is nothing in his account that would correspond with what he would be likely to see if he had gone up into Little Bay.

During the next score of years, from 1603 to 1623, when Edward Hilton and his party commenced the settlement at *Hilton Point,* it is quite probable that British and French fishermen came up the river, in the season of fishing, but such fellows never made a record of where they went, or what they saw. The river empties into Ipswich Bay, which lies between the main land and the Isles of Shoals. Newcastle (of old generally called Great Island) divides the river's mouth into two parts. The main branch makes the Lower Harbor, having old Fort Constitution on the right and Kittery Point and Gerrish Island on the left. The other exit is by way of Little Harbor, at the south end of Newcastle Island. The passage is between the historic Wentworth house, which Gov. Benning Wentworth inherited from his mother; it had been built by her father, Mark Hunking, Esq., and the Governor changed it to its present unique proportions. On the Newcastle shore is the magnificent Wentworth Hotel, built by Frank Jones, the millionaire brewer.

As to the spelling of the name, the correct orthography is evidently *Pascataqua,* notwithstanding it is generally corrupted into *Piscataqua.* Judge Potter defines the name of this river as "a great deer place," from the Indian words, *pos,* great; *attuck,* deer; and *auk,* a place. Sanford and Everts's Atlas says the Piscataqua River was so named by Capt. Martin Pring, from *piscatus,* fish, and *aqua,* water, from the abundance of the fish he found when he ascended this river several leagues in 1603. Thoreau, in his *"Maine Woods,"* says *Piscataquis* signifies, according to the definition of an intelligent Indian, "the branch of a river." Mr. Hoyt, in his notes to Tuttle's *Historical Papers,* page 101, says the word *Pascataqua* means "divided tidal place," as the river is divided at the mouth into two streams, by the island of Newcastle. The Pascataqua is, in fact, a forked river, with two great branches —one coming from East Pond in the northeast corner of Wakefield, and the other from Great and Little Bays. These unite at *Hilton's Point,* whence this confluent stream flows eastward to the Atlantic, seven miles distant.

The Hon. C. H. Bell, in his *History of Exeter,* aptly compares the Pascataqua and its tributaries to "a man's left hand and wrist, back upwards, and fingers wide apart. The thumb would stand for the Fore River; the forefinger for Back river; the second finger for Oyster river; the third for Lamprey river, and the fourth for Exeter, or Squamscot river, while the palm of the hand would represent the Great Bay and Little Bay, into which most of these streams flow, and the wrist the Pascataqua proper." A branched river as the name signifies.

Between the mouth of Back River and Newington are the *Horse Races,* where the current of the Pascataqua is very rapid and turbulent. At *Hilton Point,* otherwise commonly called *Dover Point,* the Pascataqua unites with the Newichawannock, forming what the old records call the *Main River,* which flows thence in a direct course towards the Atlantic ocean. This straight portion of the river, between *Dover Point* and the Narrows, below Boiling Rock, is called the *Long Reach.*

The chief points and coves along the Newington shore, beginning at Fox Point, the most prominent headland, at the lower side, is *Hen Island;* below is *Broad Cove.* Midway along the shore of this cove is *Rocky Point,* otherwise *Carter's Rocks.* At the lower side of Broad Cove is *Stephen's Point,* sometimes called *Bean's Point.* Next below is *Coleman's Creek;* then comes *Zackey's Point,* otherwise *Orchard Point,* so called, when there was a large orchard on it for a hundred years. On the lower side of this is

Trickey's Cove; below is *Nancy Drew's Point,* a subdivision of *Bloody Point.* Here was the landing-place of the ferries that were run between Dover and Newington until the present railroad bridge was built. There was also another ferry across from *Dover Point,* to Eliot, by which travel was carried on for two centuries. The senior President Adams travelled over these ferries, when he was a young lawyer, and went from Boston to Saco to attend courts; he makes mention of one trip he made, when he called on his uncle, Joseph Adams, then minister of the Newington Church. *Bloody Point* is the terminus of the railroad bridge. The origin of the name has been explained in previous pages of this book. In the river below Bloody Point, perhaps thirty rods from the shore, are the *Langstaffe Rocks,* dangerous to shipping, and there, for more than a half century, preceding the building of the bridge, was seen a wrecked schooner. The wreck was visible for a number of years after the bridge was built.

Going down the shore from Bloody Point may be noted the following coves and places: *Pickering's Cove,* otherwise *Whidden's Cove* and a creek, which once divided the Bickford and Cater lands, and ran a mill. The point of land below that is *Birch Point,* anciently known as *Pine Point,* before the primeval pines of the forest were cut by the first settlers, and the birches took their place. On the shore between *Pickering's Cove* and *Birch Point* was the ship-yard of the *Great World War* period—1917-1920. The owners of the yard were duly incorporated, and the management was run on the "cost plus plan." The Government paid the bills, and the larger the pay-roll, so much the larger was the pay of the incorporators. They employed skilled engineers and carpenters to boss the work, and then employed men to work under them. The "under men" were made up of farm hands, brick makers, shoe makers, and any unskilled workman who could drive a board nail. There were more than 1,000 of them. They received nothing less than three dollars a day; so business, in other lines of work, was completely demoralized, as to wages. Before the war closed several ships were built, and interesting scenes of launching were witnessed. When the war stopped the Government refused to pay the incorporators to finish the work; the result was work stopped

—instanter! The uncompleted work of some of the frames of the ships are now standing on the "Ways." Maybe they will stand there till they rot, and fall to the ground. They are Government property. The "Shipping Board" is having a difficult problem to decide what disposal to make of the finished vessels.

It does not seem to be the place to give a complete history of the Newington Ship-Yard, in this story of the Pascataqua River. Further down on the same side of the river is *Uncle Siah's Cove,* properly *Downing's Cove,* just above *Patterson Lane.* Off shore is *Shag Rock. Ragg's Point,* otherwise *Beetle's,* is on the shore of the Rollins farm. Further down is the Upper Huntress landing-place. Below is *Paul's Creek,* the *Kenney,* or *Canney's* of early times. Then comes *Hill's Cove.* A short distance below begins the Gosling Road, which separates Newington from Portsmouth. At the lower side is the landing place called *Lower Huntress.* A ferry once ran from this point to the Eliot shore. *Boiling Rock* is off the Eliot shore, and conspicuous at low tide. Beyond are the *Narrows.* Here is *Cutt's Eddy,* the worst in the river for boatmen, especially gundalows, loaded in old times with wood, from Durham on their way to Portsmouth. On the shore is *Wentworth Point,* better known as the *Pulpit,* so called from a rock that hangs out from the shore, where sailors in passing formerly "made their manners" for the sake of good luck. On the height of land back of this is the village that grew up in the World-War-Ship-Building period. Below the Pulpit is *Cutt's Cove,* with *Freeman's Point* beyond. For two hundred years this was called *Ham's Point,* from William Ham, who had a grant of land here in 1652 and built a house on it before 1654. There was the famous World War steel ship-building yard.

Going up the Long Reach, the river boatmen, after passing *Frank's Fort,* used to sing out,—"Barn Door!" as soon as they caught sight of a barn on a distant hill in Eliot, the doors of which were never known to be shut in the season of the river traffic. This was the signal for a "dram" of New England rum, and the men would flat their oars and take their grog, the better (as they thought) to stem the strong current of the Long Reach. The Oyster River boatmen always took another dram when they had passed *Dover Point* and commenced boating up the *Horse Races,* where the current is very swift and powerful. Another had to be taken at *Half-Tide Rock,* on entering the mouth of Oyster River.

Just above the *Horse Races* is *Goat Island,* where the old Pascataqua bridge connected it with Newington, on the south, and Durham on the north, where *Franklin City* was laid out, when the bridge was finished in 1796. A plan of the proposed city is now in the Dover Public Library. It is very elaborate, and great expectations were connected with the scheme.

As regards the island: William Pomfrett, the 5th, 5mo, 1652, had the grant of "one island, lying in the river that runneth toward Oyster River, commonly called by the name of *Gooett Iland,* having *Seder (Cedar) point* on the north, and *Redding point* on the east, and *Fox poynt* on the southeastward." William Pomfrett gave the island to his grandson, William Damme, who built the historic Damme garrison, now in the Woodman Institute's care. In turn, "William Damme of Dover," and wife Martha (Nute) August 5, 1702, gave their son, Pomfrett Damme, the island "commonly called and known by ye name of *Goat Island,* lying between *Fox Point* and ye neck of land formerly granted unto Mr. Valentine Hill, deceased." It is mentioned in various other land transactions. It is forty-eight rods long. At the west end it is eleven rods wide. On this island was a tavern when the travel over the bridge was very heavy, between Portsmouth and Concord.

Cedar Creek is at the mouth of *Back River,* and is the point where the boundary of three towns meet, Durham, Madbury and Dover. There you can place your feet in all these towns at once. It is a long rock, or ledge. On the north of it is *Royal's Cove,* which is enclosed on its north side by *Clement's Point.* *Redding Point,* on the east of *Cedar Point,* is a high bluff. The channel at the entrance of Back River is quite crooked, making several turns before it begins to go straight up. Several years ago the Government dredged the channel to the lower fall of the Bellamy River, and made good landing places at the brick yards. In old times no ship-building was done on this river; the ship-yards were all on the *Fore River.* *Back Cove,* near the mouth, was the busy place of business, for loading vessels in the first century. *Hall's Spring* is on the east side of the cove. This cove was Dea. John Hall's shipping point.

IMPORTANT EVENTS IN THE HISTORY OF DOVER.

1623.—The beginning of the settlement at *Dover Point* in the spring of 1623, by Edward Hilton and his party.

1633.—The arrival of Capt. Thomas Wiggin's company in October, 1633. They organized the village on Dover Neck, and established the First Parish.

1638.—The organization of the First Church, in November, 1638, by the Rev. Hansard Knollys and Captain John Underhill. They came down here from Boston in that month and began the work of organizing.

1640.—The Combination Agreement for government of the Dover settlement, signed in 1640, Thomas Roberts being Governor.

1642.—The vote in 1641 to unite with the Massachusetts Bay Colony, which union was completed in 1642, and remained in force, practically, a half century.

1663.—The advent of the Quaker Women Missionaries in 1662, and their expulsion and whipping in 1663, by order of Major Richard Waldron.

1675.—The beginning of Indian wars in 1675, which continued fifty years, ending at Knox Marsh in 1725. The first garrisons were built in 1675. There had been no trouble with the Indians up to that date, hence no need of garrisons.

1675.—The advent of Captain John Mason, the land claimant, in 1675, who demanded rent from every land owner; and the settlements here on the Pascataqua River, were then first called "New Hampshire." So Dover is fifty years older than New Hampshire. For fifty years it was a town in Norfolk County, in Massachusetts.

1680.—The rule of the First Council of the Province of New Hampshire, beginning January 1, 1680. Then New Hampshire began to be a province, separate from Massachusetts.

1682.—The rule of Lieut.-Governor Cranfield, beginning January, 1682, and the Mason law suits, "to get control of land" that followed. All of the large owners in Dover were sued by the grandson of Capt. John Mason.

1689.—The massacre at Cochecho (present heart of the city) by the Indians, 28 June, 1689, when several garrisons were burned. Major Walderne, Richard Otis and others were killed. Twenty-nine were carried away prisoners to Canada.

1712.—The change of the seat of government from Dover Neck to Cochecho by the erection of a meeting-house on Pine Hill in 1712, in which religious services were held on the Lord's Day, and town meetings on other days until 1760. The house stood near the Cushing tomb, where the Rev. Jonathan Cushing and his family were interred. He died in 1767. It was in that house he preached forty years.

1717.—The ordination of the Rev. Jonathan Cushing as pastor of the First Church in 1717, which office he held fifty years. He was a graduate of Harvard College. The extant records of the Church begin with his pastorate. The house in which he lived stood near where the Hollingworth house stands on Stark Avenue.

1744.—Major Samuel Hale commanded a company of Dover men at the siege of Louisburg in 1644. He was a noted schoolmaster in Dover before that war, and later was far more noted as Master of the Grammar School at Portsmouth, which fitted New Hampshire boys for Harvard College. It was a great event when that company went down the river to Portsmouth and then embarked for Cape Britain.

1754.—April 22, 1754—The act for incorporating the parish of Somersworth into a town was passed by the Assembly, the town taking the name which the parish had formerly borne, and possessing the same boundaries. The parish

THE DAMME GARRISON: Now (1923) enclosed within a Colonnade at the Woodman Institute. (See page 201.)

had been incorporated in December, 1729, by act of the Assembly.

1755.—Madbury was disannexed from Dover and made a parish for the support of a minister this year; being, as they alleged, at a distance from the meeting-houses in Dover and Durham, and having some years since, at their own cost, built a meeting-house situated more conveniently.

1758.—The building of a new meeting-house in 1758 where the present brick edifice stands, which changed the place of town meetings from Pine Hill to Tuttle Square.

1762.—June 11, 1762, the First Church was incorporated as a Parish distinct from the town. After that town meetings ceased to have anything to do with appropriating money for support of the minister.

1765.—The election of Jeremy Belknap as assistant pastor of the First Church in 1765, and as pastor in 1767.

1775.—The beginning of the Revolution in 1775. Dover raised companies for the defense of Portsmouth, and for the Siege of Boston.

1776.—The reception of the news of the Declaration of Independence in July, 1776, which was celebrated, in part, by the Rev. Jeremy Belknap marching at the head of a procession of school children from the schoolhouse on Pine Hill to Col. John Waldron's residence beyond Garrison Hill, where the Page farmhouse now stands. A fife and drum furnished music. That schoolhouse stood where the brick house stood at the entrance to the cemetery, which was taken down in 1912.

1790.—The establishing of the first Post Office in Dover, 1790; Dr. Ezra Green (who died in 1847, aged 101 years) was appointed Post Master by President Washington. Dr. Green's territory extended to the White Mountains. He sent the mail along when there was anybody travelling that way.

1792.—The assembling of the Legislature (General Court) here in June, 1792. It was held in the building now used by Mr. Bradley as a garage, at Tuttle Square. That was the only year in which Dover was the Capital of New Hampshire. It was a great event in the town's history.

1817.—July 17, 1817, President Monroe visited Dover and spent the night here. A grand reception was given him. He dined at Wyatt's Inn (Old Dover Hotel). At night he was the guest of Hon. William Hale (in the Lafayette house.)

1825.—The visit of General Lafayette to Dover in June, 1825. He was the guest of Hon. William Hale and the guest chamber in which he slept is carefully preserved by the St. Thomas Parish, substantially as it was in 1825.

1825-1830.—The period of general religious commotion from 1825 to 1830, when other sects, Methodists, Baptists, Unitarians, organized societies, and the First Parish was greatly disturbed, so much so that in 1829 it tore down the wooden meeting-house, that was built in 1758, and erected the present brick edifice in place of it. The Unitarian meeting house was built the same year.

1842.—June 30, 1842, the first train of cars crossed the Cochecho River to the station on Third Street. A temporary depot was established at the Washington Street cut in October, 1841; the Directors of the Boston & Maine Railroad held their annual meeting in the new station.

1852.—The erection of a High School house in 1852.

1856.—The change from the town to the city form of government in 1856.

1860.—March 2, 1860, Abraham Lincoln visited Dover and delivered his famous New York speech, which later opened the way for him to become President.

1861.—The opening of the Civil War in April, 1861, and the speedy enlistment of a company of Dover men, who soon started for Washington. (Modern History of Dover begins here.)

A NOTED WOMAN OF DOVER, CHRISTINE OTIS BAKER.

Christine Otis, who married Capt. Thomas Baker, of Deerfield, Mass., in 1715, was born in Dover, in March, 1689, in her father's garrisoned house, which stood on the north side of where is now Milk Street, about half way between Central Avenue and Mt. Vernon street. She was daughter of Richard Otis, Esq., and his second wife, Grizel Warren, daughter of James and Margaret Warren, of Kittery, Me. The Otises and Warrens have an excellent ancestral record. When her father's garrison was burned and he was killed, 28 June, 1689, Christine was an infant, and was taken prisoner, with her mother, to Canada, by the Indians, as was also her half sister Rose, and her half brothers Stephen and John. October 15, 1693, Christine's mother, having been converted to the Romish faith, was married to a Frenchman named Philip Robitaile, and never returned to New England, dying in Montreal at the great age of 90 years. Her daughter had been baptized in the First Church at Dover, by the pastor, Rev. John Pike, as Margaret Otis, but when her mother joined the Roman Catholic Church and married a Frenchman, the priest rebaptized the daughter and gave her the name Christine, which name she retained to the end of her life, although good Parson Stoddard of Dover baptized her again when she returned and married Capt. Thomas Baker, in 1715, and gave her the old name Margaret.

In Montreal she was placed in a nunnery and educated in the Romish faith, till she was 15 years old. They tried to induce her to become a nun, and take the veils of the church, but she would not be persuaded; then they compelled her to marry a Frenchman, named La Beau, June 14, 1707; the record of her marriage is on file in Montreal. As the education of women then went she was well educated. She and her husband lived together about seven years, and then he died, leaving her with two or three children.

The first that she saw of Thomas Baker was in 1707, the year she married the Frenchman. Baker had been brought to Montreal, a prisoner, from Deerfield, Mass. He was a frisky young fellow, and tried to escape; the guard caught him, and, as he was about to be shot, a Frenchman intervened and paid a suitable ransom to save his life and permit him to return to his home in Massachusetts. Somehow, during the affair, which of course made a great commotion among the inhabitants, both French and English, Christine Otis Le Beau made the acquaintance of the young man, and gave him her sympathy and probably expressed her admiration for his courage in attempting to escape. It may have been her husband who paid the sum for Baker's ransom. Anyway, they became close friends then, and did not forget it in the seven years that followed.

Thomas Baker returned home, and in time became a Captain, and won fame in the public service. Christine remained in Canada, and in the course of seven years became the mother of three children. Then it came to pass that Thomas and Christine met again, and under circumstances entirely different from those under which they had parted in 1707.

Massachusetts sent a commission to Canada in 1714, to arrange for ransoming the English prisoners there, Major John Stoddard being at the head of it. Captain Thomas Baker was a member of the Commission, being famous now from his leadership of the Indian campaign in the White Mountain region, in which he secured the scalp of the famous Indian Sachem, Wattanummon, and by the deed perpetuated his name for ever in Baker river which joins the Pemegewassett north of Plymouth, N. H. It was near the junction of these rivers that the battle with the Indians took place. Moreover, besides having the river named for him, the General Court of Massachusetts gave him a reward of £20, *summa cum laude*.

Captain Baker, with the rest of the Commissioners, was in Montreal in March, 1714; they met the prisoners and the officials, and commenced negotiations; it does not seem necessary to speak further of the negotiations other than to say that Christine Otis Le Beau, then and there met Capt. Thomas Baker. She was a handsome widow of twenty-five years, in the bloom of health, sparkling with wit and womanly attractions; he was a bachelor, a few years older, tall, stalwart, and handsome in his military bearing; after they met and exchanged the usual formalities of such an occasion, she resolved in her own mind to return to New England; he resolved in his mind to rescue that handsome widow from the thrawls of popery, and the hated and detested Frenchmen.

Thus matters stood for awhile; negotiations made slow progress; the French would not consent for her to go; if she went, she must leave her children, and lose all of her property; she attempted to smuggle her personal property into a boat, to carry them to Quebec; the French priests discovered her work, and took everything from the boat.

About this time in the negotiations, Capt. Baker was ordered, by Major Stoddard, to go back to Boston and report progress. He attended to these duties and returned to Canada. The French continued as obstinate as ever in their refusal to let the captives go. The Captain and the widow held a council of war; she decided to leave her children, and all her property, except her wearing apparel and what she could carry in her hands; they secretly embarked on a boat and started on the voyage to Quebec, where Major Stoddard and the other Commissioners were then stationed. Just imagine that trip of 160 miles in an ordinary boat! Talk about romance! Why romance pales before the true story of heroism of this woman who so loved Old Dover, which she had seen only as a babe, and so loved the gallant captain, that she forsook all and trusted her life and her fortune to his care. It is easy enough to look back over 209 years, but what a struggle it must have been for her to look ahead sixty years.

Major Stoddard chronicles their arrival at Quebec in the summer of 1714; later they sailed with others, for Boston, where they arrived 21 September of that year.

From Boston she accompanied the Captain to Deerfield, and good Parson Stoddard took her in hand and soon made a Protestant of her; rebaptized her with her baby name, Margaret, and took her into the church.

The townspeople became interested in her welfare and enthusiastic in their praise of her noble qualities. December 14, 1714, the town granted her a valuable lot of land on condition that she marry Capt. Thomas Baker. She accepted the land and the conditions.

They were married in 1715, and set up housekeeping and farming in Deerfield, and remained there two years, leading a peaceful, quiet and happy life. Their first child was born 5 June, 1716; in due time good Parson Stoddard christened it Christine, having previously baptized the mother by her baby name of Margaret.

In 1717 they removed from Deerfield to Brookfield, where they resided on their farm till 1732. In 1718 she made a trip to Canada, with the object in view of getting her French children and bringing them to New England. Her efforts were unsuccessful. The Romish priests would not permit her to see them, much less bring them away; on the other hand they tried to persuade her to stay there; she would not listen to them, and so returned, grieved in heart but determined in spirit.

In 1719 Capt. Baker was elected Representative at the General Court of Massachusetts by the freeman of Brookfield, being the first to serve from that town. He served his town in that and various capacities, honorably and ably during the next ten years. It was in this town that most of their children were born, one of whom became one of Dover's distinguished men, Col. Otis Baker.

In 1727 Christine received a letter from the prelate who had been her priest in Canada, in which he urged her to return there and reunite with the Romish Church, presenting many theological reasons why he thought she ought to do so.

Instead of returning to Canada she turned the letter over to Gov. Burnett, who wrote an elaborate answer to the theological statements of the priest; both the letter and the Governor's answer are in print in the Massachusetts archives of that period. The French priest never ventured a reply, nor made further endeavors to get her back to Canada.

In 1732 they sold their Brookfield property, which was a comfortable estate, to a speculator, who in some way cheated them out of the whole amount of the sale, and left Capt. Baker and his family in very straightened circumstances.

They lived a while at Mendon, and next at Newport, R. I. On account of the high standing of Captain Baker, and his wife, the General Court of Massachusetts very generously aided them in their efforts to recover their fortunes. The Court was furthermore inclined to do this as Capt. Baker's health had given out, so that he could not do any work that required manual exertion. The Court granted Christine 500 acres of valuable land in York

County, Maine. She sold this land for a handsome sum of money, with which she built a house in Dover, to which they removed in 1734.

This house stood at the corner of Silver Street and Central Avenue, where now is the brick block. After she had built and furnished her house, she petitioned the General Court of New Hampshire for a license to keep a public house, which petition can be found in the published Provincial Papers of New Hampshire. Here she kept a public house for many years, and prospered in her business affairs, although her husband was an invalid all the rest of his years, till his death in 1753, while on a visit to friends in Roxbury, Mass. The record says he died of "the lethagy," which the doctors in the twentieth century would undoubtedly call appoplexy.

Christine died 23 February, 1773, aged 85 years, and her remains were interred in the Col. Baker burial lot on Pine Hill. I know not whether the spot can now be found, but be that as it may, a marker of some kind ought to be placed near the spot, if not on her grave, so that future generations may know and honor it.

Her record in Dover is of the best. Her house was a model of neatness, comfort and good cooking. When the Royal Governors passed through Dover they honored themselves by calling at her tavern; they always left with a feeling of good cheer and the highest respect for their hostess.

May 11th, 1735, she united with the First Church, Parson Cushing being pastor; she remained a devout member of this organization to the end of her life; during her last few years she was an invalid, but all her wants were kindly administered to by her son, Col. Otis Baker, and his family. Rev. Dr. Belknap, who was then pastor of the First Church, gave her that spiritual consolation which her four score years must have made her greatly enjoy; and when he closed her eyelids forever at four score and five, he performed the last sad rites over her remains.

Her son, Col. Otis Baker, lived in a house that he built several years before the Revolution where the Whidden house now stands at the corner of Silver and Atkinson streets. Of course then Atkinson Street did not exist, and Silver Street was simply the Barrington Road. It was in this house that Christine Baker passed her old age; Dr. Belknap was her next door neighbor, living where now the Belknap school house stands.

All of the Baker family in Dover are her descendants. Her career, as a whole, is undoubtedly the most remarkable of any Dover woman previous to the Revolution. Dover people, in the past, have been inclined to make too little account of its heroes and heroines, while it looked up to those in Massachusetts, because great writers and lecturers, and Boston newspapers for a hundred years, have continually talked about them and their great deeds. The heroine, Mrs. Baker, is rarely spoken of by Massachusetts writers as a Dover woman, though forty years of her life were passed here; and here her distinguished son and grandson lived, and many of their worthy descendants still reside.

Her husband, Capt. Thomas Baker, seems not to have taken an active part in public affairs after he came to Dover; he was broken in health before coming here, and appears to have been an invalid during his nearly twenty years of residence, coming in 1734 and dying in 1753. He assisted his wife in running the tavern, but from the first it was *her* tavern, not his. His record, during his vigorous years, was that of an active and honorable man, and he was held in high esteem by the authorities in Massachusetts, as also was his wife.

There ought to be a marker placed on the brick block at the corner of Silver Street and Central Avenue, designating that as the spot where Christine Otis Baker kept a tavern.

The reason she had to petition the General Court to grant her a license to keep a public house is supposed to be that the Selectmen of the town refused to grant it because they favored the proprietors of the old Dover Hotel.

EARLY LAND GRANTS.

The earliest land grant on record is of date 1642,—the Back River lots, an account of which has been given on a previous page. The following are on record of date 16 June, 1648, being the assignment of lots at "Cochecho Marsh," and arranged as follows:—

EARLY LAND GRANTS. 233

1—Antony Emery, 12 yeckeres.
2—Blank.
3—Mr. Belley, 6 yeckeres.
4—George Wallton, 6 yeckeres.
5—Ye Church, 12 yeckeres.
6—Blank.
7—John Hall, 6 yeckeres.
8—John Heard, 6 yeckeres.
9—Henry Becke, 6 yeckeres.
10—William Walldon, 6 yeckeres.
11—Mr. Nutter, 6 yeckeres. In a later hand writing:—This 11th lot is exchanged with Edward Colcord for his 6 acer lote of the marsh at the Great Bay.
12—John Newgrove, 6 yeckeres.
13—Henry Langster, 6 yeckeres.
14—John Godder, 6 yeckeres
15—James Newett, 6 yeckeres.
16—Robert Huckins, 6 yeckeres.
17—James Rallens, 6 yeckeres.
18—William Furburse, 6 yeckeres.
19—Richard Walldone, 6 yeckeres.
20—John Backer, 6 yeckeres.

Next joining to yes lotes is 10 yeckeres given to John Backer & ye rest is given to Richard Walldon by ye town meeting.

(Signed)
Hatevill Nutter
John Becker.
Richard Walden
John Hall—H—his mark.
John Godder.
James Newte.

COCHECHO MARSH.

Cochecho Marsh is at the upper side of Garrison Hill, and the larger part of it is now in the town of Rollinsford. It is otherwise called *Great Cochecho Marsh* and *Great Fresh Marsh*. It is mentioned as early as May 2, 1642, when lots of six acres therein were granted to Anthony Emery and Stephen Tedder. Twenty acre lots of the same size were granted to other Dover settlers June 16, 1648, as shown on the preceding page. A path led to this marsh as early as 1648, called the "Cartway," which is the present Garrison Hill Road, or Central Avenue. This marsh is mentioned June 17, 1677, when William Wentworth conveyed to George Ricker "a piece of marsh and swamp-land near Cochecho, near ye lower part of ye marsh commonly called 'Cochecho Marsh,' the lower end butting upon ye northern side of ye brook which doth run out of ye sd marsh upon a little pond by ye sd brook." The only brook that answers to this description is the *"Styx,"* which flows through the marsh in the vicinity of the "No-Bottom" Pond. The "Styx" has its source in the so called "Hussey Springs," at the foot of the hill at the west end of the marsh.

Peter Coffin conveyed to Maturin Ricker, December 26, 1682, twelve acres at the lower end of the marsh commonly called "Cochecho marsh" in Dover, bounded south by a brook of water which issues out of said marsh, and northeast by a small stream of water which empties itself into said brook. A final division of this marsh was made by vote of the town April 16, 1722.

In passing, it is interesting to note that the six acres granted to John Heard, in 1648, were inherited by his son, Tristram Heard (Hurd), who built a house where the present Rollins "Memorial Home for Nurses" (of the Wentworth Hospital) stands. In Indian war time it was a garrisoned house. That house and land was inherited by Judge Ezekiel Hurd, whose only daughter married Mr. Harrison Haley. After the death of Mr. Haley and his wife the property passed to the ownership of the Trustees of the Wentworth Hospital.

THE EARLIEST TAX LISTS.

In 1648, in town meeting—"A town rate of 4d on a pound was made 19th, 10 mo, on the following persons:—

	pd.	s.	d.	Rate		
Joseph Austin	91.	10.	0.	1	11	2
Charles Adams	31	10	0	0	5	4
John Ault	69	0	0	1	3	0
William Beard	76	0	0	1	5	6
Jonas Binns	42	0	0	0	14	4
John Bickford	115	10	0	1	18	6.
John Baker	92	10	0	1	10	10

EARLIEST TAX LISTS.

	pd.	s.	d.		Rate	
Henry Beck	40	16	0	0	13	7
Tho. Beard	62	0	0	1	0	8.
Geo. Branson	30	0	0	0	10	0
Tho. Canney	84	0	0	1	8	0
Philip Chasley	78	10	0	1	6	6
John Damme	104	10	0	1	14	10.
William Drew	70	0	0	1	3	4
Antho. Emery	108	10	0	1	16	0
more to pay for bull	2	10	0			10.
William Furber	81	10	0	1	7	2
Darby Field	81	0	0	1	7	0
Tho. Footman	60	0	0	1	0	0
Tho. Fursen	16	0	0	0	5	0
John Goddard	129	10	0	2	2	2
Ambrose Gibbons	86	0	0	1	8	0
Matthew Gyles	194	10	0	3	3	2.
Samuel Haines	65	10	0	1	1	10
Jno. Hall	79	12	0	1	6	8
John Hilton	46	0	0	0	15	4.
Robt. Hethersey	60	0	0	1	0	0
John Hall	42	0	0	0	14	0
Tho. Johnson	40	0	0	0	13	4.
Oliver Kent	70	10	0	1	10	0.
Henry Langstaff	75	0	0	1	5	0
Tho. Layton	156	10	0	2	12	0
Francis Littlefield	60	15	0.	1	0	3
Mrs. Mathews	139	10	0.	2	3	2.
John Martin	41	10	0	0	13	10
Hatevill Nutter	78	6	0	1	6	3
James Nute	83	0	0	1	7	8.
William Pomfrett	71	0	0	1	3	8
Mr. Roberts	69	10	0	1	3	2
William Roberts	46	10	0	0	15	2
James Rawlins	60	0	0	1	0	0
Jeffrey Ragg	4	0	0	0	1	4
William Storey	66	4	0	1	2	1
Edw. Starbuck	45	10	0	0	15	4
Tho. Stevenson	50	0	0	0	16	4
Mr. Seeley	8	0	0	0	2	8
Francis Small	10	0	0	0	3	4
George Smith	32	8	0	0	10	9
John Ture	35	0	0	0	1	8
Henry Tibbetts	87	0	0	1	9	2

	pd.	s.	d.	Rate		
John Tuttle	60	0	0	1	3	0
Thomas Trickett	104	10	0	1	8	4
Thomson point house	4	0	0	0	1	4
George Webb	46	0	0	0	12	8
George Walton	84	0	0	1	7	4
Tho. Willey	71	10	0	1	3	6
Rich. Walderne	141	0	0	2	3	4
more to pay					3	4
Richard Yorke	72	8	0	1	4	0

The tax list of 1650, for the public charges of the town, is as follows:

	Pd.	s.	d.		Pd.	s.	d.
Thomas Roberts	1	00	6	Richard Walderne	3	2	0
Ralph Hall	1	2	6	Abraham Radford	0	10	0
Thomas Beard	0	13	4	Peter Coffin	0	10	0
A. Emery	0	6	0	Valentine Hill	2	2	0
John Tuttle	0	19	0	William Beard	1	4	6
William Storey	1	0	4	Philip Chesley	1	2	0
John Hall, Sr.	1	4	6	Thomas Johnson	0	14	8
Elder Nutter	1	15	6	John Hall	0	10	0
John Roberts	0	13	8	Ambrose Gibbons	1	4	8
Anthony Nutter	0	14	6	William Roberts	0	17	2
James Nute	1	0	8	Thomas Stevenson	0	16	0
William Furber	1	14	0	William Drew	0	12	4
Thomas Canney	1	7	6	Matthew Giles	2	0	0
Henry Tebbetts	1	11	2	Oliver Kentt	0	13	2
Isaac Nash	0	10	0	Charles Adams	1	0	10
Thomas Clayton	0	10	0	Mrs. Mathes	1	0	0
Rice Howell	0	10	0	James Bines	0	14	4
John Damme	1	14	8	John Bickford	1	17	4
Thomas Layton	2	12	5	Thomas Willey	1	13	2
William Pomfrett	1	2	2	John Allt	1	3	4
Henry Langstaff	1	3	4	George Webb	0	3	4
Thomas Trickey	1	11	0	George Branson	0	10	0
John Martin	0	17	0	Philip Lewis	0	18	8
John Hall, Jr.	0	12	6	William Follett	0	10	0
John Lause	0	14	0	Thomas Footman	0	12	8
Richard Keatler	1	5	4	Richard Yorke	1	0	6
James Rawlins	0	17	2	John Hill	0	10	0
William Wentworth	1	2	8	Goodie Feild	1	0	0
Joseph Austin	1	17	4		61	12	1

EARLY TAX LISTS.

"Rate maed the 12th, 8th, (16) 58 for Mr Reyner his preuetione."

	Pd.	s.	d.		Pd.	s.	d.
Isake Nash	0	12	3	Tho. Downes	0	6	11
Job Clements	1	9	1	Mr. Roberts	0	7	1½
William Pomfrett	1	8	9	Tho. Beard	1	12	8
Tho. Layton	2	12	6	John Hall, Deacon	0	16	0
John Damme, Sr	1	11	3	John Tuttell	0	11	9
John Damme, Juner	0	11	1	left. Hal	0	13	6.
William Storey	0	16	9	Elder Nutter	1	8	1
Joseph Asten	1	5	11	Tho. Caney	1	16	2
John Roberds	1	10	10	John Hilton	0	7	2
Ralph Twomly	0	9	4	James Nutte	0	12	6
Jeremy Tebetts	0	12	½	Henry Tebbetts	1	16	2
Tho. Nocke	0	8	7	William Tomson	0	5	0

BLOODY POINT.

	Pd.	s.	d.		Pd.	s.	d.
James Rallins	0	12	6	Richard Catter	1	1	6
Tho. Trickey	1	0	4	John Bickford	0	13	10
Henry Lankster	1	11	6	William ffurber	1	4	11
Antony nutter	1	5	1	Tho. Roberds	0	12	6.
Michiell Brane	0	6	0				

COCHECHAE.

	Pd.	s.	d.		Pd.	s.	d.
Edward Starbuck	1	3	5	Phelep Cromwell	0	6	4
Peter Coffin	0	11	8	Nathaniel Starbuck	0	6	8
Henry hobes	0	5	0	Edward Paterson	0	5	0
Richard Sloper	0	1	8	William Shiffilld	0	9	0
Tho. Hanson	0	18	0	Capt. Walldern	3	3	4
Ickebod Shiffield	0	5	0	George Goldweir	1	5	2
Roberd Jones	0	19	8	Richard Otes	0	15	2
Charll Buckner	0	5	0	William haket	0	5	0
Paid in before	1	8	11½	William love	0	5	4
John heard	1	9	4	henrey magoune	0	5	2.
John lovring	0	5	0	William ffollette	9	3	4.
Elder Wentworth	1	4	10				
James Grant	0	8	4		48	19	10½
Barthellme lippincotte		5	0				
Capt. Wiggin	1	16	8				
Mr. Broughton	0	16	8				

"Oyster River prouition Rate maed the 22:9::(16)59."

	Pd.	s.	d.	The great Rate Pd.	s.	d.
Mr. Hill	2	12	8	5	5	4
Thomas umfirie the stiller	2	8	4	0	16	8
John meader	0	13	4	1	7	4
William Graues	0	5	0	0	10	0
Ens. John Daves	0	15	0	1	10	0
Juner William Williams		8	0	0	16	0
James Bunker	0	8	0		16	0
Will ffollett	1	0	0	2	0	0
Thomas Jonson	0	13	4	1	6	8
Phellep Chesley	1	12	8	3	5	4
Roberd Junkes	0	8	4	0	16	8
James Jackson	0	5	0		10	0
Walter Jackson	0	5	0		10	0
William Beard	2	7	8	4	15	4.
John Woodman	0	15	0	1	10	0
Patric Jemeson	0	15	0	1	10	0
Henrey Browne	0	10	0	1	0	0
Thomas Dowty	0	10	0	1		
James Oer	0	10	0	1		
James mellman	0	10	0	1		
Edward Arwin	0	10	0	1		
John Barber	0	5	0	0	10	0
Edward Patterson.	0	10	0	1		
Roberd Burnom	1	6	8	2	13	4.
William Pitman	0	10	0	1		
William Roberds	0	10	0	1		
William Williams, sin	1	5	8	2	11	4
Thomas Steuenson.	1	13	4	1	6	8
William Drew	0	11	8	1	4	4.
Rice howell	0	5	0	0	10	0
Joseph ffilld	0	8	4	0	16	8
Mathew Gills	1	6	8	2	13	4
	24	1	6	47	6	0
Mathew Williams	0	10	6	1	1	0
Benjamin Mathews	1	5	0	2	10	0
Charlls Adams	0	13	0	1	6	8
John Bickford	1	6	8	2	13	4
Thomas Welley	0	18	4	1	16	8
John Ault	0	19	10	1	19	8
Richard Braye	0	6	10	0	13	8

	Pd.	s.	d.	Pd.	s.	d.
John Hill	0	6	8	0	13	4.
Thomas ffootman	1	3	4	2	6	8
Richard Yorke	0	19	4	1	18	8
John Martin	0	18	0	1	16	0.
John Godder	1	14	8	3	9	4
Benjamin Hull	0	8	4	0	16	8
John Hilton	0	6	8	0	13	4
James Nutte, Juner	0	5	0	0	10	0
Ollever Kent	0	8	4	0	16	8
John Hance	0	5	0	0	10	0
John Davill	0	5	0	0	10	0
Roberd Hussey	0	5	0	0	10	0
William Risbey (Risley)	0	5	0	0	10	0
Thomas Ginn (Green)	0	5	0	0	10	0
Steuen (Westinman)	0	5	0			
Will Jones	0	5	0	0	10	0
	14	0	2	28	11	4

OYSTER RIVER RATES 1661.

The first group of figures in the following list is headed—"Oyster riuer 3d Raet. 4: 9 mo. in ye yeir 61."

The second group was probably in the same year, but another levy and is headed—"Oyster Riu—in ye yeir—."

	lb	s	d	lb	s	d
John Godder	1	14	1	1	9	5
Einsin John Davis	1	0	3	0	19	2
John Meader	1	1	0	0	14	0
John Martin	1	10	0	0	19	6
Richard Yorke	2	5	6	1	10	4
Joseph ffilld	0	10	7	0	12	5
hew doenn	0	9	9	0	6	6
Mr. Hills mill and house and lands		15	0			
Will Williams juner		12	6	0	8	4
James Bunker	0	7	6	0	5	4
william ffollett	1	17	6	1	5	0
Estat of Tho. Jonson	0	12	6	0	8	4
Phellep Chesley	2	17	6	1	18	4
Jams and wat Jackson	1	7	6	0	18	4

	lb	s	d	lb	s	d
Will Beard	3	11	1	2	7	5
John Woodman	1	7	6	0	18	4.
Patrick Jemson	1	2	6	0	15	0
henrey Browne	1	12	4	1	1	8
Thomas Dowty	1	12	4	1	1	8
James Oer	1	12	4	1	1	8
James Medlton	1	12	4	1	1	8
Edward Eirwing	1	12	4	1	1	8
John Barber	0	7	6	0	5	0
Elexsander mackdonell	0	7	6	0	5	4
Elexsander Gowen	0	7	6	0	11	0
Edward Patterson	0	15	0	0	11	0
John Hance	0	7	6	0	5	0
Roberd Burnam	2	0	0	1	6	8
William Pittman	0	15	0	0	10	0
William Roberds	0	15	0	0	10	0
William Willyans sinyer	2	2	0	1	5	8
Thomas Steuenson	1	0	0	0	13	4
William Drew	0	17	6	0	11	8
Rice Howell	0	7	6	0	5	0
matthew Willyams	0	7	6	0	5	0
mathew Gilles	2	0	0	1	6	6
Benjamin hull	0	12	6	0	8	4
Benjamin mathews	2	2	0	1	6	8
Charles Adams	0	17	6	0	11	8
John Bickford sinyer	2	0	0	1	6	8
Thomas Welley	1	5	0	0	18	4
John Allt	1	9	9	0	19	10
henrey hollawaye	0	10	10	1	6	9
John hill	0	17	6	0	11	8
Thomas ffootman	1	7	6	0	18	2
John Hilton	0	7	6	0	5	0
Olever Kent	0	12	6	0	8	4
Teackge Riall	0	7	6	0	5	0
Josephf Smeth	0	7	6	0	5	0
Dauey Danell	0	7	6	0	5	0
Steuen Jones	0	7	5	0	5	0
John Collman	0	7	6	0	5	0
John Ninell	0	7	6	0	5	0
Roberd Chesley	0	7	6	0	5	0
Steuen Robinson	0	7	6	0	5	0

LAUNCHING OF THE SHIP "DOVER," at Newington Shipyard, in 1919. Mrs. Mabelle P. Smalley, Sponsor. (See page 220.)

	lb.	s.	d	lb.	s.	d.
Will Jones	0	7	6	0	5	0
Samewell —iamin	0	7	6	0	5	0
Will Shu—	0	15	0	0	10	0

The plase———the Raet———unto is Einsin John Daues. Josephf lessen forgot 7s 6d yet down in ye Constables Rate.

A tax rate was made in 1662, over the whole town, to pay Mr. Reyner the amount due him as salary, in provisions, at the following prices:—Beef, 3½ pence per pound; Pork, 4½; Wheat, 6 shillings per bushel; malt, 6 shillings; peas, 5 shillings.

At this time 28 taxpayers lived on Dover Neck; 29 lived at Cochecho; 12 at Bloody Point; 42 at Oyster River; one at Belleman's Bank, William Follett.

"A Rate maed ye 19th of 9 Month 1662 for Mr. Rayners Prouition."

	lb.	s.	d.
Thomas Kemble	0	5	6
Capt. Walter Barefoot	0	5	6
John Dam sinyer	0	14	0
Thos Layton	1	4	6
Thomas Beard	1	4	6
Deacon Hall	0	15	6
Job Clement	0	7	0
Thomas Roberds sinyer	0	3	1½
John Tuttle sinyer	0	6	2
Thomas Umphres, stiller	0	7	6
Elder Nutter	0	14	6
Left hall	0	6	6
henrey Tebbett	0	2	6
Thomas Nocke	0	6	8
Jeremt Tebbett	0	7	10
James Newtt sinyer	0	11	9
Jam Newtt juner	0	2	0
Bartholomew leppincutt	0	2	6
humfrey Varney	0	2	11
Nicholas Vutter	0	2	6
Edward Waymeoth	0	2	9
Isakes Stikes	0	2	11
Christopher Batt	0	12	6
Thomas Roberds juner	0	10	7½
Sar John Roberds	0	16	2½

	lb.	s.	d.
Thomas Canney	0	17	6½
Jeddediah Andress	0	6	8
William Pomfrett	0	5	8
Charles Buckner	0	4	12
lasaries Permett	0	2	6
	11	13	2

"This Rate is to be payd in Beffe at 3d ½ p lb; Pork at 4½; wheat at 6 s p boshell; Mallt at 6s; Barley at 6s; Pease at 5 s.

(Margin) This rate charged to the old acc.

Cochechae 1662	lb.	s.	d.
Capt. Walderne	1	9	10
Peter Coffin	1	13	11
James Coffin, Robert Euens, John Church			
	0	12	6.
Thomas Payne	0	2	6
John Screuen	0	3	7
Josephf Sanders	0	2	0
Thomas Wiggin	0	14	3
henrey hobes	0	5	11
John louring	0	9	8
Roberd Jones	0	4	1
Richard Ottes	0	11	4
Thomas Downes	0	4	5
Elder Wentworth	0	9	0
Samewell Wentworth	0	4	2
John Heard	1	0	1
James Keyd	0	3	4
Phellep Cromwell	1	1	4
Clement Raphf	0	3	4
John Adams	0	2	6
Will horne	0	4	0
Thomas hanson	0	12	11
Tobey hanson	0	4	0
Raphf Twamley	0	3	3
George Walderne	0	2	7
Quamphegon Mill	0	16	8
Josephf Asten	0	10	4
Thomas Rallines	0	2	6
William ffollett at Bellemes banke			
	0	4	2.
	12	0	2.

EARLY TAX RATES.

Blode poynt.	lb.	s.	d.
henrey lankester	1	0	4½
Richard Catter	0	10	3.
Michill Brane	0	7	1
Thomas Trickey	0	14	8
James Rallines	0	8	2
William Shuckford	0	5	4
Sargant hall	1	5	1½
William Furber	0	16	1½
Antoney Nutter	1	2	9½
John Bickford juner	0	6	11
Richard Rooe	0	4	0
John Dam juner	0	7	6

"Prouition Rate made the 19th of the 9th month (1662) apon the inhabitants in Oyster Riuer at a penny apon the pound."

	lb.	s.	d.
Richard Yorke	0	15	1½
John martin	0	12	4½
John Godderd	1	5	6
hew Donn	0	3	4
Edward Erwin & Compey	0	3	4
Patrick Jameson	0	9	9
Walter Jackson	0	15	1
Edward Patterson	0	5	9
Roberd Burnum	0	14	2.
William Pettman	0	5	5
William Wilyams sinyer	0	13	4
Josephf Filld	0	4	2
William Roberds	0	3	7
Phellep Chesley	1	0	5
John Woed	0	6	10
John Hance	0	3	4
Thomas Johnson his estate in the hands of William Furber and William Follett	0	6	11
William Drew	0	11	2
Matthew Gills	0	13	9
Beniamin hull	0	8	7
mathew williams	0	2	11
Charles Addams	0	5	9
Dauey and Phellep Cromwell	0	9	9
Mrs. Mathews	0	1	4
Thomas Welley	0	7	3

	lb.	s.	d
John Bickford sinyer	0	16	2
Thomas ffootman	0	14	7
John Allt	0	9	10
henry holloway	0	5	3
william Perkins	0	2	10
william williams juner	0	4	8
Einsin John Daues	0	8	3
Josephf Smeth	0	6	1
William Beard	0	19	10
John Woodman	0	9	10
James Smeth	0	2	6
John Smeth	0	2	6
John hilton	0	3	7
Olluer Kent	0	1	8
Teage Reiall	0	2	11
Steuen Jones	0	2	6
William Jones	0	2	6
	20	9	3

"A Prouition Rate made ye 7th, 10th month 1663 Apon all ye Inhabitants of this township of Dover at a penny apon the pound."

	lb.	s.	d.
Mr. Thomas Wiggin	0	3	3
Capt. Barffoott	0	6	3
Thomas Roberds, siny	0	6	0
Peter Gland filled	0	3	11
William Pomfrett	0	9	1
John hall, Deacon	0	10	5
Thomas layton	1	6	7
John Dam siny	0	14	6
Elder Nutter	0	13	6
Thomas Beard	0	14	8
left hall	0	4	11
wedoew Tutell	0	3	1
Thomas Nocke	0	7	2½
Thomas whitehouse	0	2	6
Jeremie Tebbetts	0	8	1
Nichles Vetter	0	7	10
James Newtt siny	0	11	9
Thomas Caney	0	19	0
Sar John Roberds	0	18	2½

EARLY TAX RATES.

	lb.	s.	d.
Thomas Roberds juner	0	9	1
Judiae Andros	No figures.		
Isakes Stokes	0	4	7
Edward Weymoeth	0	3	3
Sarie Astin	0	3	4
Humfrey Varney	0	2	11

Blodie poynt.

	lb.	s.	d.
henrey lankster	1	2	3½
Mickell Brane	00	7	7
Thomas Trickey	00	17	10
Richard Catter	00	10	8½
John Bickford juner	00	6	4
James Rallins	00	14	10
Christafer Batt	00	2	8
William Shuckforth	00	8	2
John Dam juner	00	8	8
Antoney Nutter	00	2	1 Ano.
Richard Rooe	Figures crossed out		
William ffurber	1	0	4
sargant John Hall	00	7	10½
John Woddin	No figures		

(*Cochecho.*)

Capt walldern	1	9	2
Mr Peter Coffin	1	16	5
John heard	1	00	9
Elder wentworth	00	18	11
Richard Otes	00	13	1
Thomas hanson	00	12	9
John Scruin	00	5	6
Thomas Downes	00	3	11
James Coffin	00	5	4½
Robert Euens	00	4	5½
John Church	00	5	4½
William horn	00	4	7½
John kiniston	00	2	6
Samewell wintworth	00	3	7
Thomas Payne	00	4	2
George Walldern	00	4	7

	lb.	s.	d.
Richard Scaman	00	4	6
Josephf Sanders	00	4	6
Christin Dolac	00	6	4
lasaret Permit	00	4	6
John Addams	00	4	6
Tobey hanson	00	4	6
Raphfe Twamley	00	4	6
Thomas Rallins	00	2	6
Clement Rafe	00	4	2
Antony Page	00	2	6
John Sharpe	00	3	4
Phelep Cromwell	1	5	7
Abraham folletts man	00	2	6
william layton	00	3	4
henrey hobes	00	6	8
John louring	00	10	10
ye mill at Quamphigon	00	6	8
wm. follet at Belli-bank	0	4	2
capt. Wiggin at tollend	0	10	0
Capt. Clark at Tollend	0	4	2
mr nathaniell frier	00	4	2
	14	6	0

"Oyster River Prouetion Rate made throwe the hole towneshep ye 7th 10th month 1663."

	lb.	s.	d.
Roberd Burnum	0	17	6
william Pettman	0	5	9
William willyams siney	0	12	1
Thomas morssie	0	3	4
Tho. steuensons estat	0	4	3
William Drew	0	8	11½
matthew Giles	0	13	8
Charles Addams	0	5	10
Thomas welley	0	8	1½
John Bickford sin	0	15	6
Tho. ffootman	0	13	2
John Allt	0	1	7
William Pirkins	0	2	9
William Durgen	0	3	4
Joseph filld	0	5	9
Dauey Danell	0	8	8½
Phellep Cromet	0	3	2

EARLY TAX RATES. 247

	lb.	s.	d.
Thomas Dowty	0	13	6½
John Godder	1	9	11½
Richard Yorke	0	15	9½
John martin	0	12	4
hew Dunn	0	3	4
John hillton	0	4	0
Beiniamen hull	0	8	0½
Phellep Chesley	0	5	0½
Elexsander mack Donnell (Mackdaniel) his estate			
	0	5	3.
walter Jackson	0	12	9
Pattrick Jemison	0	9	9
Edward Patterson	0	5	10
Henrey Browne & Compeny	0	17	2
John meader	0	9	6
Thomas humfries	0	11	4
Steuens Jones	0	2	4
will willyams Juner	0	5	2
william ffollett	1	00	10
william Roberds	No figures.		
James Bunker	No figures.		
Thomas Jonson his estat	No figures.		
Steuen Robinson	0	2	6
James Smeth	0	2	6
William Beard	1	2	1
——— Smeth	0	4	7½
——— Daues	0	10	11½
	22	00	3.
John Woodman	0	9	10
Mr. Hills estat	1	5	0
Tage Riall	0	2	6
mathew Williams	0	2	1
Roberd Chapman	0	2	6
Patrick Dennmark	0	2	6
	2	5	3
	22	0	3
	24	5	6

"Theis Rate is to be payd in Beff at 3d ½ p lb.; Porke at 4d ½ per lb. Wheat at 5 s p boshell; malt at 6 s p boshell; Barley at 6s p boshell; Pease at 4 sh p boshell.- If aney shall deny to pay, ye Constabells are to take it By way of distress."

"A Prouetion Rate maed the 2d loth mo. 1666 for Mr Rayner at a penny in the pound throwe the hole towneshep."

Dover Neck	lb.	s.	d.
Thomas Layton	1	7	4½
John Hall, Deacon	1	12	10
John Damme sinyer	0	15	4½
Thomas Beard	0	15	8
Jeremie Tebetts	0	9	6½
Thomas Roberds juner	0	12	10
Thamas Caney	1	2	7
Elder Nutter	0	15	10.
henrey Tebtes	0	7	7½
John Roberds	0	14	11
James Newtt juner	0	5	9
Capt. Barefoot	0	4	2
Tho. Roberds siny	0	5	1
henrey Kerke	0	5	0
Mr. Job Clements	0	19	5
John Tuttell	0	4	2
Thomas Whithouse	0	2	8
Judediah Andros	0	3	9
John Pinkoem	0	2	6
James Newtt siny	0	12	0
Isakes Stokes	0	4	7
William Pomfrett	0	10	11

Bloody Poynt.	lb.	s.	d.
Henrey Lankster	1	6	6
William ffurber	1	17	7½
Richard Catter	0	12	1½
John hall sargent	0	15	8
James Rallins	0	12	7
Thomas Trickey	0	18	10
John Bickford jun	0	6	11
Michall Brane	0	8	10
Richard Rooe	0	5	10
John Dam juner	0	1	10
William shuckforth	0	9	10

EARLY TAX RATES.

	lb.	s.	d.
Antoney Nutter	1	4	4½
Abraham Newtt	0	3	1
Exelsander Wallden	0	2	6
Thomas Pinckom	0	2	6
Phellep Cromwell	0	15	0

COCHECHAE	lb.	s.	d.
Capt. Wallderne	5	9	2½
Leften Coffin	1	13	9
Samewell Hall	0	2	6
Nathell Steuens	0	2	6
John willson	0	2	6.
Samewell Seward	0	2	6
John Chirch	0	3	10
Antoney Page	0	2	6
Lazearus Permit	0	2	6
John ham	0	3	4
Jukin Jones	0	2	6
Clark Gilles	0	2	6
Biniamen Heard	0	3	11
Thomas Downes	0	5	3½
Wedowe hanson	0	10	0
Tobias hanson	0	4	0
Thomas hanson	0	4	2
Robert Euens	0	5	2
Ralphf Twamley	0	7	1
John winget	0	8	10
	11	19	4
Humfrey varney	0	4	11
Jeriemy hodsdon	0	4	4
John Heard	0	15	3½
Josephf Sanders	0	3	9
Thomas Payne	0	3	4
Richard Rowell	0	2	6
Thomas hamacke	0	3	7
William horne	0	8	4½
william Ceiam?	0	3	4
John Addams	0	2	6
John Scriuen	0	7	5½
Quamphigone Mill	0	16	9
John louring	0	5	8

	lb.	s.	d.
henrey hobbes	0	16	4.
John foste	0	6	8
William layton	0	4	11
Elder Wentworth	1	1	10
Samewell Wentworth	0	5	10
Mr. George Wallderne	0	5	3
Richard Otes	0	15	10.
James Coffin	0	8	4
	8	17	10

OYSTER RIVER.

	lb.	s.	d.
William ffollett	1	5	0
Will Roberds	0	3	6
Will wilyams juner	0	5	0¼
John Meader	0	5	3
Steuen Jones	0	8	1
Nicloes harris	0	3	1
Einsine John Daues	0	7	4½
henrey Browne	0	17	10
Roberd watson	0	2	6
Patricke Denmarke	0	2	6
walter Jackson	0	8	4
Matthew willyams	0	3	7
John Smethe	0	3	4
Josephf Smethe	0	2	4
James Smethe	0	2	6
William Drew	0	15	8
William Beard	0	16	8
Matthew Gilles	0	13	10.
William Pitman	0	6	0
Josephf Steunson	0	8	7
Salethel Denboe	0	2	6
William willyams sinyer	0	12	4
John Woodman	0	10	7
Thomas morise	0	5	0
william Dergin	0	5	0
John Hilton	0	3	3
Richard Yorke	0	15	10
John Martin	0	11	5½
John Godder	1	6	11½
Arter Bennett	0	2	0

PROVISION RATE.

	lb.	s.	d.
Charells Addams	0	6	5
Thomas welley	0	8	6
Thomas Edgerley	0	2	9
William Perkins	0	3	10
Abraham Collines	0	2	6
John Allt	0	2	5
John Bickford siney	0	6	5
Sachrey ffilld	0	3	4
Mickall Symonds	0	3	4
Teag Riall	0	3	2
James huggins	0	2	11
Edward lethers	0	2	6
Phellep Chesley	1	2	3
Thomas Chesley	0	4	5
Josephf filld	0	4	2
Tage Danell	0	3	4
Pattrick Jemson	0	12	3.
Roberd Burnum	0	10	0
Daucy Danell & Phellep Cromett		7	3
Thomas footman	0	15	2
Tho. feloes, John Parnill and ther men and vessell.	1	10	0
Steuen Robinson	0	2	6
	8	05	6

"This Rat made at a penny in the pound for Mr. Raners proution and is in part of his sallery for the last yeir and to be returned to his hand by the Constabell, and if in case aney shall refuse to pay apon demand, thear in his maighteys name, to Empower you to take it by was destres, witness our hands.

"Bef at 3d p lb.; Pork at 4d ½ p lb.; wheat at 5s p boshell; Indian Corne 4s p boshell; pease at 4s p boshell."

PROVISION RATE FOR 1675.

OF DOVER NECK, COCHECHO, OYSTER RIVER AND BLOODY POINT.

There are no other tax lists in the old records; the town soon after this date became one of the towns of the provnce of New Hampshire.

DOVER NECK.

Mr. Nutter
Deacon Hall
Deacon Damme
Thomas Canie, junior
Henrey Tibbit
Phellep Benmore
John Pinckham
Jeremi Tibits
Tho. Beard
Tho. Perkins
Isaac Stockes
Tho. Roberts
Joe Tuttle
Philip Crumell
Rich. Pinckham
Tho. Whitehouse.
John Roberts
Leiftenant Pomfrit
James Newtt junior
Mr Clements
Johnathan Wattson
Tho. Leighton
Thomas paine
John Daues
John Heard
Mr. George Walderne
Ralf Twamlie
Ezekiel Wentworth
William Taskett
widdow Hanson
John Church.

James Newt senior
Mr. Clements
Abraham Newt.
Richard Rich.
John Dercie
Thos. Teare?
Ralph welch
Zacharie ffield
Nathaniell Stephens
ginkin Jones
John Ham
William Horne
Tho. Hamett
John Elis
Humphire Varnie.
(Nine names missing.)
david larkin.
Tho. Austyn
Tho. Haines.
Capt. Walderne
George Ricker and brother,
Richard Otis
John Gearish
Tho: Hanson.
Robert Evens.
gershom Wentworth
James Coffen
Tho. downes
Mark Giles
Benjamin Heard.

BLOODY POYNT.

Sargant Hall
William ffurber
Antony Nutter
(Eight names are missing.)

Henerie Langster
william ffurber junior
Edward Allen

OF OYSTER RIVER.

Ensign Davis
James Huckins
John Alt
John Bickford

(————)
John Hill.
Thomas Edgerlie
John Meader.

Tho. Willie
Joseph Smith
Stephen Jones
Robert Watson
John Davis junior
William Hill
John york
Nicholas dow
Charles Adams
Joseph Stimson
Stephin Willie
Joseph ffield
Tho: Moris
Nicholas ffollett
Robert Burnum
Mr. John Cutt
   (Non Resident)
Salathie Denbow
Beenjamin Mathews
william perkins
George Goe (Gee?)

William Williams junior
Philip Cheslie senior.
Walter Jackson.
Edward Leathers.
James Smith
Tho: & Philip Cheslie
John Godard.
Benjamin york.
Samuel Willie.
Nicholas Haris.
———— Stimson.
John dow.
William Durgin.
John Woodman
William Williams senior

Nathaniel Lummack
David Daniel
ffrancis drew.
William pitmans.
William ffollett

"This provision is to be paid att ye price followeth—Wheat 5s 6d p bushel; Indian Corne 4s p bushel; pease 4 s p bushel; Beif 2 d ½ p pound; pork 4 p per pound; barley 4 p per bushel; butter 5 p per pound."

There are other names on the list to which the word "nothing" had been added, as follows:

Isaac Stokes
Rich. Pinckham
ffrancis Hyuch (of Bl. Pt.)
John Mighel (O. R.)
Teage Reall (O. R.)

Capt. Barefoot
Elder Wentworth

Joseph Bickford (O. R.)
Philip Cromell (O. R.)

The highest tax payer on the above list was Capt. Walderne, who paid Pds. 2-7-4; the second was John Roberts who paid Psd 1-16-3 1/3; the third was Job Clements, paying Pds. 1-15-6½; the fourth Richard Otis, payng Pds. 1-5-7½. The lowest on the list was John Elis and six or seven others, each of whom paid 2s, 6d.

LIST OF CERTAIN TOWN OFFICERS OF DOVER, N. H.

Rev. Alonzo H. Quint, D. D.

TOWN CLERKS.

The *list* of clerks is doubtless complete, but early *dates* are scarce.

1. WILLIAM WALDERNE. Perhaps from 1635; certainly from December, 1641, until his death, September, 1646.
2. GEORGE SMITH. Appointed by Massachusetts in November, 1646, and served one year.
3. WILLIAM POMFRETT. Chosen by the town 1 November, 1647; served certainly into 1665, and perhaps to 1670. In his writing is our oldest extant volume of our records, and it is marked "No. 7" on its parchment cover.
4. Deacon JOHN HALL. Certainly in 1670, perhaps earlier; served into 1679, doubtless later, and perhaps to 1685. He had been chosen clerk by the town 6 June, 1659, but the Court refused to swear him into office.
5. JOHN EVANS. Probably chosen early in 1686. A vote of 13 September, 1686, fixed his pay, and vote of October, 1686, orders that all the town books and papers be brought to the selectmen, to be by them delivered to "John Evans the towne clerke." He probably served until his murder by the Indians, 28 June, 1689.
6. JOHN HAM. He signed the record of the election of his successor, 12 March, 1693-4.
7. JOHN TUTTLE. Chosen unanimously, 12 March, 1693-4; was in office in 1719, and probably until his death, which took place in 1719 or 1720.
8. THOMAS TEBBETS. Chosen 25 April, 1720, and may have been a little earlier; was in office 8 September, 1727.
9. PAUL GERRISH. From 15 March, 1727-8, until his death, 6 June, 1743.
10. JOSEPH HANSON. From 27 June, 1743, until into 1758, and apparently until his death, 5 September, 1758.
11. EPHRAIM HANSON, son of the last preceding. From 18 September, 1758, until 1772, and apparently until his death, 24 March, 1772.
12. THOMAS WESTBROOK WALDRON. From 30 March, 1772, until his death, 3 April, 1785.

CERTAIN TOWN OFFICERS.   255

13. JOHN BURNAM HANSON, brother of Ephraim above. From 25 April, 1785, until his death, 17 December, 1788.

14. NATHANIEL COOPER. From 29 December, 1788, until his death, 4 March, 1795.

15. WALTER COOPER, son of the last preceding. From 30 March, 1795, until his resignation, which took effect 4 November, 1799.

16. DOMINICUS HANSON, grandson of Joseph above. From 4 November, 1799, until his resignation, 29 October, 1816.

17. ANDREW PEIRCE. From 4 November, 1816, until election of successor.

18. JAMES RICHARDSON. From 14 March, 1820, until election of successor.

19. CHARLES YOUNG. From 11 March, 1836, until election of successor.

20. GEORGE PIPER. From 15 March, 1838, until election of successor.

21. THOMAS STACKPOLE. From 18 March, 1843, until election of successor.

22. GEORGE THOMAS WENTWORTH. From 13 March, 1845, until election of successor.

23. CHARLES EMERY SOULE. From 14 March, 1850; resigned 31 December, 1852.

24. CHARLES AUGUSTUS TUFTS, great-great-grandson of Joseph Hanson above. Appointed by the selectmen 5 January, 1853; served until election of successor.

25. AMASA ROBERTS. From 12 March, 1853, until the organization of the city government, 25 March, 1856.

SELECTMEN.

1647, November. Ambrose Gibbons, William Pomfrett, Anthony Emery, Richard Walderne, Thomas Layton.

1648, November 27. Ambrose Gibbons, Richard Walderne, Thomas Layton, Anthony Emery, William Pomfrett.

1649, 1650. No record.

1651, Dec. 8. Capt. Richard Walderne, Mr. Valentine Hill, Henry Lankstaff, William Wentworth, William Furber.

1652–'4. No record.

1655. Hatevil Nutter, John Bickford, Henry Lankster, Job Clements, and probably one more.

1656. No record.

1657, March 30. Valentine Hill, Elder William Wentworth, Ralph Hall, William Furber.

1658, April 19. Capt. Ralph Hall, Thomas Layton, Thomas Canney, Thomas Footman, Robert Burnum.

1659, June 5. Lieut. Ralph Hall, James Nute, Richard Otis, Robert Burnum, Henry Lankster.

1660, June 13. Elder William Wentworth, Peter Coffin, Deacon John Hall, William Beard, Robert Burnum.

1661, June 5. Elder Hatevil Nutter, Ralph Hall, William Furber, John Goddard, Thomas Beard.

1662, June 15. William Pomfrett, William Beard, John Woodman, Richard Walderne, Ralph Hall.

1663, April 20. Capt. Richard Walderne, Ralph Hall, Ens. John Davis, Henry Lankster, John Bickford, Sen.

1664, April 28. Capt. Richard Walderne, Henry Lankster, Serg. John Roberts, Ens. John Davis, Elder William Wentworth.

1665. *The same.*

1666, April 2. Capt. Richard Walderne, Anthony Nutter, Robert Burnum, John Martin, Job Clements.

1667, April 8. Capt. Richard Walderne, Job Clements, Sarg. William Furber, Ens. John Davis, Corporal Anthony Nutter.

1668, April 20. Capt. Richard Walderne, Elder William Wentworth, Robert Burnum, Lieut. Peter Coffin, Sarg. John Roberts.

1669, May 3. Capt. Richard Walderne, Henry Lankster, Lieut. Peter Coffin, Job Clements, Robert Burnum.

1670. March 7. William Furber, William Wentworth, Philip Cromwell, Thomas Roberts, jr., John Woodman.

1671, March 13. Capt. Richard Walderne, Philip Cromwell, Thomas Roberts, jr., William Furber, Ensign John Davis.

1672, March 4. Capt. Richard Walderne, Lieut. Peter Coffin, Henry Lankster, Robert Burnum, Anthony Nutter.

1673. Month lost. Capt. Richard Walderne, Anthony Nutter, John Roberts, Robert Burnum, John Gerrish.

1674, March 2. Capt. Richard Walderne, John Roberts, Anthony Nutter, John Wingett, John Gerrish, Robert Burnum, John Woodman.

1675. Capt. Richard Walderne, Job Clements, Peter Coffin, Anthony Nutter, John Woodman.

1676. John Clements, Philip Cromwell, Anthony Nutter and doubtless two others.

1677, March 5. Capt. Richard Walderne, Job Clements, Lieut. Anthony Nutter, Ens. John Davis, Sarg. John Roberts.

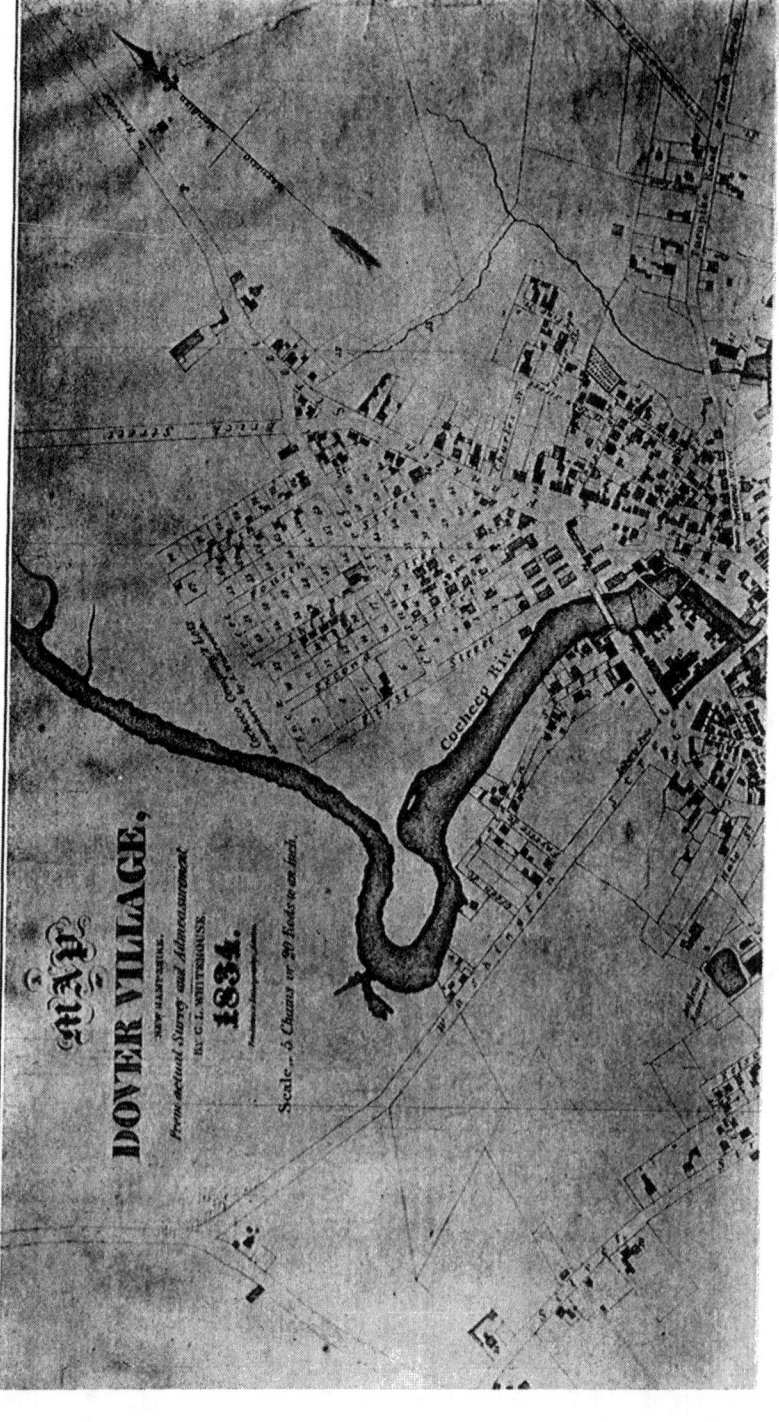

MAP OF DOVER VILLAGE, 1834.

1678-1685. No record.
1686. John Woodman, Thomas Edgerly, Nicholas Harrison, John Winget, John Tuttle.
1687, Aug. 10. John Winget, John Tuttle, William Furber, Thomas Chesley, sen., John Woodman.
1688, May 21. John Tuttle, Thomas Chesley, Wm. Furber, Tristram Coffin, Thomas Edgerly, James Huckins.
1689-1693. No record.
1694, April 16. Corporal Thomas Roberts, Samuel Heard, John Bickford, Jeremiah Burnum, Capt. John Woodman.
1695, April 22. Capt. John Gerrish, Zacharias Field, Nathaniel Hill, Thomas Chesley, sen., Joseph Meader.
1696, April 27. Capt. John Gerrish, Lieut. William Furber, Corporal Thomas Tebbets, Ens. Stephen Jones, Sarg. Thomas Downs, Thomas Bickford.
1697. No record.
1698. James Davis, Ezckiel Wentworth, Nathaniel Hill, and doubtless two others.
1699, May 30. Ens. Thomas Tebbets, Nathaniel Heard, Joseph Hill, Joseph Smith, Thomas Edgerly.
1700, 1701. Not certain. A very imperfect record *probably* belongs to one of these years, which gives John Drew, [Tristram] Heard, . . . [Sm]ith sen.,—Davis,—[B]ickford.
1702, April 6. Samuel Tebbetts, John Meader, jr., Joseph Jones, Ezekiel Wentworth, John Downing.
1703, April 5. Thomas Roberts, sen., Tobias Hanson, Joseph Jones, Francis Mathes, John Dam. Jones and Mathes refused to serve, and Samuel Chesley and Robert Huckins were chosen April 17.
1704, April 25. Sarg. Thomas Roberts, William Frost, Francis Mathes, Capt. Samuel Chesley, John Dam.
1705, April 7. Samuel Emerson, Richard Waldron, Esq., Capt. John Knight, Joseph Meader, Jonathan Woodman.
1706, April 22. Thomas Roberts, sen., Richard Waldron, Joseph Jones, Capt. Samuel Chesley, Capt. John Knight.

From this time the elections were in May, until 1717 and perhaps later.

1707, 1708, 1709, 1710. Thomas Roberts, sen., Richard Waldron, Capt. John Knight, Joseph Jones, Sarg. Francis Mathes.
1711. Sarg. Joseph Roberts, Richard Waldron, John Smith, sen., Sarg. Joseph Meader, Capt. John Knight.
1712. Joseph Roberts, Richard Waldron, John Smith, Joseph Meader, sen., John Smith, sen., Lieut. John Downing.

1713. Lieut. Joseph Roberts, Col. Richard Waldron, Sarg. Joseph Meader, sen., John Smith, sen., Lieut. John Downing.

Newington, separated from Dover, held its first meeting 6 August, 1713.

1714. Lieut. Joseph Roberts, Col. Richard Waldron, Mr. Joseph Jones, Ens. Francis Mathes, Lieut. John Downing.

1715. Capt. Thomas Tebbets, Tobias Hanson, Joseph Meader, John Amblar, Sarg. Thomas Roberts.

1716. Capt. Thomas Tebbets, Col. Richard Waldron, Ens. Paul Wentworth, Sarg. Joseph Meader, Mr. John Amblar.

1717. Capt. Thomas Tebbets, Col. Richard Waldron, Ens. Paul Wentworth, Lieut. Joseph Jones, Mr. Philip Chesley.

1718, 1719. No record.

1720, May 26. Thomas Tebbetts, Thomas Roberts, Tobias Hanson, John Smith, Francis Mathes.

1721. Joseph Roberts, Tobias Hanson, Timothy Robinson, and doubtless two others.

1722, 1723. No record.

1724. Shephen Jones, John Smith, Benjamin Wentworth, Nicholas Hartford, and probably one other.

1725. Francis Mathes, James Nute, John Smith, and doubtless two others.

1726. Nicholas Hartford, James Nute, Francis Mathes, and doubtless two others.

1727, May 5. Paul Wentworth, Nicholas Hartford, Samuel Smith, James Nute, Francis Mathes.

From this time (and perhaps earlier) the elections were invariably in March.

1728. Nicholas Hartford, Thomas Hanson, James Nute, Capt. Francis Mathes, Samuel Smith.

1729. John Canney, Capt. Paul Wentworth, Capt. Stephen Jones, Jonathan Tomson, John Wingett.

1730. Nicholas Hartford, Lieut. John Wingett, Capt. Stephen Jones, Capt. Paul Wentworth, Jonathan Thompson.

1731. Paul Wentworth, Nicholas Hartford, Lieut. John Wingett, Capt. Francis Mathes, Lieut. Samuel Smith.

1732. Capt. Thomas Millet, Liut. John Wingett, Paul Wentworth, Capt. Francis Mathes, Lieut. Samuel Smith.

Durham was separated from Dover 15 May, 1732.

CERTAIN TOWN OFFICERS.   259

1733. Nicholas Hartford, Tobias Hanson, Lieut. James Davis, Paul Wentworth, Capt. Thomas Wallingford.

1734, 1735. Capt. Thomas Millet, Lieut. John Wingett, Paul Wentworth; under vote to have but three.

1736, 1737, 1738. Capt. Thomas Millet, Lieut. John Wingett, Capt. Paul Wentworth, Eli Demeritt, jr., Capt. Tristram Coffin.

1739. Joseph Austin, John Gage, Capt. Thomas Wallingford, Lieut Thomas Davis, Joseph Hanson, jr.

1740. Capt. Thomas Millet, John Wingett, Capt. Paul Wentworth, Eli Demeritt, jr., John Wood.

1741. Capt. Thomas Millet, Lieut. John Wingett, Capt. Thomas Wallingford, Eli Demeritt, jr., Joseph Hanson, jr.

1742, 1743. Capt. Thomas Millet, Lieut. John Wingett Joseph Roberts, Capt. Thomas Wallingford, Eli Demeritt, jr.

1744, 1745. Thomas Millet, Lieut. John Wingett, Eli Demeritt, jr., Thomas Wallingford, Ephraim Ham.

1746. Thomas Millet, Capt. Joseph Hanson, Thomas Wallingford, Major Thomas Davis, Capt. John Wingett.

1747. Thomas Millett, Capt. John Wingett, Eli Demeritt, Capt. John Wentworth, Ephraim Ham.

1748. Thomas Millet, Capt. Joseph Hanson, Major Thomas Davis, Col. Thomas Wallingford, John Gage.

1749, 1750. Thomas Millet, Ephraim Ham, Eli Demeritt, Capt. John Wentworth, Capt. John Wingett.

1751. (Thomas Millet chosen, but declined to serve.) Lieut. Stephen Roberts, Capt. Thomas Westbrook Waldron, Shadrach Hodgdon, Dr. Moses Carr, Joseph Hanson, jr.

1752. Thomas Millet, Capt. John Wingett, Eli Demeritt, Capt. John Wentworth, Joseph Hanson, jr.

1753. Capt. Thomas W. Waldron, Thomas Millet, Lieut. Solomon Emerson, Capt. John Wentworth, Joseph Hanson, jr.

1754. Thomas Millet, Capt. Thomas W. Waldron, Capt. John Wentworth, Lieut. Solomon Emerson, Joseph Hanson, jr.

Somersworth was separated from Dover 22 April, 1754.

1755. Thomas Millet, Joseph Hanson, jr., James Young.

1756. Samuel Emerson, Joseph Hanson, jr., Ebenezer Demeritt, Capt. Thomas W. Waldron, James Young.

1757. Samuel Emerson, Joseph Hanson, jr., Ebenezer Demeritt, John Gage, jr., James Young.

1758. Capt. Howard Henderson, Joseph Hanson, jr., Ebenezer Demeritt, Capt. Thomas W. Waldron, James Young.

1759, 1760, 1761. Capt. Howard Henderson, Joseph Hanson, Ebenezer Demeritt, James Young, Capt. Thomas W. Waldron.

1762. Thomas Tuttle, Ephraim Hanson, John Wingett, Nathaniel Horn, Ens. Joseph Roberts.

1763. Thomas Tuttle, Ephraim Hanson, John Wingett, jr., Nathaniel Horn, Ens. Joseph Roberts.

1764. Elijah Estes, Otis Baker, John Tasker, Jacob Sawyer, Lieut. Joshua Wingate.

1765. Elijah Estes, Otis Baker, John Tasker, Jacob Sawyer, Lieut. Joshua Wingate.

1766. Clement Meserve, Solomon Hanson, Daniel Hayes, Nathaniel Horn, Capt. Dudley Watson.

1767. Lieut. Clement Meserve, Capt. John Gage, Daniel Hayes, Nathaniel Horn, Ephraim Ham.

1768. Capt. Caleb Hodgdon, Capt. John Gage, Nathaniel Horn.

1769. Lt. William Hanson, Ephraim Hanson, Ezekiel Varney.

1770. Capt. Caleb Hodgdon, John Waldron, 3d, John Kielle.

1771, 1772. 1773. Capt Caleb Hodgdon, Capt. Stephen Evans, Lt. John Wingett.

1774, 1775. Capt. Caleb Hodgdon, John Kielle, Samuel Heard.

1776. Benjamin Peirce, John Waldron, 3d, John Gage.

1777. Ephraim Ham, Col. John Waldron, Andrew Torr.

1778. Col. John Waldron, Andrew Torr, Ephraim Ham.

1779. Col. Joshua Wingate, John Burnham Hanson, Capt. John Gage.

1780. Joshua Wingate, John Gage, Andrew Torr.

1781. Major Caleb Hodgdon, Col. John Waldron, Major Benjamin Titcomb.

1782. Ens. Andrew Torr, Capt. John Gage, Col. Joshua Wingate.

1783. John Kielle, Ens. Andrew Torr, Col. John Waldron.

1784, 1785. Andrew Torr, Col. John Waldron, John Kielle.

1786. John Kielle, John Waldron, Andrew Torr.

1787, 1788, 1789. Andrew Torr, John Waldron, John Kielle.

1790. Joseph Drew, Stephen Sawyer, John Kielle.

1791, 1792. Andrew Torr, John Waldron, Ephraim Ham.

1793, 1794, 1795, 1796, 1797. Capt. Moses Wingate, Stephen Sawyer, Aaron Roberts.

1798, 1799. Deacon Benjamin Peirce, Col. John Waldron, Andrew Torr.

1800. Deacon Benjamin Peirce, Stephen Sawyer, Moses Wingate.

1801. Col. John Waldron, Capt. Moses Wingate, Dea. Benjamin Peirce.

CERTAIN TOWN OFFICERS. 261

1802. Stephen Sawyer, Tobias Tuttle, Daniel Henderson.
1803. Stephen Sawyer, Daniel Henderson, Samuel Wentworth.
1804. Tobias Tuttle, Mark Walker, Samuel Kimball.
1805. Tobias Tuttle, Stephen Sawyer, Samuel Kimball.
1806, 1807. Tobias Tuttle, Samuel Kimball, Ephraim Ham, 3d.
1808, 1809, 1810. Tobias Tuttle, Stephen Patten, jr., Jonathan Hanson, jr.
1811, 1812. John Waldron, Nicholas Peaslee, Capt. Andrew Peirce.
1813, 1814. Tobias Tuttle, Andrew Peirce, Nicholas Peaslee, Samuel Kimball.
1815. Andrew Peirce, Nicholas Peaslee, Samuel Kimball.
1816. Andrew Peirce, Nicholas Peaslee, Stephen Patten, jr.
1817. Nicholas Peaslee, Samuel Kimball, Stephn Patten, jr,
1818. Samuel Kimball, Nicholas Peaslee, Jonathan Locke.
1819. Samuel Kimball, John Kittredge, Nicholas Peaslee.
1820. John Kittredge, Samuel Kimball, Nicholas Peaslee.
1821, 1822. John Kittredge, Samuel Kimball, Joseph Tuttle.
1823. Samuel Kimball, Thomas W. Kittredge, Joseph Tuttle.
1824, 1825. Samuel Kimball, Thomas W. Kittredge, Andrew Varney.
1826, 1827. Thomas W. Kittredge, Andrew Varney, Eri Perkins.
1828. Thomas W. Kittredge, Andrew Varney, Walter Sawyer.
1829. Thomas W. Kittredge, Andrew Varney, Daniel Osborne.
1830. Thomas W. Kittredge, Andrew Varney, Walter Sawyer.
1831. James B. Varney, Ebenezer Hanson, Alonzo Roberts.
1832. Ezekiel Hurd, James B. Varney, Ebenezer Hanson.
1833, 1834. Ezekiel Hurd, Andrew Peirce, jr., Alonzo Roberts.
1835. John Riley, William Hale, jr., Ezekiel Hurd.
1836. Ezekiel Hurd, John Riley, David Peirce.
1837. Ezekiel Hurd, David Peirce, James Tuttle, jr.
1838. John Riley, Sharonton Baker, Andrew Varney.
1839. Sharonton Baker, Andrew Varney, Thomas E. Sawyer.
1840. John Riley, Sharonton Baker, Stephen Toppan.
1841. John Riley, Stephen Toppan, Samuel Howard.
1842. Samuel Howard, Joshua Banfield, Solomon Jenness.
1843. Nathaniel Wiggin, Daniel Pinkham, Ezekiel Hurd.
1844. Ezekiel Hurd, Nathaniel Wiggin, John H. White.
1845. John Tredick, Samuel Dunn, jr., William B. Wiggin.
1846. Samuel Dunn, jr., William B. Wiggin, Andrew Varney.
1847. Samuel Dunn, jr., Andrew Varney, Oliver S. Horne.

1848. Thomas E. Sawyer, Oliver S. Horne, Elijah Wadleigh.
1849. Samuel Dunn, jr., Ezekiel Hurd, Leonard S. Rand.
1850. Sharonton Baker, Samuel Dunn, Andrew Varney.
1851. Edmund J. Lane, Samuel S. Clark, Andrew Varney.
1852. Samuel S. Clark, Edmund J. Lane, Moses Gage.
1853. Jonas D. Townsend, John Clements, Samuel Dunn.
1854. Jonas D. Townsend, John Clements, Nathaniel Paul.
1855. Charles Clements, Daniel Hussey, David Steeele. The last Board.

The Act incorporating the City of Dover was signed June 29, 1855.

It was accepted by the citizens of Dover at a town-meeting held August 15, 1855.

The first mayor took the oath of office March 25, 1856, and the city government was then inaugurated.

GENEALOGY.

The following pages are made up, chiefly, from Rev. Dr. Alonzo Hall Quint's *Historical Memoranda,* as it was published in the *Dover Enquirer,* from time to time. But for Dr. Quint's work the knowledge of Dover town history would be very limited. He began in July, 1850; he was then a young man of twenty-two; his last number was published in 1888, when he was sixty years old. He was born in Barnstead (at the home of his grandparents), March 22, 1828; he died in Boston, November 4, 1896. As regards bringing to light, and the preservation, of Dover's Historical data, Dr. Quint is without a peer; he not only had much of the old town records published, but also interviewed aged persons who remembered events in their youthful days, and who had stories and traditions from old persons, and in that way Dr. Quint got the traditions from the very beginning of things in the town history.

JOHN SCALES.

Dover, February, 1923.

SOME DESCENDANTS OF DEACON JOHN DAMME, OF DOVER, N. H.

(BY JOHN SCALES, A. B., A. M.)

John Damme was born in Cheshire county, England, about 1610; he came over with Capt. Thomas Wiggin's company in 1633, and helped begin the settlement on Dover Neck; there was his home till his death, January 27, 1690. At 60 years of age he was elected second Deacon of the First Church; his neighbor, John Hall, was the first Deacon.

In July, 1911, I had published, in the *New England Historical and Genealogical Register,* an account of Deacon Damme and some of his descendants. Since then my knowledge of the family has much increased; I herein record the information. I became especially interested in the family history as Hannah Dame, my grandmother Scales, born in 1772, was grand-daughter of John (4) Dame of Newington, and he was grandson of John (2) Damme, eldest son of Deacon Damme of the First Church, who gave this son a tract of 100 acres of land, on Dame's Point, on the Newington shore of Little Bay, which land had been granted to the Deacon by the town of Dover.

According to my best information Deacon Damme's ancestors were of Cheshire County, England, and of a parish in the town of Nautwick. They were freeholders from about the time of King Edward IV. The ancient residence was known as "Red Hall Farm." One of the hills on the farm is known as "Damme's croft." Cheshire County is in that part of England east of Liverpool, and Nautwick is a town in the neighborhood of Chester, one of the historic spots in England.

One of the most interesting stories about the family in Cheshire is that about Thomas Damme, who lived to a very great age. He was born in the year 1494, and died 1648, being then 154 years old. He was buried in the Church yard of the Parish of "Church Minshall," near Middlewick, in Cheshire. The register of his death is still there, and is marked around with ink to call attention to his remarkable age. This is a copy of the inscription.

THOMAS DAMME OF LEIGHTON, BURIED ye 20th of ffebbruarie, being of the Age of seven score and fourteen. 1648.

His wife, also, is buried in the same Church yard. He is said to have been vigorous in his latest years. When he was 104 he is said to have danced a "hornpipe," at the celebration of the opening of a bridge over the river Weaver, at Church Minshall.

There is no record, or tradition, to show how Captain Thomas Wiggin happened to get John Damme for one of his party; but they came over together in the ship "James," in 1633. He appears to have been an expert carpenter, or "joiner," as the old timers called such workmen. According to the old meaning of words, a "joiner" was one who did the finer part of wood work; a "carpenter" was one who did the coarser part of the wood work in house-building, etc., hewing the logs and splitting the rails, etc. Undoubtedly he was the boss "joiner" in the construction of the garrison house now in the arcade of the "Woodman Institute," which he built, about 1675, for his youngest son, William Damme, as has been described in previous pages. He was a successful business man, and had grants of land, and timber trees, and part interest in a sawmill, at "Belle-Man's Bank" falls, and also in that with Elder William Wentworth, on Fresh Creek, in the neighborhood of the Elder's home. He was successful in business, so that during one period he was one of the largest tax-payers in the town. He assisted in organizing the First Church in 1638, and was one of its generous supporters during life; for near a quarter of a century he was one of the deacons of the Church. He does not appear to have held any other office in town affairs, not even that of road surveyor. He was simply one of the good, substantial citizens, honored and respected by all. His Will is dated May 19, 1687; was proved March 23, 1693.

In a petition to the Governor of New Hampshire, by the inhabitants of Dover, in 1689, John Damme[1] and Nicholas Damme are signers. These two are mentioned by John Camden Holton in his list of Emigration of "Persons of Quality" to America, between 1600 and 1700. I have not found any other reference to Nicholas.

John[1] Damme married about 1636, *Elizabeth Pomfrett*, daughter of William Pomfrett, who for nearly forty years was town clerk. In passing it may be well to state here that Mr. Pomfrett received numerous grants of land, one of which he gave to his grandson, Pomfrett Damme. The record is that Wm. Pomfrett had a grant of 100 acres, the 5th, 10 mo., 1652, laid out June 5, 1764. Wm. Pomfret, March 26, 1675, "out of love and affection to his grandson, Wm. Damme," then about twenty years of age, son of John Damme, sr., conveyed all the upland and meadow granted said Wm. Pomfret, 5th, 10 mo., 1652, "lying and being from ye mouth of Fresh Creek, on ye western side, towards Cochecho (River), that is to say, it runs up from Cochecho River by said creek's side from ye mouth thereof, the creek being the bounds thereof on ye eastern side. And from the mouth of Fresh creek it runs up the river, which is ye bound on ye south and by west side."—These bounds were renewed, at the request of Pomfrett Damme (son of William), June 9, 1724. And that point of land has borne the name of Dame's Point for more than 200 years.

CHILDREN.

2. 1. JOHN, b. at Dover, 8 Jan., 1636-7.
    2. ELIZABETH, b. 1 May, 1649; m. THOMAS WHITEHOUSE.
    3. MARY, b. 1651.
3. 4. WILLIAM, b. 14 Oct., 1653.
    5. SUSANNAH, b. 14 Dec., 1661.
    6. JUDITH, b. 16 Nov., 1666; d. 22 Oct., 1728; m. 6 July, 1684, THOMAS TIBBETTS of Dover. Children: 1. *John*, b. 29 Aug., 1685. 2. *Thomas*, b. 2 Nov., 1687. 3. *Ephraim*, b. 4 Mar., 1690. 4. *Elizabeth*, b. 8 Sept., 1692. 5. *Samuel*, b. 8 Oct., 1693. 6. *Elizabeth*, b. 25 July, 1696. 7. *Moses*, b. 27 Jan., 1701. 8. *Abigail*, b. 2 Sept., 1705.

2. SERGT. JOHN[2] DAM (*John[1]*), born at Dover 8 Jan., 1636-7, died there 8 Jan., 1706. He married twice: first, SARAH HALL, who died in 1663, daughter of Sergt. John of Dover; secondly, 9 Nov., 1664, ELIZABETH FURBER, daughter of Lieut. William of Dover. In the town and provincial records John Dam is called sergeant. He was an officer of the militia, and did service in the Indian wars. He resided in that part of Dover called Bloody Point, now Newington, settling upon a grant of land his father had received on the east shore of Little Bay, now known as Dame's Point, where several generations of the Dam family were afterwards born. The records show that Sergt. John Dam held various official positions.

CHILDREN, BY SECOND WIFE.

     1. JOHN, b. 11 Jan., 1666; d. in infancy.
4.   2. JOHN, b. 23 Feb., 1667-8.
     3. ALICE, b. 14 Dec., 1670.
5.   4. MOSES, b. 14 Oct., 1673.
     5. BETHIAH, b. 5 May, 1675.

3. WILLIAM² DAM (*John¹*), born at Dover 14 Oct., 1653, died there (at Back River) 20 Mar., 1718. He married at Dover, in 1680, MARTHA NUTE. He resided on the west side of Back River on land that was granted to his father by the town. His burial ground can still be seen there on the bank of the river.

CHILDREN.

1. POMFRET, b. 4 Mar., 1681; m. (1) ESTHER TWOMBLY; m. (2) at Dover, ELIZABETH TIBBETTS, dau. of Joseph and Elizabeth, of Dover. After his death she m. (2) ——— Downes, and m. (3) Richard Goodwin.
2. MARTHA, b. 29 Mar., 1683; m. JACOB ALLEN.
6. 3. WILLIAM, b. 14 Nov., 1686.
4. SAMUEL, b. 21 Mar., 1689; d. Mar. 22, 1761.
5. SARAH, b. 21 Apr., 1692; m. JOHN TWOMBLY.
6. LEAH, b. 17 Feb., 1695; m. SAMUEL HAYES.

Regarding the name of Wm. Damme's wife being Martha Nute, the following from Mr. Joseph E. Nute, of Fall River, Mass., is of interest, and settles the question beyond doubt. It is of date of Sept. 6, 1911.

"In the little Nute burying ground on the old Nute farm (next to John Damme's 20 acre lot on Back River) on the west side of the river, there are only three headstones with inscriptions. These are the graves of James Nute, founder of the Nute family in this country, and of Martha Damme and her husband, the upper part of the stone bearing his Christian name having been broken off and apparently lost. There are other graves but none marked to indicate to whom they belong. The mere fact that Martha Dam was buried by the side of James Nute is pretty good evidence that she was a pretty close relative. She was born in 1653, and it is quite evident that she must have been a daughter, as he was born apparently in 1620 or 21.

The names of her children, as shown in your genealogy is pretty good evidence to my mind that she was a Nute. The names of the first three, Pomfrett, Martha and William, are easily explained. The fourth one, Samuel, is a Nute family name, appearing frequently among the Nutes of Tiverton, England, from which family our James is supposed to have come, and was, moreover, I suspect, the name of the father of James, although as yet I have no proof on this point.

Martha's oldest brother, James[2] Nute, named his second son Samuel, Martha's fifth child, Sarah, was evidently named after the wife of James[1], and she was apparently the mother of his children, although at one time I suspected she was only the step-mother. As James[2] also had a child named Sarah[3], I think Sarah[1] was doubtless the mother of four children,—James, Abraham, Leah and Martha, who married William Damme, and they named their sixth, and youngest child, Leah, evidently named for Martha's sister, Leah Nute. The name Leah again appears as daughter of Samuel[3] Nute."

As regards the fourth child of William and Martha (Nute) Dam, Samuel[3] Dam, who was born 21 March, 1689, and died 22 March, 1761, the following information was furnished, in 1911, by Francis Herbert Dam, Esq., of San Francisco. It appears that this branch of the family has always retained the "Town Clerk" spelling of the name, "Dam."

Samuel[3] Dam was one of the early settlers on Dame's Point, at the junction of Fresh Creek with the Cochecho River. It had been given to his father by "Town Clerk" Pomfrett. It seems that Samuel[3] and his elder brother Pomfret[3] both lived there for a while. Samuel's wife's name is not known, but they had children, the eldest of whom was named Samuel, born about 1724, who married and had a family; the eldest of their children was Samuel[5] Dam, born in 1754 (probably at Dame's Point). He married Anna Nelson, of Portsmouth, and they became early settlers in Waterborough, Me., where he was a prosperous farmer, and also kept a public house, where many were entertained, who were on their way to make settlements in the Districts of Maine. Samuel Dam was a tall man, energetic, public spirited and a Christian citizen. He died in 1814, leaving three sons and four daughters. His eldest son, Joseph[6] Dam, born 17 Feb., 1780; m. 2 Nov., 1801, Sally Furlong, b. 13 Aug., 1782; d. 26 June, 1842. They had twelve children, of whom the eleventh was named Cyrus King[7] Dam, born 15 Nov., 1818; m. 29 Dec., 1840, Charlotte Gould of Boston, a descendant from the Gould family of Rowley, Mass.

Cyrus King[7] Dam emigrated to San Francisco in 1850, where he arrived Oct. 31st. He made the journey around Cape Horn, and was 219 days on the voyage. Instead of mining for gold he engaged in farming, in Yuba county. Previous to going to California Mr. Dam resided in Cambridgeport, Mass., where his son, Cyrus King[8] Dam, Jr., was born 8 Feb., 1843. In 1856 he accompanied his mother to California, via the Panama route, and joined his father, on the farm. The father died 9 May, 1865; the son succeeded him in the farming, also engaged in managing a flour mill, and was a very successful and highly respected citizen; he married, June 6, 1867, Frances L. Scott, who was born at Alton, Ill., Dec. 27, 1848. They had several children, of whom the fourth is Francis Herbert[9] Dam, Esq., attorney at law, San Francisco. Mr Dam has received the degrees of A. B. and LL. B. from the University of California, and has been successful in practice of the law in San Francisco since 1900, when he was admitted to the bar. He is married and has a family.

4. JOHN[3] DAM (*John,*[2] *John*[1]), born at Dover (Dame's Point) 23 Feb., 1667-8; married twice: first, JANE ROWE, daughter of Richard Rowe, Esq., of Dover, date of her death unknown; and, secondly, ELIZABETH HOYT. He resided at Dame's Point, was deacon of the church at Newington, also one of the proprietors of the town of Rochester. He died in 1730.

CHILDREN, BY FIRST WIFE.

7. 1. ZEBULON.
8. 2. JOHN, b. 1695.
9. 3. RICHARD, b. 26 Aug., 1699.
10. 4. ELNATHAN, b. 27 Apr., 1706.
    5. ALICE, b. 1708.
    6. ELIZA, b. ———; m. SAMUEL RAWLINS.
    7. SUSANNAH.

5. MOSES[3] DAM (*John,*[2] *John*[1]), born at Dover 14 Oct., 1673, and resided in that part which is now Newington. His wife's name was ABIGAIL HUNTRESS; m. 22 July, 1714. She was daughter of George Huntress of Bloody Point. She died before 1739, and he m., 2d, MRS. ELIZABETH WATERHOUSE, widow of Richard Waterhouse, of Portsmouth.

CHILDREN.

1. ABIGAIL, bapt. 22 Jan., 1716; m. SOLOMON LOUD.
2. JOHN, bapt. 4 May, 1717.
11.   3. ELIPHALET, bapt. 22 Dec., 1719.
4. SOLOMON, bapt. 12 Aug., 1722.
5. THEOPHILUS, bapt. 6 Dec., 1724.
6. GEORGE, bapt. 28 Jan., 1727.
7. WILLIAM, bapt. 20 July, 1729.
8. JABEZ, bapt. 4 July, 1731.
9. MARY, bapt. 17 Feb., 1734.

6. WILLIAM^3 DAM (*William,^{2} John^1*), b. 12 Nov., 1686; m. 29 July, 1708, SARAH KIMMINS; resided at Back River.

CHILDREN.

1. WILLIAM, b. 10 Feb., 1710.
2. SARAH, b. 25 Aug., 1714.
3. JOHN, b. 12 June, 1723; d. 11 Aug., 1724.
4. ABIGAIL, b. 18 July, 1725.

7. ZEBULON^4 DAM (*John,^{3} John,^{2} John^1*), b. at Dover ab. 1692; m., 16 Aug., 1716, ABIGAIL BICKFORD. He was one of the early settlers at Rochester.

CHILDREN.

1. SARAH, bapt. 13 July, 1718.
12.   2. ABNER (twin), b. 17 Aug., 1723.
3. RETURAH (twin), bapt. 17 Aug., 1723; m. in 1754, PAUL JENNESS, of Rochester.
4. JOSEPH (twin), b. 19 Sept., 1739.
5. MARY (twin), b. 19 Sept., 1739.
6. ZEBULON, b. 1740; m. MARY ———.

8. JOHN^4 DAM (*John,^{3} John, ^{2} John^1*), born 1695, died Jan., 1768-9. He married, 29 Feb., 1718, ELIZABETH BICKFORD, of Dover. He resided at Newington on the ancestral farm at Dame's Point.

CHILDREN.

13.   1. JOSEPH, b. 16 May, 1719; m. MEHITABLE HALL, 1739; d. 1807.
14.   2. MOSES, b. 2 May, 1721.

THE DAMME FAMILY.

15.   3. ISSACHER, b. 1723.
       4. JOHN, b. 1725; m. ———, and lived at Wiscasset, Me.
       5. BENJAMIN, b. 1727.
16.   6. THEODORE, b. 1728.
       7. JETHRO, b. 1730; d. in infancy.
       8. ELIZABETH, b. 1731; m. 20 Mar., 1748, JOSEPH TRICKEY.
       9. ALICE, b. 1733; m. 17 July, 1757, JOSEPH PLACE.
     10. ESTHER, b. 1736; m. 18 Dec., 1755, JAMES NUTTER.
     11. OLIVE, b. 1738; m. 10 July, 1758, SAMUEL EDGERLY.

9. RICHARD[4] DAM (*John*,[3] *John*,[2] *John*[1]), born 26 Aug., 1669; died 13 May, 1776. He married, 24 Jan., 1724, ELIZABETH LEIGHTON, daughter of Thomas of Dover (Back River), and resided at Newington.

CHILDREN.

      1. MARY, bapt. 28 Feb., 1725.
17.   2. JONATHAN, bapt. 14 Apr., 1726.
      3. MARTHA, bapt. 18 Aug., 1728.
18.   4. BENJAMIN, bapt. 2 Aug., 1730.
19.   5. JABEZ, b. 14 Aug., 1732.
      6. SAMUEL, bapt. 28 Apr., 1736.
      7. TIMOTHY, b. 30 Nov., 1736; d. 1803; m. 12 Mar., 1767, ELIZABETH ———.
      8. JOHN, b. 1738; d. 1814; m. 19 Nov., 1797, ELIZABETH FURBER; resided in Durham. Children: 1. *Betsey*; m. Jonathan Woodman; lived in Barrington. 2. *Richard*, b. 21 Sept., 1772; m. Hannah Bickford. 3. *Moses*, b. 6 March, 1775; m. Fidelia Furber, who was b. 2 May, 1771, daughter of Levi Furber, an officer in the Revolutionary War; they had three sons and two daughters; he d. 5 Sept., 1828; she d. 18 Oct., 1851. 4. *Hannah*, b. 12 April, 1776. 5. *Timothy*, b. June, 1778. 6. *Anna*, b. 15 May, 1783; m. Robert Burnham. 7. *John*, b. 25 Aug., 1785. *Katy* (twin), b. 18 Nov., 1790; m. George Johnson, in 1816. 9. *Sally* (twin), b. 18 Nov., 1790.

Descendants of MOSES[6] DAME and his wife FIDELIA FURBER: MOSES[6] DAME (*John*,[5] *Richard*,[4] *John*,[3] *John*,[2] *John*[1]), b. 6 March, 1775; m. FIDELIA FURBER, daughter of Levi Furber, who was an officer in the Revolutionary War. She was born 2 May, 1771; d. 18 Oct., 1851; he d. 5 Sept., 1828.

CHILDREN.

1. ROSAMON, b. June, 1803; m. EPHRAIM HAYES; lived in Milton.
2. ABRAHAM, b. 24 Apr., 1805; m. MARY MORRISON; lived in Farmington.
3. JOHN U., b. 3 Oct., 1807; d. 9 Oct., 1893; m. CAROLINE NELSON PARKER; they lived in Farmington.
4. SARAH A., b. 10 Feb., 1810; d. 29 May, 1863; unm.
5. RICHARD F., b. 26 March, 1815; m. SALLY TUTTLE; s. p.

The following are descendants of JOHN U. and CAROLINE NELSON PARKER DAME, who lived in Farmington, as furnished by their son, REV. JOHN E. DAME, a noted Free Will Baptist preacher.

1. ELIZABETH A.; m. JOHN H. EDGERLY; lived in Farmington.
2. JULIET; died young.
3. REV. JOHN E.; married LILLIAN MONTGOMERY, of Strafford Ridge; he d. in Dover, Jan. 29, 1914; interment in the family burial ground in Farmington.
4. JULIA F.; m. JAMES S. SANBORN; lived in Vermont.
5. CHARLES H.; m. ANNIE P. NUTE; lived in Farmington.
6. MARY C.; m. WILLIAM A. HEATH; lived in California.
7. HATTIE D.; m. SAMUEL FURBER; lived in Farmington.

Following are names of children of REV. JOHN E. and LILLIAN (MONTGOMERY) DAME, as given by him. 1. *Blanche M.* 2. *Rubie L.* 3. *Pearl F.* 4. *Faye A.* 5. *Mabel C.*

10. ELNATHAN[4] DAM (*John,*[3] *John,*[2] *John*[1]), born 27 Apr., 1706, resided at Dover. He married MARY ———.

CHILDREN.

1. SARAH, bapt. 4 Nov., 1744.
2. ISAAC, bapt. 4 Nov., 1744.
3. DEBORAH, bapt. 12 Aug., 1753.

11. ELIPHALET[4] DAM (*Moses,*[3] *John,*[2] *John*[1]), born at Newington, 22 Dec., 1719; died in 1783. He married ABIGAIL NUTTER, daughter of Hatevil and granddaughter of Anthony of Newington, where he resided.

THE DAMME FAMILY.

CHILDREN.

1. MARY FIELD, bapt. 1747.
2. TEMPERANCE, bapt. 1751.
3. SARAH, bapt. 1753.
4. BETTIE, bapt. 1756; m. 21 June, 1779, JOHN NUTTER, of Newington.
5. NANCY EMERSON, bapt. 1760.
6. JOSEPH PATTERSON.
7. SUSANNAH.
8. NABBY.
9. JOANNA.

12. ABNER[5] DAME (*Zebulon,[4] John,[3] John,[2] John[1]*), bapt. 17 Aug., 1723; died in 1783; married MARY DANA, and resided at Rochester on land he inherited from his father. He was one of the leading citizens of the town.

CHILDREN.

1. SARAH, bapt. July, 1753; m. ———— HODGDON.
2. ELIZABETH, bapt. 21 Apr., 1755.
3. MARY, b. 1759; m. 18 Mar., 1779, JOHN HAM of Rochester.
4. MERCY, bapt. 9 Mar., 1768.
5. CHARITY, bapt. 4 Sept., 1770; m. JOSEPH HODGDON, and resided at Wakefield.
6. PAUL (twin), b. 12 Feb., 1778.
7. SILAS (twin), b. 12 Feb., 1778; m. LUCY RICKER.

13. JOSEPH[5] DAME (*John,[4] John,[3] John,[2] John[1]*), born 16 May, 1718; died in Apr., 1807. He married, 1739, MEHITABLE HALL, of Dover, and there resided.

CHILDREN.

1. MARY, b. 10 Nov., 1740.
20. 2. JOSEPH, b. 24 Mar., 1743.
3. RICHARD.
4. GEORGE, b. 26 June, 1748.
5. JOHN, b. 20 Oct., 1750.
6. ESTHER, b. 28 June, 1752.

NOTE—In the fifth generation the spelling of the name became changed from Dam to Dame, and has so remained to the present time. It is said that in the ancient parish records in England the spelling is frequently Damme.

       7. BETHIAH, b. 19 Feb., 1755; m. JOHN TRICKEY of Rochester.
21.   8. SAMUEL, b. 15 Aug., 1757.

14. MOSES[5] DAME (*John,*[4] *John,*[3] *John,*[2] *John*[1]) born 2 May, 1721, at Dame's Point, Newington; died at Nottingham in 1787; married, 1743, ANNA HUNKING, daughter of Capt. Mark and Mary (Leavitt) Hunking of Portsmouth. He was a tanner and currier by trade; soon after his marriage he settled in business at Little River Falls, near Lee Hill; he had a tannery there, also was one of the stockholders in a saw-mill at the falls. He carried on business there for more than forty years. In book No. 4, page 118, date 1786, in the Register of Deeds office, is the record that—"Moses Dame of Nottingham for 50 pounds sold to his son, Hunking Dame of Lee, 6 acres of land, with the buildings thereon, with bark-house."—His wife died in 1776; he died at the home of his son, Samuel, in Nottingham (Geebig section), in 1787.

CHILDREN.

22.   1. HUNKING, b. 1744.
23.   2. SAMUEL, b. 18 Feb., 1746.
       3. MOSES, b. 1748; unm.; resided at Newington; captain of militia company.
       4. JOSEPH, b. 14 Sept., 1747; m. 30 Mar., 1783, ABIGAIL LEATHERS, and lived in Durham; they had ch.: *Timothy*, b. 16 Aug., 1784; drowned 1812. *Asa*, b. 9 Feb., 1789; m. Lucia G. Bickford. *Jason*, b. 9 Mar., 1793; m. Mary Sias, 15 Dec., 1816, b. in Epping, 8 Apr., 1794. *Moses. Sarah. Ann*, m. 6 Mar., 1817, Eliot G. Burnham. *Abigail*, b. 22 Feb., 1796; m. 22 Feb., 1817, John Fowler. *Susan*, b. 24 Apr., 1801; m. Rufus Willey. *William*, b. 19 May, 1803; d. 17 Nov., 1846; unm. *Samuel*, twin of William; m. Olive Tuttle, of Nottingham.
       5. ELIZABETH, b. 1753.
       6. MARY, b. 1756; m. ROBERT HUCKINS, of Madbury; he was b. 25 Apr., 1750; d. 1824.
       7. SUSAN, b. 1760; m. ——— EDGERLY; lived in Lee.
       8. TEMPERANCE, b. 1764; m. DANIEL EMERSON, of Lee.
       9. RUTH, b. 1768; m. ISRAEL HUCKINS; resided at Strafford; he was b. 15 Sept., 1760; d. 20 May, 1823.
24. 10. HANNAH, b. 16 Feb., 1772; m. 20 Apr., 1799, SAMUEL SCALES, of Nottingham.

15. ISACHER[5] DAME (*John,*[4] *John,*[3] *John,*[2] *John*[1]), born in 1723, married, 12 May, 1747, SARAH HODGKINS, and lived in Newington. He died there 22 Nov., 1811.

CHILDREN.

1. HANNAH, m. —— BICKFORD.
2. SARAH.
3. ELIZABETH.
4. THOMAS.

16. THEODORE[5] DAME (*John,*[4] *John,*[3] *John,*[2] *John*[1]), born at Newington in 1728 (bapt. 7 Oct., 1733); married MARY ——, surname of wife and date of marriage unknown.

CHILDREN.

1. VALENTINE, bapt. 18 July, 1756.
2. REBECCA, bapt. 23 Apr., 1758.
3. BENJAMIN, bapt. 31 Aug., 1760.
4. MARY, bapt. 6 Dec., 1772; m. WILLIAM SHACKFORD, b. 1771.

17. JONATHAN[5] DAME (*Richard,*[4] *John,*[3] *John,*[2] *John*[1]), bapt. 14 Apr., 1726; died 3 Jan., 1802. He married, 20 Nov., 1750, MERCY HANSON VARNEY, born in 1730; died in 1810; daughter of Stephen and granddaughter of Tobias. He resided at Rochester, and was town clerk continuously from 1756 to 1771.

CHILDREN.

1. JONATHAN, b. 21 Nov., 1751; d. at Kittery, Me., 11 Feb., 1840; m. HANNAH PLAISTED; lived near the navy yard. Children: 1. *Esther*, d. unm. 2. *Sally*, d. unm. 3. *Jerusha*, m. William Tibbets, of Portsmouth. 4. *Hannah*, b. 11 June, 1787; d. 26 Aug., 1869; m. Capt. John Guppy, of Dover, N. H., b. 3 July, 1768; d. 3 Apr., 1855; five sons and three daus. 5. *Joseph*, m. Olive Fernald; lived at Kittery. 6. *Mary*, d. unm. 7. *Elizabeth*, m. Joseph Litchfield.
2. MARY, m. AMOS VARNEY, of Dover, and had 8 children.
25. 3. RICHARD, b. 1756.

18. BENJAMIN[5] DAME (*Richard,*[4] *John,*[3] *John,*[2] *John*[1]), bapt. 2 Aug., 1730; died in 1810. He married JANE SIMPSON, and lived at Newington.

CHILD.

1. RICHARD.

19. JABEZ[5] DAME (*Richard,*[4] *John,*[3] *John*[2] *John*[1]), born at Newington, 14 Aug., 1732; died at Rochester, 14 Nov., 1813. He married MERIBAH EMERY, of Kittery, and lived at Rochester. He was a soldier at the siege of Louisburg, and a representative in 1781.

CHILDREN.

26.	1.	RICHARD, b. 1762.
	2.	JOSHUA, b. 1764.
	3.	DANIEL, b. 1766; d. unm., 1842.
27.	4.	SIMON, b. 28 Apr., 1767.
28.	5.	TIMOTHY, b. 21 Mar., 1770.
29.	6.	CALEB, b. Sept., 1772.
30.	7.	CHARITY, b. 1 Sept., 1775.
	8.	POLLY, b. 1778; d. 1796.
31.	9.	JABEZ, b. 1782.
	10.	MERIBAH, b. 1785; d. 15 Nov., 1856; m. REV. HARVEY MOREY, who d. 29 Oct., 1830, aged 41 years.

20. JOSEPH[6] DAME (*Joseph,*[5] *John,*[4] *John,*[3] *John,*[2] *John*[1]), born 24 Mar., 1743; died 25 Apr., 1773. He married, 1769, PATIENCE CHADBOURNE, daughter of James and Bridget (Knight), of York, Me., and lived at Barnstead.

CHILDREN.

32.	1.	JAMES CHADBOURNE, b. 25 Aug., 1770.
33.	2.	JOSEPH, b. 20 Nov., 1772.

21. SAMUEL[6] DAME (*Joseph,*[5] *John,*[4] *John,*[3] *John,*[2] *John*[1]), born 15 Aug., 1757; died at Dover, in 1798. He married, Oct., 1790, HANNAH HODGDON, and lived at Dover.

THE DAMME FAMILY.

CHILDREN.

1. MEHITABLE, b. 1792; d. unm., 1870.
2. JOSEPH, b. 1794; d. 1876; m. MEHITABLE BURROUGHS, and lived at Dover. Children: 1. *Hannah*, b. 1836; d. 1859. 2. *John Samuel*, b. 1840; m. Lydia H. Tuttle; lives at Dover; has sons: Charles H. and John Edward.

22. HUNKING[6] DAME (*Moses,*[5] *John,*[4] *John,*[3] *John,*[2] *John*[1]), born at Lee, in 1744; died there in 1827. He married, 1777, ABIGAIL HUCKINS, of Madbury. He was a tanner, and lived at Lee, N. H.

CHILDREN.

1. NANCY, b. 1780; m. (1) MOSES HUCKINS, of Madbury; m. (2) MOSES DAVIS, of Lee; had children by her first husband.
2. SARAH, b. 1783; d. at Lee in 1843; m., in 1806, WILLIAM BARTLETT, son of Josiah of Lee; lived on Lee Hill. Children: 1. *Abigail Dame*, b. 21 May, 1808; d. at Dover 29 Nov., 1890; m. Charles Ham, of Dover; children. 2. *James William*, b. 11 Mar., 1811; d. unm., 30 July, 1895. 3. *Nancy Huckins*, b. 19 Oct., 1813; d. at Lowell, Mass., 19 Sept., 1893; m. William B. Franklin; lived at Lowell. 4. *Israel Charlton*, b. 26 May, 1815; d. unm. 5. *Susan Emerson*, b. 24 Mar., 1819; d. 26 Mar., 1905; m. Benjamin F. Nealley, of Lee; lived at Lowell, Mass.; had a dau., Fannie, who m. ―――― Hill of Lowell. 6. *Sarah Whittier*, b. 31 May, 1823; d. 3 Mar., 1887; m. A. D. Cranfield, and lived at Arlington, Vt. 7. *Charles Henry*, b. May 1827; d. unm. in California, 1887.
34. 3. HUNKING, b. 16 May, 1786.
35. 4. ISRAEL, b. 26 Aug., 1788.
     5. ABIGAIL, b. 1790; m. CHARLES RUNDLETT of Durham.
     6. SUSAN, b. 1793; m. JONATHAN WATSON EMERSON.
     7. STEPHEN, b. 1796; d. unm. at Durham, in 1878.
     8. JONATHAN, b. 1798; d. 1807.

23. SAMUEL[6] DAME (*Moses,*[5] *John,*[4] *John,*[3] *John,*[2] *John*[1]), born at Lee 18 Feb., 1746; died at Nottingham 13 Sept., 1810. He married, 1780, OLIVE TUTTLE, of Nottingham, born 12 Oct., 1761; died 26 Aug., 1831. He lived at Nottingham, and was a tanner, farmer, and merchant.

CHILDREN.

36.
1. JOHN,⁷ b. 21 Apr., 1781; d. 11 Mar., 1856; m. NANCY PARSONS BARBER.
2. NABBY, b. 7 Nov., 1782; d. 7 May, 1852; m. NATHAN KNOWLTON, of Northwood; lived there and had children.
3. LOIS, b. 27 Apr., 1786; d. 11 Feb., 1861; m. ASA BURNHAM, of Nottingham.
4. SAMUEL, b. 22 Jan., 1789; d. at Manchester, 7 Dec., 1863, where he resided; m. (1) HANNAH KNOWLTON; m. (2) JANE SHEPARD; no children.
5. BETSEY, b. 9 Mar., 1792; d. 24 Nov., 1855; m. SHERBURN KNOWLTON, of Northwood.
6. POLLY, b. 21 Jan., 1798; d. 4 Aug., 1863; m. JOSEPH COLCORD, of Nottingham.
7. PERMELIA, b. 1800; d. 1802.

24. HANNAH⁶ DAME (*Moses,⁵ John,⁴ John,³ John,² John¹*), born 16 Feb., 1772, died 30 July, 1847. She married, 20 Apr., 1799, SAMUEL SCALES, of Nottingham, born 20 Apr., 1778, died 21 Sept., 1840, a farmer living at Nottingham.

CHILDREN.

1. SAMUEL SCALES, b. 18 July, 1800; d. 12 Jan., 1877; m. 28 Dec., 1828, BETSEY TRUE, dau. of Benjamin and Mary (Batchelder) True, of Deerfield, b. 11 Jan., 1805; d. 14 Oct., 1883; a farmer, captain of the militia, representative to the N. H. legislature in 1849 and 1850; lived at Nottingham. Children: 1. *True*, b. 20 Jan., 1830; d. 27 July, 1882. 2. *John*, b. 6 Oct., 1835; the editor of this article. 3. *George*, b. 20 Oct., 1840; d. at battle of Malvern Hill, Va., 2 July, 1862; one of the famous Berdan Sharpshooters.
2. MARY SCALES, b. 22 Feb., 1802; d. 1878; m. 1827, HUGH THOMPSON of Lee, and resided there until 1850, then went to San Francisco with her family. Children: 1. *Frank*. 2. *Samuel*. 3. *Henrietta*. 4. *Betsey Jane*. 5. *Warren*.
3. NANCY SCALES, b. 18 Aug., 1803; d. 1872; m. 1832, DANIEL TUTTLE, of Nottingham, and resided there. Children: 1. *Levi Woodbury*, who became a physician, resided in Mississippi, and served in the Confederate Army. 2. *Annie E.* 3. *Leonora*. 4. *Jay*, a physician in Astoria, Oreg.

THE DAMME FAMILY.

4. LEVI SCALES, b. 13 Feb., 1811; d. 4 July, 1847; m. 1835, MARTHA CILLEY BARTLETT, and lived at Nottingham. Children: 1. *Horace.* 2. *Elizabeth Ann.* 3. *Mary True.* 4. *Bradbury Bartlett.*

25. RICHARD[6] DAME (*Jonathan,*[5] *Richard,*[4] *John,*[3] *John,*[2] *John*[1]), born at Rochester, in 1756; died 19 Sept., 1828. He married, 5 Oct., 1780, ABIGAIL REED, of Smithfield, who died 10 Jan., 1832. He resided at Rochester, was Judge of the Court of Common Pleas, representative, senator, and councillor.

CHILDREN.

1. HANNAH, b. 13 Feb., 1782; m. 4 June, 1807, CHARLES VARNEY, of Rochester.
2. MOSES, b. 11 May, 1784; m. ———, and resided in Nantucket, where he and his wife d., leaving two children, who were taken to Rochester and brought up by their grandfather, Judge Dame.
37. 3. JONATHAN, b. 20 Apr., 1786.
4. MERCY, b. 30 Apr., 1788; d. 7 Aug., 1794.
5. ANNA, b. 13 Dec., 1790; d. 24 Apr., 1802.
6. RHODA, b. 18 July, 1793; d. 7 Aug., 1794.
7. JOHN REED, b. 14 June, 1795; d. 19 Dec., 1812.
8. CAROLINE, b. 19 July, 1797; d. 17 Nov., 1844; m. STEPHEN BEEDE, son of the distinguished Quaker preacher.
9. THEOPHILUS, b. 12 Apr., 1800; m. 28 Oct., 1824, MARY BAKER, dau. of Moses and Sarah Baker, of Gorham, Me., b. 15 Aug., 1804.

26. RICHARD[6] DAME (*Jabez,*[5] *Richard,*[4] *John,*[3] *John,*[2] *John*[1]), born in 1762; died 11 July, 1832; married Nov., 1786, HANNAH MCDUFFEE, born 5 Jan., 1764; died Dec., 1855, daughter of John McDuffee, of Rochester. He lived at Rochester.

CHILDREN.

1. DANIEL, b. 16 Mar., 1788; d. 1847; m. 21 Mar., 1813, RELIEF HODGDON.
2. OLIVE, b. 27 May, 1790; d. unm., 1847.
3. RICHARD, b. 4 May, 1793; d. 28 May, 1879; m. 1817, ABIGAIL PAGE. Child: *Daniel W.*, b. 8 Feb., 1820; m. Mary A. Roberts; lived in Illinois.

4. WILLIAM, b. 1 Apr., 1795; m. ANNIE FOGG. Children: 1. William. 2. Sarah A. 3. Eliza S. 4. Hannah. 5. Hattie. 6. Nathan F.
5. HANNAH, b. 6 Aug., 1797; d. Aug., 1831; m. ELIJAH MEADER; lived at Rochester.
6. JABEZ, b. 5 June, 1800; d. unm., 1832.
7. BETSEY, b. 31 July, 1832; m. LUKE FURBER.
8. LAVINIA, b. 26 Mar., 1805; m. JOHN B. DOWNING.

27. SIMON⁶ DAME (*Jabez,⁵ Richard,⁴ John,³ John,² John¹*), born 28 Apr., 1767; died 2 June, 1847. He married, 19 Dec., 1790, MARGARET HAYES, and lived at Farmington.

CHILDREN.

1. JEREMIAH, b. 26 July, 1791; d. 8 Sept., 1855; m. SUSAN HORNE; lived at Farmington; was representative and senator in the legislature.
2. BETSEY, b. 10 Feb., 1793; d. 18 Oct., 1877; m. MOSES RAND; lived at Farmington.
3. JABEZ, b. 8 Mar., 1798; d. 19 Mar., 1851; m. SARAH NOTTAGE.
4. POLLY, b. 26 Feb., 1801; d. 1802.
5. TAMSIN, b. 24 Oct., 1805; d. unm., 7 Mar., 1846.
6. JANVRIN, b. 9 May, 1808; lived in Illinois; d. unm.
7. EMERY J., b. 27 Aug., 1810; d. 16 Jan., 1857; m. LOIS GARLAND; lived at Rochester; representative.
8. LEONARD, b. 15 Feb., 1813; m. MEHITABLE ROLLINS.
9. MARY, b. 15 Sept., 1815; m. ALBERT WHEELER; lived at Lowell, Mass.

28. TIMOTHY⁶ DAME (*Jabez,⁵ Richard,⁴ John,³ John,² John¹*), born at Rochester, 25 Mar., 1770; died at Farmington, 16 Feb., 1856. He married, 19 Feb., 1795, BETSEY LOCKE, born at Rochester, 8 Aug., 1774, and lived at Farmington.

CHILDREN.

1. CHARLOTTE, b. 2 June, 1795; d. unm., 25 May, 1868.
2. EDWARD, b. 26 Apr., 1798; m. CATHERINE LEATHERS.
3. CHARITY, b. 22 Aug., 1800; m. HAM GARLAND.
4. DANIEL, b. 1 Nov., 1801; m. ABIGAIL HAM.
38. 5. MARY, b. 2 June, 1805.
6. JABEZ, b. 7 Apr., 1807; d. unm.

THE DAMME FAMILY. 281

  7. ELEANOR, b. 18 Sept., 1809; m. JOSEPH GEORGE.
  8. BETSEY LOCKE, b. 23 Jan., 1812; m. JOSIAH CROSBY.
  9. MERIBAH, b. 16 Aug., 1815; d. 24 Mar., 1819.
39. 10. ASA SEEVER, b. 8 Feb., 1818.
  11. JOSEPH, b. 27 Nov., 1820; d. unm., 20 Jan., 1835.

29. CALEB⁶ DAME (*Jabez*,⁵ *Richard*,⁴ *John*,³ *John*,² *John*¹), born in 1772; died 29 May, 1864. He married twice: first, ABIGAIL GUPPY, of Dover, and secondly, TAMMY TWOMBLY, of Rochester. He lived at Rochester.

CHILDREN BY FIRST WIFE.

 1. JABEZ, b. 1709; d. 6 June, 1863; m. ELIZABETH BICKFORD. Children: 1. *Seth*.⁸ 2. *Frank O.*, m. Mary Herrick, dau. of Joshua Herrick, M, C., from Maine.
 2. ANNA, b. 1800; d. 20 Jan., 1855; m. 9 Dec., 1827, JOHN GUPPY, of Dover. Children: 1. *Albert*. 2. *Russell*. 3. *George Fox*.
 3. MERIBAH, b. 1802; d 11. Apr., 1891; m. HENRY HALL. Child: *Harry*.
 4. JAMES, b. 1804; d. unm.; lived at Rochester; soldier in the Civil War, Co. A, 4th N. H. V.
 5. SOPHIA, b. 1806; d. 1896; m. JOHN HASKINS, of Boston.
 6. MARY, b. 21 Feb., 1808; d. 29 Mar., 1883; m. THOMAS HEALD. Children: 1. *Mary Phylura*. 2. *Louise Peabody*. 3. *Charles Thomas*.
40. 7. JOHN WESLEY, b. 26 Mar., 1813.

CHILDREN BY SECOND WIFE.

 8. CHARLES WESLEY, b. 1816; d. unm. at Fort Worth, Tex., 15 July, 1893; editor and publisher of a newspaper.
 9. MARTIN LUTHER, d. unm.
 10. AMASA, b. 1818; m. LYDIA JENNESS. Children: 1. *Taylor*. 2. *Lizzie*. 3. *Emma*.
 11. LEVI, b. 22 Oct., 1820; d. 18 July, 1880; m. OLIVE L. GARLAND. Child: *Hattie*.

30. CHARITY⁶ DAME (*Jabez*,⁵ *Richard*,⁴ *John*,³ *John*,² *John*¹), born 1 Sept., 1775; died 3 Feb., 1833. She married, 4 Mar., 1798, JOSEPH HANSON, of Rochester.

CHILDREN.

1. HUMPHREY, b. 1799.
2. MARY DAME, b. 1800; d. 1859; m. DR. J. C. FARRINGTON, of Rochester, one of the leading physicians of Strafford County, and member of Congress. Children: 1. Dr. James B. 2. Mary. 3. Joseph. 4. Walter.
3. HANNAH, b. 1801; d. in infancy.
4. JOSEPH, b. 27 July, 1803; d. unm., 21 Apr., 1828.
5. MERIBAH, b. 1805; d. 18 Nov., 1863; m. DR. JOSEPH SMITH, a prominent physician of Dover, who d. 25 Feb., 1886, aged 88 yrs. Children: 1. *Arabella.* 2. *Charles Carroll, M. D.* 3. *Elizabeth.* 4. *Herman, M. D.*
6. JOANNA, b. 1807; d. 10 Oct., 1884; m. 21 June, 1829, JOHN MCDUFFEE, of Rochester, the leading banker of Strafford County for half a century, who d. 7 Dec., 1890, aged 87 yrs.
7. HESTER, b. 1810; m. DANIEL MOONEY.
8. DOMINICUS, b. 13 Aug., 1813; d. July, 1909; m. 19 Sept., 1839, BETSEY CHASE; a merchant, and in active business. Child: *Charles A. C.*
9. ASA P., b. 1815; m. ANNA KIMBALL; lived at Dover.

31. JABEZ[6] DAME (*Jabez,*[5] *Richard,*[4] *John,*[3] *John,*[2] *John*[1]), born at Rochester in 1782; died 26 Jan., 1850. He married, 8 Dec., 1811, ELIZABETH HANSON CUSHING, daughter of Peter and Hannah (Hanson), and granddaughter of Rev. Jonathan Cushing, who was pastor of the First Church in Dover, 1717-1767. Jabez, who was a merchant-farmer, and leading citizen of Rochester, lived on the ancestral Dame farm on Haven Hill.

CHILDREN.

41. 1. PERMELIA CUSHING, b. 21 Apr., 1814.
     2. CHARLES, b. 1817; d. in infancy.

32. JAMES CHADBOURNE[7] DAME (*Joseph,*[6] *Joseph,*[5] *John,*[4] *John,*[3] *John,*[2] *John*[1]), born at Barnstead, 25 Aug., 1770; died at Concord, 10 Oct., 1859. He married, 11 Jan., 1795, PHEBE AYERS, born 12 Feb., 1772; died 30 Oct., 1854. He was a noted schoolmaster, and lived at Barnstead, where he farmed.

CHILDREN.

1. JOSEPH, b. 23 Jan., 1796; d. 1884; m. 9 Nov., 1820, URSULA HALL.
2. JOHN, b. 2 Mar., 1799; m. ANNA DREW.
3. ELIZA, b. 16 July, 1802; d. 5 Sept., 1849; m. WILLIAM NUTTER.
4. GEORGE, b. 23 June, 1809; d. unm., 1873.
5. MARY, b. 26 Aug., 1810; m. WILLIAM SHACKFORD.
6. PATIENCE HARRIET, b. 5 Jan., 1815; d. 24 Apr., 1900; a successful teacher; as a nurse in the Civil War she served continuously with the 2d Regt., N. H. V., from Apr., 1861, to Apr., 1865; received the thanks of the N. H. General Court and $500; one of the founders of the Soldiers' Home at Tilton, N. H.; clerk in the Treasury Department at Washington until 78 yrs. old; d. aged 85.

33. JOSEPH[7] DAME (*Joseph,*[6] *Joseph,*[5] *John,*[4] *John,*[3] *John,*[2] *John*[1]), born 20 Nov., 1772; died 27 Mar., 1861. He married ANNA PLUMMER, and lived at Dover; a farmer.

CHILDREN.

1. SAMUEL, b. 12 May, 1802.
2. JOHN, b. 28 May, 1803.
3. LYDIA, b. 14 Feb., 1805.
4. DANIEL, b. 17 May, 1807.
5. MARY, b. 28 Sept., 1808.
6. CHARLES, b. vb Sept., 1810; d. unm.; a graduate of Bowdoin College, 1835, and Andover Theological Seminary, 1838; was ordained 29 May, 1839; pastor of the Congregational Church at Falmouth, Me., and elsewhere.
7. FRANKLIN, b. 9 Nov., 1812.
8. ELIZABETH, b. 9 Apr., 1814; d. 16 Sept., 1878.
9. BETHIAH, b. 12 Nov., 1816; d. 12 Aug., 1842.
10. MEHITABLE, b. 23 Sept., 1818; d. 3 Nov., 1842.
11. SARAH, b. 1820.
12. JOSEPH, b. 1823; d. 26 May, 1885; soldier in the 11th N. H. V., Civil War.
13. WILLIAM (twin), b. 7 Sept., 1827; d. 8 July, 1887.
14. SUSAN (twin), b. 7 Sept., 1827; d. 20 Jan., 1889.

34. HUNKING[7] DAME (*Hunking,*[6] *Moses,*[5] *John,*[4] *John,*[3] *John,*[2] *John*[1]), born at Lee, 16 May, 1786; died at Nottingham, 16 Feb.,

1852. He married, in 1810, LYDIA C. DURGIN, born 6 Mar., 1790; died 6 Mar., 1847; daughter of Josiah Durgin, of Lee. He lived on the turnpike at Nottingham; a tavern keeper and farmer.

CHILDREN.

1. ISRAEL HUNKING, b. 29 Mar., 1811; d. 4 Feb., 1868; m. EMILY A. TUTTLE. Children: 1. *Henrietta.* 2. *Lydia.*
2. SAMUEL SCALES, b. 1816; d. 1870; m. (1) HANNAH DAME, dau. of John[7] (36, 6); m. (2) HARRIET DAME, also dau. of John[7] (36, 3); lived at Nottingham; a farmer and merchant.
3. GREENLEAF, b. 19 July, 1820; d. 19 July, 1850; m. CHARLOTTE CHISWELL.
4. JOSEPH, b. 29 Apr., 1824; d. 19 Apr., 1871; m. MARY CRAWFORD, b. 30 Apr., 1828; d. 20 Apr., 1868; lived at Nottingham.
5. LYDIA A., b. 18 Nov., 1828; d. 14 Sept., 1859; m. JOHN K. STEEL.

35. ISRAEL[7] DAME (*Hunking*,[6] *Moses*,[5] *John*,[4] *John*,[3] *John*,[2] *John*,[1]), born 26 Aug., 1788; died 3 Apr., 1872. He married HANNAH DURGIN, born 3 May, 1794, daughter of Josiah Durgin, of Lee. He was a farmer and mill owner, and lived at Lee.

CHILDREN.

1. SALLIE, b. 21 Mar., 1811; d. 28 Feb., 1860; m. WILLIAM LOCKE.
2. HANNAH, b. 5 Nov., 1814.
3. GREENLEAF CILLEY, b. 16 Apr., 1816.
4. NANCY, b. 8 Mar., 1819; m. SAMUEL GLASS.
5. CLARISSA, b. 5 Apr., 1821; d. unm., 20 June, 1878.
6. LYDIA, b. 20 Oct., 1823; d. 4 Mar., 1830.
7. ABBY H., b. 3 Mar., 1826; m. HARVEY YOUNG.
8. ISRAEL SAMUEL, b. 28 Apr., 1830; d. 22 Mar., 1893; m. 1858, MARY HANSON, of Dover; farmer; lived at Lee.

36. JOHN[7] DAME (*Samuel*,[6] *Moses*,[5] *John*,[4] *John*,[3] *John*,[2] *John*[1]), born at Nottingham, 21 Apr., 1781; died 11 Mar., 1856. He married NANCY PARSONS BARBER, of Epping, and lived at Nottingham.

THE DAMME FAMILY.

CHILDREN.

1. DANIEL BARBER, b. 17 Feb., 1810; d. 30 Oct., 1846; m. BETSEY MCKENDLY.
42. 2. SAMUEL, b. 1 June, 1812.
3. HARRIET, b. 10 May, 1814; m. SAMUEL SCALES⁸ DAME (34, 2).
4. ROBERT BARBER, b. 26 Aug., 1817; d. 26 July, 1906; m. 1844, HARRIET HILL; lived at Epping; brick mason.
5. JOHN, b. 27 Nov., 1821; m. SARAH MANNING.
6. HANNAH, b. 15 Apr., 1823; d. 7 Mar., 1845; m. SAMUEL SCALES DAME. Children: 1. *Frank H.* 2. *Hannah B.*

37. JONATHAN⁷ DAME (*Richard,⁶ Jonathan,⁵ Richard,⁴ John,³ John,² John¹*), b. on 20 Apr., 1786; died 30 Nov., 1865. He married, 9 Nov., 1828, HANNAH O. MAY. He lived at Dover, where he was cashier of the bank, and in 1841 removed to Newport, R. I., and was cashier of a bank there for many years.

CHILDREN.

1. RICHARD, b. 12 July, 1829; d. unm., 12 Dec., 1849.
2. WILLIAM, b. 18 Jan., 1831; d. 1855.
3. OWEN, b. 21 Feb., 1833.
4. ELMA MARIA, b. 23 July, 1835.
5. ELIZABETH, b. 27 Feb., 1838.
6. MARY, b. 19 Nov., 1842.

38. MARY⁷ DAME (*Timothy,⁶ Jabez,⁵ Richard,⁴ John,³ John,² John¹*), born at Rochester, 2 June, 1805; married, 1823, JONATHAN WEEKS, born at Dover, 8 Jan., 1804.

CHILDREN.

1. GEORGE LOCKE, b. 19 June, 1825; m. REBECCA PAGE.
2. RUFUS SPAULDING, b. 14 Sept., 1829; d. 1858.
3. JOHN WESLEY, b. 24 July, 1832; d. 1856.
4. JONATHAN, b. at Lowell, Mass., 7 Aug., 1835; d. 1835.
5. ORRIN FRANCIS, b. 30 Sept., 1837; d. 1842.
6. JOSEPH DAME, b. 3 Dec., 1840; d. at Pittsburgh, Pa., 26 Dec., 1898; m. MARTHA J. FOWLER; lived at Pittsburgh.
7. EDWARD FRANCIS, b. 4 Nov., 1842; d. 1861.

8. MARY ELLA, b. at Lowell, 14 Apr., 1849; d. at Cambridge, Mass., 6 Sept., 1906; m. 22 Dec., 1897, ALBERT H. LAMSON, of Elkins, N. H.; no children.

39. ASA SEEVER[7] DAME (*Timothy,[6] Jabez,[5] Richard,[4] John,[3] John,[2] John[1]*), born 8 Feb., 1818; married twice; first, ANNA NUTTER, and secondly, ARABELLA BUZZELL.

CHILDREN, BY SECOND WIFE.

1. FRANKLIN P., m. SARAH PARSONS DIXON. Children: 1. *Bessie,*[9] m. Eskar Peavy. 2. *John.* 3. *Alice,* m. Seba Smart. 4. *Arthur,* m. Edith Battey.
2. ALONZO.
3. SARAH FRANCES, m. ALLEN HALL. Children: 1. *Ossie M.* 2. *Arthur E.*

40. JOHN WESLEY[7] DAME (*Caleb,[6] Jabez,[5] Richard,[4] John,[3] John,[2] John[1]*), born 26 Mar., 1813; died 13 Mar., 1879. He married CAROLINE LORD, who died 9 Nov., 1860. He lived at Rochester, where he was a farmer.

CHILDREN.

1. CHARLES WESLEY, b. 22 Jan., 1841; m. 22 Jan., 1868, EMILY H. PERKINS; lives on Haven Hill, Rochester; a soldier in the 26th Regt., Mass. Vols., 1861-65. Children: 1. *Fannie A.* 2. *Ernest J.* 3. *Carrie M.* 4. *Lura.* 5. *Josie.* 6. *Blanche.*
2. AUGUSTA J., b. 20 Nov., 1842; m. MARTIN V. B. WENTWORTH; lived at Rochester; no children.
3. SOPHIA H., b. 25 Apr., 1845; m. JOHN BLAISDELL; lives at East Rochester. Children: 1. *Herman W.* 2. *Osmond.* 3. *B. Frank.*
4. OSMOND, b. 23 Dec., 1847; d. 1848.
5. CLARA A., b. 10 Mar., 1850; d. 1853.
6. GEORGE E., b. Oct., 1851; m. MRS. BETTIE MCCLELLAN; lives in Florida. Children: 1. *Carrie.*[9] 2. *Hattie.* 3. *Bessie.*
7. JENNIE, b. 13 Nov., 1854; m. ALBERT H. WENTWORTH; lived at Rochester. Child: *Roscoe,* m. Bessie Whitney of Portland, Me.

THE DAMME FAMILY.

41. PAMELIA CUSHING[7] DAME (*Jabez,[6] Jabez,[5] Richard,[4] John,[3] John,[2] John[1]*), born 21 Apr., 1814; died 2 May, 1854. She married, 1 Feb., 1842, STEPHEN PERKINS ESTES, born at Sanford, Me., 1810; died at Rochester 1 Jan., 1854, son of Samuel and Rhoda (Linscott) Estes. They lived at Rochester with her father on the Dame farm on Haven Hill.

CHILDREN.

1. ELIZABETH CUSHING, b. 16 July, 1843; d. unm., 8 Feb., 1909.
2. MARY MILLARD, b. 23 Dec., 1846; d. unm., 16 July, 1899. She and her sister, Elizabeth Cushing Estes, were left orphans in 1854, when they were placed under guardians and resided at Rochester Village until 1864, when they removed to Dover and resided there until their death. Soon after coming to Dover they commenced collecting the material which constitutes the larger part of this genealogy. It was a labor of love with them, and they spent much time and money in their researches. At the death of the elder sister in 1909, by order of her will, the Dame memoranda passed to the hands of Mr. John Scales of Dover, for editing and publication. Mr. Scales secured quite an additional number of families, names, and dates, which combined with the other part constitute the entire work.

42. SAMUEL[8] DAME (*John,[7] Samuel,[6] Moses,[5] John,[4] John,[3] John,[2] John[1]*), born at Nottingham, N. H., 1 June, 1812; died there 16 Nov., 1881. He married, 1836, MARY ANN GILMAN, of Newmarket, born 7 June, 1814. He lived at Nottingham, and was a farmer and active business man.

CHILD.

1. LOREN L., b. 11 Mar., 1838; d. at Medford, Mass., 1903; m. NANCY ISABEL ARNOLD, of Braintree, Mass., for many years a high school principal, the closing years of his labors being at Medford; three daughters.

THE GUPPY FAMILY OF DOVER.

The Guppy family is said to have been natives of Flanders, and came over to England and settled in Wilts County in the sixteenth century. They were cloth makers, expert weavers, some were engaged in agriculture, and some followed the sea and became famous captains. The first of the family who came to Dover was Kingwall Guppy, and at an early period he received a grant from the town of Dover, in which is the point of land since known as *"Guppy's Point."* It is the first point below St. Alban's Cove, on the Newichawannock River; it is now the burial ground of the Judge Doe family. Kingwall Guppy was uncle to James Guppy, the founder of the family that lived in the historic Guppy house, on the Guppy farm, that now belongs to the City of Dover.

About the year 1700 Joshua Guppy, brother of Kingwall, came over to New England, and settled at Beverly, Mass. He was a weaver, and brought his looms and weaving machinery with him, and set up work in that town. On the voyage he made the acquaintance of Dr. Devereaux and his wife, of Beverly; they became friends for life. In due time Joshua Guppy set up his loom and soon became engaged in a prosperous business, cloth-making. Dr. Devereaux died, and Mr. Guppy married the widow. They were then one of the well-to-do families of the town. In September, 1732, twin sons were born to them, and they were named *James* and *Joshua*. The father died when the children were small. The widow asked Kingwall Guppy, of Dover, to adopt James. Capt. Gage, of Dover, took James from Beverly to Dover and talked the matter over with Mr. Guppy; he was not so situated as to properly care for the boy, so Capt. Gage took him to his own home, and brought him up, till he was desirous of going to sea with the Captain, at the age of 14 years. James continued in the seafaring life for several years. At 18 he was mate of a vessel; and at 21 he became captain of a good ship.

In 1753, Captain Guppy married Jane Ladd, of Newcastle, and they commenced house-keeping there; he continuing in the shipping business. They had a son, Joshua, born in 1754; the mother died in 1755. In 1757, Capt. Guppy married Miss Ann

Loud, of Portsmouth, and they commenced house-keeping there, and that was his home till he came to Dover to live in 1767. Captain Guppy prospered in business; and he prospered in family affairs, having a fine, comfortable home. To them were born six children,—Sarah, James, Ann, Jane, Prudence and John; the first three died young; the others married and left descendants: *John* became the ancestor of the Dover family.

In 1767, Captain Guppy came up from Portsmouth and bought the present Guppy farm, and it remained in possession of the Guppy family untill the death of his grandson, Jeremy Belknap Guppy, 17 March, 1917, a period of 150 years. Then, by Will of Mr. Guppy, it passed to the possession of the City of Dover to be kept as a memorial of the Guppy Family. The other large property was variously distributed, by the Will.

JOHN GUPPY, the youngest child of CAPT. JAMES GUPPY, was born in Dover (in the Guppy house), 3 July, 1768; he died there 3 April, 1855, aged 87 years. He married, about 1810, MISS HANNAH DAME, daughter of JONATHAN and HANNAH (PLAISTED) DAME, of Kittery, Me., who lived near the bridge to the Navy Yard. She was born 11 June, 1787; died in that house 26 Aug., 1869, aged 82 years. It is a remarkable fact that JOHN GUPPY and his son JEREMY BELKNAP GUPPY, by their combined ages, covered a period of a century and a half, living in the same house.

HANNAH DAME was seventh in descent from Deacon JOHN DAMME, (by *Jonathan,*[6] *Jonathan,*[5] *Richard,*[4] *John,*[3] *John,*[2] *John*[1]). Her mother, HANNAH PLAISTED, was fifth in descent from Roger Plaisted, one of the early settlers in old Kittery, now Eliot, and for several years he was Representative in the Massachusetts General Court. He and son Roger were slain by the Indians 16 Oct., 1675.

THE CHILDREN OF JOHN AND HANNAH (DAME) GUPPY.

1. SARAH ANN, b. 5 Apr., 1812; d. 10 Oct., 1900, aged 88 yrs.; m. SAMUEL HOWARD HENDERSON, 5 July, 1838.
2. GEORGE FOX, b. 3 June, 1814; d. 26 Dec., 1838; m. Dec. 13, 1835, MISS ABIGAIL F. YORK, of Dover.

3. ABIGAIL, b. 19 Apr., 1817; d. 13 Apr., 1908, aged 91 yrs.; m. DR. CHARLES TRAFTON, of South Berwick.
4. ' JOSHUA JAMES, b. 27 Aug., 1820; d. (at Portage, Wis.) 8 Dec., 1893.
5. JOSEPH DAME, b. 11 Feb., 1823; d. 3 June, 1890; mayor of Dover 1879-80.
6. JOHN DEVEREAUX, b. 3 Sept., 1825; d. 1 Nov., 1844.
7. HANNAH ESTHER, b. 31 July, 1828; d. 16 Apr., 1913, aged 85 yrs.
8. JEREMY BELKNAP, b. 6 Apr., 1831; d. 16 Mar., 1917, aged 86 yrs.

This family is noted for the longevity of its members: The father, JOHN GUPPY, lived to be 87; the mother, 82; the eldest daughter, 91; the second daughter, 88; the seventh and youngest daughter, 85, and the eighth and youngest child, JEREMY BELKNAP, 86. One son, JOSEPH DAME GUPPY, was Mayor of Dover, 1879, 1880; he died at the age of 67. He held other official positions, always with credit for efficiency.

The most distinguished member of the family was JOSHUA JAMES GUPPY, who died at the age of 73, at Portage, Wisconsin. He was a tall, large, fine looking man; he fitted for college at Franklin Academy; was graduated at Dartmouth College in the class of 1843; among his seventy-four classmates were John Riley Varney, of Dover, Bradbury Poore Cilley, of Manchester, John B. Clarke, of Manchester, John L. Caverly, of Strafford, Dr. Jonathan Smith Ross, of Somersworth. In fact, a large number of his classmates won distinction for their good work. Mr. Guppy studied law in Dover and was admitted to the bar; in 1846 he went to Wisconsin, and commenced practice of law in Columbia county; soon after getting established in business he opened his office at Portage City, and that was his home the remainder of his life. In 1849 he was appointed Judge of Probate, and held the office several years; he was also Judge of the County Court eight years. He became interested in military affairs and rose to the rank of Lieut. Colonel. When the Civil War commenced he raised a regiment and was appointed Lieut. Col. of the 10th Wis. Vols.; Col. of 23d Wis. Vols.; Brev. Brig. Gen. Vols., 1865, for meritorious service. In 1866 he was again appointed Judge of the County Court, and held the office till 1882. He declined to serve longer, but continued to practice his profession. In 1883 the Guppy Guards, of Portage, the fine militia company of the city, presented him an elegant, gold-headed cane, as a token of respect. From time to time General Guppy received other gifts from the citizens, by whom he was ever held in the highest esteem. He was one of the most highly honored citizens of the State as well as the City. At his death, 8 Dec., 1893, his remains were brought to Dover and interred in the Guppy family burial lot in Pine Hill Cemetery.

The regiment that he commanded in the war had a very fine record; the following is an account of the closing scene of his gallant 23d Regiment, where took place the defeat of the Federal troops in Louisiana, Nov. 3, 1863.

It was at Bayou Bourteau. After describing how the regiments were posted for the expected battle, it says the 23d Wisconsin was assigned to guard the camp; and two paymasters were in the camp paying off the troops, and the men of the 23d Wisconsin, commanded by Col. Joshua J. Guppy, were voting for State officers. Suddenly cavalry could be seen approaching across the open prairie. It soon appeared that an overwhelming force had fallen on the camp; the cavalry on the prairie advanced in a cloud of dust against the 76th Indiana, and 23d (Guppy's) Wisconsin.

Although the Federal gunners fired their pieces until the Texas horsemen were at the muzzles of their guns, it was apparent that the command would be cut to pieces. The 76th Indiana regiment was surrounded by cavalry and surrendered. The 23d Wisconsin (Guppy's regiment) was ridden down, and out of 226 officers and men only ninety-eight escaped; Col. Guppy was wounded and taken prisoner.

The second day after the fight, Gen. Taylor, riding past the column of prisoners, noted one limping along with a bandaged leg, who wore the uniform of a colonel. It was Col. Joshua J. Guppy of the 23d Wisconsin Regiment; Gen. Taylor stopped and invited him to ride in his ambulance. Col. Guppy declined, saying the men of his regiment were all his neighbors and friends at home, and he wished to remain with them. Gen. Taylor said, in reply, that he would ride slowly with the column; at which Col. Guppy reluctantly climbed into the ambulance with Gen. Taylor.

For some miles Col. Guppy was silent, but at length Gen. Taylor tactfully put him at his ease and loosened his tongue. The Wisconsin Colonel said he feared the news of the disaster to his regiment would have a bad effect upon his family, whereupon Gen. Taylor said: "You shall start for the river tonight and go to them."

Taylor was as good as his word. Col. Guppy was released on his parole, and allowed to proceed out of the Confederate lines. Col. Guppy returned home and was not able to resume service in the army.

THE GUPPY HOUSE.

The Guppy house, now the property of the City of Dover, was built in 1690 by Capt. Benjamin Heard, son of Capt. John Heard, of Garrison Hill. In 1767, Captain James Guppy came up from Portsmouth and bought the house and farm, and retired, somewhat, from the seafaring life he had led for a number of years, and had accumulated an ample fortune for that period. Mrs. Annie Wentworth Baer, a noted local historian, and member of the Northam Colonist Historical Society, prepared and read before the society, at a meeting in 1905, the following description of the house and its contents, at that date. She said:

"It is an ordinary two-story house, built in an extraordinary way. The frame is all of white oak, and the beams and other timbers are finished off in the rooms. A beam showing a foot-wide, runs along the side of the two front rooms, a cross timber holds the house firmly together. Mortised into these is a beam, nearly eighteen inches wide, running across the ceiling in the middle of the two front rooms. Heavy corner posts are visible in each corner. The huge beams are perfectly smooth and finished on the edge with a bead.

"The southwest room or parlor, (the house faces south), is finished in clear white pine, in a very ornate style. There is a handsome buffet in the southwest corner of marvellous workmanship. The front entry is panelled from top to bottom. The stairs are winding and have a substantial oak rail.

"The living room, when Capt. Guppy bought the house in 1767, as Capt. Heard (Hurd) built it, had an immense fireplace, taking up nearly two-thirds of the west side of the room, and a small china closet was built under the stairs, at the left of the fireplace. Two bed rooms were on the east of this room.

"In 1768 Capt. Guppy took down the chimney, which he considered unsafe, and rebuilt it the same as before, from bricks and clay mortar made on the farm. The house stands on a ledge and the immense chimney is built on the solid rock.

"Capt. Guppy, to provide room for his large family, and to get the long roof which was the prevailing style then, put on the lean to and provided more rooms. In 1770 he moved from Portsmouth to the farm with his wife and seven children; five more were born here in Dover: George, Abigail, Samuel, Mary and Jeremy. Rev. Dr. Jeremy Belknap came to the house and christened these five children, at the proper age.

"When Capt. Guppy removed from Portsmouth to Dover, he had resided in the former place eighteen years; he brought the furniture, purchased in 1758, when he was first married. The six heavy mahogany parlor chairs, with heavy leather bottoms fastened with brass nails, were a wedding present from Capt. Gage. The family now have them all in good condition. The mahogany tables, secretary, with its delicate lines of inlaid work, were a part of the early house furnishings. A long mirror with heavy beveled glass, hangs between the two front windows of the southeast room, just where it has always hung. It rests on two long screws with ornamented heads. The picture on the inside of the brass rim represents a girl clothed in a loose pink robe leaning against a square monument with a pointed capital. A wreath of leaves on the plinth enclose the words 'Sacred to Friendship.'

"A comb chair of Capt. Guppy, and the armchair in which he always sat, on cold winter evenings before the open fire, are still in a good state of preservation.

"In the quaint parlor hang paintings of King George III and Queen Charlotte, which were brought from England by Capt. Guppy in 1760, the year they were crowned.

"A small curly maple table has a sea history worth recording. This table was always in the Captain's cabin, and he ate his meals from it as long as he followed the sea. It has crossed the Atlantic many times, and has made 39 round trips to the West Indies. In the house now (1908) stands a punch bowl and salver, well known to Dr. Belknap, when he made ministerial calls and baptized the children. Dr. Belknap always received his freight of foreign wines from the Captain's store.

"After the Declaration of Independence Capt. Guppy gave up going to sea, as the British cruisers made that business unprofitable for Americans. He devoted the rest of his life to farming.

In August, 1782, the U. S. Government sent him to the friendly French fleet on our coast as a competent and trustworthy pilot. He piloted five of them into Portsmouth harbor, and remained with the fleet three months, as the confidential adviser of Marquis de Vaudreuil. Mrs. Trafton says her grandfather described the Marquis as the most courteous gentleman he ever met.

"This fine old mansion house is filled with articles of virtue. Among the number are the silver candle sticks and snuffers, sugar bowl and creamer; the green Delft plates, a part of which set, the Captain bought in Delft and brought home for his young bride in 1758. What remained of the set when he died in 1826 was divided among his children. Six plates were left to his son John, who remained in the old home, having inherited the farm at the death of his father.

"Mrs. Henderson, the eldest daughter of John and Hannah (Dame) Guppy, took one of the rare plates to her home (when she was married to Samuel Hoyt Henderson in 1839), and the other five remain in the old home. The dwellers there say the plates belong with the house. A tall china coffee pot with a white ground covered with bright decorations in terra cotta, blue and yellow, has a picture on its sides: three females, representing War, Peace, and Industry. Mrs. Trafton says this pot was brought from some foreign land and given to 'Grandfather Plaisted' in 1684, and descended from him to his grand-daughter, Hannah Plaisted, who married John Guppy. Among other pieces of rare old china is a helmet cream pitcher. This and two other pieces are all that remain of the full set bought by Capt. Guppy in England.

"In the living room stands a tall, eighteenth century clock, bought by John Guppy in his early married days. In the chambers are quaint stands, bureaus, chairs, mirrors, a canopy bed, a warming pan, fire buckets, and a water set of pink Napoleon ware, a sampler and an embroidered packing case, wrought by Sarah, eldest daughter of Capt. James Guppy, when she was twelve years old, and a white linen coverlet that the Captain always took to sea with him, which has outlasted the ship and her master, and with the care it has today will be seen generations hence.

"The frame of the old house has never been repaired; new windows have been put in, but all the rest, save shingles, are as Capt. Guppy left it after repairing it in 1767."

By courtesy of Mr. William C. Henderson, Christian Science Practitioner, in Dover, for many years, and one of the founders of the Christian Science Church here, the following information is furnished, regarding Capt. Guppy's grand-daughter, Sarah Ann Guppy, who married (second wife) Mr. Samuel Howard Henderson, who was born Oct. 4, 1798, and for more than forty years was one of the leading business men in Dover, dying June 12, 1867.

Mr. Henderson married twice: (1) Delia Paul, April 11, 1827; she died Sept. 28, 1837; their children were:

1. MARY ELIZABETH, b. Apr. 19, 1828; m. SAMUEL H. DAME, June 2, 1851; she d. Dec. 7, 1887.
2. HOWARD MILLETT, b. Nov. 14, 1829; m. ELIZABETH VARNEY, Dec. 7, 1854; he d. Dec. 24, 1871; she d. Sept. 30, 1860.
3. THOMAS ALBERT, b. Dec. 1, 1833; killed in battle Aug. 16,

Mr. Henderson married (2) July 5, 1838, Sarah Ann Guppy, who was born April 5, 1812; she died Oct. 10, 1900, aged 88 years. Their children were:

4. JOHN SAMUEL, b. Apr. 22, 1839; m. SARAH FRANCES VAN ZANDT, Aug. 24, 1863; he d. Apr. 24, 1870.
5. CHARLES TRAFTON, b. Feb. 14, 1841; d. Apr. 9, 1919.
6. DELIA ANNAH, b. June 18, 1843; m. GEORGE WILLIAM NEAL, Aug. 11, 1868; she d. Sept. 17, 1914.
7. FANNY LAWRENCE, b. Nov. 5, 1845; d. Dec. 15, 1868.
8. EMMA TRAFTON, b. Jan. 21, 1848; d. Dec. 4, 1868.
9. WILLIAM CHANNING, b. Sept. 28, 1854; m. Dec. 6, 1876, LAURA E. CRAPO; she d. Jan. 27, 1896; they had no children.

Lieut. Col. Thomas Albert Henderson, third of the above-mentioned children, was graduated from Bowdoin College when he was twenty-three years old, and was one of the best scholars Dover ever produced; and was one of the finest men. He studied law and was admitted to the bar, but was called to war before he had become established in his profession. He was twenty-eight when the great rebellion commenced. He at once went to Norwich University Military School, Norwich, Vt., and took a regular course in military drill and study, to prepare himself for service in a New Hampshire Regiment. He enlisted in November, 1861, and was appointed, Nov. 4, Adjutant of the Seventh N. H. Regiment of Volunteer Infantry and was mustered in at once; August 26, 1862, he was appointed Major of that regiment; a year later, July 22, 1863, he was promoted to Lieut. Col.; he held that office till his death, a year later; he was severely wounded August 16, 1864, in the battle at "Deep Bottom." He died soon after of his wounds. This regiment has one of the best records of any of the New Hampshire Volunteer Infantry. Col. Henderson was an excellent commander, skilful in his management of his men, unflinchingly brave when danger was greatest. No better, or more capable man from Dover, served in the army of a million men that subdued the Rebellion.

BENJAMIN HEARD'S DEED TO CAPT. JAMES GUPPY.

Know all men by these presents That I Benjamin Heard of the Town of Dover, in the Prov'e of New Hampshire, in New England, yeoman, for and in Consideration of the sum of two hundred and sixty-five pounds, lawful money to me in hand before the delivery thereof well and truly paid by Jame Guppy of the town of Portsmouth, in the Province aforesaid, Mariner, the receipt whereof I do hereby acknowledge, have given, granted and sold, and by this presents do give, grant, bargain and sell, alien, enfeoff, convey and confirm unto the said James Guppy and to his heirs and assigns forever, one Certain tract of land in Dover aforesaid containing Sixty Acres (more or less) being the whole of my Homestead Farm, where I now dwell and all that I have now within fence or in my Inclosure, which sd Farm is Bounded as Followeth, vizt, Adjoyning Northerly on the Main Road leading to Fresh Creek (so called), and Easterly Adjoyning to the Road leading to Mason's Lot (so called), Southerly Adjoining, partly on land in possession of Lydia Harford & partly on Job Clements land, & westerly joining partly on Capt. Thomas W'st. Waldron's Land & partly on Col. John Gage's land, together with the house & barn & all other edfices or buildings standing on sd land,—To have and to hold the said granted premises with all the Privileges and Appurtenances to the same appertaining to him the said James Guppy & unto his Heires and Assignes forever. And I, the said Benjamin Heard hereby Covenant, Grant and Agree to and with the said James Guppy, his Heirs and Assigns, that until the delivery, I am the lawful Owner of the said premises & am lawfully seized and possessed thereof in my own Right, in Fee Simple, and have full Power and lawful Authority to grant and convey the same in manner aforesaid—That the said premises are free and clear of all and any incumbrance whatsoever, and that I, the said Benjamin Heard for me, my heirs, Executors and Administrators, shall and will Warant the same to him the sd James Guppy and unto his Heirs and Assigns against the lawful claims and Demands of any Person or Persons whomsoever. In witness whereof, I the sd Benjamin Heard have hereunto set my hand & Affixed my Seal this 16th day of April in the 7th year of his Majesty's Reign, Anno Domini 1767. And Mary, wife of the aforesaid Benjamin Heard, in token of relinquishing all her right of Dower and power of thirds to ye aforesaid premises hath hereunto set her hand & affixed her Seal the day and year aforesaid.

Signed, Sealed &
Delivered in ye presence of

Benjamin x Heard.
his mark

Mary x Heard.
her mark

John Gage } Evidences
Eph'm Hanson } for the man

Eleazer Hodgdon } Evidences
Dorcas Hodgdon } for the woman.

Province of New Hampshire, Dover, April ye 16th, 1767, the within named Benjamin Heard appeared before me the subscriber and acknowledged the within Instrument to be his free act and Deed.

John Gage, Justice of Peace.

Received and Recorded 17th April 1767.

D Pierce, Red'r.

(N. H. Province Deeds, Vol. 87, page 387.)

WILL OF LATE J. BELKNAP GUPPY.

The will of the late J. Belknap Guppy was given out for publication by Attorney Dwight Hall, who with John F. Neal, of Boston, officiated as an executor. The will contained a number of public bequests including the following:

Wentworth Home $20,000 to be used in constructing an addition to the present accommodations; $5,000 to be utilized in construction of a public swimming pool; $400 for the upkeep of grave stones in Pine Hill cemetery. The Guppy homestead and bulk of his real estate to Strafford County; three tenement houses from which to obtain revenue to maintain a free bed in the Hayes Hospital; $2,000 to the N. H. S. P. C. A.; Guppy Park to the City of Dover to be utilized and maintained as a "public park"; $1,000 to Dover Firemen's Relief Asso.; all furniture of his homestead to the New Hampshire Genealogical Society; residue of all property to the Wentworth Home, Children's Home and Hayes Hospital; $2,000 to the City of Dover to be used in caring for the city's poor.

Sixth: I give to the City of Dover the sum of two thousand (2,000) dollars, in trust, the income only therefrom to be used annually to aid the worthy poor of that city.

Seventh: I give to the City of Dover the sum of five thousand (5,000) dollars to be used towards the construction of a public swimming pool or for the purpose of maintaining a public swimming pool, upon the condition that the construction of such a pool be commenced within two years from the time of my death; and in case the construction of such a pool is not commenced within two years of my death said sum of five thousand (5,000) dollars shall become a part of the residuum of my estate.

Eighth: I give to the City of Dover the sum of four hundred (400) dollars, in trust, the income therefrom to be used for the purpose of righting, repairing and cleaning grave stones in Pine Hill Cemetery in said Dover. It is my wish that this income be expended on burial lots, for the care of which there is no other provision.

Ninth: I give, bequeath, and devise unto the City of Dover a certain tract of land situate on the westerly side of Portland Street in said Dover bounded and described as follows: viz, beginning on the westerly side of Portland Street at a stone marked "P" set in the wall at the line fence between my field and pasture and thence running westerly by the line fence between my field and pasture to the Boston and Maine railroad property; thence running southerly by the Boston and Maine railroad property a distance of four hundred and fifty-eight and forty-nine one-hundredths feet to a stone post, thence running easterly to a stone post at Portland Street, said post being marked with a letter "P"; thence running northerly by Portland Street to the point begun at, the same being a tract of land containing about thirteen acres, upon the express condition that this tract of land shall be forever used as a public park by said City of Dover.

Tenth: I give, bequeath and devise unto the County of Strafford in said State of New Hampshire, in trust, upon the conditions hereinafter set forth, the following described tracts of land—the first tract of land is situated on the westerly side of Portland Street in said Dover and is bounded and described as follows, viz; beginning at the intersection of the westerly side line of Portland Street with the southerly side line of Oak Street and running westerly by Oak Street to land of William Brown; thence running southerly by said Brown's land to land of the Boston and Maine Railroad; thence running by said railroad land to land hereinbefore given the City of Dover for Park purposes; thence running easterly by said land given said City for Park purposes to Portland Street to the point begun at. The above described tract of land contains about fifteen acres. One other tract of land situate in Rollinsford in said County and State of New Hampshire, bounded and described as follows, viz: beginning at the intersection of the northerly side line of Oak Street with the easterly side line of Portland Street and running thence easterly by Portland Street to land now or formerly of Michael McCone; thence northerly by McCone's land to land of Sarah A. Wiggin; thence westerly by said Wiggin land to Portland Street; thence southerly by Portland Street to the point begun at. This tract of land contains about eighteen acres. One other tract of land situated in said Rollinsford on the northerly side of the Fresh Creek Road bounded and described as follows, viz: beginning at the southeasterly corner of land of Albert F. R. Elliott and running thence easterly by said road to land of George H. Yeaton; thence northerly by land of said Yeaton to land of Frank Swain; thence westerly by land of said Swain and land of James McKeaver; thence southerly by land of McCone and land of said Elliott to the point begun at. Said tract of land contains sixteen acres, more or less. One other tract of land situated in said Dover on the road leading out of Dover City and commonly called the Tolend Road opposite the road leading to the Ezra Hayes place; said tract of land contains sixteen acres more or less.

One other tract of land situate in said Dover on the westerly side of Portland Street bounded as follows,—beginning at a stone post marked "P" and running westerly to a stone post at land of the Boston and Maine railroad; thence running southerly by land of the Boston and Maine railroad to Forest Street; thence easterly by Forest Street to land formerly of one McKernan; thence southerly by said McKernan's land, land of Patrick McManus, land of Avisia Rods, land of Lawrence Commonly, land of James McKeaver and land of James Quinn heirs to land of Lawrence Commonly; thence easterly by said Commonly land to the rear line of the house lots on Hancock Street; thence northerly by Portland Street to the point begun at. This tract of land contains nine and thirty-six one-hundredths acres, more or less. One other tract of land situated in said Dover on the easterly side of Portland Street bounded as follows, viz: beginning at the intersection of the southerly side line of Oak Street with the easterly side line of Portland Street and running thence southerly by Portland Street to Granite Street, thence easterly by Granite Street to land of Thomas Mason; thence northerly by land of said Mason, thence easterly by said Mason's land, land of one McKay, land of heirs of George Colbath and land of the Mainard Land Company to Oak Street, thence northerly by Oak Street to the point begun at. Said tract of land contains twenty-four acres, more or less, and includes the homestead house of the said Jeremy Belknap Guppy.

I also give to the county of Strafford upon the conditions hereinafter set forth all my farming tools, carpenter tools, harnesses, sleighs, robes, blankets, sleds, pungs, carts, wheels, machinery of all kinds and all household furniture not hereinafter disposed of which are found upon the above described property or in the buildings thereon. The condition upon which the devise and gifts contained in this section of my will are made are that the property herein devised and given shall be held in trust by said County and shall be used as a home for Protestants of good character who are descended from American ancestors and who are unable through misfortune or old age to earn their own living for whose support the said County is responsible, and upon the further condition that my homestead house shall be maintained in substantially the same condition that it is now in and shall be kept in good repair.

In case said County of Strafford shall fail to accept the above devises and gifts upon the conditions herein contained within two years of the time of the appointment of administration upon my estate, I give, bequeath, and devise all of the property mentioned in this clause of my will to the said City of Dover, the same to be held in trust and to be occupied and used in such manner as the City may see fit, meaning hereby to give said City the benefit, income, and control of said property. I request that my homestead house be maintained in the condition in which it now is.

Eleventh: I give to the Wentworth Home for the Aged, a corporation situated in said Dover, the sum of twenty thousand (20,000) dollars, said sum of twenty thousand (20,000) dollars to be used for the purpose of building an addition to the present building of said corporation or for the purpose of constructing another building for the accommodation of elderly people, and for the purpose of equipping and furnishing such addition or building. This bequest to the Wentworth Home for the Aged is made upon the express condition that all of said sum of twenty thousand (20,000) dollars, and the accumulations thereon which shall not be used for the objects above set forth within six (6) years from the time of my decease, shall upon the expiration of six (6) years from the time of my decease revert to and become a part of my residuary estate, and shall be conveyed and delivered to my executors to be distributed in accordance with the provisions of the residuary clause in my will.

Twelfth: I give, bequeath, and devise to the Hayes Hospital, a corporation situated in said Dover and existing by virtue of the laws of the State of New Hampshire and to its successors and assigns the three tenement houses numbered one and two, three and four, five and six, together with the lots on which they are located on Hancock Street in said Dover, in trust, the income therefrom to be used towards the support of a free bed in said Hospital.

Thirteenth: I give to the New Hampshire Society for Prevention of Cruelty to Animals the sum of two thousand (2,000) dollars, in trust, the income only therefrom to be used for the relief of suffering animals.

Fourteenth: I give to the Dover Firemen's Relief Association of said Dover the sum of one thousand (1,000) dollars, in trust, the income only therefrom to be used for the benefit of disabled firemen of that city.

Nineteenth: I give to the Dover Public Library any or all of my books which they may desire.

Twentieth: All the rest, residue, and remainder of my property of every name and nature wherever found, I give, bequeath, and devise in equal shares to the Wentworth Home for the Aged, the Dover Children's Home and to the Hayes Hospital, to them and their successors and assigns, in trust, the income therefrom to be used in such manner as said respective legatees see fit.

I direct my said executors to erect at my grave a stone of the same kind and design as those erected at the graves of my brothers in Pine Hill Cemetery in said Dover.

I appoint John F. Neal of Boston, Massachusetts, and Dwight Hall of said Dover, sole executors of this will.

I revoke all former wills by me made.

In witness whereof I have hereeunto set my hand and seal this eighteenth day of April, A. D. 1914.

Jeremy Belknap Guppy (S).

Signed, sealed, published, and declared by the above named Jeremy Belknap Guppy as and for his last will and testament in the presence of us who at his request and in his presence and in the presence of each other have subscribed our names as witnesses hereto.

Gilman H. Twombly,
Frank R. Bliss,
Dwight Hall.

THE ROBERTS FAMILY.

THOMAS ROBERTS was born in England about 1600, according to deposition. Rev. Dr. Everett S. Stackpole imparts the information that he had learned on "excellent authority" that Thomas Roberts was apprenticed to a fishmonger of London, as "son of John Roberts, of Woolaston Co., Worcester, 29 April, 1622, and probably came over at once, as an apprentice to Edward Hilton, and lived within a stone's throw of Hilton's house, on *Hilton Point*." He was not married at the time of coming over, but probably was married in 1627. The maiden name of his wife is not known, but there is a tradition she was sister of Edward Hilton. Further than that we know not.

As regards his ancestry the following may be of interest, and worthy of preservation in these pages. In Mckenzie's book, "Collonial Families of the United States," Vol. 2, pages 619 *et seq.* is given the genealogy of the Roberts family in England, and it is traced back to A. D. 1482, ten years before Columbus discovered his first island in the West Indies. Among the descendants is given Sir Thomas Roberts, of Glassenburg; born A. D. 1560; buried 20 Feb., 1627; Knighted 23 July, 1603; created a baronet 3 July, 1620; Sheriff of Kent, 1623; married Frances James, who died in Feb., 1648; she was daughter of Martin James, Esq., of Imarden. Their children were: Sir Walter; Thomas; Frances; William, who emigrated to Maryland, and has distinguished descendants there; Elizabeth; John; Ann. Those who have investigated the matter think there is a strong probability that the second son, Thomas, who emigrated somewhere, is the Thomas Roberts who came over and helped colonize Dover. There is no positive proof, but a strong probability, that Governor Thomas Roberts, of *Hilton Point,* was second son of Sir Thomas Roberts, who was knighted in 1603, and created a baron in 1620.

In 1640, at the March election, Thomas Roberts was chosen Governor or President of the County in place of Gov. John Underhill; he held that office until Dover (then Northam) came under Massachusetts rule in 1642. Later he held various minor town offices; he was a regular member of the church for many years, but was inclined to be liberal in his views, so when the Quaker missionaries came to Dover he favored giving them a fair hearing and opposed having the women whipped, as they were by order of the court. He died between Sept. 27, 1673, and June 30, 1674; those being the dates of his will and its probating.

When Mr. Roberts removed from *Hilton Point* to The Neck he located his house on the high bank of Fore River; Dr. Quint, in his Memoranda, describes it as follows: "He located himself on Fore River, on land now (1851) forming a part of the Jerry Roberts estate; the spot is still identified. It is nearly in a direct line, east from the house now (1851) on that estate. The land had been in the continuous possession of the Roberts faimly to that time."

This land is now (1923) owned by Mr. William M. Courser. The house was built in 1825; the former house was burned in 1824. This farm remained in possession of the Roberts family until near the close of the nineteenth century. It came down in regular line of descent from Thomas, Jr., the younger son of Governor Thomas;

their names are: Thomas,[2] Nathaniel,[3] Moses,[4] Thomas,[5] James,[6] Jerry, Sr.,[7] Jerry, Jr.,[8] who was living in the house when Dr. Quint made his Historical Memoranda.

The farm owned by the late Howard Millett Roberts's sons, Fred and Stephen W., came down to them through uninterrupted succession from father to son, as follows: Sergt. John Roberts, eldest son of Governor Thomas; his house was near the big elm tree; his son Joseph[3]; he had the tannery; his son Stephen[4]; he had the tannery and kept a public house (ordinary); his son Joseph[5]; his son Hanson[6]; his son Howard Millett Roberts, who was born August 15, 1832.

JOSEPH[5] ROBERTS, who was born in 1747, built the house about 1780, which was known as the Hanson Roberts house during the 19th century; it bore that name because Mr. Hanson Roberts was born in it in 1793, and lived there during a long life; it is one of the finest old houses in Dover, and most beautifully located. Dr. Quint, in his valuable Memoranda, which he obtained from Mr. Hanson Roberts in 1851, speaks of this house and locates the dwelling as follows: "The old house stood sixty rods northeast from the southwest corner of the new house" (Hanson Roberts house). That measurement makes the spot a few rods east of the big elm. The tannery was south of the homestead.

During many years, in early times, there was a road along the bank of the river, from the road that went from High Street down to Beck's Slip (1640), later known as Hartford's Ferry, to a point north of the Thomas Roberts, Sr., residence, as the records say, up to the "sheep pasture," and there were several houses along the road or lane, as it was called.

The oldest cemetery in Dover is in this section of Dover Neck, between the Hanson Roberts farm and High Street. Here are the graves of all the first settlers; very few of them are marked. Gov. Roberts's grave is in the northeast corner, and now has a slate stone, suitably inscribed, that marks the spot; just west of it is the marked grave of his grandson's grandson. Thomas Roberts made his will, date 27 Sept., 1673; was probated 30 June, 1674; so, he probably died in 1674, as it was the custom to probate the wills soon after the death of the testator. He had a wife, REBECCA.

AT THE GRAVE OF GOVERNOR THOMAS ROBERTS. The Oldest Burying Ground in Dover. (See page 302.)

CHILDREN.

1. JOHN² ROBERTS, b. (by deposition) in 1629; m. ABIGAIL, dau. of Elder Hatevil Nutter, of whom see below.
2. THOMAS² ROBERTS, b. (by deposition), in 1633; lived on the homestead, and filled various town offices; m. MARY, dau. of the emigrant Thomas Leighton, of Dover. He had (probably with others): 1. *Thomas*³ *Roberts*, d. unm. 2. *Nathaniel*³ *Roberts*, who lived and died on Dover Neck; m. Elizabeth Mason, of Somersworth, N. H., and had five sons and one daughter. From his son, Moses⁴, is descended Amasa⁷ Roberts, Esq., graduated at Dartmouth College, in 1838, late attorney at law, late Register of Probate at Dover, N. H. Nathaniel³ had numerous descendants.
3. HESTER² ROBERTS, m. JOHN MARTIN, of New Jersey, as early as 1673.
4. ANNA² ROBERTS, m. JAMES PHILBRICK, of Hampton, N. H.
5. ELIZABETH² ROBERTS, m. BENJAMIN HEARD, of Cochecho-in-Dover.
6. SARAH² ROBERTS, m. RICHARD RICH.

JOHN² ROBERTS, son of Thomas¹, as above, was Constable in Dover, in early life; in 1679 he was Marshal of the Province of New Hampshire; he was called "Sergeant" and filled various town offices; married ABIGAIL, dau. of ELDER HATEVIL NUTTER, and died 21 Jan., 1694-5. He had (perhaps with others):

1. JOHN³ ROBERTS, to whom his father gave marsh in Kittery (now Eliot, Me.).
2. THOMAS³ ROBERTS, who had (at least): 1. *Love*⁴ *Roberts*, who had wife Elizabeth, and had: 1. *Hannah*⁵ *Roberts*, b. 10 May, 1713. 2. *Love*⁵ *Roberts*, b. 21 Apr., 1721, who witnessed the Will of Col. Paul³ Wentworth in 1749, and who m. 9 Dec., 1741, Mary Roberts. 3. *Francis*⁵ *Roberts*, b. 12 June, 1723; m. Mary Carr, dau. of John and Elizabeth Carr, of Newbury; she was b. 4 Feb., 1721-2; d. 21 Oct., 1807; he d. 1760; she m. (2) Charles Baker, in 1761.

MARY⁶ ROBERTS, daughter of Francis and Mary (Carr) Roberts, married COL. JONATHAN PALMER, in 1771, and resided in Wakefield, N. H.

Love[5] and Francis[5] Roberts resided in that part of Somersworth, now Rollinsford, near the village of Salmon Falls, in the neighborhood of the Burial Ground at Rollinsford Junction. They are witnesses to the Will of Col. Paul Wentworth, of date, 3 Feb., 1747-8. The house is now standing in which the will was signed. These brothers were near neighbors to Col. Wentworth, who died 24 June, 1748. He was a very wealthy man and one of the most distinguished citizens of the Province of New Hampshire.

Col. Jonathan Palmer was the son of Major Barnabus Palmer, of Rochester, and his wife, Elizabeth (Hilton) Robinson; she was a great granddaughter of Edward Hilton, the first settler of Dover; also a descendant of Gov. Dudley and Gov. John Winthrop.

CHILDREN OF JOHN[2] ROBERTS CONTINUED, HAVING GIVEN JOHN AND THOMAS.

3. Hatevil[3] Roberts, of whom see below.
4. Joseph[3] Roberts; had ten children and numerous descendants. Of the descendants are Mrs. Baer and Hanson Roberts.
5. Abigail[3] Roberts, m. (1) John Hall, b. about 1649, son of Dea. John Hall, the emigrant (see "Hall" note under Bartholomew[4]—p. 310, Wentworth Genealogy—and had five children; he d. 28 Apr., 1697, and she m. (2d), 24 Oct., 1698, Thomas Downs, of Cochecho-in-Dover, who was killed by the Indians in 1711.

Hatevil[3] Roberts, son of John[2] as above, lived in what is now Rollinsford. His Will was dated 28 Oct., 1724; proved 3 March, 1724-25. He had a wife, Lydia, and children:

1. Samuel[4] Roberts, b. 12 Dec., 1686; had a wife, Sarah, and children: 1. *Samuel[5] Roberts*, b. 16 July, 1717. 2. *Benjamin[5] Roberts*, b. 1 Sept., 1719. 3. *Lydia[5] Roberts*, b. 16 May, 1721. 4. *Samuel[5] Roberts*, b. 7 May, 1723.
2. Abigail[4] Roberts, b. 22 July, 1689.
3. Benjamin[4] Roberts, b. 1692; d. 13 Oct., 1708.
4. Joshua[4] Roberts, b. 11 Oct., 1698, of whom see below.
5. Mary[4] Roberts, b. 20 July, 1701.

THE ROBERTS FAMILY. 307

JOSHUA[4] ROBERTS, son of Hatevil[3], lived in Somersworth; married SARAH, daughter of John and Mary (Tuttle) WALLINGFORD (see Wallingford note under Mary[4] Wallingford, p. 163, Wentworth Genealogy). She was sister to Col. Thomas Wallingford, of Somersworth, whose son, Capt. Samuel Wallingford, was the first husband of Lydia[6], daughter of Col. Otis Baker, whose second husband was Col. Amos Cogswell, and who was mother to Lydia[7] Cogswell, wife of Hon. Paul Wentworth. Joshua[4] Roberts had:

1. HANNAH[5] ROBERTS, b. 1735; m. —— Foss.
2. ELIZABETH[5] ROBERTS, b. 1 Apr., 1737.
3. THOMAS[5] ROBERTS, b. 1 Nov., 1740; m. ELIZABETH FALL.
4. LYDIA[5] ROBERTS, b. 31 July, 1743; m. —— KNIGHT.
5. JOSHUA[5] ROBERTS, b. 20 July, 1746; m. JOANNA WENTWORTH.
6. MARY[5] ROBERTS, b. 1748; m. JOHN ROBERTS.

JOANNA[4] WENTWORTH, daughter of Mark[3] and Elizabeth[4] Wentworth, born August, 1750; married, 8 Dec., 1766, CAPT. JOSHUA ROBERTS, of Dover, N. H., son of Joshua and Sarah Wallingford Roberts. He entered the army in 1777 as First Lieut. in Capt. James Libby's company, Col. Stephen Evans's regiment, and became Captain. She died in 1785. Her husband married (2) Widow Elizabeth Hughs Nichols, and had children. He died 19 March, 1822. They had:

CHILDREN.

1. ELIZABETH[6] ROBERTS, b. 25 Apr., 1768; m. MOSES STEVENS.
2. SARAH[6] ROBERTS, b. 26 Dec., 1770; m. a BENJAMIN WENTWORTH.
3. THOMAS[6] ROBERTS, b. 14 Dec., 1773; m. LYDIA PLUMMER, and d. at sea, having: 1. *Joanna*[7] *Roberts*, b. 30 May, 1796; m. Hubbard Goldsmith. 2. *Abigail*[7] *Roberts*, b. 29 Aug., 1797; m. John S. Wentworth.
4. JOANNA[6] ROBERTS, b. 14 Oct., 1777; m. JAMES TUTTLE.
5. MARK[6] ROBERTS, b. 12 Jan., 1779; m. SARAH THOMPSON, who d. 30 Nov., 1840; was a soldier in the War of 1812.
6. JOSHUA[6] ROBERTS, b. 7 Apr., 1780; m. SALLY POWERS, b. 8 Oct., 1787.

7. TOBIAS⁶ ROBERTS, b. 18 Mar., 1781; d. 12 Jan., 1833. He lived in Strafford. He was Selectman nine years, Representative nine sessions. He m. 5 July, 1807, LYDIA YEATON, who d. 12 Mar., 1854. They had: 1. *Joanna⁷ Roberts*, b. 13 Mar., 1811; m. 6 Nov., 1836, William Blake and had five children; she d. 28 Aug., 1750. 2. *Mercy⁷ Roberts*, b. 24 Feb., 1813; m. 6 Nov., 1836, David⁷ Hayes. 3. *Joshua⁷ Roberts*, b. 21 Apr., 1815; was Selectman of Strafford one yr.; Representative two yrs; m. 22 Aug., 1836, his first cousin, Sarah, dau. of William and Mary (Yeaton) Scruton, b. 2 May, 1815; lived in Strafford, and had:

    1. MERCY ADELINE⁸ ROBERTS, b. 9 Aug., 1837; m. 22 Mar., 1866, SAMUEL HALE of Barrington, son of William and Eliza (Shackford) Hale. They had: 1. *Nancy⁹ Hale*. 2. *Charles⁹ Hale*. 3. *William⁹ Hale*. 4. *Mary⁹ Hale*, m. Lewis H. Young, of Madbury. 5. *Samuel⁹ Hale*.
    2. TOBIAS⁸ ROBERTS, b. 30 Nov., 1839; lived with his father in Strafford; served three yrs. in 13th N. H. Vols., War of Rebellion; m. 2 Aug., 1868, LUCY PEASE, and had: 1. *Eugene⁹ Roberts*. 2. *Eddie⁹ Roberts*. 3. *Grace⁹ Roberts*. 4. *Harry⁹ Roberts*.
    3. JOHN WESLEY⁸ ROBERTS, b. 23 Aug., 1850; teacher at New Hampton Academy.

Also three others.

Rev. Dr. E. S. Stackpole's story of the Sligo Garrison, in Rollinsford, has the following in regard to the Roberts family of that section. The children of John² and Abigail (Nutter) Roberts were:

1. JOSEPH, who m. ELIZABETH JONES.
2. JOHN, who m. MARY ———, and d. before 1691, leaving sons, *John* and *William*.
3. HATEVIL, who m. LYDIA ———.
4. SARAH, who m. ZACHARIAH FIELD as early as 1677.
5. ABIGAIL, who m. JOHN HALL, 9 Nov., 1671.
6. MARY, who m. TIMOTHY ROBINSON, before 1692.

Children of Thomas² and Mary (Leighton) Roberts were:

1. THOMAS, who d. ———.
2. NATHANIEL, who m. ELIZABETH MASON, 11 Apr., 1706.
3. MARY, who m. THOMAS YOUNG, of Dover.
4. JOHN, who m. MARY JOSE, dau. of Richard and Hannah Jose.
5. JOANNA, who m. THOMAS POTTS, 24 Mar., 1689/90.
6. SARAH, who. m. HOWARD HENDERSON, 3 June, 1704.
7. LOVE, who m. ELIZABETH DREW.

Children of Hatevil^2 and Lydia Roberts were:

1. SAMUEL, b. 12 Dec., 1686; m. SARAH LORD, 20 Sept., 1716. (Tate says that a first wife was ABIGAIL PERKINS).
2. ABIGAIL, b. 20 July, 1689; m. DANIEL GOODWIN, of Berwick, 30 Dec., 1708, and lived on a portion of the Roberts Grant.
3. JOSHUA, b. 11 Oct., 1698; m. SARAH WALLINGFORD.
4. MARY, b. 20 July, 1701, who m. JAMES HEARD.

SAMUEL^4 ROBERTS, son of Hatevil^3, had twelve children. One of them was Samuel,^{5} b. 16 July, 1717, who married Judith Randall and had fifteen children. One of the fifteen was Aaron Roberts, born 1773, who married Sarah Knox, and had eleven children. One of the eleven was Aaron, born 23 Sept., 1817, who married Elizabeth Fernald and lived on the old Roberts homestead, as did Aaron's forefathers. He was interested in local history and genealogy and wrote out some account of the history of Sligo. His son, Simeon Roberts, now (1923) seventy-four years of age, lives on the ancestral acres.

NATHAN, another son of Samuel and Sarah (Lord) Roberts, married OLIVE MASON and had nine children, as recorded by Tate.

1. ESTHER.
2. HATEVIL.
3. JOHN.
4. NATHAN, who m. MISS PLUMMER.
5. SUSAN.
6. BENJAMIN.
7. DANIEL, who m. SUSAN HOBBS.
8. EUNICE, who m. CAPT. TOBIAS STACKPOLE.
9. JOSEPH.

TOBIAS and EUNICE (ROBERTS) STACKPOLE were the great grandparents of Mrs. Annie Wentworth Baer, who knows well the history and traditions of Sligo.

THE HILTON FAMILY.

EDWARD HILTON, "Father of the Settlement of New Hampshire," was probably a native of London, of good ancestry. That he was in business with the leading men of the city is shown by his being admitted to membership, in 1621, in the Aristocratic London "Fishmonger's Guild," which controlled the fishing business, to a large extent, at Newfoundland, and along the New England coast. His connection with the Guild led to his visiting the fishing territory along the coast, so he was no stranger here when he came over in 1623, in the ship *"Providence of Plymouth,"* which was owned by three merchants of Plymouth—Abraham Colomer, Nicholas Sherwell and Leonard Pomeroy—and began the settlement at *Hilton Point,* on the Pascataqua River. Mr. Hilton's house stood where the present Hilton Hall now stands. There was his home till about 1640; a little before that date he commenced building his new home at what is now Newfields village. It was then part of the territory of Exeter, of which town he was one of the leading citizens for thirty years, or more. He died there in December, 1671, aged seventy-six years. He held various offices, one of which was that of Judge, in the first court that was established by the Massachusetts General Court, after Dover, and the other towns, came under the rule of the Massachusetts Bay Colony, by the vote of the town in 1641. It seems he was not married till some date after the settlement was commenced here, probably about 1625. His first wife's name is not known, who was mother of his children; his second wife was MRS. CATHERINE TREWORGYE, widow of James Treworgye, and daughter of Alexander Shapleigh. This second marriage took place about 1650. She survived him and her Will is on record, in Vol. I of the Probate Records.

CHILDREN.

1. EDWARD, b. 1626; m. ANN DUDLEY, dau. of Rev. Samuel Dudley and granddau. of Gov. Thomas Dudley; also granddau. of Gov. John Wentworth, as her mother was dau. of Gov. Wentworth. She was b. 16 Oct., 1641; d. 16 Apr., 1699.
2. WILLIAM, b. 1628; m. REBECCA SYMONDS, dau. of John Symonds, one of Capt. John Mason's company of men that he sent over in 1634. They lived in Old Kittery, for a while, then removed to Exeter. He was a noted sea captain, and it is said he was in the expedition that made discoveries and surveys along the coast, as far south as Florida, an account of which was published in London in 1664. It is supposed that Hilton's Head, South Carolina, received its name from some act of his in the voyage.
3. SAMUEL, b. 1630. There is no record of his career; he probably d. young, but no record of death is known.
4. SOBRIETY, b. Jan., 1632-3; m. HENRY MOULTON, of Hampton; d. 31 Jan., 1718.
5. SUSANNA, b. Jan., 1634; m. CHRISTOPHER PALMER, of Hampton; d. 9 Jan., 1716.
6. CHARLES, b. 1636. There is no record of him; probably he d. when a young man, and no record of his death was kept.

Those who desire further information regarding the third generation can find it in the History of Newfields, N. H.

WILLIAM HILTON was born in 1590, probably in London; he was elder brother of Edward, and was with him in the first settlement of Dover. They were sons of *Mark Hilton, gentleman,* who gave his sons a good education, that enabled them to become leaders in business affairs of the period. He was admitted to membership in the London Fishmongers' Guild in 1616, as the record of the guild shows. That was five years before his brother Edward was admitted. They became partners in the fishing business, and otherwise. William appears to have been a very able and enterprising man, though is not so conspicuously spoken of in history as his younger brother, Edward. He was married before coming to New England. It is on record that he came over to Plymouth in 1622, and received a grant of land from the town;

he returned, and his wife and children came over to Plymouth in 1623, but he came over with his brother in the ship *"Providence of Plymouth"* and helped begin the settlement at *Hilton Point*. His wife and children came up from Plymouth in the summer of 1624. As Edward was not married, it is probable that William's wife became housekeeper for the whole family, and so continued till the younger brother married. But at an early date William went across the river and made a bargain for an old Indian cornfield, that the Indians had cultivated for many generations, in what is now Eliot. In time William built a house there, and had his family live in it, till he was dispossessed of it by the government at Strawberry Bank, as described in the early pages of this book. The famous "Laconia Company" governor, Capt. Walter Neal, played the trick. After the District of Maine came under the control of Massachusetts in 1652, Mr. Hilton obtained pay for his loss of that "corn-field," etc., from the widow of Captain John Mason, by order of the Court.

William Hilton had grants of land from the town of Dover, also of Exeter, and of the Indian Sagamore, "Tahanto of Pennacooke." Also he received grants in Old Kittery and York, where his last years were passed. He was Deputy from Dover in the Massachusetts Bay General Court in 1644, and later, as shown in the Court records. He was appointed Associate Justice for the Court, established when Dover came under control of the Bay Colony, September 26, 1642, and held the office three years. Before 1650 he had changed his residence from Dover to Old Kittery and there was his residence, on that side of the Pascataqua River, the remainder of life. He was one of the leading business men of that town and of York, where he died in 1656.

Mr. Hilton was twice married; the name of his first wife is not known; she died before 1652. His second wife's name was FRANCES, maiden name not known. After his death in 1656, the widow married Richard White. See Stackpole's History of Eliot, page 48, for additional information regarding William Hilton and his family.

CHILDREN.

1. WILLIAM, b. 1615, in England; came over with his mother to Plymouth, in 1623; came up to Dover in 1624; was a resident in Dover, and engaged in business with his father till he m. and settled in Newbury, Mass., in 1638. He remained a citizen of that town about twenty years, and then went to Charlestown, Mass., where he d. 7th 7 mo., 1675. In Newbury he was Deputy several years for that town in the General Court, at Boston; also held other offices. From his papers, and other records, he is styled "navigator and cartographer." It was through him that the exact date of the first settlement of Dover and New Hampshire was established.
2. ALICE, b. about 1617; came over in Apr., 1635, as passenger on the ship *"Ann and Elizabeth,"* aged 18. Her father was then living at Dover. She m. GEORGE WALTON, and resided at Exeter; later they resided at Great Island (Newcastle) and had charge of the ferry from that island to Kittery, in connection with her father, William Hilton, who kept an Ordinary on the Kittery side.
3. JOHN, b. about 1624; he may have been, and probably was, the infant who came over with his mother to Plymouth, in 1623, and came up to Dover in the summer of 1624. He appears to have become a good citizen of Dover, though there is no family record of him. That he was an extensive land owner is shown by his name on several tax lists, beginning in 1648 and ending in 1666. He received grants of land from the town. Two of the grants were made 4th, 10 mo., 1656. On the 5th of Sept., 1721, his nephews and nieces, who had inherited some of the land, sold it to Capt. Thomas Millett, on Dover Neck, on which Millet settled, and resided for many years. The deed is recorded in Liber 12, folio 222.
4. MAGDALINE, b. about 1630; m. 1656, JAMES WIGGIN, of Kittery, who was Marshal of the District of Maine under the Charles II. Commissioners.
5. MANWARING, b. 1636; m. MARY MOULTON, dau. of Thomas Moulton, of Hampton. He d. about 1670, and administration on his estate, in York County, was granted in 1671.
6. ANN, b. ———; m. ARTHUR BEAL; they had son, *Mannering*. Resided in York, Me.

THE NUTTER FAMILY.

(MEMORANDA No. 67.)

ELDER HATEVIL NUTTER was born in England in 1603, as appears from a deposition he made. It seems he did not come over with the first lot of emigrants in 1633, but in 1637 he bought a lot of Captain Thomas Wiggin, which was rebounded in 1640, as follows: "Butting on ye Fore River, east; and on ye west by High street; on ye north by ye Lott of Samewell Haynes; and on ye south by Lott of William Story."

His house stood on the east side of High Street, about 15 or 20 rods from the north corner of the meeting-house lot. An old pear tree stands (1923) in the hollow, which was part of the cellar. He received various grants of land from the town, and had part ownership of a saw-mill at Lamprey River. His ship-yard was on the shore of Fore River; the locality can be easily found by reference to the map. He was largely engaged in the lumber business and in ship-building. He was one of the first Elders of the First Church, and helped organize it in November, 1638. He remained a zealous and generous supporter of the Church. When the Quaker Missionaries created disturbance in 1662, he vigorously opposed them, contending they had no right to come to Dover and make a disturbance. The Quaker Historian, Sewell, speaks very harshly of the Elder. He says: "All this whipping of the Quaker women, by the Constables (in front of the meeting-house), was in the presence of one Hate-Evil Nutwell (Nutter), a Ruling Elder, who stirred up the Constables (John and Thomas Roberts) to this wicked action, and so proved that he bore a wrong name (Hate Evil)."

Elder Nutter made his will 28 December, 1674 ("being about 71 years of age"). It was proved 29 June, 1675, which shows he had died a few months before that date. To his "present wife," ANNE (AYERS), he gave the use of his house, orchard, etc., etc., all of which to go to his son Antony after her decease. Antony also received the mill property at Lamprey River, and various tracts of land. Other members of the family were properly remembered.

CHILDREN.

1. ANTONY, b. in 1630.
2. MARY, who m. JOHN WINGATE, before 1670.
3. A DAUGHTER, who m. THOMAS LEIGHTON, and was d. in 1674.
4. ABIGAIL, who m. THOMAS ROBERTS.

And probably others.

ANTONY,[2] as above, lived for a time at Dover Neck, but afterwards moved to Welch Cove, on Bloody Point side. He was a man of note as well as his father, though his genius was developed in different spheres. The father took to the Church, Antony to arms, in which, in 1667, he had reached the rank of "Corporal," in the local militia company. In 1683 he is mentioned as "Leftenant." He was admitted as "freeman" 22 May, 1662.

He was a public man also, being Selectman for several years, and Representative in the General Court, for six years, certain. He was otherwise noted as being engaged in the controversy with Gov. Cranfield. As a specimen of the free and easy manners which characterized this "tall-big-man, Antony Nutter," we refer the reader to the account of his visit, with Capt. Thomas Wiggin, to Mason, as given in the first volume of State Papers. The story says Mason got his wig burned and his teeth knocked out, and met with several other accidents. It is a very amusing story.

ANTONY married SARAH, daughter of HENRY LANGSTAFFE, who outlived him. He died 19 Feb., 1686.

1. JOHN.
2. HATEVIL.
3. HENRY.
4. SARAH, who m. CAPT. NATHANIEL HILL.

JOHN,[3] son of Lieutenant Antony, as above, resided on Bloody Point side. He had children, probably:

1. JOHN (whose Will was dated 16 Aug., 1646; proved 29 Apr., 1647; he m., but d. without issue).
2. MATTHIAS.
3. JAMES.
4. HATEVIL.

HATEVIL,³ son of ANTONY,² lived also in Newington. He was twice married, and died in 1745. His Will is of date 12 Nov., 1745; proved 25 Dec., 1745. In that he gave to his wife, SARAH, all his movables, including his "Negro Caesar." To his two sons, *Hatevil* and *Antony,* he gave all his lands in Rochester. To his sons *John* and *Joshua,* all his lands in Newington; to his five daughters, *Eleanor, Sarah (Walker), Abigail (Dam), Elizabeth (Rawlings),* and *Olive,* he gave 10 pounds each.

He therefore had children by his first wife:

1. HATEVIL.
2. ANTONY.
3. ELEANOR.
4. SARAH.

BY HIS SECOND WIFE.

1. JOHN, b. 24 Feb., 1721.
2. JOSHUA.
3. ABIGAIL.
4. ELIZABETH.
5. OLIVE.

HENRY,³ son of ANTONY,² lived also in Newington, and died about 1739-40. His Will was dated 24 Dec., 1739; proved 19 Jan., 1739-40. He gave to MARY, his wife, the use of all his estate in Newington; to his son, *Samuel,* who was also executor, all the estate, after his mother's decease, excepting that son *Valentine* was to have 50 pounds; son *Joseph* the lands in Rochester; daughter *Elizabeth (Crocket)* 10 pounds, and daughter *Mary* 10 pounds. We know of no other children but those named in his Will.

JOHN,⁴ son of HATEVIL³, and grandson of ANTONY,² was born 24 Feb., 1721; married, 17 Nov., 1747, ANN SIMS, who was born 20 Oct., 1747, and died 11 Aug., 1793. They lived in Newington. He died 19 Sept., 1776.

CHILDREN.

1. HATEVIL, b. 1 Dec., 1748.
2. MARY, b. 25 Aug., 1750.
3. HANNAH, b. 12 June, 1752; and d. 12 June, 1764.
4. DOROTHY, b. 5 Aug., 1754.

5. JOHN, b. 5 Mar., 1757.
6. ANNA, b. 6 Mar., 1760.
7. JOSEPH S., b. 3 Feb., 1762; d. 2 Feb., 1746.
8. ANTHONY, b. 17 Feb., 1764.
9. HANNAH, b. 4 July, 1767.
10. ABIGAIL, b. 21 Apr., 1769; d. 28 Aug., 1850.

THE STARBUCK FAMILY.
(MEMORANDA No. 69.)

EDWARD STARBUCK was born in 1604, and is said to have come to Dover from Derbyshire, in England. He is first mentioned as receiving, 30th, 6 mo., 1643, a grant of 40 acres of land on each side of Fresh River, at "Cutchchechoe, next above the lot of John Baker, at the little water brooke, and also one plat of marsh above Cutchechoe great Marsh, that the brook that runs out of the great river runs through, first discovered by Richard Walderne, Edward Colcord, Edward Starbuck, and William Furber."

He had other grants, at different times, and became one of the Elders of the Church at an early period. He was Representative in the General Court, in 1643 and 1646, and enjoyed various other tokens of respect that were given him by his fellow citizens. In his later career he appears to have become a heretic, as regards some of the ways of conducting Church matters. We cannot, of course, ascertain with certainty what particulars the Elder held, as an Anabaptist, but it is probable that he differed from it in the matter of the baptism of children, he supposing that immersion was the Scripture method of performing this rite, and that children were not fit subjects for its performance. But the Elder managed to get along with but little disquietude for quite a number of years.

In 1669 Elder Starbuck went off on an exploring expedition. In the course of his travels he met Thomas Macey, and his family, James Coffin, a youth of nineteen, and Isaac Coleman, a boy of twelve. These adventurers set sail in an open boat in the autumn of 1659, and in due time arrived at the Island of Nantucket. They settled first at Mantical, but afterwards moved to a more central place, now called Cambridge.

The next spring the Elder came back to Dover to get his family. His daughters, *Sarah* and *Abigail,* were married and remained in Dover; but his wife, KATHERINE, went with him; also *Nathaniel, Dorcas* and *Jethro,* the remaining children, went with him. Elder Starbuck became one of the leading and prosperous citizens of that new settlement. He died there 4th Dec., 1690.

CHILDREN.

1. NATHANIEL, b. in 1636.
2. DORCAS.
3. SARAH.
4. ABIGAIL.
5. JETHRO.

Of these, Jethro was killed 27 May, 1663, by a cart running over him. The others had families, as follows:

NATHANIEL[2] married MARY, daughter of TRISTRAM COFFIN, SR., born 20 Feb., 1645. He was a wealthy man, and of good abilities, but was outshone by the superior capacity of his wife, a woman of uncommon powers of mind. She had been baptized by Peter Folger, in Waiputequat Pond, but years after became convinced of the correctness of the Friends' principles, and became a preacher among them, as did his son *Nathaniel* and daughter *Priscilla.* A "Public Friend," who was acquainted with her, calls her *"The Great Woman."* On account of her superior judgment she was often consulted in Town affairs, as well as in religious matters. She died 13 Sept., 1717. NATHANIEL died 6 June, 1719. They had children:

1. MARY, b. 1663, the first white child b. in Nantucket; she m. JAMES GARDNER, son of Richard.
2. ELIZABETH, b. 9 Sept., 1665, who m. (1) her cousin, PETER COFFIN, JR., and (2) NATHANIEL BARKHARD, JR.
3. NATHANIEL, b. 9 Aug., 1668, who m. his cousin, DINAH COFFIN, dau. of James, and d. in 1752.
4. JETHRO, b. 14 Dec., 1671, who m. his cousin, DORCAS GAYER, and d. 12 Aug., 1770.
5. BARNABUS, b. 1673; d. 1733.

6. EUNICE, b. 11 Apr., 1674, who m. GEORGE GARDNER, son of John.
7. HEPSIBAH, who m. THOMAS HATHAWAY, of Dartmouth, Mass.
8. ANN, d. single.
9. PAUL, d. single.

DORCAS[2] married WILLIAM GAYER; she died about 1696; he died after a second and childless marriage, 23 July, 1710. Their children were:

1. DAMARIS, b. 24 Oct., 1673, who m. 17 Aug., 1692, NATHANIEL COFFIN, son of James; from them was descended *Admiral Sir James Coffin*, famous in the annals of the Isle.
2. DORCAS, b. 29 Aug., 1675, who m. 6 Dec., 1694, her cousin, JETHRO STARBUCK, as above.
3. WILLIAM, b. 3 June, 1677, who m., in England, his cousin, ELIZABETH GAYER, dau. of John, and d. in England, a wealthy man, in 1712 or 13.

SARAH,[2] is the subject of considerable difference of opinion. Tradition represents her to have married BENJAMIN AUSTIN; and the same authority says another, and nameless daughter, to have been the wife of HUMPHREY VARNEY. But from an examination of the town records we are convinced that SARAH married (1) WILLIAM STOREY, about 1658; (2) JOSEPH AUSTIN, about the year 1659-'60, who was dead in 1663; (3) HUMPHREY VARNEY. For "widow Sarah Storie" is represented to have married JOSEPH AUSTIN, when WILLIAM STORY's inventory was entered on record; and JOSEPH AUSTIN, in his Will speaks of "my brother *Peter Coffin*"; and after JOSEPH AUSTIN's death, Elder Starbuck confirms to his son-in-law, HUMPHREY VARNEY," husband of "SARAH," land formerly given by him to his son-in-law, "JOSEPH AUSTIN." If this be correct, I am inclined to think that SARAH had children in her third marriage, by which she became ancestress to a race of infinite numbers—The Varneys.

ABIGAIL,[2] married PETER COFFIN, of Dover (Cochecho), son of TRISTRAM. PETER was a noted man in his day, Councillor, Judge, etc.; had a garrison, which was burned by the Indians June 28, 1689. They had children:

1. ABIGAIL, b. 1657, who m. DANIEL DAVIDSON.
2. ELIPHALET, d. single.
3. PETER, b. 20 Aug., 1660, who m. his cousin, ELIZABETH STARBUCK.
4. JETHRO, b. 15 Sept., 1663, who m. MARY GARDNER, dau., of John.
5. TRISTRAM, who m. DEBORAH COLCORD.
6. ELIZABETH, who m. JOHN GILMAN, of Exeter.
7. EDWARD, b. 20 Feb., 1669, who m. ANN GARDNER, dau. of John, and d. childless.
8. ROBERT, who m. JOANNA GILMAN.
9. JUDITH, b. 1672.

The Starbuck family has ever been respectable, and almost invariably persons of worth. Our Dover ancestors were not perfect. The enforcing of law against theoretical opinions regarding baptism proves that, at least, they were sometimes wrong in their views; and the treatment of the Quakers increases our regret that human passions should have been suffered so far to obscure their sense of justice, and weaken their feelings of humanity.

THE PINKHAM FAMILY.
(MEMORANDA NO. 71.)

The observing Antiquarian cannot fail to be struck with the wonderful coincidence in family ancestries, which ever had any ancestors. Occasionally there were "two brothers" who settled in America, more rarely "four," but in the great majority of cases there were just "three brothers who came over," and settled here and there about the country.

Regarding the Pinkham family, of course, tradition tells of the "three brothers who came over." One, it says, settled on Dover Neck, one at Oyster River, and one on Bloody Point side—a tradition which is entirely without foundation. But it is certain that RICHARD PINKHAM, the first ancestor of the name who came over, was the gentleman who was ordered, by a vote of the town in 1648, to "beat ye drumme" on Lord's day to call the people to meeting. He was here in 1642, and perhaps earlier. The spot where he early dwelt is said to be the same on which stood the Pinkham garrison, which Richard afterwards made his habitation. The precise situation of this garrison is easily pointed out, as it continued to be a dwelling house till one side of it was blown down, nearly one hundred years ago. That event rendered it necessary for the family to move, which they did, as soon as possible, into a new house standing about five rods east of the old one. After passing the house of Hanson Roberts on Dover Neck, the traveller will notice a lane on the west side of the road, leading towards the river. On the north side of the lane is a house formerly occupied by Elijah Pinkham, a descendant of Richard, who owned land once possessed by his ancestor. About four rods directly west of this house was the garrison house, half of which was taken down about two years after the wind had demolished the other half. (It is now, 1923, marked by a stone.)

Richard[1] Pinkham lived on Dover Neck, and died there. He appears to have been a man of good character, and had his share of public offices. In 1671 he conveyed the bulk of his property to his son, John, who engaged to support him. He had children:

1. Richard.
2. Thomas; was taxed on Dover Neck in 1667 and 1668, and is seen no more.
3. John.

Richard,[2] son of Richard,[1] as above, married Elizabeth, daughter of the second Thomas Leighton. Richard was a carpenter, and lived on Dover Neck, owning a lot fronting on High Street. He conveyed to Thomas Tebbets the High Street premises 2 May, 1669; to his nephew Amos, 12 May, 1709, land which formerly belonged to the first Thomas Layton; to his son Tristram, land, 22 Feb., 1736-7; to his son Richard, lot No. 70, in the first division at Rochester, 2 Dec., 1730-31. He received land 18 April, 1699, from Thomas Layton, eldest son and heir to Thomas, deceased, grandson to Thomas the first, and brother to Elizabeth, Richard Pinkham's wife. Their children:

1. RICHARD.
2. TRISTRAM.
3. JOHN, b. 19 Aug., 1696.

JOHN,[2] son of RICHARD,[1] and the one who was to support his father, was first taxed on Dover Neck in 1665; he first assumed the care of his father legally, and took possession of the homestead in 1671, just before the time when it became necessary to build garrisons and carry guns to meeting. He married a daughter of the first RICHARD OTIS, of Cochecho, apparently named ROSE, regarding whose ancestry many curious particulars may be found in the genealogy of the OTIS family, which was published in the second number, for the year 1851, of the N. E. Genealogical Register. His children:

1. RICHARD, who had a wife, ELIZABETH, and perhaps was the Richard who, at the age of 85, m., 27 Nov., 1757, widow MARY WELCH, aged 76, at Kittery.
2. THOMAS, who had a wife, MERCY, and children: 1. *Richard*, to whom he gave property 22 Oct., 1736. 2. *Benjamin*, to whom he gave property 23 Aug., 1736. 3. *Ebenezer*, to whom he gave property 15 Mar., 1736-7.
3. AMOS, who m. ELIZABETH, widow of SAMUEL CHESLEY, killed 15 Sept., 1707, and had children: 1. *Hannah*, b. 10 Jan., 1713-4. 2. *Joanna*, b. 11 Aug., 1718.
4. OTIS, whose family will be given below.
5. SOLOMON, who had a grant of land 23 June, 1701.
6. JAMES, who m. ELIZABETH, dau. of JOSEPH[2] SMITH, and had children: 1. *James*, b. 21 July, 1714. 2. *Wesley*, b. 4 Oct., 1716. 3. *Mary*, b. 14 Sept., 1719. 4. *Lois*, b. 2 Mar., 1721. 5. *Hannah*, b. 16 Sept., 1723. 6. *Sarah*, bapt. 24 June, 1727. 7. *Jonathan*, bapt. 3 May, 1730.
7. ROSE, who m. (1) JAMES TUTTLE, (2) THOMAS CANNEY, and whose children are recorded in the Otis genealogy.
8. ELIZABETH, (probably the one who m. SAMUEL NUTE 18 Mar., 1718-19).
9. SARAH.

This JOHN[2] gave his eldest son, *Richard,* land at Cochecho 19 June, 1714; to his son *Otis,* land, 16 March, 1721-2; to his son *Amos,* 4 July, 1715, certain lands on condition that he pay each sister above named 5 pounds; this land and condition he transferred to his brother *Otis*, 8 Aug., 1720.

OTIS,[3] son of JOHN,[2] married, 22 Sept., 1721, ABIGAIL, daughter of EPHRAIM and ROSE AUSTIN TEBBETS, b. 12 June, 1701. OTIS inherited the old homestead. He died about 1763 and his inventory was entered 30 Nov., 1764, by his widow Abigail. They had children:

1. SAMUEL, b. 26 Sept., 1722, and m. SUSANNAH CANNEY.
2. ANNE, b. 30 Apr., 1724, and d. unm.
3. ROSE, b. 18 Mar., 1725-6, and m. JAMES TUTTLE, of whom we will speak under *Tuttle*.
4. PAUL, b. 3 Apr., 1730, who m. ROSE, dau. of JOSEPH AUSTIN. He d. 16 Mar., 1819, having children: 1. *Nicholas*, b. 3 Nov., 1755; d. 1 July, 1770. 2. *Joseph*, b. 14 Aug., 1757; m. Elizabeth Green, 1788, and d. 1845, having had *Nicholas*, b. 1789, and d. unm. 3. *Jeremiah G.*, b. 1791; m. Louisa Heard. 4. *Sarah*, b. 1794; m. Joseph Tuttle, known as "Friend Joseph" (who resided on Dover Neck). 5. *Elizabeth*, b. 1797, who lived in Ohio. 6. *Joseph*, b. 1800, who d. unm. 7. *Hannah*, b. 1804, who m. Levi Sawyer and lived at Garrison Hill. 8. *Rose*, b. 1807, and m. Samuel Dunn. 9. *Rebecca*, b. 1809; m. Jacob K. Purinton, and d. in 1834, leaving Mary E. and Sarah A.

OTIS,[5] son of PAUL[4] and grandson of OTIS,[3] born 25 Aug., 1759, who was lost at sea.

SILAS, born 9 Nov., 1764, who died 10 Sept., 1796.

ROSE, born 1 Dec., 1766, who married JONATHAN HANSON.

PAUL, born 1 Dec., 1768.

JOHN,[4] born 29 Aug., 1739, son of OTIS,[3] received the homestead, garrison and all, from his father; he married PHEBE TEBBETS, born 5 Apr., 1744; died 24 Jan., 1832; John died 14 Aug., 1815. They had children:

1. ELIZABETH, b. 13 Jan., 1762, and m. DAVID ROBERTS.
2. OTIS, b. 23 Mar., 1765, who m. HANNAH YOUNG, and d. in Milton, 5 Jan., 1814, leaving descendants.
3. EDMUND, b. 3 Oct., 1767, who m. MIRIAM GOULD, and went to Maine.

4. ELIJAH, b. 15 Dec., 1769, who m. EUNICE TUTTLE, and has had: 1. *Rose*, m. John Young. 2. *Phebe*, who m. Charles Thompson. 3. *Elijah*, who lived on the homestead.
5. JOSEPH and BENJAMIN, b. 18 Jan., 1772. JOSEPH m. SARAH YOUNG, lived and d. in Tuftonborough; they had children. BENJAMIN m. NANCY DAVIS. Their son, *Davis*, lived on the "Neck."
6. ENOCH, b. 14 Apr., 1774, who m. ELIZABETH, dau. of RICHARD TRIPE; he d. at sea.
7. SARAH, b. 4 Sept., 1776.
8. NICHOLAS, b. 10 Jan., 1779, who m. ABIGAIL LAMOS, and lived at Dover.
9. ABIGAIL, b. 12 Mar., 1781; d. unm.
10. PHEBE, b. 20 June, 1783, who m. JOHN JACKSON, a sea captain; they lived in Belfast, Me.; she d. 23 Oct., 1810, leaving two children, *Frank* and *Elizabeth*.
11. JOHN, b. 8 Jan., 1787; d. 29 May following.
12. SAMUEL, b. 22 July, 1788, who m. LYDIA HAM; they lived in Brookfield; had two sons, *Nathaniel* and *E. J. Pinkham*.

MAJOR RICHARD WALDERNE FAMILY.
(MEMORANDA NO. 175.)

RICHARD WALDERNE, known as Major Walderne, was born in Alcester, England, in December, 1614, and was baptized 6 January, 1615. He was son of William and Catherine (Raven) Walderne. He was the sixth child of a family of twelve children, ten sons and two daughters. Five of the sons came to New England, three of them to Dover—WILLIAM, RICHARD and GEORGE. WILLIAM was "Recorder of Dover" at the time of his death in 1646; that is, he was Town Clerk. He was baptized 18 October, 1601, eldest of the family, fourteen years older than the Major, who was seventy-five when he was killed by the Indians 28 June, 1689.

Rev. Dr. A. H. Quint's Memoranda of the Walderne-Waldron family is very long, so cannot be given entire in this volume. From what he states RICHARD came over to Dover when he was about twenty years old (1635). He remained here about a year and then returned home to make further preparations for a permanent settlement in the new colony. It appears that while at home he became engaged to a young lady. Her parents were not willing for her to come to America, at that time, so the marriage was deferred till later, and appears to have taken place about 1640, judging from date of birth of children. He had returned in 1637 and commenced his hustling, vigorous and grand career of half a century, that was before him.

His residence was on Dover Neck for about twenty years, and four of his children were born there. Following that he and his family resided in Boston, though he kept in business touch with Dover, and was very active everywhere, in public and private affairs. About 1664 he had completed his fine house at Cochecho, in the style of the best houses at Boston, of that period, and in which he and his family resided till his death, 28 June, 1689. It stood about midway of the present National block, at the east end of the Court House, on Second Street. Ten years later, 1674, he had his house surrounded with a stockade, enclosing a large yard, for protection against the Indians; but they finally caught him, unawares, and took his life.

The date of his wife's death is not given in the Memoranda, but probably it occurred about 1670. He married (2) ANNIE SCAMMON, probably sister of Hon. Richard Scammon; she died 7 February, 1685.

CHILDREN.

1. PAUL, b. about 1642. When a young man he was engaged in his father's business at Penacook, where Walderne and Peter Coffin had large dealings in trade with the Indians. Later he was engaged in his father's foreign commerce and d. at Algiers, about 1669.
2. TIMOTHY, b. about 1646, who d. while a student in Harvard College.
3. RICHARD, b. 1650. When a young man he commenced business in Portsmouth, where he was living when news of his father's murder reached him, on 28 June, 1689. He was educated as a merchant under Gov. Willoughby, at Charlestown. He was a leading man, not only in Portsmouth, but in the Province. He was a member of the convention of 1690; a Representative in 1691-92; was

Councillor in 1681; Chief Justice of C. C. P.; Judge of Probate; Colonel of the Provincial militia, for a period. He d. 3 Nov., 1730.
4. ANNA, b. about 1654; m. REV. JOSEPH GERRISH.
5. ELNATHAN, b. 6 July, 1659; d. 10 Dec., 1659.
6. ESTHER, b. 1 Dec., 1660 (in Boston); m. (1) HENRY ELKINS; (2) ABRAHAM LEE; (3) RICHARD JOSE; (4) ———. She d. in the Isle of Jersey.
7. MARY, b. 14 Sept., 1663 (in Boston); d. young.
8. ELEAZER, b. 1 May, 1665.
9. ELIZABETH, m. 8 Oct., 1666, JOHN GERRISH.
10. MARIA, b. 17 July, 1668; d. 1682.

COMMENTS.

ANNA, who married REV. JOSEPH GERRISH, of Windham, had children, but how many we do not know; her husband was son of CAPT. WILLIAM GERRISH, of Newbury, and was born 23 March, 1650; one of their children was *Elizabeth,* who married *Rev. Joseph Green,* of Salem Village.

How many children, if any, ESTHER had in the course of her four marriages, we are totally ignorant. Her first husband, HENRY ELKINS, was son of HENRY ELKINS, of Hampton. Her second husband was a "chymiat," to whom she was married 21 June, 1686; he was killed by the Indians 28 June, 1689, and she was carried into captivity by the Indians. After her return she married RICHARD JOSE, son of Richard of Portsmouth. He died and she married a man whose name is lost to history.

ELIZABETH, who married JOHN GERRISH, 8 October, 1666, resided here in Dover. His father, Capt. William Gerrish, of Newbury, was quite extensively engaged in business with Major Walderne, and this marriage pleased both families. Capt. Gerrish came here to live, and "took the oath of fidelity" in Dover 21 June, 1669. Major Walderne gave his son-in-law, 1 June, 1669, part of the mill at Belleman's Bank River, also a hundred acres of land; also a house, partly finished (which stood a short distance below the Sawyer residence, on Middlebrook farm). John was an enterprising man, being Representative in 1684; member of the Convention in 1689, and Judge. They had children:

THE RICHARD WALDERNE FAMILY.

1. RICHARD.
2. JOHN.
3. PAUL.
4. NATHANIEL.
5. TIMOTHY, b. 1684.

And probably others, of all of whom we need say nothing now, except that RICHARD became Judge Gerrish. MARIA (MARAH) died young. So that RICHARD, ANNA GERRISH and ELIZABETH GERRISH are the only children who seem to have left descendants, Richard's children being the only ones to perpetuate the name.

COL. RICHARD WALDRON, of Portsmouth, had children:

1. SAMUEL, b. 1681; d. aged about 11 mos.
2. (By Second Wife) RICHARD, b. 21 Feb., 1693-4.
3. MARGARET, b. 16 Nov., 1695; m. 18 Nov., 1721, ELEAZER RUSSELL, and d. 20 May, 1753.
4. WILLIAM, b. 1697.
5. ANNIE, b. 1699; m. HENRY RUST, of Stratham; she d. 1734. Her husband was minister from 1718 to his death in 1749.
6. ABIGAIL, b. 1702; m. JUDGE RICHARD SALTONSTALL of Haverhill in 1826, and d. in 1735.
7. ELEANOR, b. 1704; d. 1724, unm.

RICHARD WALDRON, born 21 Feb., 1693-4 (COL. RICHARD—MAJOR RICHARD). He was graduated at Harvard College in the class of 1712, receiving the degree of A. M.; he ranked third highest in his class. He lived first at Dover, but soon removed to Portsmouth, where he resided the remainder of his life. He was Councillor in 1728, and soon after Secretary of the Province; in 1737, Judge of Probate. He had a large part in the official affairs of the Province for many years; always very efficient. He married ELIZABETH WESTBROOK, 31 Dec., 1718; she was daughter of THOMAS WESTBROOK, Esq. She was born 6 Nov., 1701. He died 23 Aug., 1753. Their children:

1. RICHARD, b. 20 Dec., 1719; lost at sea, 1745.
2. THOMAS WESTBROOK, b. 26 July, 1721.
3. WILLIAM, b. 8 Mar., 1724; d. 22 Sept., 1741.
4. ELIZABETH, b. 3 Feb., 1729-30; d. 13 Apr., 1732.

5. GEORGE, b. 1 May, 1732; d. 1 Sept., 1805.
6. ELIZABETH, b. 17 May, 1734; d. 1735.
7. ELEANOR, b. 13 Nov., 1736; d. 5 Sept., 1741.
8. WILLIAM, b. 12 Dec., 1741; d. aged 17 mos.

MARGARET WALDRON, born 16 Nov., 1695 (COL. RICHARD—MAJOR RICHARD) married, 18 May, 1721, ELEAZER RUSSELL of Barnstable, who was educated at Harvard and was son of a clergyman. They had children:

1. ELEAZER, b. 21 May, 1732; d. 18 Sept., 1798.
2. ELEANOR, b. 7 Feb., 1723-4.
3. BENJAMIN, b. 13 Apr., 1729; d. master of a ship on the coast of Africa.
4. MARTHA, b. 15 Nov., 1732; d. 21 Sept., 1798.
5. ANNA, b. 6 Feb., 1734; d. 28 Feb., 1816.

WILLIAM WALDRON, b. 1697 (COL. RICHARD—MAJOR RICHARD), was a minister. He graduated from Harvard College in 1717, and was ordained 22 May, 1722, first pastor of brick church, Boston, which was afterwards merged into the Second Church. He had a distinguished career. He married ELIZA ALLEN, of Martha's Vineyard, who survived him. Their daughter, *Elizabeth,* married in 1756, *Josiah Quincy,* and they had one daughter, *Elizabeth,* who married *Benjamin Guild, Esq.*

THOMAS WESTBROOK WALDRON, b. 26 July, 1721 (JUDGE RICHARD—COL. RICHARD—MAJOR RICHARD), inherited the homestead in Dover, purchasing the rights of his brother George. He was a man of large property and extensive influence, although not so much in public office as his father and grandfather and great grandfather. He was moderator in many town meetings; selectman many years; town clerk from 1781 to 1785; and Representative 1756, '62 to 65, '68. He built, in 1763, the house that now stands in the rear of the furniture store on Second Street, opposite the Court House. Originally it stood across Second Street, fronting Franklin Square. In his day it was a very fine mansion. He married CONSTANCE DAVIS, of Dover, who was born 16 March, 1734-5, and d. 25 Sept., 1783. They had children:

THE RICHARD WALDERNE FAMILY.

1. WILLIAM, b. 8 June, 1756; d. 18 Sept., 1793.
2. ELIZABETH, b. 3 Jan., 1761; m. JOSEPH EVANS, of Dover, and d. 8 Dec., 1920, having had children: *Elizabeth, Joseph, Stephen, Vesta* and *Abigail.*
3. RICHARD, b. 27 Apr., 1762; d. 15 Oct., 1787.
4. SAMUEL, b. 17 Nov., 1764; d. 29 July, 1765.
5. ELEANOR, b. 28 May, 1766; m. JAMES SMITH, of Durham; they lived in Dover and had chidlren: *Thomas W.*, of Augusta, Me.; *Mary, James* and *Daniel.*
6. CHARLES, b. 26 Feb., 1768; d. 18 May, 1791.
7. ABIGAIL, b. 14 Dec., 1770; m. (1) DAVID BOARDMAN, and had children: *Ann (Riley), Benjamin, Olive, Harriet,* and *Thomas.* She m. (2) MARK WALKER.
8. DANIEL, b. 9 Nov., 1776.

GEORGE WALDRON, brother of THOMAS WESTBROOK, lived in Dover, was married and had children, of whom we have no record, except the names of children: *Mary, Ann* and *Jonathan,* who lived in Rye. One of the daughters married *Dr. Wigglesworth,* who lived in Lee.

Of the sons of THOMAS WESTBROOK WALDRON: *William* died 18 Sept., 1793; he married and had one daughter, who m. Samuel Ham. *Richard* died at Portsmouth, 15 Oct., 1787. *Charles,* whom his father made joint heir with *Daniel,* died 18 May, 1791. *Daniel,* by the death of his brother Charles, became sole owner, by his father's will.

DANIEL WALDRON married, 5 June, 1802, OLIVE RINDGE SHEAFE, who was born 24 May, 1777, and who died Sept., 1845. Their children:

1. RICHARD RUSSELL, who was purser in the navy and d. unm.
2. NATHANIEL SHEAFE, b. 10 Oct., 1804; m. VIRGINIA RIGGS, of Baltimore, and d. in Portsmouth in 1857, leaving two sons: 1. *Charles,* lived in Cleveland, Ohio; m. and had children. 2. *Mary Constantia,* m. Justin Dimmick, a Major in the U. S. Army, and had children. 3. *Daniel,* m. Susan Wingate, and moved to Augusta, Me. 4. *Olive,* b. 3 July, 1811; d. 1 Aug., 1811. 5. *Edmund,* b. 6 July, 1812, was a *Catholic priest,* and resided in Philadelphia. 6. *Thomas W.,* b. 21 May, 1814; d. at Hong Kong.

DANIEL WALDRON was the last owner of the great Major Walderne estate. He sold it to the Dover Manufacturing Company in 1820.

THE COL. JOHN WALDRON FAMILY.
(MEMORANDA No. 184.)

We have mentioned several generations of the descendants of old Major Richard Waldron, a distinct family of some note, and connected them with the Major's branch in England, agreeably to tradition. Of the John Waldron family we propose to record various particulars.

JOHN WALDRON is mentioned in Capt. John Heard's Will, dated 21 July, 1687, as "my prentice." A tradition communicated to us by John Waldron's great granddaughter, recites that "Master Heard," a sailor, picked him up in the streets of a seaport in England, and unceremoniously carried him off, after the fashion on the coast of Africa. Master Heard brought him to Dover, and kept him as a "chore boy." Poorly clad, and having a hard time of it generally, he excited the kind sympathies of a Mrs. Horne, past whose doors he used to drive Capt. Heard's cows to pasture, and who did him many a kindness—the last of which was to marry him, when she became a-widow, her husband being killed by the Indians, one day. She lived where the brick house now is on Horne's Hill, Sixth Street. We suppose she was widow of William Horne, who was killed by the Indians 28 June, 1689, whose property went mainly to sons, John, William and Thomas.

JOHN WALDRON acquired considerable property; probably Mrs. Horne brought him a little, and his own industry brought him more. He lived, we are informed, where *Mr. Taylor Page* later lived. He died in 1740. By his Will, which was dated 12 May, 1740, and proved 30 July following, he gave to wife MARY, (perhaps a second wife) one-half of the homestead, the whole of which was to go, after her decease, to her son *Richard*; to son *John, Jr.* (besides the 100 acres where he lived), lands in Rochester, "which I bought of the Twomblys," and "all my wearing apparel." To daughter *Elizabeth*, wife of *Ezra Kimball*, 30 pounds, and 30 acres which I bought "of Reyner." A part of "old Parson Reyner's" grant, near the present county farm, (possibly the county farm itself.) To daughter *Anne,* wife of *Timothy Roberts,* 70 acres in Rochester, 40 of which joined land which Dea. Gershom Wentworth bought of "Squire Atkinson." To daughter *Mehitable,* wife of *James Chesley,* 30 pounds and 30 acres in Dover, purchased "of Reyner." To daughter *Sarah,* wife of *Isaac Libbey,* the same as to Mehitable. To grandsons, *John Waldron, Richard Kimball, John Roberts* and *Samuel Libbey,* land in Rochester. Son *Richard* (executor) was residuary legatee.

"Reyner's brook" got its name through the grant that was made to Rev. John Reyner of Dover Neck. The brook is the one which crosses the road east of the County Farm house and runs into the Cochecho River a little above the erstwhile site of Watson's and Waldron's mills.

JOHN WALDRON had children (Family I): *Sarah, Bridget, Richard, John,* (who was born in 1698); *Elizabeth, Anne,* and *Mehitable.* These children we dispose of as follows:

SARAH and BRIDGET died in this wise: The first being seven years old and the second five; they were one day turning the calves into the pasture near the house, when nine Indians suddenly appeared and seized them, and with an axe cut off their heads, on a log in front of the house, in full view of their agonized mother. The Indians carried the heads away, but after cutting off the scalps threw them into some bushes, where their father found them some weeks afterwards.

RICHARD[2] lived on the homestead; a part of his cellar was said to be under the Taylor Page house. He inherited, as we have seen above. His wife was a SMITH, of Durham, and they had children.

JOHN (COL.) WALDRON was born 1740; HANNAH, BETSEY, MARY, JOSEPH, b. 16 May, 1744; SAMUEL, JAMES.

JOHN[2] lived in Dover; died 4 July, 1778, aged eighty, having had children:

1. JOHN.
2. WILLIAM.
3. BRIDGET.
4. EBENEZER.

Of these we know nothing further.

ELIZABETH[2] married EZRA KIMBALL; they had children. Tradition says they lived in Farmington.

ANN[2] married TIMOTHY ROBERTS and had at least one son, viz., *John* (Family 4).

MEHITABLE[2] married JAMES CHESLEY (born 18 May, 1706; died 10 Oct., 1777; son of James, grandson of Philip, great grandson of Philip of Dover. They had children as follows:

> 1. TAMSIN, who m. (1) JOHN TWOMBLY, son of John; and (2) COL. OTIS BAKER, having by her first marriage three children, viz: 1. *Lydia*, b. 12 May, 1759, and m. (1) Capt. Samuel Wallingford, and (2) Col. Amos Cogswell. 2. *Ebenezer*, b. 22 Dec. 1760 (father of Sharington Baker of Dover). 3. *John*, b. 12 Dec., 1762. 4. *Mehitable*, b. 21 Apr., 1764, and m. Capt. William Twombly. 5. *Otis*, b. 3 Aug., 1766. 6. *James*, b 15 Apr., 1768 (father to Mrs. John H. Wheeler of Dover). 7. *Thomas*, b. 21 Jan., 1770. 8. *Hannah*, who m. Rev. Avery Hall, a native of Connecticut, ordained minister at Rochester, 15 Oct., 1766; resigned 10 Apr., 1775, who had two children. 9. *Ebenezer*, who d. suddenly unm. 10 and 11. *James* and *Otis*, both of whom d. of consumption, unm.

MEHITABLE, wife of JAMES CHESLEY, died 21 Aug., 1776, and the disconsolate widower, when 70 years old, married 4 Apr., 1777, LYDIA, daughter of Isaac Horne, who had attained the venerable age of twenty-two.

SARAH[2] married ISAAC LIBBEY, and had at least one son, viz., *Samuel* (Family 6).

Those of the next generation were as follows:

COL. JOHN[3] WALDRON (of Family 2) lived on the homestead, but owned considerable other property, including the place where his grandson, Hon. Ezekiel Hurd, resided (where the Nurses' Home is in 1923); that where Jacob Clark lived, and the land where William Wendell had a farm. He was a man of note, often in public office, and possessed a wide influence, especially in the days of the old Republican party, of which he was a devoted adherent, and in which he was a leader. Records of his public office show that he was a member of the Provincial Legislature which met at Portsmouth in 1774; of the Revolutionary Convention held at Exeter in 1775, and a Representative of Dover in at least the years 1782-'3-'5-'6-'8, 1801-'3 and 1815; he was also Delegate to the Constitutional Convention in 1791, and Senator in 1788, '90, '92, and 1803, '06. It is said that he was Moderator in our town meetings, in twenty-nine out of thirty successive years.

COL. WALDRON was Colonel in the Revolutionary Army. He had held commission in the militia before, and when war broke out he was appointed Colonel to raise a regiment to go to Winter Hill, to assist General Sullivan, who was in command there, the Connecticut militia having deserted, leaving General Sullivan in danger of being overrun by the British army in Boston. Col. Waldron promptly enlisted a regiment of 700 men and went to Winter Hill, in December, 1775, and stayed there till the British army left Boston, and sailed for New York in March, 1776. He and his regiment returned home in April. His service was not long; the death of his wife recalled him to take care of his family, the youngest of which was but three weeks old when the mother died. But he rendered valiant and valuable service in other ways for carrying on the war successfully.

He married four times: (1) to JOHANNA SHEPHERD, of Salisbury, Mass., who died 1 Sept., 1775; (2) to POLLY WINN, who died 19 July, 1799; (3) to the widow of JOHN WENTWORTH, JR. (originally MARGARET FROST, of New Castle, b. 3 Dec., 1747; d. 30 Sept., 1805); and (4) to widow of REV. CALEB PRENTISS, of Reading, Mass., who died 7 Feb., 1803. Col. John died 31 Aug., 1827, at the home of his daughter, in Maine. He was buried there, as the weather was too hot to bring his remains to Dover.

By his first wife he had five children; by the second, four; by others, none. Children were:

1. ABIGAIL, who m. JOHN HURD, of Dover (uncle to Ezekiel), and who survived her; lived in New Durham, and had nine or ten children.

2. JEREMIAH, who m. MARY SCOTT, of Machias, lived in Farmington, and had children, among whom was *Elder William H.* and *George P.*
3. RICHARD, who m. MARY HANSON (aunt to Israel), lived at Long Hill, on the farm adjoining that of the Alms House, and had four children, one of whom was first wife to Lorenzo Rollins.
4. A DAUGHTER, who m. a WENTWORTH, and d. childless.
5. JOANNA, b. 1775; m. EZEKIEL HURD (who d. of fever 27 Feb., 1800, aged 27); she d. 19 Aug., 1840, having had three children, viz.: *Mary B.*, (*Hon.*) *Ezekiel* and *Eliza B.*, who d. unm., Mar., 1853.

BY HIS SECOND WIFE HE HAD:

1. TIMOTHY WINN, who moved to Bath, Me., and d., having had two children, now dead.
2. SUSANNA, m. STEPHEN HALE, of Boylston, Mass., and d. leaving children.
3. MARY B., m. ZEBADIAH WYMAN, of Woburn, and d. leaving children.
4. ELIZA, m. CAPT. BENJAMIN STANTON, of Bath, and d. leaving two children.

HANNAH[3] (of Family 2) married CAPT. JOHN HAYES, of Lebanon, Me., and had eleven children.

ELIZABETH[3] (of Family 2) married CAPT. ELISHA SHAPLEIGH, of Kittery, and had ten children.

MARY[3] (of Family 2) married, 23 March, 1768, CAPT. ELIJAH CLEMENTS, of Somersworth. They had two children.

JOSEPH[3] (of Family 2), married TAMSON TWOMBLY (born 18 Sept., 1756), daughter of Capt. John Twombly, who lived at Littleworth and married the Tamson whose second husband was Col. Otis Baker. Joseph died 8 April, 1821; his wife died 11 March, 1823. Children were:

1. MARY, b. 13 Feb., 1773; d. young.
2. MOSES, b. 7 July, 1774; later of Rochester, and left children.
3. JOSEPH, b. 10 Apr., 1776; m. BETSEY, dau. of WINTHROP WATSON (son of Col. Dudley Watson and Christine, eldest child of Christine (Otis) Baker, famous in Indian captivities), and had nine children.

4. JAMES, b. 23 Aug., 1778; d. single, in 1814.
5. SARAH, b. 13 Mar., 1781; m. GEORGE W. QUIMBY, and d. in 1855, leaving children (among whom was the wife of Joseph Morrill, Esq., of Dover).
6. OLIVE, d. young.
7. SAMUEL, d. young.
8. OLIVE, b. 4 Apr., 1787; m. JAMES HAM.
9. MEHITABLE, b. 25 July, 1789; m. HENRY QUIMBY, of Dover.
10. MARY, b. 14 Mar., 1796; m. JOHN PLUMMER; had several children, and d. in 1836.

RICHARD[3] (Family 2) married ELIZABETH CLEMENTS, born 1754, daughter of Job Clements, of Dover. Their children were:

1. JOB C.
2. RICHARD, father to Richard Waldron.
3. MRS. CANNEY (mother to Thomas J. Canney).
4. MRS. FOWLER, who lived in Durham.
5. MRS. MCDUFFEE.

SAMUEL[3] (of Family 2) married a GAGE, and died childless.

JAMES[3] (of Family 2) married BETSEY PICKERING, lived in Rochester, and had two children.

THE TIBBETS FAMILY.

(MEMORANDA No. 114.)

HENRY TEBBETS was the ancestor of probably all persons bearing the name in New England, although there was a Walter Tebbets who died in Salem, Mass., in 1651. The orthography of the name varies remarkably. This Henry[1] lived in Dover, in 1643; he owned a house lot on Dover Neck, which was near the site of the schoolhouse. A grant of land in 1656 was laid out between St. Albans and Quamphegan, which was in the family in succeeding generations. Henry was taxed in 1648, and each succeeding year to 1675, as a resident of the Neck.

He seems to have died in 1676, as in 1677 "widow Tibitt and her son Jeremiah" were taxed in his place. Henry's wife seems to have been an AUSTIN, inasmuch as on the 12th of November, 1677, it is agreed by "Mary Tippit and Jere. Tippit her son" that her youngest son shall "serve his uncle Mathew Austin." Of the children of Henry were:

1. JEREMY, b. before 1636.
2. THOMAS.
3. DAUGHTER, who m. THOMAS NOCK.
And probably others.

JEREMY[2] was taxed in Dover in 1662; he received a grant of land 10 Dec., 1658, and had other grants at various times, needless to specify. He lived at Dover Neck, and seemingly on the homestead. His Will was dated 5 May, 1677; in it he mentions his wife MARY; son *Jeremy* (under age), whose grandfather was Thomas Canney; daughter *Mary* (*Rawlins*); younger children, *Hannah, Samuel, Joseph, Benjamin, Ephraim, Martha, Elizabeth, Nathaniel, Henry;* "brother Joseph Canney," and John Roberts, executors. Jeremy married, therefore, MARY, daughter of THOMAS CANNEY, by his first wife (she was called MARY LOOME in 1700). He had children:

1. JEREMIAH, b. 5 June, 1656; he had son, *Timothy*.
2. MARY, b. 15 Apr., 1658.
3. THOMAS, b. 24 Feb., 1659; doubtless d. young.
4. HANNAH, b. 25 Feb., 1661; m. NATHAN PERKINS.
5. JOSEPH, b. 7 Aug., 1663.
6. SAMUEL.
7. BENJAMIN.
8. EPHRAIM.
9. MARTHA.
10. ELIZABETH, m. JOHN BICKFORD.
11. NATHANIEL.
12. HENRY.

Of these children, Hannah, Samuel, Joseph, Benjamin, Nathaniel and Henry, released land to Ephraim, 1? Dec., 1706.

CAPTAIN THOMAS[2] married, 6 July, 1684, JUDITH, daughter of JOHN DAM, who was born 15 Nov., 1656; died 22 Oct., 1728. Their children were:

THE WALDRON BURYING GROUND, on Chapel Street. (See page 324.)

THE TIBBETTS FAMILY.

1. JOHN, b. 29 Aug., 1685; received land near Salmon Falls, 12 Dec., 1717.
2. THOMAS, b. 4 Nov., 1687; received land near Salmon Falls from his father, 16 Dec., 1747.
3. EPHRAIM, b. 4 Mar., 1689.
4. ELIZABETH, b. 8 Sept., 1692.
5. SAMUEL, b. 8 Oct., 1693.
6. ELIZABETH, b. 25 July, 1696.
7. MOSES, b. 27 Jan., 1701.
8. ABIGAIL, b. 2 Sept., 1705.

JOSEPH,[3] son of JEREMY,[2] married (1) ELIZABETH ———; she was born 25 Dec., 1671; died 24 Feb., 1706; he married (2), in 1711, CATHERINE MASON.

CHILDREN WERE, BY FIRST WIFE.

1. ELIZABETH, b. 10 Mar., 1697; m. POMFRET DAM.
2. MARGERY, b. 18 Nov., 1700; m. JOB HUSSEY.
3. JUDITH, b. 3 Feb., 1702; m. JOHN BICKFORD.
4. LYDIA, b. 4 Aug., 1704; m. MARK GILES.
5. JOSEPH, b. 2 Feb., 1706-7.

BY SECOND WIFE HE HAD:

1. CATHERINE, b. 23 Aug., 1713.
2. MARY, b. 1 Oct., 1716.
3. HANNAH, b. 23 June, 1721.

CAPTAIN SAMUEL,[3] son of JEREMY,[2] had grant of one-half of sawmill privilege in 1701. He married, 1 Sept., 1686, DOROTHY TUTTLE, and had a son, *Samuel,*[4] whose daughter *Mary*[5] married *William Chamberlain,* and had:

1. MARY, bapt. 12 Feb., 1721.
2. REBECCA, bapt. 10 Feb., 1723.
3. EBENEZER, b. 25 May, 1729.

EPHRAIM,[3] son of JEREMY,[2] married ROSE AUSTIN, born 3 February, 1678; she was dau. of Thomas Austin; he was a blacksmith. Children were:

1. EPHRAIM, b. 31 Oct., 1694; m. 6 Sept., 1722, ANNE ALLEN.
2. ANNE, b. 8 May, 1698.

3. HENRY, b. 29 May, 1700; m. ELIZABETH, dau. of TIMOTHY ROBINSON.
4. ' ABIGAIL, b. 12 June, 1701; m. OTIS PINKHAM.
5. JOSEPH, b. 14 Oct., 1702.
6. ELISHA, b. 16 Feb., 1704.
7. AARON, b. 26 Feb., 1705.
8. MARY, b. 16 Nov., 1709.
9. ELIJAH, b. 28 Mar., 1711.
10. ROSE, b. 4 Feb., 1713.
11. ELIZABETH, b. 30 Oct., 1716.

NAHANIEL,[3] son of JEREMY,[2] had a grant of land in 1693-4; his capture by the Indians, 2 Aug., 1706, is recorded by Belknap on page 172. By his wife ELIZABETH he had *Bridget,* born 26 Sept., 1700, and probably others.

HENRY,[3] son of JEREMY,[2] lived on Dover Neck. By his wife, JOYCE, he had children:

1. BENJAMIN, b. 31 Oct., 1700.
2. EDWARD, b. 2 Feb., 1702.
3. PAUL, b. June, 1705.
4. HANNAH, b. 31 Oct., 1707.

HENRY,[4] son of EPHRAIM,[3] married, 13 March, 1730, ELIZABETH, daughter of TIMOTHY ROBINSON. Children were:

1. PETER, b. 7 Mar., 1734.
2. DAUGHTER, b. 28 Jan., 1736.

EDWARD,[4] son of HENRY,[3] born 2 Feb., 1702; removed to Rochester with his brother Benjamin. The latter settled on the Salmon Falls Road; the former on the cross road to the back road to Dover, on a farm where one of his descendants still lives. Part of the old log house of the garrison times is still occupied as a dwelling house, though the clapboards have disguised its primitive rudeness. Edward had children:

1. SUSANNA, b. 26 May, 1735.
2. HENRY, b. 26 Feb., 1737.
3. JONATHAN, b. 21 Feb., 1739.

THE TIBBETTS FAMILY.

4. CHARITY, b. 17 Mar., 1741.
5. MARY, b. 17 Apr., 1743.
6. ABIGAIL, b. 30 May, 1745.
7. EBENEZER, b. 24 Sept., 1747.
8. DEBORAH, b. 12 May, 1751.

HENRY,[5] son of EDWARD,[4] next preceding, married, 15 Sept., 1767, MARY BICKFORD, born 22 June, 1748 (N. S.). He died 22 Nov., 1795. Children were:

1. JOHN, b. 19 July, 1768.
2. EBENEZER, b. 22 Sept., 1770; d. 16 June, 1852.
3. JAMES, b. 12 June, 1772.
4. CHARITY, b. 7 Nov., 1774; d. unm.
5. SUSANNA, b. 22 Nov., 1777; m. SAMUEL CHAMBERLAIN of Rochester; d. 1851.
6. SARAH, b. 27 Dec., 1779; m. GEORGE HURD.
7. HENRY, b. 21 Feb., 1782.
8. EDWARD, b. 16 July, 1783.
9. JONATHAN, b. 11 Mar., 1787.

JAMES,[6] son of HENRY,[5] next preceding, married (1), in 1798, MARY NUTTER, who died 3 May, 1814; he married (2) WIDOW SALLY PIKE (born TOWNSEND), of Limerick, Me.

CHILDREN BY FIRST WIFE.

1. SETH, b. 10 Feb., 1799; d. unm., 20 Jan., 1829.
2. CHARITY, b. 5 Dec., 1800; m. BENJAMIN BARKER and lived in Rochester.
3. NOAH, b. 26 Dec., 1802.

BY SECOND WIFE.

1. MARY, b. 1 Feb., 1817; m. CHARLES HENDERSON; lived in Rochester.
2. SARAH, b. 8 Apr., 1818; d. unm., 1852.
3. OLIVER, b. 25 July, 1819; lived in Rochester.
4. ELIZA, b. 6 Dec., 1820; m. THOMAS M. FESSENDEN, and lived in Rochester.
5. JAMES, b. 25 Dec., 1822; d. 1836.
6. WILLIAM, b. 12 July, 1824.

Noah,[7] son of James,[6] graduated at Bowdoin College in 1821; studied law with Jeremiah H. Woodman, in Rochester; practiced law in Parsonsfield, Me., in company with Rufus McIntire until Nov. 30, 1834, when he returned to Rochester. He was elected Representative in 1842; he was appointed, in 1843, Judge of the C. C. P. He died 9 Sept., 1844.

Judge Tebbets married, 3 June, 1828, Mary Esther Woodman, of Rochester, and had children:

1. Theodore, who graduated at Harvard College in 1851, and was later an instructor at Phillips Exeter Academy.
2. Sarah Chase, b. 7 Mar., 1833; d 30 Dec., 1842.
3. James.
4. Jeremiah H. W.
5. Charles Barker.
6. Noah.

John Tebbets had wife, Tamson, and child:

1. Sarah, b. 18 Aug. 17—.

Thomas Tebbets had wife, Sarah, and son:

1. Thomas, b. 7 Jan., 1716.

Samuel Tebbets had a wife, Judith; he died 24 Dec., 1724. Children were:

1. Mary, b. 18 Nov., 1718.
2. Judith, b. 10 Dec., 1720.
3. Samuel, b. 31 Jan., 1722-3; d. 2 Mar., 1724-5.
4. Ichabod.

Judith, widow of Samuel, and the four children, were baptized 5 May, 1725.

Ichabod Tebbets had a wife, Abigail, and children:

1. Judith, b. 25 May, 1722.
2. Abigail, b. 23 Apr., 1723.
3. Ichabod, b. 25 July, 1726.
4. Nathaniel, b. 30 Aug., 1727.

They were all baptized 6 Dec., 1728.

EPHRAIM TEBBETS, JR., married, 16 Nov., 1721, ESTHER TEBBETS, and had children:

1. EPHRAIM.
2. ESTHER.
And others.

THE TAYLOR PAGE FAMILY.

In the story of Col. John Waldron's family, MR. TAYLOR PAGE was spoken of, which leads to explaining the connection of Mr. Page with Col. Waldron, as he bought the Waldron farm in 1836, and it has been in the possession of the Taylor Page descendants to the present time, a period of eighty-seven years. The Page Brothers, his grandsons, are among the best farmers of Dover, and respected citizens. Page's Corner is at the junction of Glenwood Avenue with Central Avenue, on the electric railway, between Dover and Somersworth. It is one of the historic spots in Old Dover.

TAYLOR PAGE was born in Parsonsfield, Me., in 1793; he died in Dover, July 8, 1865, aged 72. His wife, MARY HILTON (GOODWIN) PAGE, was born in Newmarket, in 1796; she died Oct. 13, 1844, aged 48. Their graves are in the Page burial ground, on the farm, north of the dwelling house, and near the Col. Waldron burial ground, where are the graves of his wives, and members of the family. Col. Waldron died at the residence of his daughter in Bath, Me., and was buried there.

TAYLOR PAGE was son of JOSEPH and SARAH (TAYLOR) PAGE, hence the origin of his Christian name (TAYLOR). Joseph Page was born in Deerfield, N. H. When a child he went to Parsonsfield, Me., with his parents, and was "brought up" there, acquiring a practical knowledge of the blacksmith trade. At some date before 1820, his son, Taylor Page, commenced practice of the same trade in Lee, N. H. He opened a shop in the village on Lee Hill, then a flourishing settlement. Mr. Page did good work, and pleased the farmers, who kept him busy making all sorts of tools, besides shoeing oxen and horses. In those days all farm tools had to be made by hand; no machine work of any kind was available. As he accumulated money he spent it in buying land, instead of high living, or hard drinking, which many indulged in. Being temperate, industrious and prudent, he prospered; so that on Jan. 21, 1822, he and MARTHA HILTON GOODWIN were united in marriage by Rev. John Osborn, minister of the Church at Lee. They commenced housekeeping on the "Hill," and there was their home for a few years.

It is on record, in the Register of Deeds office, that Jan. 15, 1823, Taylor Page bought fifty acres of land at *Wednesday Hill,* in Lee, on the east side of it. On July 18, Sept. 7, and Dec. 5 of the year 1825, he bought other tracts of land adjoining the property previously acquired, thus making a large farm, of excellent land. He soon built a house on it, and that house is now standing, as good as new, and is known as the "Taylor Page" house, though others have owned it for many years. Several of his children were born there, one of whom was *George W. Page,* who inherited the Col. Waldron homestead, and was father of the present owners. Just across the road from the house (in Lee) is the spot on which his blacksmith shop stood, in which he did blacksmithing when not engaged in farming. That was his home for a dozen years or more, till he became interested in the boom in business in Dover, and came here and purchased the Col. John Waldron farm, or a part of it.

About 1840 he had the Waldron mansion, a fine old house, removed, and built the present family residence. The old house was cut in two parts: one-half of it is now the residence of Taylor Page's grandson, *Mr. William Taylor Page,* at the *Page Corner.* In some of the rooms the fine carpenter work of the old house can be seen. Col. Waldron lived in grand style, and was a royal entertainer. Taylor Page did not do much blacksmithing after he came to Dover; he was too busy in other ways. First of all he put the farm in good condition to raise big and profitable crops, and for twenty years he was one of the leading business men of the town.

TAYLOR PAGE'S wife, MARTHA HILTON GOODWIN, was born in Newmarket, in 1796; daughter of Joseph Lawrence and Betsey (Hilton) Goodwin, who lived on what is called the *"Ash Swamp"* Road, not far from Wadleigh's Falls, in Lee. Joseph Lawrence Goodwin was great grandson of DANIEL GOODWIN, of Old Kittery (now Eliot), who was the emigrant from England, and ancestor of the Goodwin family.

MARTHA HILTON GOODWIN was grand-daughter of Col. Joseph Hilton, who was grandson of Joseph Hilton, who was grandson of Edward Hilton, *"Father of the Settlement of New Hampshire."* Joseph Hilton was son of Edward Hilton, Jr., whose wife was Ann Dudley, grand-daughter of Gov. Thomas Dudley; and Ann Dudley Hilton was grand-daughter of Gov. John Winthrop.

TAYLOR PAGE was son of Joseph and Sarah (Taylor) Page; Joseph was son of James and Dorothy (Moulton) Page, of Deerfield, and Hampton, and Parsonsfield, Me.; James was grandson of Stephen and Mary (Rawlins) Page, of Hampton; Stephen was grandson of Robert Page, the emigrant ancestor, who located in Hampton during the early settlement of that town, and was one of its leading and prosperous citizens for many years. Robert's son, Thomas, married Mary Hussey, daughter of CAPT. CHRISTOPHER HUSSEY, one of the founders of Hampton, and one of its most distinguished citizens.

TAYLOR PAGE'S mother, Sarah Taylor, was daughter of Henry Dearborn Taylor, a nephew of Gen. Henry Dearborn, the distinguished officer in the Revolution, who was Captain of the Nottingham company in the battle of Bunker Hill. The emigrant ancestor was Anthony Taylor, who was one of the first settlers in Hampton. He was a felt maker by trade, and his house was near the village in that town.

TAYLOR PAGE'S grandmother, mother of Sarah (Taylor) Page, was SUSANNA CILLEY, sister of CAPT. JOSEPH CILLEY, father of GENERAL JOSEPH CILLEY of Revolutionary fame, and one of the most distinguished citizens of Nottingham. Captain Cilley was one of the early settlers in Nottingham.

The children of Taylor Page and his wife, Martha Hilton (Goodwin) Page, were as follows. They were born at Lee.

DR. JOHN T. PAGE; did not marry; he was a practicing physician at Winchendon for several years, where he died in 1866.

MARTHA ANN PAGE was born in 1823; she married MAJOR DANIEL SMITH, who was an officer in the Seventh N. H. Volunteer regiment; he was a fine officer; he was in the campaign in

Florida, where he contracted disease, of which he died August 26, 1862. She died at Somerville, Mass., June 27, 1891.

MARY G. PAGE, born 1825; died 4 April, 1832, at Lee.

JOSEPH L. PAGE, born 1827; married ELIZA HORNE; resided in Dover. He was a soldier in the Mexican War, in the regiment commanded by Gen. Frank Pierce, who was later President of the United States. Mr. Page was also a private in Co. F of the Seventh N. H. V., which had such a fearful time with disease in South Carolina and Florida. He enlisted in Oct., 1861; discharged in Oct., 1862, on account of disease; in Jan., 1864, he again enlisted in Co. E of the Veteran Reserve Corps, and served to the end of the war, being discharged Dec. 5, 1865. He died Dec. 26, 1890, at Dover.

MARY GOODWIN PAGE, born 1835; married JOSIAH VINTON; resided at Somerville, Mass., where she died, June 18, 1914.

GEORGE W. PAGE, born Jan. 22, 1829; married JULIA A. KELLEY, daughter of William Kelley and his wife, Pamelia Demeritt. William Kelley was a tanner at the "Kelley Springs"; son of Lieut. Benjamin Kielle. Pamelia Demeritt was daughter of Samuel Demeritt, of Madbury, who was a soldier in the Revolutionary War; he was cousin to Major John Demeritt, the "Powder Major." His grave is in the William Kelley lot, Pine Hill Cemetery. His father, Capt. Samuel Demeritt, was an officer in the French and Indian War of 1757.

GEORGE W. PAGE resided on the homestead, at Page's Corner. He died there Nov. 22, 1890. His wife died April 29, 1905. Their children are:

1. SARAH KELLEY PAGE, b. Sept. 12, 1851.
2. WILLIAM TAYLOR PAGE, b. May 1, 1853; m. June 11, 1878, ELIZABETH A. FLANDERS, dau. of George H. and Asenath (Frost) Flanders, of Dover. They reside in Dover, at "Page's Corner." They have one son: *Frederick Flanders*.
3. FANNIE B. PAGE, b. Feb. 5, 1856; d. July 12, 1896.
4. GEORGE F. PAGE, b. Dec. 3, 1859; d. Sept. 7, 1864.
5. LULA E. PAGE, b. Nov. 5, 1863.

6. GEORGE F. PAGE, b. Apr. 22, 1866.
7 ' HARRY PAGE, b. May 13, 1868.
8. FANNIE B. PAGE, m. GEORGE W. BOWLIN, Feb. 22, 1883; resides in Newburyport, Mass.

FREDERICK FLANDERS PAGE, born July 5, 1882; married, June 20, 1910, CORA A. RICHMOND, dau. of R. N. and Margaret B. Richmond of Adams, Mass. Their children are:

1. MARGARET E., b. 9 Apr., 1911.
2. WILLIAM R., b. 11 Mar., 1915.

THE COFFIN FAMILY.
(MEMORANDA No. 173).

In the *Boston News Letter* of 25th March, 1715, we found the following obituary:

"On Monday the 21st Courant, Dyed at Exeter the Honourable PETER COFFIN, ESQ., in the 85th year of his age, who was late Judge of his Majesty's Superior Court of Judicature, and First Member of His Majesty's Council of this Province; a gentleman very serviceable, both in Church and State. We have a severe storm of snow."

The HONORABLE PETER COFFIN, ESQ., was long a resident of Dover. His father was TRISTRAM COFFIN, a native of the parish of Brixton, near Plymouth, Devonshire, England; a son of Peter[1] and Joanna Coffin, and born in 1609. Tristram, Sr.,[2] married Dionis Stevens, and after the death of his father came to New England in 1642, bringing with him his mother (who died in May, 1661, aged 77), his two sisters, Eunice and Mary, and his wife and five children, viz.: *Peter, Tristram, Elizabeth, James* and *John*. He at first came to Salisbury and went thence to Haverhill, the same year; thence to Newbury, about 1648; thence, in 1651, to Salisbury, where he signed his name—"TRISTRAM COFFYN, COMMISSIONER of Salisbury." In 1659 a company was formed in Salisbury who purchased nine-tenths of Nantucket, and Tristram removed there, in 1660, with his wife, his mother, and four of his children, viz.: *James, John, Stephen,* and *Mary*. There he died, 2 Oct., 1681, aged seventy-two. His children, therefore, were:

1. PETER, (our Peter), b. in 1630, of whom see below.
2. TRISTRAM, b. in 1632.
3. ELIZABETH, m. STEPHEN GREENLEAF.
4. JAMES, b. 12 Aug., 1640.
5. JOHN, b. in England; d. in Haverhill, 1642.
6. MARY, b. in Haverhill, 1645.
7. JOHN, b. in Haverhill, 13 Oct., 1647.
8. STEPHEN, b. in Newbury, 11 Feb., 1652.

As to Tristram's sisters: Eunice married William Butler; his sister Mary married Alexander Adams, of Boston.

TRISTRAM[3] was a merchant tailor, and lived in Newbury. He married JUDITH SOMERBY, widow of Henry Somerby and daughter of Captain Henry Greenleaf. He died 4 Feb., 1704, and his widow, 15 Dec., 1705, aged eighty, leaving 177 descendants. Their children were:

1. JUDITH, b. 4 Dec., 1653.
2. DEBORAH, b. 10 Nov., 1655.
3. MARY, b. 12 Nov., 1657.
4. JAMES, b. 22 Apr., 1659.
5. JOHN, b. 8 Sept., 1660.
6. LYDIA, b. 22 Apr., 1662.
7. ENOCH, b. 21 Jan., 1663.
8. STEPHEN, b. 16 Aug., 1664.
9. PETER, b. 27 July, 1667.
10. NATHANIEL, b. 22 Mar., 1669.

JAMES[3] married, 3 Dec., 1663, MARY SEVERANCE, of Salisbury. In 1659, running across Thomas Macy and his family, who, on account of Baptist notions, had found Newbury rather unpleasant, Isaac Coleman, a boy of twelve, and ELDER EDWARD STARBUCK, of Dover, whom the people of Dover had tried to reason out of his Baptist ideas, but failed on account of his uncommon obstinacy,—James and all of these took an open boat in 1659, and set sail for Nantucket. In due time they arrived at that island and prepared to make a settlement. James and his wife had fourteen children; we do not know their names, except that *Dinah* married her cousin, Nathaniel Starbuck, son of Nathaniel, and grandson of Elder Edward Starbuck.

JOHN³ married DEBORAH AUSTIN, and had seven children. He lived in Nantucket.

NATHANIEL married DAMARIS GAYER, daughter of William Gayer, who married Dorcas Starbuck, daughter of the Elder, and was the progenitor of *Admiral Sir Isaac Coffin,* famous in the annals of the Isle and the British Navy.

MARY³ married NATHANIEL, son of ELDER STARBUCK, of whom we have spoken at length in the story of the Starbuck family. She was a very able and noted Quaker preacher.

We may as well insert TRISTRAM'S³ grandchildren. JAMES⁴ married, 16 Nov., 1685, FLORENCE HOOK, and had children:

1. JUDITH, b. 17 Oct., 1686.
2. ELIZABETH.
3. SARAH, b. 20 Aug., 1869.
4. MARY, b. 16 Jan., 1691.
5. LYDIA, b. 1692.
6. TRISTRAM, b. 19 Oct., 1694.
7. DANIEL, b. 10 May, 1696.
8. ELEANOR, b. 16 May, 1698.
9. JOANNA, b. 2 May, 1701.
10 and 11. JAMES and FLORENCE, b. 1 Jan., 1705.

PETER⁴ married APPHIA DOLE, and moved to Gloucester; had children:

1. HANNAH, b. 3 Mar., 1688.
2. JUDITH, b. 9 Oct., 1693.
3. TRISTRAM, b. 10 Aug., 1696.
4. RICHARD.
5. SARAH, b. 24 Aug., 1701.

STEPHEN⁴ married, 1685, SARAH ATKINSON, and had children:

1. SARAH, b. 16 May, 1686.
2. TRISTRAM, b. 14 Jan., 1688.
3. LYDIA, b. 21 July, 1691.
4. JUDITH, b. 21 Feb., 1693.
5. JOHN, b. 20 Jan., 1695.

HON. NATHANIEL,[4] married, 23 March, 1693, SARAH DOLE, and had children:

1. JOHN, b. 21 Jan., 1694.
2. ENOCH, b. 7 Feb., 1696.
3. APPHIA, b. 7 June, 1698.
4. SAMUEL, b. 24 Aug., 1700.
5. JOSEPH, b. 30 Dec., 1702.
6. JANE, b. 7 Aug., 1705.
7. MOSES, b. June 11, 1707.
8. EDMUND, b. 7 Mar., 1708.

Before turning to Peter we might state that the descendants of Tristram[2] Coffin in 1722, numbered 1,138; and in 1728, 1,582. Of these, our Peter's descendants numbered, at the latter date, 168.

HONORABLE PETER COFFIN, ESQ.,[3] who settled in Dover, was born in England, in 1630, and came to Newbury. Tradition says his father was a Royalist and came over here with his family because he did not like the rule of OLIVER CROMWELL. The exact date of Peter's coming to Dover we cannot state; he was not here in 1648, but was taxed in 1657.

He received grants of land from the town, and bought much more, so he came to be a large land owner. One of the grants he received reads as follows:

"30, 11, 1670; 70 acres; these acres were located 17, 12, 1672:—according to that record sixty of ye sayd land lyeth on ye north side of ye great Mast Path going into ye Swamp, the south east Corner bounded by a marked tree at ye west end of Plumpudding Hill (on Lexington street) & soe by ye head of Capt. Waldens' land to ye highway that goeth to Tole End, & thence along by ye land yt sd Coffin bought of Thomas Nock, to ye bridge over ye brooke goeing to Tole End, only reserving liberty on ye sd land for a Cartway, for ye use of ye town, if required, & from sd bridge forty fower Rodd westerly if it is layed out & bounded on ye south side by the great Mast Way into ye Swamp, about seven Rodds from Plum Pudding Hill, to a rock on the top of a hill on the side of the path, & thence upon a straight line to ye northwest corner of the lot." The other ten acres laid out on the "south side of the above Mast Path, bounded N. by the mast path, E. by the land formerly laid out to sd Coffin to ye path yt goeth to Muchadoe." ("Muchadoe" is the name of the hill at the west end of Washington Street, above Arch Street.)

Whereabouts PETER COFFIN lived, at first, we have no means of ascertaining, except that it was at Cochecho, and probably where the garrison stood that was destroyed by the Indians in 1689.

Peter was a man of note. He was a Selectman in 1660, 1668, 1669, 1672 and 1675. He was Representative in 1672, 1673, 1679 and 1680. He performed various official duties. In 1666 he was one of the committee to see about fortifying Portsmouth, so as to receive great guns. In 1668 Peter experienced "great guns" himself. In June, that year, a man was slain up at Penacook (Concord) by a drunken Indian; the matter was investigated and the Indians testified that they had "several runlets of strong liquors" from Thomas Payne and Thomas Dickenson (who was killed), who sold it to them at Captain Walden's truckhouse up there, in behalf of the CAPTAIN, his son PAUL, and PETER COFFIN. This being contrary to law, which forbid selling liquors to the Indians, these three (Walderne, his son, and Coffin) were examined. All three denied any interest in the liquor selling. The General Court thereupon directed them to clear themselves by oath. The CAPTAIN and his son, PAUL, did so. PETER COFFIN declined to take the oath, and owned that he did furnish the liquor for the truck-house; so the Court fined him 50 pounds.

In 1666 the General Court made a bargain with LIEUT. PETER COFFIN for some masts which were to be a present to His Majesty, King of England; in 1668 they were delivered; on 15 May he was paid, receiving 100 pounds for the masts, and for "his own care and paynes in procuring ye same" a couple hundred acres of upland, and "thirty or forty acres of meadow," "where he can find it not laid out, which wee suppose he may well deserve & will be no less satisfying to him." PETER was Town

Treasurer several years, and serving as such was directed by the Town, in 1665, to "Agree with some workmen to build a Terret apon ye meeting house for to hang ye bell which we have Bought of Capt. Walderne." And also, in 1667, he was ordered to build a fortification around the meeting-house, which was competed before 1670.

In 1689 PETER was living in his garrison at Cochecho, which stood about sixty feet back from Central Avenue, near the corner of Orchard Street. In digging away the bank, at a later period, a sill and a metal weight were found. On June 27, 1689, some squaws asked to sleep in his house. He granted the request. In the night they opened the gate and let the Indians in, and when they left they set it on fire, and it was burned. The family escaped to their son Tristram's garrison, near the Belknap schoolhouse, and the Indians followed them and demanded admission, which was refused, at first; but the Indians threatened to kill his father, if Tristram did not let them in. Filial affection prevailed, and he opened the door. The Indians were wags, in their way, so instead of slaughtering anyone they had fun with Peter, by compelling him to open his money bag and scatter coin around for the Indians to scramble for and pick up by the firelight on the hearth. As soon as dawn of day appeared they departed, in haste, as they feared pursuit. The garrison was not harmed, and the family escaped being taken prisoners.

In 1692, after the Province of New Hampshire was established, PETER COFFIN was appointed Councillor, which position he held till he was senior at the Board. He was also Judge of a Court; he was in office at the time of the trial of Rev. Mr. Moody, at Portsmouth, for refusing to administer the sacrament to Governor Cranfield, according to the English Church Ritual. Coffin voted to condemn Moody, who was kept in jail several weeks.

PETER COFFIN married ABIGAIL, daughter of ELDER EDWARD STARBUCK, of Dover. Their children were:

1. ABIGAIL, b. 20 Oct., 1657; m. MAJOR DAVISON, of Ipswich, Mass., who moved to Newbury.
2. PETER, b. 20 Aug., 1660.
3. JOSHUA, b. 16 Sept., 1663.
4. TRISTRAM, b. 18 Jan., 1665; m. DEBORAH COLCORD.

5. EDWARD, b. 20 Feb., 1669; m. ANNA GARDNER, dau. of John Gardner.
6. JUDITH, b. 4 Feb., 1672.
7. ELIZABETH, b. 27 Jan., 1680; m. COL. JOHN GILMAN, of Exeter.
8. JETHRO.
9. PERNEL.

We come now to the families of the children of LIEUT. PETER[3] of Dover.

ABIGAIL,[4] married MAJOR DAVISON.

PETER,[4] born 20 Aug., 1660, married, 15 Aug., 1682, his cousin, ELIZABETH STARBUCK, of Nantucket, daughter of Nathaniel, and granddaughter of Elder Edward Starbuck. Their children:

1. ABIGAIL, b. July 9, 1683.
2. TRISTRAM, b. 20 Apr., 1685.
3. NATHANIEL, b. 26 Mar., 1687.
4. SAMUEL, b. 26 Feb., 1689.
5. BARNABAS, b. 12 Feb., 1690-1.

TRISTRAM[4] COFFIN, born 18 Jan., 1665; lived in Dover. He inherited the Dover estate. His wife was DEBORAH COLCORD, born 21 March, 1664, daughter of Edward Colcord, of Hampton. They had four children, viz:

1. ABIGAIL, b. 30 May, 1686; m. BARTHOLOMEW THING.
2. ELIPHALET, b. 13 Jan., 1689; m. 11 Feb., 1710, JUDITH NOYES.
3. PARNELL, m. BENJ. THING.
4. TRISTRAM, b. about 1691; m. (1) 15 Nov., 1719, JANE HEARD, of Kittery; m. (2) HANNAH SMITH.

ELIZABETH,[4] who married COL. JOHN GILMAN, of Exeter, who was born 19 Jan., 1677, had seven children; she died 7 July, 1720. Her husband married (2) Elizabeth, widow of Hon. Robert Hale, and daughter of Nathaniel Clark, of Newbury.

JETHRO,[4] married MARY GARDNER, and lived in Nantucket; they had children:

1. MARGARET, who m. REV. JOHN WILSON.
2. PRISCILLA, who m. JOHN G. GARDNER.
3. JOHN, who m. LYDIA GARDNER.
4. JOSIAH, who m. SUSANNA COFFIN.
5. ABIGAIL, who m. NATHANIEL WOODBURY.
6. PETER.
7. EDWARD.
8. ROBERT.

THE WATSON FAMILY.
(MEMORANDA NO. 120.)

JONATHAN WATSON was a resident upon the "Upper Neck," as early as 1675. Whether he was a relative of Robert Watson, of Oyster River, does not appear. Robert was born in 1641, and purchased land at Oyster River, of Walter and Jane Jackson; married HANNAH BEARD, and was killed in 1694. His inventory was entered in 1703, by said Hannah, who had previously to that date married John Amblar.

JONATHAN owned land on the Neck and also at Tole-End. He appears to have been twice married: (1) ABIGAIL, daughter of Rev. Samuel and Elizabeth Dudley; (2) to ELIZABETH ———. He gave all his property to his wife, 9 Aug., 1714, and died soon after. She conveyed the property to her sons, *David, William* and *Isaac,* the latter receiving the homestead.

Of the children of JONATHAN whose names we can ascertain were:

1. DANIEL.
2. SAMUEL.
3. DAVID.
4. WILLIAM, "of New York, mariner."
5. ISAAC.
6. DAUGHTER, m. ELEAZER YOUNG, of Dover.

Of DANIEL^2 we find no trace, except that his name occurs in a deed.

SAMUEL^2 had wife, MARY, and child, *Winthrop,* born 11 Jan., 1673, in Dover; there may have been others.

THE WATSON FAMILY.

DAVID,[2] born before 1684, had wife, MARY. He was dead in 1647. He owned land on Silver and Pleasant Streets, on the corner of which a brick building now stands. This tract was sold by his children, *Dudley, Mercy, Sarah* and *Mary,* to their brothers, *Jonathan* and *Winthrop,* 20 Oct., 1747. Children therefore are:

1. DUDLEY.
2. MERCY, bapt. 2 June, 1742; m. BENJAMIN HANSON.
3. SARAH, m. NATHANIEL DOE.
4. MARY, m. WILLIAM CUSHING (probably the fourth child of Rev. Jonathan Cushing), b. 26 Dec., 1723.
5. JONATHAN, of Exeter, 1747.
6. WINTHROP, of Exeter, 1747.

One of the sons of JONATHAN WATSON, whom we cannot ascertain, had WILLIAM, born 1737.

ISAAC[2] lived on the farm now owned and occupied by one of his lineal descendants. He married (1) ELIZABETH ———, who died before 1745; he married (2) JOANNA ———. He was dead in 1754, and his widow, Joanna, and son, Joseph, administered upon his estate, which was finally divided, in 1795. Widow Joanna became a member of the First Church in 1755. She died 28 Oct., 1784. Children were:

1. BENJAMIN, b. 3 Apr., 1734.
2. KEZIAH.
3. ISAAC, who was d. in 1795.
4. JOSEPH.
5. WILLIAM.
6. JONATHAN.
7. JOHN.
8. ELIZABETH, bapt. 5 Oct., 1755; m. FRANCIS DREW.
9. DANIEL, bapt. 5 Oct., 1755; was d. in 1799.
10. JOANNA, bapt. 16 June, 1742; m. HUMPHREY HANSON (son of Joseph and Sarah Hanson, b. 27 Aug., 1738; d. 13 Nov., 1766), and had: 1. *Dominicus,* b. 17 Mar., 1760. 2. *Joseph,* b. 18 Dec., 1764. 3. *Sarah,* b. 22 Dec., 1762. 4. *Elizabeth,* b. 12 May, 1767. 5. *David,* dead in 1795. 6. *Servia,* bapt. 5 Oct., 1765; m. Lieut. Samuel Stackpole, grandfather of Dr. Paul A. Stackpole.
11. GEORGE, bapt. 5 Oct., 1755; dead in 1795.

DUDLEY,[3] son of David and Mary Watson, married CHRISTINE BAKER, daughter of Capt. Thomas and Christine (Otis) Baker, whose captivity by the Indians, after the attack on Dover in 1689, is recorded by Belknap, and more fully by the author, in the "Otis Genealogy," in the N. E. Gen. Register, Vol. 5. DUDLEY was "Captain," and doubtless lived at Tole-End. He was baptized and admitted to the First Church 17 Oct., 1736. Children were:

1. DUDLEY, bapt. 17 Oct., 1736.
2. LUCY, bapt. 17 Feb., 1739; m. AARON HAM, and lived in Rochester; and they had five daughters.
3. DAVID, bapt. 5 June, 1731; d. young.
4. THOMAS, bapt. 7 Aug., 1743.
5. SAMUEL, bapt. 7 Apr., 1745; d. young.
6. WINTHROP.
7. MARY, bapt. 15 Apr., 1750; m. 14 Mar., 1775, HEARD ROBERTS, of Dover and Rochester, and had four sons and one daughter.
8. HANNAH, bapt. 17 May, 1752; m., 1 Aug., 1771, NATHANIEL HAM, of Dover, and had three sons and one daughter.
9. OTIS BAKER, bapt. 30 Sept., 1753.
10. SARAH, bapt. 13 July, 1756; m. RICHARD GARLAND, of Bartlett, N. H. who was b. in Rochester 28 May, 1763, and d. 17 Feb., 1814, having had five sons and three daughters.
11. LYDIA, bapt. 24 Feb., 1760; m. RICHARD HAYES, of Madbury, and had six sons and five daughters, and d. 22 Apr., 1850.

WILLIAM,[3] lived corner of Silver and Locust Streets. He married LUCY, daughter of JOSHUA and LUCY (BAKER) STACKPOLE. Children were:

1. BENJAMIN, had son, *Jeremiah.*
2. HIMEOUS, of Barrington.
3. WILLIAM, d. at sea, unm.
4. NATHANIEL, lived and d. in Danvers, Mass.
5. JOHN, d. at sea, unm.
6. FREDERICK, removed to the State of New York.
7. FENTON, d. unm., in Salem, Mass.
8. JOSEPH, d. in Dover, unm.
9. ELIZABETH, m. EZEKIEL VARNEY, of Rutland, Vt.
10. ABIGAIL, m. a TRACEY, of Dover, and d. without issue.

BENJAMIN,[3] son of Isaac Watson, lived on land received in part from his father. He married LYDIA, daughter of ISAAC and SUSANNAH HANSON, born 5 Nov., ———. He died 29 Jan., 1785; and his wife, Lydia, was appointed administratrix, 8 June, 1785. Children were:

1. SUSAN, b. 2 May, 1768; drowned in youth.
2. SUSAN, b. 15 Apr., 1770; m. (1) LEWIS WENTWORTH; (2) THOMAS BURLEIGH; and had by her first marriage, *Susan*, and one other, who d. in infancy.
3. BENJAMIN, b. 26 Jan., 1772.
4. SAMUEL, b. 7 July, 1774.
5. ISAAC, b. 21 Apr., 1777.
6. SARAH, b. 6 July, 1780; m. SAMUEL HANSON, and d. childless.
7. JOHN, b. 8 May, 1782; d. at sea, 17 Oct., 1799.

JOSEPH,[3] had wife, ELIZABETH; was dead in 1795; had children:

1. ISAAC, b. 11 Jan., 1760.
2. JAMES, b. 8 Mar., 1763.
3. SARAH, b. 2 July, 1766.

JONATHAN,[3] removed to Scarboro, Me. He married OLIVE SEAVEY, who died there before 1800. Among children born in Scarborough was:

1. JONATHAN, b. 1 Apr., 1771, who m. HANNAH MILLIKEN (b. in Buxton, 23 Apr., 1782), had *Ann* and others, and d. in 1850.

THOMAS,[4] son of Dudley,[3] married, at Dover, 31 Sept., 1770, ABIGAIL HORNE, and had children:

1. AARON (lived on the old homestead at Tole-End).
2. DUDLEY, d. in Rochester.
3. A DAUGHTER, who m. BENJAMIN HORNE.
4. ABIGAIL.
5. LYDIA, d. unm.

OTIS BAKER,[4] son of Dudley,[3] married CHARITY HORN, in Dover, and settled in Sandwich, and died there 11 March, 1815.

His wife died in Sandwich, 22 July, 1848, aged eighty-five. Children:

1. CHRISTINE, d. at the age of four.
2. POLLY, b. about 1789; m. DAVID ELDRIDGE, of Sandwich.
3. CHRISTINE, b. 23 June, 1691; m. her cousin, PAUL HORNE, and lived in Sandwich.
4. JAMES H., b. 1793; m. SARAH KEAZER, of Groton, Mass., and lived at Sandwich.
5. DAVID, b. 1792.
6. JONATHAN, b. 1796; m. (1) ADELINE TEBBETS, of Dover; (2) ELIZABETH BURNHAM, of Dover.
7. ESTHER, b. 1803; lived at Sandwich.
8. SOPHIA, b. 1806; lived at Sandwich.
9. ELEAZER H., b. 1808; lived at Sandwich.

BENJAMIN,[4] son of Benjamin,[3] married ELIZABETH WHITEHOUSE, daughter of Richard and Hannah (Goodwin) Whitehouse, of Rollinsford, born 27 July, 1772. He lived in Dover on the homestead, a part of which descended directly from his grandfather, Jonathan. He died 16 Nov., 1847. Children:

1. SETH, b. 1797.
2. JOHN, b. 13 Dec., 1799.
3. BENJAMIN, m. ——— WHITEHOUSE, and had: *Elizabeth* and *John Adams*, b. 10 Dec., 1830.
4. LYDIA, m. JEREMY PERKINS, of Dover, and they had children: *Charles Edwin, Sarah Elizabeth, Jeremy William, Lydia Augusta, Daniel Libby, John Henry, Isabella, Ann Louise, Andrew, Andrew 2d, Susan, Samuel.*

SARAH HANSON,[5] daughter of Benjamin,[4] married OLIVER L. REYNOLDS, and had children:

1. CECILIA AMANDA, b. 13 Mar., 1832; d. 1 Mar., 1850.
2. JULIETTE, b. 29 Nov., 1833.
3. BENJAMIN OLIVER, b. 3 Dec., 1836.
4. ELIZABETH WATSON, b. 4 Feb., 1813; m. HON. THOMAS E. SAWYER, and d. 1 Dec., 1847, having had: *Charles Walter, Mary Elizabeth.*
5. RUTH ANN, b. 9 July, 1835; d. 19 Aug., 1835.
6. EDWARD.
7. SARAH ELLEN, b. 2 June, 1838; d. 8 Jan., 1842.

8. THOMAS, b. 28 Oct., 1840; d. 8 Aug., 1842.
9. RUTH ELLEN, b. 9 May, 1843; d. 27 Aug., 1848.
10 and 11. ISAAC and SETH (twins), b. 1815, of whom SETH m. (1) WIDOW ANN BERRY, dau. of Jonathan and Hannah (Milliken) Watson, b. 5 Apr., 1815; she d. in Dover, having had: *Benjamin*, b. 28 Jan., 1847; d. 24 Aug., 1848; and *Benjamin Seth*, b. 11 June, 1849. SETH m. (2) LYDIA A. HORNE, of Dover.

SAMUEL,[4] son of Benjamin, married, 19 Sept., 1803, PRISCILLA, daughter of CALEB HODGDON, born 31 Jan., 1779. He died 14 April, 1847; his wife had died 31 Oct., 1822. Children:

1. NANCY, b. 1 Feb., 1804; m. 20 Mar., 1824, STEPHEN DAVIS, and d. 24 Jan., 1842, having had two children: *Ann Elizabeth* and *Horace P.*, who m. Betsey C. Ham, of Rochester.
2. SUSAN, b. 2 Oct., 1810; d. 10 Mar., 1811.
3. LYDIA, b. 21 Dec., 1815; d. 27 Sept., 1817.

We are unable to locate the following:
LILLIAN WATSON, married THOMAS SHANNON, 28 Feb., 1771.
ALICE WATSON, married THOMAS THOMPSON, 27 Sept., 1772.
ISAAC WATSON, married MARY HOGG, 31 March, 1774.

Those wishing to trace the genealogy of the Stackpole family after intermarriages with the Watsons, will find it at length in the Genealogical Register for July, 1851, commencing page 217.

THE TUTTLE FAMILY.

(MEMORANDA No. 133.)

JOHN TUTTLE, said to be a native of Wales, was in Dover in 1642, when he was granted lot No. 7, in the first division of lots on the west side of Back River. The probability is that he was here some years earlier, and perhaps he came in 1633. He was a resident of Dover Neck, and died, intestate, in 1663. The inventory of his property was entered in June, 1663; his wife was administratrix. "Widow Tuttle" was taxed in 1663 and 1664, and then disappears. Perhaps she got married. Children were:

1. THOMAS, who was killed by fall of a tree, in 1664.
2. DAUGHTER, who m. and had her portion previous to the death of her father.
3. JOHN, who was under age at the death of his father.
4. DAUGHTER.

JOHN,[2] was the only Tuttle who left children. He owned much land; had sawmills; built ships and sent them to foreign ports. He held many offices and was one of the most noted and influential citizens of Dover. He was Selectman in 1686-'87, '88; Representative in 1698; Town Clerk from 1686 to 1717; Representative in the convention of 1689; Judge of the Court of Common Pleas from 1695 to 1700. He died in 1720.

In his Will he mentions his wife, MARY, son, *Ebenezer,* and daughter, *Mary Wallingford,* and grandchildren,—*Thomas, John, Nicholas, Elijah* and *Phebe Tuttle,* and grandchildren *John* and *Peter Hayes.* Children were:

1. JOHN, b. 1671.
2. THOMAS, b. 4 Apr., 1674; d. 1699, in the "Bay of Campeacha."
3. DAUGHTER, who m. a HAYES.
4. MARY, who m. a WALLINGFORD, in 1687.
5. JAMES, b. 7 Apr., 1683.
6. EBENEZER, who received part of his father's Salmon Falls property and mill, 20 Jan., 1717-8.

JOHN TUTTLE,[3] son of John,[2] as above. He was a man of arms, being Ensign. He was murdered by the Indians, at his sawmill, 17 May, 1712. His wife was JUDITH OTIS, daughter of RICHARD[1] OTIS, who was killed by the Indians at his garrison in 1689. Their children were:

1. MARY, b. 16 Jan., 1697-8.
2. THOMAS, b. 16 Mar., 1699-1700.
3. JUDITH, b. 10 May, 1701.
4. JOHN, b. 8 May, 1704.
5. DOROTHY, b. 21 Mar., 1706.
6. NICHOLAS, b. 27 July, 1708.
7. JAMES, b. 10 Feb., 1710-11.

THE TUTTLE FAMILY.

JAMES,³ son of John,² was a "Friend." He lived on Dover Neck, where "Friend" Joseph Tuttle also lived. His wife, ROSE, was daughter of JOHN PINKHAM. After his death she married Thomas Canney. James died previous to 1711. His children were:

1. PHEBE, b. 26 Sept., 1706, who m. MOSES VARNEY.
2. ELIJAH, b. 14 May, 1708.

THOMAS,⁴ was also a "Friend." He married MARY BRACKET. His Will was dated 1 April, 1772; proved 12 March, 1777. In it *Ebenezer,* his son, was appointed executor, and to him also was given the homestead, and the *"great Bible."* The other children mentioned were: *Mary, Hope, Sarah, Abigail* and *Bathsheba.* Children were:

1. MARY, b. 29 Dec., 1723; m. DANIEL TWOMBLY.
2. HOPE, b. 25 Aug., 1725; m. ROBERT SCAMMON.
3. SARAH, b. 16 Apr., 1727; m. JOHN HANSON.
4. ELISHA, b. 14 Feb., 1729; d. unm.
5. SAMUEL, b. 3 Jan., 1731.
6. THOMAS, b. 21 Apr., 1733; m. 2 Jan., 1760, SARAH, dau. of JOHN and PHEBE (AUSTIN) HANSON, who d. 4 Apr., 1812.
7. ABIGAIL, b. 25 Feb., 1735; m. NATHAN VARNEY.
8. EBENEZER, b. 5 Feb., 1737.
9. REUBEN, b. 26 July, 1739.
10. BATHSHEBA, b. 28 July, 1741; m. JOSEPH VARNEY.
11. TABITHA, b. 18 June, 1744; d. unm.

Descendants of this branch are said to be in Windham, Me.

JOHN,⁴ probably son of John,³ made his Will 15 July, 1773; proved 9 March, 1774. Children:

1. PAUL.
2. SILAS.
3. JOB.
4. DOROTHY, who m. a JOCOBS.
5. PRUDENCE, who m. a BUNKER.
6. HANNAH, who m. a LANGLEY.
7. ANNA, who m. a LEIGHTON
8. MARTHA, who m. a JOCOBS.

JAMES,[4] apparently son of John,[3] "being advanced in years," made his Will 13 Aug., 1784; proved 7 Aug., 1790. He mentions his wife, MARY, and sons—*Stephen, David, Andrew, Elijah* and *James,* and six daughters, unmarried. Children, as enumerated above.

ELIJAH,[4] son of James,[3] was a "Friend," and married ESTHER VARNEY. He died 23 Oct., 1787; she died 8 Feb., 1802. His Will was dated 2 Nov., 1786; proved 21 Nov., 1787; leaving legacies to *Benjamin* and *Samuel.* The bulk of his property went to *James* and *William.* Children were:

1. JAMES, who m. 6 Jan., 1783, ROSE PINKHAM, and d., we believe, childless, 1816.
2. BENJAMIN, who m. MARY HUSSEY, and lived in Lebanon, Me.
3. SAMUEL, who m. MARTHA VARNEY, and lived in Somersworth.
4. WILLIAM.

EBENEZER,[5] son of THOMAS,[4] lived at Back River. He married, 30 Nov., 1768, DEBORAH LEIGHTON; died 1797. His Will was dated 29 April, 1796; proved 13 Jan., 1797. He gave to his wife the *"great Bible"*; to *Tobias,* furniture; to *Ebenezer, Thomas, Abigail* and *Hope,* certain small sums. Children were:

1. TOBIAS, b. 25 Aug., 1769; m. 24 Aug., 1796, PHEBE, dau. of ELIJAH and HANNAH (ROBERTS) AUSTIN, but had no children.
2. THOMAS, b. 1772; d. unm., 1817.
3. ABIGAIL, b. 13 May, 1775; m. SAMUEL NASON.
4. MARY, b. 15 May, 1778.
5. JOHN, b. 17 July, 1782.
6. HOPE, b. 5 Oct., 1786.
7. EBENEZER, b. ———; d. 1811.

REUBEN,[5] son of THOMAS,[4] married, 26 May, 1762, ELIZABETH, dau. of TOBIAS and JUDITH (VARNEY) HANSON. They resided first in Barrington, where their children were born. Then they went to Falmouth. Children were:

1. JUDITH, b. 16 Sept., 1762.
2. MARY, b. 24 Mar., 1765.
3. ELISHA, b. 29 July, 1767.

4. REUBEN, b. 28 Apr., 1770.
5. LYDIA, b. 30 Mar., 1773.
6. MEHITABLE, b. 2 May, 1775.
7. ANN, b. 17 May, 1778.

WILLIAM,[5] son of Elijah,[4] married, 27 March, 1782, ANNE HANSON. He died 2 Feb., 1834; she died 26 Nov., 1832. Children were:

1. PHEBE, b. 16 June, 1783.
2. JOSEPH, b. 15 Oct., 1786; m., 30 Nov., 1814, SARAH PINKHAM, dau. of Joseph and Elizabeth (Green) Pinkham, and had: *Eliza P., Asa C., Stephen, William Penn, Joseph E.*
3. ROSE, b. 29 Apr., 1791.
4. SARAH, b. 1 July, 1793.
5. IRA, b. 18 Aug., 1798; d. 3 Dec., 1839.

Mr. Elijah Tuttle, of Strafford, furnishes the following regarding Dover Tuttles. He says:

JAMES,[4] of Back River, born 10 Feb., 1719; married MARY ———, born 5 Nov., 1720. He died 9 July, 1720; she died 3 March, 1814. Children:

1. PHEBE, b. 23 Nov., 1739; m. (1) ——— JACOBS; (2) ——— HANSON; d. 7 Jan., 1819.
2. PATIENCE, b. 25 Dec., 1742; m. a JACKSON; d. 1770.
3. STEPHEN, b. 28 Nov., 1741; m. a FOSS; d. 1804.
4. ELIJAH, b. 4 Jan., 1747; m. a JOHNSON; lived in Barrington; d. 1823.
5. LOUISA, b. 24 Feb., 1749; m. (1) a DREW; (2) a FOSS; d. 1822.
6. SARAH, b. 15 Apr., 1751; m. a TASKER; she d. 1819.
7. JAMES, b. 7 Apr., 1753; m. a NUTE.
8. EUNICE, b. 8 Apr., 1755; m. a JACKSON; d. 1770.
9. DAVID, b. 10 May, 1758; m. a BUNKER.
10. ANDREW, b. 10 Jan., 1761; m. a DAME; d. 1818.
11. MARY, b. 23 Nov., 1766; m. a PINKHAM.
12. JUDAH, b. 24 Feb., 1768; m. SAMUEL DAVIS of "Pudding Hill," Madbury.

ELIJAH,[5] born 4 Jan., 1747; married a JOHNSON. He lived in Barrington and had children:

1. ELIJAH, b. 10 July, 1774.
2. SARAH, b. 20 Feb., 1776; she m. a CLARK.
3. JAMES, b. 15 Sept., 1777; m. a CLARK; d. in 1852.
4. ESTHER, b. 9 July, 1780; m. a JOHNSON.
5. LYDIA, b. 8 Nov., 1782; m. a BROCK.
6. MOLLY, b. 15 Nov., 1784; m. a FOSS.
7. JOHN, b. 20 Nov., 1787; m. a MOULTON.

ELIJAH,[6] born 10 July, 1774; married a TASKER, and lived at Bow Pond. Children:

1. SAMUEL, b. 28 June, 1799; m. a PERKINS.
2. WILLIAM, b. 9 Apr., 1802; m. a STARBARD.
3. MARY, b. 10 July, 1804; m. a GRACE.
4. JEHIAH, b. 11 Feb., 1807; m. a HALL.
5. HORATIO, b. 5 Feb., 1809; m. a FOSS.
6. SARAH, b. 13 Mar., 1811; m. a BROCK.
7. ASA, b. 12 June, 1813; m. a CAVERLY.
8. ESTHER, b. 2 Aug., 1815; m. a LIBBY; she d. in 1853.
9. HARRIET, b. 12 Apr., 1819; d. in 1836.

ANDREW,[5] son of James,[4] inhabited the homestead at Back River. He married a DAME; died in 1818. He had children:

1. JAMES, b. 12 Nov., 1782.
2. BENJAMIN, b. 23 Dec., 1784.
3. MARTHA, b. 5 Nov., 1786; m. MOSES ELLIOTT.
4. SAMUEL, b. 3 May, 1789.
5. ELIJAH, b. 16 Apr., 1791; he m. a HODGDON.
6. MARY, b. 18 May, 1793.
7. DEBORAH, b. 2 Jan., 1794.
8. ANDREW, b. 18 Nov., 1796, who was a well-known citizen of Dover.
9. JUDAH, b. 28 Oct., 1798.
10. JONATHAN, b. 10 Aug., 1800.
11. JOHN THOMAS, b. 10 Jan., 1802.
12. ABIGAIL, b. 15 Oct., 1805.

JOHN,[6] son of Elijah,[5] of Barrington, married a MOULTON. He had children:

1. LYDIA, b. 22 Jan., 1810; m. BENJ. A. WATERHOUSE.
2. ESTHER, b. 13 July, 1811; m. NATHANIEL FOSS.
3. MARGARET, b. 22 Sept., 1814; m. a GRAY.
4. JOHN, b. 24 Mar., 1816; m. a HILL.
5. ELIJAH, b. 8 June, 1818; m. a HANSON.
6. JONATHAN, b. 24 Aug., 1812; m. a WATERHOUSE.
7. JAMES, b. 20 Dec., 1823; m. a HOWARD.
8. ALVAH, b. 11 Oct., 1825; was drowned in the Pascataqua River, 4 July, 1852.
9. JOSEPH, b. 12 Nov., 1827; m. a HOWARD.
10. MARY, b. 11 Apr., 1829; d. at Dover in 1847.
11 and 12. SARAH and HANNAH, b. 1 Aug., 1832.

In 1868, Dr. Quint furnished additional matter concerning the Tuttle Family, which is here given, as it furnishes valuable information he had obtained since the preceding was published.

JOHN TUTTLE, son of JUDGE JOHN TUTTLE and MARY TUTTLE, his wife, married JUDITH, daughter of Richard and Rose (Stoughton) Otis, and had seven children. He was killed by the Indians while at work at the Tole-End saw-mill, while he was in the prime of life, leaving a widow and seven young children. He was Ensign in the military company, and is spoken of in the old records as "Ensign Tuttle." At other times he is called John Tuttle, Jr. At the time of his death he was probably residing on the Tuttle farm, on the west side of Back River, which his father later gave to his (Ensign's) eldest sons, *Thomas* and *John*. The children of Ensign John and Judith (Otis) Tuttle were:

1. MARY, b. 7 Jan., 1697 or 8; m. JAMES CANNEY; lived in Somersworth.
2. THOMAS, b. 15 Mar., 1699 or 1700; m. MARY BRACKETT, and had eleven children. He d. in Feb., 1777. He resided in the Back River District, on land his grandfather, Judge Tuttle, gave him. He and his wife were "Friends." Thomas was Selectman in Dover in 1762 and 1763. His wife d. in 1773. Tobias Tuttle, an esteemed and enterprising citizen of Dover, who built the fine brick block on the southwest corner of Tuttle Square, was a grandson. Thomas Tuttle, M. D., of Northwood, was a great grandson.
3. JUDITH, b. 10 May, 1702; was living in 1743; unm.

4. JOHN, b. 8 May, 1704; m. (1) ELIZABETH, dau. of James
and Prudence Nute, and had nine children. He m. (2)
ANNE, dau. of James and Anne (Meserve) Nute, and had
two children, viz.: *Esther*, wife of James Tuttle, Esq.,
and *James*, who m. Joanna, dau. of Capt. Joshua and
Joanna (Wentworth) Roberts. After his death his
widow m. Thomas Cushing, grandson of Parson Cushing,
and had six children. John Tuttle lived on the estate
given him by his grandfather, Judge Tuttle.
5. DOROTHY, b. 21 Mar., 1706; she does not appear to have
been living in 1717.
6. NICHOLAS, b. July 27, 1708; d. in Nottingham, in 1793. He
m. (1) DEBORAH HUNT; lived in Lee, but afterwards
moved to Nottingham (Gebig). They had children, viz.:
1. *George*, b. 1737; m. Catherine Stevens. He was Captain in the army of the Revolution; he was for many
years member of the N. H. Legislature. He d. in Effingham, 12 Apr., 1716, leaving children. 2. *Stoughton*, b.
Sept., 1739; m. (1) Lydia Stevens; (2) Hannah Sanborn.
She d. Aug., 1812, leaving children. Maj. Benjamin S.
Tuttle and his brother, Hon. B. C. Tuttle, were grandsons.
3. *Nicholas*, m. Sarah Smart; nothing further is known
of him. 4. *Judith*, m. Josiah Burleigh. 5. *Elizabeth
Stillings*. 6. *Deborah*, m. Moses Perkins. 7. *Esther*, m.
Joseph Sanborn. 8. *Keziah*, m. (1) Jeremiah Elkins; (2)
Robert Evans. 9. *Benjamin*, b. 1764. 10. *Mary*, m.
James Stokes.
7. JAMES, b. 9 Feb., 1710 or 11; d. 9 July, 1790; m. MARY, dau.
of Jacob and Martha (Dame) Allen, and had twelve children.

JAMES TUTTLE, son of JUDGE JOHN and MARY, married ROSE, daughter of John and Rose (Otis) Pinkham. He lived on Dover Neck, where his great grandson, Joseph Tuttle, subsequently lived. He and his wife were among the early members of the Society of "Friends," in Dover. They had two children:

1. PHEBE, b. 26 Sept., 1706; m. MOSES, son of Humphrey and
Esther (Starbuck) Varney, and had eleven children.
2. ELIJAH, b. 14 May, 1708; m. ESTHER VARNEY, and d. 23
Nov., 1707, leaving four children, viz.: 1. *James*, b.
1739; m. Rose Pinkham; d. in Jan., 1816. 2. *Benjamin*,
b. 1742; m. Mary Hussey, and d. 12 Dec., 1812. 4. *Samuel*, b. 1747; m. Martha Varney, and d. 8 Oct., 1807. 4.
William, b. 1750; m. Anne Hanson, and d. in Feb., 1834.

THE CLEMENTS FAMILY.

(MEMORANDA NOS. 150-151.)

ROBERT CLEMENT (or CLEMENCE), of Haverhill; b. about 1590. He came from England; was in Haverhill in 1642; Representative, 1647-53. He mar. —— ——; died 29 Sept., 1658. He made his Will 6 Sept., 1658; his wife was living. He mentions his "children's children then in England."

CHILDREN.

1. JOB, m. (1) 25 Dec., 1744, MARGARET DUMMER; (2) LYDIA ——; (3) WIDOW JOANNA LEIGHTON.
2. JOHN, m. SARAH OSGOOD.
3. ROBERT, m. ELIZABETH FAWNE.
4. ABRAHAM, living in 1658.
5. DANIEL, living in 1658.
6. SARAH, m. ABRAHAM MORRILL.
7. LYDIA, m. MOSES PENGREW.
8. MARY, b. about 1637; m. 15 Nov., 1653, JOHN OSGOOD. She was the youngest dau. who came from Coventry, Warwickshire, Eng., about 1652. She was indicted for witchcraft in 1692; living in 1695.

JOB^2 (*Robert^1*), of Haverhill and Dover; "tanner"; married (1) 25 Dec., 1644, in Haverhill, MARGARET DUMMER, daughter of Thomas Dummer, one of the founders of Salisbury. Before 1658 he married (2) LYDIA ——; he married (3) 16 July, 1673, JOANNA —— (widow of Thomas Leighton). He is supposed to have come from Ipswich to Haverhill in 1640; freeman 1647; he was the first tanner in Haverhill. He was offered a freehold in Newbury in 1649, if he would exercise his trade there; but he received a good offer from Dover, instead, and came to Dover Neck before 1655, probably in 1652. His tannery was the first one opened in New Hampshire. He at once became one of the leading business men. He was elected one of the Selectmen in 1666, and four or five years following. He was occasionally Commissioner for trying small cases. He served on grand juries. He was largely engaged in the shipping business, but his tannery products were always in great demand.

Among the deeds in which his name occurs are the following items: Job Clement, of Dover, and his wife, Lydia, convey for 80 pounds, 29 June, 1658, to Joseph Jowett, of Rowley, "my house and house lott in Haverhill," with other lands. On the 17th of March, 1657, he mortgaged, to Joseph Jowett, 150 acres of land in Dover (110 of it joining James Rawlins), and 40 more "in the Back River lotts," as security for 50 pounds "which I, the said Job Clement am to pay unto my two eldest children, had by my first wife," when the children come of age. Job Clement "of Dover, tanner," and Lydia, his wife, sold 21 Feb., 1658, to Daniel Ela, land, barn and tanhouse, situated in Haverhill. Also 23 Dec., 1653, 3½ acres of land "By ye Fore River side," bounded "in two Parsells, the one Parsell Below ye hie way that Goeth from Thomas Caney's house into ye woods, towards Tomson's Poynt, Bounding on the eastern side on the Fore River, on the northern side, on the hollowe whear the *Ship was built,* and on the western side on a drie Cove, By a hegway that goeth to the watersied;" "the other Parsell lieth fenced in on the western side the aforementioned hieway."

Among the shipping items we find the following:

That Jacob Jansen, "formerly of & belonging unto Amsterdam, in Holland, mariner & by succession of Henry Cornelius Hooke, formerly master of ye ship commonly called ye Sancta Maria, about eighty Tuns, & Master of ye said Pink, or ship," conveys to Job Clement and Dr. Henry Greenland, of Kittery, "the above sd good Pink or ship, called ye Sancta Maria, now riding at anchor neare ye Great Island, in ye River of Piscataqua," 10 Dec., 1671.

JOB CLEMENT made his Will 4 July, 1682, as follows:

"I Job Clement being weak in body but in perfect memory, do dispose of my estate as followeth.

"I make my son Job Clement my sole Heir and give to him all my housing and lands, Bils & bonds with stock in Trading, and all my other estate, except what is herein excepted.

"I give to my beloved wife Joanna Clement, the choice of my houses, for her to live in during her lifetime, together with whatsoever estate she brought with her, whether in cattle or household goods; and she shall, with the house, have the use of the accommodations of land belonging to it, and the use of a featherbed during her life.

"I give to my grandchild, Jane Kenney, the resedue of my six-acre Lott, more or less, the one-half of which was formerly given to her ffather, lying near the Watch-house on Dover Neck.

"Also I give to the sd Jane that bed which my wife has the use of during her life, to come into her hand after my wife's decease.

"I give thirty shillings to the poor of the town; and Thirty shillings to the Chuech.

"ffinally I make my son Job my sole Executor, willing him to pay my debts and funeral expenses; and request the Hon'ble Richaed Waldron, President, & the Rev. Mr. John Pike to be overseers to this Will and Testament. In witness to the premises I have set my hand and seal.

Job Clement."

"The instrument above was signed and sealed by the within mentioned Job Clements, Esq., and declared to be his last Will and Testament the day and year above written. 4, 7, 1683.

"In presence of us:
Richard Walderne
Joshua Moody."

"New Hampshire.
By the Governor.

The above named Richard Waldron & Joshua Moody came and appeared and made oath, and declared that the above named Job Clement made the above written instrument and signed & declared it to be his last Will & Testament.

Taken upon oath the 9th of Nov., 1683, before me,
Edw. Cranfield.

Entered & recorded according to ye original Nov. 25th, 1683.
Richard Chamberlain, Secr."

HIS CHILDREN.

1. A CHILD, b. 17 Nov., 1645, at Haverhill.
2. JOHN, b. 17 Nov., 1646, at Haverhill; d. young.
3. JOB, b. 17 Apr., 1648, at Haverhill. His Will, as Job Clements, Sr., of Dover, 1716, mentions wife, ABIGAIL (HEARD), and children: *Job, James, John, Daniel,* and *Margaret.* His wife was dau. of James and Shuah Heard, of Sturgeon Creek, Eliot. James was son of John Heard, of Sturgeon Creek, and wife Isabel. He was no connection of Capt. John Heard, of Dover.
4. MARY, b. 12 Dec., 1651, at Haverhill. She m., 25 Dec., 1670, JOSEPH CANNEY (THOMAS1). Hon. Job Clement mentions her (Mary's) daughter, *Jane,* in his Will.

JOB[3] appears to have been one of the substantial citizens of Dover and held some minor offices. He was Selectman several years, and largely engaged in business affairs. He lived on Dover Neck. Following is from the town records, of grants in 1714:

"Laid out 28 Oct., 1714, to Mr. Job Clement at Cochecha, which his father bought of James Kid; the land lies in the westward of James Kid's 10 acres, beginning at the head of Lieut. Heard's lot running W. by N., N. by E. by S. and return. Also same date, 20 acres which were bought of Kid joining to Cochecho River, at a place called The Gulf, beginning at a gutt of water joyning to Mr. Richard Waldrons Land running N. by E. 80 rods, then S. by E. 40 rods then S. and by W. 80 rods to the river; also 14 acres more joyning thereunto, besides the old Improvement, beginning at a hemlock, running E. S. E. 52 rods to the highway that leads to the water side, then S. S. W. to the river, leaving the highway sufficient for the Towne use and a Convenient Landing place at the river side."

Job[3] mentioned in his Will of 1716, his wife, Abigail; eldest son, Job[4]; second son, James; third son, John; fourth son, Daniel; and daughter, Margaret. In this document the name is signed "Job Clemens."

THE CUSHING FAMILY.

(MEMORANDA No. 181.)

JONATHAN[2] CUSHING, tenth minister of Dover, was son of Peter[1] and Hannah Cushing, of Hingham, Mass., where he was born 20 Dec., 1689. He was settled in Dover, Sept. 18, 1717, at a salary of 90 pounds a year, and remained pastor till his death, although for two years previous to that event he had Rev. Jeremy Belknap for a colleague. Parson Cushing graduated at Harvard in 1712. Those who knew him said he was "a grave and sound preacher, a kind, peaceable, prudent and judicious pastor, a wise and faithful friend." In personal appearance he is said to have been "a large, stout man, grave and dignified."

The meeting-house in which he preached for forty-one years, stood upon Pine Hill, a short distance from the Cushing tomb; in 1758 the new meeting-house was dedicated on the site of the present house of worship, on Court Square. Parson Cushing's dwelling house was not far from the meeting-house on the hill, about where the Chapel now stands. Parson Cushing's wife, Elizabeth, daughter of his uncle, Thomas Cushing, of Boston, came with him to Dover; she died 3 Dec., 1730, aged 30; he died 25 March, 1769, and was buried in the Cushing tomb on Pine Hill. During his ministry, not including the two years incumbency of his colleague, 1128 baptisms were recorded in the Church books; 130 persons united with the Church upon profession of faith, and nine by letter. Parson Cushing's memory deserves to be honored for the full minutes which he kept and which are the first authentic records of the First Church.

Rev. JONATHAN CUSHING had five children, viz:

1. PETER, b. 9 Oct., 1718.
2. JONATHAN, b. 24 Mar., 1720; he d. in the old French War, or immediately after his return, from disease contracted in the service.
3. DEBORAH, b. 5 Jan., 1721-2; m. DANIEL WATSON, of Dover.
4. WILLIAM, b. 26 Dec., 1723, appears to have m. MARY, dau. of David Watson, after which we know nothing of him.
5. ELIZABETH, b. 5 Jan., 1725, m. JOHN WINGATE, of Madbury, and d. in Dec., 1811.

PETER,[3] lived in Dover; married MARY BANTOM, who died 31 July, 1798, of fever, aged 84 years. He died suddenly in the street, of apoplexy, 24 June, 1780; his children were:

1. THOMAS, b. 1745.
2. ELIZABETH, b. 1747, who did not m., but is said to be the mother of Sophia Cushing, who became a famous school teacher, and possessed remarkable talent in various ways; she was a large, tall, fine appearing woman, and of commanding presence. Sophia m. (1) JONATHAN HAYES; (2) SAMUEL WYATT, who built the New Hampshire House, which stood where St. Mary's Academy now stands, on Court Square. Mr. and Mrs. Wyatt had a notable career as hotel keepers. Mr. Wyatt was a short, fleshy man, in noticeable contrast with his tall and sturdy wife. They were excellent and popular people. Mrs. Wyatt's mother d. about 1817, aged 70 years.

3. HANNAH, b. 5 Jan., 1749-50; m. JOSIAH FOLSOM; she d. in 1841.
4. DANIEL, b. 4 Jan., 1752.
5. MARY, b. 18 June, 1754; she d. unm., 1 Mar., 1835.
6. PETER, b. 22 Feb., 1757.

THOMAS,[4] married, 2 Feb., 1788, WIDOW ANNA FULLER; they had children:

1. MARY, b. ———; d. aged about 50.
2. JONATHAN, b. ———.
3. HANNAH, b. ———; m. MR. THOMAS, of Portsmouth.
4. WILLIAM, b. ———.
5. NANCY, b. ———; unm.; d. aged 45.
6. PETER, b. ———; no record of him.

DANIEL, married, 8 June, 1786, TAMSON HAYES, daughter of Lieut. Jonathan Hayes, of Dover; they lived and died in Dover. Children were:

1. JONATHAN H., b. 27 Mar., 1786; d. 22 Mar., 1836.
2. MARY H., b. 8 Mar., 1789.
3. LYDIA W., b. 18 June, 1793; m. 31 Dec., 1818, DANIEL SARGENT.
4. PETER, b. 3 June, 1796, a well known and esteemed citizen, and senior deacon of the First Church.
5. ROBERT H., b. 31 July, 1798.
6. SAMUEL W., b. 9 Apr., 1802.
7. CLARISSA W., b. 3 Sept., 1804.

PETER, married, 11 April, 1784, HANNAH, daughter of John Burnham Hanson, born in Durham, 11 July, 1766; they lived in Rochester. He died in 1804.

CHILDREN.

1. JOHN, b. 25 Oct., 1784.
2. BETSEY, b. 26 Nov., 1786; m. JABEZ DAME, and removed to Maine.
3. MARY.
4. HANNAH.
5. JONATHAN P., b. 12 Mar., 1793 (for whom see below).
6. PETER.
7. REBECCA.

JONATHAN, married HANNAH McCASLING, died 5 May, 1827, aged 38; children were:

1. ELIZA, b. 3 Dec., 1805.
2. CAROLINE, b. 3 Nov., 1807.
3. CHARLES, b. 2 Oct., 1809.
4. ALEXIS, b. 22 Feb., 1812.
5. ANNA, b. Mar., 1814; d. 1816.

WILLIAM married NANCY HAYES, of Dover, and had children:

1. THOMAS, d. aged about 21.
2. AUGUSTUS, m. RACHEL PARKER, dau. of Rev. Mr. Parker, of York, Me.; lived in Great Falls (Somersworth).
3. JARVIS, resided in Charlestown, Mass.
4. NATHAN, m. MISS PRESCOTT, of Dover.

PETER, of Dover, married SARAH AUSTIN; children:

1. JOSEPH W.
2. GEORGE W.
3. WILLIAM.
4. CHARLES.

SAMUEL W., of Dover, married ASENATH, daughter of Jacob Hyde, of Tamworth. Children:

1. LOUISA, b. 18 May, 1835.
2. ASENATH, b. 17 Mar., 1737.
3. CHARLES, b. 4 May, 1842; d. 25 Mar., 1846.

JONATHAN P. CUSHING, was born in Rochester, N. H., 12 March, 1793; in 1804 his father died; in 1806 he became an apprentice to a saddler; by extra work he purchased his time, and in 1811 went to Exeter Academy. In Sept., 1815, he entered the Junior class at Dartmouth College, and graduated in 1817. His health being feeble he went South. While in the family of Rev. Dr. J. H. Rice, of Richmond, Va., he became acquainted with a young man, tutor in Hampden-Sidney College, who being in ill health, urged Mr. Cushing to occupy his place temporarily; he entered upon his new duties in Nov., 1817, which resulted in his permanent connection with the college. In Jan., 1819, he was elected professor of chemistry and natural philosophy; in 1820 he was chosen president, pro-tem, and in 1821 was elected president. In time his health failed; in April, 1835, he started for Charleston, S. C., for its restoration, but died 25 April, 1835, at Raleigh. He married in March, 1827, LUCY JANE, daughter of Carter Page, Esq., of Cumberland Co., and left several children.

THE AUSTIN FAMILY.
MEMORANDA No. 192.

JOSEPH AUSTIN, who owned part of the mill property at Cochecho Falls, in 1649, and later, resided at Dover Neck, having come there, probably from Hampton, where a Joseph Austin resided in 1642. He moved up to Cochecho at an early date, though where his house was we have no means of knowing. In addition to the mill property he had various grants from the town; one was as follows:

A grant of 100 acres, laid out "Between quamphegon & Saynt albans Cove, partly or altogether by Nechoaneck River, on ye south east, & on the North East By henery tibbits hundred acors of Land, and partly by Tho: handsons hundred; on the South west side by a heyway that is to Ley betweene Tho: Caney & him." Also, a grant "of 50 acres at fresh creek at or near the same time, was removed & layd out to twenty acors of march, of wch medow the sd Joseph Aysten Bought tenn acors of fraynses Lettellfeeld, & the other tenn acors of anthony Emery wch was granted to them in ye year 1648."

Mr. Austin also received several other grants, recorded in the same quaint style as the above, in that section of the old town. In 1652 he received a grant of 40 acres—"Att ye head of Elder Starbucks twenty Acor Lott, on the west side of the Back River, which 20 Acor Lott, in the number of the Lotts is, the 14th Lott." This grant was laid out, 7 Jan., 1695-6, to Thomas Austin, son and successor of said Joseph.

JOSEPH AUSTIN married (probably for his second wife), SARAH, daughter of Elder Edward Starbuck, and widow of William Story; Sarah's first husband died about 1658; she married a third husband (after Austin's death), viz: Humphrey Varney, ancestor of all the Varneys hereabouts. Mr. Austin made his Will 6 June, 1662; it was proved 1 July, 1663, from which it is safe to conclude that he died between those dates; he gave his wife something, and the remainder of his estate was divided equally among all his children, save that Thomas, the oldest, according to law, had double portion; Richard Walderne, William Wentworth, and his "brother," Peter Coffin, were executors. From his choice of executors it is evident that he had a large property. Of his children we know the names of none but Thomas. There was a Samuel taxed here in 1649, who, 1 Dec., 1650, conveyed all his premises to William Furber.

THOMAS,[2] son of Joseph, and the one who inherited all the mill property, married ANN ———. They were Quakers. Their children were:

1. ROSE, b. 3 Feb., 1678; m. EPHRAIM TEBBETS.
2. SARAH, b. 1 Jan., 1682; m. JOSEPH CANNEY.
3. NATHANIEL, b. 2 Jan., 1687; m. CATHERINE NEALE.
4. THOMAS, b. 5 Apr., 1689.
5. JOSEPH, b. 30 Apr., 1692.
6 and 7. NICHOLAS and ANN, b. 6 Feb., 1695.
8. SAMUEL, b. 2 Aug., 1698; m. ABIGAIL PINKHAM.
9. BENJAMIN, b. 3 May, 1704; m. SARAH PINKHAM.

NATHANIEL,[3] married CATHERINE NEALE. They were "Friends," and had children:

1. CATHERINE, b. 12 Jan., 1715.
2. PHEBE, b. 14 Mar., 1718; m. JOHN HANSON.
3. SARAH, b. 14 Sept., 1714; m. EBENEZER PINKHAM.
4. ANN, b. 17 June, 1721; m. MAUL HANSON.
5. NATHANIEL, b. 25 Apr., 1623.
6. REBECCA, b. 23 Mar., 1725; m. SIMEON HILL.
7. NICHOLAS, b. 17 Oct., 1727.
8. MARY, b. 17 Aug., 1730; m. STEPHEN HANSON.
9. PRISCILLA, b. 4 Mar., 1732; m. CALEB HODGDON.
9. ANDREW, b. 8 Aug., 1733.
10. JAMES, b. 1 May, 1735.
11. ELIJAH, b. 3 June, 1738. This Elijah was father to *Elijah Austin, Esq.*, of Madbury.

JOSEPH,³ who received the mill property, married somebody, but records fail to tell whom. They had children:

1. ROSE, m. PAUL PINKHAM.
2. JOSEPH, d. 16 June, 1776.
3. PAUL, d. 9 June, 1776.

The son of a JOSEPH and SARAH AUSTIN is mentioned in the town records, viz:

1. THOMAS, b. 7 May, 1723.

SAMUEL,³ married, 23 Nov., 1727, ABIGAIL PINKHAM; they were Quakers, and lived in Somersworth. Their children were:

1. SAMUEL, b. 2 Oct., 1728; d. 28 Oct., 1737.
2. MARY, b. 2 Aug., 1731; d. 20 Oct., 1737.
3. STEPHEN, b. 8 Aug., 1735; d. 21 Feb., 1742.
4. SOLOMON, b. 28 Mar., 1740; d. Oct., 1760.
5. ANN, b. 21 Aug., 1741; d. 1754.
6. SAMUEL, b. 22 Nov., 1743.
7. STEPHEN, b. 3 Oct., 1754; d. 1773.

BENJAMIN,³ married, 19 Sept., 1729, SARAH PINKHAM. They were Quakers, and lived in Somersworth. Their children were:

1. EBENEZER.
2. BENJAMIN.
3. MOSES, b. 13 Apr., 1734.
4. MARY, d. young.
5. PETER.

Not a single Austin appears in the list of baptisms in the last century; the inference is that they were mainly Quakers. The Austin interest in the sawmills ceased somewhere between 1719 and 1760.

THE DEACON JOHN HALL FAMILY.

(Memoranda Nos. 297-303.)

Deacon John Hall is on the tax list of 1648, and that seems to be the earliest record we have of him, though there are other Halls having the given name, "John." It is also probable that he is the John Hall who, 18 March, 1648-9, had one of the 26 acre lots, his being No. 7; for a 26 acre lot, No. 7, in Cochecho Fresh Marsh, was relaid to John Hall, Jr., 29 May, 1722, as originally granted to John Hall, Sen.; and no other John, except the Deacon, had a descendant John. He appears on all the extant tax-lists from that date till 1670, the succeeding tax-lists being generally lost. He lived on Dover Neck, in 1652, on land joining the meeting-house lot and extending to Back River.

The deacon had various grants of land. In 1652 a lot joining the "Calves Pasture"; Oct. 19, 1656, either he, or Sergeant John, had 30 acres of upland joining Cochecho Marsh. The third lot on Newichawannock River, 100 acres upland, granted him in 1656, was laid out 12 Jan., 1660; this lot was rebounded to his grandson, John Hall, Jan., 1720-1. In 1658 he was also granted 100 acres in the third range of lots on the Newichawannock, which he sold to John Clements, in 1662. The deacon had other grants, and seems to have been held in high esteem by his fellow townsmen.

So far as the records show he was the first Deacon of the First Church, in Dover. As early as 1655, and nobody knows how much earlier, he was called "Deacon" on a list of those who took the "oath of fidelity," without date, but not before the end of 1655. He was willing to work; the records says, "Deacon John Hall, the 13th of Janewary (16) 71-2, Agried with all, By the Selleckt-men, to sweep ye meitting house and Ring the Bell, for one holl yeir, from ye date above written, and to have for that service the Some of three pounds." He was deacon, perhaps, in the days of good Parson Maud, certainly through the ministries of the Reyners, and into the time of Parson Pike.

The deacon held a few offices. He was lot layer many years, an office of constant service then, often with Ralph Hall and William Wentworth. The records mention him as such in 1657, and he was still serving in the same capacity as late as 1674. He was selectman, so far as the records show, only in 1660; occasionally "commissioner to end small cases." Town records show him as chosen to serve as grand juror in 1663, 1666, and 1668. March 30, 1657,—"John Hall, Deacon, Tho: ffootman, Peter Coffin have power to call the townsmen (selectmen) belonging to the towne to acompt for all compts belonging to the towne for the time past, and to stand till new be chosen, and that theay shall report Publickly to the inhabitants at the Publicke towne meittings." In 1666 he was on similar service by a new vote. Jan. 10, 1658-9, he was one of the three appointed to lay out the town bounds between Lamprey and Newichawannock Rivers, and to run the northern boundary of Dover. April 28, 1663, he and Lieut. Ralph Hall were to lay out the highway from Lamprey River to the water side; and he was on the same committee in 1674.

He was, for a series of years, "clerk of ye writs," for the Court. Scattering papers in Dover and at Exeter show his signature, as such, in 1663, 1668, 1669, and 1671. (The Exeter records referred to are now at Concord, in the office of the Secretary of State.)

He was chosen town clerk 6 June, 1659: "At the same time, John Hall, Deacon, chosen towne clarke." Alas, the record adds, in parenthesis, "This could not be don by reson the Court would not give the then chosen Clarke his oath." Perhaps the Court believed in civil service reform. Clerk Pomfrett was a good clerk, and seems to have held on till 1670. In 1670 Deacon Hall was elected town clerk, and doubtless such till 1680; his signature, as such, appears in 1675 and 1679. But he got into trouble. Jan. 7, 1685-6, a writ went out against the Deacon for "embezzling the records belonging to the town of Dover aforesaid, that were late in his custody." His descendants need not worry, however. It was during the Masonian controversy, when the towns hid their records as long as they could to keep them out of the Court that was trying to help Mason get possession of Dover farms.

When or where the Deacon was born is not known. A deposition makes him born about 1617, but such mentions of age were exceedingly elastic.

But in the month of Feb., 1685-6, "being in perfect health, but aged," he gave his son Ralph, "half of my house and land,

Barne, orchards and fields adjacent to my sd house, and half my Marsh near Redding Point"; and the other half, with cattle, etc., was also to go to Ralph after the old gentleman's decease. This paper was proved 4 May, 1692; recorded 2 Feb., 1694-5. The date of his death does not appear. At first glance it would seem remarkable that Parson Pike, who came here in 1678, and whose diary is quite minute, specifying the deaths of all officials in Church and State, does not record the Deacon's death. The inference is that the Deacon died elsewhere, or, which is more probable, that he died in the interval between the massacre at Cochecho, in 1689, and 1694, in which time Mr. Pike was absent from Dover, and in which there are but three Dover entries. Between January, 1690, and December, 1692, there is not a single entry. Probably he died during that period.

It does not appear who his wife was. She is mentioned but once in any deed; that is 23 June, 1662; and even then her name is not given. If the birth of "Grace, daughter of John and Elizabeth Hall," 16 May, 1664, refers to him, her name was Elizabeth. A deed from Richard and Elizabeth Pinkham, 25 Jan., 1704-5, to the Deacon's son, Ralph, speaks of the land as having once belonged to "our grandfather, Thomas Leighton (Layton)." If this means that Thomas Layton was grandfather to Ralph Hall, the Deacon's wife could not have been Elizabeth Layton; for *she* was wife of Philip Cromwell, in 1671; and Thomas Layton's Will, 21 Sept., 1671, makes no Hall allusion.

There is no list of the children, nor a date, unless Grace be an exception. If, when he was town clerk, he had made a list of all the Dover families, how we should have blessed his memory. So the best we can give is as follows:

DEACON JOHN HALL had the following children, and perhaps more:

1. JOHN, of whom see below.
2. NATHANIEL. His name appears on the Province tax-list of 1680 and 1681; also, on list of petitioners for military defence, 20 Feb., 1689-1690. June 29, 1694, he had a grant of 10 acres at the head of his 20-acre lot at the west of Back River, and it would seem that the Deacon's Back River property went to Nathaniel. He and wife, HAN-

NAH (of Dover), conveyed, 16 Nov., 1696, for 36 pounds, to Nathaniel Meader, of Oyster River, 30 acres "granted my deceased father, Deacon John Hall, as on old Book," and 10 acres on Back River. John Meader, Jr., and Nathaniel's brother, Ralph, were witnesses. And Nathaniel disappears from history.
3. GRACE, perhaps. She was dau. of Sergeant John Hall; she was b. 16 May, 1664, and we know no more of her.
4. RALPH, of whom see below.

JOHN,[2] son of Deacon Hall, is first mentioned on the 28th of July, 1655, when "John Hall deacon, John Hall Juner," and 13 others, were paid "for killing a wolfe, in the yeir 1663." This does not prove that he was of age (21). Feb. 8, 1664-5, he witnessed a deed from Thomas Beard to Parson John Reyner. In 1671-2, the Boston Register gives us a "John Hall, as constable of Dover (N. H.), aged 36, or thereabouts." There seems to be no other John Hall but the Deacon's son, but he could hardly have been born in 1636. Some things point to about 1648-49. He is on the Province tax-list of 1680. He lived on Dover Neck, and apparently, in 1693, gave bonds as a tavern-keeper, his sureties being Job Clement and Kinsley Hall.

As to land grants we find little. 19 March, 1693-4, 30 acres were granted him west of Back River, next south of 40 acres granted the same day to John Tuttle. He must have had much land from his father, the Deacon, as eldest son John conveyed to John Tuttle, 3 May, 1698, land formerly belonging to my grandfather, Deacon John Hall. He had also some from his wife's father, John Roberts, who gave to daughter, Abigail, wife of John Hall, 24 March, 1691-2, land given said Roberts by his wife's father, Hatevil Nutter,—half of a piece of 16 acres; also, at same date, land at Cochecho, which was most likely land at the second falls, which privilege John Hall owned and disposed of. He had, also, 1693-4, a grant of "100 acres east of Cochecho River," which eventually passed into the hands of John Horn, as by deeds from his sons and one grandson; it was up the river above second falls.

JOHN,[2] married 8 Nov., 1671, ABIGAIL, daughter of John and Abigail (Nutter) Roberts. Her father was son of the emigrant,

Thomas Roberts, and her mother, daughter of Elder Hatevil Nutter. After John's death his widow married, 24 Oct., 1698, Thomas Downes, of Cochecho, who was killed by the Indians in 1711.

JOHN,[2] was Representative for Dover in the N. H. Assembly, sworn 1 Nov., 1694, 1695, and 16 Sept. 1696, and died while a member. Pike's *Journal* says: "April 28, 1697, John Hall, sen., drowned coming up the River in a little float, near Green-Point." His estate was returned 1 Feb., 1700-1, by Ralph Hall and John Tuttle, at 104 pounds, 18 shillings. His sons, Thomas and Joseph, were appointed administrators, 3 Dec., 1700, their mother, Abigail Downs, having declined the trust. In the inventory the real estate comprised his homestead with 10 acres at the upper end of Dover, and sixty acres west of Back River. The administrators, with their mother, Abigail, conveyed to Samuel Emerson, 18 Dec., 1700, for 25 pounds, the 30 acres granted their father by the town 16 March, 1693-4, west of Back River. John, eldest son, had conveyed to John Tuttle, 3 Aug., 1698, land formerly belonging to his grandfather, the deacon. Jan. 1, 1727, Mary Sanders, of the Island of Nantucket, daughter of John Hall, of Dover, deceased, intestate, quitclaimed all her right in her father's estate, for 12 pounds, but the paper does not tell to whom; it was recorded 8 Dec., 1730. May 11, 1730, Richard Gooding (Goodwin) and his wife, Sarah, of Dover, in consideration of a parcel of land, "quitclaimed to Thomas and Joseph Hall" all right in her father's (John Hall) estate. Same date, Thomas and Joseph, of Dover, planters, in consideration of quitclaim just mentioned, released to Richard Goodwin and Sarah, his wife, "ye parcel of land yt Richard Gooden and Sarah, his wife, had of ye estate of their grandfather, Jno. Hall, senr. deceased, yt came to them by heirship." There is a bare possibility that this Mary and Sarah were daughters of John, brother of Thomas and Joseph, but it is very improbable.

JOHN and ABIGAIL (ROBERTS) HALL had:

1. JOHN, b. 27 June, 1673, of whom see below.
2. THOMAS, b. 19 June, 1675, of whom see below.
3. JOSEPH, of whom see below.
4. ABIGAIL, b. 24 Feb., 1679-80.

6. SARAH. She, "maiden," 9 Jan., 1718-19, conveyed to Richard Rook, or Rooks, of Dover, for 100 pounds, land granted her father, John Hall, 19 Mar., 1693-4, laid out 16 June, 1694; it was land on Salmon Falls River. She m. RICHARD GOODWIN, and quitclaimed as above, May 11, 1630. Richard Goodwin had laid out, 4 July, 1721, 60 acres of land, it being his quarter part of 200 acres of land made to Hatevil Nutter, in the year 1658, which said 60 acres was given to his dafter, Abigail Roberts, deceased," said Goodwin being the "suruiuer and owner of the above saide land," which was "on the west sied of mallego riur." This Abigail (Nutter) Roberts was the grandmother of Goodwin's wife, Sarah. Richard Goodwin, doubtless the same, had children baptized, as by Church records: 1. *Elizabeth*, b. 15 Oct., 1721. 2. *Richard*, b. 19 Apr., 1721. 3. *Hannah*, b. 7 Aug., 1726.
7. MARY, m. a SANDERS, and moved to Nantucket.

RALPH,[2] the youngest son of Dea. John, first appears on record 1 Feb., 1685-6, when his father, the Deacon, conveyed to him one-half of his Dover Neck homestead, the other half to be his on death of the Deacon. 11 July, 1694, he had a grant of twenty acres on Fresh Creek. This land was lost, with a number of other grants, in a lawsuit with Richard Walderne, who claimed it by a prior grant, but in whose dealings considerable chicanery existed, if the allegations in the State papers are to be believed. The town gave grants elsewhere to all the sufferers, or their heirs. 25 Jan., 1704-5, Ralph received a 10 pound quitclaim of Richard and Elizabeth (wife) Pinkham, of a lot of 3½ acres once belonging to our grandfather, Thomas Leighton, "now in ye tenure and occupation of ye aforesaid Ralph Hall, bounded west on Back River, north by the land formerly John Dam's; east on "ye Low street"; south on lane running down to Back Cove. This proves to be the identical house lot of Thomas Leighton, taken of Capt. Thomas Wiggin in 1636, or thereabouts. How it came into Ralph Hall's hands does not appear. Ralph was Auditor in 1702, Constable in 1705.

Pike's *Journal* says: "13 Nov., 1706, Ralph Hall, sen., of Dover, deceased after six days illness, with grevious pain in his side, together with the fever."

He must have married twice. The name of his first wife is not ascertained. He married (2) 26 May, 1710, MARY, daughter of the emigrant Philip Chesley; 23 Dec., 1713, "we, Mary Hall (evidently widow of Ralph), John Hall and Esther Hall, ye only daughters of Philip Chesley, sen., late of Dover," conveyed to "couzzen Philp Chesley (evidently their nephew), 12 acres, part of their father's home plantation, or neck of land at Oyster River, granted by the town," and which their father reserved when he deeded land to his sons, Thomas and Philip; consideration 15 pounds.

But Widow MARY HALL married again. "John Foy and Mary, his wife, 26 Feb., 1717-18, quitclaimed to John Hall (evidently son of Ralph by his first wife), all her right in lands that my former husband Ralph Hall left to me his widow, Mary Hall." Some of this land was on Dover Neck. The paper was proved 5 July, 1727, and Benjamin Peirce was a witness.

The widow, MARY, declining to administer, Ralph Hall's sons, John and James, were appointed 4 March, 1706-7. In the division of his estate 15 pounds were reserved for Jonathan, "a sick and weak child," and the remainder was divided between the seven sons mentioned below, the eldest having a double share. Of the twenty acres granted in place of that lost in the Waldron lawsuit, sons Benjamin, Ralph, Joseph, and the heirs of James (by uncle Joseph, their attorney), conveyed their four-eighths, 21 Nov., 1735, to "Joseph Hanson, Jr., inn-holder." A similar deed conveys similar property to William Twombly, of Dover, 1 Nov., 1735.

RALPH had seven sons. But where were the daughters? The sons were, by his first wife:

1. JOHN, of whom see below.
2. JAMES, of whom see below.
3. JONATHAN, the "sick and weak child."
4. ISAAC, said to have settled in Massachusetts.

By his second wife, MARY CHESLEY, RALPH had:

5. BENJAMIN, b. 2 June, 1702, of whom see below.
6. RALPH, of whom see below.
7. JOSEPH, b. 26 Mar., 1706, of whom see below.

In giving the next generation we shall be obliged to close the account of each son and daughter, giving hints of the localities of their descendants.

JOHN, son of John and Abigail, born in Dover, 27 June, 1673. In earlier papers he was regarded as the John who married ESTHER CHESLEY, and was ancestor of the Somersworth Halls, but it was later found, by a chance record, that that John was son of Ralph. *This* John appears to have lived in the Oyster River part of Dover. On 3 Aug., 1698, John Hall, "eldest son and heir" of John, deceased, with Elizabeth, his wife, and his mother, Abigail, conveyed to John Tuttle, 10 acres of land (then in possession of said Tuttle), formerly belonging to grandfather, John, the Deacon, being "west to the road to Cochecho,"—the purchase of June 8, 1675. On 16 Dec., 1700, his younger brothers, Thomas and Joseph, were appointed to administer to their father's estate, and no allusion to him is made; nor in any subsequent transaction on record. It is barely possible, but not probable, that the Sarah (who married a Meader), and Mary (who married a Sanders), mentioned in account of his father, were his children. Probably this John was dead in 1700. He had wife Elizabeth. Further, "widow Elizabeth Hall of Dover,"married 7 Sept., 1705, (Rev. John Buss, of Oyster River, officiating), Benjamin Peirce, of Watertown, Mass., who appears to have come here to live. They had two children, as by our records, viz:

1. BENJAMIN, b. 11 Dec., 1706.
2. JOSEPH, b. 26 Oct., 1709.

This wife of Peirce died, and he married (2), 30 May, 1714, Hannah Ash, and had seven more children, all of whose births are on Dover records. Who knows but the Barrington Peirce family comes from the same Benjamin?

JOHN and ELIZABETH had:

1. SARAH, b. 21 July, 1696.

But we are completely perplexed to know who was the John Hall who had wife Sarah, and had son John, born at Oyster River, 17 Dec., 1720.

THOMAS,³ son of JOHN,² and ABIGAIL, was born in Dover, 19 June, 1675; in manhood he lived at Oyster River. He was administrator, with his brother Joseph,³ of the estate of their father, who had much to do with real estate on the Cochecho River about Reyner's brook.

THOMAS,³ must have married tolerably early, as his son James,⁴ gave a deed, in 1722, when Thomas³ was not 47 years old. The name of his wife does not appear, except that it was Mary. He was dead in 1732. James,⁴ eldest son, refused to administer, 2 Sept., 1732, his mother, Mary, having previously refused, he desired that his brother Thomas⁴ be appointed. Three children only appear, viz:

1—JAMES,⁴ eldest, born about 1700. He was of Durham. He signed deed for 6 pounds to John Hall, 20 April, 1722, of all interest in grant "to my father, Thomas Hall, of Dover, at ye brook above ye head of Jonathan Woodman's." He, then called "senior," with his wife, Tabitha, of Durham, 2 April, 1735, conveyed to Joseph Atkinson, of Durham, for 25 pounds, all his right in the common or undivided lands in Durham. He and wife Tabitha sold their house and land to Timothy Emerson. No more heard of him.

2—THOMAS,⁴ has but little to his record, of land transactions, to show where he lived and what he did. He acted as administrator of his father's estate. Thomas⁴ and Otis⁴ conveyed to Otis Pinkham, of Dover, 20 acres on the west side of Back River, adjoining the river "near Back Cove." Thomas, and his wife, Elizabeth, appear in other land transactions.

3—JOSEPH,⁴ born 13 April, 1707. He (of Dover) conveyed to John Hall, 22 April, 1728, for 5 pounds, all interest in a certain grant to "my father, Thomas Hall of Dover." Also in other land transfers. Doubtless he is the one referred to, when Thomas Hall, of Dover, husbandman, quitclaims 12 Dec., 1741, to "my brother

Joseph Hall, of Dover, husbandman," a "tract of land where Joseph Hall now lives, containing all his homestead land in Dover," on the "westerly side of Dover Neck, adjoining to Back River, bounded southerly on land of Capt. Thomas Tebbets; westerly on Back River; northerly on land commonly called 'The Calves Pasture'; easterly on the highway that leads from said Hall's house to that of Capt. Thomas Tebbetts," including the dwelling house. He must have had children. Joseph Hall, of Dover, mariner, 11 Dec., 1752, for 50 pounds conveyed to Joseph Dam, of Durham, all his right in the estate of his father, Joseph, late of Dover, yeoman, deceased; it being two-fifths of his father's estate. A Mehitable Hall (who owned the covenant and was baptized 3 March, 1734), married Joseph Dam (baptized 26 Sept., 1719). It is possible that this mariner and Mehitable were children of Joseph[3], who married Esther Beard.

JOSEPH,[3] son of JOHN,[2] and ABIGAIL, was variously associated with his brother, Thomas,[3] as above. He married, 3 Nov., 1707, ESTHER BEARD. Possibly he had children, but certainly he had:

1. ABIGAIL, b. in Dover, 5 July, 1708.

HATEVIL,[3] son of JOHN.[2] It was formerly supposed that he was the son of John[1], but the following shows he was the son of John[2]. On 17 Nov., 1733, Hatevil[4] Hall gave a quitclaim deed of land to John Horn, of all interest that his father, Hatevil,[3] had in the 100 acres granted to "my grandfather, John Hall of Dover, yeoman, in ye yeir 1693-4." Deacon Hall was dead before that date, so the "grandfather" must have been John[2] Hall. HATEVIL[3] married, 14 March, 1706-7, MERCY CROMWELL, and lived on the west side of Back River. The tradition among the descendants of Hatevil[3] is, that he was drowned in early manhood, and left but one son. But Rev. Samuel R. Hall, LL. D., of Brownington, Vt., a descendant, of the Medford, Mass., Halls, says, that his father, Rev. Samuel R. Hall, married Elizabeth Hall, and that said Hezekiah was grandson of Hatevil Hall, of Dover. Hezekiah lived in Uxbridge, Mass., and afterwards in Tyringham, Mass., and had nine daughters and one son. Rev. Dr. Hall had his information from a son of Hezekiah, who ought to have known who his great grandfather was. Nor did Rev. Dr. Hall have any knowledge of this Hatevil Hall, except through this tradition. But we cannot name any other son, and we, therefore, have but one.

1. HATEVIL, b. 15 Feb., 1707-8.

JOHN,³ son of RALPH,² (by first wife), was born in Dover as early as 1685; he lived at first, on Dover Neck, but as early as 1730, was of Somersworth, where he had land which evidently came to him from his father's estate, and originally from his grandfather, the Deacon. There are on record five deeds of land transfers of his property on Dover Neck and Back River, of dates between 1716 and 1726. They are signed by him and his wife, Esther. He conveyed to Gershom Downs, 20 Sept., 1724, for 11 pounds, the 6 acres in Cochecho Marsh, originally granted to Deacon John Hall, and which John³ had had bounded 29 May, 1722.

He had rebounded, 23 Jan., 1720-1, the 100 acres in Rollinsford, which had been granted to his grandfather, the Deacon, in 1666. In 1656 it was the third lot on the tract of land between St. Alban's Cove and Quamphegan; in the rebounding, it was said, to begin at a tree by the water side, "at a poynt Comanly Called Curriell Poynt;" and there he lived. That is to say, he lived in a house which he built on some good plot of land, on the grant, which ran back a mile, or more, from the Newichawannock River. The name "Curriell" seems to have been derived from Edward Cowel, who acquired the Magoon land, afterwards conveyed by his grandson, Jethro Furber, to Benjamin Weymouth, and now forms part of the Garvin lands. Various land transfers of his, in Rochester, and various parts of Dover, are on record. He was known as "Sergeant John." Some of his Rollinsford land is still in the possession of his descendants. The date of his death is unknown.

JOHN,³ son of RALPH,² (by first wife), married, 9 August, 1705, ESTHER, (the records give the old English pronunciation, Hester) CHESLEY. He and his wife, Hester and her sister Mary, who married Ralph Hall, 23 Dec., 1713, quitclaimed to Philip Chesley, as "only daughters" of Philip, Sen. Philip Hall, of North Berwick, wrote in 1877: "My great grandfather, John³ Hall, married with Esther Chesley, who escaped from the Indians (in 1694, at Oyster River,) by jumping from the upper story of her father's house, with a babe in her arms, when most of the family were killed, at Durham Falls."

1. JOHN, b. 1706. He lived in Rollinsford on land now partly owned by his descendants. He m. (1.) ANNA MORRILL, of Kittery; (2) 17 Oct., 1743, SARAH STACKPOLE, of Somersworth, who d. Jan., 1804, aged 86. He d. suddenly, 19 Oct., 1789, and was buried in the Carr burial ground. He had eleven children. His son, *Capt. William*, went to North Berwick, and settled, and left numerous descendants. *Ruth*, dau. of JOHN, m. Bartholomew Wentworth.
2. SAMUEL, received land from his father, in Rollinsford, 4 July, 1732. Samuel and Lydia Hall, of Somersworth, 12 Nov., 1736, for 135 pounds, conveyed to Ens. Jeremiah Rollins and Ebenezer Roberts, 16 acres in Somersworth, reserving wood for his father, John Hall; there was a road between said land and Benjamin Wentworth's.
3. JAMES, who received land from his father, as above. James Hall, of Somersworth, conveyed to Thomas Hodgdon, of Berwick, for 10 pounds, a certain part of a sawmill at Quamphegan, commonly called "old Briggs," "which part is three days, in each month in the year, which part was purchased by me of my father, John Hall, and is the shore saw on Dover side, with all the iron work and other utensils that belong to the part."
4. KEZIAH.[4]
5. ESTHER.[4]
6. BETSEY.[4]

One of these daughters m. an EVANS.

JAMES,[3] son of RALPH,[2] (by first wife), was dead when the final settlement of his father's estate was made, in 1735, on 21 Nov., 1735. Ralph's[2] sons, Benjamin, Ralph, Joseph, and the heirs of James, made a conveyance already mentioned. On 31 July, 1734, Rowland Green, tailor, and wife, Elizabeth, of Portsmouth, and Mary Hall, spinster, of Rye, make "our trusty and well beloved uncle, Joseph Hall, jun., of Dover," their attorney to convey. "Mary, widow of James Hall," married in Portsmouth, 14 March, 1716-17, Joseph Holmes; quite clearly widow of James[3]. He had:

1. ELIZABETH,[4] m. ROWLAND GREENE.
2. MARY,[4] single in 1734.

BENJAMIN,[3] son of RALPH,[2] (by second wife), born in Dover, June, 1702, was apprenticed to William Dam, weaver, 16 July, 1709. On 9 Nov., 1726, Benedictus (and Leah) Torr sold to Benjamin and Ralph Hall, of Dover, 20 acres on the westerly side of the mast way that leads to the Hook. He lived in Madbury till 1755, when he removed to Barrington. He was one of the petitioners for the incorporation of Madbury, in 1743. Parson Cushing baptized, at Madbury, 30 Dec., 1741, "Benjamin Hall & Frances Hall, his wife, and their children, viz: Benjamin, Isaac, Joseph, John and Abigail." "1772, Benjamin Hall's house burned in Spring" is a record in Pike's *Journal*. He died in Barrington, in 1789 or '80. He married Frances Willey, of Lee, and had Family:

1. BENJAMIN,[4] b. 12 Dec., 1730. He lived in Barrington, was a soldier of the Revolution, commencing at Cambridge, and brought home a remarkable musket. He m., in 1756, SARAH, dau. of James Huckins, of Madbury, and had 10 children. He d. 30 Oct., 1810; she d. 7 Apr., 1821. Joseph D. Hall, of Barnstead (on the Province Road), was a descendant.
2. ISAAC[4] lived and d. in Barrington on his father's farm. He m. his cousin, ELIZABETH WILLEY, of Lee, and had 15 children.
3. JOSEPH,[4] d. young.
4. JOHN,[4] b. 18 Jan., 1739; lived at Bow Pond; m. his cousin, DEBORAH, dau. of his uncle, Ralph[3] Hall, and had nine children. He d. in Strafford, 2 Dec., 1824; his widow, b. 1 May, 1748; d. 29 Oct., 1839. "At her funeral four of her sons, *Winthrop, Israel, Samuel* and *Daniel*, followed her remains to the grave, each on a crutch and a cane, from effects of rheumatism." E. Melvin Hall, of Barrington, is a descendant.
5. ABIGAIL, d. young.
6. SAMUEL,[4] b. 19 May, 1744; unm.; d. 1776.
7. MARY,[4] b. 22 Dec., 1755; m. EBENEZER (or SAMUEL?) KELLEY, and lived at Strafford Ridge.

RALPH,[3] son of RALPH,[2] (by second wife), born in 1704, lived in Madbury; then removed to Barrington, in 1753; in the latter part of his life he went to live with his son, Joseph,[4] who lived at Crown Point, Strafford. His grave is there. He married ELIZABETH WILLEY of Lee, and had:

1. ELIZABETH,[4] m. JOSEPH DANIELS, of Barrington, and had:
2. FRANCES,[4] m. SAMUEL FOSS, son of Samuel and Mary Downs Foss, and had five children and numerous descendants.
3. SOLOMON,[4] lived in Barrington. He m. (1) ABIGAIL DAVIS, of Barrington; (2) WIDOW TAMSEN AYERS; (3) CHARITY JOHNSON. He d. Sept., 1818. Hon. Daniel Hall and Hon. Solomon H. Foye, of this city, were descendants.
4. RALPH,[4] m. a DAVIS, and moved to, or near, Jackson, N. H.
5. LOIS,[4] d. young.
6. JOSEPH,[4] b. 11 Dec., 1741. He owned the farm later occupied by his great grandson, John,[7] in Strafford. He was a Revolutionary soldier; he was a ruling elder in the Church; m. 4 Aug., 1764, MARY, dau. of Samuel and Mary (Dowse) Foss, b. 25 Mar., 1745; they had nine children. He d. in Strafford, in 1826. She d. in 1822. Among his descendants were Joseph[6] Hall, of Barnstead, and Alonzo[7] Hall Quint.
7. DEBORAH, b. 1 May, 1744; m. her cousin, JOHN[4] HALL, son of Benjamin,[3] whom see.
8. ABIGAIL,[4] m. SAMUEL BERRY, of Barrington, and had a large family, of whom five grew up. Her son, John[4] Berry, was father of the late Samuel G. Berry, of the Governor's Council, and of William[6] Berry, formerly State Treasurer. Her son, Jonathan,[5] was ancestor of the Berrys of "Felker's Mills," in Barrington.
9. SOBRIETY,[4] m. 19 June, 1777, NICHOLAS BROCK, of Barrington, and had six children; from whom are the Brocks of Strafford.

JOSEPH,[3] son of RALPH,[2] (by second wife), born in Dover, 26 March, 1706; lived in Dover. He married, 19 Dec., 1734, Peniel Bean. He died in Dover, 14 Nov., 1782. He had:

1. ANNA,[4] bapt. 29 July, 1735; m. (1) REUBEN DANIELS, of Wolfeboro; (2) PHILIP KELLEY, of Wakefield. She had three children by her first husband, and four by her second.

THE HALL FAMILY.

2. MARY,[4] bapt. 23 May, 1736; m. PAUL HUSSEY, and had four children.
3. JOSEPH,[4] bapt. 5 Nov., 1738; went from Dover to the vicinity of Portland, Me., but afterwards to Bartlett, N. H. He m. MARY CQE, in 1763. They had eight children.
4. DANIEL,[4] bapt. 22 Aug., 1742; moved to Wakefield. He m. WIDOW PATIENCE TAYLOR, of Sanbornton, and had one daughter, *Hannah*,[5] who m. John Sanborn, of Wakefield.
5. ABIGAIL,[4] bapt. 7 Oct., 1744; m. a HAWKINS.
6. SAMUEL,[4] bapt. 19 Mar., 1747; moved to Wakefield about 1768; about 1800 moved to Athens, Me., where he d., 19 Apr., 1831. He m. (1), 26 Aug., 1763, BRIDGET GILMAN, b. 4 Nov., 1748; d. 18 June, 1781; m. (2), 1795, HANNAH, dau. of Isaac Leighton, of Barrington, N. H.; she d. in Athens, Me., 7 May, 1845, aged 89. He had three children by his first wife, and six by the second. Hon. Dwight Hall, of this city, is his great grandson.
7. HANNAH,[4] bapt. 2 Apr., 1749; m. REUBEN LANG, of Wakefield, and had two children.
8. JOHN,[4] b. 4 Nov., 1752; lived in Dover. He m. MARY GAMMONS, of Portsmouth, b. Apr., 1755; d. 10 July, 1826. He d. 19 Apr., 1828. They had three children.
9. PENIEL,[4] m., 10 Mar., 1775, JOHN SCRIBNER, and had six children.

HATEVIL,[4] son of HATEVIL,[3] and MERCY, was born in Dover, 15 Feb., 1707-8; married April 1, 1738, SARAH FURBUSH, of Kittery. On 17 Nov., 1733, he sold to John Ham, of Dover, all the right his father, Hatevil[3], had to 100 acres of land, formerly in the possession of John Hall, Deacon. April, 1734, Daniel and Sarah (Field) conveyed to Hatevil Hall, chairmaker, 10 acres west of Back River, on the southward of the country road from Dover to Durham. He had other land transfers. About 1753, or a little later, he removed to Falmouth, Me. He was a "Friend." He died 28 Nov., 1797. He had ten sons and three daughters. All that we can give here is a list of his children.

1. DOROTHY,[5] b. 23 Aug., 1733; m. GEORGE LEIGHTON, and had eight children.
2. DANIEL,[5] b. 23 Mar., 1735; m. LORANA WINSLOW, and had nine children. Winslow Hall, of this city, was a descendant.

3. HATEVIL,[5] b. 24 Mar., 1763; m. (1) RUTH WINSLOW; (2) ANN JENKINS, and had thirteen children.
4. MERCY,[5] b. 6 Oct., 1738; m. JOSEPH LEIGHTON, and had thirteen children.
5. ABIGAIL,[5] b. 12 Feb., 1740; m. ISAAC ALLEN, and had seven children.
6. EBENEZER,[5] b. 20 July, 1741; m. HANNAH ANDERSON, and had seven children.
7. WILLIAM,[5] b. 6 Dec., 1742; m. (1) BETSEY COE; (2) ELIZABETH WILSON, and had ten children.
8. JOHN,[5] b. 19 June, 1744; m. GRACE SPRAGUE, and had sixteen children.
9. JEDEDIAH,[5] b. 21 Jan., 1748; m. (1) HANNAH HUSSEY; (2) ELIZABETH CLOUGH, and had eleven children.
10. ANDREW,[5] b. 15 Sept., 1750; m. JANE MERRILL, and had eight children.
11. NICHOLAS,[5] b. 8 Mar., 1753; m. (1) EXPERIENCE STONE; (2) EMMA SAWYER, and had ten children.
12. PAUL,[5] b. 15 Dec., 1755; m. (1) SARAH NEAL; (2) KEZIAH (NEAL), widow of TIMOTHY HANSON, and had eleven children.
13. SILAS,[5] b. in 1758; m. (1) MARY GOULD; (2) HANNAH NEAL, and had sixteen children.

THE HAYES FAMILY.

(MEMORANDA No. 277.)

We can only start this genealogy, and leave its continuance to this widespread and highly respectable family.

JOHN HAYES, the ancestor, is said to have emigrated from Scotland, about 1680, and to have settled at *"Dover Corner."* The tradition also says that a brother, Ichabod, settled "South," as to which we know nothing. John had a grant of 20 acres between Tole-End and Barbadoes, 19 March, 1693-4, laid out 4 Nov., 1702. Doubtless most of his possessions came by purchases. He married, 28 June, 1686, MARY HORNE. Tradition says she was but thirteen years old, of which we confess painful doubt. The date of his death we have not found. He had children—order not clear:

1. JOHN, b. 1686, of whom see below.
2. PETER, of whom see below.
3. ROBERT.
4. ICHABOD, b. 13 Mar., 1691-2, of whom see below.
5. SAMUEL, b. 5 Mar., 1694-5, of whom see below.
6. WILLIAM, b. 6 Sept., 1698.
7. BENJAMIN, b. Sept., 1700, of whom see below.

And three daughters, who married, respectively, a Phipps, an Ambrose, of Salisbury, and an Ambrose, of Chester. Perhaps there were other children.

SECOND GENERATION.

JOHN,[2] son of JOHN,[1] and MARY, was born in 1686, and lived at Tole-End. He was Deacon of the First Church. He died June 3, 1759, and his gravestone stands on Pine Hill at the present time. He married twice, (1) TAMSEN, widow of James Chesley, daughter of Deacon Gershom Wentworth, of Somersworth. She died 30 Sept., 1753, aged 66. He married (2) MARY (ROBERTS), widow of Samuel Wingate. His children, all by his first wife, were:

1. JOHN, b. 19 Oct., 1711; lived in Barrington; d. 7 May, 1776. Apparently he was never m. His Will, dated 3 May, 1776, divided his property among brothers and sisters, nephews and nieces.
2. PAUL, b. 16 Sept., 1713. He lived in Barrington; was Justice of the Peace. He d. 9 Apr., 1776. *Paul*, of Alton, was his son. So was *James*, a rich man of Barrington, whose only son, Paul, m. a Horne, and had children: Elizabeth and James.
3. THOMAS, b. 29 Sept., 1715; see below.
4. ELIHU, b. 16 Dec., 1717; lived at Tole-End; d. 12 Mar., 1751; had son, *John*.
5. HEZEKIAH, b. 2 Feb., 1719-20.
6. ELIZABETH, b. 5 Apr., 1722; m. her cousin, ICHABOD, son of Ichabod, and grandson of John.[1]
7. ABRA, b. 17 Feb., 1723-4; m. JOHN MONTGOMERY, of Strafford, N. H.; she had son, *Jonathan*, and other children.
8. ROBERT, b. 21 Mar., 1725-6; was of Green Hill, Barrington. He d. 17 May, 1769. His son, *Joshua*, of Barrington, m. a Locke, and had five children.

9. WENTWORTH, b. 27 Jan., 1727-8. See below.
10. SAMUEL, b. 12 Mar., 1729-30; was of Barrington; d. 22 Apr., 1776. His son, *Samuel*, had sons: Capt. John, of Barrington, and Deacon Samuel, who lived in Durham, but was deacon of the Newmarket Church.
11. JONATHAN, b. 17 Apr., 1732. See below.

PETER,² son of JOHN,¹ and MARY, lived at Tolend. He married SARAH, daughter of John Wingate, and granddaughter of John¹ Wingate. They had children:

1. ANN, b. 3 June, 1718.
2. REUBEN, b. 8 May, 1720. He owned the "Dr. Green place," in Dover. He m. ABIGAIL SHACKFORD. He d. in 1762, and his only child, *Susanna*, m. Dr. Ezra Green, and had 13 children.
3. JOSEPH, b. 17 Mar., 1722.
4. BENJAMIN, b. 17 Mar., 1723-4; was of Barrington.
5. MEHITABLE, b. 11 Dec., 1725.
6. JOHN, was of North Yarmouth, Me.
7. ELIJAH, was of Berwick, Me.
8. ICHABOD, was of Berwick, Me.

ICHABOD,² son of JOHN,¹ and MARY, was born 13 March, 1691-2; lived at Littleworth. He was killed by a mill-log, 1 June, 1734. His wife's name was ABIGAIL, and they had:

1. SARAH, b. 13 Sept., 1776; m. NATHANJEL HORNE, of Dover.
2. ICHABOD, b. 13 Dec., 1718; see below.
3. EZEKIEL, b. 21 Feb., 1720; d. young.
4. DANIEL, b. 26 May, 1728; m. SARAH, dau. of Richard Plumer, of Madbury.
5. MOSES, b. 30 Jan., 1725-6; see below.
6. AARON, b. 23 Mar., 1727-8; was of Nottingham.
7. ABIGAIL, b. 27 Aug., 1730; supposed to have d. young.
8. HANNAH, b. 5 Jan., 1734; m. WILLIAM WENTWORTH, of Milton. She had eight children, and d. in Aug., 1808.

SAMUEL,² son of JOHN,¹ and MARY, born 16 March, 1694-5; lived at Back River. He married, 23 Nov., 1720, LEAH, daughter of William and Martha Pomfrett Dam, who was born 16 Feb., 1695-6. They had:

1. MARY, b. 12 Aug., 1728; m. JOTHAM NUTE, of Dover.
2. ABIGAIL, m. TRISTRAM PINKHAM, of Dover.

WILLIAM,² son of JOHN,¹ and MARY, born 6 Sept., 1698; lived somewhere about the "Corner." He married, 23 Nov., 1720, HANNAH SANBORN. They had:

1. MARY, b. 23 Oct., 1721.
2. HANNAH, b. 21 Oct., 1723.
3. WILLIAM, was of Dover.
4. PATIENCE, m. a HALL.

BENJAMIN,² son of JOHN,¹ and MARY, born 6 Sept., 1700; moved to Rochester. He married JANE (SNELL), widow of Tristram Heard. Children:

1. BENJAMIN, b. 19 Dec., 1726; see below.
2. ABIGAIL, bapt. 9 June, 1728.
3. GEORGE, bapt. 30 June, 1730.
4. ELIZABETH, bapt. 14 May, 1732.
5. HANNAH, bapt. 28 Oct., 1733.

THIRD GENERATION.

THOMAS,³ son of JOHN,² and TAMSEN, born 29 Sept., 1715, lived at Tolend. He was deacon. His wife was HANNAH. He died 7 April, 1774. His children were :

1. EZEKIEL, b. 14 Oct., 1742.
2. SUSANNAH, b. 11 Oct., 1745.
3. ABIGAIL, b. 5 Mar., 1748-9.
4. THOMAS, was of Gilmanton, N. H.

HEZEKIAH,³ son of JOHN,² and TAMSEN, born 2 Feb., 1719; lived in Barrington. He married MARGARET CATE. He died 24 Feb., 1790. His children, in part:

1. WILLIAM, of Poland, Me.
2. ELIHU, of Madbury, who had four children, viz.: *Sarah A.*, m. Nicholas Pike. *Elizabeth*, m. cousin, Dea. Solomon Hayes. *Reuben*, of Alton. *Jonathan*, of Madbury.
3. HEZEKIAH, of Barrington. He m. his cousin, SOPHIA CATE. His son, *Dea. Solomon*, of New Durham, m. his cousin, Elizabeth, just mentioned.

WENTWORTH,[3] son of JOHN,[2] and TAMSEN, born 27 Jan., 1727-8; lived in Rochester. He married (1), 28 Feb., 1753, MARY, daughter of Rev. Amos Main, of Rochester. She was born 9 Sept., 1732; died 14 Jan., 1744. He married (2), 13 March, 1777, WIDOW SUSAN (BURNHAM) ROBERTS. She was born 17 Jan., 1741; died 5 Aug., 1815. He died 11 Jan., 1802. Children by first wife:

1. AMOS MAIN, b. 25 Oct., 1754; settled in North Yarmouth, Me., and had five children.
2. BETTY, b. 25 July, 1757; m. TIMOTHY ROBERTS, son of her father's second wife. He was a soldier in the Revolution. Lived in Milton, after war.
3. JOHN, b. 10 May, 1760; d. 14 Oct., 1760.
4. ELIHU, b. 16 Jan., 1763; m. his cousin, and left children.
5. THEODORE, b. 13 Mar., 1766; settled in Belgrade, Me., and had six children.
6. MOLLY, b. 16 Aug., 1768; d. 10 July, 1773.
7. TAMSEN, b. 11 Apr., 1772; m. SAMUEL LOCKE, of Barrington, and they lived near Lee Hill. Their dau., *Abigail Page Locke*, m. Gorham W. Hoitt, and lived near them. Mr. Hoitt was formerly Sheriff for Strafford County, and officiated at the hanging of the murderer, Howard, at Dover, in 1846.

By the second wife:

8. JOHN, b. 20 June, 1780.

By her first marriage SUSANNA (BURNHAM) ROBERTS had the following Roberts children:

1. TIMOTHY, b. 5 Aug., 1759; m., as above, and had eight children. One of these, *Amos Main Roberts*, was father of Charles Wentworth Roberts, of Bangor, who was the Democratic candidate for Governor of Maine in 1875.
2. JOHN, b. 16 Mar., 1761; d. 22 Jan., 1764.
3. JOSEPH, b. 19 Sept., 1762; m. a DAM, of Rochester.
4. SUSANNAH, b. 7 Nov., 1764; d. young.
5. RELIEF, b. 22 Jan., 1767; m. DANIEL HORNE, of Farmington. *Timothy*, late of New Durham, and others were her children.

JONATHAN,³ son of JOHN,² and TAMSEN, was born 17 April, 1732. He was Lieutenant, and lived on the homestead at Tolend. He married MARY WINGATE, daughter of his father's second wife. He died 15 April, 1787. His children:

1. MARY.
2. ROBERT.
3. JONATHAN.
4. TAMSEN, who m., 8 Jan., 1786, DANIEL CUSHING, and had eight children, one of whom was *Deacon Peter Cushing*, of the First Church.
5. NANCY, m. WILLIAM CUSHING, and had three children.
6. SARAH, m. SAMUEL JACKSON, of Rochester, N. H
7. ROBERT, was of Bolton, Vt.
8. BETSEY, m. STEPHEN JACKSON, of Rochester.

ICHABOD,³ son of ICHABOD,² and ABIGAIL, married ELIZABETH, daughter of John,² and grand-daughter of John,¹ the emigrant. She died 28 Oct., 1795. He died 15 Oct., 1794. Children:

1. ABIGAIL, b. 9 May, 1742; m. ICHABOD HANSON, of Windham, Me.
2. ICHABOD, b. 17 Jan., 1744; was of Farmington, N. H.
3. EZEKIEL, b. 19 Feb., 1746; was of Dover.
4. DANIEL, b. 24 June, 1748; was of Farmington.
5. MOSES, b. 15 June, 1750; was of Farmington.
6. AARON, b. 19 Jan., 1752; was of Dover.
7. JAMES C., was of Milton.
8. TAMSEN, d. young.
9. ABRA, b. 2 Aug., 1757; d. single.
10. BETTY, b. 10 Mar., 1762; m. MAJOR JOSEPH MOONEY, of Alton.
11. JOHN, b. 11 Sept., 1764; was of Saco, Me.

MOSES,³ son of ICHABOD,² and ABIGAIL, born 30 Jan., 1725-6; was Ensign, and lived in Rochester. He had:

1. SARAH, b. 13 Jan., 1750.
2. ANN, b. 19 Dec., 1753.
3. PETER, b. 24 Feb., 1755.
4. ENOCH, b. 27 Aug., 1757.
5. ABIGAIL, b. 9 July, 1760.

6. MOSES, b. 10 Aug., 1763.
7. JOSHUA, b. 9 Dec., 1765.
8. JACOB, b. 28 May, 1769.
9. HANNAH, b. 9 Aug., 1771.
10. MARY, b. 13 May, 1774.

BENJAMIN,[3] son of BENJAMIN,[2] and JANE, was born 29 Dec., 1726; lived in Rochester. He had, at least:

1. GEORGE SNELL, b. 23 Nov., 1760, and others.

The following from the Rochester town records we cannot connect:

ICHABOD HAYES had children:

1. BETSEY, b. 20 Oct., 1771.
2. MARGARET, b. 27 Mar., 1773.
3. ICHABOD, b. 8 Mar., 1775.
4. DANIEL, b. 29 Sept., 1776.
5. HEZEKIAH, b. 7 Sept., 1779.
6. TAMSEN, b. 6 Dec., 1780.
7. HANNAH, b. 17 Nov., 1783.
8. EZEKIEL, b. 4 Apr., 1786.
9. POLLY, b. 23 Aug., 1787.

MOSES HAYES had children:

1. HEZEKIAH, b. 7 Nov., 1778.
2. ELIZABETH, b. 9 Aug., 1780.
3. MOLLY, b. 2 June, 1782.
4. JOHN, b. 5 Apr., 1785.
5. STEPHEN, b. 29 Oct., 1788.

THE GAGE FAMILY.
(MEMORANDA NO. 231.)

JOSEPH GAGE was son of Moses Gage, who lived at Dover Neck, and was brother of CAPT. JOHN GAGE, and to Jonathan, of the Dover Hotel. Of his ancestry we give the following account, which we insert in the language of John Paul Robinson, Esq. He says:

"The family of GAGE derives its descent from De Guaga, who accompanied William, the Conqueror, into England, and after the Conquest was rewarded with large grants of land in the forest of Dean, County Gloucester, adjacent to which forest he fixed his abode, and erected a mansion at Chrenwell; he also built a large Mansion House in the town of Chester, where he died, and was buried in the Abbey. His descendants remained in the county for many generations, of whom there were barons in Parliament in the reign of Henry II.

"JOHN GAGE, 1408, had a son, *John*, who married Joanna Sudgrove. Their son was knighted, in 1454, and died 30 Sept., 1486. His heir, William Gage, Esq., married Agnes Bolney. Their son, Sir John, married Philippa Guilford, and was made Knight, 22 May, 1641. He died April 28, 1657, aged seventy-seven years, leaving four sons and four daughters. Sir Edward, his eldest son, was knighted by Queen Mary, and had nine sons and six daughters. JOHN GAGE, EsQ., the eldest son, was thirty years old at his father's death, and heir to fifteen manors, with many other lands in Sussex; but having survived all his brothers, and leaving no issue, the estate descended to his nephew, JOHN, the second son of Sir Edward, who was advanced to the degree of baronet, 22 March, 1622. This John Gage married Penelope, daughter and co-heir of Thomas Darcey, Earl Rivers. She was the widow of Sir George Trenchard, by whom she had four sons and five daughters. He died Oct. 3, 1633. His estate descended to his eldest son, Sir Thomas Gage.

"His second son, JOHN GAGE, of Stoneham, County Essex, came to America with JOHN WINTHROP, JR., in 1633, and they, with ten others, were the first settlers of Ipswich. In June, 1658, his wife, Ann, died at Ipswich. He married (2) a Keyes. He removed to Rowley as early as 1664. He had by his first wife: Benjamin, Samuel, Daniel, Jonathan and Thomas."

Mr. Robinson received the above account from Mr. Somerby, who obtained it from Lord Gage, in England. Whether it is authentic or fabulous, we have no means of knowing. (There is no reason to doubt its correctness.)

That the Gages of Dover are undoubtedly lineal descendants of John Gage, first settler of Ipswich, is not to be doubted. The pedigree is as follows:

The first Gage who appears in Dover records is COL. JOHN. He was the son of Moses and Sarah Gage, of Beverly, born April 7, 1702; William, born Sept. 23, 1703; Mary, born Aug. 15, 1705. The Beverly records says:

"Family of MOSES and SARAH GAGE:—Sarah, b. April 3, 1692; Hannah, b. Sept. 18, 1694; John, b. April 7, 1702; William, b. Sept. 3, 1703; Mary, b. Aug. 15, 1705."

This MOSES was probably the grandson of JOHN,[1] of Ipswich, and the tradition was that all his brothers, four in number, were killed by the Indians, but when or where is unknown. They were young men, and left no issue.

COL. JOHN GAGE, who was born in Beverly, in 1702, came to Dover prior to 1725, and married ELIZABETH HUBBARD, widow (she had two children by her first marriage), daughter of Joseph[3] Roberts (son of John[2] Roberts), Marshal of New Hampshire in 1680. By her he had four children:

1. CAPT. JOHN GAGE, b. in Mar., 1729, and d. Oct. 19, 1799, aged 70.
2. JONATHAN, b. in 1734; d. in 1800, aged 66.
3. SARAH, m. a HORNE, of Rochester.
4. COL. JOHN GAGE, d. June, 1773. See notice of his death in the *New Hampshire Gazette*, July 2d and 9th, 1773.

CAPTAIN JOHN was born in 1729; married JUDITH TWOMBLY, born in 1730; died in 1827, aged 97. Their issue were:

1. ELIZABETH, b. in Sept., 1754; d., at Alton, July, 1846, aged 92. She m. FREDERICK M. BELL, in 1773, who was killed at Stillwater, N. Y., in 1777. She then m. BENJAMIN BENNETT, of Alton.
2. HANNAH, b. in 1756; m. (1) SAMUEL WALDRON, in 1776. He d. soon, without issue; she then m. (2) DANIEL ROGERS, of Rochester. She d. Mar. 19, 1809.

THE GAGE FAMILY.

3. LYDIA, b. in 1758; m. JOHN BENNETT, ESQ., of New Durham; she d. in 1845, aged 87.
4. SALLY, b. in 1764; m. COL. JANVRIN FISHER; she d. in 1795, aged 31.
5. LOUISA, b. in 1766; m. ISAAC BROWN, of Rochester; d. in 1836.
6. NANCY, b. in 1769; m. PAUL ROBINSON; d. in 1850, aged 81.
7. JOHN, b. in 1771; went to sea—never heard of after 1797.

MOSES, who was born in 1732, had issue by his first wife:

1. JOHN, b. in 1756; d. without issue, in 1800.
2. MARY, b. in 1758; m. ROBERT VARNEY; d. in 1850, aged 92.

By his second wife:

3. MOSES, who lived in Wakefield.
4. JOSEPH, who lived in Dover.
5. JONATHAN, who lived in Dover.
6. ABIGAIL, d. unm.
7. LYDIA, m. a CURTIS.

JONATHAN, born in 1734, married REBECCA HANSON, daughter of Joseph Hanson. They had children, as follows:

1. SUSANNA, m. THOMAS FOOTMAN.
2. HANNAH, m. COL. JOHN RAWSON.
3. ELIZABETH, m. SHADRACH HODGDON.
4. PEGGY, d. unm., 1811.

JOSEPH, son of MOSES, as above, was twice married: (1) to a WINGATE, and had his only child, *Mary W.*; he married (2) a daughter of David Copp, of Wakefield. JOSEPH made his Will March 30, 1802, which was proved April 13, following. By his Will, after giving his wife, ESTHER, $500.00, in lieu of dower, he gave to his sister, Abigail, certain household furniture and one share in N. H. Bank, and to his sisters, Mary Varney, Elizabeth Chase, Hannah Roberts, and Lydia, each $100.00. He gave the bulk of his property to his only child, *Mary W.* William Shannon and Olive Crosby were executors. He died of consumption, in 1802.

Mary Wingate, his daughter, was placed under the guradianship of her uncle, Moses Gage, of Wakefield. She married Charles Woodman, Esq., a young lawyer of Dover, who was born in 1792, graduated at Dartmouth College in 1843; was Representative in the Legislature; Speaker of the House; and a brilliant young man in every way. He died in 1822, aged 30.

THE EDGERLY FAMILY.

(Memoranda No. 240.)

Thomas Edgerly was received as an inhabitant at Oyster River 19 Jan., 1665. He took the oath of fidelity 21 June, 1669, and was made freeman 15 May, 1672. He was a Justice of the Peace in 1674. His garrison house was burned by the Indians in the raid of 1694. At this time he was taken prisoner, but soon escaped. He deeded all his remaining land in 1715. He married 28 Sept., 1665, Rebecca, widow of Henry Hallowell, daughter of John and Remembrance Ault. Children:

1. Thomas, b. 1666; m. Jane Whidden.
2. Samuel, b. 1668; m. Elizabeth Tuttle.
3. John, b. 1670; m. Elizabeth Rawlins.
4. Zachariah, b. 1673; killed by Indians, 1694.
5. Rebecca, b. 1675; m. Aaron Hutcote, 2 June, 1718-9.
6. Joseph, b. 1675; m. Mary Greene.

Thomas,[2] son of Thomas,[1] born 1666; married 3 Dec., 1691, Jane Whidden. He moved to Exeter in 1700, and died in 1719. Children:

1. John, b. 1693; killed by Indians, 1694.
2. Abigail, b. 1695; m. John Huckins.
3. Mary, b. 1697; m. Thomas Kelley, of Brentwood.
4. Samuel, b. 1700; m.; lived in Brentwood.
5. Joseph, b. 1702; m. (1) Sarah Rawlins; (2) Widow Sanborn; (3) Judith Currier. He lived in Stratham.
6. Hannah, m. 28 Jan., 1724-5, James Urin, of Greenland.

THE EDGERLY FAMILY.

SAMUEL,[2] son of THOMAS,[1] born 1668, married 1695, Elizabeth Tuttle, daughter of Capt. John Tuttle, of Dover Neck. He died at Oyster River in 1724. She married (2), 1725, Dea. John Ambler. His children:

1. DOROTHY, b. 1697; m. JAMES DURGIN.
2. JOHN, b. 1700; m. ELIZABETH WAKEHAM.
3. JAMES, b. 1704; m. (1), 1730, ELEANOR SAWYER; (2) RACHEL STANWOOD.
4. JUDITH, b. 1707; m. JONATHAN DURGIN.
5. SAMUEL, b. 1713; d. 1733.
6. MOSES, b. 1716; m. MARY KENT.
7. SUSANNA, b. 1717.

MOSES, born 1716; married MARY, daughter of John Kent, of Durham, and had several children, among whom was *Moses, Jr.*, and *Ebenezer*, who married Tamson Smith.

MOSES EDGERLY, JR., resided for a time at Newmarket, where he married ELIZABETH, daughter of John Wedgwood, but afterwards lived in Durham, and had seven children:

1. JOSEPH, b. at Durham; after 1800 lived at Wolfeboro, where he d. in 1828. His wife was SARAH COLBATH, dau. of Dr. Joseph Colbath, of Wolfeboro, and they had children: 1. *Curtis C.*, of New Durham. 2. *Moses*, of New Durham. 3. *Bradbury*, of Dover. 4. *Statira*, who m. Stephen Giles, of Wolfeboro. 5. *Nathaniel G.*, of Indiana. 6. *Dudley*, of Wolfeboro.
2. NATHANIEL, of Durham, m. WIDOW CRUMWELL, dau. of Daniel and Eliza.
3. EBENEZER, of Durham, m. BETSEY DURGIN, and had children: *Nathaniel, Richard* and *Mary*.
4. MOSES, of Durham, m. (1) LOUISE THOMPSON; (2) a DAVIS. He had several children, among whom were: *Jacob* and *Joseph M.*, of Durham, and *Oliver*, of Newington.
5. DOROTHY, m. RICHARD KENT, of Durham.
6. POLLY, m. SAMUEL DREW, of Durham.
7. ANN ELIZABETH, m. BRADBURY JEWETT, of Sandwich.

EBENEZER, of Durham, brother of Moses, Jr., married WIDOW TAMSON SMITH, maiden name, Daniels. Their children were:

1. JAMES S., d. at sea.
2. ELIPHALET, who d. while a prisoner to the British, in the War of 1812.
3. MARY, m. a SEWARD.
4. SUSAN, m. a HALL.
5. REBECCA, m. a PRESBY.
6. EBENEZER, m. BATHSHEBA, dau. of Moses Wasgatt, of Eden, Me. He settled at Sebec, Me., and had six children.
7. ROBERT, b. 13 June, 1785; m., 11 Nov., 1808, SARAH WASGATT, sister of the foregoing; he lived in Eden, Sebec, and Hampden, Me. They had twelve children. He d. in 1835.

JOHN, of Durham, son of Samuel, married 1730, ELIZABETH WAKEHAM, of Durham. He lived on the homestead in Durham till his death, 11 April, 1784. His wife, Elizabeth, died Aug. 1, 1774. Their children were:

1. ABIGAIL, b. 19 July, 1732; d. unm.
2. SAMUEL, b. 13 Apr., 1735; m. OLIVE DAME.
3. JAMES, b. 13 Apr., 1737; m. (1) JENNIE PHILIPS; (2) WIDOW RACHEL KENT.
4. JOTHAM, b. 11 Apr., 1730; m. SARAH DOE.
5. JUDITH, b. 26 June, 1741; m. THOMAS GEORGE, of Lee.
6. CALEB, b. 20 Dec., 1743; m. ABIEL SYLLY.
7. THOMAS, b. 6 Jan., 1745; m. AGNES PHILLIPS.
8. ELIZABETH, b. 18 Dec., 1747; m. JOSEPH DURGIN, of Durham.

SAMUEL, son of JOHN, married OLIVE DAME, of Newington; lived in Durham; Olive died in 1803, after which he lived in Northwood, with his son Samuel, and there died. They had children:

1. JAMES, b. 13 Dec., 1764; m. TEMPERANCE KNIGHT, dau. of George Knight, of Durham. They removed to Woodstock, in 1790 (then called Peeling), where he d., leaving a large family of children.

SAMUEL, son of SAMUEL and grandson of JOHN, as above, married BETSEY, daughter of Jacob Crumwell, of Durham, and settled in Northwood, and died there about 1824.

THE EDGERLY FAMILY.

JETHRO, born 28 Feb., 1770; married July, 1797, ABIGAIL, daughter of Jacob Crumwell, of Durham; they lived in Wolfeboro, and Acton, Me., where he died in 1848; they had children:

1. RICHARD, b. in 1797.
2. SARAH, b. 1801.
3. BETSEY, b. 1808.
4. JACOB, (twin), b. 1811.
6. JOHN (twin), b. 1811.
7. HANNAH, b. 1813.

GEORGE, born 30 Nov., 1773; married, 1798, ABIGAIL C., daughter of Capt. Joseph Thomas, of Durham. He died at Lowell, in 1856; they had children:

1. ADDISON S., b. 1799.
2. OLIVE, b. 1803.
3. LOVE T.

JONATHAN, born 19 Sept., 1777; married 1808, SARAH W., daughter of John Edgerly, of New Durham; resided at New Durham, Woodstock, and Alton, died at Lowell, 1857. They had children:

1. MARIA C.
2. LOUISA R.
3. BETSEY B.
4. SARAH A.
5. MARY J.
6. DANIEL W.
7. ALICE O.
8. CHARLES E.
9. CLARA A.

JAMES, son of JOHN, married (1) JENNY, daughter of Andrew Phillips of Kittery; she died in 1772; married (2) RACHEL KENT, of Durham; her maiden name was CARLILE; they lived in Milton, Brookfield, and Wolfeboro, where he died in 1815. They had children:

1. TAMSON.
2. DEBORAH.
3. AGNES.
4. JUDITH.
5. ELIJAH.
6. JANE.
7. DANIEL.

JONATHAN, son of JOHN, married SARAH DOE, and lived in Durham, and died there about 1783. They had children:

1. SAMUEL.
2. MEHITABLE.
3. SARAH.
4. LYDIA.
5. HANNAH.
6. MARTHA.

CALEB, son of JOHN, married ABIEL, daughter of Benoni Sylley, of Salisbury. He purchased, in 1772, 200 acres of land in New Durham, of Valentine Marges, of Durham, and settled there about 1777. He died in Alton, 1825. Their children were:

1. JOHN, b. 1766.
2. BENJAMIN, b. 14 May, 1769; settled in Candia.
3. DANIEL, b. 21 Sept., 1771; d. young.
4. ELIZABETH, b. 15 Aug., 1773.
5. JEREMIAH, b. 13 May, 1776; lived in New Durham and Alton.
6. MERCY, b. 11 Jan., 1782; m. (1) DR. JOHN GILBERT; (2) JOSEPH FERREN.

THOMAS, son of JOHN, married AGNES, daughter of Andrew and Miriam Phillips, of Kittery, Me., lived in Durham, till he moved to New Durham, in that part now called Alton, in 1788. After the death of his wife he moved to Farmington, and there he died in 1815. Children:

1. JOSIAH, who m. MARY, dau. of Col. Thomas Tash.
2. JUDGE JAMES H.
3. SYLVESTER.
4. MARY.
5. MARTHA A.
6. SARAH A.

ANDREW, born 13 March, 1772; married 1794, ELIZABETH TASH; settled in Exeter, Me., in 1830. Children:

1. JOHN.
2. ANDREW H.
3. WILLIAM.

THOMAS C., born 4 Dec., 1773; married 1797, HANNAH LIBBEY; lived in Alton and Milton; died in 1844. Children:

1. GEORGE W.
2. MARTHA W.
3. MARY C.
4. LYDIA M.

JOHN, "weaver," son of Thomas, lived at Oyster River; he married ELIZABETH ———, and had children:

1. ELIZABETH.
2. JOHN.
3. ZACHARIAH.
4. JOSEPH, was of Durham.

THE WALLINGFORD FAMILY.
(MEMORANDA No. 250.)

WALLINGFORD is the surname of respectable families in Dover for more than 200 years. The following is a mere sketch of the first families, gathered from records while searching for material for genealogies for other old families of Dover.

Whether JOHN WALLINGFORD, the ancestor of this family, was born abroad, or was of a family settled at Bradford, Mass., as early as 1675, remains to be ascertained. But certain it is that on the 6th day of Dec., 1687, JOHN WALLINGFORD was married to MARY, daughter of Judge JOHN TUTTLE, of Dover, by Rev. John Pike. She was living in 1727, when her father gave her a legacy in his Will of that date. Who were the children of John and Mary (Tuttle) Wallingford?

HON. THOMAS WALLINGFORD, of Somersworth, Judge of the Supreme Court of the Province of New Hampshire, from 1721 to the time of his death in 1771, was one son. The Will of Ebenezer Wallingford, of Dover, made Aug. 19, 1721, proved Sept. 6, 1721, throws some light on the question of other children living at that date.

THOMAS, who had wife MARGARET, had:

1. HANNAH, b. 5 May, 1720.
2. JUDITH, b. 25 March, 1722.
3. EBENEZER, b. 21 July, 1724.
4. ABIGAIL, b. Sept., 1726.

EBENEZER WALLINGFORD was apparently married; he gave sixty acres of land in Dover, which he bought of Israel Hodgdon, to Susanna Cotton, of Portsmouth; the rest of his estate he divided among his beloved brothers, viz: John Wallingford, Thomas Wallingford (the Judge), and James Clement, who married a daughter; he was probably son of Job Clement, and grandson of Councillor Job Clement, and was born March 6, 1693. The Judge was born in 1696, and died in 1771, leaving numerous descendants.

JOHN WALLINGFORD, the first named brother of Ebenezer, lived in Rochester. His Will, made Oct., 1761, was proved Jan. 7, 1762. In it he mentions his wife, Charity, and sons, Peter and William; he also mentions daughters Mary Dore; Phebe Weymouth; Patience; Hannah and Frances Clement.

The following facts were obtained from the Bradford, Rowley and Newbury Town Records, and the County records at Salem, Mass.

NICHOLAS WALLINGFORD, a boy, came over in the ship *Confidence* from London, in 1638, to Boston. He settled in Newbury. He married, 30 Aug., 1654, SARAH, daughter of Henry and Briget

THE WALLINGFORD FAMILY.

Travis, or Travers, of Newbury. Sarah was born in 1646. Nicholas was captured at sea, and never returned. His estate was settled among his children and his widow, in 1684.

The children of Nicholas and Sarah (Travis) Wallingford were:

1. JOHN, b. 16 Sept., 1655; d. 6 Jan., 1656.
2. NICHOLAS, b. 2 Jan., 1657; m., 4 Dec., 1678, ELIZABETH PALMER.
3. JOHN, b. 7 Apr., 1650; m., 6 Dec., 1687, MARY TUTTLE, of Dover, N. H.
4. SARAH, b. 20 May, 1661; m., 25 Nov., 1669, CALEB HOPKINSON.
5. MARY, b. 5 Aug., 1663.
6. JAMES, b. 6 Oct., 1665; he had a wife, DEBORAH.
7. HANNAH, b. 27 Nov., 1667.
8. WILLIAM, b. 16 Feb., 1670.

These children appear under the name WALLINGFORD in the records.

JOHN WALLINGFORD, who married MARY TUTTLE, daughter of Judge Tuttle, of Dover, lived in Bradford, anciently a part of Rowley. Their children:

1. JOHN, b. 14 Dec., 1688.
2. NICHOLAS, b. 2 Oct., 1691.
3. SARAH, b. 3 Sept., 1693.
4. EBENEZER, b. 30 Sept., 1695.
5. THOMAS, b. 28 July, 1697. He was JUDGE WALLINGFORD, of Somersworth.
6. JUDITH, b. 16 Mar., 1699.
7. ABIGAIL, b. 27 Sept., 1702.

These children appear to have emigrated to Dover, probably attracted here on account of its being the home of their mother, Mary Tuttle. Nicholas had wife Rachel, and daughter Margaret, born 4 April, 1714.

JOHN WALLINGFORD, who was born 14 Dec., 1688, and settled in Rochester, became an extensive landowner there. His Will, dated 7 Oct., 1761, was proved 17 Jan., 1762. He gave his son, Peter, the homestead, and land in Milton, then a part of Rochester.

PETER WALLINGFORD made his Will 18 April, 1771, which was proved 24 Aug., 1773. He gave his son, DAVID WALLINGFORD, the land in Milton, and on that he settled when a young man. He died in 1815, and the homestead passed to his son.

SAMUEL WALLINGFORD, who married Sallie Worcester; they had four children, one of whom was:

ZIMRI SCATES WALLINGFORD, who was born 7 Oct., 1816. He was a distinguished citizen of Dover, and for many years Agent of the Cochecho Manufacturing Company. His father died in 1825, leaving his widow with four children, of which, Zimri was the eldest.

The Dover town records furnish the following:

NICHOLAS, who had wife RACHEL, had:

1. MARGARET, b. 4 April, 1714.

SAMUEL, of Somersworth, married 22 July, 1775, LYDIA BAKER, of Dover.

LAVINA, married, 5 Dec., 1816, DANIEL PIKE, of Wolfeboro.

LYDIA, married, 13 Nov., 1785, AMOS COGGSWELL, of Dover.

THE EVANS FAMILY.

(MEMORANDA NO. 244.)

ROBERT[1] EVANS is said to have come from Wales, which is very probable. But the story accompanying the tradition, that "three brothers came over, one settling in Dover, one in Salisbury and one in Pennsylvania," is doubtless no more correct now than it ever was.

It appears by the old records that there was a JOHN EVANS, who had a dwelling house in Dover in 1672, as shown by deed of Major Walderne. No doubt he was brother of Robert, and so, probably, "two brothers came over" and settled here, at Dover, before 1665. No member of the Evans family appears at Newbury till twenty years later, when Thomas Evans (parentage unknown), married Hannah Brown, 30 Sept., 1686. (Hoyt's Old Families of Salisbury.) The probability is that Thomas was son of John Evans, above mentioned, as he was born about 1665, and may have gone to Salisbury, where he lived and raised a family of eight children. (See Hoyt's Old Families, etc.)

In the *Journal of Reverend John Pike,* date June 28, 1689, appears a list of those who were killed by the Indians, when they captured the Walderne garrison. The record says: "Killed 23 persons, principal of wch Maj: Waldron, Mr. Leigh, *Mr. Evans,* Richard Otis, etc."

Now it is evident the "Mr. Evans" mentioned was JOHN EVANS; because in Mr. Pike's *Journal,* "Feb. 27, 1696-7, Robert Evens, Sen., died of a Cancer, after nine moenths painful exercise." And the Probate record shows that Edward Evans, son of Robert, made return of the inventory of Robert Evans' estate, 4 Nov., 1697.

ROBERT EVANS was "received an inhabitant, 19, 1 mo. 1665;" and he "took the oath of fidelity" 21 June, 1669. He was on the Cochecho tax-list until his death, as his residence was at Bellamy.

ROBERT[1] married ELIZABETH ———; their children:

1. ROBERT, b. 30 Sept., 1665.
2. EDWARD, b. 20 June, 1667.
3. JONATHAN, b. 10 Apr., 1669.
4. ELIZABETH, b. 28 June, 1671.
5. BENJAMIN, b. about 1673. He is mentioned, where Edward, son of Robert,[1] "deeds to brother Benjamin, 30 acres in Cochecho, Ash Swamp, 4 April, 1709."

CAPTAIN ROBERT lived and died in Dover. A document speaks of him, 19 Sept., 1753, as "aged about 88," when he testified that he was one of the committee to run the line between Dover and Rochester. Others testified at the same time. The testimony is interesting, but need not be given here.

CAPTAIN ROBERT[2] had wife ANN, and they had children, born in Dover:

1. JOSEPH, b. 4 June, 1682.
2. SARAH, b. 9 Nov., 1685.
3. BENJAMIN, b. 2 Feb., 1687.
4. HANNAH, b. 21 June, 1690.
5. PATIENCE, b. 5 Sept., 1693.

EDWARD[2] had wife DORCAS; their children:

1. ELEANOR, b. 3 Mar., 1700.
2. RACHEL, b. 6 Apr., 1703.
3. JOSEPH, b. 20 Oct., 1704.

JOSEPH,[3] son of CAPTAIN ROBERT,[2] had wife MARCY (Mercy);. their children:

1. ROBERT, b. 11 Jan., 1704; lived for some time in Madbury, but later moved to Strafford, and had a farm above Parker Mountain (Blue Hill), and d. there, leaving children,. one of whom, *William*, had a son, Lemuel.
2. JOHN, b. 3 Feb., 1705; he resided and d. in Madbury; when living in Madbury the Indians caught him one day, near where Benjamin Twombly lived, in Littleworth, 15 Sept., 1725, and scalped him; he was thought to be dead (by the Indians), but recovered. He was m. and had three children: 1. *Jonathan*. 2. *Moses*, who went to New Durham. 3. *Abigail*, who m. Benjamin Buzzell, of Barrington.
3. JOSEPH, b. 28 Mar., 1708; for whom see below.
4. WILLIAM, b. 9 Feb., 1711.
5. DANIEL, b. 28 June, 1715.
6. MARCY, b. 6 Dec., 1717.
7. ———, b. 6 Mar., 1720.

BENJAMIN,[3] son of CAPT. ROBERT,[2] had wife MARCY, and was killed by the Indians 15 Sept., 1725, as was William Evans and Benjamin's son Benjamin. The children of Benjamin and Marcy were:

1. BENJAMIN, b. 18 June, 1713.
2. ELIZABETH, b. 17 June, 1716.
3. JOSEPH, b. 7 Mar., 1719.
4. JONATHAN, b. 17 June, 1722.
5. (COL.) STEPHEN, b. 13 Nov., 1724; of whom see below.

THE EVANS FAMILY.

JOSEPH,[4] son of JOSEPH,[3] and MARCY, lived in Madbury and inhabited his father's farm. He married ELIZABETH HANSON; their children:

1. BENJAMIN, of Meaderborough, who left children.
2. JOSEPH, of New Durham Ridge, who left children.
3. SOLOMON, b. Aug., 1743; for whom see below.
4. MARCY, who m. SAMUEL HUSSEY, and d. in Rollinsford.
5. ELIZABETH, d. unm., 1 Nov., 1829.
6. ———, b. 1831; d. young.

COLONEL STEPHEN,[5] born 13 Nov., 1724, was married three times, (1) ELIZABETH ROBERTS, in 1749; they had:

1. EPHRAIM, b. 24 June, 1750.
2. MOLLY, b. 21 June, 1752.
3. JOSEPH, b. 13 Oct., 1754.
4. MARY, b. 31 July, 1757.

His wife died in 1760, and he married (2) SARAH ROBERTS, in 1762; children:

5. BENJAMIN, bapt. 20 May, 1764.
6. BETTY, bapt. 22 Sept., 1765.
7. SARAH, bapt. 8 Mar., 1767.

COL. EVANS's second wife died in 1768; he married (3) LYDIA CHESLEY; their children:

8. TEMPERANCE, bapt. 27 Apr., 1771.
9. ELIZABETH, bapt. 25 Oct., 1772.
10. LYDIA, bapt. 25 Oct., 1772.
11. ICHABOD CHESLEY, b. 29 Jan., 1777.
12. PATTY, b. 20 Feb., 1780.

His son JOSEPH, born 13 Oct., 1754, graduated from Harvard College in 1777; he married ELIZABETH WALDRON, daughter of Col. Thomas Westbrook Waldron, April 6, 1786; he died Aug. 30, 1797. No children. The house in which he lived stood on the corner of Washington and Payne streets, where the Cochecho Block stood.

412   HISTORY OF DOVER, N. H.

SOLOMON,[5] son of JOSEPH,[4] received the homestead in Madbury. He married CATHERINE HANSON, who died 13 July, 1849, at the advanced age of 102 years, lacking 5 days; Solomon died 2 May, 1832; their children:

 1. TOBIAS, b. 11 Feb., 1770; he lived on the homestead in Madbury, an esteemed member of the Society of Friends. He m. SARAH AUSTIN, sister of Elisha Austin, Esq., of Madbury. Their only child married Lorenzo Rollins, of Rollinsford.
 2. ELIZABETH, b. 10 Mar., 1774.
 3. DAVID, b. 24 May, 1778.
 4. AARON, b. 17 July, 1781.
 5. JOHN, b. 15 Oct., 1785.

COL. STEPHEN lived in a house that stood a few feet northwest of the "Jenness House," on School street; that is, it was on the northwest corner of Main and School streets, and his store was on the southwest corner, opposite his house; his house faced the south; it was many years after his death, in 1808, that School street was opened. In Col. Evans's day it was a fashionable, as well as a business section of the town.

Col. Evans was a man of wealth, and was busily engaged in trade and ship-building. During the Revolutionary war he lost much of his property. He was a soldier in the army that captured Louisberg. During the Revolution he was Dover's most distinguished officer in the army. He commanded a regiment of New Hampshire soldiers at the surrender of Gen. Burgoyne's army in 1777, at Saratoga. He was also in command of a regiment in the Rhode Island campaign, under Gen. Sullivan. He was often in office in time of peace, and was a prominent member of the First Church.

THE NUTE FAMILY.

(MEMORANDA No. 225.)

NUTE, Newt, Newtt, Newtte and Newte are some of the ways this family name is written in the public records of New Hampshire. JAMES, the great ancestor of this family in this State, wrote his name NEWTE, which corresponds with the English surname borne by a family of distinction living in Tiverton, Devonshire, in the reign of Elizabeth. The members of this English family were zealous loyalists during the civil wars. Many of them were Clergymen, in the Church of England, in the 17th and 18th centuries.

In this country the name is now universally written, NUTE. This form appears to have been generally adopted by the third generation of the first settler.

JAMES NUTE, or NEWTE, came to Portsmouth in 1631, being one of the company of planters which came from England under the auspices of Capt. John Mason to settle his Laconia Patent. There can be hardly any doubt of his connection with the Tiverton family. He was in Dover in 1648, and perhaps earlier, in which year he had a grant of land and was taxed. Like the early settlers he resided on Dover Neck, his house being westerly or northwesterly of the meeting-house on Meeting-House Hill; his house was on Low Street. He was Selectman in 1659. The records indicate that he was a man of character and influence among his fellow citizens.

In 1656 the town granted him forty acres of land on the west side of Back River, at the head of Lot No. 10, of the "Twenty-Acre" lots. He previously had bought No. 10 of John Newgrove, to whom it had been allotted in 1642.

Feb. 15, 1671, in consideration of "natural love and affection," he gave his son James "three score acres of land" on the west side of Back River, being the same previously mentioned; at the same time he gave his son Abraham "twelve acres" on the east side of Back River, that is on Dover Neck,—these lands to be enjoyed, after the decease of one "ye said James Nute and my now wife Sarah." It is a remarkable fact that the Back River farm has remained in continuous possession of their descendants in the Nute name, the present owner (1923) being Mr. Herbert Nute. It is one of the best farms in Dover, always kept up in good condition. Mr. Nute is one of our respected citizens.

JAMES, JR., son of JAMES,[1] as above, was a tax-payer in 1662. He married ELIZABETH, daughter of Capt. John and Elizabeth (Hull) Heard. He lived on the Nute farm on the west side of Back River. He died intestate, leaving Widow Elizabeth, and four young children. His widow married 13 Aug., 1694, WILLIAM FURBER, who died in 1707, leaving her a widow the second time. She was administratrix of James Nute's estate. She is called, in one or two places in the writings relative to the settlement, MARY, which has occasioned some confusion. Children of James and Elizabeth (Heard) Nute, were:

1. JAMES, b. 27 July, 1687.
2. SAMUEL.
3. SARAH, m. WILLIAM FURBER, son of her step-father.
4. LEAH, m. HATEVIL NUTTER, of Newington.

In 1725, Samuel Nute and wife Elizabeth, and Sarah, wife of William Furber, and Leah, wife of Hatevil Nutter,—joined in a deed releasing their "interest to 60 acres of land which our honored grandfather, James Nute, mentioned and gave by deed to his son, James, our father, said deed bearing date Feb. 15, 1671." This recital establishes the relationship of these persons. Dec. 16, 1699, James Nute, "being 13 years old," chose John Layton, of Dover, his guardian.

JAMES,[3] son of JAMES,[2] married PRUDENCE ———. He lived on the homestead of his father, the Court having decreed him "two thirds of all the house and lands and one cow, two steers of three-year old, when he comes of age." He was an active, enterprising man and held many important trusts. He was Selectman in 1725, 1726, 1728. His Will was dated July 14, 1752; proved Oct. 31, 1759. He gave his son, James, the homestead, and eighty acres of land in Rochester; to his son Paul, the land where Paul then lived, also a dwelling house in Rochester. He gave legacies to daughters, Elizabeth Tuttle and Anne Allen. His wife, Prudence, not being mentioned, she was probably dead at the time of making of the Will. Children of James and Prudence:

THE NUTE FAMILY.   415

1. ELIZABETH, b. 1706; m. JOHN, son of Ensign John and Judith Tuttle.
2. JAMES, b. 12 Mar., 1712-13; m. ANNE, dau. of Daniel and Deborah Meserve.
3. PAUL, b. 19 Aug., 1714; m. ———, and had dau., *Comfort*, who m. Thomas Tuttle, of Lee; also a dau. who m. a Davis, of Durham.
4. ANNE, b. 21 Mar., 1721, who m. an ALLEN.

SAMUEL,[3] son of JAMES,[2] married 18 March, 1718, ELIZABETH, daughter of John and Rose (Otis) Pinkham, and lived on the north side of the road leading from the main road to the old Pascataqua bridge to Capt. Thomas Nute's. His Will was dated March 9, 1764; admitted to probate June 26, 1765. He gave his son, John, sixty acres of land in Rochester; to his son, Jotham, his dwelling house and land in Rochester; also legacies to his daughters. Children of Samuel and Elizabeth Nute were:

1. JOHN, m. and lived in Rochester. *Capt. Samuel Nute*, who served in the Revolutionary War, was his son; he was Lieut. in the Army.
2. JOTHAM, m. (1) MARY, dau. of Samuel and Leah (Dam) Hayes; (2) WIDOW MARY CANNEY.
3. SARAH, of whom there is no record.
4. MARTHA, b. in Mar., 1734; m. BENJAMIN DAME, of Rochester; she d. 12 Feb., 1783.
5. ELIZABETH, of whom there is no record.

JAMES,[4] son of JAMES,[3] and PRUDENCE NUTE, married ANNE, daughter of Daniel and Deborah Meserve. He lived on the homestead given by his father. He died 4 April, 1776. His widow, ANNE, survived him, and died 14 Jan., 1796. The children of James and Anne Nute were (order of ages uncertain):

1. JAMES, m. LEAH PINKHAM, and lived in Madbury.
2. PAUL, of whom see below.
3. SARAH, who m. JOB TUTTLE, her cousin, and d. in Lebanon, Me., Feb., 1724.
4. DANIEL, m. LUCY, dau. of John Tuttle, Jr., brother of Job Tuttle, and removed to Bartlett, N. H.
5. ANNE, m. (1) JOHN TUTTLE, being his second wife, and on his death m. (2) THOMAS CUSHING, grandson of Jonathan Cushing. She d. 27 July, 1819.

Paul,[5] son of James,[4] and Anne (Meserve), held the commission of Lieutenant in the army of the Revolution. He lived and died on the old homestead. He married Hepzibah, daughter of Thomas and Elizabeth (Tebbets) Canney, who lived on Dover Neck, and who were members of the Society of Friends. Thomas Canney was descended from Thomas Canney, who came from England with James Nute, in 1631. Lieut. Paul Nute died 6 June, 1812. His children were:

1. Thomas, m. Eunice, dau. of Robert Varney, and removed to Wolfeboro.
2. Elizabeth, who d. young.
3. Joseph, who d. young.
4. Meserve, b. 24 Dec., 1767, of whom see below.
5. Anne, b. 1769; m. Daniel Drew, son of Francis and Elizabeth (Watson) Drew.
6. Ephraim, b. 1771; he was a sailor, and d. at sea.
7. Paul, b. 1773; he was a sailor, and d. at sea.
8. Rosanna, b. 1775; she m. Samuel Stackpole, of Rochester, and one of their sons was *Dr. Paul Stackpole*, of Dover.
9. James, b. 1777; he was a sailor and d. at sea.
10. Abigail, b. 9 Oct., 1783; m. Philemon Chandler, of Dover.
11. Elizabeth, b. 28 May, 1785; m. Isaac Pinkham, son of James and Abigail (Meserve) Pinkham.

Meserve,[6] son of Paul,[5] married Elizabeth Ames, and lived and died on the homestead of his ancestors, at Back River. Their children were:

1. Ephraim, b. 14 Apr., 1796; m. Mary Bancroft, of Boston. *Rev. Ephraim Nute,* the well-known Unitarian clergyman, was a son.
2. Clarissa, b. July, 1801; m. Jeremiah Drew, of Durham.
3. Greenleaf, b. 20 Oct., 1804; m. Susan Bock, of Strafford, dau. of Paul Bock.
4. Mary, b. 27 Nov., 1806; m. (1) Elisha Murdock; (2) William Chandler.
5. Elizabeth, b. 23 Jan., 1808; m. James Clark, of Strafford.
6. Paul, b. 4 July, 1812, of whom we have no record.
7. James, b. 13 May, 1815, of whom we have no record.

8. (CAPTAIN) THOMAS, b. 10 Nov., 1817; m. MARIA BROCK, sister of Susan; lived on the homestead at Back River; Captain of militia company; held various town offices, etc.
9. JOSEPH, b. 25 Feb., 1820; m. HANNAH CUSHING, youngest dau. of James and Joana (Roberts) Tuttle. He d. 17 June, 1847, at the early age of twenty-seven years. He was Captain of a militia company at the time of his death. He was a young man of energy and ability.

ABRAHAM,[2] son of JAMES,[1] has his name on the tax-lists for several years. He made his Will May 31, 1756, in which he mentions wife RACHEL, and children *Isaac, Abraham, Joanna, Sarah,* and *Mary.* Descendants of this branch live on Dover Neck on lands owned by the first settler.

THE MESERVE FAMILY.

(MEMORANDA No. 253.)

MESERVE, MESSERVE, MESSERVY, MESSERVEY, and MISHARVIE, are some of the ways in which this family name is spelled in the old records of New Hampshire. This diversity of spelling the surname obviously came from the way it was pronounced; not being an English name, it was written and pronounced by the English, at their pleasure, after it became Anglicised. It is often written in the ancient records, "MESSERVY." This is the correct way, being in conformity with the original surname as it was written in the Isle of Jersey, whence the first settler came to this country. Clement Messervy was a rather common name in that Isle two hundred years ago.

The present mode of spelling this surname "MESERVE," has long been followed by the members of the family in this country. It is worthy of note that while there is a uniformity of spelling the name, there is a diversity in pronouncing it. For example, Nicholas D. Meserve, of Lee, and Charles R. Meserve, of Dover (a noted Jail-keeper), were often spoken of as "Harvy"; Nick Harvy was a common expression in Lee. This, evidently, was a survival of the old spelling, "Misharvy." In some families the "Mis" was dropped, and "Harvy" remained.

In 1678, Clement Meserve lived in Portsmouth, where he had a family and owned a house. How and when he came there remains to be determined. He is undoubtedly the Clement which, a family historian says, came from the Isle of Jersey, and became the ancestor of the family in New Hampshire. In 1693, Clement Meserve and his family occupied a pew in the North Church, at Portsmouth. In 1710, Clement Meserve, of "Welch Cove," (Newington), conveyed his home lands, house, orchards, etc., to his son, Clement, in consideration of his son's engaging to provide for the grantor and his wife, Elizabeth, during their lives. Clement, the father, was dead in 1721. Their children were:

1. ELIZABETH, who m. MICHAEL WHIDDEN, of Portsmouth, 6 June, 1694.
2. CLEMENT, who m. ELIZABETH JONES, of Dover, Sept. 4, 1702.
3. DANIEL, who m. DEBORAH ———, and settled in Dover, being the first person of this surname to locate here.
4. TAMSON, or THOMASINE, who m. JOSEPH HAM, and had a large family.

CLEMENT,[2] son of CLEMENT,[1] appears to have removed to Scarborough, Me., about 1727, having previously sold part of the Newington homestead, given to him by his father, to John Vincent. His descendants have been numerous in Scarborough, and throughout that section of Maine.

DANIEL,[2] son of CLEMENT,[1] had a grant of land from the town of Dover in 1701, and therein is called "husbandman." In 1725 he purchased thirty acres of the Starbird estate, "it being near that part of Dover called Madbury." His Will is dated May 1, 1747, being then "aged and well stricken in years." (Born about 1670.) His Will was proved Jan. 30, 1757. In it he mentions wife, DEBORAH, and children:

1. DANIEL, to whom he devised the 30 acres granted to him by the town of Dover; also 30 acres adjoining, bought of the Starbird estate.
2. ELIZABETH, who m. a LIBBY.

THE MESERVE FAMILY.

3. MARY, who m. DANIEL MEADER.
4. JOHN, to whom he devised 30 acres on the south side of Oyster River.
5. ANNA, who m. JAMES[4] NUTE, and lived on the ancestral Nute farm.
6. TAMSON, who m. STEPHEN PINKHAM.
7. CLEMENT, who was executor of the Will, and had the rest and residue of his father's estatee "in Dover and Rochester."

DANIEL,[3] son of DANIEL,[2] had wife ABIGAIL. His estate was divided Nov. 6, 1783, among his children:

1. JOSEPH, b. 4 Oct., 1729; we have no record of him.
2. DEBORAH, b. May 14, 1732; m. CAPT. JAMES GILMAN.
3. DANIEL, b. Mar. 18, 1734; we have no record of him.
4. JONATHAN, b. Mar. 4, 1738; m. MARY DAVIS; Gen. George P. Meserve, of Bartlett, N. H., was a grandson.
5. CLEMENT. b. Jan. 23, 1741; m. LOIS TORR; Isaac H. Meserve, Esq., of Roxbury, Mass., was a grandson.
6. ABIGAIL, b Aug. 27, 1745; m. (1) NICHOLAS' (DUDA) DURELL, of Lee, N. H. *Hon. Daniel Meserve Durell*, of Dover, Member of Congress, and Chief Justice of the Court of Common Pleas, was a son. Judge Durell's son, Edward Henry Durell, was a distinguished Judge of the United States District Court for the Eastern District of Louisiana. A daughter of Judge Durell m. James D. Green, of Cambridge, Mass. Upon the death of Nicholas Durell, his widow m. (2) ANTHONY PICKERING.

CLEMENT,[3] son of DANIEL,[2] lived and died in the old Meserve "garrison," on the north side of the highway leading from the Back River School house to Durham. He was selectman of Dover in 1766-67, and interested in military affairs. He was commonly styled "Lieut. Meserve." He died July 18, 1800, aged 84 years. He married ABIGAIL, daughter of Joseph and Tamson (Meserve) Ham; their children:

1. EBENEZER, m. EUNICE TORR. Gen. John Smith Meserve and Col. Henry Meserve were grandsons.
2. CLEMENT, m. LYDIA, dau. of John Tuttle, Jr., who was the eldest son of John and Elizabeth (Nute) Tuttle. He removed to Bartlett, N. H. *Hon. Silas Meserve* and *Capt. Isaac Meserve* were sons.

3. STEPHEN, m. ABIGAIL YEATON.
4. ABIGAIL, m. JAMES PINKHAM.
5. DEBORAH, m. MICHAEL EMERSON.
6. PAUL, m. MARY PINKHAM.
7. ISRAEL, m. SARAH GERRISH.

THE WIGGIN FAMILY.

(MEMORANDA NOS. 261-262.)

The name WIGGIN is a common one only in New Hampshire, and is seldom met with out of New England. The neighboring town of Stratham has, for nearly two centuries, been the home of the family. THOMAS WIGGIN was the first of the name in this country. He was the business manager of the first settlement on Dover Neck, in 1633. He was styled GOVERNOR, just as Walter Neal was called Governor at Strawberry Bank.

GOVERNOR THOMAS WIGGIN had two sons, ANDREW and THOMAS. The maiden name of his wife is not known; her Christian name was CATHERINE. He was probably married about 1636. He lived on Dover Neck for several years, until he changed his residence to what is now Stratham, on the shore of Great Bay. After that his son Thomas occupied the homestead on Dover Neck, and was in business with Dr. Barefoot, later known as Lieut. Gov. Barefoot, when New Hampshire was made a separate province after having been a part of the Massachusetts Bay Colony for forty years. The exact date of the birth of his sons is not known, but it would appear that Andrew was born about 1635, and Thomas about 1640. This appears by their respective depositions taken in 1700, which are preserved.

Upon the union of Dover with Massachusetts in 1642-3, Wiggin was appointed a Magistrate. He was Deputy for Dover in the General Court, in 1645; and from 1650 to 1664, was one of the Assistants to the Massachusetts Governor, the only one during that time for New Hampshire. He was one of the leading men of the Massachusetts Bay Colony during life. Gov. Wiggin died about the year 1667.

ANDREW, the eldest son of Gov. Thomas, was born, as above stated, about the year 1635. He married HANNAH BRADSTREET, daughter of Gov. Simon Bradstreet, of Andover, Mass., about the year 1659. Her mother was Ann Dudley, daughter of Gov. Thomas Dudley. Her mother was celebrated for her accomplishments, and poetical genius. A small volume of her poetry was published, and was the first effort of the American Muse to be given to the public through the press; the work was highly praised in England.

On the 4th of June, 1663, Thomas Wiggin and Catherine, his wife, gave to their son, Andrew, "in consideration of his late marriage with Hannah, daughter of Simon Bradstreet, of Andover, Esquire," a deed of "all that our land" called or known by the name of Quamscutt, being three miles square, or thereabouts."

Mr. Wiggin was not much in public life, but in private life he appears to have been highly regarded, and considered as a sort of Patron of Squamscot, now Exeter. As such and especially as one who guarded his own interests as well as the interests of the colonists, he was occasionally in collision with Mason, and his friends, who were trying to get control of the land. Walter Barefoot (the first doctor on Dover Neck), was one of Mason's friends, and so connected, by marriage, with Mr. Wiggin's brother, Thomas, as to make the controversy between them very bitter. In June, 1667, Barefoot entered a complaint against Wiggin, for beating and bruising him in the public highway, and robbing him of a pistol and several writings of great concernment. Both parties were bound over to appear at Court, one to prosecute, the other to answer. In September there was a solemn trial, which left the whole case, and the whole Court, very much in the dark, as appears from the record: "The Court finds that the charge is not proved in all the particulars of it; but finding that the said Andrew Wiggin thrust the said Barefoot into a gully, and did after that, in another place, upon some words passing between them, turn towards said Barefoot and face him, and suddenly thereupon both were seen upon the ground scuffling, and said Barefoot demanding his pistol of said Wiggin, which said Barefoot said he had taken from him, and which this Court doth suspect the said Wiggin did take from him, the Court judges the said Wiggin to have broken the peace." They sentenced Wiggin to pay a fine of ten pounds, which was immediately afterwards reduced to five pounds and costs.

Mr. Wiggin died in 1710, at the age of 75. His wife died about three years before him. His children were:

1. SIMON.
2. THOMAS.
3. ANDREW.
4. JONATHAN.
5. ABIGAIL.
6. MARY.
7. DOROTHY.
8. SARAH.
9. A DAUGHTER, who was the wife of SAMUEL WENTWORTH; Christian name unknown.

SIMON,[3] son of ANDREW, and grandson of GOV. THOMAS, was born 17 April, 1764. The name of his first wife, who was mother of his children, is not known. His second wife was CATHERINE, widow of Robert Tufton, grandson of Captain John Mason, who took the name MASON. She was his cousin, being daughter of his uncle, Thomas Wiggin, and granddaughter of Gov. Wiggin. Prior to the marriage, Capt. Simon Wiggin entered into a marriage contract with Catherine, which is duly recorded in the County Records. By this contract, dated 29 Oct., 1703, he agreed to take her "out of pure love," and "without anything beside her person," and relinquished all claim upon the property of her first husband. Capt. Wiggin died about the year 1720. His last wife survived him and died about 1738. In her Will she mentioned her daughter, Elizabeth, wife of Walter Philbrick, and her grandsons, John Tufton, Thomas Tufton, and Tufton Philbrick. The children of Capt. Simon Wiggin by his first wife were:

1. HANNAH, who probably m. either WILLIAM COGSWELL, 15 Mar., 1722, or GEORGE VEAZEY, 17 Dec., 1719. Her cousin, Hannah, dau. of Thomas, before mentioned, presumably m. the other.
2. DEBORAH.

3. SIMON (LIEUT.), b. 12 Aug., 1701; d. 11 Aug., 1757. He m. SUSANNAH SHERBURNE, who was b. 13 Mar., 1703; d. 9 July, 1763.

THEIR CHILDREN.

1. SIMON, ESQ., b. 4 Mar., 1734; m. HANNAH MARBLE, of Bradford, Mass., 22 July, 1756; d. 11 Oct., 1823. His wife d. 9 Nov., 1811, aged 75. Their children were: 1. *Captain Simon*, b. 5 Jan., 1749; m. Joanna Thurston, of Exeter, who was b. 15 Sept., 1765, and of their children were: William Henry, who m. Mary Ann Shackford, and Sarah Jane. 2. *Ann*, b. 15 Apr., 1760, wife of Noah Robinson, Esq., of North Hampton. 3. *Sarah*, b. 5 Jan., 1762, wife of Daniel Holton, of Newmarket, and mother of Nancy, and of Charlotte, wife of Dr. Odell. 4. *Hannah*, b. 24 Sept., 1764, wife of John Smith, of Exeter. 5. *Betty (Elizabeth)*, b. 1766; wife of Benjamin Clark, and mother of Daniel and David Joseph Clark, of Manchester. Daniel graduated at Dartmouth College in class of 1834, and David J. in class of 1836; and Daniel was U. S. Senator, and Judge of the U. S. District Court. 6. *David*, b. 17 June, 1769, of Newmarket. His wife was Mehitable Robinson, and of his children were: Henry, Simon, Charles, Jeremiah, Robert, Deborah, and Ann. 7. *Jane*, b. 20 May, 1771, wife of Bradbury Robinson, of Greenland, and of Corinth, Me.

2. JOSEPH, of Concord, whose children were: *Sherburne*; *Sarah*, who m. a Herbert; *Nancy*, and others.

3. SARAH, wife of WILLIAM PERKINS, of Newmarket, had daughters: *Mary* and *Sarah*.

4. SUSANNAH, who m. a PRESBY, of Newmarket.

5. MARY, wife of HARVEY MOORE.

6. HENRY, of Newmarket, and of Tuftonborough. His first wife was a SHUTE, and his second, a HERRICK. Of his children were: 1. *Michael*, who m. Deborah Perkins. 2. *Henry, Esq.*, of Newmarket, who had three wives: Hannah Hill and Aphia Hill, daus. of Gen. Hill, and Olive Smith, by each of whom he had children. 3. *Lydia*. 4. *Betsey*, who m. a Copp.

7. THOMAS; he d. in the Revolutionary Army, in 1777. His wife was dau. of ——— JEWELL, ESQ., and his son was *Thomas*, of Newmarket.

HANNAH,³ daughter of ANDREW, was born 10 Aug., 1666, and was probably the one who married SAMUEL WENTWORTH, son of Elder William Wentworth. She died prior to the year 1704, and is not named in her father's Will; but her son, Samuel, had a legacy. This son was a merchant in Boston, and died about the year 1715, and his father administered on his estate, a part of which was inventoried land given to the deceased by his grandfather, Andrew Wiggin.

MARY,³ daughter of ANDREW, was born in 1668. She married CAPT. JEREMY GILMAN, son of Moses, and grandson of Edward Gilman, of Exeter. Among his descendants were Col. Samuel Gilman, of Newmarket, afterwards of Tamworth, who was trustee of Gov. Wentworth's estate on his leaving the State of New Hampshire in 1776; Israel Gilman, of Newmarket, David Gilman, of Tamworth, and Dea. Samuel Gilman, of Exeter.

ABIGAIL,³ daughter of ANDREW, married WILLIAM FRENCH, of Stratham.

DOROTHY,³ daughter of ANDREW, married a GILMAN.

SARAH,³ daughter of ANDREW, married WILLIAM MOORE; they had children: *William, Mary,* and *Jacob B.*

JONATHAN,³ son of ANDREW, married, and had children:

1. SARAH, m. a HILL.
2. ANN, m. JOSEPH JEWETT.
3. MARY, m. a PERKINS.
4. HANNAH, d. unm.
5. ANDREW, ESQ., who was b. 7 Mar., 1719; m., 12 Sept., 1751, DOROTHY SWEAT, who was b. 25 Jan., 1727. He d. in 1774. His children were: 1. *Andrew*, b. 14 July, 1752; d. 22 Jan., 1836; m. Mary Brackett, of Greenland, on the 29th of Jan., 1774. Their daughter, Mary, b. 9 Oct., 1780, was wife of George Hilton, Esq., of Newmarket, and mother of George O. Hilton. The second wife of Andrew was Mary, dau. of Hon. Payne Wingate, and of their children were: Capt. Caleb, who m. Eliza Adams, and Andrew P. 2. *Dorothy*, b. 13 Dec., 1757; wife of Rev. James Milti-

more, of Stratham. 3. *Levi*, b. 8 Nov., 1760; had wife, Jane, and children: Caleb M. and William. 4. *Caleb*, b. 4 Jan., 1763. He was lost at sea, leaving no children. 5. *Aaron*, b. 12 Jan., 1776. 6. *Mary*, b. 26 Nov., 1767, wife of Thomas Boardman.

HON. ANDREW,[3] son of ANDREW, and grandson of Gov. THOMAS, was born 6 Jan., 1671-2. He married twice; name of his first wife is not known. He married (2) RACHEL (CHASE) FREESE, widow of James Freese, 4 Jan., 1737; she survived him. He was speaker of the House of Representatives; Judge of Probate; Judge of the Superior Court of the Province. Judge Wiggin died in 1756. His children were:

1. HANNAH, who m. a BURLEY.
2. MARTHA, who m. a RUST.
3. ABIGAIL, wife of ———— DOE, of Newmarket.
4. MARY, wife of THEOPHILUS SMITH, ESQ.
5. MERCY, who m. a SHERBURNE.
6. JONATHAN. Of his children was: 1. *Capt. Jonathan Wiggin*, b. 19 Jan., 1740; m., 10 Oct., 1761, Mary Little, of Newbury, Mass., and his children were: 1. Elizabeth, b. 10 Oct., 1762, wife of Stephen Thurston. 2. Mary, b. 30 July, 1767; wife of Levi Barker. Capt. Wiggin m. (2) Mehitable Thurston, and his children by her were: 1. Edmund, of Thomaston, Me., b. 1772. 2. Mehitable, b. 1773; wife of Samuel Marble. 3. Abigail, b. 1775; wife of Thomas Chase. 4. William H., of Thomaston, Me., b. 1776. 5. Sally, b. 1778; wife of a Sinclair. 6. Clarissa, b. 1780; wife of Stephen Boardman. 7. Augusta, b. 1782. Mrs. Wiggin d. 14 Nov., 1784. After her death, Capt Wiggin m. (3) Mary ————, who survived him. He d. in 1810.
7. BRADSTREET,[4] son of HON. ANDREW, m. PHEBE SHERBURNE; he was a prominent citizen of Stratham. They had six children: 1. *Andrew*, b. 5 May, 1737. 2. *Mary*, b. 5 Apr., 1739. 3. *Abigail*, b. 20 Feb., 1741. 4. *Martha*, b. 20 Feb., 1743. 5. *Bradstreet*, b 18 Apr., 1745. Of these:

ANDREW,[5] married, 15 Oct., 1760, MARY JEWETT WEEKS, widow of Walter Weeks. She was daughter of Joseph and Anna Wiggin Weeks, and Anna Wiggin was daughter of Jonathan Wiggin; she was born 6 Oct., 1733. Her husband died, 16 Sept., 1778. She survived him, and died 24 Jan., 1834, aged 100 years, plus three months. Their children were:

1. ANNA, b. 26 July, 1762; m. THEOPHILUS SMITH, ESQ.
2. NATHAN, (ESQ.), b. 20 Feb., 1763; m., 12 Mar., 1786, MEHITABLE NORRIS, of Pembroke, dau. of Capt. Benj. Norris and Sarah, his wife, who was dau. of Capt. Thomas Wiggin, of Stratham. Mrs. Wiggin was b. 5 Mar., 1766. They had children: 1. *Zebulon*, postmaster of Stratham, who m. Mary Odell. 2. *Mary*, wife of Nicholas Chase. 3. *Nathan*, who m. (1) Hannah Fellows, of Bridgewater; (2) Mary Cross, of Andover. 4. *Benjamin*, who m. Mary Hoag. 5. *Mehitable*, of whom there is no record. 6. *James J.*, of Exeter, whose wife was Nancy P., dau. of Daniel Wiggin. 7. *Walter*, who m. Charlotte, widow of Dr. James Odell. 8. *Andrew N.*, who m. Sarah Messer, of Salem. 9. *Mark*, of whom there is no record. 10. *Hiram*. 11. *Sally Ann*, wife of Mark Roberts. 12. *Nancy W*. 13. *Uriah*, whose wife was Ruhamah Clark, of Petersham, Mass.
3. PHEBE, b. 1 Mar., 1765; wife of PHINEAS MERRILL, ESQ., of Stratham.
4. ANDREW, ESQ., b. 8 Oct., 1768; m., 31 May, 1798, DOLLY WIGGIN; d. 28 July, 1838. His wife was dau. of David Wiggin, of Greenland, b. 11 Nov., 1777. Their children were: 1. *Dolly W.*, wife of David Smith, of North Hampton. 2. *Andrew M*. 3. *Josiah B., Esq*.
5. LYDIA, b. 8 Mar., 1771; m. NATHANIEL HOYT, of Moultonborough.
6. JEWETT, b. 7 Oct., 1775; m. DEBORAH, dau. of Jonathan Piper. Their children were: 1. *Mary*, wife of John Lucy. 2. *Olive L.*, wife of Benjamin Moulton. 3. *Martha*, wife of John T. G. Cate, of Northwood. 4. *Benjamin F.*, who m. Ruth Davis, of Lee. 5. *Sarah B*. 6. *Abner*. 7. *Edwin*, who m. Mary Ann Jones, of South Hampton. 8. *Jonathan*.

MARY,[5] daughter of BRADSTREET and PHEBE, born 5 April, 1739; was wife of DANIEL WILSON.

ABIGAIL,[5] daughter of BRADSTREET and PHEBE, born 20 Feb., 1741; was wife of TIMOTHY MURRAY, of Newmarket.

MARTHA,⁵ daughter of BRADSTREET and PHEBE, born 20 Feb., 1743; was wife of JOHN STOCKBRIDGE.

BRADSTREET,⁵ son of BRADSTREET and PHEBE, born 18 April, 1745. He married JUDITH HARDY, who was born 8 Jan., 1746, and their children were:

1. PHEBE, b. 10 Aug., 1769.
2. POLLY, b. 1 Mar., 1771.
3. NANCY, b. 29 Nov., 1772.
4. PATTY, b. 4 Jan., 1774.
5. HENRY, b. 14 Aug., 1776.
6. THOMAS, b. 11 Mar., 1778.
7. SHERBURNE, b. 22 Sept., 1780.
8. JOHN, b. 17 Apr., 1783.
9. JUDITH, b. 8 June, 1785.
10. DOROTHY, b. 17 June, 1787.
11. BETSEY, b. 1789.

HANNAH,⁵ daughter of BRADSTREET and PHEBE, born 5 Feb., 1752.

BRADSTREET,³ son of ANDREW, was born 25 March, 1675-6; he married 21 Aug., 1697, ANN CHASE, daughter of Joseph Chase, of Hampton. She was born 9 Jan., 1676-7. Mr. Wiggin died 18 Jan., 1708-9; their children were:

I. CHASE. b. 19 Oct., 1699; m., 9 Jan.. 1723, MARTHA WEEKS, dau. of Joshua Weeks, of Greenland; he d. 24 July, 1733. His widow m. Col. Winthrop Hilton, of Newmarket, 9 Dec., 1736; d. 31 Mar., 1769, aged 65. The children of CHASE and MARTHA WIGGIN were:

1. BRADSTREET, b. 25 Nov., 1724; m. MARY COKER. Their children were: 1 *Coker.* 2. *Winthrop,* of Greenland, b. 17 Mar., 1749. 3. *Chase,* b. 1 Sept., 1751; he m., 10 Nov., 1774, Molly Perkins, who was b. 17 Sept., 1775, and they had children: 1. Bradstreet, b. 3 May, 1776. 2. Chase, b. 21 Sept., 1778. 3. Winthrop, b. 19 Apr., 1781. 4. Martha R., b 14 Nov., 1783. 5. Richard R., b. 23 Jan., 1786. 6. Molly, b. 12 Apr., 1788. 7. Joshua P., b. 2 June, 1790. 8. Comfort, b. 15 May, 1792.

2. COMFORT, born 5 Dec., 1727, m. BRADSTREET GILMAN, of Epping, and of her children were: *Dudley*, of Gilmanton; *Chase*, of Epping; *Bradstreet*, unmarried; *Martha*, m. —— Peas; *Comfort*, m. —— Merrill.
3. CHASE, born 12 July, 1730; married 19 May, 1757, MARY PERKINS, a grand-daughter of Jonathan Wiggin. They had children:

  1. BRADSTREET, b. 24 July, 1762; lived in Bradford, Vt.
  2. CHASE, b. 19 Dec., 1764. Had children by first wife: *Martha, Mary*, and *Samuel;* by second wife: *Charlotte, Nancy* and *Sarah*.
  3. MARY, m. GILMAN GALE, of Kingston, and afterwards m. GEORGE HALLIBURTON, of Exeter. Her children by her first husband were: 1. *John*, surgeon in U. S. Army. 2. *Enoch*, of Albany, N. Y. 3. *Amos*. 4. *Charles C. P.*, of Yale College, 1826.
  4. MARTHA, m. SAMUEL CALEF.
  5. NANCY, m. REV. JOHN PRENTICE, of Northwood. Children: 1. *Matilda*, m. Samuel B. Buzzell, of Northwood. 2. *Mary Ann*, m. Abraham Perkins, of Durham. 3. *Martha H.*, m. Dudley F. Tucker, of Deerfield. 4. *Hannah*, m. Rev. Samuel Merrill. 5. *Tryphene C.*, m. Greenville Remick.

4. JOSHUA, born 13 July, 1773, married ELIZABETH LYFORD; their children were:
  1. BETSEY, m. JOHN GIDDINGS.
  2. THEOPHILUS, who d. at Philadelphia, in the Revolutionary War.
  3. DEBORAH, m. EDWARD HILTON, of Newmarket.
  4. ANN, m. CALEB THURSTON.
  5. JOSHUA, m. COMFORT WIGGIN, dau. of Jonathan. Children: *Joshua, John, Chase, Stephen, Albert, Elizabeth* m. Nathan Morrill, of Corinth, Me.
  6. DOLLY, m. SAMUEL DOE, of Parsonsfield, Me.
  7. MARTHA, m. BENJAMIN HALEY.

II. MARTHA, m. (1) DR. RUST, and (2) JOSHUA WEEKS, by whom she had children:

  1. GEORGE W.
  2. MARTHA, m. THOMAS PICKERING.
  3. MARY ANN, who married a PICKERING.

III. THOMAS born, 15 March, 1701-2. Of his children was Mark, who married a daughter of Capt. Brackett, of Greenland, and removed to Wolfeboro.
IV. ELIZABETH, born 23 Aug., 1704; she married BENJAMIN TAYLOR.
V. JOSEPH, born 30 March, 1707; died suddenly, in 1788. His first wife was SUSANNAH BAKER, and their children were:

1. JOSEPH, of Greenland, b. 10 Sept., 1788; m. MERCY ODELL, and left but one child, *Chase*, of Greenland, b. 26 Feb., 1765.
2. DAVID, of Greenland, b. 27 Aug., 1741; d. 9 Feb., 1814; m. DOROTHY WINGATE, dau. of Joshua Wingate, of North Hampton. She was b. 26 Dec., 1741; d. 10 Aug., 1800. Their children: 1. *Susannah*, b. 9 Mar., 1766; wife of John Dearborn. 2. *Love*, b. 14 Feb., 1768; wife of Levi Clark. 3. *James*, b. 30 July, 1771; m. Betsey Brown. 4. *Dolly*, b. 11 Nov., 1777; wife of Andrew Wiggin, Esq. 5. *Benjamin*, Esq., b. 30 Nov., 1779; d 21 Jan., 1815; m. Elizabeth Chase, of Stratham, and lived in Alton. Children: Benjamin, Elizabeth, and Mary J., wife of Dr. Beech, of Sharon, Ohio.
3. BENJAMIN, ESQ., of Hopkinton, b. 14 Feb., 1743. He had three wives: (1) MARY CLEMENT; (2) ELIZABETH CLEMENT; (3) DOROTHY HOLT. Of his children were: *Benjamin* and *Timothy*, eminent merchants of the city of London; *Joseph*; *Ellen*, m. Baruch Chase; *Betsey*, m. William Little; *Mary*, m. Samuel Greenleaf.
4. CHASE, b. 14 June, 1745; m. TABITHA PIPER. Their children: *Ezra* and *Joseph*. Mr. Wiggin and some of his family joined the Society of SHAKERS, and d. among the Brethren of that society.
5. MARTHA, b. 9 Jan., 1748; m. DANIEL FRENCH.

JOSEPH,[4] son of BRADSTREET and ANN, married (2) PATIENCE PIPER, and they had nine children:

1. PAUL, b. 10 Feb., 1754; m. a HILL, and had children: *Mark*, *Joseph*, and *Phebe*, who m. Francis Piper of Tuftonborough.
2. NOAH, b. 28 Sept., 1755. He was of London. His wife was LYDIA GOSS, of Greenland; they had: *Nathaniel*, *Lydia*, *Joseph*, *Thomas*, and *Mary*.

3. SUSANNAH, b. 11 May, 1757; m. STEPHEN WIGGIN.
4. ANNA, b. 12 July, 1759.
5. JONATHAN, b. 20 Apr., 1763. He was of Warner, and d. about 1840.
6. WILLIAM, b. 10 Sept., 1764. He was of Warner, and afterwards of Bradford.
7. ELIZABETH, b. 25 July, 1767; wife of ZEBULON DOE, of Newmarket. She was afterwards of Warner. Her children were: *Deborah, Nancy* and *Elizabeth*.
8. THOMAS, b. 31 Mar., 1768; m. ELIZABETH LEAVITT, and had children: 1. *Nancy*, wife of Samuel Hatch, Jr., of Greenland. 2. *Mary H.*, wife of Nathan Brown, of New York. 3. *Deborah*, wife of Amos Davis. 4. *Eliza*, wife of Josiah Brown, of Boston. 5. *Jane*. 6. *Dolly*. 7 and 8. *Two sons*.
9. PATIENCE, b. 26 May, 1769, of whom there is no further record.

DESCENDANTS OF THOMAS[2] WIGGIN.

THOMAS,[2] son of GOV. THOMAS, was born at Dover Neck about the year 1640. He married SARAH BAREFOOT, sister of Dr. Walter Barefoot; for several years they (Thomas and Walter) were in partnership in the sawmill and lumber business, while Thomas was resident of "Captain's Hill," on Low Street, on Dover Neck. In a deed from Walter Barefoot to Thomas[2] Wiggin, dated 27 June, 1762, the grantor speaks of the grantee as his brother, and again, in another deed, he speaks of him as his "brother-in-law." The tradition is that Thomas's wife was a strict observer of Christmas, and other Church of England festivals, and was a zealous friend of that Church.

It is interesting to note the account, in the first volume of Provincial Papers, that while Barefoot was Deputy Governor, and Mason the Governor, and they were in the Governor's residence at New Castle, Thomas[2] Wiggin and Anthony Nutter visited the Governor, to protest against his prosecuting his claims, as Proprietor of New Hampshire. At that time the brothers-in-law took opposing sides of that question; Wiggin was violently opposed to Mason's claim. The report says that Wiggin and Nutter called to see the Governor, for the purpose of discussing the matter. After supper, being in the kitchen, they talked the question over; finally, Wiggin treated the Governor with so little deference, that the Governor ordered him out of the house. Instead of going, he told Mason he had no business in the Province, owned not a foot of land in it, and never should own any; whereat the Governor was so much provoked that he opened the door, and took Wiggin by the arm to thrust him out, but Wiggin, being, as the Governor afterwards deposed, "a tall, big man," took Mason by the collar and threw him upon the fire, in the big fireplace, and held him there till the live coals scotched his feet and stockings, as well as his periwig. Upon Barefoot's interfering, to get the Governor out of the fire. Wiggin released the Governor, who was sufficiently roasted, and thrust the Deputy under the forestick; in which operation two of his ribs were broken, and one of his teeth knocked out. The Governor ordered the house-servant to bring his sword but Nutter snatched it out of his hands, and kept walking around, laughing at the sufferers, while Wiggin was toasting them in the fireplace.

Mr. Wiggin resided on Captain's Hill, Dover Neck, the larger part of his life, but in later years resided at Sandy Point, Great Bay, where, it is supposed, his father died, and where he also died in 1700, or early in 1701. His children were:

1. CATHERINE, who m. ROBERT TUFTON; after his death she became the wife of her cousin, CAPT. SIMON WIGGIN.
2. SARAH, wife of HENRY SHERBURNE.
3. SUSANNAH, wife of ―――― JOHNSON.
4. THOMAS, of Sandy Point, who d. 7 Mar., 1726-7. He was m., name of wife not known. They had children: 1. *Elizabeth.* 2. *Deborah*, m. ―――― Doe. 3. *Sarah*, m. ―――― Stevens. 4. *Bridget*, m. ―――― Evans. 5. *Joseph*, who d. about the year 1749, leaving a widow, and two children: John, b. 3 Nov., 1743, and Joseph, b. 7 Nov., 1747. 6. *John*, who d. 11 Mar., 1749, aged 49 yrs. His wife was Martha Savory, of Bradford, Mass. She d. 2 Jan., 1803, aged 85 yrs. Their son:

STEVEN[4] was born 9 May, 1746; died 4 Nov., 1820. He married twice: (1) SUSANNAH, daughter of Joseph Wiggin. She died 27 June, 1808. Her children were:

1. LYDIA (SCAMMON), b. 28 Feb., 1777.
2. JOHN, b. 9 Feb., 1779.
3. SUSANNAH (SINKLER), b. 13 Apr., 1782.
4. JOSEPH, b. in Mar., 1785.
5. STEPHEN, b. 20 July, 1787.
6. HENRY, b. 24 Nov., 1789.
7. BENJAMIN, b. in 1791.

STEVEN married (2) HANNAH, daughter of Nathaniel Wiggin; their children were:

1. AMMI RUHAMA.
2. ANDREW JACKSON.
3. MARTHA ABIGAIL.

WALTER,[3] son of THOMAS and SARAH, was born about the year 1701. His wife was MARY RAWLINS, a sister of Andrew Rawlins; their children were:

1. JONATHAN, was of Newmarket.
2. WALTER, b. 27 Mar., 1733. His first wife was MARY THOMAS, of Boston, and his children by her were: 1. *Sarah*, b. 18 Oct., 1736; married Joseph Cate, of Greenland. 2. *Mary*, b. 16 Feb., 1700. 3. *Rachel*, b. 9 Apr., 1762; m. Wm. Boardman, of Newbury. 4. *Ann*, b. 4 June, 1764; m. Andrew Cate, of Greenland. 5. *George*, b. 27 June, 1776, was of Chelsea, Mass. 6. *Charlotte*, b. 12 Oct., 1768; m. Thomas Durgin. WALTER WIGGIN's second wife was DEBORAH NEAL. Children by her were: 7. *Deborah*, b. 15 Nov., 1771. 8. *Olive*, b. 4 May, 1773.

HENRY,[3] son of THOMAS, lived for sometime near the powder mill, at Exeter. Name of wife unknown. Of his children were:

1. JOSEPH, who went to Vermont.
2. JOSHUA, a blacksmith, who also went to Vermont.
3. NATHANIEL, was of Stratham.

ANDREW,[3] son of THOMAS, was of Newmarket. His wife was ELIZABETH RAWLINS, and they had at least:

1. WINTHROP, b. 26 Dec., 1744; was of Kensington. He was a soldier in the Revolution. He m. WIDOW ELIZABETH JONES, originally ELIZABETH THORNDIKE, of Beverly, Mass. Their children were: 1. *Olive.* 2. *Winborn Adams,* m. Emma Hobbs, of Portland, and their only child, Caroline, m. Mr. Gove. 3. *Hepsibah,* m. Moses Brown, of Newburyport.

MOSES,[4] son of ANDREW, was of Wolfeboro, married COMFORT FOSS, of Stratham. Their children were born in Stratham, before they removed to Wolfeboro, and were:

1. BETSEY, b. 23 Feb., 1767.
2. ISAAC, b. 16 June, 1769.

CHASE,[4] son of ANDREW, was of Wolfeboro; married ELIZABETH CHAPMAN, of Newmarket, and had son *Chase,* and probably others.

ANDREW,[4] son of ANDREW, was of Wolfeboro, and married ZERUIAH GOODWIN, of Newmarket; their children were:

1. JAMES.
2. ANNA.
3. PAUL.
4. SUSANNAH.
5. MOSES.
6. ANDREW.

DAVID,[4] son of ANDREW, was of Lee. By his first wife, ABIGAIL DUTCH, of Newmarket, his children were:

1. CHARLES.
2. RUFUS.
3. DAVID.
4. ANDREW.
5. ABIGAIL.

By his second wife, MARTHA ROWE, his children were:

6. WARREN.
7. ASA.

GIDEON,[4] son of ANDREW, was a soldier in the Revolution, and died at Watertown, during the war, leaving no children.

TUFTON,[4] son of ANDREW, died probably about the first of the year 1779, as his Will was proved 31 March, 1779. His first wife was MARY CALLEY; they had children:

1. TUFTON, one of whose daughters was wife of Joseph Leavitt, of Exeter, and another dau. m. Mr. Bartlett, of Lee.
2. RICHARD, whose children were: *Theodore* and *Daniel*.
3. BENJAMIN, of Tuftonborough.

TUFTON's second wife was SARAH DARLING, and his children by her were:

4. JUDITH, b. 5 Feb., 1768.
5. MEHITABLE, b. 28 Aug., 1773.
6. SALLY, b. 1774.
7. SAMUEL, b. 20 June, 1776.

SAMUEL,[3] son of THOMAS; his wife's name is not known; his children were:

1. MARY, b. 12 May, 1751.
2. ANN, b. 1753.
3. PHINEAS, b. 1757.
4. ELIJAH, b. 1760.
5. ANDREW, b. 1762.
6. ABIGAIL, b. 1765.
7. LYDIA.
8. HANNAH, b. 1771.

CAPTAIN THOMAS,[3] son of THOMAS, married SARAH PIPER, 17 Dec., 1719; and had at least:

1. THOMAS, b. 13 Sept., 1720. His wife was DOLLY, and of his children were: *Joshua, Thomas, Herbert, John*, of Northwood, whose wife was a Durgin, and whose children were: 1. John, whose wife was Charlotte Batchelder, and their son, Henry Batchelder, was b. at Northwood, 23 May, 1813; graduated at Dartmouth College in 1838; in 1840 he became principal of Glasgow Academy, Ky.; became Baptist minister in 1843, serving in the church at Union, Ky.; later he was principal of the Acad-

emy at Green River, Ky.; in 1867 he was at Rochester, N. Y. He m. Jane M. Mohon, of Butler, Ky., Mar. 3, 1842. 2. Polly, m. Joseph Durgin. 3. Lydia, m. John Moore. 4. Betsey, m. Miles Durgin. 5. Andrew. 6. Sarah. 7. William. 8. Elijah.

NATHANIEL,[4] son of CAPT. THOMAS, was born 16 Oct., 1729. He married HANNAH FIFIELD, who was born 17 March, 1734, and died 29 March, 1782. He died 25 Nov., 1824. His children were:

1. DAVID, b. 16 Nov., 1756. His wife was HANNAH, dau. of Nicholas Rollins, Esq., and their children were: 1. *Hannah*, b. 1784. 2. *Sally*, b. 1785. 3. *David*, b. 1786. 4. *Thomas*, b. 1788 He was of Northwood; deacon of the church; m Abigail Lane; d. 1838. 5. *Nancy*, b. 1790. 6. *Daniel*, b. 1791. 7. *Shadrach*, b. 1793. 8. *Betsey*, b. 1794. Mrs. Wiggin d. 23 Dec., 1794. Mr. Wiggin m. (2) Elizabeth Huntress; their children were: 1. *Lydia*, b. 1797. 2. *Mary*, b. 1798. 3. *Abigail*, b. 1801. 4. *George*, b. 1803. 5. *Olive*, b. 1805. 6. *Nathaniel*, b. 1806. 7. *Gideon*, b. 1809. 8. *Martha*, b. 1811. 9. *Levi*, b. 1814. 10. *Sarah*, b 1816. 11. *James*, b. 1818. Mr. Wiggin d. in June, 1824, aged 68 yrs., leaving 19 children.
2. LYDIA, dau. of Nathaniel and Hannah, was b. 30 Sept., 1758. She m. THOMAS VEAZEY.
3. ABIGAIL, b. 11 Mar., 1761; never m.
4. SARAH, b. 8 Nov., 1763; never m.
5. NATHANIEL, b. 11 June, 1766; m. NANCY SIMPSON, of Greenland; d. in 1803, leaving one child, *Ira W.*, of Durham.
6. STEPHEN, b. 7 Dec., 1768; m. NANCY, widow of his brother, Nathaniel.
7. HANNAH, b. 19 Feb., 1778; was second wife of STEPHEN WIGGIN, son of John Wiggin.
8. POLLY, b. 13 Mar., 1782; never m.

JOSIAH,[4] son of CAPT. THOMAS, was of Newmarket, and his children were:

1. LEVI.
2. JOSIAH.
3. MARY.
4. BETSEY.
5. NANCY.

HENRY,⁴ son of CAPT. THOMAS, was of Parsonsfield, Me.

SAMUEL,⁴ son of CAPT. THOMAS, married ANNA PARKS of Bradford; he died in 1797. His children were:

1. SAMUEL, of Ossipee.
2. THOMAS, of Vermont.
3. ANNA, wife of ———— URIN.
4. DANIEL, b. 1759; d. July, 1832. His wife was MARY, dau. of Walter Wiggin. She was b. in 1760, and their children were: 1. *Anna P.*, m. James J. Wiggin. 2. *Mary*, m. Daniel Wiggin.

ABIGAIL,⁴ daughter of CAPT. THOMAS, was born 28 Aug., 1737, and married STEPHEN PIPER, 20 June, 1754.

SUSAN,⁴ daughter of CAPT. THOMAS, married JONATHAN JEWETT.

MARY,⁴ daughter of CAPT. THOMAS, married JOHN DOE, of Newmarket; they afterwards removed to Parsonsfield, Me.

SARAH,⁴ daughter of CAPT. THOMAS, married BENJAMIN NORRIS, of Pembroke.

Soon after Gov. John Wentworth came into office and commenced his work of starting Wolfeboro, the various branches of the Wiggin family began to migrate to that town, and to Tuftonborough, Moultonborough and Ossipee, and many of their descendants live there at the present time. One of the families was SAMUEL⁴ and his wife ANNA (PARKS), of Bradford, Mass. They were married about 1756, and settled in Ossipee before the beginning of the Revolution. Their youngest son was SAMUEL, born about 1775; Dec. 8, 1805, he was united in marriage with Miss Susan Fisher, daughter of Col. Janvrin Fisher, of Dover. The marriage ceremony was performed at Rochester, by Rev. Joseph Haven. Haven's record says "both of Dover," but they resided in Ossipee, on the home farm; and there their children were born, viz:

1. SALLY FISHER, b. Sept. 6, 1806; d. Dec. 10, 1862.
2. JANVRIN FISHER, b. July 30, 1809; d. Mar., 16, 1880.
3. SAMUEL L., b. July 14, 1814; d. Feb. 26, 1860.
4. JOSEPH HENRY, b. June 6, 1817.
5. CHARLES WILLIAM, b. July 17, 1822; d. May 8, 1894.

By courtesy of Mr. Harry Mortimer Wiggin, of Dover, the only surviving member of this line of the Wiggin family, we are permitted to complete the genealogy of the family.

SAMUEL,[5] who was born about 1775, and married SUSAN FISHER, in December, 1805, resided in Ossipee, where all his children were born, the youngest of whom was Charles William Wiggin, born July 17, 1822. The father appears to have died before 1830, and when this youngest son was about ten years old the family removed from Ossipee to Dover, which had then become a flourishing manufacturing town. In the Directory of 1837, the elder brothers are recorded as "saddle, harness and trunk makers, at 101 Main Street," and their mother, Susan Wiggin, widow, was "inn-keeper at Garrison Hill." She occupied a large, fine old mansion, standing in the early years of the twentieth century, and known as the "Wiggin house." In a later Directory, it is called "Wiggin's Hotel, Garrison Hill, Susan Wiggin, widow," proprietor. Her sons became merchants, and were among the leading business men of the town.

CHARLES WILLIAM, the youngest son, born in 1822, was educated in the public schools and Franklin Academy. He got his business training in the store of his brother, Samuel, so that, in 1848, the Directory reads: "Charles W. Wiggin, firm of S. L. Wiggin & Co." He was then 26 years old, and was so well established in business that he became united in marriage with MARY ABBA BROOKS, daughter of Oliver and Susan (Horn) Brooks; the marriage ceremony was performed August 17, 1848, by Rev. I. G. Foreman, assisted by Rev. E. G. Brooks, brother of the bride; his portrait is in the Woodman Institute; their elder brother was the great and famous locomotive builder, in New York. Mrs. Wiggin was born Nov. 18, 1823; she died Sept. 17, 1913, aged 89 years and ten months. Mrs. Wiggin was a most excellent woman and remarkably vigorous to the very last year.

Charles William Wiggin remained in business with his brother for a while, then set up business for himself, and so continued till his death, May 8, 1894; for more than a half a century he was one of the leading business men of Dover, the later years being engaged in the furniture business. Most of the time he was located on the corner of Main and Chapel Streets, where (in 1923) Lothrop Brothers have their piano store and warehouse. Mr. Wiggin had the building erected about 1860, taking the place of two older buildings, which his elder brothers occupied prior to 1840. Mr. Wiggin's mother, daughter of Col. Janvrin Fisher, of Dover, died March 8, 1862, aged 74 years. For more than thirty years she had been a widow, but possessed so much vigor and business capacity that she was not only of great assistance in the management of her sons' affairs, but possessed of a good estate at her death.

The children of CHARLES WILLIAM and MARY ABBA (Brooks) WIGGIN, were:

1. ALICE FISHER, b. May 15, 1850; d. Aug. 12, 1889. She m. SPENCER K. SEWELL, Sept. 2, 1874; no children.
2. FRANK BROOKS, b. Apr. 6, 1853; d. July 15, 1874.
3. HARRY MORTIMER, b. June 7, 1858; m., Mar. 28, 1883, CARRIE BROOKS TUFTS, in Buffalo, N. Y. She d. Jan. 17, 1890. He m. (2), at Alton, Oct., 30, 1901, EUNICE LEILA HANSON; he has no children, and is the last of the Wiggin family, in his line.
4. EMMA GERTRUDE, b. Dec. 30, 1860; d. June 27, 1863.

THE RANDALL FAMILY.
(MEMORANDA No. 202.)

Early Randalls were found both in Massachusetts and New Hampshire. The New Hampshire branch settled at Great Island (New Castle).

1667, Jan. 14, Edward Randall had a grant of land there, on the usual terms, viz: that he should build a house upon it within a year. In 1670 it appears he had not complied with that provision, and was therefore to pay twenty shillings for the land. He, or another Randall, bought house and land of Nathaniel Frier, Oct. 8, 1712.

JAMES RANDALL was on the minister's tax-list at Strawberry Bank, in 1671, and in 1672 was on a committee to consult about getting a minister. On Aug. 30, 1672, he agreed to build for Nathaniel Frier "six frames for dwelling houses," for which Frier conveyed to him certain land at the head of Sagamore Creek. In 1688 he was one of the Selectmen. In 1689 he had charge of building a pound. In 1698-9 he was appointed administrator of his brother's estate; the brother was Peter Randall, of New Castle. In 1712 he was Representative from New Castle. In 1719, by Will, he gave his estate to his only son, JAMES, and his daughters, MARY (Talton) and CATHERINE (Jordan). A Rye record says it was Elias Talton, of New Castle, who married a Randall, of New Castle, and inherited a hundred acres of land, moved to Long lane, and had a son, Elias; that Mary's sister married a Jordan, and inherited another hundred; also, Mrs. Talton's brother, James, had a son who had three sons, viz.:

1. MARK, who m., 24 Nov., 1748, ABIGAIL PHILBRICK, and moved to Moultonborough, having children: 1. *James*, b. 1750. 2. *Moses*, b. 1751. 3. *Elizabeth*, b. 1755. 4. *Mark*, b. 1757. 5. *Simeon*, b. 1760. 6. *John*, b. 1762. 7. *Deborah*, b. 1764. 8. *Samuel*, b. 1766. 9. *Daniel*, b. 1770. 10. *Olly*, b. 1772. 11. *Hannah*, b. 1778. 12. *Sally*, b. 1780.
2. WILLIAM, m., 24 Apr., 1745, HANNAH MARSTON, a schoolmistress; lived in Rye, and had children: 1. *James M.*, b. 1746. 2. *William*, b. 1748; lived in Greenbush, N. Y. 3. *Mary*, b. 1750; m. Joseph Morse, and lived in Chester. 4. *Stephen*, b. 1753. 5. *Joseph*, b. 1756, who lived in Deerfield, and had son, Francis D. 6. *Jonathan*, b. 1759; m. Elinor Osgood, and went to Cabot, Vt. 7. *Lucy*, b. 1767; m. a Carr, and lived in Chester. 8. *Samuel*, b. 1670.
3. PAUL, m., 4 Feb., 1752, HANNAH ADAMS, and had: 1. *Paul*, b. 1751. 2. *Hannah*, b. 1759. 3. *Abigail*, b. 1762.

The following is taken from the Rye records: JOHN RANDALL had children:

1. JOHN, b. 1745.
2. ABIGAIL, b. 1747.
3. JAMES, m. MARY SHERBURNE, 15 Nov., 1748.

GEORGE RANDALL married, 18 July, 1751, SARAH BERRY, and had children:

1. SARAH, b. 1752.
2. SARAH, b. 1754.
3. EDWARD, b. 1758, who was lost at sea in time of the Revolution.
4. GEORGE, b. 1762; m. ELIZABETH BERRY.
5. RACHEL, b. 1765; m. JOHN MACE.
6. ABIGAIL, b. 1769; m. JOHN, son of Levi Goss.
7. WILLIAM B., b. 1771; m. DEBORAH, dau. of Joseph Yeaton.

GEORGE, son of GEORGE, married ELIZABETH BERRY, and had children:

1. MARY, m. JOSEPH HALL.
2. EDWARD, d. at sea.
3. BETSEY, who m. (1) ROBERT MATHES; (2) JOHN DAVIS.
4. SAMUEL, who m. BETSEY SMITH.
5. WILLIAM, who m. SALLY JOHNSON.
6. LOVE, who m. (1) SAMUEL HEALEY; (2) SAMUEL ROBINSON.

These are evidently descendants of James. The Exeter records also show that a James Randall (probably the son named in the first James's Will), was dead in 1731; that his widow, Deborah, was appointed to administer, and that Deborah, widow of James, conveyed property, in 1771, to James Marston Randall, of Rye.

SAMUEL RANDALL, of Dover, bought, 21 Feb., 1726-7, land at Salmon Falls, of Joseph and Elizabeth Roberts. Samuel married Elizabeth Mayfield, in Dover, 30 Nov., 1720.

RICHARD RANDALL, of Dover, deeded to Richard Tozer, of Berwick, 15 Aug., 1711, "all claims in behalf of my wife, Elizabeth Torr," daughter of Richard Torr, deceased. On 21 Jan., 1712-13, he conveyed land in Kittery to his sons, Richard and William.

THE RANDALL FAMILY.

Who Elder Benjamin Randall's grandfather was, no record shows. Benjamin stated that his grandfather came from England. The Elder's father was:

BENJAMIN RANDALL, whose mother appears to have been Mary, daughter of Shadrack Walton, who was Colonel, Chief Justice, and for many years senior member of the Provincial Council. He was born in New Castle, 13 Jan., 1726. He was a sailor, and for many years a shipmaster, in foreign trade. In the latter part of his life he removed to Ossipee, N. H., where he died 22 Jan., 1790. His wife was Margaret, daughter of Benjamin Mordantt, who was a native of either Jersey or Guernsey, and a shipmaster. She was born in New Castle, 17 Oct., 1730. After the death of her husband she went to New Durham and lived with her son, Elder Benjamin Randall. Their children were:

1. BENJAMIN, b. 26 Feb., 1749.
2. MARY, m. DANIEL RANDALL.
3. SALLY, d. unm.
4. JACOB, m. NANCY HARTFORD.
5. BETSEY, b. 1761; m. JOHN BUZZELL.
6. JOHN, lost at sea; unm.
7. WILLIAM, lost at sea; unm.
8. MARGARET, m. (1) WILLIAM LYONS, who d. in 1801; (2) EPHRAIM LEIGHTON; she d. without issue, at the house of Mr. Joseph Hall, in Barnstead, 24 Feb., 1838.
9. MIRIAM, m. THOMAS DAVIS, and had six children.
10. SHADRACK W., whom we suppose to be named for his great grandfather, Shadrack Walton, who m. POLLY BERRY, of Lemington, Me.

BENJAMIN, the Elder, who early in life was a sail-maker, and afterwards a minister and founder of the *Free Will Baptist* Denomination, was born in New Castle. He removed to New Durham, worked on his farm, and preached until his death, Oct. 22, 1808. His wife was JOANNA, daughter of Robert Oram, a shipmaster, at New Castle; she was born in Kittery, Me., Feb., 1748, and died in New Durham, 12 May, 1826. They were married 28 Nov., 1771. Their children were:

1. ROBERT ORAM, b. in New Castle, 3 Dec., 1772.
2. MARY SHANNON, b. 24 Feb., 1774; m. JOSEPH HALL, of Barnstead.
3. BENJAMIN WALTON, b. 4 May, 1776.
4. MARGARET F., b. 8 Aug., 1778; m. STEPHEN PARSONS.
5. URSULA PINKHAM, b. 15 Oct., 1780; m. SAMUEL RUNNELLS.
6. WILLIAM, b. 30 Oct., 1782; m. LOVE MURRAY.
7. JOANNA, b. 24 Oct., 1785; m. TIMOTHY HORNE, of New Durham.
8. HENRY ALLEN, b. 10 Feb., 1788.

MARY, sister of the Elder, married (1) her cousin, DAVID RANDALL, and had children.

1. BETSEY.
2. ABIGAIL, who m. ELIJAH JACKSON, of Canterbury, and had: *Mary* and *David*. Mary m. (2) Henry Munsey, and had Henry, who m. Olive Davis.

JACOB, brother to the Elder, lived and died in Saco. His wife was NANCY HARFORD. Their children were:

1. BENJAMIN, who d. at sea.
2. JOHN, a sailor.
3. JOSEPH.
4. JACOB.
5. NANCY, who m. JAMES MAXWELL, of Saco.
6. DOLLY, who m. (1) ROBERT BROOKS (and had *Margaret, Harriet,* and *Ann*); and m. (2) a SHUTE.

BETSEY, sister of the Elder, married JOHN BUZZELL, who was born about 1760, and died in 1841. She died in Effingham, in 1805. They had:

1. MARY, b. 26 Dec., 1790; m. ISRAEL LEIGHTON, and had children: 1 and 2. A *son* and *daughter*, who d. young. 3. *John Buzzell*, b. 24 Aug., 1826. 4. *James Twombly*, b. 22 Apr., 1829. 5. *Mary Elizabeth*, b. 24 Nov., 1832. 6. *Elizabeth*, b. 8 June, 1834; m. John Sanders; d. 26 Dec., 1850, having had eight children.

THE RANDALL FAMILY.

ROBERT ORAM, eldest child of the Elder, removed to Hardwick, Vt., then to Danville, then to Ohio. He died at Morgan, Ind., 23 Oct., 1848. His first wife was HANNAH DAVIS, born in Nottingham, N. H., Feb., 1771; died 7 Jan., 1826. His second wife was WIDOW HANNAH WEBBER, of Ohio, who died before him.

MARY SHANNON, second child of the Elder, married JOSEPH HALL, of Barnstead, N. H.; he was born in Strafford, 8 July, 1767, and died in Barnstead, 27 April, 1844. She died in Barnstead, 23 Feb., 1845. Their children were:

1. BENJAMIN RANDALL, m. (1) SUSAN MASON; (2) SARAH VANCE, having children: *Oram R.*, *Lorenzo*, and *Joseph Varney*.
2. SALLY WILLIAMS, m. GEORGE QUINT, ESQ., of Dover, N. H., and had one child: *Alonzo Hall Quint*.
3. ABIGAIL, m. JOSEPH DREW, and had two children.
4. SUSAN MASON.
5. JOSEPH, of Barnstead, who m. ELIZABETH DREW, and had four children.
6. JOANNA R., b. 1 May, 1808; m. DEA. HENRY GRAY, of New Durham.
7. URSULA R., b. 17 Aug., 1811; m. DARIUS WINKLEY, of Barrington.

BENJAMIN WALTON, third child of the Elder, lived in New Durham; married 12 March, 1801, SALLY PARSONS; he died in New Durham, 24 Sept., 1843. Their children were:

1. JOSIAH PARSONS.
2. SARAH SEWELL.
3. WILLIAM SWEET.
4. MARY SAVAGE.
5. BENJAMIN.
6. JOANNA ORAM.
7. HENRY SARGENT.
8. JAMES JENKINS.
9. SEWELL.

MARGARETTA F., fourth child of the Elder, married 29 Oct., 1801, STEPHEN PARSONS, of Edgcomb, Me. Their children were:

1. LYDIA D.
2. LUCY KNIGHT.
3. URSULA R.
4. STEPHEN.
5. JOSIAH P.
6. SARAH SEWELL.
7. MARGARETTA F.
8. JOANNNA ORAM.
9. HARVEY.
10. QUINCY ADAMS.

URSULA PINKHAM, fifth child of the Elder, born 15 Oct., 1780, married SAMUEL RUNNELS. They had children:

1. MARGARET.
2. URSULA.
3. SAMUEL DANA.
4. BENJAMIN PAUL.
5. JOANNA.
6. MARY.

WILLIAM, sixth child of the Elder, married LOVE MURRAY, and was a resident of Dover, where he died 28 Jan., 1845, and had:

1. MARY, m. JOSEPH HAM, and lived at Garrison Hill. Children: 1. *Marie Teresa.* 2. *Edward.* 3. *Joanna*, m. William Gray. 4. *Love.*

JOANNA, seventh child of the Elder, married TIMOTHY HORNE, lived at New Durham; had seven children.

HENRY ALLEN, eighth child of the Elder, married (1) ELIZA SHEPARD; (2) MARY ANN CLARK; they had seven children. He resided in Charlestown, Mass.

THE HEARD FAMILY.

(MEMORANDA No. 331.)

JOHN HEARD signed the DOVER COMBINATION of 1640. In March, 1648-9, John Heard had lot No. 8, in Cochecho Fresh Marsh assigned him. He does not appear on the tax-list of 1648, but does appear on that of 1657, and on lists following. During that time there was another John Heard living in Old Kittery, now Eliot, who made his Will, which was proved in 1676, but John Heard, of Dover, did not die till 1689. This shows that there were two Heards by the name of "John." They lived on opposite sides of the Newichawannock River.

JOHN,[1] of Kittery, made Will 3 March, 1657; probated Feb., 1676-7. Mentions wife ISABEL; gives portions to grandchildren, Mary and Elizabeth, daughters of his deceased son, James, and three younger grand-daughters, Katherine, Abigail and Ann, all of whom were under 18 years of age; gives farm to grandson John, then not married; mentions his daughter-in-law, widow of James. His son:

JAMES,[2]. The last known record of him is in 1668, and his wife was certainly a widow in 1676. The Will of his father calls James's wife, Susanna, but she is also called Shuah. She married, before 5 Nov., 1677, the first Richard Otis, of Cochecho; for on that date, "Richard Otis, husband of Shuah, formerly widow of James Heard, son of John Heard, of Piscataqua," and James Chadburne, undertook to administer on estate of said James Heard. Yet York County records show that John Clements, of Dover, 16 May, 1695, was appointed to administer on the estate of his father-in-law, James Heard. James[2] appears to have had:

1. JOHN, b. 1667.
2. MARY.
3. ELIZABETH, m. SAMUEL SMALL.
4. KATHERINE.
5. ABIGAIL, who m., 28 Feb., 1688-9, the second JOB CLEMENTS, of Dover.
6. ANN.

JOHN,[3] son of JAMES, had Richard Otis for his guardian. Pike's *Journal* says he was wounded, in Kittery, by the Indians, 4 July, 1697, when his first wife, PHEBE, and others, were killed. He married (1) PHEBE LITTLEFIELD, killed as above; married (2), July, 1698, JANE, daughter of Nicholas Cole, and widow of Joseph Littlefield. She died, and he married (3), ANN WINGATE, widow of Capt. John[2] Wingate. At that marriage he is called Captain. He made his Will 16 Jan., 1739, being "aged and weak."

It was probated in 1751. He died on his grandfather's farm, at Sturgeon Creek. He left property to children of James[4], deceased; to daughters, Dorcas (Tucker), Shuah (Bartlett), Phebe (Stevens) and Abigail (Hubbard); to children of his daughter, Jane (Coffin) deceased; and to grandsons, John Heard Bartlett and John Heard Hubbard. Son-in-law, Nathan Bartlett, executor.

JOHN[3] had by first wife:

1. DORCAS, b. 26 Feb., 1690; m. HUGH TUCKER.
2. PHEBE, b. 25 Jan., 1692-3; m. THOMAS STEVENS.
3. SHUAH, b. 25 Jan., 1694-5; m. NATHAN BARTLETT, and had twelve children.
4. JAMES, b. 21 Jan., 1696-7; m., and d. before 1739, leaving *Sarah* and *Phebe*.

JAMES[3] had by his second wife:

5. JANE, b. 18 June, 1699; m., 15 Nov., 1719, CAPT. TRISTRAM COFFIN, of Dover, son of Tristram and Deborah (Colcord) Coffin. She was his first wife; his second wife was mother of Debby Coffin.
6. MARY, b. 24 Aug., 1700; m., 1 July, 1722, HENRY BAXTER.
7. ABIGAIL, b. 15 Apr., 1702; m. a HUBBARD.

THE HEARD FAMILY OF DOVER.

JOHN[1], 5 Dec., 1662, received a grant of 50 acres of "upland under ye Great Hill at Cochechae, on ye soueth sied of the great Hill, beloe the Cartway, at the secont desent of the great hill, and soe to the southward fiftie poell in Breathe and Eightie scoer in lenkth." Also, 26 Feb., 1665, 40 acres, "to the northward of the half-way swampe, on the north side of which is a 20 acre lot granted to James Ordway, and soe forty Roedd in Breadth, by the Cartway, or paeth wich goeth to ye marsh, and 168 Roed in lenketh." This must be the date of laying out, inasmch as a grant of 40 acres, to Elder Wentworth, 5 Dec., 1652, on the north side of this John Heard lot, mentions Heard, cartway and swamp, and all. Capt. Heard gave it to his son Benjamin.

CAPT. JOHN[1] built his house on the grant first mentioned above. He was called "Captain" Heard because he was commander of ships in the foreign trade of Dover, while in business connection with Capt. Richard Walderne. While he was in the shipping business his residence was on Dover Neck, where Capt. (later Major) Walderne, lived twenty years, till he moved his family to the house he had built on the hill, where National block now stands. Capt. Heard appears to have come up here about 1655, having built his house and retired from the foreign shipping business. By ancient tradition it stood on the brow of Garrison hill, where a brick house now stands (1923). About 1675, when the Indians began to be dangerous, he had a stockade placed around it, and it became known as "Heard's garrison." The next garrison below was that of Richard Otis. The next was the Waldron garrison.

Of the five garrisons near the falls, that of Capt. Heard was the only one saved in the massacre of 28 June, 1689. By some incredible folly two squaws were allowed to sleep before the kitchen fire, in each garrison, although fears of Indian troubles had sent many persons into the garrisons each night for safety. Early in the morning the squaws opened the gates of the stockades, and let the Indians in, while the families were fast asleep. Elder Wentworth, and his family, were at Heard's garrison. Just as the Indians were about to enter a dog barked, and awakened Elder Wentworth; he arose and closed the gate, just as the Indians were about to enter; he fell upon his back and held the gate closed till other members of the household came to his aid. The Indians fired several bullets through the door, but no one was hit.

This garrison-house was long the frontier post. A letter dated 26 March, 1690, says: "Heard's garrison at Cochecho being the frontier & only Garrison on the North side of the river, having left three men, one killed and two wounded in the late fight at Salmon Falls, etc."

Pike's *Journal* says: "Jan. 17, 1688-9, Master Heard deceased after a short sickness." His Will, made 2 April, 1687, was proved in 1692. He mentions his wife, Elizabeth, and children, Benjamin, Tristram, Samuel, Dorcas, Nathaniel, Mary (Ham), Abigail (Jones), and Elizabeth (Nute). There was trouble about this will, afterwards. Tristram petitioned, 7 March, 1703-4, being the only surviving son, saying that his father, John[1] "left no legal Will"; but Sarah, wife of William Foss, formerly widow of Nathaniel Heard, asserted that the estate had been divided according to the Will.

CAPT. JOHN[1] married, about 1643, at York, Me., ELIZABETH, daughter of Rev. Joseph Hull. She is said to have been born at the rectory, at North Leigh, Devonshire, England. Mr. Hull was at one time minister at Oyster River (1662). Elizabeth was a "brave, gentle woman." Her remarkable escape, when she came up the river at night, June 28, 1689, "with one daughter and three sons, & all masters of families," is narrated by Cotton Mather. Although urged to secure safety at Portsmouth after the massacre, she continued stoutly to hold her frontier garrison all through the war. She died, 30 Nov., 1706. Pike's *Journal* says: "Old widow Heard (commonly called Dame Heard) deceased after a short illness with fever. She was a grave and pious woman, even the mother of virtue and piety." Her children were:

1. BENJAMIN, b. 20 Feb., 1643-4.
2. WILLIAM, d. about 1675. His property went half to his widow and half to Edward Leathers. We know of no children.
3. MARY, b. 26 Jan., 1649-50; m. the first JOHN HAM, of Dover.
4. ABIGAIL, b. 2 Aug., 1651; m. JENKON JONES, of Dover.
5. ELIZABETH, b. 15 Sept., 1653; m. (1) JAMES NUTE, JR.; m. (2) WILLIAM FURBER, JR.
6. HANNAH, b. 22 Nov., 1655; m., 6 Nov., 1674, JOHN NASON.
7. JOHN, b. 24 Feb., 1658-9; not mentioned in his father's Will.
8. JOSEPH, b. 4 Jan., 1661-2; not mentioned in his father's Will.
9. SAMUEL, b. 4 Aug., 1663.
10. TRISTRAM, b. 4 Mar., 1666-7.
11. NATHANIEL, b. 22 Sept., 1668; he d. 3 Apr., 1700, "after four days sickness with violent fever." His grave stone is standing in the Waldron burial ground, east of the Methodist church. It is the oldest marked stone in Dover burial grounds. His widow, SARAH, m. William Foss, 26 Apr., 1703. Nathaniel had son, *James*, b. 1696; m., Mar. 22, 1720, Mary Roberts.
12. DORCAS, b. 1670; m. JABEZ GARLAND.

BENJAMIN², son of CAPT. JOHN, was admitted freeman (given the right to vote) 21 June, 1669; he was 26 years old; probably he got married about that time, to ELIZABETH ROBERTS, daughter of Gov. Thomas Roberts, of Dover Neck. And probably he had a house ready for the bride near where the present Guppy house stands, as his father had a grant of that land from the town, before 1652. In due time he gave it to his son Benjamin. In place of the first cabin he built the present Guppy house, in 1690. He lived there till his wife died, and his son Benjamin got married. In 1697, Benjamin, Sr., removed to Salisbury, Mass. He may have married there, but that is not probable; he was then 54 years old. Benjamin, Jr., was left on the farm. Pike's *Journal* says Benjamin, Jr., died "of violent fever, 10 Feb., 1698-9," aged 24 years. It is reasonable to suppose his father came back and took care of the property. Benjamin, Sr., died in February, 1710; in his Will, dated Jan. 20, 1710-11; probated Feb. 21, 1710-11, he gave to his son, James, "all his lands and livings at Dover, located at Fresh Creek, provided he pay all debts appearing against him (Benjamin) in New Hampshire." Benjamin, Sr., had received the land, by his father's Will, described as follows: "the 40 acres of land where he now lives, and is possessed of according to the right and title I have to said land by virtue of the town grant." The town grant describes it as follows: "Forty acres to the northward of the halfway swamp, on the north side of which is a 20 acre lot granted to James Ordway, and soe forty Roed in Breadth, by the cartway, or path wich goeth to ye Marsh and 160 Roed in lenketh." On March 10, 1665, James Ordway and wife, Ann, had sold this lot to John Heard, thus making it a part of the Guppy farm.

BENJAMIN² and wife, ELIZABETH, had, at least, three children:

1. BENJAMIN, b. in 1673. *Pike's Journal* says: "John Heard, Jun., died of malignant fever 10 Feb. 1696-7," only 24 years old.
2. ANNA, b. 1675; she was captured by the Indians, 25 Jan., 1691-2, being on a visit at York; she returned later, but we have no further record of her.

3. JAMES, b. about 1680; he d. in 1748; his Will was proved 31 Jan., 1749, in which he mentions wife, DEBORAH, and children: 1. *Benjamin.* 2. *Mary*, m. William Twombly. 3. *Lydia*, m. Paul Harford. 4. *Hannah*, m. Thomas Peirce.

On page 12, Vol. 1, of "Dover Historical Collections," is recorded:

"1. BENJAMIN HEARD, son of JAMES HEARD, by his wife Deborah, borne August 2, 1715.
2. MARY HEARD, dafter of James Heard, borne in September, 1717.
3. LYDIA HEARD, Dafter of James Heard, by his wife Deborah, born Feb., 1720.
4. PHEBE HEARD, Dafter of James Heard and wife Deborah, born 13 Dec., 1722.
5. JAMES HEARD, son of James Heard and wife Deborah, born May 6, 1725.
6. HANNAH HEARD, Dafter of James Heard and wife Deborah, bapt. June 14, 1730."

SAMUEL,[2] son of CAPT. JOHN, married in 1686, EXPERIENCE OTIS, daughter of Richard[1] Otis; she was born in 1666. His father, 20 March, 1685-6, conveyed to him thirty acres. "Whereas there is an intention of marriage between Samuel Heard, son of John Heard, of Cochecho, yeoman, and Experience Otis, spinster, daughter of Richard Otis, etc." On the same day Richard Otis, for the same reason, conveyed to his daughter, Experience, twenty acres of good upland. They had several children, one of whom was John.

Pike's *Journal* says that Samuel[2] Heard died of malignant fever, 20 Feb., 1695-6; and his widow, Experience, was scalped by the Indians, 26 July, 1696. She recovered, and married William Jenkins, by whom she had one child. She died Feb. 8, 1699, "chiefly from her wound bleeding."

JOHN[3], son of SAMUEL, born 1692, was but four years old when his father died, and but eight when his mother died. July 2, 1706, when he was 14, he chose his uncle, Tristram, as his guardian. No more is recorded of him.

TRISTRAM[2] lived, we think, northeast of the Great Hill; he owned land over there. There was an ambush "betwixt Tristram Heard's and Ephraim Wentworth's, upon the north side of the Hill," 28 May, 1703. In 1711, on a Sabbath day, several people fell into an ambush, as they were returning from meeting, and John Horn was wounded and Humphrey Foss was taken captive, "but by the determined bravery of Tristram Heard he was recovered out of the hands of the enemy." He had wife, ABIGAIL. The notes to Farmer's Belknap says he was killed by the Indians, in 1723, but this is a mistake; his son *Tristram,* was the one killed. TRISTRAM made his Will 18 April, 1734; probated 3 June, following. He gave property to wife ABIGAIL; to sons *Joseph, John,* and *Samuel,* and to daughters, *Elizabeth (Knight), Mary (Warren),* and *Keziah (Wentworth);* to daughter-in-law, *Jane,* who afterwards married Benjamin Hayes, formerly widow of his son, *Tristram;* to grandchildren, *John, Jane, Tristram,* and *Reuben,* all children of his deceased son, *Tristram,* and to grandchildren, *Mary* and *Nathaniel,* children of his son, *Nathaniel.* Wife, and son, *Samuel,* executors. He had children:

1. JOSEPH, b. 15 Feb., 1692-3; living in 1734. A Joseph Heard, in Newington, m., 9 Aug., 1722, REBECCA RICHARDS, of Newington.
2. TRISTRAM, b. 26 Mar., 1695.
3. NATHANIEL, b. 26 Jan., 1696-7.
4. JOHN, b. 1 Jan., 1700.
5. ABIGAIL, b. 15 Apr., 1702; not mentioned in her father's Will.
6. SAMUEL, b. 28 Feb., 1703-4.
7. ELIZABETH, b. 8 Feb., 1706-7; m. a KNIGHT.
8. MARY, b. 10 June, 1709; m. a WARREN.
9. KEZIAH, b. 1 Dec., 1712; m. (1) SPENCER WENTWORTH, of Dover; m. (2) CAPT. THOMAS PEIRCE, of Portsmouth.

SAMUEL,[2] son of CAPT. JOHN, had wife RUTH, and they had children, baptized in First Church: *Experience, Elizabeth, Jane,* and *Samuel;* nothing further is known concerning the family.

TRISTRAM,[3] son of TRISTRAM, and wife ABIGAIL, married JANE SNELL; he was killed by the Indians in the summer of 1723.

His widow married, as early as 1726, Benjamin Hayes, and had six children. The children of TRISTRAM and JANE were:

1. JOHN, b. 20 July, 1718.
2. JANE, b. 12 Nov., 1719.
3. REUBEN, b. 9 Mar., 1721.
4. TRISTRAM, b. 5 Dec., 1723.

NATHANIEL,[3] son of TRISTRAM and ABIGAIL, was dead in 1734; perhaps he was the Nathaniel Heard who died in Salem, 9 Feb., 1730. He was married, but his wife's name is not known. His children were:

1. MARY; date of birth not known; but she was living in 1734.
2. NATHANIEL; date of birth not known, but he was living in 1734.

BENJAMIN,[4] son of JAMES and DEBORAH; was born August 2, 1715; he married MARY ———; they resided on the home farm of his grandfather, Capt. Benjamin,[2] it having been bequeathed to him by his father's Will; it does not appear they had children. April 16, 1767, he and Mary sold the house and farm to Capt. James Guppy.

BENJAMIN[2] gave his farm to his son, BENJAMIN, who died in a few years; then it was given to his brother, James, who, by will, gave it to his eldest son Benjamin; in April, 1767, this Benjamin sold the property to Capt. James Guppy.

The following, on record, cannot be connected with preceding generations:

May 9, 1782, JONATHAN HEARD married SARAH YEATON.

Jan. 6, 1785, TIMOTHY HEARD married MARY DAME, both of Rochester.

May 2, 1803, ABRAHAM HEARD married PATTY MCDUFFEE, both of Rochester.

June 25, 1815, ISAAC HEARD married MARY HUSSEY, both of Rochester.

Feb. 27, 1817, JOHN HEARD, JR., married ELIZABETH KNOWLES, both of Rochester.

Feb. 1, 1818, TRISTRAM HURD married SARAH HURD.

Dec. 3, 1818, JOHN HURD, of Tuftonborough, married SUSANNA HURD, of Rochester.

May 3, 1792, JONATHAN HEARD, JR., married HANNAH JENNESS.

Nov. 28, 1799, WILLIAM HURD married MARY GARLAND.

Oct. 20, 1805, REUBEN HURD, JR., married MOLLY VARNEY.

Feb. 20, 1812, WILLIAM HURD married FANNY BAKER.

When TRISTRAM^2 built his house is not known, but as he was born in March, 1667, and married in 1690, he probably built the house before that date. When Tristram made his Will, in 1734, he appears to have been living on the ancestral homestead on the west side of Garrison Hill, and his son John, who was born in 1700, was living in the house on the north side of the hill.

JOHN^3 married CHARITY DAY, and had children:

1, 2, 3. (TRIPLETS), WILLIAM, PAUL, and EBENEZER, b. 24 Oct., 1735; d. in infancy.
4. JOHN, bapt. 31 Oct., 1736.
5. WILLIAM, bapt. 15 Oct., 1738.
6. JOSIAH, bapt. 27 Sept., 1741.
7. DAVID, bapt. 10 Oct., 1745.
8. JOSHUA, bapt. 14 May, 1749.
9. JACOB, bapt. 10 July, 1753.

JOHN^3 died in 1765, and his son JOHN was appointed administrator, 24 April, 1765; the appraisers reported the estate valued at 7,239 pounds and 10 shillings. On 27 Feb., 1760, JOHN^3 deeded to JOHN^4 "39 acres of land, laid out in Dover to my honored father, TRISTRAM HEARD." It is on record that JOHN^4 sold land in Rochester, to his brother, Josiah, in 1765.

JOHN,^{4} son of JOHN, married ABIGAIL WALDRON, sister of Col. John Waldron; they had several children, one of whom was:

EZEKIEL,[5] who was born in 1773, married his cousin, JO-ANNA WALDRON, daughter of Col. John Waldron, by his wife, Joanna Waldron, was born Sept. 1, 1775. EZEKIEL HEARD died 27 Feb., 1800, "of fever, aged 27 years." Their son:

EZEKIEL,[6] known as "Judge" Hurd, was born 3 Oct., 1797.

JUDGE EZEKIEL,[6] (a change of spelling the family name took place in his generation) was but two years and four months old when his father died, but he was well brought up, and when a good sized boy he was apprenticed to learn the "joiner's trade." He became a good workman, and when master of his trade engaged in house building. He was a large, fine looking man, resembling his grandfather, Col. John Waldron, of Revolutionary fame.

January 26, 1827, when he was in his thirtieth year, he was united in marriage with Miss MARY PICKERING HENDERSON, daughter of Thomas and Elizabeth (Hoyt) Henderson. About the same time he was appointed Justice of the Peace and Quorum, also deputy sheriff, which office he held several years, and was then made High Sheriff. About 1850 he was appointed Associate Judge of the Court of Common Pleas, in Strafford County. He held this office with dignity and efficiency, till he became cashier of the Cochecho State Bank, at its organization. He held this office till his death, 29 Oct., 1870.

In the Presidential campaign of 1828 there were two papers published in Dover,—the *Dover Gazette* and the *Strafford Inquirer;* the *Gazette* took the stand for Gen. Andrew Jackson, for President, and the *Inquirer* supported the re-election of President J. Q. Adams. John Tuttle Gibbs was editor of the former. Richard Kimball was editor of the latter, of which Samuel C. Stevens was publisher. Mr. Gibbs had been publishing the *Gazette* four years; Mr. Stevens commenced publishing the *Inquirer* Feb. 26, 1828, with Mr. Kimball as editorial writer. Of the two men, probably, Mr. Kimball was the better educated, but Mr. Gibbs had a sharp and crisp way of putting arguments into popular form. Mr. Kimball was a lawyer, and farmer, and late in life was known as Judge Kimball, being the first Judge of the municipal court. He was a good lawyer, just judge and progressive farmer.

Speaking of the *Strafford Inquirer* it seems well to state that in August, following its beginning, 26 February, Mr. Stevens sold the plant to George W. Ela & Co., and Mr. Ela changed the name to *Dover Enquirer*. It is not quite clear why Ela changed the spelling from *"Inquirer"* to *"Enquirer,"* as *"In"* is the correct way, instead of *"En,"* according to the derivation from the Latin language.

What has all that to do with Judge Ezekiel Hurd? Consider a moment and you will understand. Mr. Gibbs, in the *Gazette*, valiantly supported the election of General Jackson; Mr. Kimball just as valiantly supported the re-election of President Adams. Previous to this an aristocracy, and the intellectuals, alone, had determined the governmental personnel. Men went into training for the Presidency, and, as in a lodge, passed as a matter of course, from the Cabinet to the Vice-Presidency, and thence to the Chief Magistracy; so an office-holding class had grown up that felt secure in the life tenure. The discussions in the Dover papers were very sharp, and decidedly personal. The presidential campaign in New Hampshire commenced at the State election on March 11, when the Dover men lined up, in voting, as follows, For Governor John Bell (Adams man), 517; Benjamin Pierce (Jackson man), 235. The vote in Dover was the largest ever thrown here up to that time, as it was the largest ever thrown in the State. The whole number cast was 39,897, of which Pierce received 18,672, and Bell 21,149, with 76 scattering.

In the political drama of that portentious period of America's political history, Ezekiel Hurd took his stand with the Jackson party; he remained a Jackson Democrat to the end of life. He was always more of a business man than a politician; he was a success in business. He voted for Benjamin Pierce, for Governor; he voted for Benjamin' son, Frank Pierce, for President. He was Moderator in town meetings; chairman in Democratic party conventions; Selectman several times, when his party was in power; State Senator one term; and always a gentleman; *"suaviter in modo, fortiter in re."*

JUDGE HURD married (2) widow of Thomas Hanson Cushing, the noted bridge builder; the Judge died, 29 Oct., 1870. His stepdaughter, daughter of Mrs. Cushing, is the wife of Hon. John H. Nealley, ex-Mayor of Dover.

THE OTIS FAMILY.

The following story of the OTIS Family, in Dover, is a brief of the Genealogy of the Otis Family in general, as given in Vol. V of the New England Historical and Genealogical Register, in the year 1851, by Hon. Horatio N. Otis, of New York.

The emigrant ancestor was RICHARD OTIS, son of Stephen, and grandson of Richard Otis, of Glastonbury, County Somerset, England. He was born before 1626; he came over when he was about thirty years old and was admitted an inhabitant of Boston, in 1655; he then came to Dover, where he settled for life. By trade he was a blacksmith, and a good one, who could do all sorts of iron work. The town of Dover gave him a grant of ten acres in 1655. It was laid out on the south side of what is now Hill street, and between Central avenue and Park street. He built his house about where the present large, two-story house stands, a short distance in from Central avenue. After 1655, the town gave him a grant of 100 acres on the south side of Garrison Hill, then called the Great Hill. The present old house, known as the "Ham house," and the Garrison Hill green houses, are on that grant. Later he had a grant of fifty acres, on the west side of Central avenue, then called the "cart way." That grant covered the land on which the Christian Science Church stands. On this grant he built his second house, which stood where the house stands, on Mt. Vernon street, south of the church. When the Indian wars began he made it a garrison, by surrounding it with a high stockade, which enclosed a large yard, in which he had his blacksmith shop, etc. He resided there several years preceding the massacre of June, 1689; and his son, Stephen, lived in the house between Central Avenue and Park Street, it having been given to him by his father.

RICHARD OTIS was thrice married. (1), In England, ROSE STOUGHTON, daughter of Anthony Stoughton, and sister of Sir Nicholas Stoughton; their children:

1. RICHARD; date of birth not known; wife was SUSSANNA.
2. STEPHEN, b. 1652; m. MARY PITMAN, 16 Apr., 1674.
3. SOLOMON, b. 1663; d. 1664.

THE OTIS FAMILY. 457

 4. NICHOLAS, m.; was killed by the Indians, 26 July, 1696.
 5. EXPERIENCE, b. 1666; m. SAMUEL HEARD.
 6. JUDITH, m. ENSIGN JOHN TUTTLE, JR.
 7. ROSE, m. JOHN PINKHAM.

RICHARD married (2) SHUAH HEARD, widow of James Heard, of Old Kittery, who became a widow in 1676. No children by her.

RICHARD married (3) GRIZET WARREN, daughter of James Warren, of Kittery. Mr. Otis had his third marriage in 1685, when he was 60 years old. Had children:

 8. HANNAH, b. 1687; killed by the Indians, June 28, 1689.
 9. CHRISTINE, b. Mar., 1688-9; m., in Canada, ——— LE BEAU;
  (2) CAPT. THOMAS BAKER, of North Hampton, Mass.

RICHARD[2] was wounded by the Indians on Sunday, 26 July, 1696, as he, with others, was returning from public worship, when about at the junction of Milk Street and Central Avenue. The Indians were in ambush, shot upon them, and killed his brother, Nicholas, carrying away captive, Nicholas, Jr., to Penobscot.

He had a grant of land in Dover in 1694; he was a blacksmith. He was a member of the society of "Friends," having joined it after the birth of his second child. He is the ancestor of all those of the Otis name, who are descendants of Richard[1]. He was dead in 1701; his wife, SUSANNA, administered on the estate in 1702. His widow married, in 1703, JOHN VARNEY, but left no children by him. Children by first husband were:

 1. ROSE.
 2. RICHARD, who m. REBECCA ———, and was in Charlestown, Mass., about 1720.
 3. REBECCA.
 4. STEPHEN, b. 12 June, 1698; m. (1) MARY YOUNG, 30 Jan., 1719-20; m. (2) CATHERINE AUSTIN, July 30, 1736, dau. of Nathaniel and Catherine (Neal) Austin, who was b. 12 Jan., 1715; m. (3) ELIZABETH ———.
 5. NICHOLAS, b. 8 Feb., 1701; he settled in Newport, R. I.

STEPHEN[2] OTIS, born 1652; married MARY PITMAN, daughter of William Pitman, of Oyster River. He lived in the home place, between Central Avenue and Park Street. He was killed by the Indians June 28, 1689 (in the garrison fight). Children:

1. STEPHEN; carried prisoner to Canada in 1689; never returned.
2. NATHANIEL; carried to Canada and sold to the French; he m. a French girl, and had a family; never returned.
3. MARY; she was taken prisoner and carried as far as Conway, with the other prisoners, and there was rescued and brought home. She m. EBENEZER VARNEY, about 1693, and they built what is now known as the "Ham house," at the west side of Garrison Hill, about 1694 or 1695. The interior of the house has been remodeled, the big chimney having been removed. The papers are on file by which her brothers, in Canada, released, and transferred to Mary, all the rights they had in the property in Dover. These transactions fix the date of the building of the house.

NICHOLAS,[2] son of RICHARD, had a grant of land in Dover in 1694; as previously stated he was killed in 1696, on his way home from meeting on Sunday. His son:

NICHOLAS[3] was taken prisoner, when his father was shot by the Indians, and was carried to the Penobscot River, where the Indians had their camp; he soon made his escape and came back. No further record of him.

EXPERIENCE,[2] daughter of RICHARD. She married SAMUEL HEARD; see the Heard Genealogy. He died in 1696; she married (2) —— JENKINS. Her son, by HEARD, was named *John*.

JUDITH,[2] daughter of RICHARD, married Ens. JOHN TUTTLE, JR. He was murdered by the Indians, 17 May, 1712. For their children see Tuttle Genealogy.

ROSE,[2] daughter of RICHARD, married JOHN PINKHAM, son of RICHARD, the first of the name to settle in Dover. They had eight children. See Pinkham Genealogy.

CHRISTINE,[2] youngest child of RICHARD, was an infant of three months when he was shot by the Indians. She was born in the garrison, on Mt. Vernon Street, in March, 1688-9; she was carried prisoner in her mother's arms, to Canada; later, her mother married a Frenchman, in Montreal (named "ROBETAIL," the English pronounced it as if spelled "Rubetoy.") She never returned, but raised up a family of French children. The French priests took the child, and had her educated to become a nun; she declined to take the veil; at the age of sixteen she married a Frenchman, and had two or three children, then he died. Capt. Thomas Baker, while in Canada, on business of getting prisoners released (persons who had been captured by the Indians), met CHRISTINE, and secured her release; soon after that they were married, and returned to his home in Northampton, Mass. An extended biographical sketch of Mrs. Baker can be found elsewhere, in this volume.

The children of CAPT. THOMAS and CHRISTINE (OTIS) BAKER, were:

1. CHRISTINE, b. 5 June, 1716; m. CAPT. DUDLEY WATSON, of Dover.
2. EUNICE, b. 1718; m. DR. CHENEY SMITH, of Dover.
3. LUCY, b. 1720; m. JOSHUA STACKPOLE, of Somersworth, now Rollinsford.
4. CHARLES, b. 1722; m. (1) LOVE ———; (2) SARAH CARR, of Newbury, Mass., and widow of Francis Roberts, of Somersworth; d., at Somersworth, 26 Sept., 1784. His wife d. 21 Oct., 1807, aged 85.
5. MARY, b. 16 Feb., 1725-6; m. CAPT. BENJAMIN BEAN, of Epping, in 1753. She d. at Conway, 6 Feb., 1826.
6. OTIS, b. 1727. His full name was Otis Archelaus Sharrington, but when he became of age he dropped the two middle names. He m. (1) LYDIA, dau. of Dea. Gershom Wentworth; m. (2) TAMSEN, dau. of James and Mehitable Chesley, and widow of John Twombly. He d., at Dover, 27 Oct., 1801. She d. 6 Nov., 1801.
7. ALEXANDER DOUGLAS, b. 1729; did not m.; d. 23 Sept., 1756.

RICHARD,[3] son of RICHARD.[2] The probate record says Richard Otis, of Charlestown, Middlesex County, Mass., conveyed to Stephen Otis, his brother, of Dover, N. H., "all my right to land of my father, Richard Otis, or of my grandfather, Richard Otis, or of my uncle, Nicholas Otis." The date is 30 Oct., 1722. From the town and church records of Charlestown, it is found that his wife, GRACE, died 9 Dec., 1721; that a young child died 11 Dec., 1721. Where or when he died has not been ascertained.

REBECCA,[3] married RICHARD CANNEY, of Dover, and had:

1. OTIS, b. 23 Jan., 1718.
2. RICHARD, b. 11 Mar., 1720-21.
3. JUDITH, b. Mar., 1723.

STEPHEN,[3] son of RICHARD; married (1) MARY YOUNG, 30 Jan., 1719-20; married (2), 30 July, 1736, CATHERINE, daughter of Nathaniel and Catherine (Neal) Austin, born 12 Jan., 1715; married (3), ELIZABETH ———. He received, in 1721, at Dover, land granted to his father in 1694; and in 1722, all his brother Richard's right and title in the old estate. In 1733, measures were commenced by himself and brother, to recover some portion of the old estate, which they claimed by right of inheritance, and which from some cause had passed out of their hands. "Stephen Otis, of Dover, and Nicholas Otis, of Newport, R. I., tailor, for the recovery of lands belonging to our father, Richard Otis, and our grandfather, Richard Otis." They agreed to share in the expense. He lived in Madbury. Children by his first wife were:

1. JOSHUA, b. 1720; m. JANE HUSSEY, of Dover; settled in Barrington.
2. STEPHEN, b. in 1731; m. MOLLY ELWELL, of Barrington.
3. JOHN, b. 1735; did not m.; was soldier in the Revolutionary army.
4. SUSANNA, b. 1737; m. AARON DAVIS, of Madbury.

NICHOLAS,[3] was a ship-caulker, at Newport, R. I. He came to be commander of a ship, and was lost at sea. His son, *Nicholas*, was taken to Dover when a child, and brought up by relatives. He became a school teacher in Onondaga County, N. Y. He married CYNTHIA WINDSOR, of Providence, R. I.; they had several children.

MARY,[3] daughter of STEPHEN, married EBENEZER[2] VARNEY, son of HUMPHREY[1], who was son-in-law of Elder Edward Starbuck, by marriage to his daughter Esther. From records it is evident that Ebenezer Varney took possession of the Garrison Hill part of the Richard[1] Otis estate, about 1696, and built the house that now stands there. His wife secured her title through her father, fortifying her title by deeds from her brothers, in Canada. Title to the property was in dispute from 1689 to 1694, or 1695, caused by the Indian massacre. The house and farm remained in possession and occupation of the Varney family, 150 years, and then was sold to John Ham, who gave it to his son, Joseph Ham; from him it passed to his daughter, Theresa Ham, who sold it to her uncle, John Thomas Wentworth Ham. He permitted his niece to live in the house till her death, in 1917. Then Mr. Ham sold it to Mr. Charles Luke Howe.

It may be of interest to note that Hon. Job^6 Otis, of Strafford, who was one of the most noted men of his time, in that town, after it became separated from Barrington, in 1820, was son of Elder Micajah Otis, who was one of the founders of the Free Will Baptist Denomination; he was son of Joshua^4; Stephen^3; Richard^2; Richard^1.

The following are the facts, in brief, of the destruction of Richard Otis's garrison on the morning of 28 June, 1689, when Major Walderne's garrison, and others, were destroyed, and Richard Otis, and twenty-two others were killed, and twenty-nine persons taken away captives to Montreal, Canada, and sold to the French; they were the first persons ever sold by the Indians to the French. To get them back, their friends here had to go to Canada and pay the French a large sum for each individual prisoner.

While one party of Indians were ransacking Major Walderne's place, other parties were attacking the other garrisons, to which they had gained admittance by the Indian squaws, who unfastened the gates.

These garrisoned houses were surrounded with timber walls, the gates of which, as well as the house doors, were secured with bolts and bars. The neighboring families resorted to these houses at night, for safety. Two squaws were allowed, by Mr. Otis, to lodge in his yard. At some time between midnight and early dawn, the squaws opened the gate, and the Indian warriors entered. One account says Richard Otis was killed as he was rising up in bed, his son, Stephen, shot dead, and a child, Hannah, two years old, killed by their dashing her head against the brick chimney. Another tradition is, that Richard Otis was shot while looking out at a window, on the first alarm. Those of the family who were not killed, on the spot, were taken away prisoners. The prisoners appear to have been taken to Canada by different routes; Mr. Otis's wife, with her infant daughter, Christine, and two grandsons, Stephen and Nathaniel, were carried by one route, direct to Montreal; the other members of Mr. Otis's family, Judith and Rose, and his grand-daughter, Mary Otis, daughter of Stephen (who was killed), were taken by another route; at Conway this party was overtaken, and the prisoners were rescued, by a company of men who collected and pursued them.

As time passed on, later generations forgot where the garrison stood; tradition always held that it was in the vicinity of the west end of Milk Street, and on Mt. Vernon Street. In April, 1911, when workmen were digging a cellar for the house which stands near the Christian Science Church, on the south, various material came to light, which, on examination, proved to be relics of the burned garrison of Mr. Otis. Mr. Chester Snell Wendell, (who lived just across Mt. Vernon Street), took the matter in hand and made a careful examination of the debris of the workmen, and found a very interesting collection, which he later placed on exhibition in the Woodman Institute. One very remarkable relic was an ear of corn, which had been completely roasted; the kernels were perfect on the cob, bright and clean. Another gruesome relic was a bone of the leg of the child that was slain by the Indians, as above stated; one of the best informed surgeons in the city examined it, and said it was undoubtedly a bone from the limb of a child.

Those who are desirous of tracing later generations of the Otis family, are respectfully referred to Vol. V of the New England Historical and Genealogical Register, published in 1851.

THE SCALES FAMILY IN DOVER.

The SCALES FAMILY has been in Dover fifty-four years (1869-1923). JOHN SCALES, and his wife, ELLEN TASKER SCALES, took charge of Franklin Academy in May, 1869. The school was under their management for fourteen years. During that time the Academy reached its highest membership, one hundred students. During the fifteen years following, they were engaged in newspaper work, publishing (in partnership with Mr. Fred E. Quimby) the

Daily Republican and *Dover Enquirer,* until its sale in 1899 to Cook & Stone. Mr. Scales was editor, Mrs. Scales proof-reader and bookkeeper, and Mr. Quimby business manager.

After retiring from newspaper work, Mr. and Mrs. Scales were engaged in various literary activities, till her death, Dec. 29, 1920.. Mrs. Scales was a woman of marked ability; a first-class teacher, especially in mathematics; an accurate proof-reader; a good writer on historical and literary topics. Many valuable papers from her pen were read before the Northam Colonist Historical Society. She was member of the School Committee eight years, being the first woman to serve on the Dover Board. When the Wentworth Home was established, in 1898, Mrs. Scales was appointed one of the women Managers, and held the office continually till her death; during the last six years of her connection with the institution, she was President of the Board. She exercised a large influence in organizing The Wentworth Home, and in the management of its household affairs.

To Mr. and Mrs. Scales were born four children; three sons and one daughter; the daughter and youngest son died in childhood; the eldest son, *Burton True Scales,* was born August 10, 1873; he died Jan. 31, 1922, at his home in Philadelphia. Mr. Scales was prepared to enter Dartmouth College by pursuing the regular course in the Dover High School; he entered college in 1891, and graduated with his class in 1895, with honors. He was President of the class at the time of his death. In college he was managing editor of *The Dartmouth,* during the junior and senior years; member of the editorial staff of the *Dover Daily Republican,* 1895-97; made special study of music in Boston and New York, and was graduate of New School Methods in Public School Music. He was secretary of the N. H. Music Teachers' Association, 1896-9; instructor in music at the Plymouth, N. H., Normal School's summer sessions, 1898-1908; director of music, and aid to the headmaster of the William Penn Charter School for Boys, Philadelphia, Pa., from 1899 to 1914; director of music in Girard College, Philadelphia, 1914, till his death, 1922; director of the University of Pennsylvania Glee Club, and Mask and Wig Glee Chorus, 1910, till his death; lecturer at the Institute of Musical Art, New York City; instructor in the Music Department of the New York

University Summer School, 1908-1913; instructor in music at Cornell University Summer School, 1914-1920; in this way he became associated with the leading music teachers, directors and publishers in the Eastern Cities; he was highly esteemed by all and they were shocked by his sudden death.

In college, Mr. Scales was member of the D. K. E. Fraternity; Casque and Gauntlet Society; in Dover, of Moses Paul Lodge, A. F. and A. M.; in Philadelphia, of the Musical Art Club, and the Presbyterian Church. Received Degree of A. M. in 1920.

MR. SCALES married, Sept. 10, 1900, at Dover, MISS KATE HUBBARD REYNOLDS, daughter of Capt. Benjamin Oliver Reynolds, and his wife Catherine White, daughter of Hon. (Judge) John Hubbard White, and wife, Rebecca Peirce, daughter of General Andrew Peirce, the first Mayor of Dover. To Mr. and Mrs. Scales were born two children: *Catherine Bradstreet,* born Jan. 11, 1903; *Benjamin,* born 24 March, 1907; he is in the William Penn Charter School for Boys, and preparing to enter Dartmouth College in 1925, for which his father had him registered in 1920. The daughter is a graduate of the Holman School for Girls, Philadelphia; and the New York University School of Music, where she prepared to engage in the work of director of music, in public schools, following the vocation of her father.

ROBERT LEIGHTON SCALES, younger son of Mr. and Mrs. John Scales, was born 20 May, 1880; he died 31 Oct., 1912, at Roswell, New Mexico, where he and his wife, Laura Wolsey Lord, daughter of Prof. John K. Lord, were residing, in an endeavor to recover his health. He fitted for college in the Dover High School; was president of his class; during his senior year he edited and published a school newspaper; a copy of it was bound, and is on file in the Dover Public Library; he conducted the paper with marked ability and good judgment, as can be seen by reference to it in the library. Its name was *The Garrison.* His teachers rated him as one of the brightest and best members of his class.

Mr. Scales entered Dartmouth College in 1897, and graduated in the class of 1901; he pursued the classical course, and held high rank during the four years. He was especially noted for his unusual ability as writer and ready debater. On March 4, 1900, he delivered an original oration before the college, which won the

1866 prize for oratory. Professor Emerson said it was a delight to hear him roll off the words and express, with power, the sentiments of his topic. He was chief speaker in several debating contests with other college teams. For a season he was a member of the Dartmouth Dramatic Club, taking one of the leading parts in the plays that were rendered. Like his brother, he was member of the Delta Kappa Epsilon fraternity, and the Casque and Gauntlet Society. He did not engage in athletic sports. In his vacations and leisure hours he gave some attention to music, so that he could play the piano well, and sing with fine voice. Of his classmates were President Hopkins, of Dartmouth, and Gov. Cox, of Massachusetts.

For two years, 1902-1904, he was instructor in English, in Dartmouth College, following which he entered Harvard Law School, from which he was graduated in 1907, receiving the degree of LL. B. While an instructor at Dartmouth he gave much attention to training the boys to win in debates with other colleges, by which the Dartmouth men won more often than they lost. During the time he was instructor, in collaboration with Professor Laycock, he prepared a text-book on *Argumentation and Debate,* which was published in 1904, and became the text-book in Dartmouth College, that year, and in other colleges and universities later. It is still in use as a standard text-book on that subject. His phrasing of the text shows a remarkable command of the English language.

In 1907, Mr. Scales became a member of the law firm of Powers and Hall, in Boston, and remained connected with that firm one year. He then received a more lucrative offer to engage in work with the law firm of Hutchins and Wheeler, of Boston. He remained connected with the latter firm one year, when he was advised to give up office work, to recuperate his health, which had become somewhat impaired by trouble in one lung. During those two years of law practice he met with good success in cases that were given him to try.

During the summer vacation of 1908, Mr. Scales visited England, and some of the countries of Europe, in company with the son of Mr. Hutchins, as tutor, to complete his fitting to enter Dartmouth College. In the course of their travels they visited *The Hague,* at the time the great *Arbitration Court* was in session, and saw the great men of that period, at work.

On the 6th of October, 1908, he was united in marriage with Miss LAURA WOLSEY LORD, only daughter of Professor and Mrs. John King Lord, of Dartmouth College. The wedding ceremony took place in the College church, in the presence of a large assembly of students, and neighbors of the Lord family. It was one of the notable events of the year, in the social life of the college. They commenced housekeeping on Mt. Vernon Street, in Boston, and he was engaged in law practice during the year following.

During the summer of 1909, Mr. Scales had a slight attack of tuberculosis, the top of his left lung being affected. An expert in treatment of that disease advised him to try the Adirondack treatment. He did so, during the winter of 1909-10. The treatment improved the condition, but not sufficiently to warrant his resuming his law practice. During 1910-11, Mr. and Mrs. Scales spent the larger part of the year in the health resorts of Switzerland and Italy, closing with spending the summer in the west of England. During that time he pursued the study of text books on *Political Science,* and had prepared himself to enter upon the work as instructor in some college, or university, in case his health was not sufficiently recovered to resume the practice of law. On arriving home he was not sufficiently recovered to engage in law practice, or to take charge of college work, as instructor in *Political Science.* His mind was as active and vigorous as ever, so he concluded to pursue a course of study, at Hanover, which would secure for him the Degree of Master of Arts. He had nearly completed the course, but was not able to receive the honor at Commencement, in 1912. In the fall of 1912, Mr. and Mrs Scales went to Roswell, New Mexico. He died there October 31, of that year.

THE SCALES FAMILY IN ENGLAND.

The SCALES FAMILY in England is one of the oldest on record, following the Norman Conquest. At the time of The Conquest, A. D. 1066, there were no surnames. The *Conqueror* himself was simply *William.* A commander of one division, or army corps, of King William's Norman invaders, was named *Hugh;* to distinguish him from others who might be called "Hugh," he was known as *Hugh de Scalerius,* because he was commander of the soldiers whose duty was to climb over the fortress walls, as soon as the men, with battering rams, had opened a breach sufficiently large for entrance. After the battle of Hastings, A. D. 1066, King William rewarded his officer, *Hugh de Scalerius,* by various grants of land, and the rights given him were entailed on the eldest son of succeeding generations; as governments changed, from time to time, the eldest sons were advanced in power. When the first parliament was called, *Baron Robert Scales,* A. D. 1299, was summoned to be a member; as time passed on there were six Barons, in succession, named *Robert.* When the Crusades began, one Baron Scales was in command of a division of the army, on the march to Jerusalem; for his service and valor he was granted a coat of arms, it being one of the first that was granted by the King of England. In the course of years the surname became anglicized, and *Scalerius* (Climber-over), became *Scales;* so *Hugh de Scalerius* came to sign his name *"Hugh de Scales."* In the next century the *"de"* was dropped, and the name came to be used uniformly as now. The elder sons retained the titles, but the younger sons retained the family name, Scales, and, from time to time, made good report of themselves, in official stations, as good citizens, and as soldiers and officers in the King's army.

Berke's Extinct Peerage book gives a long and interesting account of "SCALES-BARONS." The story closes as follows: "Lord Scales is said by Story, to have been murdered, on the 25th of July, 1460, but Dugdale merely says that he departed life (naturally). After his lordship's decease, the second husband of Elizabeth (his only daughter and heiress), Anthony Widvile, was summoned to Parliament as *Lord Scales,* and upon the death of said Elizabeth, without issue, the *Barony of Scales* fell into Abeyance (that is, the name Scales, dropped out), between the descendants of Margaret, Lady Howard, and Elizabeth, Lady Febbrigg (refers to issue of Robert, third Baron), as it still continues with their representatives (not in the Scales name). The noble family of *Scales* resided, for many generations, in great splendor and power, at the castle of Middleton, near Lynn, in the county of Norfolk."

THE SCALES FAMILY IN ROWLEY, MASS.

WILLIAM SCALES was the ancestor who came over in 1638, and the Scales families in New England are descendants of his son, JAMES SCALES, who was born in Rowley, about 1650; married SARAH CURTIS, 7 Nov., 1677; she was born in 1654; he died in the winter of 1686; she died in the winter of 1690-91; April 23, 1691. John Harris, of Ipswich, was appointed guardian of their children, "there being no other relative living to begg ye same." (Court record.) There are two families in Dover whose children are descendants of this James and Sarah Curtis Scales; they are those of John Scales, and of Fred E. Quimby, by Mrs. Quimby (nee Marietta Scales, daughter of Earl C. Scales, 8th in descent from William Scales, the emigrant ancestor). Mrs. Quimby's line is from James, the eldest son of James and Sarah; that of Mr. Scales, is from Matthew, youngest son of James and Sarah. The children of Mrs. Quimby are: *Edward Harold Quimby,* born Oct. 2, 1880; *William Leroy,* born June 29, 1883.

WILLIAM SCALES, the emigrant, was born about 1610; the place of his birth is not known, but according to tradition he was born in London, and was son of William and Margaret (Greene) Scales; Margaret was daughter of Robert Greene, who is mentioned in the Will of "Dame Bennett, widow of Sir William Webb, sometime Alderman and Mayor of London," dated 14 Jan., 1602, with a codicil, dated 1604, proved 9 July, 1604, which makes numerous bequests, one of them being "to uncle Robert Greene, and William Scales, his son-in-law, and to cousin Margaret, wife of William Scales." (N. E. H. & G. Register, vol. 48, p. 393.) William Scales was a descendant from a younger son of one of the Barons Scales, and so got his family name, as previously described, from *Hugh de Scales,* who came over from Normandy with William the Conqueror.

WILLIAM,[1] and wife, ANN, were parishioners of Rev. Ezekiel Rogers, pastor (rector) of the Church at Rowley, near Hull, England. Mr. Rogers, and twenty families "of good estate," came over to New England, in 1638, in the ship *"John,"* of London. Rev.

Joseph Glover, the "Father of the American Press," was a fellow passenger, bringing with him the first printing press ever shipped to America. Like thousands of Puritans who had come before them, they were at once conscientious and thrifty. They arrived in December, and wintered at Salem, and looked about for a desirable locality in which to settle. During the winter, Mr. Rogers asked leave of Mr. Willson's Church, in Boston, to commune with them. His request was cordially granted, and just before the communion, at the desire of the Elders of the Church, he made a clear cut statement of the religious position of his company. They acknowledged the special presence of God, in the Church of England, as shown in its soundness of doctrine, and in the excellence of its ministerial gifts, so that there was more good religion in England than in all the known world besides. Still, Mr. Rogers said, he and his parishioners could no longer, with safe conscience, commune with those of the Church of England, because of their antichristian hierarchy; their dead (that is "read") service; their receiving all to the seals (the sacraments); and their abuse of the power of excommunication.

While Mr. Rogers was looking around for land, New Haven made the new colonists a tempting offer to settle in Connecticut; but they finally chose the shore between Newbury and Ipswich, buying out some previous claims, at a cost of 800 pounds. Here the work of clearing the ground was commenced in the spring of 1639, and in 1640 they had the village laid out and houses ready for occupancy. During this interval other persons had come over from Rowley, so that they numbered about sixty families. The new settlement was laid out with admirable taste and judgment. Hardly a change in the streets, which the settlers made, has been found needful to the present day; and their common, or training ground, has always been admired. On the 13th of May, 1640, the General Court gave the town its name, "Rowley," and the heads of families were made "freemen" of the Massachusetts Bay Colony. That is to say, they were given the right to vote.

WILLIAM[1] was granted one acre and a half on Whethersfield Street, on which he built his house, in which he lived, as did also his son, James, following the death of his parents, whose deaths are recorded as follows: "William Scales, buryed July ye tenth, anno:

1682"; "Ann, widow of William Scales, buryed ye 26 day September, anno: 1682." Mr. Scales received several other grants of land, and was engaged in the lumber business, farming, and stock-raising, having the best breeds of cattle, sheep and swine. He appears to have been too deeply occupied in business affairs to accept any public office, either of the town or colony. He was a staunch supporter of Parson Rogers. His children:

1. WILLIAM,[2] killed by the falling of a tree, 26 Jan., 1670. (Court record.)
2. MATTHEW, private in Capt. Thomas Lathrop's company; killed by Indians, at Hatfield, Mass., 24 Aug., 1675. (Register, Vol. 44, p. 355.)
3. JAMES, b. about 1650.

JAMES[2] was born in Rowley, Mass., about 1650; married, Nov. 7, 1677, SARAH CURTIS, who was baptized 15 Feb., 1654, daughter of Zaccheus and Joanna Curtis, of Boxford, Mass. James inherited his father's estate; he died there in the winter of 1686; his wife died in the winter of 1690-91; April 23, 1691, the Court record at Salem, says: "John Harris, of Ipswich, prays to be appointed Admr. of Estate of William Scales, of Rowley, dec'd, there being no other relative living to begg ye same." Granted. Children:

1. JAMES, b. 30 Mar., 1679.
2. SARAH, b. 18 July, 1681.
3. WILLIAM, b. 1 Mar., 1683-4.
4. MATTHEW, b. 29 Mar., 1685.

Mrs. Marietta (Scales) Quimby's line of descent is from William,[1] James,[2] James,[3] John,[4] James,[5] James,[6] William Angel,[7] Earl C.,[8] Marietta.[9]

WILLIAM,[3] third child, as above, married and settled at Yarmouth, Me. His wife was SUSANNAH AYERS, of Ipswich, Mass. They had six sons and three daughters; the third son was JAMES, born at Ipswich, Mass., 6 August, 1713; he went south and settled at Savannah, Georgia, later in North Carolina; one of his descendants, Alfred Moore Scales, who was born at Reedsville, N. C., Nov. 27, 1827, was a General in the Confederate Army; later member of Congress several terms, and Governor of the State, 1884-1888.

MATTHEW,³ youngest son of JAMES, married SARAH ———, of Ipswich, Mass., about 1712; they settled in Portsmouth, before 1714. He was a "joiner" by trade; they became members of the North Church, in which their children were baptized as follows:

1. MATTHEW, bapt. 25 Apr., 1714; did not m.; d. at Durham, N. H., 1742.
2. JAMES, bapt. 18 Apr., 1715.
3. JOHN, bapt. 10 June, 1716.
4. MARY, bapt. 2 June, 1717.
5. ABRAHAM, bapt. 1 Sept., 1718.

MATTHEW SCALES appears to have resided in Portsmouth about ten years, and then removed to North Yarmouth, Me., where he engaged in business with his brother, William, having their houses on land that had been granted to their father, by the Massachusetts General Court. William Scales was the first Representative for the town in the General Court; he was also one of the Selectmen of the town several years. His house was made a garrison, as soon as it was built. Col. Thomas Westbrook had soldiers stationed there, in 1723. The brothers were both killed by the Indians, 24 April, 1725. At Alfred, Me., 5 Oct., 1725, their widows, Susannah and Sarah, were appointed Administratrixes of their husbands's estates.

The widow, SARAH SCALES, appears to have taken her children to Ipswich, Mass., and resided there the rest of her life. At a suitable age her sons, *Matthew* and *Abraham,* were apprenticed to learn the "joiner's trade." They worked in Boston till about 1740, when they settled in Durham, N. H., engaged in the "joiner" business, in general, and house-building, in particular. The elder brother died in 1742, and the younger brother administered on his estate; Matthew did not marry.

ABRAHAM⁴ married, 8 July, 1747, SARAH THOMPSON, born 5 Jan., 1724, daughter of John and Mary (Davis) Thompson, of

Durham. Soon after marriage Mr. Scales bought land in Nottingham, and built a house there in 1750, and that became his home the rest of his life. The house is yet standing, as good as new, only a new and smaller chimney has been placed where the original one was built. The house and the farm (300 acres), remained in possession of the Scales family for more than one hundred years. Abraham's house was the first two-story house built in Nottingham; the burial ground has the graves of five generations of the family. The children of Abraham and Sarah were:

1. JOHN, b. 9 Sept., 1748; d. Sept., 1754, of diphtheria.
2. SARAH, b. 8 Aug., 1750; d. Sept., 1754, of diphtheria.
3. ABRAHAM, b. 17 Aug., 1752; d. Sept., 1754, of diphtheria.
4. SAMUEL, b. 9 Sept., 1754.
5. JAMES, b. 1 May, 1757; d. Sept., 1760, of diphtheria.
6. MARY, b 19 Oct., 1759; d. Sept., 1760, of diphtheria.
7. HANNAH, b. 2 Aug., 1761; m., 10 Dec., 1784, NATHAN CLOUGH, of Loudon.
8. ABIGAIL, b. 29 Jan., 1764; m., 13 July, 1786, ELIJAH CARTland, of Lee.
9. EBENEZER, b. 6 Nov., 1766; m. ANNA MATHES, dau. of Gideon and Anna, of Lee.
10. LOIS, b. 20 Dec., 1769; d. 2 Mar., 1849; m., 4 Jan., 1790, GIDEON MATHES, JR., and lived in Lee.

ABRAHAM, by trade, was a "joiner," and was generally known as "joiner" Scales; he had a cousin, who lived at Lee Hill village, two miles away, named Edward Scales, who was a tailor by trade; he was known as "tailor" Scales. That was the fashion, in those days, by which persons were familiarly known. Abraham was a noted house-builder, but more than that he could, and did, make all kinds of household furniture. His wedding presents for his daughters, Hannah, Abigail and Lois, were articles for furnishing their households, and he made the furniture with his own hands, using bird's eye maple, for hard wood, and old timber pine, for the soft wood. Mr. Scales participated in town affairs, somewhat, being Moderator in some town meetings, and was Selectman a few years; but most of his energy was spent in cultivating his farm, and in the practice of his trade.

EBENEZER[5] was born 6 Nov., 1766; his father trained him to be a good "joiner," and good farmer, but his chief life work was that of *Elder* in organizing the *Free Will Baptist* denomination, and in speading the faith in the District of Maine. He remained on the farm in Nottingham, with his father, till that parent died in 1797. He married, 17 Feb., 1789, ANNA MATHES, daughter of Gideon and Anna Mathes, of Lee. In 1796, he became interested in the *Free Will Baptist* denomination. In 1800 he was made an Elder of the Church, and began preaching; first, at Kearsarge, N. H.; next, at Farmington, Me.; finally, he located at Wilton, Me., in 1805; there was his home till his death, 18 Feb., 1855. Elder Scales became a noted Evangelist, in Maine. His children:

1. HANNAH, b. 17 Feb., 1790; m. THOMAS ALLEN, farmer, at Joy, Me.
2. ABIGAIL, b. 17 Feb., 1792; m., 7 July, 1817, CHARLES MORSE, of Wilton, Me. Mr. Morse owned several gristmills and sawmills; he was Colonel of a regiment of Maine militia; a member of the convention which drafted the constitution of Maine, under which it was admitted into the Union, in 1820; he was representative in the first legislature, under the constitution, and later was State Senator. He was postmaster for Wilton for 20 years. He was b. 27 Oct., 1785; d. 20 May, 1845. They had three sons: 1. *Samuel Butterfield*, b. 15 June, 1818. 2. *Charles M.*, b. 21 July, 1820. 3. *Moses Leland*, b. 9 May, 1822. This son was the first Principal of the Dover High School, and is well remembered by some of his pupils, still living in this city. He was a perfect gentleman, a fine scholar, and an excellent teacher, so his pupils bear witness. The school was opened in 1854. Mr. Morse was twice m.; (1), at Franklin, N. H., 6 Feb., 1851, to Louise Jane Clarke, b. 1826; d. at Dover, 1856; by whom he had two sons: Charles Leland, and Edward Leland; he m. (2) Lucy M. Bryant, of Dover, by whom he had one son, Warren Morse, b. at Dover, 9 July, 1860.
3. JOHN, b. 14 Dec., 1793.
4. ANNA, b. 1 Dec., 1795; d., at Wilton, Me., 1880; m. there, 18 Nov., 1823, CHARLES EMERSON COLBURN, b. at Weare, N. H., 9 Dec., 1800.
5. ABRAHAM, b. at Kearsarge, 3 Sept., 1798; d. at Galveston, Texas, 1856. He was a prominent citizen of Wilton;

Colonel of a regiment of Maine militia; in 1838, he went to Texas, and became largely engaged in stock raising, and was a successful business man. He did not m.

6. GIDEON, b. 2 Sept., 1800; d. unm., 1827.
7. SARAH, b. 27 Nov., 1802; d. at Wilton, 1880; m, 16 Mar., 1823, SETH ALLEN, a farmer, at Wilton. They had seven children, of whom the sixth, b. 24 Sept., 1834, was named *John Scales Allen*, and has descendants living in Dover, N. H., at this time (1923).
8. JAMES BUTTERFIELD, b. 4 Feb., 1804; d. at Chesterville, Me., 1885. He was an Elder in the Free Will Baptist denomination. He served as pastor of the church at West Milton, N. H., and at Chesterville, Me.
9. ENOCH, b. 20 Jan., 1808; d. 12 Dec., 1885. He m., 11 Aug., 1849, OCTAVIA W. WOODMAN, b. 8 Jan., 1829; she d. 10 May, 1885. For many years he was known as Col. Scales, and was a man of wide influence in town and state. He was a prosperous merchant; postmaster several years; Justice of the Peace, and officiated in settling many cases; Representative in the State Legislature, several terms; Colonel of a regiment, in the days when those commanders were held in high respect. Col. Scales did not m. till he was 41 years old. He had one son, *Otto Clifford*, b. 21 Sept., 1868, who was graduated from Bowdoin College in 1891; and from Harvard Law School in 1894. He practiced law in Boston, and held good rank in the profession; he did not m.; he d. in 1921.
10. LOIS, b. 29 June, 1810; d. in 1865; m. THOMAS E. WEBSTER; they had one son, *Henry*, and three daus.: *Mary, Sarah,* and *Elizabeth*.
11. LORINDA, b. 27 Jan., 1818; m. RODNEY CHASE, of Deering, N. H.; no issue.

SAMUEL[5] was born at Nottingham, 9 Sept., 1754; died 20 March, 1778; married, in 1774, HANNAH LANGLEY, daughter of Samuel and Hannah (Reynolds) Langley, who resided at Wednesday Hill, in Lee, N. H. Like his father, he was an expert "joiner," and a good farmer. He was a private soldier in Capt. Smith Emerson's company of Minute Men, Col. Joshua Wingate's regiment, in service in the Revolutionary War. He was but 23 years and 6 months old when he died; his death occurred one month before his only son was born. His children:

1. MARY, b. 1776; d. 1777.
2. SAMUEL, b. 20 Apr., 1778; d. 21 Sept., 1840.

SAMUEL[6] born as above stated; married HANNAH DAME, 20 April, 1799, at the home of her brother, Hunking Dame, at Lee; it was Mr. Scales's 21st birthday anniversary; Hannah Dame was born 16 Feb., 1772, hence was nearly six years older than Samuel.

Mr. Scales was "brought up" by his grandfather, and uncle, Elder Ebenezer Scales, who remained on the farm till Samuel was 18 years old. His wife was daughter of Moses and Anna (Hunking) Dame; Moses Dame was fourth in descent from Deacon John Damme, of Dover Neck, who was the second deacon of the First Church in Dover. Anna Hunking was daughter of Capt. Mark Hunking, of Portsmouth, a kinsman of the wife of Lieut.-Gov. John Wentworth, and mother of Gov. Benning Wentworth, the first governor of the Province of New Hampshire. Their children were:

1. SAMUEL, b. 18 July, 1800; d. 12 Jan., 1877.
2. MARY, b. 22 Feb., 1802; d. 18 Apr., 1874, in San Francisco; m., 1826, HUGH THOMPSON, of Lee; they had three sons and two daughters; one dau., *Betsey Jane*, b. 1834, m., at San Francisco, 27 June, 1855, Edward H. Palmer, a native of New Bedford, Mass.; their son, Samuel Harding Palmer, was a graduate of the University of California, and subsequently one of the great railroad managers of California.
3. NANCY, b. 18 Aug., 1803; d. at San Francisco, 17 Apr., 1871; m. DANIEL TUTTLE, in 1828; they resided in Nottingham; for many years he was one of the leading citizens of that town; he was 6th in descent from Judge John Tuttle, of Dover Neck. They had two sons and two daughters; the eldest son, *Dr. Levi Woodbury Tuttle*, b. 24 Jan., 1829, settled in Mississippi, at Satartia, Yazo Co., and was surgeon in the Confederate Army; he d. in 1870; he was a very brilliant man; his descendants are residents of that State. The younger son, *Dr. Jay Tuttle*, of Astoria, Oregon, was b. 21 Dec., 1841; he was twice m; had one son by his first wife; two daughters by second wife.

SAMUEL[7] was born at Nottingham, 18 July, 1800; died at Lee, N. H., 12 Jan., 1877; married, 23 Dec., 1828, at Nottingham

Square, BETSEY TRUE, daughter of Benjamin and Mary (Batchelder) True, of Deerfield, N. H., who was born 11 Jan., 1805; died at Dover, N. H., Oct. 14, 1883; her father, was 4th in descent from Captain Henry and Jane (Bradbury) True, of Salisbury, Mass.; Jane Bradbury was daughter of Captain Thomas Bradbury, one of the most distinguished men of Salisbury, and the Massachusetts Bay Colony. Betsey True's mother was grand-daughter of Judge Jonathan Longfellow, of Deerfield, and later of Machias, Me., where he settled in 1765. In 1768, he was appointed Judge of the first court held in Maine, east of the Kennebec River. He held court there till his death, in 1674.

SAMUEL inherited the Scales farm in Nottingham; he was Captain of a militia company; Justice of Peace; Selectman; Representative in the Legislature of 1849-1850 (two sessions). He was a schoolmaster in his early years; leader in the church choir a number of years, having a fine bass voice. He was about six feet tall; large of body; strong of muscles; a good mechanic, as well as an up-to-date farmer. He was one of the Charter members of Sullivan Lodge, A. F. and A. M., whose lodge room was at Lee Hill village; he was Master of the Lodge; and was also an officer in the Grand Lodge of New Hampshire. His children:

1. TRUE[8] SCALES, b. 20 Jan., 1830; d. July 7, 1892, in Cambridgeport, Mass.; m., 4 Oct., 1853, MARY BIRD SHATTUCK; she was b. in St. Albans, Vt., 10 Dec., 1828; d. in Cambridgeport, 10 Nov., 1905. They had two sons: 1. *Burton*, b. Mar. 1, 1856; d. 23 Dec., 1856. 2. *Frank*, b. 26 Sept., 1859; m., 24 Oct., 1886, Nellie Doyle, and resided in Cambridge. They have three children: 1. Marion Bird, b. 28 Aug., 1889. 2. Walter Francis, b. 18 Sept., 1895. 3. George Burton, b. 3 May, 1903. Walter Francis was a soldier in the World War, saw service in the front line of battle in France, and returned uninjured.

   TRUE SCALES was, by trade, a brick-mason; he became a contractor and builder, in Cambridge, and Boston; he also did contract building outside of those cities; one of his buildings is the Walker block, in Dover, corner of Washington and Locust Streets. It has the credit of being one of the best constructed in the city. Mr. Scales held high rank in the Masonic Fraternity. In the Cambridge

Lodge he became Worshipful Master; in Parkman Commandery he became Eminent Commander; he had the credit of being a very efficient presiding officer.

2. JOHN,[8] b. 8 Oct., 1835; graduated from Dartmouth College, in the class of 1863; teacher; editor; author; m. ELLEN TASKER, as before stated, in the beginning of this article.
3. GEORGE,[8] b. 20 Oct., 1840; was graduated from Colby Academy (New London, N. H.), in 1861; he was about to begin the study of law when the Civil War commenced; he enlisted, and served in the Berdan Sharp Shooter Regiment. His company was in the forefront of service in the Siege of Yorktown; he marched with McClellan's Army to the Potomac, to capture Richmond; he participated in four of the seven battles that were fought; he was shot dead, on the evening of July 2, 1862, in the last charge the Confederate Army corps made up Malvern Hill; only a few of the company came out of that battle alive.

LEVI,[7] was born 13 Feb., 1811; died 4 Aug., 1847; married, 28 Nov., 1835, MARTHA CILLEY BARTLETT, daughter of Judge Bradbury and Polly (True) Bartlett, of Nottingham; her grandmother was Sarah Cilley, daughter of Gen. Joseph and Sarah (Longfellow) Cilley; her grandfather was Gen. Thomas Bartlett, of Revolutionary fame. Mr. Scales, like his father and grandfather, was a "joiner," by trade; he was also engaged in the lumber business, and had charge of a large sawmill, where much lumber was manufactured into shingles, clapboards, etc. Their children were:

1. HORACE,[8] b. 29 Mar., 1836; d. 30 Nov., 1895; m., in 1866, OREANNA McLANATHAN, of Cambridge, Mass; she d. in 1890; they had dau., *Martha Fitzjames.* Horace Scales was a soldier in the Berdan Sharp-Shooters, in the Civil War. He resided in Cambridge, Mass., and engaged in the insurance business.
2. ELIZABETH ANN, b. 18 Feb., 1840; d. Aug. 22, 1915; m., 13 May, 1863, HON. JOHN C. BARTLETT, of Lee. Mr. Bartlett was b. 4 Nov., 1838, son of Hon. Josiah and Hannah (True) Bartlett; grandson of Gen. Thomas Bartlett, of Revolutionary fame; and great grandson of Gen. Joseph Cilley, who was Col. of the First New Hampshire Regiment, three years, that did such gallant service in the

Revolutionary army. Mr. and Mrs. Bartlett celebrated their Golden Wedding, 13 May, 1863; two years later Mrs. Bartlett passed on. He inherited the home farm, which his father bought in 1822; for a century the father and son managed the farm, and it is now one of the best in the town of Lee. Their children:

1. GRACE, b. 1865; m. GEORGE ALBERT DUDLEY, and had four children: *Albert Bartlett, Marion Grace, Alice Evelin*, and *Leon Kennett*. The younger son is a student (1923) in the Dover High School; the daughters graduated from New Hampshire College. The elder son m., and had four children.
2. JOSIAH, b. 1868; m. AMY FOLSOM, of Dover; resides in Arlington, Mass.; engaged in the watch and jewelry business, at 515 Washington St., Boston. They have one son, *John Minot*, graduate of Worcester Academy; he was a soldier in the volunteer army that served on the Mexican border, during 1913-1914; he served in the World War, 1915-1918; he attained the rank of Captain. He m. and has one son.
3. BRADBURY BARTLETT, b. 7 Mar., 1842; m., 1876, ARIANNA BARTLETT, dau. of Edward St. John and Almira (Sawyer) Bartlett; resides at Exeter; retired. Children: 1. *George Levi*, b. 26 Sept., 1877, who is m. and has a son; he was student at Dartmouth College two years, 1900-1902. He is a civil engineer and resides in Michigan. 2. *Betsey True*, b. 4 May, 1880; resides at home with parents.
4. MARY TRUE, b. 17 Sept., 1844; m., 14 Mar., 1878, Mr. GEORGE B. TAYLOR, of Quincy, Mass., coal merchant. They had one son, *Horace Scales Taylor*, b. 5 Sept., 1879; d. 1896. George B. d. in 1885; Mrs. Taylor continued to reside at Quincy, till her death, 22 Nov., 1916.

THE DORE FAMILY.

(MEMORANDA No. 256.)

RICHARD DORE, or DOOR, as it was often written in olden times, of Portsmouth, made his Will, 16 Feb., 1715-16; proved 17 March, following. In it he mentions wife, TAMSEN, to whom he devised certain real estate to be sold by her, and after paying debts, etc., the balance to go to his children. He was a pew holder in the Church at Portsmouth, in 1681. (See Rambles about Portsmouth.)

At the time of the division of common lands about Portsmouth, among the inhabitants in 1699, his share of the land was fourteen acres. A "Mr. Door" served as a soldier at "Her Majesty's Fort, William & Mary, at New Castle," from Aug. 9 to Aug. 19, 1708. This person was probably son of Richard Dore, of Portsmouth.

It is not easy to make out the children of Richard and Tamsen Dore. In 1714, Richard speaks of his daughter, "Jou Boole Whidden," whom he had previously invested with certain rights in some real estate. *Mary Dore* married James Houston, Dec. 20, 1692. *Philip Dore,* of Portsmouth, married a *Miss Child,* May 20, 1709. There may have been other children.

Henry, Frances, Elizabeth and *John Dore,* children of PHILIP and SARAH DORE, of Newington, were baptized by Rev. Joseph Adams, the first three in 1727, and *John,* in 1730. *Philip,* son of PHILIP and ELIZABETH DORE, of Newington, was baptized 11 March, 1728. William Dore, of "Cochecho," married Mary, daughter of John and Charity Wallingford, of Newington, 25 April, 1740.

PHILIP DORE was owner of land, in the first division of lots, in Rochester, in 1729, and was a resident there later; he died before 1771. He gave his son, Philip Dore, Jr., one-half of the Rochester lot, in 1735, and the other half to son Henry, in 1742.

The children of PHILIP and SARAH DORE were as follows, but the order of births is not known:

1. HENRY; he had wife, MARY; removed from Rochester to Lebanon, Me.
2. ELIZABETH.
3. FRANCES, m. ABIJAH STEVENS, of Lebanon; d. in 1804; has descendants.
4. JOHN, m. CHARITY WENTWORTH, and lived in Lebanon; d., 1800.
5. PHILIP, m. LYDIA MASON; removed to Shapleigh, Me., about 1770; he d. there about 1796, leaving descendants. He speaks of sons, *Philip, Jr.,* and *Henry Dore*; perhaps he had second wife, ELIZABETH.

6. WILLIAM, m. MARY WALLINGFORD.
7. JONATHAN; he was captured by the Indians, in Rochester, in 1746; carried to Canada, where he remained till 1763, when he was released and came home. He then m. DOROTHY VARNUM, and settled in Lebanon, near his brother, John; he d. about 1797, without issue.

The children of JOHN and CHARITY (WENTWORTH) DORE were:

1. DANIEL.
2. JOHN.
3. JONATHAN.
4. HANNAH.
5. ELIZABETH.
6. CHARITY.
7. JOSEPH.
8. BENIAH.
9. PHILIP.
10. WENTWORTH.
11. PAUL.
12. SARAH.
13. ANDREW.
14. DOROTHY.

Children of PHILIP and LYDIA MASON DORE, born in Rochester:

1. RICHARD, m. HANNAH WEBBER.
2. ELIZABETH, m. PAUL FARNUM.
3. MARY, m. JOSEPH, son of Samuel and Abigail Merrow, of Rochester.
4. JOSEPH, m. PATIENCE HUSSEY.
5. JAMES, m. HANNAH HUSSEY.
6. OLIVE, m. EBENEZER TEBBETTS.
7. LYDIA, m. JACOB HERSOM.
8. PHILIP, m. MARY, dau. of James and Mercy (Foss) Lock, of Barnstead.
9. PHEBE, m. ELDER TOZIER LORD, a famous minister in his day.
10. BENJAMIN, b. 9 Jan., 1756; d. 2 Apr., 1843; m. SARAH, sister of Mary Locke; she was b. 1 Jan., 1758; d. 1850.

BENJAMIN settled in Lebanon, but removed to Shapleigh, and had the following children:

1. MEHITABLE, b. 2 May, 1778; m. LIEUT. JOSEPH MERROW, son of Joseph and Mary (Dore) Merrow; she d. Sept. 4, 1865.
2. SARAH, b. 31 Aug., 1780; m. MOSES TWOMBLY, of Alton.
3. ISAAC, b. 3 June, 1782; m. SARAH GILMAN; d. 12 Mar., 1833.
4. JAMES, b. 10 July, 1784; m. ABIGAIL YOUNG; d. 24 Sept., 1854.
5. PATIENCE, b. 25 June, 1786; m. CURTIS TAYLOR.
6. CHARLES, b. 16 Oct., 1789; m. PHEBE HOBBS.
7. EZEKIEL, b. 7 Feb., 1792; m. ABIGAIL CLARK; d. 31 Dec., 1865; *Hon. John C. Dore*, graduate of Dartmouth College, 1847, and former President of the Board of Trade, of Chicago. was his son.
8. JOHN, b. 25 Dec., 1794; m. MARY HANSON, of Rochester.
9. MASON, b. 16 Aug., 1797; m. SARAH MARSTON; d. 2 Apr., 1839.

JAMES LOCKE, referred to above, was son of Edward and Hannah (Jenness) Locke, of Rye, and was born in Rye, 4 Oct., 1709; he settled in Barnstead, about 1750; died there in 1796; his grandfather was Capt. John Locke, of London, who settled in Portsmouth, as early as 1652. The children of James and Mercy (Foss) Locke were:

1. MERCY, m. a BARBER.
2. MEHITABLE, m. CAPT. JOHN GOODWIN.
3. EDWARD, m. ELEANOR ———.
4. HANNAH, unm.
5. MARY, m. PHILIP DORE.
6. JAMES, m. MARY BEAN.
7. SUSAN, m. RICHARD HODGDON.
8. PRUDENCE, m. SAMUAL AVERY.
9. SARAH, m. BENJAMIN DORE.

THE TWOMBLY FAMILY.

(MEMORANDA No. 243.)

RALPH TWOMBLY, at first, was a resident at Dover Neck, where he had land laid out 10 April, 1656, that had previously been granted to him by the town. He was first taxed in 1657, and then appears to have changed his residence from the Neck to "Cochecho," as he had land there also. At the Neck he was a near neighbor to Governor Thomas Roberts, on the bank of Fore River.

His Will was dated 28 Feb., 1684; proved 7 August, 1686. ELIZABETH, his wife, and son *John*, were executors. If son John should live with his mother, then they were to occupy the homestead, jointly; if not, then his wife to have the estate for life, after which John should have one-half. If son *Ralph* lived with his mother till he was twenty-one, then he was to have ten pounds in money, or goods equivalent thereto. To son *Joseph*, a heifer; to daughter *Mary* (*Tebbetts*), five shillings; to each of the other children, *Elizabeth, Sarah, Hope, Esther* and *William*, when 18 years of age, a cow. Mr. Twombly appears to have been born in England, about 1630, and came over when he was about 20 years old; there is no mention of "three brothers" coming on the same ship. The children of RALPH and ELIZABETH were:

1. JOHN, b. about 1658, at Dover Neck.
2. JOSEPH, b. 1661.
3. MARY, b. 1663; m. a TEBBETTS.
4. RALPH, b. 1665; he m., and had a son, *Ralph*.
5. ELIZABETH, b. about 1666.
6. HOPE.
7. SARAH.
8. ESTHER.
9. WILLIAM, b. about 1677.

JOHN^2 married RACHEL ———. He made his Will 18 July, 1724; gave to his wife, RACHEL, one-half of the homestead, lying on the south side of the road leading down to Joseph Hanson's, and so to the Neck (back road); after her decease it was to go to son *William;* to son *John,* 20 acres in Littleworth, as by deed; to sons *Joseph* and *Samuel,* certain land, they to pay legacies to their uncles and aunts, as provided in the Will of their grandmother, Elizabeth; to son *Benjamin,* five pounds; to *William,* half of the homestead; to daughters *Sarah, Rachel, Esther, Mary* and *Anna,* five pounds each; *William* to support his mother; his wife, Rachel, and son, Joseph, were named executors. Their children were:

1. JOHN.
2. JOSEPH.
3. SAMUEL, b. 10 Mar., 1699.
4. BENJAMIN.
5. WILLIAM.
6. SARAH.
7. MARY.
8. RACHEL.
9. ESTHER.
10. HANNAH.

SAMUEL,[3] married, 26 Sept., 1723, JUDITH HANSON, daughter of Tobias and Ann (Lord) Hanson, born 12 July, 1703. They lived at Cochecho, and had children:

1. ANN, b. 23 Aug., 1724; m. JAMES NOCKS.
2. SAMUEL, b. 18 Mar., 1726.
3. ———, b. 21 Oct., 1727.
4. TOBIAS, b. 24 Oct., 1728; d. 25 Nov., 1809.
5. JUDITH, b. 25 July, 1730; m. CAPT. JOHN GAGE.
6. REBECCA, b. 31 July, 1737.
7. ISAAC, b. 23 Mar., 1739; d. 21 Aug., 1824.

We have not sufficient proof to connect the following families with the families preceding:

JOHN, married SARAH, daughter of William and Martha Dame; she was born 21 April, 1692. Their children were:

1. JOHN, b. 28 Oct., 1712.
2. SARAH, b. 21 Feb., 1714; m. a HANSON.
3. DANIEL, b. 18 Jan., 1716.
4. MARTHA, b. 25 Feb., 1719.

This John made his Will, 20 Dec., 1747; it was proved 27 April, 1748; it was a joint Will of John, and his wife, Sarah. They mention son *John,* who was executor; daughters *Sarah* (*Hanson*) and *Martha,* "and daughter-in-law, *Mary,* widow of son *Daniel,* now with child."

It is highly probable that this *John* was son of JOHN[2].

JOHN, son of JOHN, lived in Dover. His wife's name was MARY. His Will was dated 5 May, 1764. To sons *John* and

David, he gave the homestead formerly belonging to "my honored father and mother, John Twombly and Sarah Twombly, deceased." Both of these sons were then under age; he gave something to daughters *Lydia* (*Runnels*); *Anna* (*Purington*); *Sarah* (under age); to sister Martha; to nephew, Daniel (under 21); and to wife, who was executor with his father-in-law, Joseph Bunker. Their children were:

1. JOHN.
2. DAVID.
3. LYDIA.
4. ANNA.
5. SARAH.

Of these—

JOHN TWOMBLY was a Quaker; married 30 Jan., 1734, MARTHA, daughter of Ebenezer Varney, and had:

1. ANNA, b. 10 Mar., 1740.

WILLIAM married MARY ———. He made his Will in Dover, 14 Sept., 1763; proved 29 Oct., 1763; he gave to his son, *Isaac,* the homestead in Madbury; to *William,* land in Madbury, Barrington, and elsewhere; to daughter, *Elizabeth,* wife of Benjamin Pearl, of Barrington, land in Barrington; something to grand-daughter, Tamson, daughter of son *John,* deceased; to sons, *Ralph, Isaac, William,* and son-in-law, *Ichabod Hayes,* a saw-mill; he named his son, *Ralph,* as executor, and gave him much land in Dover, and elsewhere. The children were:

1. RALPH, b. 13 Sept., 1713.
2. ISAAC, b. 18 Dec., 1715.
3. WILLIAM, b. 25 July, 1717.
4. MARY, b. 25 Feb., 1721.
5. ELIZABETH, b. 1 Nov., 1723; m. BENJAMIN PEARL.
6. JOHN, b. 19 Sept., 1725; was dead in 1763.
7. ELEANOR, b. 1727; m. NICHOLAS RICKER.

It is probable that William was son of Ralph,[3] son of Ralph.[2]

BENJAMIN lived in Somersworth; his Will was dated 29 Dec., 1721; proved, 30 March, 1762; he gave to his wife, HANNAH, half of estate for life; to son *Benjamin,* all of estate, except as above, he to pay certain legacies, viz: to daughters *Hannah (Hayes), Tamson (Hodgdon), Abra (Woodbridge),* 100 pounds, old tenor, each; to *Abigail* (daughter), 250 pounds; to daughters *Sarah* and *Abigail,* one room while single; *Benjamin,* executor. Children:

1. HANNAH, b. 16 May, 1722; m. a HAYES.
2. TAMSON, b. 1725; m. a HODGDON.
3. ABRA, b. 23 June, 1728; m. a WOODBRIDGE.
4. SARAH.
5. BENJAMIN.
6. RACHEL, bapt. 26 Apr., 1735; m. a HAYES.

WILLIAM, who settled in Madbury, was born 25 July, 1717. His children were:

1. NATHANIEL.
2. JOSHUA.
3. JOHN, who was b. 24 Nov., 1755.

The children of the last named were:

1. PETER.
2. JOHN.
3. HURD.
4. MARY.
5. SARAH.

JOSHUA, who was born 1750, married HANNAH WILLEY, and settled in Strafford; their children were:

1. SAMUEL.
2. JACOB.
3. POLLY.
4. AARON.
5. JOSHUA.
6. SUSAN.
7. SALLY.
8. HANNAH.
9. JOHN.

10. NATHANIEL.
11. ABIGAIL.
12. WILLIAM.
13. MEHITABLE.

The sons grew up; married, and had children.

JOSHUA, born in 1750, died 20 Feb., 1837. His wife died 30 Jan., 1835, aged 79 years. *Samuel,* son of Joshua, settled in Vermont; he moved from there to Illinois, in 1816. *Jacob* married Tamson Hill; she died 24 Jan., 1868, aged 96 years, 5 months. He died 15 Dec., 1852, aged 77. Their children:

1. DANIEL.
2. SAMUEL.
3. WILLIAM.
4. SALLY.
5. ANDREW.
6. SUSAN.
7. JOHN.

POLLY, daughter of Joshua, married JAMES GREY; they settled in Vermont.

AARON, settled in Strafford; wife's name not known; their children:

1. SMITH.
2. SALLY.

HANNAH, daughter of Joshua, born 13 Feb., 1789, married WILLIAM E. EVANS, who was born 13 Sept., 1786. They lived in Barrington, and had children:

1. JOHN.
2. RHODA.
3. SAMUEL.
4. JOSEPH.
5. ELIZA.
6. WILLIAM.
7. MARY.
8. SARAH.

THE TWOMBLY FAMILY. 487

NATHANIEL, son of Joshua, lived in Strafford; his children were:

1. IRA.
2. NATHANIEL.

ABIGAIL, daughter of Joshua, born 31 Aug., 1795, married PETER HACKETT; they settled in Rochester, and had children.

WILLIAM, youngest son of Joshua, married, and lived in Dover; they had three children:

1. MARY J.
2. ELIZABETH A.
3. WILLIAM K.

MEHITABLE married URIAH HENDERSON; they settled in Holderness; their children were:

1. ALFRED.
2. RICHARD.
3. HIRAM.
4. WARREN.
5. ABIGAIL.
6. LYDIA.

JOHN, born 24 Nov., 1755, son of William, who was born 25 July, 1717; son of William; son of John; son of Ralph, the emigrant; married ANNA HURD, who was born 24 May, 1749. Their children were:

1. MARY, b. 7 June, 1776.
2. SARAH, b. 3 June, 1777.
3. PETER, b. 11 Oct., 1778.
4. ANNA, b. 15 Feb., 1780.
5. PHEBE, b. 1 Mar., 1782.
6. JOHN, b. 19 Mar., 1787.
7. HURD, b. 31 Dec., 1789.
8. MARY, b. 10 Jan., 1791.

HURD, born 31 Dec., 1789, married SARAH C. CAVERNO, in 1812; she was born 25 June, 1792; died in August, 1827; their children were:

1. JOHN, b. 2 Aug., 1813.
2. MARY, b. 9 Feb., 1815.
3. JEREMIAH, b. 15 Feb., 1817; d. 3 July, 1859.
4. NATHANIEL, b. 7 Mar., 1819.
5. HANNAH, b. 2 Dec., 1822; d. 26 Apr., 1843; not m.
6. GEORGE W. K., b. 19 Nov., 1824.

HURD, married (2) widow, Mrs. LAVINIA TUTTLE; she died in Jan., 1881; he died 1 March, 1872. Their children were:

7. JAMES T., b. 2 Sept., 1829.
8. SARAH C., b. 22 Jan., 1831.
9. LAVINIA H., b. 1833.
10. WILLIAM HENRY HARRISON, b. 16 Oct., 1840.

JOHN,[7] HURD,[6] JOHN,[5] WILLIAM,[4] WILLIAM,[3] JOHN,[2] RALPH,[1] married (1) SUSAN COLBATH, who died 24 Nov., 1839, leaving twenty children; he married (2) CHARLOTTE DREW, who was born 8 Oct., 1818; they were married 7 Jan., 1842; she died 7 Dec., 1859. *Their* children were:

1. HERBERT A., b. 18 Apr., 1845; d. Sept., 1848.
2. JOHN HERBERT, b. 17 Oct., 1848.
3. CHARLES A., b. 7 Sept., 1859; d. 2 Oct., 1868.

MARY,[7] daughter of Hurd,[6] married SAMUEL DAVIS, JR., 1 Jan., 1837; he was born 11 Aug., 1799; died 11 Jan., 1853; their children were:

1. MARY E., b. 1 Apr., 1838; d. 16 June, 1842.
2. SAMUEL C., b. 15 Mar., 1842.
3. JUDITH A., b. 15 Mar., 1842 (twin with Samuel).
4. MARY A., b. 28 Apr., 1847.
5. JAMES J., b. 4 Jan., 1851; d. 20 Mar., 1851.
6. WILLIAM L., b. 24 Sept., 1852.

JEREMIAH,[7] son of Hurd,[6] married JANE MALTBY, of Illinois, who died, leaving one daughter, *Martha J.;* he married (2) LOUISA L. KEMBRICK; he died 3 July, 1859; their children were:

1. BENJAMIN T., b. 19 June, 1854.
2. MARY A., b. 24 Oct., 1857.
3. KATIE, b. 5 Apr., 1859.
4. SARAH C., b. 24 Dec., 1860.

NATHANIEL,[7] son of Hurd,[6] born 7 March, 1818; married, 13 June, 1842, MARY A. DREW; she was born 18 Feb., 1824; died 2 Aug., 1897; their children:

1. HELEN F., b. 24 June, 1845; d. 30 Oct., 1850.
2. MARY E., b. 22 Oct., 1846; d. 21 Oct., 1853.
3. FRANK H., b. 20 Sept., 1851.
4. MARY H., b. 20 Oct., 1853; d. 29 Aug., 1854.
5. NATHANIEL A., b. 20 June, 1857.
6. JAMES WALTER., b. 2 Aug., 1859.
7. WILLIAM D., b. 3 Feb., 1863; d. 2 Sept., 1864.
8. MARTHA L., b. 4 Dec., 1866; d. 13 Mar., 1874.

BENJAMIN H.,[7] son of Hurd,[6] married ROWENA L. BOONE, 26 May, 1842; she died 14 April, 1854; he married (2) AUGUSTA A. KELLOW, 21 Oct., 1855; their children:

1. ALICE A., b. 11 May, 1859.
2. BENJ. H., b. 7 Dec., 1862.

GEORGE W. K.,[7] son of Hurd,[6] married MARY A. LANGLEY, in 1846; she died in 1856; he died, 1 July, 1872. Their children were:

1. GEORGE, b. 15 Dec., 1848.
2. HURD W. C., b. 22 Sept., 1852.
3. JOHN C., b. 2 Feb., 1854.

JAMES T.,[7] TWOMBLY, son of Hurd,[6] married HATTIE RAYMOND; they had one son:

1. CHARLES E., b. 11 May, 1878; d. July 2, 1880.

SARAH C.,[7] daughter of Hurd,[6] married Hon. JACOB D. YOUNG, of Madbury, who was born 28 Dec., 1823; their children were:

1. LILLIAN L., b. 4 July, 1858.
2. EDWARD L., b. 21 June, 1860.
3. ' LEWIS H., b. 10 Dec., 1863.
4. ESTHER L., b. 14 May, 1868.

LAVINIA H.,[7] daughter of Hurd,[6] married DANIEL DREW; they had children:

1. ROWENA L.
2. NELSON U.
3. ALICE.

WILLIAM HENRY HARRISON,[7] son of Hurd,[6] married 4 June, 1865, MARY ESTHER HALL, daughter of Gilman Hall, Esq., and youngest sister of the late Col. Daniel Hall; their children were:

1. ROSCOE R., b. 22 June, 1866.
2. GEORGIE E., b. 24 June, 1868.
3. JOHN H., b. 23 May, 1870.
4. GILMAN H., b. 18 Feb., 1872.
5. HARRY L., b. 10 Dec., 1873.
6. WALTER T., b. 7 Mar., 1876; d. 17 Jan., 1874.
7. LAVINIA H., b. 13 May, 1878.
8. WINFIELD H., b. 19 Jan., 1880.
9. FRED C., b. 21 June, 1883.

THE MERROW FAMILY.

(MEMORANDA No. 257.)

DR. SAMUEL MERROW, of Oyster River, (Durham), is the ancestor of the Merrow families in New Hampshire. He was born in Reading, Mass., 9 Oct., 1670; son of Henry and Jane (Wallis) Merrow, who were married 9 Dec., 1661. His father,

HENRY MERROW, was born in Scotland. Merrow is the name of a parish, in the Hundred of Woking, county of Surry, England. A "hundred" is the name of a division in each county, in England. He came over about 1660, and settled in Woburn, Mass. In 1664, he purchased land in Reading, Mass., and resided there the remainder of his life. He died 5 Nov., 1685. According to his deposition, on file among the old Court records in Cambridge, he was born in 1625. He was made freeman, 23 May, 1677. His family consisted of eleven children, of whom the sixth was *Dr. Samuel Merrow*, of Rochester, N. H. There were five sons and six daughters. The record of them is found in Massachusetts.

Dr. Merrow's residence in Durham appears to have been near that of Col. James Davis, on the north side of Oyster River. They were contemporary citizens. While he was resident there he made purchases of land in Rochester, on which he settled later, and was the first resident doctor for the families in that new town. Most of his children were born in Reading, before he settled at Oyster River. His wife's name was MARY. Their children:

1. MARY, b. 13 Sept., 1696.
2. JOSEPH, b. 1 Aug., 1698.
3. BENJAMIN, b. 3 Sept., 1700.
4. JONATHAN, b. 1 Jan., 1702.
5. RUTH, b. 14 Aug., 1705.
6. RACHEL, b. 16 Aug., 1707.
7. SAMUEL, b. 7 May, 1710.

BENJAMIN, second son of Dr. Merrow, lived in Rochester, where he died about 1764. Name of his wife is not known. He had the following children, baptized in Rochester:

1. BENJAMIN, 20 Mar., 1748.
2. JOHN, June, 1750.
3. DANIEL, 8 Sept., 1754.
4. MOSES, 24 Apr., 1757.

George Merrow, Esq., of Madison, and Hon. Josiah Merrow, of Bowdoinham, Me., are his grandsons.

JONATHAN, third son of Dr. Merrow, settled in Somersworth; he had wife, ELIZABETH. The names of his children have not been obtained. His daughter *Abigail*, married Nicholas Canada. *Jonathan Merrow, Jr.*, of Somersworth, and married (1) Phebe Heard; their children were:

1. THOMAS.
2. ANNE.
3. JONATHAN.
4. JAMES.

After the death of his wife, he married (2) Hannah Wentworth, and they had:

5. ISAAC.
6. PHEBE.
7. SALLY.

SAMUEL, fourth son of DR. MERROW, lived in Rochester, where he died about 1786. His first wife was ABIGAIL ———, and they had children:

1. SAMUEL, who m., wife's name not known, and had children: *Edward, Joshua, Susan, Stephen, Joseph* and *Ruth*.
2. JOSEPH.
3. MARY.
4. JONATHAN.
5. RUTH.
6. JOSHUA.
7. WILLIAM.

JOSEPH, second son of Samuel and Abigail, was baptized in Rochester, in 1739; he married MARY, daughter of Philip and Lydia (Mason) Dore, and settled in Shapleigh, Me. He died about 1799; she died about 1822. He was a soldier in the French and Indian War. Children:

1. JONATHAN, b. 1762.
2. LYDIA, b. 1764; she m. (1) DANIEL BRACKET; (2) SAMUEL TASKER, both of Ossipee.
3. MARY, b. 1766; m. ZACHARIAH KNOX.
4. ABIGAIL, b. 1768; m. BENJAMIN GUPTIL. Their dau., *Phebe*, m. Capt. Thomas Bond, only brother of the celebrated astronomer, William C. Bond, late Director of the Astronomical Observatory of Harvard College.
5. JOSEPH, b. 4 Jan., 1778; m. MEHITABLE, eldest dau. of Benjamin and Sarah (Locke) Dore, of Lebanon. She was b. 2 May, 1778, and d. Sept., 1865. He settled in Newfields, Me., in 1802. He was in the War of 1812-15, and held

the commission of Lieutenant. He d. 15 May, 1856. Hon. Augustus D. Merrow, M. D., and brother, James M. Merrow, M. D., and Mr. Horace P. Tuttle, of the Cambridge Observatory, were grandsons.

6. ABEL, b. Sept., 1780; m. PATIENCE, dau. of John James, of Shapleigh.
7. PHEBE, b. 16 Apr., 1782; m. AMOS MERROW; she d. 8 Dec., 1866.

JOSHUA, fourth son of Samuel and Abigail, married MARGARET GARLAND, and settled in Rochester. He entered the army of the Revolution and was promoted to the rank of Lieutenant. He made a fine record, which is to be seen by any one consulting Vol. VII, of the N. H. Historical Collections. He died in 1808, leaving a son, *Joshua*, who married Nancy, daughter of Moses Hodgdon, of Dover. Lieut. Merrow had the honor of being one of the original members of the *Order of Cincinnati*, in New Hampshire.

WILLIAM, fifth son of Samuel and Abigail, married MARY, daughter of William Haley, of Winter Harbor, Me., and settled in Hollis, Me. Their children were:

1. MARY, b. 1775; m. ISAAC YORK.
2. CHARITY, b. 1779; m. SAMUEL BOOLTER.
3. AMOS, b. 14 May, 1780; m. PHEBE, dau. of Joseph and Mary (Dore) Merrow, and d. 23 May, 1868.
4. OLIVE, b. 1783; m. WHITS DYER.
5. JOSEPH, b. 1787; m. ISABELLA HUTCHINSON.
6. SARAH, b. 1790; m. WILLIAM HANSCOM, of Newfield, Me.

THE CHURCH FAMILY.

(MEMORANDA No. 337.)

JOHN CHURCH (according to deposition) was born about 1641; was received an inhabitant of Dover, 19 March, 1665-6. A family tradition says that he had red hair, also, that he was a nephew of that great Indian fighter, Capt. Benjamin Church, but, unluckily, Capt. Benjamin's brother, Joseph, the only one older, married in 1660. John was on the grand jury, 8 April, 1667, petit jury, 4 March, 1671-2; on the tax list, 1675, and doubtless on lost lists. On a contract to take care of "Neamy's child," 3 Oct., 1667, the town voted him sixty acres of land; and voted, 5 March, 1667-8, to confirm this grant and make it seventy, if he take care of the waif (a girl) till she were twenty years old. And he did so.

John Church bought, of Peter Coffin, 1 Jan., 1668-9, for 13 pounds, 75 acres, "near Cochecho," "bounded E. and S. E. by Thomas Downs," and W. by somebody's swamp. Likewise he had land from the town, 3 April, 1678, near "Campin's rocks," and every boy knows where the rocks are, down the river, below the Gulf. Tradition says he lived close to the site of the jail, on Silver Street, where the Brown house now (1923) stands, on the south side of the street and west of the railroad bridge.

In the memorable massacre of 28 June, 1689, Church was carried off a prisoner, but he managed to escape before reaching Winnipesaukee, and came home. He was killed, however, 7 May, 1696, and scalped. Pike's *Journal* says, "John Church, Sen.: slain by the Indians, as he traveled to seek his horse upon a little hill betwixt Cochecho and Tole-end." That road is the present Arch Street, from Silver to Washington Street. Belknap, in his History, says Church was killed near his house. One tradition says he was killed in Coffin's woods, at the top of "Much-a-do-Hill," at the west end of Washington Street.

JOHN,[1] married, in Salisbury, Mass., 29 Nov., 1664, ABIGAIL, daughter of John Severanc , born 25 May, 1643. They had:

1. JONATHAN, b. 12 Apr., 1666, of whom we find no further mention.
2. JOHN, b. 12 Apr., 1668.
3. EBENEZER, b. 25 Feb., 1669-70, of whom we know nothing more.
4. ABIGAIL, b. 12 Aug., 1672; m., 23 Apr., 1694, SAMUEL PIPER, probably son of Nathaniel Piper, of Ipswich.
5. DEBORAH, m., 26 Oct., 1704, JOHN ROBERTS, and lived in Somersworth. The connection of this John with the Roberts family, of Somersworth, is not definitely known; but probably he was son of Sergt. John Roberts, and grandson of Gov. Thomas Roberts, of Dover Neck. Deborah had five children, all girls, who left many descendants in the Wentworth, Tuttle, and Ricker families. She d., and John m. again.

6. SARAH, m., 29 Sept., 1699, NATHAN FOLGER, son of Ebenezer Folger, of Nantucket, b. 1678, and had seven children. He was a blacksmith, and also used to keep tavern. He d. 2 July, 1747; she d. 23 Feb., 1745; they were members of the Society of Friends. Sarah had plenty of descendants. One of them was Walter Folger, who was in Congress, 1817-21.

JOHN,[2] son of JOHN,[1] born 12 April, 1668, lived in Dover. He was lot layer in 1702. He married, 1 Dec., 1699, MERCY HANSON, daughter of Thomas Hanson. The Hansons lived westward of the Church family, about a mile towards Knox's Marsh. John was killed by the Indians, in 1711. Thomas Downs, a near neighbor, in what is now known as the Ricker field, and three others, were killed at the same time by the savages. He had children:

1. ABIGAIL, b. 16 May, 1702.
2. JOHN, b. 7 Apr., 1704.
3. ELIZABETH, b. 2 Dec., 1706; bapt. 17 June, 1729.
4. JONATHAN, b. 25 July, 1708.
5. MERCY, b. 4 Aug., 1710; bapt. 30 Apr., 1732.

JOHN,[3] son of JOHN,[2] had wife MARY, and lived in Dover; he died in 1775; he had children as follows:

1. JOHN, d. young.
2. DANIEL, d. young.
3. JOHN, bapt. 6 Aug., 1738.
4. BENJAMIN, b. 5 Apr., 1740; m., 21 Sept., 1780, EUNICE, dau. of Dr. Cheney Smith, of Dover. She was bapt. 18 Sept., 1743. They lived on what is known as the Faxon farm, at Tole-End. He d. childless, in 1812. His Will, dated 7 Apr., 1812, proved 30 Sept., following, mentions wife, Eunice, and *John, Ephraim*, and *Daniel Young*. His widow m. (2) Miles Evans; and m. (3) Frank Drew.

JONATHAN,[3] son of JOHN, born 25 July, 1708, signed a petition, as citizen of Dover, in 1732; was enrolled in a militia company, in 1740. He moved into Barrington, and represented that town in the General Court in 1762, 1765, and 1767; he died in 1774. His wife was ABIGAIL HANSON. We do not know what line; but if his mother was daughter of the second Thomas Hanson, then Jonathan had a cousin Abigail, born 23 Feb., 1721-2, daughter of the second Thomas Hanson's son, Thomas.[3] He had the five first named, certainly, born in Barrington.

1. EBENEZER b. 9 Jan., 1742-3, who had land given him on the Kennebec River, by his father, and moved thither. He m., 4 Oct., 1770, SARAH WINSLOW.
2. JOHN, b. 30 Oct., 1745; was captured in an American privateer, by the British; carried into Halifax, and d. there of yellow fever.
3. JAMES, b. 20 Jan., 1747-8.
4. ANN, b. 6 Oct., 1749; m. WILLIAM ROBINSON.
5. NATHANIEL, b. 28 Sept., 1741.
6. BENJAMIN, under 14 in 1774.
7. HANNAH, m. CHARLES BABB.
8. MERCY, m. ISIAH FELKER.
9. ABIGAIL, m. a SCRIBNER.
10. CHARITY, m. JAMES TASKER.

JAMES,[4] son of JONATHAN,[3] born 20 Jan., 1747-8, lived in Barrington, on the homestead of his father. He married a Cate, doubtless of Barrington. The Cates had a garrison at "Hard Scrabble," near the meeting-house. James died about 1821; she died in 1848, aged 93 years. They had children:

1. JONATHAN, b. in 1776.
2. JOSEPH, b. 1778.
3. JOHN, studied medicine under Dr. Jabez Dow, of Dover; practiced a short time in the West Indies, then settled in the State of Maine; he did not m.; was accidentally drowned, 14 July, 1809, in Wiscasset, Me.

NATHANIEL,[4] son of JONATHAN,[3] born 28 Sept., 1751, lived in Barrington, and later in Ossipee. He was a soldier in the war of the Revolution, in Capt. Drown's Co., and lost a leg in Rhode Island. He married MARY LEIGHTON; he died 18 Feb., 1826. They had children:

1. MARTHA, b. 21 Jan., 1786; m. JOHN NEAL, and d. 22 Jan., 1879.
2. BENJAMIN, b. 28 Jan., 1788.
3. NANCY, b. 10 Nov., 1790; m. (1) JOHN MARDEN; m. (2) ICHABOD CANNEY.

4. MARY, b. 1 Jan., 1793; m. ISAAC HANSON, of Madbury.
5. ABIGAIL, b. 22 Oct., 1796; m. FRANCIS WINKLEY, of Barrington.
6. NATHANIEL, b. 8 Sept., 1799.
7. PRUDENCE, b. 2 June, 1803; m. MARK THOMPSON.

BENJAMIN,[4] son of JONATHAN,[3] born 31 Dec., 1766; went from Barrington to Hallowell, Me., in 1795, and thence to Hartland, Me., in 1811. In 1813 he enlisted in the U. S. Army, and died in the service, at Sackett's Harbor, 10 Sept., 1813. He married MARTHA NUTE. Children:

1. JAMES, b. 10 July, 1795; m. HANNAH MCCAUSLAND; had three sons and two daughters; he d. in Hartland, 10 Oct., 1875.
2. HANSON, b. 6 Apr., 1797.
3. POLLY, b. 23 Apr., 1800; m. DAVID SIBLEY, and had four sons and two daughters; all m.
4. ABIGAIL, b. 14 June, 1802; m. WILLIAM COGSWELL, and had one son and three daughters.
5. HARRIET, b. 18 May, 1805; m. STEPHEN S. ROBINSON, of Kent's Mills, Readville, Me.; had two sons and four daughters.
6. GREENLEAF, b. 3 May, 1807; m. ELIZABETH FINSON.
7. DRUSILLA, b. Nov., 1809; m. DAVID PRIEST; they had a son and a daughter.

JONATHAN,[5] son of JAMES,[4] born in 1776; married, in 1815, NANCY MORRILL, and lived in Barrington, on the homestead of his grandfather, Jonathan.[3] He died, Dec., 1848; he had children:

1. ELIZABETH, b. 8 May, 1816; never m.
2. JONATHAN, b. 1818; never m.; he was a sea captain; d. in California, in 1848.
3. CHARLES, b. 8 Apr., 1820; lived on the homestead in Barrington; unm.
4. JAMES, b. 1822; d. 1832.
5. MARY ANN, b. 1824; d. 1831.
6. JOHN, b. 1826; m. NANCY MORRILL, of Northwood; he d. in 1853, leaving son, *John E.*
7. HORATIO, b. 1828; d. 1833.
8. SAMUEL, b. 1830; lived on the homestead; did not m.

JOSEPH,[5] son of JAMES,[4] born 1778; lived in Barrington, and kept tavern near the Congregational meeting-house, at "Hard Scrabble"; he married HANNAH, daughter of Benjamin Balch, the Barrington minister from 1784 to 1812; he died at his son's house, in Bridgewater, Mass., in 1850. His children:

1. LUCY, m. a WRIGHT.
2. LOUISE, d. single.
3. JOSEPH, m. and lived in Boston, Mass.; unm.
4. CHARLES, m. a DOWSE, and lived in Sherburne, Mass.
5. ANDREW JACKSON, lived in Sherburne, Mass.
6. HANNAH, d. young.
7. JULIA.

BENJAMIN,[5] son of NATHANIEL,[4] born 28 Jan., 1788; lived in Lee, N. H.; married 28 May, 1818, ABIGAIL, daughter of Israel and Abigail (Hall) Peirce, of Barrington; he died 19 April, 1845; she died in Dover, 14 May, 1864. They had children:

1. CATHERINE, d. single.
2. ISRAEL PEIRCE, b. 1 Mar., 1843; m. (1) LYDIA S. BROWN; m. (2) ANNE C. LOCKE; lived in Durham, and had three children.
3. TAMSON PEIRCE, m. 15 July, 1849, JEFFERSON FORD; she d. at South Berwick, in 1871, leaving seven children.
4. MARY, lived in Dover; unm.
5. ABBIE, twin with Mary; lived in Dover; unm.
6. LUCETTA, b. 17 Mar., 1833; d. 28 May, 1855.
7. NATHANIEL, d., aged three years.

NATHANIEL,[5] son of NATHANIEL,[4] born 8 Sept., 1799; married PATIENCE HANSON, and lived in Madbury; died 22 Feb., 1850. His children were:

1. JOHN H., b. 6 Feb., 1822; lived single, on the homestead in Madbury.
2. LYDIA V., b. 22 Oct., 1833; m. IRA LOCKE, of Madbury.
3. MARY, b. 24 Nov., 1836; m. SAMUEL ROBINSON.
4. ISAAC, b. 3 Feb., 1839; lived single, in Madbury.
5. ELIZABETH H., b. 12 Oct., 1840; m. JOHN WOODHOUSE.
6. ELLEN M., b. 23 June, 1843; lived single, in Madbury.
7. NATHANIEL B., b. 6 June, 1846; lived single, in Madbury.

HANSON,[5] son of BENJAMIN,[4] born 6 April, 1797; lived in Hartland, Me., on a farm formerly his father's. He married FANNY BOWLEY. They had children:

1. JOSEPH B., b. 9 Sept., 1827; lived in Hartland, Me.; m.
2. LYDIA, b. 6 Apr., 1831; m.; d. in California.
3. MARY, b. 26 Apr., 1835; m.; lived in Virden, Ill.
4. MARTHA, b. 13 Apr., 1838; m.; lived in Hartland, Me.
5. SILAS B., b. 1 June, 1840; d. in Hartland, Me.; single.
6. JOHN A., b. 23 June, 1842; m.; lived in California.
7. CALVIN B., b. 20 Oct., 1845; lived in California; single.
8. WINFIELD SCOTT, b. 15 Jan., 1849; lived with his father; single.
9. FRANCES E., b. 25 July, 1852; lived at home; single.

INDEX

The following is a complete name index to both the historical and genealogical portions of this book, and replaces the partial index to the historical section which appeared in the original edition. Titles such as Capt., Lt., Mr., etc., have been omitted when the person is identified by a given name, but are otherwise retained. The designations Jr. and Sr. have been retained, but the reader should be cautioned that they are transitory designations. Wives have been indexed under both maiden and married surnames when possible. Indians and Negroes lacking surnames have been placed at the end of the index.

ADAM Joseph 55
ADAMS Alexander 346 Charles 234 240 253 Charlls 238 Eliza 424 Hannah 439 Hugh 178 J Q 454 John 55 242 Joseph 220 479 Mary 346 Mr 56 President 220
ADDAMS Charles 243 246 251 John 246 249
ALFORD Benjamin 72
ALLEN Abigail 390 Anne 337 414 415 Benja 89 Edward 252 Eliza 328 Hannah 473 Isaac 86 390 Jacob 204 205 206 214 267 John 93 John Scales 474 Joseph 86 Martha 204 205 206 214 267 Mary 206 214 Robert 158 Sarah 474 Seth 474 Thomas 473 William 86
ALLEY John 87 Samuel 87 Samuel Jr 87
ALLT John 240 244 246 251
ALT John 252
AMBLAR John 258
AMBLER Elizabeth 401 John 401
AMBROSE 391 Alice 128 130 131 132 133 176
AMES Elizabeth 416
ANDERSON Hannah 390
ANDRESS Jeddediah 242
ANDREWS Jedediah ix
ANDROS Judediah 248 Judiae 245
APPLETREE Millett vii
ARCHDALE Col 192 John 189 190
ARGALL Samuel 9
ARNOLD Nancy Isabel 287
ARWIN Edward 238
ASH Hannah 382 Thomas 85
ASTEN Joseph 237 242
ASTIN Sarie 245
ATKINSON Joseph 383 Sarah 347 Theo 153 154 162 181
AULT John 183 234 238 400 Rebecca 400 Remembrance 400
AUSTIN 335 Andrew 373 Abigail 373 374 Ann 138 373 374 Benjamin 319 373 374 Catherine 373 457 460 Ebenezer 374 Elijah 360 373 Elisha 412 Hannah 360 James 373 Joseph viii 117 179 234 236 259 319 323 372 373 374 Mary 373 374 Mathew 336 Moses 374 Nathaniel 86 457 460 Nicholas 373 Paul 374 Peter 374 Phebe 359 360 373 Priscilla 373 Rebecca 373 Rose 323 337 373 374 Samuel 373 374 Sarah 319 371 372 373 374 412 Solomon 374 Stephen 374 Thomas 206 337 372 373 374
AUSTYN Tho 252
AVERY Prudence 481 Samuel 481
AYERS Anne 314 Phebe 282 Susannah 470 Tamsen 388
AYSTEN Joseph 372

BABB Charles 496 Hannah 496
BACKER John 233
BACON William 164
BAER Annie 310 Annie Wentworth 292 Mrs 306
BAKER Alexander Douglas 459 Capt 229 230 Charles 305 459 Christine 229 230 231 334 354 457 459 Christine Otis 227 232 Col 231 Ebenezer 332 Eunice 459 Fanny 453 Hannah 332 James 332 John 184 234 317 Love 459 Lucy 354 459 Lydia 307 408 459 Mary 279 305 459 Mehitable 332 Moses 279 Mrs 232 Otis 230 231 260 307 332 334 459 Otis Archelaus Sharrington 459 Sarah 279 459 Sharonton 261 262 Susannah 429 Tamsen 459 Tamsin 332 Thomas 227 228 229 232 332 354 457 459
BALCH Benjamin 498 Hannah 498
BALLEW William 164
BAMPTON Ambros 89
BANCROFT Mary 416
BANFIELD Joshua 261
BANGS Edward 65
BANTOM Mary 369
BANTUM Ambrus 86
BARBER John 238 240 Mercy 481 Nancy Parsons 278 284
BAREFOOT 197 198 199 Capt 248 Dr 142 186 192 193 194 195 420 John 191 Lieut Gov 420 Sarah 185 191 430 Walter ix 20 141 184 185 186 189 191 200 241 421 430
PAREFOOTE Capt 192 Dr 196 Mr 192
BARFFOOTT Capt 244 248 253
BARKER Benjamin 339 Charity 339 Levi 425 Mary 425
BARKHARD Elizabeth 318 Nathaniel Jr 318
BARNUM James 161 Jere 157
BARTHOLOMEW Henry 25

BARTLETT Abigail Dame 277
  Almira 478 Arianna 478
  Bradbury 477 Charles Henry
  277 Edward St John 478
  Elizabeth Ann 477 Hannah 477
  Israel Charlton 277 James
  William 277 John C 477 John
  Heard 446 Josiah 277 477
  Martha Cilley 279 477 Mr 434
  Nancy Huckins 277 Nathan 446
  Polly 477 Sarah 277 477 Sarah
  Whittier 277 Shuah 446 Susan
  Emerson 277 Thomas 477
  William 277
BATCHELDER Charlotte 434 Mary
  278 476
BATT Christafer 245 Christopher
  241
BATTEY Edith 286
BAXTER Henry 446 Mary 446
BEAL Ann 313 Arthur 313
  Mannering 313
BEAN Benjamin 459 Mary 459 481
  Peniel 388
BEARD Esther 384 Hannah 352
  Thomas viii 76 117 179 216 235
  236 237 241 244 248 252 256
  378 Will 240 William 234 238
  244 247 250 256
BECK Ann 118 Henry viii 117 118
  202 235
BECKE Henry 233
BECKER John 233
BEECHDr 429 Mary J 429
BEEDE Caroline 279 Stephen 279
BELKNAP Dr 145 146 Jeremy 27 70
  225 293 368 Rev Dr 231
BELL Elizabeth 398 Frederick M
  398 John 455
BELLEY Mr 233
BELLINGHAM Mr 94 163 166
BENMORE Phellep 252
BENNECK Abraham 161
BENNETT Arter 250 Benjamin 398
  Dame 468 Elizabeth 398 John
  399 Lydia 399
BENNICK Abraham 161
BERRY Abigail 388 Ann 357 John
  388 Jonathan 388 Polly 441
  Samuel 388 Samuel G 388 Sarah
  440 William 388
BIBER James 88
BICKFORD Abigail 270 Charles 86
  Elizabeth 270 336 Hannah 271
  275 Henry 88 John 85 176 203
  211 234 237 238 252 255 257
  336 337

John Jr 243 245 248 John Sr
  240 244 246 251 256 Joseph 86
  253 Judith 337 Lucia G 274
  Mary 339 Thomas 87 257
BINNS Jonas 234
BLACKSTON William 37
BLACKSTONE William 50
BLAISDELL B Frank 286 Herman W
  286 John 286 Osmond 286 Sophia
  H 286
BLAKE Joanna 308 William 308
BLAXTON William 32
BLISS Frank 302
BOARDMAN Abigail 329 Ann 329
  Benjamin 329 Clarissa 425
  David 329 Harriet 329 Mary
  425 Olive 329 Rachel 432
  Stephen 425 Thomas 329 429
  William 432
BOCK Paul 416 Susan 416
BODGE Benjamin Jr 86
BOLNEY Agnes 397
BOND Phebe 492 Thomas 492
  William C 492
Boolter Charity 493 Samuel 493
BOONE Rowena L 489
BOSWELL Mr 94
BOWDITCH William 72
BOWLEY Fanny 499
BOWLIN Fannie B 345 George W
  345
BRACKET Daniel 492 Lydia 492
  Mary 359
BRACKETT Capt 429 Mary 363 424
BRACKSTONE William 206
BRADBURY Jane 476 Thomas 476
BRADFORD Gov 14 16 17 22 45 50
BRADLEY Mr 226
BRADSTREET Ann 421 Hannah 421
  Mr 147 Simon 421
BRADSTREETE Mr 103 163
BRANE Michall 248 Michiell 237
  Michill 243 Mickell 245
BRANSON Geo 235
BRAYE Richard 238
BREWSTER Elder 43 45
BROCK Lydia 362 Maria 417
  Nicholas 388 Sarah 362
  Sobriety 388 Susan 417
BROOKE Baron 101 Lord 92 94 95
  100 101 102
BROOKIN William 206
BROOKS Ann 442 Dolly 442 E G
  437 Harriet 442 Margaret 442
  Mary Abba 437 438 Oliver 437
  Robert 442 Susan 437
BROUGHTON Mr 237 Thomas 179

BROWN Betsey 429 Eliza 430
    Hannah 409 Hepsibah 433 Isaac
    399 John 87 Josiah 430 Louisa
    399 Lydia S 498 Mary H 430
    Moses 433 Nathan 430 William
    299.
BROWNE Henrey 238 240 247 250
BRYANT Lucy M 473
BUCKFORD Elizabeth 281
BUCKNER Charles viii 113 117 145
    237 242
BUDEY Ezariah 87
BUNKER 361 Daniel 85 James 210
    238 239 247 John 210 Joseph
    484 Love 84 Prudence 359
    Zachariah 86
BURBOUGHS Gov 99 George viii 94
    103 105 109 127 149 171 Mr 107
    146
BURGOYNE Gen 412
BURLEIGH Josiah 364 Judith 364
    Susan 355 Thomas 355
BURLEY Hannah 425
BURNAM Roberd 240
BURNETT Gov 230
BURNHAM Ann 274 Anna 271 Asa 278
    Eliot G 274 Elizabeth 356 Lois
    278 Robert 271 Susan 394
    Susanna 394
BURNOM Roberd 238 Robert 176
BURNUM Jeremiah 156 257 Roberd
    243 246 251 Robert 253 256
BURTON Tho 164
BUSS John 177 382 Mr 178
BUSSEL John 87
BUSSY Henry 85
BUTLER Eunice 346 John 164
    William 346
BUZZELL Abigail 410 Arabella 286
    Benjamin 410 Betsey 441 442
    John 441 442 Mary 442 Matilda
    428 Samuel B 428

CALEF Martha 428 Samuel 428
CALLEY Mary 434
CAMMOCK Thomas 38
CANADA Abigail 491 Nicholas 491
CANE Mr 110
CANEY Thamas 248 Thomas 237 244
    366 372
CANIE Thomas Jr 252
CANNE Thomas 181
CANNEY Elizabeth 416 Grace 217
    Hepzibah 416 Ichabod 496 James
    363 Jane 367 John 258 Joseph
    336 367 373 Joshua 85 217
    Judith 460 Mary 336 363 367
    415 Mrs 335 Nancy 496 Otis
    460 Paul 85 Rebecca 460
    Richard 460 Rose 322 359
    Samuel 217 Sarah 373 Susannah
    323 Thomas viii 66 86 138 179
    216 217 235 236 242 256 322
    336 359 367 416 Thomas J 335
    Thomas Jr 86 217
CANNING Thomas 53 175
CANNY Thomas 132
CARD Henry 57 Thomas 58
CARL Samuel 156
CARLILE Rachel 403
CARR 189 195 Elizabeth 305 John
    305 Lucy 439 Mary 305 Moses
    259 Sarah 459
CARTER John 87
CARTLAND Abigail 472 Elijah 472
CARTWRIGHT 189 195
CARVER Robert 72
CATE 496 Andrew 432 Ann 432
    John T G 426 Joseph 432
    Margaret 393 Martha 426 Sarah
    432 Sophia 393
CATTER Richard 237 243 245 248
CAVERLY John L 290
CAVERNO Sarah C 487
CEIAM William 249
CENNEY Ichabod 88
CHADBOURNE Bridget 276 James
    276 Patience 276 James 445
CHAMBERLAIN Ebenezer 337 Mary
    337 R 79 Rebecca 337 Richard
    367 Samuel 339 Susanna 339
CHAMPERNOWNE 191 Arthur 200 C
    Elliott 190 Capt 192 193 195
    Francis 189 199 200 Gawen 199
    200 Mrs 190
CHANDLER Abigail 416 Mary 416
    Philemon 416 William 416
CHAPMAN Elizabeth 433 Roberd
    247
CHASE Abigail 425 Ann 427
    Baruch 429 Betsey 282 Ellen
    429 Elizabeth 399 429 Joseph
    427 Lorinda 474 Mary 426
    Nicholas 426 Rachel 425
    Rodney 474 Thomas 425
CHESLE Philep 74
CHESLEY Daniel 213 Elizabeth
    322 Esther 381 382 385 386
    George 158 James 87 331 332
    391 459 Lydia 332 411 Mary
    380 385 Mehitable 331 332 459
    Phelep 74 75 Phellep 238 239

243 247 251 Philip vii 104
235 258 332 381 385 Roberd
240 Samuel 86 159 257 322
Tamsen 391 459 Tamsin 332
Thomas 251 257 381 Thomas Sr
257
CHESLIE Thomas 253 Philip 253
 Philip Sr 253
CHEVALIER John 53
CHILD Miss 479
CHIRCH John 249
CHISWELL Charlotte 284
CHURCH Abbie 498 Abigail 494 495
 496 497 498 Andrew Jackson 498
 Ann 496 Anne C 498 Benjamin
 493 495 496 497 498 499
 Calvin B 499 Catherine 498
 Charity 496 Charles 497 498
 Daniel 495 Deborah 494
 Drusilla 497 Ebenezer 494 496
 Elizabeth 495 497 Elizabeth H
 498 Ellen M 498 Eunice 495
 Fanny 499 Frances E 499 Green-
 leaf 497 Hannah 496 497 498
 Hanson 497 499 Harriet 497
 Horatio 497 Isaac 498 Israel
 Peirce 498 James 496 497 498
 John 242 245 252 493 494 495
 496 497 John A 499 John E 497
 John H 498 Jona 88 Jonathan
 494 495 496 497 Joseph 493
 496 498 499 Julia 498 Louise
 498 Lucetta 498 Lucy 498
 Lydia 499 Lydia S 498 Lydia V
 498 Martha 496 497 499 Mary
 495 496 497 498 499 Mary Ann
 497 Mercy 495 496 Nancy 496
 497 Nathaniel 496 497 498
 Nathaniel B 498 Patience 498
 Polly 497 Prudence 497 Samuel
 497 Sarah 495 496 Silas B 499
 Tamson Peirce 498 Winfield
 Scott 499
CUSING Jonth 88
CILLEY Bradbury Poore 290 Joseph
 343 477 Sarah 477 Susanna 343
CLARK Abigail 481 Abraham 157
 Benjamin 423 Betty 423 Capt
 246 Daniel 423 David Joseph
 423 Elizabeth 351 416 423
 Jacob 332 James 416 Levi 429
 Love 429 Mary Ann 444
 Nathaniel 351 Richard 88 159
 Ruhamah 426 Samuel S 262 Sarah
 362
CLARKE John B 290 Louise Jane
 473

CLAYTON Thomas 236
CLEMENS Job 368
CLEMENT Abigail 367 368 Abraham
 365 Daniel 88 365 367 368
 Elizabeth 365 429 Frances 406
 James 367 368 406 Joanna 365
 366 Job vii viii 66 87 113
 117 179 217 241 365 366 367
 368 378 406 Job Jr 89 Job Sr
 113 John 85 365 367 368 Lydia
 365 366 Margaret 367 368 Mary
 365 367 429 Robert 365
 Samuel 87 Sarah 365
CLEMENTS Abigail 445 Charles
 262 Elijah 334 J Wesley 113
 122 Job 237 248 253 255 256
 296 335 445 John 58 122 256
 262 375 445 Margaret 365 Mary
 334 Mr 252 Robert 165 William
 58 122
CLEMMENTS Elizabeth 335
CLOUGH Elizabeth 390 Hannah 472
 Nathan 472
COE Betsey 390
COFFEN Enoch 346 James 252
COFFIN Abigail 319 320 350 351
 352 Ann 320 Anna 351 Apphia
 347 348 Barnabas 351 Damaris
 319 347 Daniel 347 Debby 446
 Deborah 320 346 350 351 446
 Dinah 318 347 Dionis 345
 Edmund 348 Edward 320 351 352
 Eleanor 347 Eliphalet 320 351
 Elizabeth 318 320 345 346 347
 351 Enoch 348 Eunice 345 346
 Florence 347 Hannah 347 351
 Isaac 347 James 242 245 250
 317 318 319 345 346 347 Jane
 348 351 446 Jethro 320 351
 Joanna 320 345 347 John 320
 345 346 347 348 352 Joseph 348
 Joshua 350 Josiah 352 Judith
 320 346 347 348 351 Leften
 249 Lydia 346 347 348 352
 Margaret 352 Mary 318 320 345
 346 347 351 Moses 348
 Nathaniel 319 346 348 351
 Parnell 351 Pernel 351 Peter
 120 121 123 134 208 234 237
 242 245 256 319 320 325 345
 346 347 348 349 350 351 352
 373 376 494 Peter Jr 318
 Priscilla 352 Richard 347
 Robert 352 Samuel 348 351
 Sarah 347 348 Stephen 345 346
 347 Susanna 352 Tristram 89
 257 259 318 319 320 345 346

347 348 350 351 446
COGGSWELL Amos 408 Lydia 408
COGSWELL Abigail 497 Amos 307
 332 Hannah 422 Lydia 307 332
 William 422 497
COKER Mary 427
COLBATH George 300 Joseph 401
 Sarah 401 Susan 488
COLBURN Anna 473 Charles Emerson
 473
COLCORD Deborah 320 350 351 446
 Edward viii 201 233 317 351
 Joseph 278 Polly 278
COLE Amias 8 30 Jane 445
 Nicholas 445 William 8
COLEMAN Anna 130 133 137 Calvin
 83 Isaac 317 346 James 57
COLLINES Abraham 251
COLLMAN John 240
COLOMER Abraham 5 12 19 310
COMMONLY Lawrence 300
CONNOR Joseph 87
COOK Ezekiah 88 John 88
COOPE Nathaniel 255
COOPER Walter 255
COPP Betsey 423 David 399
COPPUR Pet 37
CORBETT Abraham 197
COTTON Susanna 406
COURSER Mr 116 William M 39 58
 81 303
COWEL Edward 385
COX Gov 465
CQE Mary 389
CRAMLAN Florence 30
CRANFIELD Edw 367 Gov 315 350
 Lieut Gov 224
CRAPO Laura E 295
CRAWFORD Mary 284
CRETCHET Elias 161
CROCKET Elizabeth 316
CROMET Phellep 246
CROMETT Phellep 251
CROMWEL Joseph 86
CROMWELL Dauey 243 Elizabeth 377
 John 86 Mercy 384 Oliver 348
 Phelep 237 246 Phellep 242 243
 249 Philip vii 117 253 256 377
 Samuel viii
CROSBY Betsey Locke 281 Josiah
 281 Olive 399
CROSS John 203 211 Mary 426
CRUMELL Philip 252
CRUMWELL Abigail 403 Betsey 402
 Daniel 401 Eliza 401 Jacob
 402 403
CROSSE John 202

CURRIER Judith 400
CURTIS Joanna 470 Sarah 468 470
 Zaccheus 470
CUSHING Alexis 371 Anna 370 371
 Anne 364 415 Asenath 371
 Augustus 371 Betsey 370
 Caroline 371 Charles 371
 Clarissa W 370 Daniel 370 395
 Deborah 369 Eliza 371
 Elizabeth 369 Elizabeth
 Hanson 282 George W 371
 Hannah 282 368 370 371 417
 Jarvis 371 John 370 Jonathan
 224 282 353 368 369 370 371
 415 Jonathan P 370 371 Joseph
 W 371 Louisa 371 Lucy Jane
 372 Lydia W 370 Mary 353 369
 370 Mercy 118 Nancy 370 371
 395 Nathan 371 Nathaniel 373
 Parson 231 387 Peter 282 368
 369 370 371 395 Rachel 371
 Rebecca 370 Rev 180 Robert H
 370 Samuel W 370 371 Sarah
 371 Sophia 369 Tamson 370 395
 Thomas 118 364 369 370 371
 415 Thomas Hanson 455 William
 353 369 370 371 395
CUTT John 195 253 Richard 195
 Robert 190
CUTTS 200

DALTON Mr 147
DAM 394 Abigail 269 270 272 316
 Abner 270 Alice 266 269 271
 Anna 268 271 Benjamin 271
 Bethiah 266 Betsey 271 Bettie
 273 Charlotte 268 Cyrus King
 268 269 Cyrus King Jr 269
 Deacon 202 Deborah 272
 Elinathan 272 Eliphalet 270
 272 Eliza 269 Elizabeth 266
 267 269 270 271 337 Elnathan
 269 Esther 267 271 Fidelia
 271 Francis Herbert 268 269
 Frances L 269 George 270
 Hannah 271 Isaac 272 Issacher
 271 Jabez 270 271 Jane 269
 Jethro 271 Joanna 273 John
 201 202 205 211 257 266 269
 270 272 336 380 John Jr 243
 245 248 John Sr 117 241 244
 Jonathan 271 Joseph 86 268
 270 384 Joseph Patterson 273
 Judith 336 Katy 271 Leah 204
 205 206 212 267 268 392 415
 Mr 207 Martha 202 204 205 206
 212 267 271 Martha Pomfrett

392 Mary 270 271 272 Mary
Field 273 Mehitable 270 384
Moses 266 269 270 271 272
Nabby 273 Nancy Emerson 273
Olive 271 Pomfret 267 268 337
Returah 270 Richard 269 271
Sally 268 271 Samuel 87 267
268 271 Sarah 266 267 268
270 272 273 Solomon 270
Susannah 269 273 Temperance
273 Theodore 271 Theophilus
270 Timothy 271 William 202
203 204 205 206 208 211 212
267 270 387 392 William Jr
204 205 William Sr 205 Zebulon
269 270

DAME 361 Abby H 284 Abigail 274
277 279 281 Abner 273 Abraham
272 Alice 286 Alonzo 286 Amasa
281 Ann 274 Anna 274 279 281
283 286 475 Annie 280 Annie P
272 Arabella 286 Arthur 286
Asa 274 Asa Seever 281 286
Augusta J 286 Benjamin 275
276 415 Bessie 286 Bethiah
274 283 Betsey 278 280 285
370 Betsey Locke 281 Bettie
286 Blanche 286 Blanche M 272
Caleb 276 281 286 Caroline 272
279 286 Carrie 286 Carrie M
286 Catherine 280 Charity 273
276 280 281 Charles 282 283
Charles H 272 277 Charles
Wesley 281 286 Charlotte 280
284 Clara A 286 Clarissa 284
Daniel 276 279 283 Daniel
Barber 285 Daniel W 279 Edith
286 Edward 280 Eleanor 281
Eliza 283 Eliza S 280
Elizabeth 273 274 275 281 283
285 Elizabeth A 272 Elizabeth
Hanson 282 Elma Maria 285
Emery J 280 Emily A 284 Emily
H 286 Emma 281 Ernest J 286
Esther 273 275 Fannie 286 Faye
A 272 Fidelia 271 Frank H 285
Frank O 281 Franklin 283
Franklin P 286 George 273 283
George E 286 Greenleaf 284
Greenleaf Cilley 284 Hannah
264 274 275 276 277 278 279
280 284 285 289 294 475
Hannah B 285 Hannah O 285
Harriet 284 285 Hattie 280 281
286 Hattie D 272 Henrietta 284
Hunking 274 277 283 284 475

Isacher 275 Israel 277 284
Israel Hunking 284 Israel
Samuel 284 Jabez 276 279 280
281 282 285 286 287 370 James
281 James Chadbourne 276 282
Jane 276 278 Janvrin 280 Jason
274 Jennie 286 Jeremiah 280
Jerusha 275 John 264 273 274
275 276 278 279 280 281 282
283 284 285 286 287 John E
272 John Edward 277 John Reed
279 John Samuel 277 John U
272 John Wesley 281 286
Jonathan 275 277 279 285 289
Joseph 273 274 275 277 281
282 283 284 Joshua 276 Josie
286 Judge 279 Julia F 272
Juliet 272 Lavinia 280
Leonard 280 Levi 281 Lillian
272 Lizzie 281 Lois 278 280
Loren L 287 Lucia G 274 Lucy
273 Lura 286 Lydia 281 283
284 Lydia C 284 Lydia H 277
Mabel C 272 Margaret 280
Martha 415 483 Martin Luther
281 Mary 272 273 274 275 279
280 281 283 284 285 452 Mary
A 279 Mary Ann 287 Mary C 272
Mary Elizabeth 295 Mehitable
273 277 280 283 Mercy 273 275
279 Meribah 276 281 Moses 271
274 277 279 283 284 287 475
Nabby 278 Nancy 277 284 Nancy
Isabel 287 Nancy Parsons 278
284 Nathan F 280 Olive 274
274 275 277 402 Olive L 281
Osmond 286 Owen 285 Pamelia
Cushing 287 Patience 276
Patience Harriet 283 Paul 273
Pearl F 272 Permelia 278
Permelia Cushing 282 Phebe
282 Polly 276 278 280 Rebecca
275 Relief 279 Rhoda 279
Richard 272 273 275 276 279
280 281 282 285 286 287
Robert Barber 285 Rosamon 272
Rubie L 272 Ruth 274 Sallie
284 Sally 272 275 Samuel 274
276 277 278 283 284 285 287
Samuel H 295 Samuel Scales
284 285 Sarah 272 273 274 275
277 280 283 285 483 Sarah A
280 Sarah Frances 286 Sarah
Parsons 286 Seth 281 Silas
273 Simon 276 280 Sophia 281
Sophia H 286 Stephen 277

Susan 274 277 280 283 Tammy 281 Tamsin 280 Taylor 281 Temperance 274 Theodore 275 Theophilus 279 Thomas 275 Timothy 274 276 280 285 286 Ursula 283 Valentine 275 William 274 280 283 285 483 Zebulon 273
DAMME Deacon 252 264 Elizabeth 265 266 John viii 179 203 235 236 263 264 265 266 267 289 475 John Jr 237 John Sr 237 248 Jonathan 289 Judith 266 Martha 214 222 267 Mary 266 Nicholas 265 Pomfrett 265 Richard 289 Susannah 266 Thomas 264 William 203 211 222 265 266 268 William Jr 214 William Sr 214
DANA Mary 273
DANELL Dauey 240 246 251 Tage 251
DANFORTH Thomas 25
DANIEL David 86 253 Jacob 86 John 85 Jonathan 86 Joseph 85
DANIELS Anna 388 Elizabeth 388 Joseph 388 Reuben 388 Tamsen 401
DARCEY Penelope 397 Thomas 397
DARLING Sarah 434
DAUES 247 John 176 241 244 250 252
DAVES John 238
DAVIDSON Abigail 320 Daniel 320
DAVILL John 238
DAVIS 388 401 Aaron 460 Abigail 388 Amos 430 Ann Elizabeth 357 Betsey 440 Betsey C 357 Constance 328 Deborah 430 Elezir 88 Ensign 252 Hannah 443 Horace P 357 James 159 257 259 491 James J 488 John 160 239 256 440 John Jr 253 Joseph 178 Judah 361 Judith A 488 Mary 419 471 488 Mary A 488 Mary E 488 Miriam 441 N W 203 Nancy 324 357 Nathl 87 Olive 442 Ruth 426 Samuel 87 361 Samuel Jr 88 488 Samuel C 488 Stephen 357 Susanna 460 Thomas 158 259 441 William L 488
DAVISON Abigail 350 351 Maj 350 351
DAY Charity 453
DEAN Charles 28
DEANE Charles 10 12 19 Mr 12
DEARBORN John 429 Susannah 429

DEMERET Eli Jr 85 William 87
DEMERIT John 87
DEMERITT Ebenezer 259 260 Eli 259 Eli Jr 259 John 344 Pamelia 344 Samuel 344
DEMERRET Ely 160
DENBOE Salethel 250
DENBOW Salathie 253
DENMARKE Patricke 250
DENNMARK Patrick 247
DEPUTY Mr 103
DERCIE John 252
DERGIN William 250
DERING 198 199 Henry 197
DERRY John 206
DEVEREAUX Dr 288
DICKENSON Thomas 349
DIMERREST Eli 157
DIMMICK Justin 329 Mary Constantia 329
DIXON Sarah Parsons 286
DOE Abigail 425 Deborah 430 431 Dolly 428 Elizabeth 430 John 436 Mary 436 Nancy 430 Nathaniel 353 Samuel 428 Sarah 353 402 404 Zebulon 430
DOENN Hew 239
DOLAC Christin 246
DOLE Apphia 347 Sarah 348
DONN Hew 243
DORE Abigail 481 Abijah 479 Andrew 480 Beniah 480 Benjamin 480 481 492 Charity 479 480 Charles 481 Daniel 480 Dorothy 480 Elizabeth 479 480 Ezekiel 481 Frances 479 Hannah 480 Henry 479 Isaac 481 James 480 481 John 479 480 481 John C 481 Jonathan 480 Joseph 480 Jou Boule 479 Lydia 479 480 492 Mary 406 479 480 481 492 493 Mason 481 Mehitable 481 492 Olive 480 Patience 480 481 Paul 480 Phebe 480 481 Philip 479 480 481 492 Philip Jr 479 Richard 478 479 480 Sarah 479 480 481 492 Tamsen 478 479 William 479 480 481
DOW Jabez 496 John 253 Nicholas 253
DOWNE James 37 93
DOWNES 267 Elizabeth 267 Tho 237 252 Thomas 242 245 249
DOWNING Emanuel 170 John 257 258 John B 280 Lavinia 280
DOWNS Abigail 306 379 Gershom

385 Thomas viii 117 257 306
378 494 495
DOWSE 498 Mary 388
DOWTY Thomas 238 240 247
DOYLE Nellie 476
DREW Abigail 443 Alice 490 Anna
  283 Anne 416 Charlotte 488
  Clarissa 416 Daniel 416 490
  Edwin Plaisted 212 Elizabeth
  309 353 416 443 Eunice 495
  ffranic 253 Francis 206 207
  353 416 Frank 495 Jeremiah 416
  John viii 89 203 206 207 257
  John Jr 89 John Sr 204 Jos 89
  Joseph 86 204 205 206 212 214
  260 443 Joseph Jr 203 Lavinia
  H 490 Leah 204 206 212 214
  Louisa 361 Mary A 489 Mishack
  157 161 Nelson U 490 Polly 401
  Rowena L 490 Samuel 401 Sarah
  206 Thos 161 Thomas Jr 86
  William 235 238 240 243 246
  250 William Plaisted 204 212
DROWN Capt 496
DRU Clement 88 David 88 Francis
  87 Meshack 88
DUDLEY Abigail 352 Albert Bart-
  lett 478 Alice Evelin 478 Ann
  311 343 421 Elizabeth 352
  George Albert 478 Gov 306
  Grace 478 Leon Kennett 478
  Marion Grace 478 Samuel 165
  311 352 Thomas 311 343 421
DUMMER Margaret 365 Thomas 365
DUNN Hew 247 Rose 323 Samuel 262
  323 Samuel Jr 261 262
DURELL Abigail 419 Duda 419
  Daniel Meserve 419 Edward
  Henry 419 Nicholas 419
DURGEN Jonathan 89 William 246
DURGIN 434 Betsey 401 435
  Charlotte 432 Dorothy 401
  Elizabeth 402 Hannah 284 James
  401 Jonathan 401 Joseph 402
  435 Josiah 284 Judith 401
  Lydia C 284 Miles 435 Polly
  435 Thomas 432 William 253
DUTCH Abigail 433
DYER Olive 493 Whits 493

EDGERLEY Thomas 251 252 257 400
  401 402 404
EDGERLY Abiel 402 404 Abigail
  400 402 403 Abigail C 403
  Agnes 402 404 Alice O 403
  Addison 403 Andrew 405 Andrew
H 405 Ann Elizabeth 401
Bathsheba 402 Benjamin 404
Betsey 401 402 403 Betsey B
403 Bradbury 401 Caleb 402
404 Charles E 403 Clara A 403
Curtis C 401 Daniel 404
Daniel W 403 Deborah 404
Dorothy 401 Dudley 401
Ebenezer 401 402 Eleanor 401
Elijah 404 Eliphalet 402
Elizabeth 400 401 402 404 405
Elizabeth A 272 George 403
George W 405 Hannah 400 403
404 405 Jacob 401 403 James
401 403 James H 404 James S
402 Jane 400 404 Jennie 402
Jenny 403 Jeremiah 404 Jethro
403 John 400 401 402 403 404
405 John H 272 Jonathan 403
404 Joseph 400 401 405 Joseph
M 401 Josiah 404 Jotham 402
Judith 400 401 402 404 Louisa
R 403 Louise 401 Love T 403
Lydia 404 Lydia M 405 Maria C
403 Martha 404 Martha A 404
Martha W 405 Mary 400 401 402
404 Mary C 405 Mary J 403
Mehitable 404 Mercy 404 Moses
401 Moses Jr 401 Nathaniel
401 Nathaniel G 401 Olive 271
402 403 Oliver 401 Polly 401
Rachel 401 402 403 Rebecca
400 402 Richard 401 403 Robert
402 Samuel 271 400 401 402
404 Sarah 400 401 402 403 404
Sarah A 403 404 Sarah W 403
Statira 401 Susan 274 402
Susanna 401 Sylvester 404
Tamson 401 404 Temperance 402
Thomas C 405 William 405
Zechariah 87 400 405
EDLING David Ludecas viii
EIRWING Edward 240
ELA Daniel 366 George W 455
ELIS John 252 253
ELKINS Esther 326 Henry 326
  Jeremiah 364 Keziah 364
ELLIOTT Albert F R 299 Martha
  362 Moses 362
ELWELL Molly 460
EMERSON Deborah 420 John 84
  Jonathan Watson 277 Michael
  420 Prof 465 Samuel 257 259
  379 Smith 474 Solomon 87 259
  Susan 277 Temperance 274
  Timothy 383

EMERY A 236 Anthony vii 179 233 235 255 372 Meribah 276
ENDICOTT Gov 104 108 John 50 108 Jno 67
ERWIN Edward 243
ESTEARS Joseph 88
ESTERS Elisha 88
ESTES Elijah 260 Elizabeth Cushing 287 Mary Millard 287 Pamelia Cushing 287 Rhoda 287 Samuel 287 Stephen Perkins 287
EUENS Robert 242 245 249
EVANS 386 Abigail 329 401 Ann 409 Benjamin 77 409 410 411 Betty 411 Bridget 431 Catherine 412 Daniel 410 Dorcas 410 Edward 409 410 Eleanor 410 Eliza 486 Elizabeth 329 409 410 411 Ephraim 411 Eunice 495 Hannah 409 410 486 Ichabod Chesley 411 John 207 254 409 410 489 Jonathan 409 410 Joseph 329 410 411 412 486 Keziah 364 Lemuel 410 Lydia 411 Marcy 410 411 Mary 411 486 Mercy 410 Miles 495 Molly 411 Moses 410 Patience 410 Patty 411 Paul 415 Rachel 410 Rhoda 486 Robert 77 364 408 409 410 Robert Sr 77 409 Samuel 486 Sarah 410 411 412 486 Solomon 411 412 Stephen 70 260 307 329 410 411 412 Temperance 411 Thomas 409 Tobias 412 Vesta 329 William 410 486 William E 486
EVENS Danie 88 John 88 Joseph 3rd 88 Robert 252 Robert Jr 88
EVERETT William 3
EYRES 195

FALL Elizabeth 307
FARNUM Elizabeth 480 Paul 480
FARRINGTON J C 282 James B 282 Joseph 282 Mary 282 Mary Dame 282 Walter 282
FAURBISH William 131
FAWNE Elizabeth 365
FAY John Jr 87
FAYER John 53 174
FEBBRIGG Elizabeth 467
FELKER Isiah 496 Marcy 496
FELLOWS Hannah 426
FELOES Tho 251
FERNALD Dr 185 Elizabeth 309 Joseph 57 Olive 275 Renald 184
FERREN Joseph 404 Mercy 404

FESSENDEN Eliza 339 Thomas M 339
FFIELD Joseph 253 Zacharie 252
FFILD Joseph 239
FFILLD Joseph 238 Sachrey 251
FFOLLETT Nicholas 253 Will 238 William 202 239 242 247 250 253
FFOLLETTE William 237
FFOOTMAN Thomas 239 240 244 246 276
FFURBER William 117 176 237 245 248 252 William Jr 252
FFURSEN Thomas 53
FFURSON Thomas 174
FIELD Daniel 389 Darby 235 John Jr 86 Joseph 161 Sarah 308 389 Zach 210 Zachariah 206 308 Zachius 210
FIENNES William 102
FIFIELD Hannah 435
FILLD Joseph 246 Josephf 243 251
FINSON Elizabeth 497
FISH Mr 111
FISHER Janvrin 399 436 438 Mary 138 Sally 399 Susan 436 437
FISKE Mr 61
FLANDERS Asenath 344 Elizabeth A 344 George H 344
FLECHER Mr 175
FLOYD Capt 208
FOGG Annie 280
FOLGER Ebenezer 495 Nathan 495 Nathaniel 318 Peter 318 Priscilla 318 Sarah 495 Walter 495
FOLLET John 86 William 246
FOLLETT Abraham 246 John viii Nichilas 78 William viii 241 243
FOLSOM Amy 478 Hannah 370 Josiah 370
FOOTMAN Susanna 399 Tho 235 251 256 399
FORD Benjamin 57 George W 57 Jacob 57 Jefferson 498 Tamson Peirce 498
FOREMAN I G 437
FOSS 361 Comfort 433 Esther 363 Frances 388 Hannah 307 Humphrey 451 Louisa 361 Mary Downs 388 Mercy 480 481 Molly 362 Nathaniel 363 Samuel 388 Sarah 448 William 448
FOSTE John 250
FOWLER Abigail 274 John 274

Martha J 285 Mrs 335
FOY John 381 Mary 381
FOYE Solomon H 388
FRANKLIN Nancy Huckins 277
  William B 277
FREESE James 425 Rachel 425
FRENCH Abigail 424 Daniel 429
  Martha 429 William 424
FRIER Nathaniel 439 Nathaniell
  246
FROST Asenath 344 Margaret 333
  William 257
FRYER Nathaniel 195
FULLER Anna 370
FURBER Elizabeth 266 271 414 448
  Fidelia 271 Hattie D 272
  Jethro 385 Levi 271 Samuel 272
  Sarah 414 William viii 155 160
  164 179 184 235 236 243 255
  256 257 266 317 373 414
  William Jr 448
FURBURSE William 233
FURBUSH Sarah 389
FURLONG Sally 268
FURSEN Tho 235

GAGE Abigail 399 Agnes 397 Ann
  397 Benjamin 397 Capt 293
  Daniel 397 David 57 Edward
  397 Elbridge 57 Elizabeth 398
  399 Esther 399 Hannah 398 399
  Joanna 397 John 118 217 259
  260 296 297 396 397 398 399
  483 John Jr 259 Jonathan 396
  397 398 399 Joseph 396 399
  Judith 398 483 Louisa 399
  Lydia 399 Mary 398 399 Mary W
  399 Mary Wingate 400 Mr 58
  Moses 57 262 396 398 399 400
  Nancy 399 Peggy 399 Penelope
  397 Philippa 397 Rebecca 399
  Sally 399 Samuel 397 Sarah
  398 Susanna 399 Thomas 397
  William 397 398
GALE Amos 428 Charles C P 428
  Enoch 428 Gilman 428 John 428
  Mary 428
GAMMONS Mary 389
GARDNER 195 Ann 320 Anna 351
  Christopher 107 Eunice 319
  George 319 James 318 John 319
  320 351 John G 352 Lydia 352
  Mary 318 320 351 Priscilla
  352 Richard 318
GARLAND Charity 280 Dorcas 448
  Ham 280 Jabez 88 448 Lois 280
  Margaret 493 Mary 453 Nathan

88 Olive L 281 Richard 354
  Sarah 354
GAYER Damaris 319 347 Dorcas
  318 319 347 Elizabeth 319
  John 319 William 319 347
GEARICH John 252
GEE George 253
GELLS Mark 88
GEORGE Eleanor 281 Joseph 281
  Judith 402 Thomas 402
GERRISH Anna 326 327 Elizabeth
  326 327 Joseph 326 327 356
  357 Maria 327 Nathaniel 327
  Paul 153 207 254 327 Paul Jr
  89 Richard 79 327 Sarah 420
  Samuel 88 Timothy 327 William
  326
GIBBENS Ambrose 164
GIBBONS Ambrose 5 235 255
GIBBS John Tuttle 454
GIBONS Edward 170
GIDDINGS Betsey 428 John 428
GILBERT Humphrey 199 John 404
  Mercy 404
GILES John 86 Lydia 337 Mark
  252 337 Matthew 246 Statira
  401 Stephen 401
GILLES Clark 249 Mathew 240 250
GILLS Mathew 238 Matthew 243
GILMAN Bradstreet 428 Bridget
  389 Chase 428 Comfort 428
  David 424 Deborah 419 Dorothy
  424 Dudley 428 Edward 424
  Elizabeth 320 351 Israel 424
  James 419 Jeremy 424 Joanna
  320 John 320 351 Moses 424
  Martha 428 Mary 424 Mary Ann
  287 Samuel 424 Sarah 481
GINN Thomas 239
GLAND Peter 244
GLASS Nancy 284 Samuel 284
GLOVER John 469
GODARD John 53 174
GODDARD John 235 253 256
GODDER John 233 239 243 247 250
GOE George 253
GOLDSMITH Joanna 307
GOLDWEIR George 237
GOODING Richard 379 Sarah 379
GOODWIN Abigail 309 Betsey 342
  Daniel 309 342 Elizabeth 267
  380 Hannah 356 380 John 481
  Joseph Lawrence 342 Martha
  Hilton 342 343 Mary Hilton
  341 Mehitable 481 Richard 267
  379 380 Sarah 379 380 Zeruiah
  433

GORGE F 147 Robert 47
GORGES Ferdinando 5 6 7 41 93
  188 189 200 Robert 15 33 41
GOSS Abigail 440 John 440 Levi
  440 Lydia 429
GOULD Charlotte 268 Mary 390
  Miriam 323
GOVE Caroline 433 Mr 433
GOWEN Elexsander 240
GRACE Mary 362
GRANT Capt 95 James 179 237 Mr
  95
GRAUES William 238
GRAY Henry 443 Joanna 444 Joanna
  R 443 Margaret 363 William 444
GREEN Elizabeth 323 326 361 386
  Ezra 225 392 James D 419
  Joseph 326 Rowland 386
  Susanna 392 Thomas 239
GREENE Elizabeth 367 Margaret
  468 Mary 400 Robert 468 Row-
  land 387
GREENLAND 195 Henry 189 194 366
GREENLEAF Capt 208 Elizabeth 346
  Henry 346 Judith 346 Mary 429
  Samuel 429 Stephen 346
GREENOWAY Mary 84
GRENLEFE Edmond 164
GREVILLE Robert 101
GREY James 486 Polly 486
GUILD Benjamin 328 Elizabeth
  328
GUILFORD Philippa 397
GUNNISON Hugh 164
GUPPY Abigail 281 290 293
  Abigail F 289 Albert 281 Ann
  288 289 Anna 281 Capt 288 289
  293 294 295 Col 292 George
  293 George Fox 281 289 Hannah
  275 289 294 Hannah Esther 290
  J Belknap 298 James 288 289
  292 294 296 297 452 Jane 288
  289 Jeremy 293 Jeremy Belknap
  289 290 300 302 John 275 281
  289 294 John Devereaux 290
  Joseph Dame 290 Joshua 288
  Joshua J 291 Joshua James 290
  Kingwall 288 Mary 293 Prudence
  289 Russell 281 Samuel 293
  Sarah 289 294 Sarah Ann 289
  295
GUPTIL Abigail 492 Benjamin 492
  Phebe 492
GYLES Matthew 235

HACKETT Abigail 487 Peter 487
HAINES Samuel viii 118 235 Tho
  252
HAKET William 237
HALE Charles 308 Eliza 308
  Elizabeth 351 Mary 308 Mercy
  Adeline 308 Nancy 308 Robert
  351 Samuel 224 308 Stephen
  334 Susanna 334 William 215
  226 308 William Jr 261
HALEY Benjamin 428 Harrison 234
  Martha 428 Mary 493 William
  493
HALL Abigail 306 308 332 378
  379 382 383 384 387 388 389
  390 443 498 Allen 286 Andrew
  390 Ann 390 Anna 386 388
  Arthur E 286 Bartholomew 306
  Benjamin 381 386 387 388
  Benjamin Randall 443 Benjn 87
  Betsey 386 390 Bridget 389
  Charity 388 Daniel 213 387
  388 389 490 Deacon 241 252
  Deborah 387 388 Dorothy 389
  Dwight 298 302 389 E Melvin
  387 Elizabeth 377 382 383 384
  387 388 390 443 Emma 390
  Esther 381 382 384 385 386
  Experience 390 Frances 387
  388 Gilman 490 Grace 377 378
  390 Hannah 332 377 389 390
  Harry 281 Hatevil 86 384 385
  389 390 Henry 281 Hester 385
  Hezekiah 384 Isaac 381 387
  Israel 387 James 381 383 386
  387 Jane 390 Jedediah 390
  Joanna R 443 John vii 115 117
  119 120 126 179 202 222 233
  235 237 244 245 248 254 256
  263 266 306 308 375 376 377
  378 379 380 381 382 383 384
  385 386 387 388 389 390 John
  Jr 236 375 378 John Sr 236
  375 Jonathan 235 381 Jonathan
  Sr 379 Jose Joseph 88 Joseph
  379 381 382 383 384 386 387
  388 389 441 443 Joseph Jr 86
  Joseph D 387 Joseph Varney
  443 Keziah 386 390 Kinsley
  378 Lois 388 Lorana 389
  Lorenzo 443 Lydia 386 Mary
  375 380 381 382 383 385 386
  387 388 389 390 Mary Esther
  490 Mary Shannon 441 443
  Mehitable 270 273 384 Mercy
  384 389 390 Meribah 281
  Nathaniel 377 Nicholas 390
  Oram R 443 Ossie M 286 Otis
  383 Paul 390 Patience 389

Peniel 388 389 Philip 385
Ralph vii 87 117 179 236 256
375 376 377 378 379 380 381
382 385 386 387 388 Raphfe 176
Robert vii Ruth 386 390 Sally
Williams 443 Samewell 249
Samuel 386 387 389 Samuel R
384 Sarah 266 380 382 386 387
389 390 443 Sarah Frances 286
Sargant 243 252 Silas 390
Sobriety 388 Solomon 388
Susan 402 443 Susan Mason 443
Tabitha 383 Tamsen 388 Thomas
379 382 383 384 Ursula 283
Ursula R 443 William 386 390
Winslow 389 Winthrop 387
HALLIBURTON George 428 Mary 428
HALLOWELL Henry 400 Rebecca 400
HAM Aaron 354 Abigail 419
  Abigail Dame 277 Benjamin 89
  Betsey C 357 Charles 277
  Clement 86 Daniel 87 Dodefer
  89 Edward 444 Epherem 87
  Ephraim 259 260 Ephraim 3rd
  261 Hannah 354 James 335
  Joanna 444 John 249 252 273
  389 448 461 John Jr 85 John
  Thomas Wentworth 461 Jonathan
  87 Joseph 88 89 160 418 419
  444 461 Love 444 Lucy 354
  Lydia 324 Marie Teresa 444
  Mary 273 444 447 448 Nathaniel
  87 354 Olive 335 Samuel 329
  Tamson 418 419 Theresa 461
  Thomasine 418 William 221
HAMACKE Thomas 249
HAMETT Tho 252
HANCE John 239 240 243
HANDSON Tho 372
HANSCOM Sarah 493 William 493
HANSON Abigail 395 495 496 Ann
  373 483 Anna 282 Anne 361 364
  Asa 282 Benjamin 353 Benjamin
  Jr 89 Betsey 282 Catherine
  412 Charity 281 Charles A C
  282 David 353 Dominicus 255
  282 353 Ebenezer 261
  Elizabeth 353 360 411 Ephraim
  254 260 297 Eunice Leila 438
  Hannah 282 370 Hester 282
  Humphrey 282 353 Ichabod 395
  Isaac 88 355 497 James 157
  Joanna 282 353 John 88 159 359
  373 John Jr 87 John Burnam 255
  John Burnham 260 370 John P 64
  Jonathan 88 89 323 Jonathan Jr
  261 Joseph 254 259 260 281 282
  353 399 482 Joseph Jr 88 259
  381 Joseph 3rd 88 Judith 360
  483 Keziah 390 Lydia 355 Mary
  284 334 373 481 497 Mary Dame
  282 Maul 89 373 Mercy 353 495
  Merirah 282 Nathaniel 78 88
  Nathaniel Jr 88 Patience 498
  Phebe 359 361 373 Rebecca 399
  Rose 323 Samuel 88 Sarah 353
  359 483 Servia 353 Solomon 88
  260 Stephen 373 Susannah 355
  Thomas 87 179 237 242 245 249
  252 258 495 496 Thomson 78
  Timothy 88 390 Tobey 242 246
  Tobias 249 257 258 259 360
  483 Wedowe 249 Widdow 252
  William 260
HARDY Judith 427
HARFORD Lydia 296 450 Nancy 442
  Nicholas viii 118 161 Paul
  450
HARIS Nicholas 253
HARRIGAN Mr 65
HARRIMAN Jonathan 86
HARRIS John 468 470 Nicloes 250
  Thomas 88
HARRISON Nicholas 156 257
HARTFORD Nancy 441
HARTHORNE William 137
HARVEY Clement 86 Daniel 87
  John 86 Richard 194
HARVY Nick 417
HASKINS Sophia 281
HASSAM John T 35
HATCH Nancy 430 Samuel Jr 430
HATHAWAY Hepsibah 319 Thomas
  319
HATHORNE William 136
HAVEN Joseph 436
HAWKINS Abigail 389 Stephen 86
  Thomas 68
HAYES Aaron 392 395 Abra 391
  395 Amos Main 394 Ann 392 395
  Benjamin 391 392 393 396 451
  452 Betsey 395 396 Betty 394
  395 Charles W 112 Daniel 260
  392 395 396 David 308 Elihu
  391 393 394 Elizabeth 391 393
  395 396 Enoch 395 Ephraim 272
  Ezekiel 392 393 395 396 Ezra
  299 George 393 George Snell
  396 Hannah 334 392 393 396
  485 Hezekiah 391 393 396
  Ichabod 390 391 392 395 396
  484 Jacob 396 James 391 James
  C 395 Jane 393 396 451 452
  John 334 358 390 391 392 393

394 395 396 John Jr 88
Jonathan 369 370 392 393 395
Joseph 392 Joshua 391 396
Leah 204 205 206 212 267 392
415 Lydia 354 Margaret 280 393
396 Mary 205 390 391 392 393
394 395 396 415 Mehitable 392
Mercy 308 Molly 394 396 Moses
392 395 396 Nancy 371 395
Patience 393 Paul 391 Peter
88 358 391 392 395 Polly 396
Rachel 485 Reuben 392 393
Richard 354 Robert 391 395
Rosamon 272 Samuel 86 204 205
206 212 214 267 391 392 415
Sarah 392 395 Sarah A 393
Solomon 393 Sophia 369 393
Stephen 396 Susan 394 Susanna
392 Susannah 393 Tamsen 391
393 394 395 396 Tamson 370
Theodore 394 Thomas 391 393
Wentworth 392 394 William 391
393
HAYNES Samewell 115 202 314
HEALD Charles Thomas 281 Louise
Peabody 281 Mary 281 Mary
Phylura 281 Thomas 281
HEALEY Love 440 Samuel 440
HEARD Abigail 367 445 446 447
448 451 453 Abraham 452 Ann
445 Anna 449 Benjamin 252 292
296 297 305 446 447 448 449
450 452 Biniamen 249 Capt 446
447 Charity 453 David 453
Deborah 450 452 Dorcas 446
447 448 Ebenezer 453 Elizabeth
305 414 445 447 448 449 451
453 Experience 450 451 457
458 Ezekiel 454 Hannah 448 450
453 Isaac 452 Isabel 367 445
Jacob 453 James 132 309 367
445 446 448 449 450 452 457
Jane 351 393 445 446 451 452
Joanna 454 John vii 89 233
234 237 242 245 249 252 292
330 367 414 444 445 446 447
448 449 450 451 452 458 John
Jr 453 Jonathan 452 Jonathan
Jr 453 Joseph 448 451 Joshua
453 Katherine 445 Keziah 451
Lieut 368 Louisa 323 Lydia 450
Mary 297 309 445 446 447 448
450 451 452 Nathaniel 257 447
448 451 452 Patty 452 Paul
453 Phebe 445 446 450 491
Rebecca 451 Reuben 451 452
Ruth 451 Samuel 88 257 260

447 448 450 451 457 458
Samuel Jr 89 Sarah 448 452
Shuah 367 445 446 457
Susanna 445 Timothy 452
Tristram 160 234 257 393 447
448 450 451 452 453 William
448 453
HEARN Richard 88
HEATH Mary C 272 William A 272
HEAYS Benja 89 Elihu 87 Ezekiah
88 Ichabod 88 Joseph 88
Reuben 88 Thomas 88
HENDERSON Abigail 487 Alfred
487 Charles 339 Charles
Trafton 295 Daniel 261 Delia
295 Delia Annah 295 Elizabeth
295 454 Emma Trafton 295
Fanny Laurence 295 Hiram 487
Howard 54 55 58 259 260 309
Howard Sr 64 Howard Millett
295 John H 58 John Samuel 295
Laura E 295 Lydia 487 Mary
339 Mary Elizabeth 295 Mary
Pickering 454 Mehitable 487
Mrs 294 Richard 487 Samuel
Howard 289 295 Samuel Hoyt
294 Sarah 54 309 Sarah Ann
289 295 Sarah Frances 295
Thomas 57 58 64 454 Thomas
Albert 295 Uriah 487 Warren
487 William 54 William C 294
William Channing 295
HERRICK 423 Joshua 281 Mary 281
HERSOM Jacob 480 Lydia 480
HESELRIG Arthur 94
HETHERSEY Robt 235
HEWELL Mr 94
HICKS Joseph 87
HIGGINS Bryant 158 Robt 160
HILL 429 Aphia 423 Fannie 277
Hannah 423 Harriet 285 John
202 239 240 252 Joseph 257 Mr
238 239 247 Nathaniel 178 257
315 Rebecca 373 Sarah 315
Simeon 373 Tamson 486 Val 182
Valentine 166 222 255 256
Vallintine 176 William 87 157
160 253
HILLTON John 247
HILTON Alice 313 Ann 311 313
343 Betsey 342 Catherine 310
Charles 197 198 199 311
Deborah 428 Frances 312
George 424 George O 424 Ed 36
Edward 1 5 7 8 14 15 17 19 20
21 22 23 24 26 27 28 30 34 35
36 37 38 39 40 43 44 46 49 80

90 92 93 94 101 103 109 218
223 302 306 310 311 312 343
428 Edward Jr 343 Elizabeth
306 John 22 235 237 239 240
244 250 313 Joseph 343
Katharine 193 Magdaline 313
Manwaring 313 Mark 311 Martha
427 Mary 313 424 Mr 39 51 196
Pawl 35 Rebecca 311 Samuel
197 311 Sobriety 311 Susanna
311 William 1 5 14 15 19 21 22
23 24 25 26 27 28 34 35 37 38
93 311 313 William Jr 22 24 25
26 28 William Sr 202 203 211
Winthrop 427
HOAG Mary 426
HOBBES Henrey 250
HOBBS Emma 433 Phebe 481 Susan 309
HOBES Henrey 242 246 Henry 237
HODGDON Caleb 260 357 373
 Charity 273 Dorcas 297 Eleazer
 297 Elizabeth 399 Hannah 276
 Israel 206 406 Israel Jr 88
 Joseph 273 Moses 493 Nancy 493
 Priscilla 357 373 Relief 279
 Richard 481 Sarah 273
 Shadrach 86 259 399 Susan 481
 Tamson 485 Thomas 386
HODGKINS Sarah 275
HODSDON Jeremy 249
HOGE Samuel 88
HOGG Mary 357
HOITT Abigail Page 394 Gorham W 394
HOLDEN Samuel 85
HOLLAWAYE Henrey 240
HOLLOWAY Henry 244
HOLMES Joseph 387 Mary 387
HOLT Dorothy 429
HOLTON Charlotte 423 Daniel 423
 John Camden 265 Nancy 423
 Sarah 423
HOOD Hope 208 209
HOOK Florence 347
HOOKE Henry Cornelius 366
HOOTEN Elizabeth 134
HOPKINS President 465
HOPKINSON Caleb 407 Sarah 407
HORN Charity 355 John 87 378 384
 451 John Jr 87 Nathaniel 87
 260 Susan 437 William 87 245
HORNE 391 Abigail 355 Benjamin
 355 Christine 356 Daniel 88
 394 Daniell Jr 89 Eliza 344
 Giles 58 Isaac 88 332 Joanna
 442 444 John 330 Lydia 332

Lydia A 357 Mary 390 Mrs 330
 Oliver S 261 262 Paul 356
 Relief 394 Samuel 57 58 Sarah
 398 Susan 280 Thomas 330
 Timothy 394 442 444 Will 242
 William 249 252 330 William Jr 89
HOUSTON James 479 Mary 479
HOWARD Margaret 467 Samuel 261
 Sarah 54
HOWE Charles Luke 461
HOWEL Rice 236 240
HOWELL Rice 238
HOWES Edward 94
HOYT Elizabeth 269 454 Lydia
 426 Nathaniel 426
HUBBARD Abigail 446 Elizabeth
 398 John Heard 446 Joseph 86
 Mr 27 29 William 14 26 28
HUCKINS Abigail 277 400 Israel
 274 James 87 252 257 387 John
 86 400 Mary 274 Moses 277
 Nancy 277 Robert ix 233 257
 274 Ruth 274 Sarah 387
HUGGINS James 251 Robert 202
HUGHS Elizabeth 307
HULL Beiniamen 247 Beniamin 243
 Benjamin 239 240 Elizabeth
 414 448 Joseph 176 448
HUMFRIES Thomas 247
HUNKING Anna 274 475 Mark 70
 218 475 Mary 274
HUNT Deborah 364
HUNTRESS Abigail 269 Elizabeth
 435 George 269
HURD Abigail 333 Anna 487 Eliza
 B 334 Ezekiel 234 261 262 332
 334 454 455 Fanny 453 George
 339 Joanna 334 John 333 453
 Mary 453 Mary B 334 Mary
 Pickering 454 Molly 453
 Reuben Jr 453 Sarah 339 453
 Susanna 453 Tristram 234 453
 William 453
HUSINGS Joseph 88
HUSSEY Christopher 343 Daniel
 262 Hannah 390 Jane 460 Job
 337 Marcy 411 Margery 337
 Mary 343 360 364 389 452
 Patience 480 Paul 389 480
 Richard 157 Roberd 239 Samuel
 411
HUTCHINS Mr 465
HUTCHINSON Ann 109 148 Anne 167
 Isabella 493 Mrs 148 William
 167
HUTCOTE Aaron 400 Rebecca 400

HYDE Asenath 371 Jacob 371
HYNCH ffrancis 253

JACKSON Abigail 442 Andrew 454
  Benja 89 Betsey 395 David 442
  Elijah 442 Elizabeth 324
  Ephraim 211 203 Eunice 361
  Frank 324 Gen 455 James 86 238
  Jams 239 Jane 352 John 324
  Joseph 87 Mary 442 Patience
  361 Phebe 324 Samuel 395 Sarah
  395 Stephen 395 Walter 238 243
  247 250 253 352 Wat 239
JACOBS Dorothy 359 Martha 359
  Phebe 361
JAMES Frances 303 John 88 493
  Martin 303 Patience 493
JAMESON Patrick 243
JANSEN Jacob 366
JEFFREY Jam 154
JEFFRIES William 37
JEMESON Patric 238
JEMISON Pattrick 247
JEMSON Patrick 240 Pattrick 251
JENKINS Ann 390 Experience 450
  458 Jos 158 Joseph 159
  Stephen Jr 89 William 450
JENNESS Hannah 453 481 Lydia 281
  Paul 270 Returah 270 Solomon
  261
JEWELL 423
JEWETT Ann 424 Ann Elizabeth 401
  Bradbury 401 Capt 55 Jonathan
  436 Joseph 424 Susan 436
JOANES Joseph 159
JOBE M 10 Mr 6 10 18
JOHNSON 361 Charity 388 Esther
  362 George 271 James 53 174
  Katy 271 Sally 440 Susannah
  431 Thomas 235 243
JONEN Stephen 257
JONES Abigail 447 448 Anthony 86
  Elizabeth 308 418 433 Frank
  217 Ginkin 252 Jenkon 448
  Joseph 257 258 Jukin 249 Mary
  Ann 426 Richard 89 Roberd 237
  242 Rufus 190 Shephen 258
  Stephen 178 253 258 Steuen 240
  244 250 Steuens 247 Will 239
  241 William 53 174 244
JONSON Thomas 238 239 247
JORDAN Catherine 439
JOSE Esther 326 Hannah 309 Mary
  309 Richard 309 326
JOWETT Joseph 366
JUNKES Roberd 238

KEATLER Richard 236
KEAZER Sarah 356
KELLEY Anna 388 Ebenezer 387
  James 88 Julia A 344 Mary 387
  400 Pamelia 344 Philip 388
  Samuel 387 Thomas 400 William
  77 344
KELLOW Augusta A 489
KEMBEL Nemiah 87
KEMBLE Thomas 241
KEMBRICK Louisa L 488
KENNARD E P 58 59
KENNEY Jane 367
KENT Dorothy 401 John 401 Mary
  401 Olever 240 Oliver 235
  Ollever 239 Olluer 244 Rachel
  402 403 Richard 401
KERKE Henrey 248
KEY James 208 John 208
KEYD James 242
KEYES 397
KEYSER Thomas 70
KID James 368
KIELLE Benjamin 344 John 260
KIMBALL Anna 282 Elizabeth 330
  332 Ezra 330 332 Mr 455
  Richard 331 454 Samuel 261
  Thomas 117
KIMBEL Ezora 87
KIMMINS Sarah 270
KINCKAD David 160
KINISTON John 245
KITTREDGE John 261 Thomas W 261
KNIGHT Bridget 276 Capt 54
  Elizabeth 451 George 402 John
  53 257 Lydia 307 Robt 164
  Temperance 402
KNOLLY Mr 147
KNOLLYS Hanserd viii 107 109
  125 126 127 145 149 167 168
  170 223 Mr 126 146 148 150
  169 171 172
KNOWLES Elizabeth 453
KNOWLTON Betsey 278 Hannah 278
  Nabby 278 Nathan 278 Sherburn
  278
KNOX Mary 492 Sarah 309
  Zachariah 492

LA BEAU Christine 227 457
LADD Jane 288
LAFAYETTE Gen 226
LAIGHTON Hatevil 86
LAMOS Abigail 324
LAMSON Albert H 286 Mary Ella
  286
LANDERS Nathanl 156

LANE Abigail 435 Edmund J 262
LANG Hannah 389 Reuben 389
LANGDON John 178
LANGLEY Hannah 359 474 Mary A
  489 Samuel 474
LANGSTAFF Henry 235 236
LANGSTAFFE Hanry 174 315 Sarah
  315
LANGSTAR Henry 179
LANGSTER Henerie 252 Henry 233
LANKESTER Henrey 243
LANKSTAFF Henry 255
LANKSTER Henrey 245 248 Henry
  237 255 256
LARKHAM Mr 126 147 148 150
  Thomas viii 21 99 125 127 146
  149
LARKIN David 252
LATHROP Thomas 470
LAUSE John 236
LAWSON Xtopher 164
LAYCOCK Prof 465
LAYTON Elizabeth 377 John 414
  Thomas 202 235 236 237 241 244
  248 255 321 377 William 246
  250
LE BEAU Christine Otis 228
LEATHERS Abigail 274 Catherine
  280 Edward 253 448
LEAVITT Elizabeth 430 Joseph 434
  Mary 274
LEBBEY Isaac 89
LECHFORD Mr 150
LEE Abraham 326 Esther 326
LEIGH Mr 409
LEIGHTON Anna 359 Deborah 360
  Dorothy 389 Elizabeth 271 321
  442 Ephraim 441 George 389
  Hannah 389 Isaac 389 Israel
  442 James 86 James Twombly 442
  Joanna 365 John 85 John
  Buzzell 442 Joseph 390
  Margaret 441 Mary 305 308 442
  496 Mary Elizabeth 442 Mercy
  390 Thomas vii 85 117 252 271
  305 315 321 365 377 380
  William 3
LEPPINCUTT Bartholomew 241
LETHERS Edward 251
LETTELLFEELD Fraynses 372
LEVERICH Caleb 105 Eleazer 105
  Mr 106 127 William viii 94 95
  101 105 111 125 127
LEVETT Capt 33 43 47 49
  Christopher 41 46
LEVITT Christopher 15
LEWIS Philip 53 117 174

Thomas 37 93
LIBBEY Hannah 405 Isaac 331
  Samuel 331 332 Sarah 331 332
LIBBY Elizabeth 418 Esther 362
  James 307
LIDDAL John 137
LINCOLN Abraham 226
LINSCOTT Rhoda 287
LIPPINCOTTE Bathellme 237
LITCHFIELD Elizabeth 275 Joseph
  275
LITTLE Betsey 429 Mary 425
  William 429
LITTLEBURY 196 Capt 195
LITTLEFIELD Francis 235 Jane
  445 Joseph 445 Phebe 445
LOCK James 480 Mary 480 Mercy
  480
LOCKE 391 Abigail Page 394 Anne
  C 498 Betsey 280 Edward 481
  Eleanor 481 Hannah 481 Ira
  498 James 481 John 481
  Jonathan 261 Lydia V 498 Mary
  480 481 Mehitable 481 Mercy
  481 Prudence 481 Sallie 284
  Samuel 394 Sarah 480 481 492
  Susan 481 Tamsen 394 William
  284
LONGFELLOW Jonathan 476 Sarah
  477
LONGSTAFFE Henry 53
LOOME Mary 336
LORD Ann 483 Caroline 286 John
  K 464 John King 466 Laura
  Wolsey 464 466 Phebe 480
  Sarah 309 Tozier 480
LORIMORE Thomas 67
LOUD Abigail 270 Ann 289 Solomon
  270
LOURING John 242 246 249
LOVE Capt 9 William 237
LOVRING John 237
LUCAS Isaac L 57
LUCY John 426 Mary 426
LUMMACK Nathaniel 253
LUSHER Elea 25
LYFORD Elizabeth 428
LYONS Margaret 441 William 441

MC CASLING Hannah 371
MC CAUSLAND Hannah 497
MC CLELLAN Bettie 286
MC CONE Michael 299
MC DUFFEE Hannah 279 Joanna 282
  John 279 282 Mrs 335 Patty
  452
MC INTIRE Rufus 340

MC KEAVER James 299 300
MC KENDLY Betsey 285
MC LANATHAN Oreanna 477
MC MANUS Patrick 300
MACE John 440 Rachel 440
MACEY Thomas 317
MACK DONNELL Elexsander 247
MACKDANIEL Elexsander 247
MACKDONELL Elexsander 240
MACY Thomas 346
MAGOUN Henry 179
MAGOUNE Henrey 237
MAIN Amos 394 Mary 394
MALTBY Jane 488
MANING John 164
MANNING Sarah 285
MARBLE Hannah 423 Mehitable 425 Samuel 425
MARCH Col 55
MARDEN John 87 496 Nancy 496
MARGES Valentine 404
MARSHAL Henry 88
MARSTON Hannah 439 Sarah 481
MARTIN Hester 305 John 235 236 239 243 247 250 256 305
MASON 201 Ann 23 38 Capt 7 36 Catherine 337 Elizabeth 305 309 John 5 6 7 18 21 23 30 33 34 35 38 90 92 93 109 188 199 223 224 311 312 413 422 Joseph 189 Lydia 479 480 492 Mrs 189 Olive 309 Robert 189 196 Susan 443 Thomas 300
MATHER Cotton 448 Dr 55
MATHES Anna 472 473 Betsey 440 Francis 257 258 Gideon 472 473 Gideon Jr 472 Hamilton A 178 Lois 472 Robert 440
MATHEWS Beenjamin 253 Benjamin 238 240 Mrs 235 243
MAUD Daniel viii 127 174 Mr 166 Parson 375
MAVERICK 195 Amias 31 Samuel 31 50
MAXWELL James 442 Nancy 442
MAY Hannah O 285
MAYFIELD Elizabeth 440
MAYS Samuel 105
MEADER Daniel 419 Elijah 280 Hannah 280 John 238 239 247 250 252 John Jr 257 378 Joseph 77 257 258 Joseph Jr 257 258 Mary 419 Nathaniel 378 Sarah 382
MEDLTON James 240
MELIMAN James 238
MERRILL Comfort 428 Hannah 428 Phebe 426 Phineas 426 Samuel 428
MERROW Abel 493 Abigail 480 491 492 493 Amos 493 Anne 492 Augustus D 493 Benjamin 491 Charity 493 Daniel 491 Dr 492 Edward 492 Elizabeth 491 Hannah 492 Henry 490 Isaac 492 Isabella 493 James 492 James M 493 Jane 490 John 491 Jonathan 491 492 Jonathan Jr 491 Joseph 480 481 491 492 493 Joshua 492 493 Lydia 492 Margaret 493 Mary 480 481 491 492 493 Mehitable 481 492 Moses 491 Nancy 493 Olive 493 Patience 493 Phebe 491 492 493 Rachel 491 Ruth 491 492 Sally 492 Samuel 480 490 491 492 493 Sarah 493 Stephen 492 Susan 492 Thomas 492 William 492 493
MESERVE Abigail 416 419 420 Anna 419 Anne 364 415 416 Charles R 417 Clement 260 418 419 Daniel 415 418 419 Deborah 415 418 419 420 Ebenezer 419 Elizabeth 418 Eunice 419 George P 419 Henry 419 Isaac 419 Isaac H 419 Israel 420 John 419 John Smith 419 Jonathan 419 Joseph 419 Lois 419 Lydia 419 Mary 419 420 Nicholas D 417 Paul 420 Sarah 420 Silas 419 Stephen 420 Tamson 418 419 Thomasine 418
MESSER Sarah 426
MESSERVY Clement 417
MIGHEL John 253
MILLARD Jane 137
MILLER John 203 211
MILLET Capt 85 John 84 Love 84 Mary 84 Thomas 82 83 114 258 259 Thomas Jr 84 Thomas Sr 84
MILLETT Thomas vii 313
MILLIKEN Hannah 355 357
MILTIMORE Dorothy 424 James 424
MOHON Jane M 435
MONROE President 226
MONTGOMERY Abra 391 John 391 Jonathan 391 Lillian 272
MOODEY Joshua 195
MOODY Rev Mr 350 Joshua 367
MOONEY Betty 395 Daniel 282 Hercules 77 Hester 282 Joseph 395

MOORE Harvey 423 Jacob B 424
  John 435 Lydia 435 Mary 423
  424 Sarah 424 William 424
MORANG James 57
MORDANTT Benjamin 441 Margaret
  441
MOREY Harvey 276 Meribah 276
MORIS Tho 253
MORISE Thomas 250
MORRILL Abraham 365 Anna 386
  Elizabeth 428 Jane 390 Joseph
  335 Nancy 497 Nathan 428 Sarah
  365
MORRISON Mary 272
MORSE Abigail 473 Charles 473
  Charles Leland 473 Charles M
  473 Edward Leland 473 Joseph
  439 Louise Jane 473 Lucy M 473
  Mary 439 Moses Leland 473
  Samuel Butterfield 473 Warren
  473
MORSSIE Thomas 246
MORTON Thomas 22 28 50
MOSES Timothy Jr 86
MOULTON Benjamin 426 Dorothy 343
  Henry 311 Mary 313 Olive L 426
  Sobriety 311 Thomas 313
MOWBRAY Geoffry 96
MUCKELAROY John 87
MUNSELL Robert 9
MUNSEY Henry 442 Mary 442 Olive
  442
MURDOCK Elisha 416 Mary 416
MURRAY Abigail 426 Love 442 444
  Timothy 426

NANNY Robert 76
NASH Isaac 236 Isake 237
NASON Abigail 360 Hannah 448
  John 448 Samuel 360
NEAL Capt 172 Catherine 460 457
  Deborah 432 Delia Annah 295
  George William 295 Hannah 390
  John 496 John F 298 302
  Keziah 390 Martha 496 Sarah
  390 Walter 3 7 23 30 38 312
  420
NEALE Catherine 373
NEALLEY Benjamin F 277 Fannie
  277 John H 455 Susan Emerson
  277
NELSON Anna 268
NEWETT James 233
NEWGROVE John 233 413
NEWHOUSE Thomas 137
NEWT Abraham 252 James Sr 252
NEWTE James 233

NEWTT Abraham 249 Jam Jr 241
  James Jr 248 252 James Sr 241
  244 248
NICHOLAS Timi 37
NICHOLS Elizabeth 307 Gov 112
NICOLLS 189
NINELL John 240
NOCK Ebenezer 89 Sylvanus vii
  Thomas 75 336 348
NOCKE James 483 Thomas 241 244
NOCKS Ann 483
NORRIS Benjamin 426 436 Mehit-
  able 426 Sarah 426 436
NOTTAGE Sarah 280
NOYES Judith 351
NUTE 361 Abigail 416 Abraham
  viii 86 268 413 417 Anna 419
  Anne 364 414 415 416 Annie P
  272 Clarissa 416 Comfort 415
  Daniel 415 Elizabeth 322 364
  414 415 416 419 447 448
  Ephraim 416 Eunice 416 Green-
  leaf 416 Hannah 417 Hepzibah
  416 Isaac 417 James viii 117
  160 202 203 205 207 208 212
  235 236 256 258 267 268 364
  412 413 414 415 416 417 419
  James Jr 89 448 Joanna 417
  John 415 Joseph 416 417
  Joseph E 267 Jotham 393 415
  Leah 204 206 212 214 268 414
  415 Lucy 415 Martha 202 212
  222 267 268 415 497 Mary 205
  393 414 415 416 417 Meserve
  416 Paul 86 414 416 Prudence
  364 414 415 Rachel 417
  Rosanna 416 Samuel 268 322 414
  415 Sarah 413 414 415 417
  Susan 416 Thomas 415 416 417
NUTTE James 237 James Jr 239
NUTTER Abigail 272 305 308 315
  316 317 378 380 Ann 316 Anna
  286 317 Anne 314 Anthony 256
  317 430 Antoney 243 245 249
  Antony 237 253 314 315 316
  Bettie 273 Dorothy 316 Elder
  117 119 236 237 241 244 248
  Eleanor 316 Eliza 283
  Elizabeth 316 Esther 271
  Hannah 317 Hatabell 202
  Hateevil 183 Hateevill 164
  Hatevil vii 92 115 116 126
  135 255 256 272 305 314 315
  316 378 379 380 414 Hatevill
  233 235 Henry 315 316 James
  236 271 315 John 273 315 316
  317 Joseph 316 317 Joshua 316

Leah 414 Mary 315 316 339
Matthias 315 Mr 233 252 Olive
316 Samuel 316 Sarah 315 316
Valentine 316 William 283

OATS Stephen 88
ODELL Charlotte 423 426 Dr 423
    James 426 Mary 426 Mercy 429
ODIORNE Jotham 153 Mr 154
OER James 238 240
OLDHAM John 108 Mr 74
ORAM Joanna 441 Robert 441
ORDWAY Ann 449 James 446 449
OSBORN John 342
OSBORNE Daniel 261
OSGOOD Elinor 439 John 365 Mary
    365 Sarah 365
OTES Richard 176 237 245 250
OTIS Catherine 457 Christine 227
    334 354 457 458 459 460 462
    Cynthia 460 Elizabeth 457 460
    Experience 450 457 458 Grace
    459 Grizel 227 Grizet 457
    Hannah 457 461 Horatio N 456
    Jane 460 Job 461 John 460
    Joshua 460 461 Judith 358 363
    457 458 462 Margaret 227 Mary
    456 457 458 460 462 Micajah
    461 Mr 462 Molly 460 Nathaniel
    458 462 Nicholas 457 458 459
    460 Nicholas Jr 457 Rebecca
    457 460 Richard 224 227 252
    253 256 322 358 363 409 445
    447 450 456 457 458 459 460
    461 Rose 322 363 364 415 456
    457 458 462 Shuah 445 457
    Solomon 456 Stephen 456 457
    458 459 460 461 462 Sussanna
    456 457 460
OTTES Richard 242

PAGE Abigail 279 Antoney 249
    Antony 246 Carter 372 Cora A
    345 Dorothy 343 Eliza 344
    Elizabeth A 344 Fannie B 344
    345 Frederick Flanders 344 345
    George F 344 345 George W 342
    344 Harry 345 James 343 John
    T 343 Joseph 341 343 Joseph L
    344 Julia A 344 Lucy Jane 372
    Lula E 344 Margaret E 345
    Martha Ann 343 Martha Hilton
    342 Mary 343 Mary G 344 Mary
    Goodwin 344 Mary Hilton 341
    Rebecca 285 Robert 343 Sarah
    341 343 Sarah Kelley 344
    Stephen 343 Susanna 343 Taylor
    330 331 341 342 343 Thomas
    343 William R 345 William
    Taylor 342 344
PAINE Thomas 252
PALMER Barnabus 306 Betsey Jane
    475 Christopher 192 193 196
    311 Edward H 475 Elizabeth 306
    307 Jonathan 305 306 Mary 305
    Samuel Harding 475 Susanna 311
PARKER Caroline Nelson 272
    Rachel 371 Richard 164 William
    118
PARKS Anna 436
PARLE James 57
PARNILL John 251
PARSONS Harvey 444 Joanna Oram
    444 Josiah P 444 Lucy Knight
    444 Lydia D 444 Margaret F 442
    Margaretta F 443 444 Quincy
    Adams 444 Sally 443 Sarah
    Sewell 444 Stephen 442 443 444
    Ursula R 444
PARTRIDGE Richi 37
PATERSON Edward 237
PATTEN Stephen Jr 261
PATTERSON Edward 238 240 243 247
PAUL Delia 295 Nathaniel 262
PAYNE Thomas 242 245 249 349
PEARL Benjamin 484 Elizabeth 484
    John 86 Samuel 207
PEAS Martha 428
PEASE Lucy 308 Samuel 68
PEASLEE Nicholas 261
PEAVEY Bryant 212 Ellen S 212
PEAVY Bessie 286 Eskar 286
PEDDOCK Leo 9
PEIRCE Abigail 498 Andrew 255
    261 464 Andrew Jr 261 Benjamin
    260 381 382 David 261 Eliza-
    beth 382 Hannah 382 450 Israel
    498 Joseph 382 Keziah 451
    Rebecca 464 Thomas 450 451
PENDLETON Brian 195
PENGREW Lydia 365 Moses 365
PEREY William 87
PERKINS Abigail 309 Abraham 428
    Andrew 356 Ann Louise 356
    Charles Edwin 356 Daniel Libby
    356 Deborah 364 423 Emily H
    286 Eri 261 Isabella 356
    Jeremy 356 Jeremy Williams 356
    John 86 John Henry 356 Joseph
    87 Joshua 85 Lydia 356 Lydia
    Augusta 356 Mary 423 424 428
    Mary Ann 428 Molly 427 Moses
    364 Samuel 159 356 Sarah
    Elizabeth 356 Solomon 86

Susan 356 Tho 252 William 244
251 253 423
PERMETT Lasaries 242
PERMIT Lasaret 246 Lazearus 249
PERRY 197
PETERS Hugh 147
PETTMAN William 243 246
PHILBRICK Abigail 439 Anna 305
  Elizabeth 422 James 305 Tufton
  422 Walter 422
PHILIPS Jennie 402
PHILLIPS Agnes 402 404 Andrew
  403 404 Jenny 403 Miriam 404
PHIPPS 391
PICKERING Abigail 419 Anthony
  419 Betsey 335 Martha 428 Mary
  Ann 428 Thomas 428
PIERCE Benjamin 455 Frank 344
  455
PIKE Daniel 408 Dr 155 James 180
  John 53 155 210 227 367 405
  409 Lavinia 408 Maj 142 194 Mr
  377 Nicholas 393 Parson 375
  377 Sally 339 Sarah A 393
PINCKHAM John 252 Rich 252 253
PINCKOM Thomas 249
PINKEM Benjn 89
PINKHAM Aaron 57 Abigail 323 324
  338 373 374 393 416 420 Amos
  160 322 Anne 323 Benjamin 322
  324 Daniel 58 127 148 261
  Davis 324 E J 324 Ebenezer 88
  322 373 Edmund 323 Elijah 128
  321 324 Elizabeth 321 322 323
  324 361 377 380 415 416 Enoch
  59 324 Eunice 324 Hannah 322
  323 Ira A 59 Isaac 416 James
  322 416 420 James Jr 86
  Jeremiah G 323 Joanna 322 John
  vii 159 321 322 323 324 359
  364 415 457 458 John E 57 59
  Jonathan 322 Joseph 323 324
  361 Leah 415 Lois 322 Louisa
  323 Lydia 324 Mary 322 361 420
  Mercy 322 Miriam 323 Nancy 324
  Nathaniel 324 Nicholas 323 324
  Otis 86 322 323 338 383 Paul
  323 374 Phebe 323 324 Rebecca
  323 Richard vii 117 119 120
  126 127 128 202 320 321 322
  377 380 458 Richard Jr 88
  Richard A 59 Rose 322 323 324
  359 360 364 374 415 457 458
  Samuel 323 324 Sarah 322 323
  324 361 373 374 Silas 323
  Solomon 322 Solomon Jr 86
  Stephen 86 419 Susannah 323
Tamson 419 Thomas 321 322
  Thomas Jr 86 Tristram 321 322
  393 Tristrum 86 Wesley 322
PINKOEM John 248
PIPER Abigail 436 494 Deborah
  426 George 255 Jonathan 426
  Nathaniel 494 Patience 429
  Samuel 494 Sarah 434 Stephen
  436 Tabitha 429
PIRKINS William 246
PITMAN Derey 87 Mary 456 457
  William 238 250 471 Zachariah
  206 Zechariah 87 Zeeberiah 87
PITMANS William 253
PITTMAN Francis 156 Nathl 158
  William 240
PLACE Alice 271 Joseph 271
PLAISTED Hannah 275 289 294
  Roger 289
PLUMER Daniel 87 Richard 86 392
  Sarah 392
PLUMMER 309 Anna 283 John 335
  Lydia 307 Mary 335
POMEROY Leonard 4 5 12 17 19 34
  310 Mr 14
POMFRET Lt 202
POMFRETT 268 Elizabeth 265
  William viii 117 126 151 162
  201 202 211 222 235 236 237
  242 244 248 254 255 256 265
POMFRIT Leiftenant 252
POTTS Joanna 309 Thomas 309
POUND Thomas 68
POWERS Sally 307
PRAY William 53 174
PRENTICE Hannah 428 John 428
  Martha H 428 Mary Ann 428
  Matilda 428 Nancy 428 Tryphene
  C 428
PRENTISS Caleb 333
PRESBY Rebecca 402 Susannah 423
PRESTON George 128 129 176
PRIEST David 497 Drusilla 497
PRING Capt 218 Martin 46 217 218
PURINGTON Anna 484
PURINTON Jacob K 323 Mary E 323
  Rebecca 323 Sarah A 323

QUELCH Capt 67
QUIMBY Edward Harold 468 Fred E
  462 468 George W 335 Henry 335
  James 468 Marietta 468 470
  Mehitable 335 Mr 463 Sarah 335
  468 William Leroy 468
QUINCY Elizabeth 328 Josiah 328
QUINN James 300
QUINT Alonzo Hall 263 388 443

Dr 122 207 251 303 George 443
Rev Dr 127 Sally Williams 443

RAFE Clement 246
RAGG Jeffrey 235
RALEIGH Walter 199
RALLENS James 233
RALLINES James 243 Thomas 242
RALLINS James 237 245 248 Thomas 246
RAND Betsey 280 John 159 Leonard S 262 Moses 280
RANDAL John 86 Tobiea 86
RANDALL Abigail 439 440 442 Benjamin 441 442 443 Benjamin Walton 442 443 Betsey 440 441 442 Catherine 439 Daniel 439 441 David 442 Deborah 439 440 Dolly 442 Edward 438 440 Elinor 439 Eliza 444 Elizabeth 439 Francis D 439 George 440 Hannah 439 443 Henry Allen 442 444 Henry Sargent 443 Jacob 441 442 James 439 440 James Jenkins 443 James M 439 James Marston 440 Joanna 441 442 444 Joanna Oram 443 John 439 440 441 442 Jonathan 439 Joseph 439 442 Josiah Parsons 443 Judith 309 Love 440 442 444 Lucy 439 Margaret 441 Margaret F 442 Margaretta F 443 Mark 439 Mary 439 440 441 442 444 Mary Ann 444 Mary Shannon 442 443 Mary Savage 443 Miriam 441 Moses 439 Nancy 441 442 Olly 439 Paul 439 Peter 439 Polly 441 Rachel 440 Richard 440 Robert Oram 442 443 Sally 439 440 441 443 Samuel 439 440 Sarah 440 Sarah Sewell 443 Sewell 443 Shadrack W 441 Simeon 439 Stephen 439 Ursula Pinkham 442 444 William 439 440 441 442 444 William B 440 William Sweet 443
RANDOLPH 191 Edward 189
RANER Mr 251
RANSOM Thomas 86
RAPHF Clement 242
RAVEN Catherine 162 324
RAWLINGS Elizabeth 316 432 400
RAWLINS Andrew 432 Eliza 269 Ichabod 210 James 235 236 366 Mary 336 343 432 Samuel 269 Sarah 400
RAWSON Edward 25 163 164 166 184

Hannah 399 John 399
RAYMOND Hattie 489
RAYNER Priest 489
RAYNERS Mr 241
REALL Teage 253
REED Abigail 279
REIALL Teage 244
REMICK Greenville 428 Tryphene 428
RENDALL Nathanl 159 Nathaniel Jr 89 Richard 159
REVERE Paul 124
REYNER John vii viii 116 127 137 331 378 Mr 127 241 Parson 119 129 143 217 Rev 237
REYNOLDS Ann 357 Benjamin 357 Benjamin Oliver 356 Benjamin Seth 357 Cecilla Amanda 356 Edward 356 Elizabeth Watson 356 Hannah 474 Isaac 357 John Hubbard 464 Juliette 356 Kate Hubbard 464 Lydia A 357 Oliver L 356 Rebecca 464 Ruth Ann 356 Ruth Ellen 357 Sarah Ellen 356 Sarah Hanson 356 Seth 357 Thomas 357
RIALL Tage 247 Teackge 240 Teag 251
RICE J H 371
RICH Richard 252 305 Sarah 305
RICHARD James 88
RICHARDS Josh 160 Rebecca 451
RICHARDSON James 152 255
RICHMOND Cora A 345 Margaret B 345 R N 345
RICKER Eleanor 484 George 234 252 Lucy 273 Maturin 234 Nicholas 484
RIGGS Virginia 329
RILEY Ann 329 John 261
RINES Samuel 78
RISBEY William 239
RISLEY William 239
ROBARTS Benja Jr 89 Stephen 89
ROBERDS John 237 241 244 245 246 Tho 237 Thomas Jr 241 245 248 Thomas Sr 241 244 Will 250 William 238 240 243 247
ROBERTS Aaron 57 86 260 309 Abigail 305 306 307 308 309 315 378 380 Alonzo 57 58 261 Amasa 255 305 Amos Main 394 Ann 303 332 Anna 305 Anne 331 Benjamin 306 309 Betty 394 Charles 117 Charles Wentworth 394 Daniel 309 David 323 Deborah 494 Ebenezer 386 Eddi

308 Elizabeth 303 305 307 308
309 323 398 411 440 449
Esther 309 Eugene 308 Eunice
309 310 Frances 303 Francis
305 306 459 Fred 58 304 Gov
106 Grace 308 Hannah 305 307
360 399 Hanson viii 57 58 118
304 306 321 Harry 308 Hatevil
306 307 308 309 Heard 354
Hester 305 Howard 122 Howard M
58 Howard Millet 80 83 304
James 304 Jerry 57 58 303
Jerry Jr 304 Jerry Sr 304
Joana 417 Joanna 307 308 309
364 John 75 80 120 132 138 179
236 252 253 256 302 303 304
305 306 307 308 309 314 331
332 336 378 394 398 497 John
Sr ix John Wesley 308 Joseph
ix 57 58 81 118 257 258 260
304 306 308 309 394 398 440
Joshua 306 307 308 309 364
Judith 309 Love 305 306 309
Lucy 308 Lydia 306 307 308 309
Mark 307 426 Mary 305 306 307
308 309 354 391 448 Mary A
279 Mercy 308 Mercy Adeline
308 Mr 235 237 Moses 304 305
Nathan 309 Nathaniel 86 304
305 309 Olive 309 Rebecca 304
Relief 394 Sally 307 Sally Ann
426 Samuel 86 306 309 Sarah
54 305 306 307 308 309 411 459
Simeon 309 Stephen ix 259 304
Stephen W 304 Susan 309 394
Susanna 394 Thomas 1 5 14 39
49 80 81 86 132 133 134 138
146 149 157 201 223 236 252
257 258 302 303 304 305 306
307 308 309 314 315 379 449
482 494 Thomas Jr 256 Thomas
Sr ix 80 117 257 304 Timothy
331 332 394 Tobias 308 William
235 303 308
ROBETAIL 459
ROBINSON Ann 423 496 Bradbury
423 Elizabeth 306 338 Harriet
497 Jane 423 John Paul 396
Love 440 Mary 498 Mehitable
423 Nancy 399 Noah 423 Paul
399 Samuel 440 498 Stephen S
497 Steuen 240 247 257 Timothy
86 258 308 338 William 496
ROBITAILE Grizel 227 Philip 227
ROBORDS William 176
RODS Avisia 300
ROGERS Daniel 398 Daniell 89

Ezekiel 468 Hannah 398 Mr 469
Rev 180
ROGGERS Richard 201
ROLLINS Edward W 57 Hannah 435
Ichabod 161 Jeremiah 386
Lorenzo 334 412 Mehitable 280
Nicholas 435
ROOE Richard 243 245 248
ROOK Richard 380
ROOSEVELT Theodore 111
ROSS Jonathan Smith 290
ROUNDS Ellen S 203 212 Holmes B
212 Mr 212 213 Mrs 211 212
213
ROWE Jane 269 Martha 433 Richard
269
ROWELL Richard 249
RUBETOY 459
RUNDLETT Abigail 277 Charles 277
RUNNELLS Samuel 442 Ursula
Pinkham 442
RUNNELS Benjamin Paul 444
Joanna 444 Lydia 484 Margaret
444 Mary 444 Samuel 444
Samuel Dana 444 Ursula 444
Ursula Pinkham 444
RUSSELL Anna 328 Benjamin 328
Eleanor 328 Eleazer 327 328
Margaret 327 328 Martha 328
RUST Annie 327 Dr 428 Henry 327
Martha 425 428

SALTONSTALL Abigail 327 Mr 103
163 Richard 94 327 Robert 94
SAMEWELL __iamin 241
SANBORN 400 Esther 364 Hannah
364 389 393 James S 272 John
389 Joseph 364 Julia F 272
SANDERS Elizabeth 442 John 442
Josephf 242 246 249 Mary 379
380 382 Daniel 370 Lydia W
370
SAVORY Martha 431
SAWYER Almira 478 Charles Walter
356 Eleanor 401 Elizabeth
Watson 356 Emma 390 Hannah
323 Jacob 260 John 64 Levi
323 Mary Elizabeth 356
Stephen 260 261 Thomas E 261
262 356
SAY Lord 92 94 95 100 101 102
SCALERIUS Hugh de 467
SCALES Abigail 472 473 Abraham
471 472 473 Alfred Moore 471
Amy 478 Ann 468 470 Anna 472
473 Arianna 478 Benjamin 464
Betsey 278 476 Betsey True

478 Bradbury Bartlett 279 478
Burton 476 Burton True 463
Catherine Bradstreet 464 Earl
  C 468 470 Ebenezer 472 473 475
Edward 472 Elizabeth 467
Elizabeth Ann 279 477 Ellen
477 Ellen Tasker 462 Enoch 474
Frank 476 George 278 477
George Burton 476 George Levi
478 Gideon 474 Grace 478
Hannah 274 278 472 473 474 475
Horace 279 477 Hugh de 468 467
James 468 469 470 471 472
James Butterfield 474 John 112
278 287 462 464 468 470 471
472 473 477 John Minot 478
Josiah 478 Kate Hubbard 464
Laura Wolsey 464 466 Levi 279
477 Lois 472 474 Lorinda 474
Margaret 468 Marietta 468 470
Marion Bird 476 Martha Cilley
279 477 Martha Fitzjames 477
Mary 278 471 472 475 Mary Bird
476 Mary True 279 478 Matthew
468 470 471 Mr 463 464 465 Mrs
463 Nancy 278 475 Nellie 476
Octavia W 474 Oreanna 477 Otto
Clifford 474 Robert 467 Robert
Leighton 464 Samuel 274 278
472 474 475 476 Sarah 468 470
471 472 474 Susannah 470 471
True 278 476 Walter Francis
476 William 468 469 470 471
William Angel 470
SCAMAN Richard 246
SCAMMON Annie 325 Hope 359 Lydia
  432 Richard 325 Robert 359
SCAMMONS Richard 88
SCOTT Frances L 269 Mary 334
SCREUEN John 242
SCRIBNER Abigail 496 John 389
  Peniel 389
SCRIWEN John 249
SCRUIN John 245
SCRUTON Mary 308 Sarah 308
  William 308
SEAVEY Olive 355
SEELEY Mr 235
SEVERANCE Abigail 494 John 494
  Mary 346
SEWALL Stephen 67
SEWARD Mary 402 Samewell 249
SEWELL Alice Fisher 438 Spencer
  K 438
SHACKFORD Abigail 392 Eliza 308
  Mary 275 283 Mary Ann 423
  William 275 283

SHAKESPEARE William 96
SHANNON Lillian 357 Thomas 357
  William 399
SHAPLEIGH Alexander 310
  Catherine 310 Elisha 334
  Elizabeth 334 Katharine 193
  Maj 132 143 144 190 195 Mr 196
  Nicholas 142 189 194
SHARPE John 246 Samuel 37 93
SHATTUCK Mary Bird 476
SHEAFE Olive Rindge 329
SHEPARD Eliza 444 Jane 278
SHEPHERD Johanna 333
SHERBORN Capt 208
SHERBURNE Henry 153 162 431
  Mary 440 Mercy 425 Mr 154
  Phebe 425 Sarah 431 Susannah
  423
SHERWELL Mr 18 Nicholas 5 12 19
  310
SHERWOOD M 10 Mr 6 10
SHIFFIELD Ickebod 237
SHIFFILLD William 237
SHUCKFORD William 243 245 248
SHUTE 423 Dolly 442
SIAS Mary 274
SIBLEY David 497 Polly 497
SIMPSON Jane 276 Nancy 435
SIMS Ann 316
SINCLAIR Sally 425
SINKLER Susannah 432
SLOPER Richard 237
SMALL Elizabeth 445 Francis 235
  Samuel 445
SMART 286 Sarah 364 Seba 286
SMEG Barthey 201 203
SMETH James 244 247 John 244
  Josephf 240 244
SMETHE James 250 John 250
  Josephf 250
SMITH 331 Anna 426 Arabella 282
  Carroll 282 Charles 282
  Cheney 459 495 Daniel 329 343
  David 426 Dolly W 426 Eleanor
  329 Elizabeth 282 322 Eunice
  459 495 George 151 235 254
  Hannah 351 423 Herman 282
  James 70 253 329 John 27 41 42
  43 257 258 423 John Sr 257 258
  Jos Jr 158 Joseph 253 257 282
  322 Martha Ann 343 Mary 329
  425 Merirah 282 Olive 423
  Samuel 258 Tamson 401
  Theophilus 425 426 Thomas W
  329
SMYTH Edward 165 George 103 163
  164 183 184

SMYTHE George 166
SNELL Jane 393 451
SOMERBY Henry 346 Judith 346
SOULE Charles Emery 255
SOUTER John 193
SPRAGUE Grace 390
SQUEBB Capt 9
STACKPOLE E S 308 Eunice 309 310
  Everett S 302 Joshua 354 459
  Lucy 354 459 Paul 416 Paul A
  353 Rosanna 416 Samuel 353 416
  Sarah 386 Servia 353 Tobias
  310 Thomas 255 309
STAGPOLE Joshua 89 Samuell 89
STANDISH Miles 17 22 32 44 45 46
STANTON Benjamin 334 Eliza 334
STANWOOD Rachel 401
STARBACK Edward 202
STARBOARD Samuel 86 Stephen 86
STARBUCK Abigail 318 350 Ann
  319 Barnabus 318 Dinah 318
  Dorcas 318 319 347 Edw 235
  Edward ix 126 165 237 317 346
  347 350 351 372 460 Elder 319
  372 Elizabeth 318 320 351
  Esther 364 460 Eunice 319
  Hepsibah 319 Jethro 318 349
  Katherine 318 Mary 318 347
  Nathaniel 237 318 347 351 Paul
  319 Sarah 318 319 372
STEEL John K 284 Lydia 284
STEELE David 262
STEPHENS Nathaniell 252
STEUENS Nathell 249
STEUENSON Thomas 238 240 246
STEUNSON Josephf 250
STEVENS Abijah 479 Catherine 364
  Dionis 345 Elizabeth 307 John
  B 122 Lydia 364 Mr 455 Moses
  89 307 Phebe 446 Samuel C 454
  Sarah 431 Thomas 446
STEVENSON 160 Tho 235
STIKES Isakes 241
STILEMAN Elias 195 199
STIMSON 253 Joseph 253
STOCKBRIDGE John 427 Martha 427
STOCKES Isaac 252
STODDARD John 228 Maj 229 Parson
  227 229
STOKES Isaac 66 253 Isakes 245
  248 James 364 Mary 364
STONE Experience 390
STOREY Sarah 319 William vii 235
  236 237 319
STORY Sarah 372 William 115 201
  314 372
STOUGHTON Anthony 456 Nicholas
  456 Rose 363 456
STYLES William 89
SUDGROVE Joanna 397
SULLIVAN Gen 333 412 John 178
SWEAT Dorothy 424
SWEET George 198
SYLLEY Abiel 404 Benoni 404
SYLLY Abiel 402
SYMONDS Harlakenden 187 192
  John 311 Mickall 251 Rebecca
  311 Samuel 187
SYMONS Mr 103

TALTON Elias 439 Mary 439
TASH Elizabeth 405 Mary 404
  Thomas 404
TASKER Charity 496 Ellen 477
  James 496 John 87 211 260
  Lydia 492 Samuel 88 492 Sarah
  361 William 87
TASKETT William 252
TAYLOR Anthony 343 Benjamin 429
  Curtis 481 Elizabeth 429 Gen
  291 292 George B 478 Henry
  Dearborn 343 Horace Scales 478
  Mary True 478 Patience 389 481
  Sarah 341 343
TEARE Thos 252
TEBBETS Aaron 338 Abigail 323
  337 338 339 340 Adeline 356
  Anne 337 Benjamin 336 338
  Bridget 338 Catherine 337
  Charity 339 Charles Barker
  340 Deborah 339 Dorothy 337
  Ebenezer 339 Edward 338 339
  Elijah 338 Elisha 338 Eliza
  339 Elizabeth 336 337 338 416
  Ephraim 323 336 337 338 373
  Ephraim Jr 341 Esther 341
  Hannah 336 337 338 Henry 201
  335 336 338 339 Ichabod 340
  James 339 340 Jeremiah 335
  336 Jeremiah H W 340 Jeremy
  179 336 337 338 John 337 339
  340 Jonathan 338 339 Joseph
  336 337 338 Joyce 338 Judith
  336 337 340 Lydia 337 Margery
  337 Martha 336 Mary 336 337
  338 339 340 Mary Esther 340
  Moses 337 Nathaniel 336 338
  340 Noah 339 340 Oliver 339
  Paul 338 Peter 338 Phebe 323
  Rose 323 337 338 373 Sally
  339 Samuel 336 337 340 Sarah
  339 340 Sarah Chase 340 Seth
  339 Susanna 338 339 Tamson
  346 Theodore 340 Thomas 254

257 258 321 336 337 340 384
Thomas Jr 89 Walter 335
William 339
TEBBETT Henrey 241 Jeremt 241
TEBBETTS Ebenezer 480 Ephraim 85
Henry 179 236 237 Jeremie 244
John Jr 89 Mary 482 Olive 480
Samuel 257 Thomas 153 258
TEBETTS Jeremie 248 Tho 237
TEBTES Henrey 248
TEDDER Stephen 233
TENITS John 87
THING Benj 351 Parnell 351
THOMAS Abigail C 403 David 6
Hannah 370 Jos 89 Joseph 403
Mary 432
THOMPSON Alive 357 Betsey Jane
278 475 Charles 324 Frank 278
Henrietta 278 Hugh 278 475
John 471 Jonathan 258 Louise
401 Mark 497 Mary 278 471 475
Mary P 216 Phebe 324 Prudence
497 Samuel 278 Sarah 307 471
Thomas 357 Warren 278 William
11
THOMSON Amias 8 30 31 David 4 5
6 7 8 9 10 11 12 14 15 16 17
18 19 20 21 22 23 27 28 30 31
32 33 34 38 43 50 90 92 John
30 31 32 Michael 8 Mr 9 11 15
16 17 29 33 47
THORNDIKE Elizabeth 433
THRASHER Benjn 88
THURSTON Ann 428 Caleb 428
Elizabeth 425 Joanna 423
Mehitable 425 Stephen 425
TIBBETS Capt 157 159 161 Henry
86 Jerusha 275 John Jr 88
Nathaniel 156 Samuel 155 156
Thomas 155 156 William 275
TIBBETT Henry 217 Jeremiah 193
TIBBETTS Abigail 266 Charles W
30 Elizabeth 266 267 Ephraim
266 Henry vii 235 Ichabod 86
Jeremiah 117 192 Jerry 136
John 266 John Sr vii Joseph 86
267 Judith 266 Moses 266
Samuel 266 Thomas vii 266
TIBBIT Henry 372 Henrey 252
TIBBITS Jeremiah 88
TIBITS Jeremi 252
TIPPIT Jere 336 Mary 336
TITCOMB Benjamin 260 Daniel 85
TOMKINS Mary 128 129 130 131 132
133 176
TOMSON Florence 30 Jonathan 258
Richard 30 William 237

TOPPAN Stephen 261
TORR Andrew 260 Benedictus 387
Elizabeth 440 Eunice 419 Leah
387 Lois 419 Richard 440
Vincent 86
TORREY William 67 166
TORRY William 25
TOWNSEND Jonas D 262 Sally 339
TOZER Richard 440
TRACEY Abigail 354
TRAFTON Abigail 290 Charles 290
Mrs. 294
TRAVERS Briget 406 Henry 406
Sarah 406 407
TRAVIS Briget 406 Henry 406
Sarah 406 407
TREDICK John 261
TRELAWNEY Robert 31 40
TRENCHARD George 397 Penelope
397
TREVORE William 32
TREWORGYE Catherine 310 James
310
TRICKETT Thomas 236
TRICKEY Bethiah 274 Elizabeth
271 John 274 Joseph 271
Thomas 52 53 174 236 237 243
245 248 Zachariah 52 53
TRIMINGS Oliuer 53 Oliver 174
TRIPE Elizabeth 324 Richard 324
TRUE Benjamin 278 476 Betsey
278 476 Hannah 477 Henry 476
Jane 476 Mary 278 476 Polly
477
TUCKER Dorcas 446 Dudley F 428
Hugh 446 John 203 Martha H
428
TUFTON Catherine 422 431 John
422 Robert 189 422 431 Thomas
422
TUFTS Asa A 146 Carrie Brooks
438 Charles Augustus 255 Rev
180
TURE John 235
TURNER John 67
TUTELL Wedoew 244
TUTTELL John 237 248
TUTTLE Abigail 359 360 362 Alva¹
363 Andrew 360 361 362 Ann 361
Anna 359 Anne 361 364 415
Annie E 278 Asa 362 Asa C 361
B C 364 Bathsheba 359
Benjamin 360 362 364 Benjamin
S 364 Capt 85 155 156
Catherine 364 Comfort 415
Daniel 278 475 David 360 361
Deborah 360 362 364 Dorothy

337 358 359 364 Ebenezer 86
358 359 360 Elejah 89 Elijah
358 359 360 361 362 363 364
Elisha 359 360 Eliza P 361
Elizabeth 360 364 400 401 414
415 419 Elizabeth Stillings
364 Emily A 284 Esther 360 362
363 364 Eunice 324 361 George
364 Harriet 362 Hope 359 360
Horace P 493 Horatio 362 Ira
361 James 86 204 205 206 214
307 322 323 358 359 360 361
362 363 364 417 James Jr 261
Jay 278 475 Jehiah 362 Joana
417 Joanna 307 364 Job 359 415
Joe 252 John vii 53 84 86 114
157 201 209 236 254 257 357
358 359 362 363 364 378 379
382 401 405 415 475 John Jr
415 419 457 458 John Sr vii
117 207 241 John Thomas 362
Jonathan 362 363 Joseph 261
323 359 361 363 364 Joseph E
361 Judah 361 362 Judith 358
360 363 364 415 457 458 Keziah
364 Lavinia 488 Leonora 278
Levi Woodbury 278 475 Louisa
361 Lucy 415 Lydia 361 362 363
364 419 Lydia H 277 Margaret
363 Martha 359 360 362 364
Mary 206 214 307 358 359 360
361 362 363 364 405 407
Mehitable 361 Molly 362 Nancy
278 475 Nicholas 86 358 364
Olive 274 277 Patience 361
Paul 359 Phebe 358 359 360
361 364 Prudence 359 Reuben
359 360 361 Rose 322 323 359
360 361 364 Sally 272 Samuel
359 360 362 364 Sarah 323 359
361 362 363 364 415 Silas 359
Stephen 360 361 Stoughton 364
Tabitha 359 Thomas 86 260 358
359 360 363 415 Tobias 261 360
363 William 360 361 362 364
William Penn 114 361
TWAMLEY Ralphf 249 Raphf 242
  Raphfe 246
TWAMLIE Ralf 252
TWOMBLEY Sarah 267
TWOMBLY Aaron 485 486 Abigail
  485 486 487 Abra 485 Alice A
  489 Andrew 486 Ann 483 Anna
  482 484 487 Augusta A 489
  Benjamin 410 482 483 485
  Benjamin H 489 Benjamin T 489
  Charles A 488 Charles E 489
Charlotte 488 Daniel 359 483
484 486 David 484 Ebenezer 332
Eleanor 484 Elizabeth 484
Elizabeth A 487 Esther 267 482
483 Frank H 489 Fred C 490
George 489 George E 490 George
W K 488 489 Gilman H 302 490
Hannah 483 485 486 488 Harry L
490 Hattie 489 Helen F 489
Herbert A 488 Hope 482 Hurd
485 487 488 489 490 Hurd W C
489 Irs 487 Isaac 88 483 484
Jacob 485 486 James T 488 489
James Walter 489 Jane 488
Jeremiah 488 John 267 332 334
459 482 483 484 485 486 487
488 John Jr 89 John C 489 John
H 490 John Herbert 488 Joseph
482 483 Joshua 485 486 487
Judith 398 483 Katie 489
Lavinia 488 Lavinia H 490
Louisa A 488 Lydia 332 484
Martha 483 484 Martha J 488
Martha L 489 Mary 359 450 482
483 484 485 487 488 Mary A 489
Mary E 489 Mary Esther 490
Mary H 489 Mary J 487
Mehitable 332 486 487 Moses
481 Nathaniel 485 486 487 488
489 Nathaniel A 489 Peter 485
487 Phebe 487 Polly 485 486
Rachel 482 483 485 Ralph ix 89
179 237 481 482 484 487 488
Rebecca 483 Roscoe R 490
Rowena L 489 Sally 485 486
Samuel 482 483 485 486 Sarah
481 482 483 484 485 487 Sarah
C 487 488 489 Sharington Baker
332 Smith 486 Susan 485 486
488 Tammy 281 Tamsen 459
Tamsin 332 Tamson 334 484 485
486 Tobias 483 Walter T 490
William 332 381 450 482 483
484 485 486 487 488 William Jr
88 William D 489 William Henry
Harrison 488 490 William K 487
Winfield H 490

UGOVE John 201
UGROVE John 203
UMFIRIE Thomas 238
UMPHRES Thomas 241
UNDERHILL Capt 108 109 111 112
  147 148 149 168 Gov 169 John
  viii 39 107 109 110 126 145
  146 148 167 223 303 Mr 171
URIN Anna 436 Hannah 400 James

VANCE Sarah 443
VANE Harry 109 148 Henry 108 167
  Mr 110
VARNEY Abigail 359 Amos 275
  Andrew 58 261 262 Bathsheba
  359 Charles 279 Ebenezer 458
  460 484 Elizabeth 295 354
  Esther 360 364 Eunice 416
  Ezekiel 260 354 Hannah 279
  Humfrey 241 245 249 Humphrey
  vii 117 319 364 373 460 James
  R 261 John 87 John Riley 290
  Joseph 359 Judith 360 Martha
  360 364 484 Mary 275 399 458
  460 Mercy Hanson 275 Molly 453
  Moses 86 364 Nathan 359 Nathn
  87 Nicholas 58 Phebe 364
  Robert 58 399 416 Samuel 88
  Sarah 319 373 Stephen 87 275
  Susanna 457 Tobias 275
VARNIE Humphire 252
VARNUM Dorothy 480
VAN ZANDT Sarah Frances 295
VAUDREUIL Marquis de 294
VEAZEY George 422 Hannah 422
  Lydia 435 Thomas 435
VETTER Nichles 244
VINCENT John 418
VINTON Josiah 344 Mary Goodwin
  344
VOSE Roger 156
VUTTER Nicholas 241

WADLEIGH Elijah 262 G H 124
  George 124 Mr 125 Robert 187
WAITS Samuel 86
WAKEHAM Elizabeth 401 402
WALDEN Capt 348 349 Deputy 131
  Paul 349 Richard 134 135 233
  William 201
WALDERN Isaac 54 Richard 20 182
WALDERNE Anna 326 Annie 325 Capt
  66 67 120 242 252 253 350
  Catherine 162 324 Edward 162
  Eleazer 326 Elizabeth 326
  Elnathan 326 Esther 326 George
  162 242 252 324 Maj 210 224
  326 408 461 Maria 326 Mary 326
  Paul 325 Richard vii 66 101
  119 120 123 130 141 143 162
  163 166 176 184 185 216 217
  236 255 256 317 324 325 373
  380 447 Timothy 325 William
  vii 103 126 151 162 163 164
  201 254 324

WALDRON Abigail 327 329 453 Ann
  329 332 Anne 331 Annie 327
  Betsey 331 334 335 Bridget
  331 Charles 329 Col 333
  Constance 328 Daniel 329 330
  Ebenezer 331 Edmund 329
  Eleanor 327 328 329 Eliza 328
  334 Elizabeth 327 328 329 330
  331 332 334 335 411 George 328
  329 George P 334 Hannah 331
  334 398 James 331 335 Jeremiah
  334 Joanna 334 454 Job C 335
  Johanna 333 John 87 225 260
  261 330 331 332 341 342 453
  454 John Jr 330 John 3rd 260
  Jonathan 329 Joseph 331 334
  Maj 194 409 Margaret 327 328
  333 Mary 329 330 331 334 335
  Mary B 334 Mary Constantia
  329 Mehitable 332 335 Moses
  334 Nathaniel Sheafe 329 Olive
  329 335 Olive Rindge 329 Polly
  333 R 154 Richard 89 223 257
  258 327 328 329 330 331 334
  335 367 368 Richard Russell
  329 Samuel 327 329 331 335
  398 Sarah 331 332 335 Susan
  329 Susanna 334 Tamson 334
  Thomas 296 Thomas W 260 329
  Thomas Westbrook 254 259 327
  328 329 411 Timothy Winn 334
  Virginia 329 William 327 328
  329 331 William H 334
WALFORD Thomas 50
WALKER Abigail 329 Mark 261 329
  Sarah 316
WALLDEN Exelsander 249
WALLDERN Capt 237 245 George 245
WALLDERNE Capt 249 George 250
WALLDON William 233
WALLDONE Rochard 233
WALLINGFORD Abigail 406 407
  Charity 406 479 David 408
  Deborah 407 Ebenezer 406 407
  Elizabeth 407 Frances 406
  Hannah 406 407 James 407 John
  307 405 406 407 479 Judith
  406 407 Lavina 408 Lydia 307
  332 408 Margaret 407 408 Mary
  307 358 405 406 407 479 480
  Nicholas 406 407 408 Patience
  406 Peter 406 407 408 Phebe
  406 Rachel 407 408 Sallie 408
  Samuel 307 332 408 Sarah 307
  309 406 407 Thomas 259 307
  406 407 William 406 407 Zimri
  Scates 408

WALLIS Jane 490
WALLTON George 233
WALTON Alice 313 George vii 236
  313 Mary 441 Shadrack 441
  Shedrech 89
WAMOUTH Benja Jr 89
WARDELL Eliakim 131
WARNERTON Mr 103
WARREN Grizel 227 Grizet 457
  James 227 475 Margaret 227
  Mary 451
WARWICK Ro 37
WASGATT Bathsheba 402 Moses 402
  Sarah 402
WATERHOUSE Benj A 363 Elizabeth
  269 Lydia 363 Richard 269
WATSON Aaron 355 Abigail 352
  354 355 Adeline 356 Alice 357
  Ann 355 357 Benjamin 353 354
  355 356 357 Betsey 334 Charity
  355 Christine 334 354 356 459
  Daniel 352 353 369 David 352
  353 354 356 369 Deborah 369
  Dudley 89 260 334 353 354 355
  459 Eleazer 356 Elizabeth 352
  353 354 355 356 416 Esther 356
  Fenton 354 Frederick 354
  George 353 Hannah 352 354 355
  357 Himeous 354 Isaac 88 352
  353 355 357 James 355 James H
  356 Jeremiah 354 Joanna 353
  John 353 354 355 356 John
  Adams 356 Jonathan 89 352 353
  355 356 357 Joseph 353 354 355
  Keziah 353 Lillian 357 Lucy
  354 Lydia 354 355 356 357 Mary
  352 353 354 357 369 Mercy 353
  Nancy 357 Nathaniel 354 Olive
  355 Otis Baker 354 355 Polly
  356 Priscilla 357 Roberd 250
  Robert 253 352 Samuel 88 352
  354 355 357 Sarah 354 355 356
  Sarah Hanson 356 Seth 356
  Sophia 356 Susan 355 357
  Thomas 354 355 William 352 353
  354 Winthrop 334 352 353 354
WATTSON Johnathan 252
WAYMEOTH Edward 241
WEARE Nathaniel 153 154 162
WEBB George 236 William 468
WEBBER Hannah 443 480
WEBE George 201
WEBSTER Elizabeth 474 Henry 474
  Lois 474 Mary 474 Sarah 474
  Thomas E 474
WEDGWOOD Elizabeth 401 John 401
WEEKS Anna 425 Edward Francis

285 George Locke 285 George W
  428 John Wesley 285 Jonathan
  285 Joseph 425 Joseph Dame 285
  Joshua 427 428 Martha 427 428
  Martha J 285 Mary 285 Mary Ann
  428 Mary Ella 286 Mary Jewett
  425 Orrin Francis 285 Rebecca
  285 Rufus Spaulding 285
  Walter 425
WELCH Mary 322 Ralph 252
WELLAND William 89
WELLEY Thomas 238 240 243 246
  251
WENDELL Chester Snell 462
  William 332
WENTWORTH 334 Abigail 307 333
  Albert H 286 Annie 310
  Augusta J 286 Bartholomew 386
  Benjamin 258 307 386 Benning
  85 218 475 Bessie 286 Charity
  479 480 Elder 237 242 245 250
  253 446 447 Elizabeth 307
  Epherem 87 Ephraim 451 Ezek
  157 Ezekel 87 Ezekiel 252 257
  George Thomas 255 Gershom 252
  331 391 459 Gov 56 Hannah 392
  424 492 Jennie 286 Joanna 307
  364 John 259 311 333 436 475
  John Jr 333 John S 307 Keziah
  451 Lewis 355 Lydia 307 459
  Margaret 333 Mark 307 Martin
  V B 286 Mary 305 Mehitable 331
  Paul 258 259 305 306 307
  Roscoe 286 Ruth 386 Samewell
  242 250 Samuel 261 422 424
  Sarah 307 Spencer 451 Spencor
  89 Susan 355 Tamsen 391 Will
  120 William 119 168 179 234
  236 255 256 265 373 375 392
  424
WESTBROOK Elizabeth 327 Thomas
  327 471
WESTELL John 202
WESTINMAN Steuen 239
WESTON Thomas 9 16
WEYMOETH Edward 245
WEYMOUTH Benjamin 385 Edward 135
  Phebe 406
WHARTON Edward 128 135 136 137
  143 176 194
WHEELER Albert 280 John H 332
  Mary 280
WHEELWRIGHT John 109 148 167 Mr
  168
WHIDDEN Elizabeth 418 Jane 400
  Jou Boole 479 Michael 418
WHIGHTHOUSE John 88

WHITE Frances 312 John H 261 Richard 39 312
WHITEHOUSE Elizabeth 266 356 Hannah 356 Pomfrett 78 Pumphret 157 Richard 356 Thomas 244 248 252 266 William 87
WHITING Mr 94
WHITNEY Bessie 286
WHITTIER John Greenleaf 141
WHITTY Mr 9
WIBIRD Capt 162
WIDVILLE Anthony 467 Elizabeth 467
WIGGANS Thomas 51
WIGGIN Aaron 425 Abigail 422 424 425 426 433 434 435 436 Abner 426 Albert 428 Alice Fisher 438 Ammi Ruhana 432 Andrew 102 420 421 422 424 425 426 427 429 432 433 434 435 Andrew Jackson 432 Andrew M 426 Andrew N 426 Andrew P 424 Ann 324 424 427 428 429 432 434 Anna 425 426 430 433 436 Anna P 436 Aphia 423 Asa 433 Augusta 425 Benjamin 426 429 432 434 Benjamin F 426 Betsey 423 427 428 4269 433 435 Betty 423 Bradstreet 425 426 427 428 429 Bridget 431 Caleb 424 425 Caleb M 425 Capt 52 94 94 99 103 104 106 109 113 115 164 165 172 237 246 Caroline 433 Carrie Brooks 438 Catherine 102 420 421 422 431 Charles 423 433 Charles W 437 Charles William 437 438 Charlotte 426 428 432 434 Chase 427 428 429 433 Clarissa 425 Coker 427 Comfort 427 433 Daniel 426 434 435 436 Daniel C 64 David 423 426 429 433 435 Deborah 422 423 426 428 430 431 432 Dolly 426 428 429 430 434 Dolly W 426 Dorothy 422 424 427 429 Edmund 425 Edwin 426 Elijah 434 435 Eliza 424 430 Elizabeth 423 425 428 429 430 431 432 433 435 Ellen 429 Emma 433 Emma Gertrude 438 Eunice Leila 438 Ezra 429 Frank Brooks 438 George 432 435 Gideon 434 435 Hannah 421 422 423 424 425 426 427 432 434 435 Harry Mortimer 437 438 Henry 423 427 432 436 Henry Batchelder 434 Hepsibah 433 Herbert 434 Hiram 426
Ira W 435 Isaac 433 James 313 429 433 435 James J 426 436 Jane 423 425 430 Jane M 435 Janvrin Fisher 437 Jeremiah 432 Jewett 426 Joanna 423 John 427 428 431 432 434 435 Jonathan 422 424 425 426 428 430 432 Joseph 423 429 431 432 Joseph Henry 437 Joshua 428 432 434 Joshua P 427 Josiah 435 Josiah B 426 Judith 427 434 Levi 425 435 Love 429 Lydia 423 426 429 432 434 435 Magdaline 313 Mark 426 429 Martha 425 426 427 428 429 431 433 435 Martha Abigail 432 Martha R 427 Mary 422 423 424 426 427 428 429 432 434 435 436 Mary Abba 437 438 Mary Ann 426 426 Mary H 430 Mary J 429 Mary Jewett 425 Mehitable 423 425 426 434 Mercy 425 429 Michael 423 Mrs 192 Molly 427 Moses 433 Nancy 423 427 428 430 435 Nancy P 426 Nancy W 426 Nathan 426 Nathaniel 261 429 432 435 Noah 429 Olive 423 432 433 435 Olive L 426 Patience 429 430 Patty 427 Paul 429 433 Phebe 425 426 427 429 Phineas 434 Polly 427 435 Rachel 425 432 Richard 434 Richard R 427 Robert 423 Rufus 433 Ruhamah 426 Ruth 426 S L 437 Sally 425 434 435 Sally Ann 426 Sally Fisher 437 Samuel 428 434 436 437 Samuel L 437 Sarah 185 191 422 423 424 426 428 430 431 432 434 435 436 Sarah A 299 Sarah B 426 Sarah Jane 423 Shadrach 435 Sherburne 423 427 Simon 422 423 431 Stephen 428 430 432 435 Steven 431 Susan 436 437 Susannah 423 429 430 431 432 433 Tabitha 429 Theodore 434 Theophilus 428 Thomas viii 3 20 21 37 52 90 93 94 95 101 102 104 151 162 165 168 185 186 216 223 242 244 263 264 314 315 380 420 421 422 423 425 426 427 429 430 431 432 434 435 436 Thomas Jr 185 186 191 Timothy 429 Tufton 434 Uriah 426 Walter 426 432 436 Warren 433 William 425 430 431 William B 261 William H 425

William Henry 423 Winborn
Adams 433 Winthrop 427 433
Zebulon 426 Zeruiah 433
WIGGINS Capt 182 Thomas 136 137
WIGGLESWORTH Dr 329
WILLE Benjamin 86 Robert 86
WILLEY Elizabeth 387 388 Frances
  387 Hannah 485 Rufus 274
  Stephen 86 Susan 274 Tho 236
WILLIAMS Gov 126 148 172 Mathew
  238 243 247 Mr 103 147 Roger
  108 167 Saml 87 Will Jr 239
  William Jr 238 244 253 William
  Sr 238 253
WILLIE Samuel 253 Stephen 253
  Tho 253
WILLIS Mr 94
WILLOUGHBY Gov 325
WILLSON John 249 Mr 469
WILLYAMES William 176
WILLYAMS Matthew 240 250 Will Jr
  247 250 William Sr 246 250
WILLYANS William Sr 240
WILSON Daniel 426 Elizabeth 390
  John 352 Margaret 352 Mary 426
WILYAMS Will Jr 250 William Sr
  243
WINDSOR Cynthia 460
WINGATE 399 Ann 445 Dorothy 429
  Elizabeth 369 Joanna 78 John
  77 315 369 392 445 Joshua 260
  429 474 Mary 315 391 395 424
  Moses 78 260 Payne 424 Samuel
  391 Sarah 392 Simon 78 Susan
  329
WINGET John Jr 88 89 249 257
  Joseph 88 Joshua 206 Saml 88
WINGETT John 123 256 258 259 260
  John Jr 260
WINKLEY Abigail 497 Darius 443
  Francis 497 Ursula R 443
WINN Polly 333
WINSLOW Gov 50 Lorana 389 Mr 29
  Ruth 390 Sarah 496
WINTER John 40
WINTHROP Gov 26 51 74 93 94 95
  108 148 168 171 John 11 51 93
  99 107 109 125 148 163 192 306
  343 John Jr 397 Mr 12 148 169
  Robert C 11 28
WINTWORTH Samewell 245
WISE Rev 180
WITHREL James 87
WOED John 243
WOLLASTON Capt 50
WOOD John 259
WOODBRIDGE Abra 485

WOODBURY Abigail 352 Nathaniel
  352
WOODHOUSE Elizabeth H 498 John
  498
WOODIN John 245
WOODMAN Betsey 271 Charles 400
  Jeremiah H 340 John 53 238 240
  244 247 250 253 256 257
  Jonathan 257 271 383 Mary
  Esther 340 Mary Wingate 400
  Octavia W 474
WORCESTER Sallie 408
WRIGHT Lucy 498 Peter 105
WYATT Samuel 369 Sophia 369
WYMAN Mary B 334 Zebadiah 334

YEATON Abigail 420 Deborah 440
  George H 299 Joseph 440 Lydia
  308 Mary 308 Sarah 452
YORK Abigail F 289 Benjamin 253
  Isaac 493 John 253 Mary 493
  Richard viii
YORKE Richard 183 236 239 243
  247 250
YOUNG Abby H 284 Abigail 481
  Abner 157 Benjn 88 Charles 255
  Daniel 495 Ebenr 157 Edward L
  490 Eleazer 352 Elezer 88
  Ephraim 495 Esther L 490
  Hannah 323 Harvey 284 Isaac 88
  Jacob D 489 James 88 259 250
  John 85 324 495 John Jr 89
  Jonathan 87 Lewis H 308 490
  Lillian L 490 Mary 308 309 457
  460 Natha 87 Rose 324 Samuel
  88 Sarah 324 Sarah C 489
  Thomas 88 309

INDIANS Hopehood 121 Kankamagus
  121 Mesandowet 121 Passaconaway 121 Pummadockyon 168
  Robinhood 121 Tahonto 23 24
  312 Wahowah 121 Wehanownuwit
  168 Wituwamat 44 Wonolancet
  121

NEGROES (no surnames) Caeser 81
  Julia 70 Pompy 81 Richard 70

www.ingramcontent.com/pod-product-compliance
Lightning Source LLC
Chambersburg PA
CBHW060907300426
44112CB00011B/1373